DRAGON BONES

Published by Avalonia

BM Avalonia
London
WC1N 3XX
England, UK

www.avaloniabooks.co.uk

Dragon Bones – Ritual, Myth and Oracle in Shang Period China
Copyright © 2012 Jan Fries

ISBN 9781905297627

First Edition, 2013
Design by Satori

Cover collage by Astrid Bauer, based on photos by Jan Fries
and from the United College Library. The Dragon Graces, a
well at Heilongtan Temple near Kunming, Yünnan.

British Library Cataloguing in Publication Data. A catalogue
record for this book is available from the British Library.

Other Books by Jan Fries

Visual Magick: a Handbook of Freestyle Shamanism, Mandrake, 1992 & 2001
Helrunar:Manual of Rune Magick, Mandrake, 1993 & 2002
Seidways: Shaking, Swaying and Serpent Mysteries, Mandrake, 1996
Living Midnight: Three Movements of the Tao, Mandrake, 1998
The Cauldron of the Gods: Manual of Celtic Magick, Mandrake, 2003
Kali Kaula: A Manual of Tantric Magick, Avalonia, 2010
Nightshades: A Tourist Guide to the Nightside, Mandrake, 2012

The author welcomes you to write to him:

Jan Fries
c/o Avalonia
BM Avalonia
London
WC1N 3XX
United Kingdom

Disclaimer

Although both Avalonia and the author of this book have taken great care to ensure the authenticity of the information and the techniques contained therein, we are not responsible, in whole or in part, for any injury which may occur to the reader or readers by reading and/or following the instructions in this book. It is understood that many of the techniques, rituals and meditations are only discussed for scholarly purposes, and that there exists a potential for injury when using the techniques or practices described in this publication, especially when the full text is not carefully studied.

It is essential that before following any of the activities, physical meditative or otherwise, herein described, the reader or readers should first consult his or her physician for advice on whether practising or using the techniques, rituals or meditations described in this publication could cause injury, physical, mental or otherwise. Since the techniques and physical activities could be too demanding or sophisticated, it is essential that a physician be consulted. Also, local, state or federal laws may prohibit the practice of phyiscal activities, rituals or exercises described in this publication. A thorough examination must be made of the federal, state or local laws before the reader or readers attempt to try or practice any of the exercises, techniques, rituals, meditations or any other activity described in this publication.

Neither Avalonia nor the author guarantees the legality or the appropriateness of the techniques, acts, rituals, exercises or meditations herein contained.

Small Shang Ding Vessel
Today in Nanjing Museum. Height 21.8 cm

Dragon Bones

Ritual, Myth and Oracle
in Shang Period China

Jan Fries

Published By Avalonia
www.avaloniabooks.co.uk

Acknowledgements
and Rites of Thanksgiving

First of all, I would like to thank all those dear friends, teachers, parents, relations, ancestors, gods and spirits of this and former lifetimes whose support, laughter, effort and encouragement made this book possible.

To begin with, let me express my gratitude to the late Professor Chang, Tsung-Tung, originally from Taiwan, who spent much of his life teaching sinology at Frankfurt University. In the late seventies I enjoyed a few months of Chinese lessons with him. At the time, I was not aware that he was one of the leading oracle bone scholars. I recall watching him drawing modern characters and ancient pictograms on a blackboard. It amazed me that the Bronze Age Chinese developed a system of writing that was not only functional but also strikingly beautiful. True enough, Chinese writing developed a lot since those early days, and the contemporary characters have their own fascinating beauty. Nevertheless, it made me wonder why anyone would wish to turn perfectly good pictures of a mountain, cloud, fire or river into much more abstract glyphs. Tree, Ding cauldron, a person sitting under a roof awaiting orders, Dragon and Phoenix ... each of them has a magical intensity that speaks directly to the deep mind. Chinese could be a lot easier if tigers would still look like tigers.

Many years later, Professor Chang's brilliant study of the religious inscriptions of the Shang was recommended to me. (Thank you, Norbert!) It changed my life. In the next years, I filled many notebooks with variations of the ideograms. They grew bigger and bigger, as I chanced upon volume after volume of Chang's original oracle bone library. After his death, the books had gone to other sinologists, upon whose demise they ended up in my favourite second hand bookshop. I went through many crates of fascinating material. Professor Chang had not only gathered a superb collection of oracle bone catalogues and studies, but also books on Taijiquan, mythology, history and comic book versions of the *Daodejing*, the *Zhuangzi*, Sima Qian and the *Liao Zhai*. With each gem I uncovered I had a distinct sensation of his spirit's presence. Scholars like him are a rare gift to the world.

Chang, Tsung-Tung: wherever your soul is: blessings!

Professor Chang's study afforded a good start for my research, but as it had been completed in 1970 I was soon busy looking for newer literature. I found several good books thanks to the internet, some were ordered from China by good friends, and others came my way when I was in China myself.

Writing books has the advantage that the personal spirits and deities become acutely book conscious, and provide useful material from the unlikeliest sources. The gods and spirits of ancient China were obviously keen to manifest. Nevertheless, I was in much need of help. My (contemporary) Chinese is so dismal that I can barely handle a taxi ride (the trick is not to listen to what the driver says, and better still, to ignore everything until the cab stops and you can set your trembling legs on the ground, breathe a sigh of relief and wait for the adrenaline rush to pass). Anyway, equipped with so many books in Chinese I frequently enervated my Chinese friends with questions and appeals for translation.

Let me assure you that the errors in this volume are all my own.

Thanks are due to Xiaonan whose curiosity, enthusiasm and boundless good humour encouraged this book. She translated several important texts and poems and put me in touch with her friends who contributed more.

This project would have been impossible without the patience and encouragement of Qing, who spent many hours translating dictionary entries and commentaries. Always fascinated by the prehistory of her culture and ready to laugh about people then and now, she supplied the enthusiasm that made writing easy and pleasant.

Yuan told me much about Chinese music, and provided new strings for my guzheng and a xun bass ocarina. It taught me about the ritual music of ancient China under the influence of too much oxygen.

Jing happily supplied lots of travelling tips while her wild and wonderful daughter Xinyue reminded me of what is really important in life.

Norbert of the Zeil Antiquariat and Ren Damin of the China Culture Service were exceptionally helpful. They managed to obtain a wide range of obscure and rare books for me: without their help, this book wouldn't have happened.

Many thanks are due to the wonderful people I met in China. You made me feel very much at home.

I am very grateful to those who followed the development of this book with so much interest.

Astrid, Gavin, Julia, Tina, H.H. and Volkert all made their unique own contributions to the research and cheered me up when I began to wonder whether anyone will ever read this. Special thanks are due to Astrid, who designed the cover with much enthusiasm. Avalonia did a wonderful job editing the text without messing it (or me) up; Holger, Christiane and Dagmar asked questions and reminded me to keep things simple. It didn't always work.

All of you are a rare blessing.

My thanks are due to the many oracle bone scholars who devoted their lives to the understanding of the magnificent Bronze Age cultures of China and their history. Shang studies are still a fairly young art. I have learned a lot from your research, from your highly varied approaches and the many unique interpretations. Your work is a pleasure and an inspiration. As my book is just a simple introduction to the topic, I very much recommend that all readers consult the specialist literature to explore the topic in full depth. It is fascinating, exciting and highly stimulating. And though I cannot always agree with all of your interpretations (sorry) I am glad that so many possibilities exist and that we can view the Shang from many different points of view.

Let me insist that the errors of this book are my responsibility, and ask all readers to do their own research and thinking.

During the last stage of the writing; I was briefly in contact with David Keightley; alas, due to serious health problems he could not contribute much. Nevertheless, I am grateful he replied.

Next I got in touch with Sarah Allan, whose remarkable and ground-breaking studies have much influenced my way of understand the Shang. Sarah Allan kindly replied at length, supplied data on grammar, discussed difficult subjects like the ritual of the king erecting the centre and even sent an essay on the meaning of Di, a tricky subject that has perplexed a wide range of researchers. Some of her insights were so close to what I had learned during trances and meditations that I was delighted and relived to hear of them. I am very thankful for Sarah Allan's support and wish to point out that she is not responsible for my more exuberant speculations.

Finally, my thanks go to the gods and spirits who accompanied this project: Xiwangmu as ever, Fuxi and Nüwa for signs and creativity; Di, Taiyi and Hundun as three manifestations of One Consciousness and especially the deified spirits of Fu Hao and Bi Xin (period three). May you be remembered.

And all of you, this is you, who woke and are waking, for I am talking to you now, as the ancient gods return and reform and the dreaming transforms life: Thank you.

"Sky merges with cloudy waves
And blends with early morning mist.
The River of Heaven wants to turn
And a thousand sails dance.
As in a dream, my soul returns to Di
I hear the voice of Heaven ask politely:
Where do you return? I reply:
Alas, the road is long and the sun is sinking,
Long time in vain I studied poetry
And astonished people with my verses.
Bird Peng is flying easily on a wind,
Ninety thousand li high.
Wind, do not stop, blow my light boat
To the Three Mountain Peaks."

Song by Li Qingzhao (1084-c.1151),
poetess, archaeologist, historian and lay Daoist,
to the tune *'The Honour of the Fisherman'*

Dragon Bones is dedicated to the memory of
Li Qingzhao
and all enthusiasts
who combine research with spiritual practice.

Table of Contents

Ancestor Monkey

First Words:
Reading the Past

It is one thing to write about a culture long past and another to allow the people of the time to speak for themselves. When I planned to write this book, I thought it should be a simple, easy to understand introduction to early Chinese ritual, myth and divination. The words *'short and simple'* floated through my mind. I naively assumed that a few brief chapters and a handful of inscriptions would suffice. However, oracle bone inscriptions can be highly addictive. For a start, they are beautiful. You get used to reading them and soon enough you marvel at the magnificence and enchantment of the divinations. At first glance, this fascination is not very evident. Most oracle bone fragments are small and offer merely a few words of what may have been a much longer question. Repetitions are numerous; again and again the diviners are inquiring about rain, weather, hunting and whether a given night or indeed the next ritual week will be free of disaster. Much of this is dull and tedious, or at least it would be, if the calligraphy were not so varied. Such divinations form the bulk of the surviving scripture of the Shang. There are no myths, no poetry, no songs and few commemorations of historical events. Where other cultures eulogised how their great king slaughtered enemies, built cities and pronounced laws, Shang inscriptions tell us that their regents worried as they went to war. We learn that King Wu Ding divined whether he should follow one general or another, whether his health was up to the effort, whether to send his queen with her armies and if a lot more offerings to gods and ancestors were required to ensure success. The war itself, and if and how it was won, eludes us. Even when we encounter longer or more original divinations, each topic is treated in a dry and sparse style with little narrative to liven up the day.

However, when you study many inscriptions a strange thing happens in your mind. The shreds of information conglomerate into a fantastic collage, which, like a broken mirror, reflects the light in all sorts of angles and directions. They reflect the Shang, they reflect life in the Bronze Age, they reflect our modern beliefs, assumptions and prejudices and finally they reflect you, and how you are thinking what you assume to be true. Used carefully, you can discern your own culture in this mirror, and how your own belief shapes your reality. It was the grand historian of the Han Dynasty, Sima Qian, who pointed out that *"those who do not forget the past are the masters of the future"*. There is much to be learned from the Shang, and more to be learned about yourself.

Shang oracle bone inscriptions may not contain much in the way of story-telling, but when you read enough you realise that each of them is a glimpse of reality, an insight into the world-view entertained by a highly successful Bronze Age culture that became one of the major civilisations on this planet. It is the Chinese past, but, in a strange way, it shares much with the past of Europeans and other cultures. When I compare, say, Celts with the Shang, I see regents who make much of head-trophies, animal totems and divination, who venerate a wide range of ancestral and natural gods and spirits, who have an elaborate system of offerings, who drink more than is good for them and who like to take the chariot into the grave. The Celts did not leave much record of their spiritual life but luckily the Shang did. Their world view was imbued with spirituality. True enough, it wasn't always the spirituality that suits our own era, or should be encouraged in your worship. The Shang, like so many Bronze and early Iron Age cultures, had no hesitation when it came to sacrificing captives and prisoners of war, and many aristocrats went into the otherworld in the company of a large group of ministers, servants, concubines and grave guardians. Such acts seem cruel and possibly insane to us, as our age defines reality and religion in a different way. No doubt the Shang would have had similar thoughts about the customs that characterise our own, and any other culture. However, some of the spiritual and religious practices of the Shang retain their relevance, and when you seek for a culture which boasted several intensely religious regents, you will learn much about how they maintained their mind-space and cultivated magical power (de). As you consider Shang thought, you may wonder about the parameters that define your reality, your ideas about the divine, about the otherworlds, about fate and choice and the decisions that shape your journey through life.

To trace early Chinese religion, I have combined historical accounts, myths, practical meditation and the oracle bone inscriptions at my disposal. From maybe 15000 inscribed bone and shell fragments I have selected more than 400 inscriptions and attempted to provide word by word translations, plus a beginner's dictionary, so you can enjoy the variations of early Chinese writing and consider different readings. Given that many of the characters are still under discussion, and that the inscriptions are frequently enigmatic, in shorthand or employ odd grammar, I would not dream of claiming that my reading is the final word.

Each of my translations is provisional, based on educated guesswork and has some likeliness to be relatively reliable...until the next and better interpretation comes along.

Where it comes to peculiar innovations, I have taken the liberty to translate the names of diviners and people, if possible, into English. Here, I have made much use of T.T. Chang's translations. Professor Chang generally wrote the names of people and states in Chinese, but gave clear translations wherever possible. Contemporary oracle bone scholars tend to give names only in Chinese, which may give rise to some misconceptions. For one thing, it suggests that we know how the names were pronounced, and this is not the case. For another, it blinds the non-Chinese reader to the fact that these names had meanings, or were written with meaningful characters.

In many cases, it is useful to deliberate how meaningful they were. I am sure General Panther made much of his name. That prince Yang, whose name reads Shoulderpack, actually identified with this item is less likely. However, he may have heard quite a few puns about it. Chinese, with its limited range of syllables, is simply made for puns. Diviners named Great, Bell-Stroke, Drum, Command (Commander?) or To Show (i.e. maybe '*Revealer*') may have been proud of their names. A general written See-Far Climb-High could have considered his name a great good omen. Whether General Wash-Feet Shield thought the same is not so certain, let alone General Little Bird (or: Sparrow) whose name is, as with many Shang worthies, a clan name.

Maybe the ethnic group written Chin-Beard State (Gongfang) was indeed characterised by special beards, or maybe the character was simply chosen as it sounded like what this group called themselves. The Horse State may have bred great horses, the Dragon State could have been characterised by a dragon totem. Or, once again, the characters were used due to phonetic similarity. Let others be the judge of that. However, I believe that meaning should be considered. In very doubtful cases, like the name of diviner Zheng *'To Quarrel'*, a question mark was added.

The only exception to this rule is temple names. It is not very convenient to write *'Ancestor worshipped on the Yi day of the ten-day week who has the title Grandfather just like all males of his generation'* when a simple Zu Yi will do the job. I could have added that Yi probably meant *'river, water or flood'*, and that Zu is usually translated Grandfather, only that it doesn't have to be a real grandfather; but once in a while it's good to keep things simple.

In translating these inscriptions; I have made much use of T.T. Chang's interpretations, and of the vocabulary outlined in *Jia Gu Wen Zi Dian* (JGWZD). Both sources made wide use of earlier research, and no doubt contemporary sinologists will find that some of their readings are out of date. I look forward to further advances in oracle bone research. Until that time, this plain book may serve as a simple introduction to a vast and wonderful field of research and inspire sinologists, ethnologists, mythographers, enthusiasts, mind-explorers and practical ritualists to explore the wonders of an early civilisation that has much to offer.

Enjoy!
Chinese New Year, Year of the Dragon

Introduction:
Three Dynasties plus Extras

The Chinese literati divided the ancient history of their ancestors into a pre-dynastic phase and into Three Dynasties. It is a tale of steady devolution. The first regents are godlike culture heroes who govern whole phases of human development. Then follow five sage like thearchs, who are models of virtue and conduct, but nevertheless a lot more human than their predecessors. And finally the rulers are entirely human and prone to make a mess out of everything. Where other cultures imagine a success story leading from crude tents to villas with swimming pools, Chinese history has a golden age right at the beginning, when people were just getting used to agriculture, and from then on, things got worse.

The predynastic phase can be divided into the age of the Three Sovereigns and the Five Sage Emperors. The **Three Sovereigns** are the regents of Heaven, Earth and the Human Realm, if we can trust Sima Qian. It's a very cosmic concept. While the three were usually represented in human form, they were not entirely confined to it. Modern Chinese religion assigns them a rather remote position in time and space. But if (or when) you practice Daoist inner cultivation (neidan) meditation, you can encounter the three as the embodiment of the purest principles. Right in your body. The heavenly sovereign resides in the head and above it, the earthly sovereign in belly, legs and underworld and the sovereign of the human realm in the heart. There are numerous descriptions and images of the three, but I am sure you'll get much further when you simply relax, close your eyes, introvert, and seek them out in the cavities of the inner void. They'll appear just as it suits you. And what suits you suits them too.

The *Yundou Shu* and the *Yuanming Bao* calls the three Fuxi, Nüwa and Shennong.

They were no regents in our modern sense. Deities or culture heroes is much closer to the mark. You'll read more about them further on. Their regency was not really limited to dynastic progression and statecraft. Think of them as representations of the first stages of human evolution.

Then followed the **Five Emperors**. Here we come to sage like, superhuman thearchs. They are not quite as primordial as the three sovereigns. On occasion, they could be quite human. First of them was Huangdi (the Yellow Emperor), then followed

Zhuanxu, Ku, Yao and Shun. Not all sources agree on this point. Sometimes, Shaohao appears instead of Huangdi. And while the three Sovereigns are placed in a vertical model (above, below and the human sphere in between), the five sage-emperors can be assigned to the directions. Here we have Shaohao in the east, Fuxi in the south, Shennong in the west and Zhuanxu in the north. Huangdi, the Yellow Emperor, resides in the centre. And again this is just one model. Another popular map is used in ritual Daoism. Here Fuxi, the Green Emperor is in the east. The Red Emperor Shennong, also known as the Fire Lord (Yandi), is in the South. In the West is Shaohao, the White Emperor. The Black Emperor, Zhuanxu resides in the north. Huangdi, representing the rich ochre ground of the north Chinese plains, is in the centre.

Both of these models are useful in a magical sense. The emperors can be imagined as great deities who guard the quarters of the world. They can be evoked to control the energy and consciousness of each realm. Their essence can be visualised as a colourful vapour which you can breathe into your body for special power and awareness, store within your organs for health and exhale for sorcery and enchantment. All of this is practical. So please don't complain that these systems do not quite fit official history. I'm sure you noticed that neither Yao nor Shun got a place in the circle. It's probably because they were too human.

The period of the Five Emperors ended in a devastating flood. Chinese myth records several floods, as do so many other mythologies around the world. And after this flood Yü the Great starts a period of much more mundane history.

Yü founds the **Xia Dynasty**, allegedly the first dynasty of China. The Xia, so it was recorded, ruled from 2205 to 1766 BCE. It sounds like precise time-keeping but is really imaginative chronology. The Grand Historian of the Han, Sima Qian, even recorded the names of their regents, though he had very little to say about most. Other sources provided snippets of myths, vague hints, remarks about rituals and very little reliable information. Most of the data on the Xia was recorded or, more usually, made up more than a thousand years after they ceased to govern. Provided they ever did. There is, at the time being, very little reliable evidence for the House of Xia. Archaeologists have unearthed many impressively palace foundations, city walls and settlements from their period, but whether these belong to the Xia or anybody else remains an open question. Early China was characterised by a wide range of distinct cultures. A few scholars cling to the term 'Xia' for this period. More common are the terms Yangshao period for the earlier Neolithic and Longshan for the later Neolithic and the early Copper and Bronze Age. Yangshao and Longshan sound reassuringly like large, unified cultures, but this is misleading. Each of them consisted of many sub groups with their own, frequently independent developments and characteristics. Some of these cultural groups lived in well organised cities with pounded earth foundations and walls. They had distinct professions, skilled manufacturers, artisans, metal casters, traders, soldiers, ritual specialists and hereditary aristocrats. Others inhabited farming villages, subterranean houses, dwelled near rivers or swamps or spent their lives as nomadic sheep herders. The very idea of a single dominant *'dynasty'* may be completely wrong. If the House of Xia really existed, it was not an empire nor was it ruled by an emperor. You had better think of them as a bunch of wealthy cattle-breeders, farmers and aristocratic warlords. But no matter what they really were, their power came to an end. The last regents were thoroughly corrupt, or so we are told by much later historians, and Heaven decided that government should go to a more capable ruler.

He was Tang the Successful, and began the **Shang Dynasty**. Much later, the house of Shang acquired the name **Yin**. It's by no means certain whether the Shang ever used that name for themselves. But nowadays, many Chinese scholars prefer it, especially for the last phase of the Shang, when the capital was in Anyang, Henan. The **Yin Period** is a technical term for the reign of the last Shang kings from Pan Geng to Zhòu Xin. The Shang Dynasty wasn't a proper dynasty either. Its rulers were kings, not emperors, though a few of the last ones received the title posthumously. And once again, the European term *'emperor'* misleads. Those dead kings were worshipped as Di, which in this context means superhuman, godlike thearch. It was such an exalted title that no living regent would have dared to assume it. And these kings were not almighty dictators. They were religious figureheads of an alliance of clans and vassal tribes. Government and war were part of their duties, but even more important was participation in numerous religious rituals. Over the centuries, their power waxed and waned repeatedly, depending on how much influence the central court had over the lords of the periphery. Just as the regents were no emperors, their royal house, or rather the Zi clan, was no dynasty. It's another misleading term. Inheritance followed several tricky regulations and did not automatically go from father to son. So instead of 'dynasty' I much prefer to speak of the Shang period. Where it comes to facts, we can be sure the Shang had maybe 29-32 regents. The actual number is under discussion, as some of those kings never lived long enough to govern, and received the title posthumously. Dating the Shang remains problematic. Classical literature generally favours the period between 1766 and 1122 BCE. But the texts disagree. The *Zuozhuan* claims that the Shang lasted six hundred years. Mengzi (Mencius) recorded *more than* *five hundred years*, while a third source speaks of 29 kings and a total of 496 years. Now the start is impossible to decide, but the end of the Shang and the beginning of the Zhou period are only slightly better documented. Once again, the sources disagree. As a result, for many centuries Chinese scholars argued that the Shang ended in 1122, 1111 or 1027 BCE. Contemporary scholars had their say, and you'll be delighted to know that the Shang ended in the year 1122, 1116, 1111, 1076, 1075, 1070, 1067, 1066, 1057, 1050, 1049, 1047, 1046, 1045, 1030, 1029, 1027, or 1025 BCE (K. C. Chang 1983:2). This didn't make anybody happy. To settle the matter, a number of leading experts decided on 1045 BCE, which is the official date at the moment. It was a majority decision.

The Shang period ended, just like the house of Xia, when the last kings became thoroughly corrupt. The Mandate of Heaven went to another noble family, the House of Zhou, who founded the **Zhou Dynasty** after killing the last Shang king. The Zhou had been enemies, vassals and allies of the Shang, and had adopted many of their customs. Like the Shang, the Zhou kings were heads of an alliance of clans and vassal states. Once they had become kings, they put their own relations in charge over vast ranges of the north Chinese plain and gradually extended the domain. In the beginning, they retained a number of Shang customs, but roughly after a hundred years of rule they began to make up their own religious system. The first part of the Zhou period is called the Western Zhou, as their capital was close to their old homeland in Shaanxi. By the year 800 BCE their power was swiftly fading, and numerous lords did not bother to attend the court any more. Around 771 BCE the Quan Rong (Dog Barbarians), coming from the west, sacked the capital and killed King You. The aristocracy beat a hasty defeat from the Wei river homeland to the east, where they set up a new capital. It started the Eastern Zhou Dynasty (c. 770-221 BCE), a period characterised by nominal government and incessant warfare. While Zhou kings tried their best to conduct rituals and ceremonies, their many relations and neighbours fought it out among themselves. First during the **Spring and Autumn Period**, when several hundred small statelets fused into seven (c. 770-481 BCE). At the same time, Chinese thought underwent considerable changes. In a time of almost continuous warfare, few intellectuals retained much faith in deities or the power of the ancestors. Faced by so much bloodshed, Kongzi (Confucius) developed a secular code of conduct that attempted to make life safer and happier by emphasising virtues like humanity, love, self-refinement, respect, ritual and obedience. Other philosophers had their say, and said quite a lot, much of it disagreeing with each other. Next followed the **Warring States Period** (481-221 BCE) when the seven remaining states struggled among themselves until one, the state of Qin, assimilated the others by being especially violent. In the process, religious custom transformed again. Confucian lore became increasingly popular, and began to influence the aristocratic way of life and the administration of states. Not that it really stopped the lords from fighting. In the religious sphere, the wu ritualists (or *'shamans'*) gradually lost power and prestige, the fang shi (method masters) combined ritual sorcery with writing, a growing number of better placed people began to seek for life extension and immortality by using earlier ritual, shamanic or alchemical means and finally around the fourth and third century BCE Daoism developed by taking the best from all of these. Much of it emphasises the great idea that life might be happier in the mountain wilderness or on remote islands, in fact anywhere but central China. The Zhou Dynasty ended after a final climax of atrocities and China was unified for a mere fifteen years by the **Qin Dynasty** (221-206 BCE) of the self-styled *'First Emperor'* in 221 BCE. Qin Shihuangdi grandly styled his name on Huangdi, the Yellow Emperor of prehistory, and ruled the freshly unified China with such cruelty that all scholars and regents of the future cursed him. In the process, he instituted a great book burning, buried scholars alive and worked malcontent intellectuals to death in his grandiose building projects. The First Emperor believed that excessive punishment is the best form of government. He simply executed scholars who bored him with old histories and reminded him to cultivate virtue. To everyone's relief the First Emperor died at the early age of 49, after governing united China for a mere twelve years, and was buried in a megaolmanic mausoleum. He was followed by an incompetent son and a crafty minister who thought that harsher laws might be an improvement. They simply resulted in rebellion, and the dynasty came to a sudden end. The Qin Dynasty left behind a range of major tourist attractions and the exciting idea that a unified China could be created and maintained by centralised administration. The **Han Dynasty**. (206 BCE-220 CE) went to great lengths to revive the traditional values. Under the Han, virtue became important again. More so, many thinkers were trying to compose an ultimate state-philosophy by blending Confucianism with Daoism. It was a great period, when the grand idea of a centralised China was aligned with the tatters of the histories and virtues of the past. Scholars went to great lengths to compile lost books and documents, or to make them up for the very best reasons. Most of the earlier literature of the Zhou period was thoroughly edited at this time. Sima Qian, the grand historian of the Han, composed the first proper history of China, and remarkable linguists compiled the first Chinese dictionaries, like the famed *Shuowen Jiezi*, that structured and unified Chinese writing and did much to gloss old and obscure terms. In the process, the scholars created a version of the past that was great propaganda and slightly remote from reality.

So much for a very brief look at the Three Dynasties and the dynasties that followed. The first (Xia) is mythical or not properly discovered, the second (Shang) left a huge amount of inscriptions on oracle bones and some bronze vessels, while the third, the Zhou, did the history writing and left behind a wide range of classical books proving beyond doubt that virtuous Zhou regents had been justified in overthrowing the Shang. They also recorded tales, documents and speeches which allegedly dated from earliest proto-history. Maybe some of these items contain ancient lore and history. But certainly a lot of other things were reconstructed, transformed or simply invented for the sake of political correctness.

Our topic is early China. We have early Chinese documents from the Shang, early Chinese histories, from the Zhou and Han, and early Chinese myths of uncertain age recorded during the Zhou or Han, or even later. What you find in this book is a combination that encompasses material from all periods. There is archaeology, good, trusty, reliable but always open to discussion and never complete. Archaeological evidence is a matter of luck. You can discuss what has been found, but you will never be sure what remains undiscovered or happened to be lost. Such as nuclear powered mobile phones, neutrino generators and flying pyramids. Sure, they are not likely. But unless we uncover every square inch of Chinese soil to a depth of at least a hundred metres we can't be sure. Like it or not, it's impossible to exclude anything. Early history has less to do with facts than with estimating probabilities. Worse yet, when little has been found, scholars tend to believe that these fragments are especially important. Simply because they are the only ones they have. Lack of evidence invites generalisation. It's a very human thing.

As far as we know at the moment (and I hope this is wrong), neither the Yangshao, the Longshan nor the hypothetical Xia people left us any written documents.

The Shang did. On their bronze vessels, rare inscriptions appear. Sadly, they are exceedingly short and not very helpful. At the same time, an enterprising monarch, King Wu Ding, ordered that all divinations had to be recorded. In those days, divination was made by exposing shoulder blades (scapula) of cattle and belly plates of turtle shells (plastrons) to heat. A ritual was performed, a question asked (or a statement made) and when the item cracked, the shape of the crack provided affirmation or denial. Later, the bone or shell was carefully inscribed and stored away. Eventually, thousands of these documents ended up carefully stacked in pits. While divination records were an everyday manner for the Shang, the scholars of the Zhou were hardly aware of them. By the Han period, the entire corpus of oracle bone writing was forgotten. Fragments of inscribed bone and shell turned up from time to time. They were traded to apothecaries, who sold them as **Dragon Bones**. Crushed to powder, the dragon bones were sure to settle queasy stomachs.

Unlike the contemporary inscriptions of Egypt, Mesopotamia and elsewhere, the oracle bone inscriptions give an honest picture of history. It's a partial account, as it only deals with matters of divination. However, it does not contain inventions or deliberate falsification, nor is there glorification of regents or propaganda. Luckily, King Wu Ding was an enthusiastic supporter of divination. He employed more than fifty diviners and ruled for a long time. We know more about him and his court than about most regents of the Bronze Age. So far, so good. But when you look at the single divinations or characters you will find plenty of open questions. Often, inscriptions are abbreviated, many characters are unidentified, and neither grammar nor spelling were standardised. Often, a given inscription can be read in several ways, and generally is. Those who read the bones live an exciting life at the very edge of the unknown.

And finally there are the books of the Zhou historians. Around the year 800 BCE, Zhou scholars began to record history. Or maybe they did so earlier and we simply don't have copies of their work. Be that as it may, by the Warring States period they not only documented their own time but also copied or invented documents of much earlier times. Some of these works survived the ages, but a lot of others were re-assembled from fragments by the historians of the Han Dynasty around the first century BCE. These texts are our best sources for early myth and legend. They purport to be factual and had a status much like holy writ for the last two millennia of Chinese history. But as you'll soon see, much in them disagrees with the archaeological record and the oracle bones. Essential elements of Shang life were completely unknown to the Zhou historians. Some contemporary scholars, especially in the West, are so distrustful of the Zhou classics that they prefer to ignore them. Others, especially in China, believe that there are genuine ancient elements hidden in them, and that we should carefully judge each item for its quality. I very much agree. For this reason, though this book is focused on the Shang period, you will find a lot of Zhou, Qin and Han time material in this book. You will find speculation, questionable mythology, hypothetical reconstruction and a lot of anachronism. Some items will be useful to illustrate life and ritual in the Shang world. Other pieces will be way off the mark. When we try to understand early cultures we are bound to make mistakes. I am sure this book contains plenty, and hope they are interesting ones. However, asking stupid questions and making errors is hard work and, much as I want to, you can't expect me to get everything wrong. It would be nice if you could get a few things wrong, too, for the only way to avoid errors is to hide under the bed and turn the brain off.

Prehistory is not just the study of old cultures. Some believe that research should yield facts and that scholars are paid for being right. Sure, it's nice to be moderately certain once in a while. However, the more you know the more you will realise how little you know for certain. Perhaps you will come to appreciate the value of questions. In this sense, each ancient culture acts like a mirror for our own time. You can look at the Shang and you will learn a lot. But you can also look at yourself looking at the Shang, and look at yourself looking at yourself looking at the Shang. There is so much to be discovered. You can discover a fascinating Bronze Age culture with unique ideas about religion, reality and the world at large. You can watch the seeds of culture sprout and grow, and marvel how people's thinking transformed in the process. The late Shang culture is characterised by remarkable changes between intense devotion, wild ritual, excessive divination and the development of organised and bureaucratic religion and statecraft. During the Yin period, religion and society transformed again and again. It's a story full of drama and excitement. As you explore the ruins of the Yin and the oracle bone inscriptions, you will come to know the kings and queens personally. They were formidable people, and terrifying ancestors, and in a sense they are still very much alive. You can also discover how you react to various types of religiosity, meet some of the earliest deities in evidence, and find out how a magnificent beautiful script suits itself to writing, divination, meditation and ritual.

To ensure that you understand some of the basics of early religion practically, this book includes exercises in meditation, visualisation and divination. It's an anachronistic approach, as the Shang did not leave written records about their meditative rites, their celestial flights, their meetings with ancestors and gods. However, practice will allow you to understand the mindset of people for whom ritual and magic were of overwhelming importance, and supply you with tools to contemplate Shang culture in depth. I would like to offer two invitations. One is for my usual readers, many of whom are practically involved in trance and ritual of various sorts. Here is a chance to get a glimpse at ancient religion and ritual, and at a world that was totally dominated by the otherworldly ones. It is also a journey through the evolution of spirituality and an opportunity to give scientific research and scholarly studies a chance. A few centuries ago, magic was still a branch of the academic world. It was studied at famous universities, like Cracow (where the historical Dr. Faust got a degree), Vincennes near Paris, Salamanca, Toledo and Bologna. There is a lot that ought to be shared between those who study and excavate, and those who explore consciousness and practically interact with the spiritual world.

The other invitation is for all those wonderfully dedicated oracle bone scholars whose work has provided the foundation for this book and for the coming generations of sinologists, archaeologists and historical ethnologists. Your studies are an excellent approach to the Shang. As you know, the Shang themselves had a mindset that was far from academic. Many of them were extremely religious and dedicated their lives to meditate between ancestors, deities and the people. Are you serious enough about your work to explore meditation, trance and divination practically?

Ouroboros Images from the Hongshan culture (3500-3000 BCE) Longshan Culture (3300-2100 BCE) Shijiahe culture (2500-2000 BCE) and the Shang (bottom right, from Fu Hao's tomb)

Taotie Designs 1

Chaotic Beginnings

In the South Sea dwelled an emperor called Brief. In the North Sea was the emperor Sudden. In the Middle World was the emperor Hundun (Primordial Chaos). Once in a while the emperors of the north and south met in the central realm and were entertained with great virtue (de) by Hundun. The two wondered how they could repay the virtue. They said *'all humans have seven apertures through which they see, hear, eat and breathe. Hundun is the only being which has none. Let's go and bore some.'* Every day they made another hole and on the seventh day, Hundun died.

This true story appears in *Zhuangzi* (ch. 7). It shows how the undifferentiated chaos of the beginning disappeared once there were separate senses to sort out the world. Here, separation implies order. By literally *'making sense'*, the grand unity of the ancient chaos came apart. While we won a lot when we learned to tell one thing from another, we also lost our simplicity. It may give you an idea why so many Daoists close their mouths, eyes and senses in order to return to the state of the primal chaos. They shut up, introvert and return to primordial simplicity in the realm of no-difference. For chaos is the world in potential, it is the great creative unity out of which the ten thousand things appeared. When you enter this indescribable state, you lose your shape, your face, your name and nature. But you also attain a highly magical consciousness from which you may transform the world of names, shapes and appearances. By going inwards you leave the outside, and transform it from within.

It's a magical metaphor, now for a psychological one. Think of a really young baby. Or better yet, remember what life was like when you were freshly born. You had no words in your mind. Shapes held no meaning. You did not know that the wriggly things at the ends of those long things were fingers and toes. Nor did you know they were yours. You could not tell the difference between sound and sight and feeling. You couldn't tell the difference between close and far away. You didn't know how to estimate time. All was sensation. Some of it was nice and some made you cry, but in either case you could not understand how or why. Loud sounds startled you, rhythmic movements soothed you. Singing and dancing were fascinating. Digestion was hard work and not much fun. And if it were not for the deeply rooted instinct to respond to faces, preferably with laughter, we all might have given up then and there.

Well, if the Hundun state resembled that of a baby, the Dao corresponds to the fact that someone was there for you. Someone looked after you, fed you, cleaned you, offered warmth and company and laughter. Maybe the Daoist who returns to the simplicity of the Hundun enjoys the state where the universe acts like a mother. It's a charming thought, for essentially, all is really whole.

Laozi had a similar idea. Or rather, it was the person or persons who wrote the *Laozi* around the third or fourth century BCE. Their thinking was very poetic and abstract. Unlike Zhuangzi, who loved sarcasm and weird humour, the *Laozi Daodejing* reflects Daoist thought in its primal purity. Let's have a passage on the beginning. First the standard version recorded by Wang Bi, which everybody has been reading since the early third century:

"There was something fused and structured
before Heaven and Earth were formed.
Tranquil and empty
it remains independent, unchanging,
turning the Universe without ever tiring,
regard it the Mother of All Under Heaven.
I do not know its name,
so I call it the Dao" (25)

Here's the much earlier and somewhat shorter version of the Mawangdui manuscripts. These texts, inscribed on silk, were excavated in 1973. They date sometime before 168 BCE:

"There is a thing
completed in Chaos
alive before Heaven and Earth.
What silence, what emptiness!
It remains alone and does not change,
it can be Mother of Heaven and Earth.
I do not know its name.
They call it Dao." (69)

The term Dao has a wide range of meanings. It is generally translated as way, approach, method, system, meaning or even speech. All of these are correct, and each of them is too limited and partial to reflect the amazing totality of it. If taken for *'way'* it can imply a path, a road or, much better, a water way. We are on dangerous ground here. As Sarah Allan shows, the term *'way'* is full of associations that are far from early Chinese thought. *"We tend to find something on the road, be it God or ourselves. The dao, however, has no connotations of spiritual encounter or self-awakening. It is a course that one follows naturally. A person does not encounter God or the inner self by following the dao, but fulfils his highest potential as a human being."*(1997:68) Western mysticism and religion emphasise the way as a journey through life. They make much of pilgrimage, of choosing the right way, of

30

undergoing danger, tribulation, suffering and ordeal. In Western thought, the way implies choice and effort. By contrast, the Dao is a flow. It is not a single way but every way, and all beings and things follow it naturally. Laozi compared the Dao with flowing water, and in the stone ages, long before roads were made, long distance journeys were often made by boat. It was a lot easier than struggling through tangled forests, wading through swamps or plodding along muddy tracks. Water is supremely magical. It moves effortlessly along the way of least resistance, it relaxes into its path, it fills every hollow and cavity, it feeds the ten thousand beings and things, it moves past and through all obstructions, it clears up naturally by becoming still, it reflects everything without judgement or interference and merges in rivers, streams and the great ocean by following its inherent nature. Water evaporates, water moves invisibly through the air, it moistens like dew and pours like rain; it disappears in the underworld, travels through the dark realm of the dead and reappears from the nine springs in fresh glory. When earth formed, water was trapped within the atmosphere. Hardly any of it disappears. The water you see in a spring or pool has been around since the beginning. It has moved through lichens, plants and fungi, through animals and people, through rivers and oceans, it has rested in ice and moved along the airways. In each glass of water are molecules from all rivers and seas that ever existed on earth. Trilobites swam in it, dinosaurs lapped it up, mammoths walked through it. Each glass of water contains molecules that moved through every single person who lived before the Renaissance and of many who came later. Taking a drink you share with everyone. Like dragons, water is a miracle. It has been everywhere and has experienced everything. In practical magick, water is easily charged with any consciousness and feeling you like. As a symbol, it is a perfect representation of One Consciousness.

We are exceptionally lucky that in 1993 an even earlier version of the *Laozi* was discovered. This one, called the *Zhujian Laozi* (Bamboo Strips Laozi) came from a tomb at Guodian in Hubei and dates from sometime around 300 BCE. This version is much shorter than the standard text, its arrangement is somewhat questionable as the bamboo strips were partly rotten and not in their proper order, and finally, it shows some significant differences from the later versions. With regard to early cosmology, the famous line

"The things of the world arise from being, and being comes from non-being"

can alternatively be read

"The things of the world arise from being, and they arise from non-being."

It is such a major difference that not all Daoist scholars are happy about it (see Henricks 2000: 77).

More surprising is an addition to the *Laozi* which is completely absent in later literature. It's the *Taiyishenshui*, a brief text which details how Taiyi, the Great One, or Great Unity, made the cosmos appear. Let's have a look at this. Our text does not tell us how everything began. It starts with Taiyi, the Great One, who gives birth to water. Water, released from the all-inclusive unity, emerges and returns to it. Water assists the Taiyi, and their union creates Heaven. Heaven emerges, expands and returns to Taiyi to assists it, which creates earth. Now the elements of the world have enough substance to get along on their own. Heaven and earth assist each other repeatedly, and this creates the gods above and below. The gods above and below assist each other; which creates yin and yang. Next, yin and yang assist each other, which produces the four seasons. The seasons assist each other, which results in cold and hot. Cold and hot assist each other, this creates moist and dry. Moist and dry assist each other and they create the year. This is the last stage of emanation and completes the world, and a cycle of manifestation.

"This being so, the Great One is concealed in water and moves with the four seasons. Completing a cycle (it starts) over again; (we regard this beginning as) the mother of the ten thousand things. .."

Here, earliest (surviving) Chinese myth shows some independence from the classical Daoist teachings recorded in the next centuries.

Strangely enough, it is very close to ancient Sumerian myth, where everything begins with the goddess Nammu, who is the primordial water which contains everything in its chaotic, surging, swirling, all-inclusive flow. Out of this cosmic ocean arises the cosmic mountain. The cosmic mountain implies the idea of height and depth. It separates, its upper half becomes the god An (Heaven) and its lower half becomes the goddess Ki (Earth). Out of their union, the god Enlil (*'Lord Air'*) is born. Enlil separates the two deities. An rises upwards, where he creates his attendant deities, the Anunnaki, while Enlil and his mother create the phenomena that constitute the planets, landscapes, animals, plants, people, and everything needed to start civilisation. Any Sumerian could have told you that earth floats over a watery abyss. Indeed, the word abyss derives from the Sumerian word abzu, the primordial watery realm deep below the earth where the great secrets and cosmic laws are guarded by Nammu's son, the lord of water, Enki, priest and shaman of the gods. (S.N. Kramer, 1981:81-83 & 1972: 72-75; Leick, 2003:12-16). What you just read is the earliest recorded cosmogony and dates around 2500 BCE. If the proto-Sumerians, as is likely from their peculiar non-Indo-European and non-Semitic language, entered Mesopotamia from Central Asia, it might be possible that they once had contact to the people who became the Chinese. The early Chinese myths agree with the Sumerians that there is a watery realm deep under the earth. The Chinese called it the Yellow Springs, and identified it as a or the realm of the dead. Under the heavy ochre soil, the secret watercourses flow and the sun makes its passage from west to east. Common roots or cultural crossover? In the thousands of years between the Sumerians and the early Chinese mythmakers, all sorts of myths got around.

Let's return to the Taiyi. The Great One is a basic principle of Daoist literature and often equated with the Dao. It is also frequently used as a synonym for the Hundun. Indeed, Great Unity and Primordial Chaos have a lot in common. If you think of it as a unifying principle it appears as one being, one consciousness, one all-ness, but when you examine the contents of this vast, all inclusive continuity it appears chaotic and overwhelmingly incomprehensible. Much depends on your point of view. If you look for sameness, you behold the Taiyi, if you search for difference, say welcome to the Hundun. It's a perceptual choice. You can observe it, right here, as you go for a walk on planet earth.

Both Taiyi and Hundun may be vast and cosmic, but this does not mean that we are only dealing with abstractions. As you'll read soon, the Hundun also appeared as a sack like, yellow, winged, dancing entity without a face. Well enough, the Taiyi appears on a picture from tomb 3 of Mawangdui. The painting is badly damaged (see Allan and Williams 2000:164). Taiyi is in the company of the gods Leigong (Lord Thunder) and Yushi (Rainmaster), who stand beneath to either side of it. It has a human body, a red face, and red legs, zigzaging horns or antlerlike emanations emerge from its head, arms which might be slim wings and possibly, as Henricks proposes, a mouth that could be a birds beak. Henricks sees antlers as a symbol for a dragon. In his opinion, the combination of dragon and bird goes back to the imagery of the Shang. Now I'm not so sure about antlers being a symbol for dragons, as they are primarily a symbol of deer. The dragons of Shang imagery do not necessarily exhibit any. More often dragons and birds appear in company with each other. And of course the taotie monsters have characteristics of both, and any other animal conceivable. So we have the Taiyi as an abstract principle and as an anthropomorphic personification. Whatever sort of hybrid creature the Taiyi may have been, in the Warring States and Han periods the term also referred to a number of stars and constellations. All of them were close to Polaris and sections of Ursa Minor and Draco. The exact location seems to have shifted due to the precession of the equinoxes. In short, the Taiyi may have been a term for the centre of heaven. Here, it occupied the same position as the Shang Di, the highest god/s of the late Shang period.

In the main text of the *Laozi*, the concept of Taiyi is absent. There is reference to yi, as the One, but not to the specific form Taiyi. However, the term appears in the very early Daoist chapters hidden in the *Guanzi*, which date from the middle of the fourth century BCE. Here we are on ancient territory. The fourth century BCE was the period when Daoism was disentangling itself from what generally may be termed shamanism. Unlike the later *Laozi, Zhuangzi* and *Huainanzi,* these core texts were primarily concerned with self-cultivation. Political ideas and sage advice for rulers are still absent. Indeed they may be among the first manifestations of Daoist practice in written history. (Roth 1999). The Taiyi is also mentioned by Lü Buwei in the *Lüshi chunqiu* (midsummer chapter) and in the *Liji* (chapter *Li yun*). Both references are to the origin to the world, but neither of them contains the idea that the first emanation is water, which I for one find a useful thought. Hydrogen is one of the essentials if you want to assemble a universe and develop life. Another idea that seems to have faded is the notion that some gods were responsible for creating yin and yang. It appears in a passage of the *Huainanzi* (see below), but otherwise, early Daoist literature does not seem to have been overly keen on deities. Maybe the idea that upper and lower gods could produce the primal energies of the cosmos was too close to earlier wu *'shamanism'*.

However you look at it, Daoist cosmogony does not appear as a unified theory but as a range of original visions which were later streamlined and simplified. And while the importance of water as a primal manifestation disappeared, it still remained a favourite metaphor for the Dao.

Here is another early Daoist model of the beginning. It comes from the *Tianwen* (*Heavenly Questions*) of the *Chuci*, an enigmatic song dating between fourth to second century BCE:

"Who can reveal the beginning of things in earliest antiquity?

How can you know what existed before heaven was formed above and earth was formed below?

Who can explore the murk before darkness and light were divided?

What can you tell of the chaos of formless preconception?

What is darkness? What is light?

How did yin and yang unite?

How do they create things and how do they transform them?

The sky is round and has nine gates,

whose compass measured them and who created them in the beginning?

What connects the ladle and the measuring line,

who has erected the axis?

Where do the eight pillars support heaven,

and why does it tilt to the southeast?"

Liu An, king of Huainan (180-122 BCE), assembled scholars favouring Daoist thought (plus extras from other philosophies) and complied the amazing *Huainanzi* around the year 139 BCE. He was certainly familiar with the *Heavenly Questions*, and his account of creation reads much like a direct answer to them.

"When Heaven and Earth were yet unformed,
All was ascending and flying, diving and delving.
Thus it was called the Great Inception.
The Dao began in the Nebulous Void.
The Nebulous Void produced spacetime;
Spacetime produced the primordial qi.
A shoreline (divided) the primordial qi.
That which was pure and bright spread out to form Heaven,
The heavy and turbid congealed to form Earth.
It is easy for that which is pure and subtle to converge,
But difficult for the heavy and turbid to congeal.
Therefore Heaven was completed first, and Earth fixed afterwards.
The conjoined essences of Heaven and Earth produced yin and yang."

(*Huainanzi* 3, 1-13, translation John S. Major).

As the *Huainanzi* is not an entirely streamlined work, it contains several references to this primordial process. Here is a quotation from Anne Birrel's magnificent *Chinese Mythology* (1993:32):

"Long ago, before Heaven and earth existed, there were only images but no forms, and all was dark and obscure, a vast desolation, a misty expanse, and nothing knew where its own portals were. There were two gods born out of chaos who wove the skies and designed the earth. So profound were they that no one knew their lowest deeps, and so exalted were they that no one knew where they came to rest. Then they divided into Yin and Yang and separated into the Eight Poles."

From these appeared the hard and the soft, and they, in turn gave rise to the myriad of things. Please observe that this cosmogony involves two gods. It would be nice to know which ones.

Another early writer, Lü Buwei (Midsummer, chapter 2) gives a brief synopsis in a text entitled *Great (Classical) Music*. His book dates around 239 BCE:

"The origin of music lies far away. It appears out of due measure and has its origin in the Tai Yi. The Tai Yi generated the two poles, the two poles generated the forces of the dark and the bright. The forces of the dim and the bright transformed; one rose to the height, the other sank into the depth; they united, moving in waves and surges and formed the material shapes. When they are separate, they reunite; when they are united they separate once more. This is the eternal motion of Heaven. Heaven and Earth are

moving in a cycle. On every ending a new beginning follows, on every excess follows reversion." (after Wilhelm's German translation, 1979:56)

Several of these accounts have a cosmogony without the activity of any creator deity. The universe simply happens. Things develop naturally when given a chance to do so. Nor is there a real beginning. There is simply an incomprehensible, nameless state of chaos, and we don't read where it came from. Perhaps it was always here. As it was undifferentiated, it existed outside of time and space, and far beyond human comprehension. But we have more than the attempt of Daoist cosmologers to explain the beginning of it all.

Daoist thought is practical. It shapes itself on natural processes, but it aims at a transcendence which is nameless, undefined and undifferentiated. The primal chaos is not just the beginning but also the goal of Daoist effort. Provided we can speak of origin and goal when the whole crazy muddle has neither beginning nor end.

The Hundun, like the pre-create universe, goes beyond what you may think or say about it. It is original awareness, and the aim of plenty of Daoist meditation. Now there are a wide range of techniques various adepts employed to attain this formless state. Some pioneers favoured starvation, drugs, practised minimal (*'embryonic'*) breathing, introverted, emptied the heart (mind) or used complicated rituals to exteriorise the spirits (faculties of consciousness). They shut their eyes, closed their ears, ate little, breathed lightly, relaxed and allowed awareness to sink into the belly. They forgot the world, forgot themselves and dissolved in the primal formless emptiness of the central void. And this void is not just empty. The void within the empty body is your self. Like the Hundun, it contains everything in potential. Within the emptiness, whole universes revolve. And from the core of central chaotic formlessness, new shapes are born all the time. By going within you can transform the outside world. At this point, what looks like a mystic return to lost unity, the process reverts and changes the world by magic. For when you return from the primal beginning, the whole wide world is new and fresh for you. You see things as you never saw them. You think fresh thoughts without the clutter of knowledge, history and habituation. You enjoy the very simple things which make life so delightful. And you carry in your heart/mind a wordless wisdom which transforms the people whom you meet. Here mysticism becomes magical.

All these methods, plus a huge range of complicated visualisations favoured by later generations, are simply means to return to the Hundun. The primordial Chaos, the Mother of heaven and earth, the Dao, are all approximations for an awareness which does not suffer from limitation, strain, worry or old age. As sage-poet Han Shan (7th century?) in his mountain solitude expressed so beautifully

"How happy we were in the age of Hundun (Primordial Chaos)
we needed no food nor did we piss.
Who came after us with a drill,
to equip us with nine apertures?
Day after day we have to eat and dress,
and worry over taxes every year,
a thousand of us fighting over a small coin,
knocking our heads together, screaming loud."

Yes, there is something comforting to the Hundun. It's certainly simpler than everyday life on Planet Idiot. The Daoists loved it. They recalled (or imagined) a time of pure, natural chaos when things were much simpler than today. *Huainanzi*, chapter 2 (quoted by Girardot, 1988:268) says that the people of the Hundun period *"did not know directions. They ate and wandered about in complete freedom, drumming their bellies and rejoicing."*

Of course such visions of Paradise Lost did not find the favour of the Confucians. In a biting passage of the *Zhuangzi* (12), Kongzi (Confucius) assures a student that *"As for the arts of Mr. Chaos* (Hundun), *you and I need not bother to find out about them."* (trans. Burton Watson, 1971:136).

But just how old are such cosmologies? Here, the answer is not very satisfying. Whether the Xia or Shang told such tales remains unknown. However, both had great regard for water. The Xia people are often characterised as being fond of watery symbols, such as dragons, fish, toads. According to the Zhou scholars, their most highly esteemed ritual drink offering was *'black wine'*, i.e. water drawn at midnight from a well. Shang symbolism was more concerned with solar and fiery motifs, but as the oracle bones and the many tomb goods show, they favoured ritual washing and ritual baths, and dedicated many sacrifices to springs, and rivers. The yin and yang concepts, in their Daoist form, were invented during the Zhou period. The character for qi had several entirely different meanings. The Shang used it to write *'to ask, to ask the gods'*, *'to receive, to take'* and *'finishing, completing'*. Its image seems to show horizontal motion, maybe the flow of the winds as they move clouds and fogs. It was many hundred years later that the literati attached it to such ideas as *'primal essence'*, *'cosmic stuff'*, *'basic substance'*, *'subtle energy'*, *'breath force'* or *'vitality'*. Qi became one of the most complex ideas of Chinese thought.

When we look at the Hundun, there is something ancient and weird lurking behind the serenely abstract appearance. Maybe the Daoists reinterpreted an elder deity called Hundun when they made up their refined cosmology. Zhuangzi was closer to this than the abstract philosophers. For in the *Shanhaijing* (c. 3 century BCE) we read about a very different Hundun:

"Three hundred and fifty leagues further west is a mountain called Mount Sky. It has a great amount of gold and jade, and green male-yellow. There is a god here who looks like a yellow sack. He is scarlet like cinnabar fire. He has six feet and four wings. He is Muddle Thick (Hundun). He has no face and no eyes. He knows how to sing and dance. He is in truth the great god Long River." (Book 2, ch. 3, translation Anne Birrell). Birrell's translation calls Hundun a *'god'*, but the original reads shen-niao, god-bird. It prompted Izutzu to propose that the Hundun symbolises a shaman in a feather-cloak (Girardot, 1983:82). Early Daoists were sometimes referred to as *'Feather-cloaked Ones'*, a term with a distinct shamanistic origin. But if the Hundun is the whole universe in its primal form, it is also a divine bird. This is not a contradiction. In Chinese religion, Heaven, Rain, Thunder, Lightning, Wind and so on can all be natural phenomena, abstract principles and still have an anthropomorphic statue standing in the temple. It makes communication so much easier.

As you'll read further on, the Shang traced the origin of their Zi clan to a dark and mysterious bird, out of whose egg their primal ancestor was born. More so, the Shang organised their ten-day week into *'ten suns'*, each of which appears prominently in late Zhou and Han art as a raven or crow. And to this day a three-legged raven/crow is the symbol of the sun, just as the three legged toad represents the moon. Shang art especially favours bird emblems, while their religion made much of the posthumous naming of each king and queen after one of the ten suns (or days). It might be proposed that the Hundun represents such a yellow or red sunbird, if it were not for its odd shape. Think of a faceless, yellow sack. It's not quite the picture of a popular deity or bird. N.J. Girardot compared it to the calabash, the bottle shape gourd. Brilliant! For one thing, there is a wide range of creation tales among Chinese minorities which relate how a primal couple survived a cataclysmic flood by floating in a hollow gourd. For another, gourds feature prominently in alchemical Daoism as they resemble the human body. A good bottle gourd has a huge belly and another sphere in the heart region, while the head is represented by the thin bit which is attached to the vine the gourd grew out of. Gourds, like the Hundun, look much like a sack and have a warm yellow colour. While normal people have used such bottle gourds to carry water or wine, Daoist sorcerers and immortals use them to carry pills of immortality, magical vapours, spirits or lucky bats. And when you study Daoist meditation, or, much better, actually do it, you will soon learn that much of it consists of getting into the depths of the gourd. You'll learn this in the practice section further on.

Top: Three Jade Tigers

Middle: One of the few naturalistic faces of Shang Art (Bronze). According to Hentze, the head is not a pendant but a face-sized mask.

Bottom: A large shovel for ceremonial purposes. Is this item connected with the character Bi and was it used to measure earth for the Earth altar?

Creation reconsidered: a Primal Giant

Long, long ago before the beginning of things, Heaven and Earth were one misty, fluent swirling chaotic mixture shaped much like a chicken's egg. It took eighteen thousand years for Heaven and Earth to divide. Yang energy, which is light and subtle, rose upwards, while yin energy, dark and heavy, sank down. In between, Pangu appeared. Pangu went through nine transformations every day, his head moved Heaven and his feet stabilised Earth. Each day the sky rose ten feet, Earth became ten feet thicker and Pangu grew ten feet. After another eighteen thousand years lofty Heaven had reached its highest limit, thick Earth had sunk to its deepest depth and an amazingly tall Pangu extended in- between. And the time of the Three Sovereigns began.

As you recall, they were the deities or intelligences of Heaven, Earth and the Middle World. When they appeared, they imposed order on the universe. You'll read about them soon.

But Pangu did not last forever. When he was dying, Pangu transformed. His breath turned into winds and clouds, his voice became thunder, the arms and legs fixed the four dimensions of space and the five sections of his body became the Five Sacred Mountains. His blood and sperm poured over the earth and formed the flowing rivers, his veins became roads, his flesh and skin turned into the rich ground of the fields, his hair and his beard became stars, the tiny hairs on his hide became trees and plants, his teeth and bones turned into metals and stones, his marrow transformed into jade and pearls, his sweat fell like rain and fertilised the world. And the insects in his flesh, exposed to the winds, turned into men and women.

This is how creation happened. It's a popular Chinese myth, compiled from the *Yi Wen Lei Ju* and the *Yi Shi*, but its age is enigmatic. Around the early third century the first written accounts appear. Compared to the earlier myths, it is pretty late. There is no trace of Pangu in the Shang oracle bones nor in the writing of the Zhou literati. And regarding the Pangu myth, a lot of conflicting interpretations abound. For one thing, though the Pangu story was recorded at such a late time, it still became the most popular creation myth for the Chinese literati. On the other hand, modern researchers tend to disregard it as a foreign import.

Myths and Literature

All of this is not entirely satisfactory. Perhaps we should take a brief look at mythology in general. People speak of *'Chinese Myth'*, *'Greek Myth'*, *'Nordic Myth'* and so on, as if these concepts were real and meaningful. They are not. Such terms are modern labels which we make up to discuss things. Take *'Greek Myth'*. The expression should read *'myths related by some people in what we nowadays term 'Greece' which happened to be recorded, a process involving literary refinement, editing and plenty of elimination, in a specific period, and which had the exceptionally good luck to survive.'* There is no such thing as *'Greek Myth'*. Nor is there *'Greek Religion'*. Greece was a melting pot of cultures. Out in the provinces, there may have been scores, if not hundreds of gods, cults and myths which never caught the attention of an educated city dweller. Hence, what could have been the widest range of Greek religious activity, out there in the illiterate countryside, may have long been forgotten. For what we find in Homer, Hesiod, Apollodorus and later in Ovid are refined and edited literary masterpieces. They were composed for an educated, cultivated audience. And they were streamlined in the process. Homer, whoever that may have been, composed highly refined poetry. Apollodorus tried to include all variations of a tale in his account, which makes the result a little less convincing. Hesiod used remarkable style to relate soap-operas. We can be happy that we have their works. Had their style and rendering been cruder, their books would not have been copied often enough, and would have disappeared long ago. But imagine our knowledge of Greek mythology without Homer and Hesiod! Or imagine *'North Germanic myth'* without Snorri Sturlason! We would be facing shards and fragments.

Now take a look at China. To begin with, what we consider *'China'* is a vague name covering a much greater terrain and a much wider range of cultures than ancient Greece. For another, early literature was produced and read by the literati and administrators who tended to live close to the court. Few of them had much interest in the customs of the countryside, let alone of different ethnic groups. Confucian scholars did not approve of myths they didn't make up themselves. And finally, we lost so much during the great book burning of Qin Shihuangdi. As a result, the amount of surviving ancient mythology is very small. It appears here and there, scattered through a wide range of books, and in many cases we cannot even be sure if an author was recoding elder lore or making up a distorted new version of it. Nor is it easy to date such pieces of myth. Maybe ancient China had its great mythmakers, but if they ever lived, their works have long been lost. Hence we are looking at a wide range of fragments. In one sense this is an advantage. Mythology is very much alive. Stories move around, they are told and retold, and they take different shapes in separate districts and distinct periods. Just look at the variations in the Gilgamesh songs as recorded by Sumerian scribes. Then, some centuries later, some great writers come along and compress the oral tales into one or two literary masterpieces. It ensures the survival of the tale, but in the process, a huge amount of variation is eliminated. When the Assyrian scholars fused the Sumerian *Gilgamesh* poems into a single epic work, they discarded a vast amount of fascinating material. And they gave us the illusion that their work, the *Epic of Gilgamesh*, was really popularly known in this single and enduring form. Chinese myth, lacking such a unifying literary rendering, is a lot truer to the many different things that people really believed.

Pangu's Relations

The Pangu story has some similarities to the Hundun tales. Out of an egglike something, a threefold world appears. You might wonder about the later Pangu stories, where Pangu appears as a horned, tusked giant who shapes the world by excavating valleys and heaping up mountains. He used hammer and chisel to knock the universe into its present shape. Seated on his high throne he lectured about chaos and order, until one fine day he had enough and simply disappeared.

Third or fourth century, sure enough. Maybe Pangu is a Chinese myth which only appeared in literature at a late date. Or maybe the tale was imported. Pangu really extended everywhere. And when you consider how wide Pangu spread, you can only marvel at the age of his tale. Think of Ymir, the primal giant of the *Eddas*, out of whose dead body the whole living world was created. The similarity is amazing. Ymir came to exist between the ancient glaciers of Niflheim (Home of the Fog) and the firestorms of Muspelheim (Home of Parched Earth), right in the centre of the Great Gaping Void, while Pangu appears in the middle of a yin / yang polarity. While the Icelandic tale moves the polarities sideways, to the north and south, the Chinese version divides between up and down. But for all that, the story is too close for coincidence. Now the *Eddas* give more detail than the Chinese tale. We read how Ymir brought forth children, and how Odin and his brothers killed Ymir and created the world out of the carcass, making mountains out of bones, oceans out of blood, forest of hair, clouds of brains and arranged the middle world right on the eyebrows of the dead giant.

And when we look at the countries between China and Iceland, other versions appear. One is the Babylonian tale how Marduk slew the Chaos-mother Tiamat. The story dates from sometime between 1500 and 1200 BCE, but the most complete version is the Neo-Assyrian form recorded in the Semitic Akkadian language during the reign of Assurbanipal (668-626 BCE), and from which I shall quote here. There are, however, indications that the Neo-Assyrian version is a retelling of much earlier material. Some (but not all) protagonists have Sumerian names. A parallel myth was told by the Assyrians, only that they replaced the Babylonian god Marduk with their own national god Ashur. Earlier Sumerian myth also provides several dragon fights.

"When up in the height Heaven was unnamed
and firm matter below had no name,
when Apsu, the primal, creator of all,
Mummu, Tiamat, mother of all beings,
with their waters combined and united,
when dry land was unknown and no swamp could be found,
when not a single one of the gods was alive,
nor any was named, nor fate was decided,
the gods were formed within the centre,
Lachmu and Lachamu came into being."

In the next lines more and more gods appeared, the seasons were ordered, and finally the gods came to an agreement and organised.

"They disturbed Tiamat, they scoffed about the guardians,
they confused the mind of Tiamat:
suddenly her omnipotence was taken away."

(after the German translation of Ungnad, 1921:27)

So the three primordial ones, Apsu, Tiamat and Apsu's messenger Mummu, wage war against the gods. Probably they are, as most scholars assume, the oceanic water (Tiamat) and the sweet water (Apsu). In the Sumerian prototypes of the story, the draconic monster is called Kur. Kur originally signified the dangerous mountains surrounding the fertile land of Sumer, and all the threatening foreigners, beasts and plagues which came from them. In this sense, Kur signified everything alien and dangerous. But Kur is also a name for the otherworld, the realm of the dead, the subterranean world and the void space between the crust of the earth and the lethal dark waters flowing beneath it. (Kramer 1981:154, 168-171 and 1972:76-83). In one song, Kur fights the god Enki by hurling the primal waters against his boat. In another, the slaying of Kur by the warrior-god Ninurta results in a flood of rising underworld waters which effectively block the flow of sweet water and destroy the entire arable land. In a third song, of which only fragments survive, the goddess of love, war and high heaven, Inanna fights against the Kur, and threatens to dry it up. Here, Kur appears as a mountain, a culture, and as a being whose throat the goddess attacks. It may remind you of the water symbolism we discussed earlier. Or, just as a guess, the embryonic fluids of the womb. Kur and Tiamat have much to do with the primordial waters.

But let us continue. In her rage, Tiamat, the Shining One, Mother of Chaos, spawns legions of dragons, poisonous snakes, basilisks, mad dogs, storm-winds, tempests, scorpion-men, fish-men, seagoats, altogether eleven breeds of chaos creatures, and raises Kingu to lead the battle. In the meantime the gods arm Marduk, the city god of Babylon, to fight against the Ancient Ones. There is an extended battle which ends when Marduk releases a devastating evil wind and follows up with a deadly arrow. It blows Tiamat to pieces, and Marduk leaps around, splitting her skull, tearing out her heart and offering her blood to the north-wind. The story ends with Marduk lifting one half of Tiamat's body *like a shell*, which becomes the sky, while the other half becomes earth. Out of Tiamat's eyes, the rivers Euphrates and Tigris are born, which make Mesopotamian civilisation possible. It goes on like this. Marduk puts sun and moon in their places, measures the year, gives habitations to the gods, assigns stars to them, and finally creates humans.

"Blood I will gather and bones I will add,
"I will raise mankind, Man be his name,
I will create him, will create man,
and dedicate him to the worship of the gods...
the ways of the gods I will change with wisdom,
equally worshipped, but divided in two parts (heaven and underworld)".

This is straight Sumerian thinking: humans were created to worship the gods.

Marduk blames Kingu for inciting Tiamat to war, cuts his veins open and bleeds him dry. The blood is used to fashion mankind. Then he graciously pardons the other chaos creatures. For the Babylonians this story related how it all began. But creation is never over. In the final verses Marduk is implored

"Like sheep he herds the gods,
he shall conquer Tiamat and shorten her life,
in the future of mankind, in the age of all time,
shall this remain binding, full of power without end."

May we assume that the Chaos Mother remained alive? And that you see her, feel her, hear her, smell her, eat her, each day you walk between heaven and earth?

It's an uplifting and exciting meditation. Go for a walk and enjoy your senses. Whatever you experience, say *'this is Tiamat, the Mother of Chaos. And she is very much alive.'*

This song contains many elements which you read about earlier.

But let us look further to the east.

Much closer to Ymir and Pangu, the *Ŗg Veda* (book 10, hymns 90 & 130) tells of Puruṣa, who was The Man, or maybe The Giant, but certainly the very first sacrifice. Puruṣa was born in the beginning of all things. It had a thousand eyes, a thousand feet, and pervaded the earth to all sides. Puruṣa who was all that had been and all that will be, who grew greater with food, was the very Lord of Immortality. The gods sacrificed Puruṣa, whose body became the four seasons, and the creatures of the earth, and the sacred chants and offerings. His mind became the moon and his heart became the sun. The sky was shaped out of his head, his navel formed the middle world, his feet became the earth. His limbs, his sense organs, his breath became the gods, and the classes of society.

This hymn dates around the ninth or eighth century BCE, a time when the seers of India were beginning to wonder about the beginning of things. They made up several distinct myths, just as the Chinese did. It's the same idea all over again, a great living unity divided for the sake of separate existence. For neither Ymir nor Tiamat, Puruṣa or Pangu ever really die. As long as the trees grow, as flowers blossom, as people and animals move across the land, as clouds fly, winds blow and the sparkling waves of the oceans come surging against the shore, the primal Chaos giant/ess is alive. We all partake of its essence. Though the great unity was divided it can be reunited. In your awareness, in your experience, as soon as you embrace every thing as your own vast self.

Greenwood Mysteries: Fuxi and Nüwa

Long, long ago dense forests covered the face of the earth. Animals moved stealthily through the vegetation, gibbons called, lizards sat baking on sunwarmed rocks and bamboo leaves rustled gently in the breeze. Strange colourful birds winged through the foliage, serpents slid through shady, tangled undergrowth and in the green forest pools, elephants bathed, trumpeting with delight. Rhinos sought fruit under shady trees, crocodiles dozed on the sandbanks of uncharted rivers, and spiders built webs of art and cunning, sparkling with dewdrops in the morning sun. It was the time before time-keeping, the age before the beginning of men.

In the centre of the primeval world, a huge mountain soared into the height. It was there, ages ago, and it still is. The mountain has nine levels and rises far above the clouds to the very centre of heaven. It is surrounded by a river of water, so soft that nothing can swim through it. Countless caves and grottoes, each of them a world in itself, cut like wormholes through the multi-coloured rock. And on the peak, framed by otherworldly blossoms, an azure lake shines upwards like an eye of heaven. Welcome to Mount Kunlun, triple peaked central axis of the universe, bridge between heaven and earth, foundation of tranquillity, source of timeless immortality. Here are the nine gates and triple peaks of the macrocosmic body.

In the time before, after and beyond time, Fuxi and Nüwa dwelled on Mount Kunlun. They were all alone, and as there were no others around, they wondered whether they should marry. But as they were brother and sister, they felt shy about the idea. So Fuxi and Nüwa ascended to the mountaintop to pray. They vowed *'If it is the will of Heaven that we should be husband and wife, the sacrificial smoke (or mist) shall rise narrowly entwined.*

45

Nüwa Transforming Seventy Times a Day

And if it is not permissible, may winds scatter the clouds in all directions.' Heaven entwined the rising smoke, and Fuxi and Nüwa married. As they still felt a bit shy, they wove grasses to make fans to hide their faces. Hence, in marriage rites, the bride used to hold a fan. It allowed her to hide her face or to avoid looking at her husband, if necessary. The custom is attested from the Han Dynasty and was at its most popular during the Tang. We find the marriage myth in the *Duyi Zhi* by Li Rong, a Tang Dynasty account of the ancestors of mankind.

Let's return to the early past when the world was young, fresh and unknown. Fuxi, otherwise known as Pao Xi or as the Green Emperor and his sister / wife Nüwa (Nügua, Nükua) have oddly reptilian and amphibian connotations. Nü means girl or woman, while gua or wa can be translated, depending on the writing of the name, as snail, frog or pond (Schafer, 1967:255-256). Both of them appear prominently in Han period art from central, southern and southwestern China. They are easy to recognise, as they have serpent bodies but human faces. Often, they appear entangled, just like snakes or snails in courtship, and a couple of times they form a trinity with the ancient shaman's goddess Xiwangmu. Shang oracle bones refer to a pair of serpents who may have been gods or extremely remote ancestors.

Fuxi and Nüwa may be the primal creative forces in early Chinese myth. Their magical tools are an angular ruler (the carpenter's square) and a compass, signifying the angular (earth) and the round (heaven). They are also frequently shown holding pieces of string. The string could be a reference to the strings involved in marriage symbolism (the god of love, residing in the moon, likes to tie lovers up with red string), but the string also appears in their much earlier myths. Fuxi and Nüwa were the first couple who measured the sky and the earth with compass and angle. This is one of the answers for the *Heavenly Questions* (see above). But their coiling also resembles the twists and turns of the DNA. Almost two meters of spiralling information, coded on atomic crystals so slim that it is almost two dimensional, in each of our cells. The double serpents get around.

Fuxi and Nüwa were there when it all began. Both are ancient gods, but maybe they did not start out as a couple. The earliest known texts refer to each of them separately. Contemporary scholars argue that they were two distinct deities who became connected during the Han Dynasty. I would propose that, given so many gaps in our knowledge, we have to be very lucky to draw conclusions from lack of evidence.

Here is something early. This little text comes from a commentary to the *Zhouyi* (otherwise known as *Yijing* / *I Ching*) entitled Dazhuan or Xicizhuan, the oldest surviving manuscript having been found in the grave library of Mawangdui. It dates around 195 BCE, but possibly earlier versions existed.

Scholarship used to ascribe this text to King Wen of Zhou (who definitely did not compose it) or to Kongzi, who is also an unlikely author. It has been claimed that Kongzi was fond of the Yijing, as he once said that, if he had another eighty years to live, he would devote them to *'the changes'*. The changes of what? Changes is yi, and the Zhouyi (Changes of Zhou) nowadays called the *Yijing* (Classic of Changes) were accordingly classed as a favourite interest of the sage. Sorry, but it's an unlikely story. Kongzi never referred to divination, nor was he likely to have approved of it. And even if he had a secret fondness for the topic, we wouldn't know what book he was talking about. In Kongzi's time, several versions of the *Yijing* existed.

The Culture Hero and the Creatrix

"When in early antiquity Pao Hsi (Fuxi) ruled the world, he looked upward and contemplated the images in the heavens; he looked downward and contemplated the patterns on earth. He contemplated the markings of birds and beasts and the adaptations to the regions. He proceeded directly from himself and indirectly from objects. Thus he invented the eight trigrams (bagua) in order to enter into connection with the virtues of the light of the gods and to regulate the conditions of all beings." (*Ta Chuan*, the *Great Treatise*, translation Wilhelm / Baynes, 1977: 328-329). Fuxi had a vision when he was walking on the banks of the Yellow River. He saw a striped dragon-horse emerging from the flood, which carried a diagram on its back. This was the famous Hetu, a chart ascribing numbers to the directions, which became fundamental to Chinese divination. Sadly, the earliest pictures of this chart date from the Song Dynasty. The *Great Treatise* shows Fuxi as a remarkable seer and visionary, a shamanic sage walking the earth, perceiving meaning in the signs of the universe. He structures his system on the natural, and the world speaks to him. Perhaps it might remind you of consciousness states when the entire world seems freshly formed, amazing, new and beautiful. When you look at a tree for the first time and see the qi flow in its growth. When the pebbles on the ground and the clouds in the sky are unique, impressive, perfectly arranged and amazingly meaningful. This is the beginning of awareness. Fuxi moved through the new world delighting in signs and significance.

The bagua, the eight signs of the *Yijing* were invented by Fuxi. They are a brilliant model of the world, the mind and all that moves between them. Due to his invention, the *Yijing* is occasionally called the *Xijing*, the *Classic of Fuxi*.

As you recall, there were no people around when heaven and Earth separated. But when things had settled, Nüwa was sitting there, in the damp green forests beneath the slopes of Kunlun Mountain, and no doubt she was beginning to feel bored. In her idleness she began to knead human figures out of the rich, yellow loess soil, the very earth which gave the name to the *'Yellow'* river, and allowed the northern Chinese civilisations to flourish. Loess is colourful, fertile and very sticky. Each little human began to breathe and move. Fascinated, the goddess made more and more. It was a difficult job and eventually she found herself exhausted. So she invented mass-production. She pulled a vine (or a string made of plant fibres) through mud and lifted it. The lumps of mud that flew from the vine also turned into men. The ones she carefully handmade from good yellow soil looked well shaped, and became rich and cultured people. And the ones who dropped from the vine and splattered into the vegetation were the poor and lowly. Says the *Tai Ping Yu Lan,* a collection dating from the northern Song Dynasty. The original account, however, comes from the latter Han Dynasty, and was composed by Ying Shao around the year 200. Once again, the vine (or string) might remind you of the DNA.

A fairly late tale says that she baked the first humans in an oven. The ones who came out too early where white, the ones who stayed inside burned black and only the people of the Middle Kingdom ripened properly and developed a beautiful tan.

While Nüwa people the world with little humans Fuxi gave them the crafts and skills for survival. It started the first world age. People lived in the wild, green forests and ate whatever they found. Unless it ate them first. Fuxi, the Green Emperor, decided to improve conditions. As a culture hero, he invented many things which have been with us for thousands of years. He taught how to build shelters, to make fire and to cook food. It improved digestion remarkably. He showed how string can be made from fibres, sinews and hide. Ge Hong (*Baopuzi*) tells us that Tai Hao (Fuxi) observed spiders and learned from them how to make nets. Tai Hao was originally an independent deity (the name means Great Brilliant Light) about whom very little is known. At the end of the Han Dynasty he became identified with Fuxi, indeed, Tai Hao became an honorary title of Fuxi. He invented knots of all sorts, the net, and even a script of knotted strings. And as string was one of his favourites, he also discovered bows and arrows and made the first string instruments. It might make you think of music bows, such as were played by Palaeolithic sorcerers, but Fuxi didn't always start simple. Allegedly he invented the very first guzheng. It had a huge rectangular wooden box, three meters long, and was equipped with 35 strings. Later generations thought that things can be improved by reduction, so the modern type is only 1.60m long and has a mere 21 strings. People learned to sew clothes and built boats to travel the waterways. But as they had barely transformed from purely instinctive animal existence, they did not know much about life. Fuxi and Nüwa gave them marriage ceremonies, taught groom and bride to give

Double Serpents

pieces of fur to each other and brought order and peace to humanity.

Fuxi is also closely connected to the invention of ritual. As the primary seer and diviner, he taught people how to relate with the gods and spirits and all the visible and invisible forces. More can be learned from his names. Fuxi's name was written with a range of distinct characters. Anne Birrell (1993:45) records:

"The most common is Fu Hsi, which may mean Prostrate Breath. There are also Fu Hsi, or Silent Sacrificial Victim; P'ao Hsi, or Kitchen Sacrificial Victim; Pao Hsi, or Embracing Breath; Pao Hsi, or Embracing the Victim; P'ao Hsi or Roasted Sacrificial Victim; and Fu Hsi, or Hidden Play..."

Sima Qian's descendant Sima Zhen, who lived around 720, summarised a lot of mythical material and several odds and ends about Fuxi. Like all scholars after the second century, he identified him with Taihao, but he also claimed that Fuxi's surname was Feng (Wind). This fits nicely with the names relating to breathing. *"He had a serpent's body, a man's head and the virtue of a sage."* Allegedly he was conceived after his mother accidentally stepped into the footprint of a giant (you'll find the same story told about the ancestor of the House of Zhou further on). The event happened at Thunder Lake. Like Green and Wind, Thunder is a reference to springtime: good symbolism, as Fuxi's period was the springtime of humanity. As the age was ruled by wood, east and spring, he made dragons his officers. As Sima Zhen tried hard to record serious history, he also claimed that Fuxi reigned eleven years and that his descendants bore the name Feng.

You probably noticed that this world needs a deity for computers. Fuxi is an excellent candidate. As you recall, he invented the eight signs of the *Yijing* when he studied the marks and signs of the animals. Each of the signs consists of three lines, which may represent the three levels of heaven, middle world and earth, as I proposed in *Living Midnight*. Each level is characterised by an open yin or a closed yang line. Welcome to the binary system. You meet it wherever things are digital. Later generations worked out combinations of the trigrams, and produced sixty four hexagrams, i.e. signs composed of six open or closed lines. Some enterprising shamans, sages or mathematicians invented an order of the sixty four hexagrams which shows them in a circular arrangement of the numbers 0-63 in binary order. They called it the Fuxi Arrangement. Much later, in backward Europe, Wilhelm Leibnitz (1646 – 1716) was struggling to invent binary mathematics. He thought they should be based on the numbers one and two, and didn't get anywhere. Hellmut Wilhelm relates that a friend of Leibnitz, Father Joachin Bouvet, who was a Jesuit missionary in Beijing, wrote that the Chinese had something that looked like binary maths, and sent a chart showing the Fuxi arrangement. Leibnitz was not aware of the *Yijing* nor did he know about Fuxi. However, when he examined the arrangement of the hexagrams he realised that the proper combination is zero and one. On this foundation, he tried to build a sophisticated calculation machine, employing balls that rolled through slots, and wasted his entire income on a device that couldn't be built by the craftsmen of his time. After his death, his family inherited a frustrating machine that didn't work and a huge amount of debts. It was the start of the computer industry.

Nüwa: World saviour

Nüwa is famous for her deeds during one of those floods. Every good story needs a cataclysm once in a while. It is said that there was a terrible battle in heaven when Gong Gong and Zhuanxu (the Black Emperor) fought for supremacy. Gong Gong (or maybe both of them) crashed against Incomplete Mountain. He, or they smashed the pillars which supported the sky. Heaven tilted dangerously to the north-west, while the earth became empty in the south-east (*Huainanzi* ch. 3). That's why all Chinese rivers eventually flow to the south-east. Maybe it was an accident and maybe it happened on purpose. The *Huainanzi* also alludes to the collapse of heaven in chapter 6. Here, you find all four supports of heaven collapsing, and a vast cataclysm shakes the earth. And you meet Nüwa, who saves the world.

Long ago, the four pillars of Heaven collapsed and the Nine Regions of Earth burst apart. Heaven could no longer cover the earth, and neither could the earth support all beings living on it. A devastating firestorm surged over the land and would not cease, a thundering flood followed and would not abate. Wild beasts devoured innocent people and violent birds seized the aged and the weak.

But Nüwa took gems of five colours. She melted them and mended the cracks in heaven. Then she cut the legs of a huge turtle and used them as pillars to support the corners of Heaven. She slew a black dragon, thus saving the people living in the central square (district) of the earth. And finally she built dikes of reeds (or their ashes) to dam the surge of the waves.

Heaven was repaired; the corners of heaven supported, the central plain saved, dangerous beast and birds destroyed and people resumed a peaceful life under the shelter of heaven. Even wild animals, birds, insects and snakes no longer dared to use their teeth or claws or toxic stings, as in their hearts they no longer desired to hurt weaker beings.

Nüwa's great success extended from the height of heaven to the depths of the yellow earth. Her name became famous through all later generations, and her blessing appeared everywhere. She rides in a thunder-chariot drawn by three dragons, one two winged and two hornless green ones, holding auspicious objects of life and death in her hands, sitting on a mat and surrounded by golden vapours. A white dragon is her vanguard and a snake flies in her trail. Coursing over the clouds she leads gods and ghosts to Ninth Heaven to meet Shang Di and dwell in tranquillity and silence. She does not show her achievements, she never displays her fame. She conceals the way of the sage in accordance with the motion of the universe.

What could be greater than this? Nüwa's deeds earned her a position in many tales, including the preamble of the magnificent *Dream of Red Mansions*.

Her myth blends many elements that are crucial to ancient myths. You get cataclysms of fire and water, reflection a time of chaos when yin and yang, out of balance, were threatening to destroy cosmic harmony. You have exorcistic elements, such as the rushes and reeds which were prominent sacred objects for at least two thousand five hundred years. Reeds were once used to wrap the sacred earth from the capital, which empowered a noble to govern a fief (*Shujing*). Then there are references to a time of paradise directly after the cataclysms are over. There is the huge turtle whose legs support the sky. It might be a memory from the Shang period, as Sarah Allan argued so convincingly. Another ancient element may be the idea that the flood surged all the way to Hollow Mulberry, a place of great significance to Shang myth (*Huainanzi* ch. 8). And finally Nüwa engages in heavenly flight, a magical trance technique favoured by many wu, Daoist sages, a few specially blessed kings and emperors, and a number of poets who went up and out to visit Shang Di, the Supreme Deity/s. To top it off and much in line with the *Huainanzi's* Daoist philosophy, you can observe that the great serpentine saviouress remains humble and modest and avoids the snares of honour and fame.

Of course many literati added to the tale. Some intuitively picked up on the fact that when Heaven is damaged (i.e. spirituality is inhibited), body hardens up or tenses in what Wilhelm Reich called character armour, an exoskeleton of cramped muscle restricting the ability to feel and pulse freely.

Li He, that wonderfully mad poet of the Tang Dynasty may have alluded to this effect, when he wrote

"Where Nü Gua smelted stones
to weld the sky,
Stones split asunder, sky startles, ·
Autumn rains gush forth."

(translation Frodsham, 1983:3).

It's a wonderful mantra to dissolve tension. Sometimes it's just essential to let go of effort, strain, ambition and to surrender oneself to the flow.

But Nüwa also had other myths, many of them recorded in such small fragments that their meaning is lost. The *Shanhaijing* hints that when Nüwa died, her guts transformed into ten gods, who went to live in the western wilderness. The gods are called Guts of Nüwa. Ten gods might be a reference to the ten suns of the Shang. But this is just silly old me guessing. For so much of the universal order started with chaotic transformation. As Guo Pu remarked in his commentary to the *Shanhaijing* (late 18th century), Nüwa was a great goddess, literally a Di. She transformed seventy times a day and her belly transformed into the ten gods. If the gods correspond to the ten suns and the ten days of the week, she is right at the beginning of measured time-keeping. And while her grave is allegedly in the western wonderland, there was also a grave of hers near the Yellow River. Schafer (1985:256) relates that the river flooded her grave during a violent rainstorm in 754. But her spirit did not rest. In the night, she appeared to the dreaming (future emperor) Su Zong. *"Her arms were scaly, and she carried a pair of carps. Later, the prince realized her identity because of a simultaneous apparition by the side of her tomb. On June 29 of 758 the tomb suddenly reappeared from the water, adorned with two willows. The court ordered official paintings to be made of this gracious scene."*

As far as dead gods go, this is pretty much alive. And to this day her birthday is celebrated on the 15th day of the third lunar month. Nowadays this is usually between April and May, the season of spring when the world has turned freshly green. The goddess is also associated with the hulusi reed organ. This is a gourd (o yes, a gourd again) from which bamboo pipes emerge. The reeds within the gourd produce a highly enchanting, magical drone. Such instruments have a long history. The Warring-States period Dian people of Yunnan left us a bronze gourd with holes for a set of reed pipes. Evidently, some musician was not satisfied with the easily available, but fragile bottle gourd any more. From the simple type with the bottle-gourd body, more sophisticated instruments such as the sheng pipes were developed. In 1780, a French missionary, Père Amiot, obtained several reed instruments in China and sent them to Paris. The local instrument makers picked up the principle, replaced the reeds with metal, and by the early nineteenth century, Europe was discovering a deeply enchanting sound that had previously been restricted to east Asia. Harmonium, melodicas and mouth harps are direct descendants of Nüwa's favourite instrument.

The Primal Pair

Finally, let's take a look at some myths which combine elements of the creation tales. Two are cited by Girardot, who quotes them from James Hillman (1968). The Hmong (also: Miao) people (Vietnam, Laos, Thailand, Yunnan) relate that long ago,

Heaven decided to punish mankind. A great flood surged over the earth. But Heaven sent a messenger to Fuxi and Nüwa, who found refuge in a hollow gourd. The gourd floated on the waves. It stranded them on Kunlun Mountain. Here, the two lived in complete loneliness. Bamboo stalks and the tortoise shell oracle told them to marry. Nüwa gave birth to a bloody mass (or a gourd) which Fuxi cut into pieces to form men.

The Zhuang Miao of Yunnan relate that after the great flood, only a single couple remained alive. They were called Mi Long and Tu Nyi, and were brother and sister. They asked heaven's permission to marry and brought forth a son called Hundun. He was like a piece of wood without a head or any orifice. The two chopped him up and threw pieces onto a peach tree, a willow tree, and onto other trees and objects. The next dawn there was smoke from heath-fires rising everywhere, for the two gods had made people.

A related tale, involving humans made from clay and a primal incestuous couple, is told by the Lolo of Yunnan. After much hesitation, brother and sister married. The sister gave birth to a gourd, which contained the first ancestors of the Lolo. They were an elder brother and a younger sister who had neither face nor shape. The deity Kedze gave them faces and hands. Then the elder brother became the sun and created day, the younger sister turned into the moon and made the night. (Prunner in *Die Religionen Südostasiens*, 1975: 143-144)

The Lisu of Yunnan have a similar tale. In the earliest antiquity, a brother and sister, both of them orphans, were warned by a flock of birds that a flood was coming. The two hollowed out a gourd and spent 99 days inside, being tossed about by the waves; until the birds told them they could safely come out. The waters had abated and they found themselves stranded on a mountaintop. But life on earth had changed a lot. There were nine suns in the sky which scorched everything, and seven moons which didn't allow the night to go dark. Everything was too hot and bright. To improve this situation, the two descended to the dragon king beneath the waves, from whom they obtained a bow and arrows, much against his will. They shot eight suns and six moons, and made life on earth much easier. Now they were left with an entire world all to themselves. The birds told them that they should marry. The two were much against this idea. But then they saw one omen after another, each of them insisting that their marriage was a must. Finally, they obeyed the will of heaven and became a couple. They had six daughters and six sons, who married. The couple which moved north became Tibetans, the couple who moved south the Bai. In the west are the Keqin, in the east the Han. Another pair followed river Nu and became the Nu people. Those who remained in the centre became the Lisu. (Miller 1994: 78-84)

Now perhaps these are ancient myths. All of them come from minorities living at the south-western fringe of the dominant Han civilisation. South-west China is the homeland of most myths relating to Fuxi and Nüwa. Up to the last century, Yunnan was a place that few Han Chinese would travel to. The emperors had some officials in the cities, who did much to spread Confucianism and control the Silk- and Tearoads, and with them came soldiers, administrators and traders. Their sphere of influence was mainly confined to urban areas. And when the emperors wanted to punish someone, they exiled him to the rugged south west, where strange cultures dwelled among towering mountains and fever-haunted jungles. To the Chinese aristocrats, the entire south was a dreaded land haunted by weird spirits and exotic diseases. This served the locals very well. They retained many of their ancient traditions intact. Nowadays, much of their heritage is celebrated and protected by the government. In Yunnan, you can find dozens of distinct cultures out in the country, and all of them are justly proud of their magnificent cultural traditions. Many of them have retained a form of animism and practice shamanic rites of some sort. And when you go for a walk in the forest or mountains, you discover little sacrificial sites at rocks, springs, lakes and trees wherever you go. At least I did. It made me feel very much at home. So perhaps the Miao and Lisu retained independent knowledge of some very ancient tales. But just as possibly, perhaps they were influenced by Han scholars who had read the odd book or two. Stories get around. Myth starts from word of mouth, is written (or laid) down as legend, and retold by word of mouth again. It happens all the time. The old can be new and old again. The reason that it happens, however, is that there is a substratum of magical truth to it. It's not a factual truth but one that makes sense.

But let us take another look at Fuxi. In southwest China, a wide range of nature spirits and deities have serpent shape. In Buddhist scriptures, these beings appear as Nāgas, Tibetan: klu, Naxi: lū-mun, Lolo: lo, Chinese: long-wang etc. The Naxi of Yunnan and Sichuan have five categories of these deities: ssu (serpents of the water), nyi (tree serpents), dtü (stone- and rock serpents), ssaw-ndaw (earth- and underworld serpents) and the lü (no information available). Chief of them is great deity who is called Shu (Ssu-ssü-szi). Shu is the god of wild nature, and just like Fuxi, he is half human and half serpent. In the Dongba religion of the Naxi, Shu is one of the greatest deities. North of Lijiang, an entire lake (Hei Long Tan, the Black Dragon Lake) is dedicated to Shu. Its crystal clear waters come streaming from the glaciers of Jade Dragon Range. As I learned at the Dongba museum and research institute, Shu is the brother of the deity who created mankind, (or, in some versions, Shu and mankind are brothers). It turned out to be a difficult situation. In Joseph

Rock's study (1952), Ssu-ssü-szi and the god Ts'o-zä-llü-ghügh were half brothers. They had different fathers but the same mother.

When, in elder times, the realms of the earth were divided, Ssu received the mountains, mountain meadows, and the responsibility for all wild animals. Ts'o received the fertile valleys between the mountains, the houses and all domesticated animals. Ts'o created mankind, but mankind was not content to stay in the lowlands between the towering mountain ridges. As soon as people roamed the mountains and forests, they began to cut plants, dig earth and molest wild animals. They hunted, cleared forests, built settlements and polluted the water. Their deeds disrupted the cosmic harmony and made the world ritually impure. Ssu would not bear this. He sent his minions, the small Ssu (a host of semi-serpentine nature spirits) to punish mankind. The small Ssu are troublemakers. They bring bad luck, poisonous animals, plagues, diseases, storms, floods and earthquakes. So nature and mankind waged war, and neither would grant peace. Then, maybe a thousand years ago, religious pioneer Dongbashiluo had a vision. He reformed the much earlier Dongba religion, invented rituals to harmonise life and uphold peace, taught the Naxi to respect nature, to keep damage at a minimum and to sacrifice to Ssu and all spirits of the world. Animals that have been killed by hunting are painted on wooden slabs and receive offerings, so that their essence can return to nature. Dongbashiluo is also famed for his alleged invention of the wonderful Naxi script, the last surviving hieroglyphical script on earth. So the Naxi made peace with nature, and Ssu grants them his blessing. Every year during the second lunar month, when spring is coming to the mountains, Ssu is venerated in a great ritual.

How closely is Ssu/Shu related to Fuxi? Apart from having serpent-shape and being brother of the deity who made humans? Just take a brief look at Naxi history. The Naxi ('Black Persons') belong to the Yi branch of the ancient Diqiang group. This relates them to the Qiang people. Some branches of the Qiang used to live in northern China, where they became the archenemies of the Shang people. They were nomadic sheep-herders who roamed around the Yellow River. The ancestors of the Naxi are distant relations, whose homeland was near Mount Kailash. Approximately two thousand years ago, they emerged in Yunnan. Moving south through Sichuan, they passed the Yalong, Anning and Yinsha rivers and settled at the edges of Yunnan, Sichuan and Tibet. To this day, the souls of dead Naxi follow the same route when they return to their ancestral homelands. It is not quite clear how the ethnic relationship is, but the Naxi believe themselves related to the Tibetans and the Ba people, with whom their language and mythology shows some similarity. Like the Ba, the Naxi believe that their creation involved several primal, incestuous couples. And when we look into the *Shanhaijing*, most of which assumed form during the later Han Dynasty, we find the Ba people in Sichuan tracing their descent from Tai Hao. At this time, Tai Hao had already become a title of Fuxi.

Nüwa is still venerated in modern Chinese temples. She is sometimes shown holding a child, for though she had none, she created mankind, and is hence empowered to make couples fertile. In some places, she has entire temple structures dedicated to her cult, such as in Shexian, Hebei, on the sheer Cliffside of Zhonghuangshan, the Mountain of the King of the Middle Realm.

But Fuxi and Nüwa also found a permanent place in San Huang Three Emperors Daoism, a form of ritual Daoism that remains especially popular in southern China. In this creed, which began to emerge around the middle of the Han, maybe two thousand years ago, the emphasis is on the first three sagelike thearchs, the first emperors of Chinas mythical prehistory. Fuxi, as the green, or more precisely blue-green emperor, was identified with the Emperor of Heaven, who dwells in the height but also in the head of the adept. Nüwa was turned into a man and became the Emperor of Earth (and the underworlds). Her/his realm is in the belly. The third is the Emperor of Mankind, Shennong, the Divine Farmer, whom you'll meet further on. His realm is in the heart. Another interpretation has Fuxi as Heavenly Emperor, Shennong as Earthly Emperor and Huangdi, The Yellow Emperor, as the Emperor of Mankind. When you stand before the statues of the three, you will find it hard to see a hint of their original appearance. As well dressed, courtly aristocrats they wear rich robes (green/blue, yellow/brown and red) and sit on lavish thrones, surrounded by a selection of popular local deities. Before them are offerings, incense sticks, bottles, vases full of plastic flowers and the odd statue of Guanyin for good measure. Not a sign of snake bodies, bull heads or tiger faces. But I recall discovering a beautiful wooden statue of primordial Fuxi in a corner of the grand hall of Golden Temple, near Kunming. Facing the elaborate and refined three worthies, this Fuxi looked like a wild man from the forest. Imagine a semi-nude man clad in a crude dress of leaves. Our culture hero had just invented clothes and was proudly exhibiting his creation. I sat down in front of the statue and tranced off.

Now round it off. What happens when you superimpose all these basic myth-types? What are their similarities? Far from being separate accounts, the versions seem to match each other admirably, and share a good many similarities. And while none of these versions can be directly traced to the Shang or early Zhou, their shared essence may have come a long, long way.

But let us also take a look at conflicting material. The *Liezi*, containing such a lot of divergent items dating from maybe the fourth century BCE to the fourth CE mentions Nüwa in book 5,1, recording that Nüwa collected colourful stones to repair Heaven, and broke off the legs of a giant tortoise to stabilise the sky. Well and good. But you also read that the Gong Gong incident happened after Nüwa's time. Not a bad idea, clearly, the author is referring to the two references in the *Huainanzi*. Now for a surprise: he also tells us that Nüwa was a man. It might be a writing mistake, or an entirely different tradition. But it is certainly perplexing.

The other reference to Fuxi and Nüwa appears in 2.18, which you'll read in the chapter on animal and divine transformations.

Let's take another look at the work of Sima Zhen, the eighth century descendant of the famous Grand Historian Sima Qian. In his late, Tang period account, Nüwa is also a man, who followed Fuxi on the throne. The two are not a couple; they are one king, and indeed one dynastic family, following the other. As we are still in the age of very plain woodland habitations, Nüwa was known as the Wood King. Sima Zhen does not have much praise for him. Unlike Fuxi, who created the sophisticated ghuzheng zither, Nüwa only invented the reed organ. It did not earn him a place among the great inventors. For the literati, the reed organ was a low status instrument associated with the barbaric people of the south west. In the last years of Nüwa's regency, a certain Prince Gong Gong usurped power, installed himself as an independent tyrant and had a fight with his rival Zhuanxu. It destroyed Incomplete Mountain, but Nüwa restored Heaven and Earth, just as the *Huainanzi* says.

So much for Sima Zhen's strained attempts to turn myths into history. I just mention them to make things a little more confusing. For as Mengzi mentions, if medicine does not make you giddy, it probably doesn't work.

And as I'm sure you really prefer experience to reading, I suggest a little exercise now. Sit down comfortably in a quiet place and relax. Make yourself feel good. Relax your arms, relax your legs, take a few deep breaths, and enjoy the pleasant mixture of peace and excitement which is building up in you right now. Then close your eyes and tell each story to yourself. Speak slowly and go slowly. Just a few calm words with each breath, steady and regular. Use a gentle and peaceful voice. There's time to explore. Things will sort themselves out as you go along, and what you do now is excellent preparation for the trances sure to follow. Tell each myth and make it happen in your mind. Use all your inner senses. Hear the sounds, see the visions, make them large and bright and colourful, and feel what you are talking about, feel what happens. Go to the point of origin where chaos congeals, spins, whirls, transforms and outfolds into the world of energies and shapes. See yang rising and yin sinking, find the world appearing from potential. Remember the world-mountain and the dense green forests, where mists swirl, tangled roots coil through rich yellow and reddish earth, where heavy blossoms release their stunning perfumes and bright birds play in the moist and dripping foliage. Go through each story, feel it, see it, hear it and sense it with your whole heart. Fill in the details you find lacking. Make it your story. And as you speak (or imagine you are speaking), you will find the story comes to life. It gets better every time. When you have told each story (or version) to yourself three times, it will become very vivid indeed. You might like to do it more often. There is so much to discover. And you'll come to understand what chaotic beginnings are all about.

Advent of Agriculture

Either Fuxi and Nüwa were a pair. Or Nüwa followed Fuxi on the throne. Regardless what the historians say, after them came the age of Shennong (Divine Farmer), who also has the name Yandi (Firegod). He appears in ritual Daoism as the Red Emperor, his direction is south and his season is summer. Originally, Shennong and Yandi were separate deities. But by the Han Dynasty they had fused, and Yandi became a name of Shennong, just as Tai Hao had become a name of Fuxi. Now Shennong is god of agriculture, but he is not the only one. A similar deity, called Lord Millet, Hou Ji or Qi the Abandoned, was revered by the Zhou. You will meet him further on. In all likeliness, there was a whole range of agricultural gods before the scholars of the late Zhou and Han streamlined prehistory.

Shennong got the people out of the forest. Just as fire destroys wood, the people of China learned how to clear wide ranges of forest by setting fires. They burned down the densely tangled growth and cleared the ash-covered land for cultivation. Shennong instituted the Neolithic revolution when he invented the plough and taught the people how to cultivate the five grains. It was a tough task. The first ploughs were huge wooden forks. They were entirely moved by manpower. According to Sima Zhen's eight century account, Shennong's mother was impregnated by a dragon (i.e. the last world-age) and brought forth a brightly blazing boy with the head of a bull. Sparky grew up and became the Red Emperor. The *Yijing* commentaries state that he taught how to till the soil and how to domesticate and breed animals. In his age, the first roads were cut and people learned to build houses. House clung to house and settlements developed. Shennong taught mankind to have markets and to exchange goods in a civilised manner. In his age, the harvest sacrifices at the year's end were instituted. And just like his predecessors, Shennong invented a musical instrument. It was the five stringed qin 'lute'. Let's take a look at this. As you recall, Fuxi had invented the large guzheng-zithers earlier on. Shennong's instrument was smaller and portable. Nowadays, the qin looks like a black, rectangular zither with seven silk strings. It may appear like a primitive lyra, but as the strings are quite close to the surface on one side of the instrument, they can be pressed against the wood, creating a wide range of different tones. Hence, this qin is much closer to lutes and guitars than to harplike instruments. It became a favourite of the literati, who played it, accompanied by bamboo flutes, preferably drunk, in full moon nights, to accompany sad songs. It would be nice to know if the qin was an independent Chinese invention. It certainly doesn't look like any other lute instruments. The lute family has quite a history where it comes to sacred music. The first known lutes appear on Sumerian roll-seals sometime before 3100 BCE. That's at least five hundred years before the Egyptians copied them. They were used for sacred music and associated with the goddess Inanna. Mind you, one such roll-seal shows a lute playing woman on a sacred bark facing a bull. It brings us back to Shennong. The bull-faced culture hero improved the eight signs, the bagua, which Fuxi had invented, by multiplying them. The result is the sixty-four signs of the *Yijing*. They leave the triple-layer symbolism of the first age (heaven, middle world and earth) and replace them with six lines looking like a ploughed field.

But there are more stories about him, and some are earlier. Zhuangzi (22) makes him a simple and somewhat stupid student of the Dao, who throws a fit when he hears that his master has died. In chapter 28 the same (or another?) Shennong is praised as a capable regent.

"...he performed the seasonal sacrifices with the utmost reverence, but he did not pray for blessings. In his dealings with men, he was loyal and trustworthy and observed perfect order, but he did not seek anything from them. He delighted in ruling for the sake of ruling, he delighted in bringing order for the sake of order. He did not use other men's failures to bring about his own success; he did not use other men's degradation to lift himself up. Just because he happened along at a lucky time, he did not try to turn it to his own profit."

(Translation Burton Watson. A very similar passage appears in *Lüshi Chunqiu* 12,4.) But Zhuangzi went beyond this.

He wrote that the people of Shennong's age went peacefully to sleep and woke up refreshed. They were aware of their mothers but did not know their fathers, and lived side by side with deer and elk. They tilled the land for a living, wove their own clothes and did not think of harming each other: perfect virtue indeed (ch. 29). The people led simple lives, and though they did not own much, they desired little and enjoyed life.

Lü Buwei relates (2.3) that in his actions, Shennong held life to be important, and encouraged the natural instincts. He calmed the desires and the fashions in the population, and instilled them with beauty. All beings and all things were treated with justice and equality (17, 8). Shennong (and Huangdi) relied on virtue and justice. Hence, during their reigns, punishment and rewards were unnecessary. Their virtue extended to the four oceans, and as they remained humble, truthful and just, the people followed their example, without even knowing by whom they were influenced. So the sage rulers of antiquity remained hidden and obscure, but their deeds shone forth. *"What need was there for harsh punishment and great rewards? Harsh punishments and rich rewards are the political tools of a time of decline."* (19.3)

"*Shennong taught: If a man does not plough in the right age of his life, he will make someone in the world suffer from hunger. If a woman does not spin and weave in the right age of her life, she will make someone in the world suffer from cold. Hence he personally dedicated himself to fieldwork and his wife personally span and wove, to set an example for the benefit of mankind.*" (21.5 after Wilhelm's German translation).

Shennong is also a god who innovated medicine. Fuxi had made the first steps when he studied the marks of plants and animals and decided which of them were nourishing and worth eating. Shennong turned it into a science. He had the ability to look right into his own body, where he could see the five greater and lesser organs do their job. Once, on a journey, as he was drinking his hot water, a couple of leaves fell into his cup. The Divine Farmer studied how they tinted the fluid, took a sip and liked the taste. Since this moment, tea has been popular in China. This is a late and not very true tale (sorry about this, it won't happen again) as tea did not become really popular till the sixth century. The first writers who bothered to mention it compared its taste with piss.

Shennong experimented with different soils, he tried the waters of rivers and springs, and taught the people what to do and what to avoid.

But Shennong also went out of his way to test every other type of herb, tree, root, berry, animal, mineral and weird creatures dwelling under rocks. He took a dose and then had a good look inward to find out what it was doing to him. Then he wrote it down, creating, so they say, China's first classic of applied medicine.

Of course, once in a while the stuff he ate was toxic. It didn't bother him much. He just looked into his belly, said *'hello, my liver shrinks and my heart explodes'* and took some drugs to counter the effect. According to the *Huainanzi*, he poisoned himself seventy times a day. I'm sure he had an exciting life. He also developed a more esoteric way of experimentation. As the *Suo Shen Ji* by Gan Bao relates, he used to strike plants with a red whip. It taught him the qualities of each, and allowed him to classify it as safe or toxic, cold or hot and revealed what disease might be cured with it. After many, many years of happy exploration he ate something called *'thousand legged vermin'*. Perhaps it was a centipede. Or he ate *'bowel breaking weed'*. And it finished him off.

The Yellow Emperor

So far we had the Mesolithic and the early Neolithic. But things were becoming increasingly complicated. The early settlements turned into villages, towns and cities. More and more of the primal forest was cleared to win arable land. Roads criss-crossed the country and people moved, travelled, explored, organised and fought each other. We are at the beginning of a new age: we had culture, but now we get civilisation. We also observe how a deity is transformed into a model emperor. Welcome to the next culture hero. After Shennong, Huangdi, the Yellow Emperor took charge. The age of the Three August Ones was over, we are entering the time of the Five Sovereigns. Allegedly, Huangdi reigned from 2497 BCE to 2398 BCE, which gave him a neat hundred years to reform everything. Or it was from 2699 to 2588 BCE, which provides 111 years. Such dates were made up mainly by Han time historians who wanted to date the early thearchs with scholarly precision. Some claim that there was war between Shennong and Huangdi. Lü Buwei hints at such a conflict, and says the armies of the regents fought each other with fire and water (7.2). But he does not supply further insight. Luckily, we can turn to China's Grand Historian here, to the incomparable Sima Qian, who practically invented serious historical studies, wrote a huge history from Huangdi's reign to the Han period (his own lifetime), and set an example that influenced Chinese historians to the present. Sima Qian worked with numerous lost texts, and collected material which had survived the censorship and book burning of the *'First Emperor'* Qin Shihuangdi. And where he found gaps in the material, he made up his own story. More so, he created a history that included commentaries and ethical lessons. History, in traditional Chinese thought, should not only be factual but educational. It usually is, but so is everything in life. Sima Qian began his account with the reign of Huangdi, the Yellow Emperor. It was a wise choice. The earlier *'emperors'* are basically deities, and their *'government'* is minimal. With Huangdi we are meeting the first human regent of a unified China. He still retains some divine traits, and his reign is a miracle of virtue and prosperity, but still, the person is more of a historical figure than Fuxi, Nüwa and Shennong could ever hope to be.

The Yellow Emperor was a child prodigy. Barely born, he was already able to speak, and of course he grew up to be an intelligent, sincere and virtuous character. Before he became emperor, he had the name Gongsun Xuanyuan. In his age, Sima

Qian wrote, wars were fought everywhere. Here, his estimate shows a marked difference to the peaceful Daoist paradise ascribed to Shennong's reign by other sources. According to Sima, when Shennong grew old, he could no longer control the lesser regents and officials. They began to wage war among each other. With some effort, Shennong brought them under control. It cost him the sympathies of the warmongers, who eagerly flocked together and selected Xuanyuan as their leader. Xuanyuan fought three battles against Shennong, and became emperor. It might be worth noting that the *Yishi* (*Book of History*) tells us that Yandi (Shennong) and Huangdi were half-brothers. Huangdi ruled virtuously and Yandi didn't. And when their armies met on the Plain of Zhulu, they shed so much blood that weapons floated on it. It's not an exaggeration. As metal hadn't been invented yet, most weapons were made of wood.

Only the wicked Chiyou refused to offer obedience. Huangdi battled Chiyou for many years. In these wars, the Yellow Emperor employed black and brown bears, foxes, panthers, lynxes and tigers. These animals were his officers. In all likeliness, his leaders represented clans that identified themselves with animals. It is also possible that the animal spirits obsessed the fighters, much in the same way that elite berserk warriors were obsessed by their fylgiar spirits, who usually had the shape of a fierce animal. Huangdi's own tribe, the Youxiang (*'bear-owners'*) identified with a bear totem. Likewise, it is likely that Shennong's clans identified with a bull totem. In one of its earlier sections, the *Liezi* refers to this episode: the vanguard of Huangdi's army consisted of black and brown bears, wolves, panthers, cats and tigers, while his banners and flags were formed by falcons, pheasants, eagles and kites.

Chiyou turned out to be a problem. He was accompanied by his seventy-two brothers. As the *Shu Yi Ji* claims, each of them had a copper head and an iron forehead. They also had whiskers like swords and horns emerged from their heads. These monsters were so fierce that they ate iron and stones. When they fought, they hid themselves in clouds and fog. In Zhulu, (modern Jizhou) where Chiyou was slain, much of his memory remained alive. He used to appear to the locals as a god with a human body and the hooves of an ox. He had four eyes and six hands. Much later, during the reign of Emperor Han Wudi, the deity appeared at daytime exhibiting a serpent head and turtle feet, and spread pestilence. The locals built a temple for him. And in the Plain of Zhulu, the farmers found human bones, as hard as iron and unbreakable, including teeth 5cm long, which were considered the bones of Chiyou. In memory of the great battle, the locals performed a dance and fight ritual called *'Chiyou's game'*, which involved horn-bearing men attacking each other.

Ceremonial Axe from Fu Hao's Tomb (Note her name inscription). The motif is, once again, two tigers with a human head between them.

How the battle between the Yellow Emperor and Chiyou went is a matter of some dispute. One tradition (*Shanhaijing*) claims that Chiyou had power over the deities Rainmaster and Windgod.

Whenever he wanted, he could soak and flood the armies of the Yellow Emperor. The Yellow Emperor retaliated by sending the Responding Dragon and the Goddess Drought against him. More about her in the chapter on drought sacrifices. The two put a stop to the havoc of the water. The rainfalls ceased, the earth dried up, and Huangdi marched against his enemy. A text included in the Song Dynasty *Taiping Yu Lan* (it dates from the fourth century) has it that Huangdi and Chiyou fought nine battles. Then Huangdi received strategic advice from Xuannü, the Dark or Mysterious Woman, and mastered the art of war. More on her later on.

After killing Chiyou, Huangdi did much to pacify the country. The *Taiping Yu Lan* contains a text dating from the third century. It claims that Huangdi, after establishing himself as a regent, cultivated himself, showed benevolence to his subjects and abstained from further warfare. There were four chieftains, styled the Green-Blue, Red, White and Black emperors, who saw this as a sign of weakness. Each of them attacked Huangdi from the direction of his colour. As they lacked strength to fight the emperor directly, they harassed the frontiers and killed wherever they saw a chance. Huangdi sighed, mumbled something about giving his enemies too much freedom and gathered his armies to crush them.

Huangdi also caught a Kui monster. Imagine a one legged, dragon like creature looking much like a hornless blue bull. Kui dwelled in the eastern Ocean, deep beneath the waves. Whenever they emerged, severe storms followed. Huangdi killed one, and used its hide to make a drum. Its sound echoed for over five hundred miles (*Shanhaijing*). More on the Kui further on. If we take this story to mean that Huangdi invented the drum, it connects him to the earlier regents and musical pioneers.

Things got more peaceful afterwards. From now on we meet the Yellow Emperor as a culture hero. According to Sima Qian, he was constantly moving across the land, venerating the spirits and gods of rivers and mountains and instituting a wide range of ceremonies.

One such custom is mentioned in the *Shanhaijing*. Huangdi once learned that out in the great ocean, a mountain called Dushuo rises from the waves, where a gigantic peach tree grows. Its branches extended in all directions and covered 1500km. North of it is the Ghost Gate, the doorway to the Spirit world. Two gods, Shenshu and Yulü guard this gate. They are entitled to direct and supervise all ghosts. When a ghost works evil, the two gods catch him, tie him up with reeds and feed him to tigers. Huangdi contemplated this and invented a ritual. To protect households from malevolent ghosts, he had a figure carved out of sacred peach wood. On the doors, pictures of Shenshu, Yulü and tigers were painted, and some reeds were tied to them.

Huangdi refined the hierarchical structures of army and government and installed a wide range of new posts to make things run smoothly. His administrators directed the people in their rituals and sacrifices, regulated the times of sowing and harvesting, of hunting and fishing and public works. He made records of the motion of the sun, moon and stars, invented a calendar, and did much to explore the qualities of stones, gems, soils and metals. *"Once, heaven made a huge rainworm and a huge molecricket appear. Huangdi said: 'The force of earth is victorious.' As the earth-force was victorious, he selected yellow as the supreme colour and took the earth as an example for his deeds."* (*Lüshi Chunqiu*, 13, 2) As his reign was under the sign of the yellow earth, he acquired the title Yellow Emperor. He levelled the ground, cleared forests, built roads and streets, and founded cities wherever he went. He sent his music master Ling Lun to the bamboo forests of the mountains. The musician cut a perfect pipe and built up a scale from its tone. From the basic note, he created twelve tones. When he heard the male and female phoenix sing to each other, he developed the twelve scales, six of them male and six female. The music master also had twelve bells cast, from which the harmonious five tones were selected according to each month. (*Lüshi* 5,5) Huangdi was good at finding exceptionally people. His historian Cang Jie, a modest person with four eyes, is credited with inventing the first Chinese characters. Lü Buwei (after the German translation of Wilhelm) referred to Huangdi frequently.

"Huangdi said: regarding tones, avoid profusion; regarding beauty, avoid profusion; regarding clothes, avoid profusion; regarding scents, avoid profusion; regarding food, avoid profusion; regarding your home, avoid profusion." (1.5)

"Huangdi said: 'The Regent may have no specific place. When he has a place, he has no place'. This means that he may not become attached to anything. It is part of the Round Way (of Heaven)." (3.5)

"Huangdi said: There is a great ruler above
There is a great square below,
If you can take them as your example
You will be father and mother of the people." (end remark of section 12)

"Huangdi said: 'Be unlimited and wide,
Rest on the glory of Heaven,
And be united with the Origin in your use of force.'" (13.2)

"Huangdi gave orders to search for sages in all directions." (14.2)

"*Huangdi said: 'There are some things which one does not carry out in the right season, but field cultivation has to be done punctually.'*" (26.6)

Huangdi's wife Lei Zu is noted for her inventiveness. It is said that she invented silkworm breeding, and thereby started Chinas enduring silk industry. Historically, this is quite a good idea. Silkworm cocoons have been found in Neolithic Chinese settlements, and by the time of the Shang Dynasty, silk manufacture was well developed. Much later, during the late Zhou Dynasty, noble women were still busy breeding silkworms. It had become a ritual duty. The fine silks they made were essential to make garments for the ancestors. Huangdi had 25 children (or sons), of whom fourteen were allowed to chose their own surnames. It was the start of many complicated genealogies. A wide range of noble families of Zhou time and later periods traced their origin to the mythical First Emperor. And when the so called '*First Emperor*' of the Qin unified China for a few years of terror, bloodshed and suppression, he gave himself the grand title '*Huangdi*' to emphasise his link to the regent of prehistory. It was a unique gesture, as before him, no living regent had dared to assume the title Di (deity, thearch, superhuman) while alive.

In late Zhou and Han time histories, Huangdi became a figure of much greater importance than the Three August Ones who preceded him. Where it comes to Chinese deities, Huangdi was almost a newcomer. He does not appear in the early texts. The historians built up the myth of Huangdi and made him the first real regent of a China which allegedly reached all the way south to the Yangzi. They also made him a model for a regent, researcher, scholar and inventor. Allegedly, Huangdi was the first to write systematically about warfare and strategy. Likewise, the first guidebooks on sexual hygiene, refinement of inner energies and the cultivation of immortality are ascribed to him. The same goes for that classic work on medicine, the *Huangdi Neijing*, the *Yellow Emperor's Classic of Internal Medicine*. The early Daoist made him a patron of their craft. In the *Zhuangzi*, he is busy cultivating the Dao and practicing non-action. Numerous works on inner alchemy are related or ascribed to Huangdi. Of course it was claimed that Huangdi became an immortal after his death. Indeed, some made the Yellow Emperor a pioneering founder of Daoism. This tradition blended with the cult of a somewhat fictional Laozi, their fusion producing early Huang-Lao Daoism. Some manuscripts of this school survived in the grave library of Mawangdui, just like the earliest known copy of the *Huangdi Neijing*. Huangdi's fight against Chiyou also provided a model for close combat tactics, hence, Huangdi became a patron of several martial arts systems. In later literature, Huangdi became a role model for all emperors that followed.

Ba, Goddess Drought

Shaohao

The next two regents remain obscure figures. Here we observe the influence of late Zhou, Qin and Han time symbolism. In this period, the system of the Five Movers (Wuxing) reached an amazing degree of refined complication. The Five Movers are the forces which are occasionally (and wrongly) identified with the *'elements'*. They look similar, but they are different in their effect. We owe the elements to the Greek pre-Socratic philosophers. These thinkers were fascinated by the question what material the universe consists of. Their elements are basic substances. The Five Movers are not substances but forces and energies. They are symbolised by fire, water and so on, but these metaphors were selected for their dynamic interaction. Our Chinese thinkers of the late Zhou and early Han were eager to describe the transformation of qi, here considered the basic substance of the universe. They started the cycle with wood and springtime. This corresponds to the age of Fuxi and Nüwa. Wood nourishes or even creates fire; hence the next world age was ruled by Shennong/Yandi, the Fire Lord. Fire nourishes earth, just as ashes nourish the fields, hence, the next aeon was symbolised by the Yellow (earth) Emperor. So far things were neat and meaningful. But how was the cycle to continue? Our next two emperors had to signify metal (earth nourishes and creates metal) and water (metal nourishes and produces water). This gives a whole cycle, for water, in turn, nourishes wood. So two regents were needed to manifest the qualities of metal and water. At this point, history becomes a little strained. Huangdi had invented and done so much that anyone who followed him would have a hard time doing anything remarkable. Our accounts show some variation and very little detail. One ruler who followed Huangdi was his son Shaohao, otherwise called Jin Tian and Xuanxiao. Not all historians agreed. In Sima Qian's history, he was not an emperor, but only a king of some minor district. Huangdi had many sons, and they received fiefs if capable to govern them. But as he did not deem them very capable, he chose a grandson as the next emperor. Here we have an important point: Huangdi did not believe in imperial succession. He wanted a capable emperor; even if this implied that none of his sons got the job.

Unlike Sima Qian, Lü Buwei believed that Shaohao was the next emperor after Huangdi. In the Zhou time ritual calendar, Shaohao is the White Emperor and rules over metal and autumn.

He was granted the title *'God of the Western Heaven'*.

Zhuanxu

The next emperor was Zhuanxu, otherwise known as Gaoyang. He is called the Dark or Mysterious (zhuan) Emperor. Dark connects with black, the traditional colour of water, wintertime and the north, hence Zhuanxu was known as the

Black Emperor. Sima Qian recorded that Zhuanxu was a calm, unfathomable and highly skilled character whose main characteristic was virtue. He relied on the spirits when it came to making laws, calculated the motions of the planets and stars and sacrificed with a pure heart and a sincere mind. Humans and spirits were subject to him. Lü Buwei has it that when Zhuanxu ascended the throne, the world was in perfect balance and the winds came from their proper directions. The regent loved the sound of the winds and discerned three different qualities in them: the sound of the human voice, the sound of rain and gale and the sound of things that collide. He commanded Flying Dragon (Fei Long) to imitate them, and to develop the sounds of the eight winds. These were related to the cardinal directions and to the eight signs (bagua) of the *Yijing*. Zhuanxu also uttered the remarkable order, that the salamander should beat the rhythm for the music masters. The salamander sat and beat its tail against its belly. (5.5) And in case you are thinking of a tiny amphibian: in China, the few surviving giant salamanders reach a length of almost two metres. They are sometimes called babyfish, as their call is said to resemble a weeping infant.

Zhuanxu also appears in the cosmic battle when he and Gonggong knocked each other around as each wanted to be a deity (Di), until a heavenly pillar broke and the sky tilted dangerously (*Huainanzi*). It's an odd tale. According the *Guanzi*, Gonggong used to be a regent. In his age, a great flood covered the earth, and seventy percent of the earth surface was submerged. Gonggong governed the remaining part with strict discipline. The *Guoyu* adds that he did much to win land. He built dams, levelled the high ground and extended the low ground, but as he was lacking in virtue, he damaged the realm and his people would not support him. So his reign ended in disaster and chaos.

It's a strange tale. Chinese myth knows several floods, and it also has several regents or deities who tried to cope with them. Gonggong seems to have come from another myth cycle. It did not fit the pattern of the (known) historians of the Zhou and Han, and hence, he disappeared into obscurity.

Zhuanxu was something of a religious reformer. The *Guoyu* records that in old times, Heaven and Earth were separate. In those days, it was only a highly gifted, qualified and dedicated class of people, namely the female wu and male xi, who were able to ascend to Heaven, and to whom the gods could descend on earth. This changed under the reign of Shaohao, when virtue and order declined. At the same time, the Nine Li disrupted the cosmic balance. Gods and humans enjoyed such close relations that their worlds merged and one could hardly be told from the other. In the process, anyone could do rituals and perform sacrifices, and many people lost their respect for the spirits and gods. Each family produced its own wu and xi ritualists and interfered with the pattern of the cosmos. The result was chaos, bad weather and a government crisis. When Zhuanxu became emperor, he decided that things should be sorted out properly. He ordered his ministers to put the people in one place, and to assemble the gods in another. He re-established the old religious relations, and this was called *'to sever the connection between Heaven and Earth'*. Henceforth, only qualified wu and xi were able to interact with the gods, and the world returned to order.

It sounds like a fascinating period, and makes me wonder whether this lone fragment represents an entire forgotten myth cycle. Sadly, everything else is lost. And that's pretty much all there is to say. Zhuanxu could have been a fascinating figure, if only we knew more about him. When he died, his three sons lived a disgraceful life and, after dying became ghosts. One son became a fever ghost, the other moved into a river and became a water-monster, while the third haunts palaces and houses and loves to scare children.

Diku

A grandson of Zhuanxu became the next emperor of China. This was Emperor Ku, also known as Diku. Diku was another child prodigy who began to speak wisdom when he was still a baby. Sima Qian related that he was highly intelligent, understood practically everything, selflessly served the people, refined himself, practiced humility and virtue, improved the calendar, knew everything about the spirits, performed the rites faithfully, instructed the people and governed wisely. He also dressed well. It's nice to know. But as to his period and just what really happened, our emperor was a model of restraint. None of his achievements or reforms is recorded in any detail. Lü Buwei attributes the first orchestras to his reign. Ku had his music master write new songs, he had the people clap their hands and perform on hand-drums, bass-drums, bells, jade sound-stones, flutes, panpipes, xun-okarinas, clarinets, wooden clappers, rattles and hammered bells. The music was so enchanting that it attracted the great bird Peng, who descended from heaven, beating its wings in tune with the music. The music, so Master Lü commented, served to ensure the influence of the regent. (5.5) Henceforth, when flying pheasants, phoenixes or storm god Peng appeared, it was taken as a sign that heaven was bestowing blessings on an emperor. We could understand it as a confirmation of divine grace. Or we could wonder if these regents used their orchestras to invoke animal spirits.

Yao

The next regents appear in many histories. The first of them is virtuous Yao. Yao is already a long way from the semi-divine regents of prehistory. As a single un-human characteristic he exhibited two pupils in each eye. It's just the thing when you need to look in every direction at once. Yao is a popular but rather shadowy figure. The first document of the *Shujing* is ascribed to his period (in reality, it was written much later during the Zhou Dynasty). Sima Qian leaned on it when he wrote his history. Yao was a highly intelligent regent, virtuous, humble, courteous and thoughtful, he was benevolent like heaven and wise like a god, and he accomplished his work with natural grace. His character was so refined that its influence radiated through all lands, and the people became intelligent, well-behaved, cuddly and loveable, just like the emperor. He united the many distinct cultures in his domain and caused universal accord. To harmonise the day, he selected four administrators who were settled in the four cardinal directions. Each had to record the sun's motion and to perform a ceremony to his quarter of the day, and to the season it corresponded with. Yao also re-calculated the calendar, and introduced an intercalary month. When Yao ascended the throne, he ordered his music master to define the basic note. Most ancient Chinese emperors followed this custom. Each new reign requires the careful calculation of its basic sound, which specifies the relations between Heaven and Earth. Yao's music master found the basic note in the sound of forests and mountain streams. He also improved drum music and played the jade chimes as if they were the voice of the Highest God. All the animals (or their spirits) assembled and danced. (Lü Buwei 5.5).

But no matter how virtuous Yao was, his age was one of unrest. Another huge flood threatened China. Vast ranges of land were submerged, the waves rushed up the mountainsides and people lost their lives and homes. Yao urgently needed a man to control the flood. His administrators suggested that Gun should do the job. Yao said: *'Gun? Is he suitable? He is perverse, he disobeys orders and tries to harm other nobles'.* The Chief of the Four Mountains, however, insisted on him, and Yao reluctantly gave his consent. Gun laboured for nine years but got nothing done. We will get back to him. When Yao had been on the throne for seventy years, he wanted to retire. He had ten sons but knew that none of them would be a capable emperor. Hence, some later commentators claimed that Yao acted without love for his offspring. Instead, Yao asked the highly capable Chief of the Four Mountains to accept the job. The Chief of the Four Mountains graciously refused. Next, Yao asked his administrators to suggest a good replacement. The courtiers told Yao that there was a virtuous man of humble birth who might be fit to become emperor. *'There is a man called Shun of Yü'.* Shun and his servants ploughed at Lishan Mountain, made clay vessels at the shore of the Yellow River and fished in Thunderlake. He laboured with his men, he dug earth and wove nets until his fingers were callused and worn. All people who met him became his friends (*Lüshi*, 14.6). Shun was a dutiful, self sufficient farmer with an excellent reputation. Yao said: *'I have heard his name, tell me about his qualifications'*. The courtiers replied: *'He is the son of a blind man. His father was stubborn and lacked principles, his mother was untrustworthy and insincere and his brother arrogant. Shun showed such virtuous conduct that he managed to live peacefully with all three of them, and they have all been refined by his conduct, so nowadays they are not extremely wicked anymore.'*

Yao was delighted. *'I shall test him further'* he announced, and passed an imperial decree that Shun had to marry the two daughters of Yao. Shun accepted the marriage and treated his wives with all courtesy. They performed, against all tradition, a secret marriage ceremony. Shun knew better than to involve his family in such a delicate ritual. Yao, who was watching Shun closely, was delighted. Next, he ordered Shun to travel through wild forests and rugged mountains, to cross surging rivers and malarious swamps, and Shun did not miss the way. Yao tested him for three years, and resigned happily, decreeing that Shun should follow him. Shun wanted to refuse, but Yao forced him accept the duty in the temple of Yao's ancestors.

Shun

Shun did not change much after he became emperor. He worked as hard as before, and sought for talented administrators wherever he went. More so, he was skilful at employing markedly different characters. Not all of his ministers were models of virtue, but each of them received tasks that were exactly suited to their abilities. Hence, Shun was able to employ almost anyone. Shun made pilgrimage to the sacred Taishan Mountain, he sacrificed to the gods and spirits and assigned talented administrators to oversee the many tasks of the government. According to the *Shjing*, he reformed the judicial system, introduced banishment as a milder alternative to execution, and admonished the judges to be compassionate.

Alas, the flood problem was far from solved. In Yao's time, some rivers had been dredged and a lot of dams were built, but none of them was sufficient to break the fury of the waters. It was Gun's job to control the flood, and he made a mess of it.

Gun is a complex character. In some myths he has a trickster nature, in others he appears as an insolent criminal, or at best, a failure. Our Gun is the product of several conflicting myth-streams. One common tradition claims that Gun spent nine years building dams and earthworks, as he hoped to resist the flood. Water, however, proved to be stronger than firm earth. The effort was in vain, and Gun had to admit his failure. It's a good question just where Gun went wrong. The *Tianwen* ask: if Gun was incapable of controlling the flood, why was he assigned to the task? True enough; Yao had his doubts about him. But just why did he allow Gun to mess around for nine years? It's one of the things we'll never know. An entire myth cycle seems to be hidden here. The *Tianwen* hint that Gun journeyed to the west and that somehow he passed through the heights. It could mean that he died, as the west was traditionally associated with the sunset, hence, the end of the day. The heights may be the mountain chains that ridge parts of China. Or maybe he just tried to leave the flooded country for higher ground. But let us continue. "*Gun transformed into a yellow bear. How did the wu (ritualists) restore him to life? They sowed black millet and the dry soil became a field. But as they planted simultaneously, how is it that Gun grew so fast, so tall and so lush?*"The answers to this riddle are lost. Things become even trickier when we consult the *Shanhaijing*. Here we read that the floods surged to the height. Gun knew that Di, the High God, had something mysterious. It was the self-renewing earth. Gun wanted it to stop the flood, but being in a hurry he didn't to ask for permission, but simply took it. Di was not amused and ordered a fire god to kill Gun. Gun, dead but not decaying, lay on Feather Mountain, and finally, Yü was born from his belly. The High God granted Yü the right to use the self-renewing earth to stop the flooding of the Nine Provinces.

As Anne Birrell points out, this myth has an almost promethean quality. She rightly connects it to a wide range of Native American tales, involving ducks, waterbirds and other primal entities who raise a self-renewing earth from the bottom of the primal ocean. Once this soil surfaced, it extended in every direction, and became the whole wide earth (1993:79-81). If these myth cycles are related, they may date from earliest prehistory. Sadly, the whole background of the self-renewing earth episode has long been forgotten. It does not appear in any other written source.

According to the *Shujing*, Gun was banished to Mount Yü, where he had to dwell until his death. It's the most prosaic interpretation. Let me add that Gun's name is related to the character for '*fish*'. His transformation into a yellow bear is just one animal aspect; other sources claim that he became a yellow dragon or turtle after his death. His corpse lay on Feather Mountain and did not decompose.

Then, after three years Yü the Great (Da Yü) was born from his belly.

Yü

Shun made Yü the minister of works. He gave him the same task that Gun had failed at, and Yü immediately went to work. First of all, he joined forces with his friend Yi, who was Shun's forester. The two began their task by cutting trails through the forests and across the mountains, and by building roads. It made it so much easier to move people and equipment. Having crisscrossed the country with a network of streets, they turned their attention to the surging waters. Gun had tried to block the water, and wasted much strength and many lives in the futile effort. Yü had a different method. His main skill was in building canals. He had the rivers deepened and the narrow mountain gorges opened, so that the waters could flow away easily. In his work, he transformed the entire landscape of China. He had his men break mountains, level hills, cut gorges, drain swamps; elsewhere he opened canals so that lakes could take the excessive water. As if this wasn't enough of a job, he also organised supplies for starving communities, assessed land for its fertility and value and did much to improve the economy. It was the toughest job in Chinese prehistory. Yü worked frantically, until his entire body was chafed and sore, his hands were callused, his legs were without hair and his fingers without nails, and his entire figure stooped. Diseases shrivelled him and he was hardly able to set one foot past the other. This peculiar gait became known as '*Yü's walk.*' The *Lüshi* gives a long account of Yü's travels, which led him pretty much anywhere in China. Yü was so anxious to help the people that his face was burned black by the sun, his orifices and vital organs gave up their proper function and his feet were staggering. For ten long years Yü fought the hungry waves. In this time he passed his home several times, but allowed himself no rest, nor did he waste time seeing his family. He performed his rituals in the same tattered clothes that he wore while shovelling mud and it is said (Sima Qian) that in the meantime "*his wretched hovel fell in ruins in the ditch*" (Herbert Allen's translation). If we trust the Mawangdui manuscripts on Huanglao sexual hygiene, he exhausted himself, lost the use of his limbs and ruined his family life. Noticing that this did not seem auspicious, he asked a sage for advice. His advisor told him to allow the brain to relax, to eat varied food, to use work as an exercise, to stretch and bend the body and to draw qi into his genitals before going to bed. Yü followed this method, drank plenty of milk and made his wife happy. (Cleary, 1994) More serious texts omit this interesting episode.

You probably noted that Yü was very committed, dedicated and terribly virtuous. Many Confucian scholars would have approved. Let's consider Yü's labour from a Daoist point of view. His strategies to control the flood have an admirably Daoist character. Instead of opposing the waters, as Gun had done, Yü managed to channel them, and allowed them to exhaust their violence without doing harm. This is excellent thinking, and sound advice. It is also excellent gongfu. On the other hand, Yü worked himself into the ground. In this matter, he showed great dedication but very little common sense. Many Daoist texts, including the *Laozi*, insist that a sage ruler should care for the health of his body first of all. Only one who is able to care for his well being can ensure the well being of the state. This sounds like an invitation to self-indulgence but it isn't. When you are healthy, you have a better outlook on life. Important matters should be decided when you feel well. It's not such an obvious idea at all. Many people tend to make important decisions when they feel bad. They decide about their future when they are sick, or a relationship has just disintegrated, or when they are disappointed, worried, overworked or fed up. That's exactly the times when people make most mistakes. When you feel good, as Richard Bandler emphasised, you are more likely to make good decisions than when you feel stressed, overworked or troubled. Sure, you can still be wrong. But it won't happen so often. So when you wish to decide something important, first make yourself feel good. Don't wait for a good feeling to come. This is another essential Chinese lesson. In the Chinese language, feelings are easily MADE. One of my Chinese friends, she teaches music, keeps saying: *'and now we take the instrument and make joy'*. European languages, by contrast, show a highly passive attitude. In German and English, people HAVE feelings. Or they ARE feelings, such as happy, sad, joyous, frustrated and so on. It sounds as if feelings fell from heaven and you can't do a thing about them. Westerners even *'fall in love'*, instead of going there voluntarily. Sorry folks, you go into love, and you use a lot of specific thinking and specialised brain chemistry for the job. Love is not a ditch or rabbit hole, it's a highly developed trance state. And you have to do something really good, and make wonderful thoughts and feelings, to maintain it.

Once you realise that making feelings is simple, and that you have unconsciously done so all of your life, you can assume responsibility for them. Why wait for a feeling? Why buy all sorts of rubbish in the hope that it would make you feel better? You can make feelings by the way you think, the things you are aware of, by your memories, your hopes, your imagination, by what you do and how you think about it. You can use your breathing and your posture and do it now, right now, and much better for a change. When we look at Yü the Great from this point of view, he sure got some things terribly wrong.

But when we look at a more mythical and less historical Yü, we find him doing plenty of magical things. In digging channels, he employed the help of a dragon, who split up the soil. And when the mountains inhabited the flow of the floods, Yü assumed the shape of a bear to claw his way through earth and rock. Let's call it shapeshifting. His bear transformation inspired an exorcistic dance which is performed in Daoist rituals to this day. The dance uses the ground plan of a square of nine spaces (which correspond to the Nine Provinces) and the Daoist, identifying him- or herself with the bear-shaped Yü, dances across them. (Saso,1978). The basic diagram for the dance was revealed to Yü when he stood on the banks of River Luo. Presumably he was cursing at the rushing waves when a huge turtle rose from the foam and proudly displayed a diagram on its shell. Sadly, this image does not go back to 2000 BCE. Its numerology is strictly Han and its visual form emerged only a thousand years ago during the Song Dynasty. Sometimes, life is disappointing.

Another attraction of the Yü tale are his associates. The Shang and the Zhou both claimed that the ancestor of their clans personally helped Yü to dam the flood.

Finally, Yü managed to fulfil his task. Shun was mightily pleased. He decided that Yü should be his heir. At a grand feast, the nine airs of Shun were played, the spirits of the ancestors and the nobles celebrated, the phoenixes descended, the many animals joined in a merry dance and the officers were happy and content. Shun was so overjoyed that he composed the ode *'On being appointed by Heaven, we must be cautious and circumspect at all times and in all matters.'* (Sima Qian). Seventeen years later, Shun died in the south while he was waging war against the Miao people, who would not respect his exalted rule. Yü was greatly upset and spent three years with the traditional mourning rites. Then he declared that he was unfit to become emperor. Hence, a son of Shun ascended the throne. The nobles were unhappy about this choice. They flocked to Yü and practically forced him to become regent. He assumed his position, facing south, and gave imperial decrees. It started Yü's own dynasty. Earlier rulers had chosen their heirs for reasons of virtue, but Yü passed the throne to a son, who did the same, until imperial regency became hereditary. And in doing so, Yü became the primal ancestor of China's first semi-historical *'dynasty'*, the Xia. Here we leave the land of semi divine mythical figures and enter the realm of semi historical regents.

A Word on Virtue

Let's take a look at the virtue (de) of the early regents. Virtue is a difficult concept. In its earliest form, as Duyvendak points out, the term simply referred to magical power, and had no ethical connotations. Instead, it described the quality of the sage or ruler to get things done. Call it charisma, or enchantment, or true will if you like. In the Confucian sense, de requires love for humanity, precise observation of rituals and social distinctions, dutiful conduct towards superiors and a constant striving for self refinement. In the Daoist interpretation, de is the natural conduct which enables a sage or regent to acquire and apply magical power and the charm required to influence others. Here the idea was not necessarily to do *'good'* but to do what was right, and necessary in the grand transmutations of the world. While Confucian virtue requires plenty of conscious effort, Daoist virtue means following inherent self nature. This virtue was not regulated by laws or ethical consideration, but by the true nature of Heaven's motion, Earth's qualities and human's essential true self. The Daoists sought to pattern their behaviour on the natural development flow of the Way. Sometimes virtue required acting before things grew out of control, but just as often it was the skill of letting them behave and develop spontaneously, without interference. Now the myths and proto histories you just read may have some relation to the earliest Chinese myths, but the way they were assembled, edited, recorded and refined mirrored the worldview of the late Zhou and the Han dynasties. This goes especially for the cosmology of the Five Movers, the idea of a divine Heaven (a Zhou innovation) and the modes of government, which show a blend of Kongzi's ethics and Laozi's natural spontaneity, plus elements from Mozi and other philosophers.

It's worth considering what the emperors excelled at. One such skill was to believe in high goals. Yao sought to unify all lands under the sun and moon. He failed at the task, but he got further than anyone before him. Shun was less ambitious. He simply wanted to extend the domain and pacify the lands beyond the four steppes. He failed at the task, but he made a better job of pacifying the foreign barbarians than anyone before him. Both sage emperors were aware that their goals could not be achieved. But by applying themselves to great tasks, they were successful in their failure. And as they cultivated humility, failure did not frustrate them.

More important than the deeds of an emperor is the work of those around him. The regents made themselves images of the Perfect Man, and of the incarnated divinity. Their virtue extended far beyond the habit of being humble, courteous, measured, cautious and a shining example to everyone. The most important skill of an emperor is to remain 'round', i.e. undefined, while all ministers have to be 'square', i.e. assigned to specific and particular duties. The round way is the mysterious and unlimited motion of Heaven; the square way the special and limited activity of the ten-thousand things on this bonny earth. Each has its shapc; cach has its qualities, limits, beginning and end. The emperor can't understand or handle them all. A good regent excels in finding and attracting capable administrators. Such a regent knows that he is not all knowing, and does not try to be best. Indeed, his skill is to find the best specialists and to allow them to do their job properly. The sage emperors did not meddle, nor did they try to be clever, or to solve all problems on their own. In fact, the less they actively interfered, the better could their administrators do their jobs. It was more important for an emperor to radiate tranquillity, honesty and benevolence than to dabble in things he didn't understand anyway. All of this reads like state craft but it also applies to magick. The conscious mind should know its limits. The heart knows how to beat, the lungs know how to breathe, the guts know how to digest, and they usually work best when you don't interfere. When things get out of balance, your conscious mind may tell the deep mind that some job needs to be done, but it should leave the doing to the deep mind. The same goes for healing, consciousness changing and anything that transforms your personality and reality from within. A vast amount of magick is simply getting the deep mind (gods, spirits, ancestors etc) to do a special job without conscious interference. For this reason sigils, symbols, stories, hypnotic suggestions etc work their enchantment but leave the human ego in blissful ignorance. The self-styled *'ruler'* of the mind, the ego, is simply incapable of dealing with all the complexities the subconscious handles with such ease. Think of the sage emperors. If you want an ego that does its duty for the whole, keep it simple, humble, virtuous, and make it delegate the skilful tasks to the subconscious parts of the mind. Here, the sage emperors represent the conscious mind, the ego and the personality. They were never proud, haughty or self important. They considered themselves ritual foci of a much vaster phenomenon, and they saw their task as a sacred duty for the whole. And while we can consider ourselves the sage regents of our own state, we can also act as administrators for the greater state, the All Self, Great Unity, the One.

A Daoist Model of Evolution

Let's devote a little thought (if you have one) to the Daoist model of evolution. In the first world age, so Zhuangzi believed, people lived in nests high up in the trees and had few cares apart from gathering firewood for winter. And when we look at the reign of Fuxi and Nüwa we don't see any government. The two made a couple of innovations and provided simple rituals for the people, which barely elevated them from animal life, but they did not bother to rule over them. It wasn't necessary. Communities were small, travelling difficult, and infrastructure non-existent, what with all the trees getting in the way. And with regard to property, everyone owned pretty much the same. People got along without government: welcome to Daoist paradise. This made the Green Emperor the best ruler of them all. Next we have the age of agriculture, and once people organise and clear the forest, they could make roads, produce their own food and have as many children as possible. In this period, settlements grow and government becomes an issue. It is still a gentle and cautious government based on example and virtue, and as people are fundamentally innocent and good, not much more is needed. But the world has become a more complex place and was becoming more so. The time of the three Sovereigns was passing.

With Huangdi, the Yellow Emperor, we arrive in the time of the five sage-rulers when things were not quite that innocent and happy. The villages have grown, the fields are large, people are greedy for property and soon there is conflict. Huangdi spent much of his reign imposing order and waging war against evildoers. By this time, innocence has disappeared. And though the regent is still more virtuous and benevolent than later ones, people begin to wonder whether it wouldn't be nice to live on trees again. Next follows the obscure and possibly chaotic period when Heaven and the human realm intermingled and it was hard to tell humans, spirits and gods apart (it still is). Then the connection between the worlds was cut (or restricted) and life resumed its normal path. In the ages of the sage rulers Yao and Shun, government becomes an organised, hierarchical machine, and people are confused, greedy and increasingly wicked. Great catastrophes befall the earth. Yü fights the flood but almost kills himself in the process; obviously he has lost the natural grace of the first regents. And when he sets up his own dynasty, realpolitik begins and the fun is over for good. We get regents after regents, and few of them are good at the job or have the grace to let the people do their thing without interference. What western thinkers call progress is a sad story of corruption and restriction for the Daoists. Laozi summed it all up in a few brief lines (ch.17).

"In earliest antiquity, people did not even know there were regents.

Next they loved them and praised them.

Next they feared them.

Next they were despised.

If the prince does not trust the people, the people will not trust the prince.

The ancient sage-kings were cautious and sparing in their words.

When a task was accomplished and everything worked well,

the people said; 'We have done it ourselves.'"

Likewise, Zhuangzi (ch.16) argues that in the primal period, people lived in chaos, crudeness and simplicity. In that age, yin and yang alternated in harmony, the seasons were in order, ghosts and spirits did no evil and the ten-thousand things knew no injury, nor was there early death. People had knowledge but did not misapply it. Later, when Sui Jen and Fuxi ruled the world, the people co-operated but unity was lost. When Shennong and Huangdi ruled, people enjoyed security but lost agreement. Virtue declined, and when Yao and Shun took charge, they instituted order and destroyed purity and simplicity. The Way, Dao, was mistaken for goodness, and virtue (de) was taken for right conduct. People forgot their inner nature, their heads began to spin with new thoughts, schemes, tricks and cunning inventions, and the stability of the world disappeared. People developed civilisation (another strange idea), and soon enough the Way was lost.

Luckily, it does not have to be that way. The decline of innocence is paralleled by the way a child grows up. And when you are old enough to understand what you have lost, you can reverse the flow. Daoism means turning back. Turning from the outside to the inside to the side-less, from the difficult to the simple to the inestimable, from the artificial to the natural to the truly appropriate. And just as we acquire loads of rubbish as we grow up, we can grow young when we turn back and get rid of the lot. The decline of the world can be reversed. When you realise that you are the state, you are the people, the land, the animals and plants and the regents who rule over them, you can change everything. You can simplify the politics within your own head, you can replace strict laws with natural grace, and find your primal nature in the state where no ruler is known or needed.

Dynastic History

Flight of a Dark Bird

Shang history can be divided into three phases. The first is the predynastic phase, starting with the mythical origin of the Zi clan and its rise to power and wealth. The second is the dynastic phase, beginning when Tang the Successful overthrew the last regent of the Xia Dynasty and continuing to the downfall of the last Shang regent, Zhòu Xin. The third phase began when the Zhou Dynasty rose to power and the descendants of the Shang were granted fiefs which they governed under the control and supervision of the Zhou kings. In the process they attempted to revolt, were soundly beaten, relocated and became the state of Song.

Let's begin this story with a bit of confusion and a myth.

We begin with a nebulous regent called **Di Ku**. According to Zhou period history books, Di Ku was the earliest ancestor of the Shang. That is, if he happened to be the father of his son. Or maybe it was a black bird. Or the bird did the spiritual impregnation while Di Ku supplied the sperm. We'll get to that point soon. Whatever it may be, Di Ku is a candidate for primal ancestor in the history books. In oracle bone inscriptions, the earliest ancestor is written with the character *'monkey'*. Darwin would have been delighted. Hence, it may be possible that Di Ku was written as *'monkey'*. Monkey has been transcribed variously as Nao, Kui and Jun, depending on scholarly reasoning; some even suspected that the character *'monkey'* might refer to the Xia Dynasty, though this idea never really made it. Sarah Allan makes a point of identifying Di Ku with Jun, and I recommend you read her reasoning in *The Shape of the Turtle* (1991:51-54). If the proper transcription is Jun, we have left the human realm and are talking religion. Jun was the husband of two goddesses, Xihe, who gave birth to the ten suns and Chang Xi, the mother of the twelve moons. It may or may be not the case that these two mothers are related or even identical with two early Shang goddesses, the eastern and the western mother. The matter is rather complicated and, given that the speculations are based on very little data, I wouldn't wish to propose an opinion. Be that as it may, and it may be in plenty of ways, given that mythology is not logical, reasonable and involves plenty of variations, Shang history began with people who also happened to be deities. To complicate things further (or to make them more attractive to the

Flight of a Dark Bird

dreaming mind) let me just add that Jiandi's husband appears under the name **Gao Xin**. Here we leave human history entirely, for according to David Hawkes (1985: 91), Gao Xin was probably a sky god.

Well and good. We've had the mythical confusion, now for plain truth, facts and cold realism.

One day in mythical prehistory, the High Lady **Jiandi** and her two sisters went for a ritual bath. Jiandi was secondary wife (concubine) of King **Di Ku**. On the way, they observed a mysterious black bird (xuan niao). The bird dropped (or laid, more likely) an egg right in front of them. Jiandi was amazed. She picked up the egg and ate it. And soon enough she found herself pregnant. Her son was named **Shang Xie**, but he also appears simply as Shang and as Xuan Wang (Black King). Xie was a contemporary of Yü the Great. In this age, a great flood was devastating the Middle Kingdom, and in its wake followed plague, starvation, violence and misery. Emperor Shun courteously asked Yü to still the surge of the waters, and Yü worked at it day and night. One of his assistants was Xie, and Xie did such a good job that Yü recommended him to Shun. Shun spoke: "*The people are lacking in affection to one another, and do not care about the five regulations of relationship. As Minister of Instruction, you should teach the duties belonging to those five orders, and you should do so with gentleness.*" (Sima Qian).

So Xie received a task, but he also received a fief and the right to found his own clan. It was the **Zi clan**, written with a character meaning *'child; son, prince'*, which became the core of the royal family of the Shang.

Now there are a few interesting points about this story, which has come to us in a few variations. In one, briefly alluded to in the *Chuci*, Lady Jiandi was kept locked up in a jade tower. The black bird came flying through the window. Mysterious birds simply go anywhere. Another version appears in *Lüshi*, 6.3. Here, Jiandi and her sister were locked up in a nine story tower. Whenever they ate and drank they made music. The High God (Shangdi) sent a swallow to look after them. Its call sounded: ai, ai. The sisters caught the bird and kept it in a nephrite basket. After a while, the swallow laid two eggs and flew away, heading north. The girls composed a song entitled: Swallow, you have flown away. It was the first song in Northern Music. Lü Buwei adds: "*All music is born from the human heart. What moves the heart outfolds as tone, and what sounds outside of us moves the heart within.*" He continues to discuss music without a further comment on the sisters and their swallow. Perhaps the tale was too well known to need repeating. The rest is history.

Need I point out the similarity to the tale of Danae in Greek myth? Or mention that in ancient Palestine, a girl was impregnated by a dove? But what is this black bird? According to the Third Ode of Shang in the *Shijing*,

"Heaven gave a task to the swallow
it descended and caused the birth of the father
of the Shang, who were to rule the domain of Yin."

These lines of a sacrificial hymn chanted by the Song (the descendants of the house of Shang) tell us that the black bird was a swallow. Swallows return from the south in springtime, and later variations claim that before Lady Jiandi bathed she went to sacrifice and pray for a son on the day of the spring equinox. Personally, I am not sure whether the bird was really a swallow. The term xuan means dark or black, but it can also mean mysterious. We have a sign for swallow in the oracle bones, which does appear as a happy omen. The Kings were concerned about the date when the first swallows arrived, and asked the oracle about its meaning. We also have a sign showing a raven or crow which was specifically associated with the bird star, perhaps the only known constellation to which the Shang sacrificed. It is possible that the rising of the bird star signified the beginning of spring. It would be nice to settle this for certain. However, the *'bird star'* inscription, as you will see further on, has caused plenty of scholarly disagreement and is my favourite for an inscription that can be interpreted in many ingenious and contradictory ways.

The ideogram for *'bird'* (niao) in oracle bone script shows a raven or crow. Today, the word for the crow family is wu, but its sign is simply the same old niao with a tiny extra dot to mark the difference. In early Chinese thought, the crow or raven is closely connected with the sun, and hence with the cycle of time. As you'll read in the chapter on the Shang ritual calendar, the week had ten days, or really, ten suns, and from their names the nobility received their posthumous temple names and the specific day on which sacrifices were offered to them. The ten suns are a common element in the art of the Zhou and Han period, where they usually shown as ravens or crows. The raven became the animal of the sun, and I would guess it became black cause of being too close to it. By Han times there was also a toad representing the moon.

The nature of the black bird remains mysterious. But there is another echo of the xuan bird. In the *Laozi Daodejing* 6 we encounter the xuanpin, the black (or mysterious) woman, who is the essential source of the Dao. Pin literally means mare, female, or female animal, it can also mean keyhole, but is usually interpreted as woman.

"'The valley spirit never dies'.
This is called the gate of the dark female.
'The gate of the dark female';
this means the root of heaven and earth.

Penetrating everything, always present,
its activity cannot be exhausted."

In the earliest version of this text, found in the tomb library of Mawangdui (168 BCE), the word for *'valley'* is written with an ideogram meaning *'to bathe'*. It was supposed to mean valley, but it read, literally, the *'bath-spirit'*. Welcome! Is this another link to Jiandi?

The xuan bird has another appearance in early literature. In early prehistory, the Yellow Emperor Huangdi was struggling to control the Middle Kingdom. His many enemies beset him, and his troops frequently suffered defeat. Huangdi sought the fault with himself. The *Quan Shang gu san dai qin han liuchao wen* (*Anthology of Ancient Literature*) tells us:

"Huangdi had many battles with Chiyou, but won none of them. He withdrew to Taishan Mountain (Shandong), which became veiled in heavy fog for three days and three nights. Before him appeared a woman who had the head of a human but the body of a bird. He dropped to his knees and did not dare to rise. The woman spoke: 'I am Xuannü. What do you want from me?' Huangdi said: 'I desire to win ten thousand victories even if I have to fight so many battles, and I desire to win ten thousand times even if I have to wait in ambush as frequently. How do I begin?' And Xuannü taught him war strategy."

Other texts, dealing with the arts of the bedchamber, go beyond this. Here we have Xuannü teaching the Yellow Emperor how to cultivate jing (here: sexual secretions) to extend life.

In Daoist literature, Xuannü was soon identified with the dark female of the *Daodejing*. And a little later, during the Tang Dynasty, when Daoism had become the state religion, the dark and mysterious female was identified with Xiwangmu, the Queen Mother of the West, who became the supreme goddess and the perfect embodiment of the Dao. Others thought that Xuannü was really identical with primal creatrix Nüwa.

Which was quite a development. All we began with was a dark and mysterious bird. And quite honestly, we have no evidence what it really signified to the Shang. All we can be sure of is that the Shang had a deep reverence for birds. You find them in the oracle bones and on the ritual bronze vessels. Even the tempestuous storm god was a huge bird. And like so many royal houses all over the world, the Shang attributed their origin to a divine source. A mysterious bird is a good start for the founding of a dynasty. Like the clans who founded the Xia and the Zhou dynasties, the Shang needed an ancestor who was there at the very beginning of things. All of the three great royal houses had an ancestor helping Yü to control the flood. When the land was divided into nine sections, when balance between heaven and earth was restored and Yü taught order and civilisation to the survivors of the cataclysm, the royal houses of the future were already in the making. Or so they said, believe it who may.

The Zi Clan

Things become a little more realistic when we look at the next generations. As you can see in the appendix, the genealogy of the Shang kings (and many of their queens) can be reconstructed. Sure, at some points the experts disagree. There are several kings on record who may or may not have received the title posthumously, as they never made it to the throne. Here and there the sequence isn't quite certain. And there are a few candidates, such as Yang Jia, who are difficult to place. Also, there are two kings with remarkably similar titles Qiang Jia and Xiang Jia. These titles refer to victories over the Qiang nomads. Personally, I find them suspiciously similar, and wonder whether they were one person. However, much of the genealogy is based on Professor T.T. Chang's study, and I wouldn't dream of arguing with such a formidable ancestor. In the table you can find a few samples how their names were written. I have limited my effort to inscriptions I came upon. No doubt there are many more. However, I did not want to make up variations just as I have read that they exist somewhere. So what you can find in the genealogy table is a convenient help for classification. It is not complete, it is not perfect, but maybe it will be useful for you.

After **Xie** followed **Wang Hai**. Perhaps he was his son. More likely there were a few generations between them. Sima Qian lists five regents between Xie and Wang Hai. He had no information on any of them. Some of the early ancestors who appear in the oracle bones may fit in here. If we are talking of early ancestors, that is. Some bones simply record entities who received sacrifices. Call them ancestors or deities if you like: the ancient Chinese did not make much of a difference between them. But things are more complicated than that. Maybe Wang Hai is another name of Xie, as Sarah Allan suspects. One way of writing the name Wang Hai in oracle bone script shows a bird above the sign for grass-root. He might have been *the* bird-child, but of course he could also be a simple bird-descendant, like any other clan member.

The name Hai is an unusual one. To begin with, it is a posthumous temple name. Unlike all other temple names of the Shang, it comes from the twelve signs that are known as the Earthly Branches today. The other kings and queens have temple names with signs of the ten day xun week. Wang Hai hasn't. So perhaps in Wang Hai's time, there was a religious reform including a change in the choice of posthumous names. Wang Hai also appears under the names Zhen and Xin Hai. Xin Hai combines names of the ten and twelve sign cycles, indicating that his sacrifices were performed on the Xin day.

Unlike his ancestors, Wang Hai was very much a human being. For a start, he probably wasn't a king (wang) at all. The title wang was often given posthumously. The other part of his name, Hai, is more interesting. According to the *Shuowen* dictionary, hai could mean grass-root. And with Wang Hai we are at the start of a pastoral tradition. Legend claims that Wang Hai invented cattle breeding. Let's look into this. Wang Hai lived in the early second millennium BCE.

The Chinese Neolithic began around 8,000 BCE, when small groups of hunter gatherers began to improve their diet by planting and later seeding plants. In northern China around the Yellow River the first farmers planted several types of millet while the southern realm of China, around the Yangzi basin, developed rice cultivation. Simultaneously, pottery was developed; permitting the farmers to store and cook their food. Animal domestication and husbandry developed much later, starting with pigs and dogs. It was an easy step: both animals are highly intelligent and are attracted by human leftovers. One of the earliest known Chinese culture that kept bovines (here: water buffaloes), plus plenty of pigs and dogs was the Hemudu Culture, Zhejiang, (5,000 – 3,500 BCE) in the lower ranges of the Yangzi (Yan Wenming in K.C. Chang, 2005:39). The excavators uncovered human figurines, bone whistles and flutes, xun ocarinas, drums, engraved black pottery vessels (many with animal images) engraved ivory and jade jewellery. For an early farmer community, their lifestyle was pretty refined. However, living far to the south/east of the Shang territory, they may not have exerted a strong influence on Wang Hai's contemporaries.

Around the Yellow River plain, the Yangshao cultures (5,000 – 3,000 BCE) appear in many variations.

The Banpo culture, developing out of the earlier Laoguantai culture in the future heartland of the Shang around 5,000 BCE subsided on millet, leaf mustard and cabbage farming. Again, these farmers were by no means primitives. The excavations uncovered densely settled villages with round and square house foundations, and stone tools like shovels, spades, axes, hoes. The Banpo people produced pottery knives and sophisticated ceramic vessels on the potter's wheel, beautifully painted with fish, frogs, insects, birds, deer and strange masked human/fish faces. They also had impressive cemeteries. At the Yuanjunmiao cemetery, child burials were mixed with adult burials. Unexpectedly, all buried children were female and many had impressive grave goods. As Zhang observes: *"...a family level of private ownership existed and wealth was transmitted from mother to daughter."* It is likely that at least some branches of the Banpo culture were matricentristic, possibly matriarchal. Their rituals are still fairly unknown. However, beneath one building the excavators discovered two small, buried vessels of millet, while a large house

Ancestors

had skulls and a covered jar under the foundation and walls. Banpo animal husbandry started with pigs and dogs, while cattle and chicken were raised by later generations (Zhang Zhongpei in K.C. Chang, 2005).

So whatever Wang Hai did, he certainly didn't invent cattle breeding. But maybe he was rather good at it. Cattle meant wealth and Wang Hai had plenty of it. I would guess that he had forests cleared and brush burned to create large pastures for his ever increasing herds, and wherever the trees disappeared, grasses flourished. King Grass-Root was not alone in cattle breeding. Other nobles had their herds, and there were frequent conflicts about grazing grounds. Maybe Wang Hai formed alliances with a few other cattle breeding clans, bonds as strong as the grass roots that were extending over the rich loess plains of his homeland.

One day, it wasn't his lucky day, Wang Hai drove a herd to the pastures of Lord Yi and went to visit him. Mian Chen, lord of You Yi, received him with lavish generosity, and for a while it seemed as if the two would get on well. Wang Hai even performed a feather-and shield dance for his host. Then, however, they had a disagreement, which ended when Yi had Wang Hai killed. Modern scholars suspect that the quarrel was about grazing grounds, territory or maybe a bit of cattle theft. People of our days think like that. They attribute economic reasons to conflict. The Chinese historians of antiquity preferred a touching story about ethics and moral virtue. As the *Chuci* (*Tianwen* 109) hint, Wang Hai's little dance won him the heart of Mian Chen's wife. A few herders observed them flirting and Mian Chen ordered his warriors to catch the couple in the act. They stormed into the bedroom while Wang Hai ran out, and cut him down outside the chamber. And Mian Chen, lord of You Yi, confiscated the cattle Wang Hai had brought with him.

With Wang Hai being very dead very fast, his family, the Zi clan, rose in anger. First Wang Hai's brothers interfered. Heng won the confidence of the lord of You Yi and retrieved the cattle by false promises and treachery. In the meantime, the other brother, Dark Wei, engaged in some unspecified act of incest. How, asks the *Tian Wen*, could the Shang clan rise to glory if it began with such ignoble acts?

Wang Hai's heir, **Shang Jia**, collected armed men from all neighbours, formed new alliances, made treaties and finally marched against the Lord of You Yi. After slaying him, the wealth of Yi went into the hands of Shang Jia. Equipped with an armed force and more cattle than before, Shang Jia set about to make his family and friends more formidable. Soon he was extending the borders of his domain and gaining more and more influence at what may have been the court of Xia.

The Shang had much veneration for these early ancestors. Wang Hai and Shang Jia frequently received large sacrifices. They were violent men and became dangerous angry ghosts. Whenever great calamities threatened the Shang, they immediately suspected that Wang Hai or Shang Jia were angry with them.

Neolithic China and the Xia Dynasty

With the reign of Yü the Great we enter a period of semi-reliable prehistory. The kings are no longer mythical wonder beings. Some of them appear like venerable thearchs, but a greater part of them are people, pure and simple. As you remember, it was Yü himself who founded the House of Xia and started the *'dynasty'*. Sima Qian did his best to reconstruct the kings of the Xia, just as he listed the kings of the Shang who followed them. Alas, his lists are very brief and he had very little to say about the individual regents. The kings at the beginning and end of both dynasties get most attention. The dynasty founders are usually virtuous, humble and competent, and the ones under whose reign the dynasty ends tend to be immoral, irresponsible, cruel and corrupt. It allows the next dynasty to overthrown them for ethical reasons. Sima Qian's history was considered a highly reliable document until the end of the nineteenth century. In the early twentieth, China was undergoing massive crisis and the intellectuals, exploring new methods of scholarship and historical research, began to doubt the venerable wisdom of the ancients. The new scholars used the catchword *'Show your proof!'* when they examined elder histories, and soon discovered a lot of highly suspect material. In particular they had their doubts about the reign of the Three Sovereigns, the Xia and Shang dynasties, as all documents purporting to come from these periods turned out to be fabrications of the Zhou. Many radical thinkers refused to believe in these dynasties at all and proposed that the first real (i.e. provable) dynasty was the Zhou. Then the oracle bones were discovered, and after some quarrelling about their authenticity, the Shang Dynasty was acknowledged as something real. And when a few dedicated scholars worked out the royal succession of the Shang from the oracle bones, it turned out that Sima Qian had almost been right. It's an amazing thing. In Sima Qian's time (the early Han Dynasty, roughly a thousand years after the fall of the Shang), most details regarding the Shang had long been forgotten. Sima had no idea about the oracle bones, nor did he know about the astonishing religious changes that happened during the last two centuries of Shang rule. But he got the royal succession almost right. He clearly had access to documents that have long disappeared.

But what about his king list of the Xia? Here we get into deep and murky waters. At the time being, there is no archaeological evidence for a dynasty that called itself Xia. There is evidence for a number of pre-Shang cultures, and some highly advanced people who began to experiment with bronze casting before the Shang period, but that does not mean that these cultures are identical with the Xia, let alone that they formed a dynasty. None of these early cultures left a written record. We have no idea who they were, how they named themselves and into which cultures they developed. And there is certainly more than one.

When you explore the histories of the late Zhou and early Han historians, you might get the impression that Chinese prehistory is a matter of one grand culture following each other. First the Xia, then the Shang and third the Zhou, who recorded (or invented) this historical succession. For two millennia, Chinese historians believed in linear succession. They believed in three great royal houses, one after the other, and in three great states, and saw them as the stem out of which Chinese culture grew and flourished. Then the archaeologists moved in and upset everyone. It turned out that there were far more early high cultures than anyone had expected. The Shang were not an island of civilisation surrounded by a sea of barbarians, they had several neighbours, near and far, who had similar states, large cities, cast bronze and had a very similar level of refined art and civilisation. Some of these cultures lived near the Yellow River, and were in touch with the Shang, while others were so far in the remote south that the Shang had very little contact with them. The Zhou historians were completely ignorant of their existence. Now it might be that one of the early cultures around the Yellow River appear as the Xia in recorded history.

Here we are on difficult terrain. As far as the oracle bones can be read, no sign for the Xia has been identified. This may appear remarkable, as allegedly the Shang did not destroy the House of Xia but left its nobles, in a reduced position, to govern smaller fiefs and continue with their ancestral worship. If this story (coming from Zhou period history books) is true, the House of Xia ought to appear among the many state names that can be found in the oracle bones. So far, it has not been identified. This may say a lot or very little, as there are many oracle bone characters which can't be read. Several such state names have been proposed for 'Xia', but none of them could be proved. They even include the glyph of the primordial ancestor Monkey (Wolfgang Behr, *Asiatische Studien/Études asiatiques*, LXI, 3, 2007:727-754) Likewise; the very name Xia remains inexplicable.

According to the Zhou historians, the original realm of the Xia was somewhere in the country around Mount Wei where the Zhou settled during the Shang period. By all accounts (you'll find more detail further on) the Zhou had started as a fairly simple and small group of clans which were considered barbarian by the Shang. They moved into the territory that had been Xia land much earlier, and immediately identified themselves with the cultural heritage of the Xia. The *Shujing* has several documents which imply that the Zhou believed themselves to be the natural successors of the exalted Xia, a belief that seems to have come up very early in the Zhou period. It looks like a case of a rugged newcomer trying to fabricate a high class background for his clan. Such a legitimisation may have been direly needed. Sure, the Zhou overthrew the Shang. But on closer examination it turns out that the Zhou were merely a small tribal unit with a charismatic leader. They needed a lot of reinforcement from other clans, tribes and noble families to fight the Shang, and when they had won, found themselves figureheads of a highly shaky alliance of differing cultures. Some of their allies had a much better pedigree and a lot more refinement regarding art, technology and civilisation. Hence, we might consider the story of the Zhou continuing the Xia tradition as a useful fable. Likewise, during the late Zhou, the House of Qin declared itself the descendant of the House of Xia to legitimize its claims of supremacy. And finally, the famous tale of the wicked last Xia regent who was justly overthrown by the virtuous Shang regent Tang (you'll read the story further on) was a highly useful model for justified rebellion. The Zhou could point at this story, praise Tang, and insist that their own rebellion against the wicked last Shang regent was justified by the precedent. The legend of the Xia Dynasty was very useful for the Zhou. So useful that we may wonder whether the Xia existed at all.

How about the historical record? Northern China had several enterprising Neolithic cultures which are loosely classed as the Yangshao Cultures (5,000-3,000 BCE). Some of them developed into the more advanced Longshan Cultures, which lasted from 3,000 BCE to the beginning of Shang history around c. 1750 BCE. Unlike the Yangshao cultures, who seem to have existed more or less independently, the Longshan cultures show an increase in trade and information exchange. The Longshan cultures are characterised by major advances. Here, I would just like to point out that they formed the first real states in Chinese history. Among the indications are increasingly differentiated burials, reflecting a stratification of society into classes, the accumulation of greater wealth among somehow privileged individuals and a style of building that made much use of hangtu style pounded earth terraces, house foundations and defensive walls. Many Longshan cultures increasingly waged war among each other, resulting in a refinement of weapon and defence technology. Simultaneously, scapulamancy develops, providing a new form of oracular advise for ritualists, shamans and regents. In this stage, cities grow and distinct professions develop. The Longshan people went beyond individual production: in several sites we can discern specific workshops, manufactories or small settlements of clan groups specialised in the production of distinct types of pottery, bone handicrafts (arrow points, hair pins, ornaments), jade carvers and so on. Simultaneous to the emergence of a ruling class appear ritual specialists who professionally mediate between the government, the people, the state and the invisible world of gods, ancestors and nature powers. Whether these ritualists belong to the budding aristocracy remains unknown. At the time, several distinct religions were practiced, but as the evidence is still too fragmentary, I wouldn't like to generalise about anything.

In the last phase of the Longshan culture we find a possible candidate for the Xia. It's the Erlitou Culture, excavated at various places in southern Shanxi and northwest Henan, provisionally dated 1,900–1,350 BCE. In 1959, archaeologists discovered this culture at Yanshi, east of Luoyang in western Henan. Here we encounter a mixture of Neolithic and Bronze Age elements. Simple people made use of items that had been around for millennia. They had stone tools, like hoes, knives, sickles and made spades with stone, shell or bone blades. Harpoons and fish-hooks were usually made of bone, arrowheads of bone or stone. At the same time, wealthier people started using bronze arrowheads and fish-hooks. The Erlitou people were among the first in China who experimented with bronze casting. Graves include typical dagger axes (a type of halberd) with jade or bronze blades. Sacral vessels such as the three legged jue and jia and the four legged ding cauldrons appear in their old pottery form but also cast in bronze; the result, though somewhat crude compared to later development, is still impressive. At the time, bronze vessels had very few ornaments; often, a mere arrangement of dots and lines was enough. On the other hand, the same bronze casters produced magnificent metal plates which were carefully inlaid with turquoise, and show animal (wolf or fox?) designs. Aristocrats wore cast bronze knives, items of great value, and were buried with impressive treasures. Among them is an early bronze bell.

Most impressive were the large buildings, built on pounded earth foundations. One such hall measured 30m east-west and 11m north-south, with an unroofed porch. As Bagley points out (in Loewe and Shaughnessy, 2006:158-165), *"If the compound was a setting for ceremonies performed on the porch of the wall, an audience of several thousand could have watched from within the enclosure."* Around the hall, several sacrificial pits containing skeletons were discovered. A tomb at a second compound, only 150 from the large pillared hall, provides a few insights into burial customs. Though covered by 6m of rock-hard pounded earth, the grave had been thoroughly plundered. Enough remained to show that the interior of the tomb contained cinnabar, possibly used for decoration, and the remnants of two lacquered wooden coffins, one of them containing the skeleton of a dog. Other, but smaller tombs in the neighbourhoods show that the Erlitou people already made sacrificial pits beneath the floor of the tomb chamber. Floors showed cinnabar deposits, coffins were lacquered and grave goods included ceramic and bronze vessels, weapons, and jade ornaments. Other finds include jade knife and knife-axe blades, jade disk-axe rings, cowrie shells, turquoise and numerous ceramic cultic vessels, including tripods, basins, ding cauldrons, beakers, bowls and specialised vessels for drink offerings. Like the later Shang, the Erlitou people had a highly specialised range of ritual equipment. Pottery of the Erlitou culture is frequently ornamented with animal designs, especially fish, dragons, serpents and even taotie monsters. The Erlitou ritualists frequently made cracks on sheep and bovine scapula, but they did not prepare the bones much, nor did they inscribe them. While it remains unproved that the Erlitou people constituted the Xia, people like them may certainly serve as models for the high cultures that preceded the Shang. The name Xia, though not verified so far, is a convenient description.

During the reign of Shang Jia, the house of Shang was still accumulating power. The house of Xia (no matter whether it was a bunch of alliances or a dynasty) was the strongest force in the country and the Zi clan just a minor group of nobles. The Xia gave them a fief in the periphery of the country, to keep them at a distance from the court, and made it a small fief, so the Zi would not gain too much power. Now the advantage of being far from the court was a certain amount of independence. The Shang used their location to scheme and intermarry with other clans. They also fought with nomads and settlers dwelling outside the middle kingdom. It was their duty to guard the country from invasions, but it was also their chance to gain a bit of extra wealth. Five generations followed. After Shang Jia came **Bao Yi**, **Bao Bing**, **Bao Ding**, **Zhu Ren** and Queen *Bi Geng* and **Zhu Gui** with Queen *Bi Jia*. Bi, by the way, does not mean queen but grandmother, woman of grandmother's generation or ancestress. Grand Historian Sima Qian lists the same regents but has a slightly different order to them. During this period, the power of the Zi clan was steadily growing. And they knew their time was coming fast.

The historians of the Zhou period tell us that the Xia Dynasty lost its virtue. Every dynasty does, eventually. They start with headstrong achievers and end in degenerate invertebrates.

Sima Qian has it that a king of the Xia, **Kong Jia**, was passionately fond of magic, but thoroughly lacking in virtue. He could not keep his domain unified, and one clan after the other rose in rebellion.

Heaven sent down two dragons, a male and a female. Kong Jia could not feed them, and could not find a dragon-keeper, as the

Dragon Images

Dragon Raising Clan refused to support him. One of Yao's descendants, Liu Lei, learned the art of dragon keeping at the Dragon Raising Clan. He went to serve Kong Jia, who gave him the tile *'dragon tamer'* and gave him the people of a clan to govern. But in spite of all care, the female dragon died. On Kong Jia's order, the trainer prepared a meal out of the flesh of the dragon and sent it to the king. Kong Jia sent someone to fetch more, and Liu, seized with fright ran away.

Soon afterwards, Kong Jia died.

Sarah Allan (1991: 72-73) offers another tale regarding the decline of the Xia. In the *Guben Zhushu Jinian* (*Old Bamboo Annals*) Kong Jia is missing. Instead, there is a Xia regent called **Yin Jia**, who does not appear in Sima Qian. When Yin Jia made his capital at the Western River, Heaven sent a terrible disaster. The ten suns appeared at the same time. In the same year, for whatever reason, King Yin Jia died. The ten suns appear in several myths. What they have in common is devastating heat, scorching brightness, wildfire and drought all over the country.

After these ominous incidents, the Xia came to a terrible end. According to their history books, the last king of the Xia, one **Jie**, was a thoroughly corrupt character. He cared nothing for the ancestors, for the misery of the common people or for the decrees of heaven. Jie, we are told, excelled in cruelty and arrogance, wasted the wealth of his country, oppressed the righteous, exploited the weak and generally made a mess out of things. He was addicted to drinking and festivity, forced his enemies to drink themselves to death in a lake of wine and set up a forest of meat where he staged midnight parties. When not waging wars he tortured his upright ministers and, I'm sure you expected this, he was misled by his corrupt, immoral and sex-crazed wife **Mo Xi**. He had acquired her, as a spoil of war, after his victory over Meng Shan, and as she was equally alluring and perverse, he soon became completely dependent on her.

This made it practically the duty of the Zi clan to put an end to the Xia and to reinstall virtue.

The term virtue (de) is at the heart of Confucian thinking. Originally, the word de used to mean power, magical power and charisma. De was the quality that kept heaven and earth in harmony, that kept government functional and allowed the regents to fulfil their tasks with grace. Thanks to the writings of Kongzi (Confucius), de acquired a moral meaning and became an ethical quality. In his teachings, de is primarily virtue, the virtue which upheld tradition, honoured the ancestors and deities, gave significance to the correct execution of the rites and generally kept society ordered and stable. Good manners, measured conduct, strict hierarchy, just laws, perfect order and everybody satisfied. Stay in line, do as you are told and no funny business. That's Kongzi for you.

By contrast, early Daoist writings interpreted de in its ancient form, as a quality of magical power which is gathered, cultivated and perfected by rulers and sages. Hence the *Daodejing* is basically about cultivating the de in accord with the Dao. And while the classical version of the good book starts with the understanding of Dao, the Way, the much earlier Mawangdui version reverses the order of the chapters and begins with the cultivation of de. Unless you cultivate magical power, charisma, and a bit of virtue in your life, you simply cannot comprehend the Way.

However we look at it, everybody knew that Jie had lost his de. The regent of the Zi clan, Tang the Successful, was full of it. Or so we are told by the Zhou historians, who had good reason to say so. Approximately twelve generations after the founding of the Zi clan, Tang and his associates overthrew the reign of Jie and began the Shang Dynasty.

The Rise of Tang

The Zhou scholars had a lot to say about Tang the Successful, and all of it is favourable.

Cheng Tang, otherwise known as **Da Yi**, **Tai Yi**, **Zi Lü**, and **Tai Zu**, began his career as the lord of a small fief on the edge of the Xia domain. His rule extended over a bare 35 km, a good sign that his overlord did not trust him much. He was granted the title fang bo, which means *'lord of a semi-foreign vassal-state'*, and of course Tang had to pay tribute for the honour. Whatever the reason, he soon had trouble with **Jie**, the last of the Xia kings. And he was imprisoned in a tower in Cong Quan for a couple of years. When he was eventually released (presumably his family had paid for this mercy) he returned to his fief in a very bad mood. And he began a series of eleven wars. Here our history books disagree. They date some wars before, others after his conquest of Jie. Whatever it may be, Tang needed troops, wealth, allies and used every chance to get them. It sounds like a violent upstart with a grudge in his heart. Our Zhou historians, however, insist that Tang was a model of virtue. Again and again Tang was praised as a just and noble ruler, honourable, trustworthy, generous, responsible and a model for all the kings and emperors to come. We find him like this in the *Shujing*, *Shijing*, *Mengzi*, *Liji*, in Kongzi's aphorisms and a few later works, such as the *Lüshi Chunqiu* and Sima Qian's *Shiji*. So let us try to be a bit naïve for a while.

Tang's first war was against the state of Gu. The people of Gu did not worship in the same way as Tang's people did, and Tang felt offended. The regent of Gu, we read, was not offering proper sacrifices to the ancestors. Tang complained about this to the Lord of Gu, but the latter replied that he would lack appropriate sacrificial animals. Tang in his generosity sent cattle to the Lord of Gu. Instead of sacrificing, the people of Gu ate it. Again Tang enquired why the people of Gu would not sacrifice properly. *'We have no grains'* replied the lord of Gu. So Tang supplied a large amount of millet and vegetables, carried by a strong force of farmers and labourers, accompanied by women and children. Tang claimed that these should help the people of Gu to clear the land and grow grains. The Lord of Gu did not approve of agriculture, and he disliked the invasion of foreigners even more. He had them slaughtered and took the millet by force. This was all that virtuous Tang needed to wage war. He made a famous speech bemoaning the death of men, women and innocent children, all of whom had been sent in a gesture of goodwill and neighbourly help. So Tang, the Zi clan and their associates waged war against Gu. Mengzi (Mencius) informs us that the entire domain of Xia supported Tang's war, and praised Tang for taking revenge for common peasants and children.

Perhaps the people of Gu were a semi-nomadic herder culture which lived on hunting, fishing, gathering and possibly bred sheep or goats, and Tang merely exploited the cultural difference to add Gu to his domain. The people of Gu had a different religion, a different world-view and simply did not know what to do with cattle and grains. Apart from eating them. But then, I wouldn't dream of criticising a regent who was praised by the cream of Chinese literati.

Ten more wars followed, each of them entirely justified on ethical principles. Soon virtuous Tang had gained so much power that many nobles thought him a good alternative to the famously corrupt and inefficient Jie of Xia.

Yi Yin's Tale

Tang had the support of an eminently cunning statesman. Here we meet **Yi (steward) Yin**, also known as **Yi Zhi**. Time for another true story.

When Yi Yin's mother was pregnant with him, she had a remarkable dream. A deity appeared and told her: *'When water comes rushing out of the stone mortar, start walking to the east and never turn back!'* The next day she saw water flowing from the mortar and began walking. After 20 li (10 km) she felt exhausted and sat down. And as she could not control her curiosity any longer, she turned her head and looked back. Her whole city had disappeared under a lake. There was water everywhere, and the shock was so much that she instantly became a hollow mulberry tree. Yi Yin, the unborn baby in her womb, grew up in a cavity of the tree. One day a woman was plucking mulberry leaves for her silkworms and she discovered the baby. She carried the boy to the lord of You Xin, who appreciated the mysterious event, told her to raise Yi Yin and had him trained as a cook. Yi Yin excelled at the art and proved to have a very cunning head for politics. Tang heard of Yi Yin and desired to have him as a counsellor. He sent a message to the lord of You Xin and asked whether he might borrow Yi Yin for a while. The lord would have none of it. Only when Tang asked to marry one of his daughters, thus fixing a firm alliance between the two families, permission was reluctantly granted. As a humble cook without family, Yi Yin accompanied the young bride to Tang's court. And Tang, overjoyed by Yi Yin's skill, made him his prime minister. (*Lüshi Chunqiu*, 14,2). But there is much more in the learned Lü Buwei's amazing compilation. When Yi Yin arrived at the court of the Zi clan, Tang took him to the ancestral temple. Some sort of initiation occurred, and Tang blessed Yi Yin by smearing him all over with the blood of a sacrificial pig. On the next day, the two met in conference. Tang, ever subtle and polite, asked Yi Yin about fine cuisine and the art of cooking. Yi Yin lectured at great length about the most refined and rare delicacies of the most distant provinces, and concluded that only a great king would have sufficient influence and far-reaching power to acquire the best ingredients. Tang was impressed and acquired an insatiable appetite.

Now for a brief look at the origin of our mulberry tree child. The mulberry appears frequently in elder Chinese myth. Its leaves are the sole food of the silkworm, so when you wish to produce silk, you need plantations of the tree. But the mulberry is also a sacred tree. The oracle bones relate occasional sacrifices to sacred trees, usually without telling us which sort. But there is an ancient myth which found its way into Han literature, such as the *Huainanzi*, where we learn that in the very east of the world a sacred mulberry rises near the sea. From the water, the ten suns arise, one after the other, over the span of the ten-days ritual week. The suns have the shape of ravens and they fly to the top of the mulberry to dry their feathers. Then they fly south, where they rest in another sacred mulberry. From the south they fly west, where a sacred Paulownia tree with white and violet blossoms stands next to a watery abyss. The ravens cast their feathers into this chasm, drop into the deep, dark waters and disappear. Through the night they travel the underground waterways, such as the Yellow Springs, the place of utter death and dissolution, and by morning they have returned to the east to rise and shine once more.

In all likeliness, this myth has come to us from the Shang period, when they cult of the ten suns (or days) was of eminent importance. If we trust this legend, Yi Yin was a child of the suns, or the tree of the rising suns. Maybe we should also see the mulberry as a world tree, an axis mundi connecting heaven and earth. Numerous Eurasian shamans use such trees (or sacred mountains) to rise to heaven and to descend to earth and even to the underworlds. Their journeys parallel the sun's journey in

Shang myth. If the mulberry was a world tree, I can only wonder at the unusual child that grew up in its core. Chinese myth makes Yi Yin a sage and statesman. By contrast, the early oracle bone inscriptions ascribe more power to him than to many early ancestors. If we only had these inscriptions, we might even wonder whether he was originally a deity.

In another sense, the mulberry could be a sinister omen. The ideogram for mulberry in the oracle bones, a tree with many hungry mouths, signifies waning, loss and death. But it is also a place name, and maybe Yi Yin grew up there. There were several settlements called Hollow Mulberry in ancient China.

Another legend claims that Yi Yin was a humble peasant before becoming prime minister. Whatever the truth, when Yi Yin got the job Tang set a precedent which had repercussions through Chinese history. Quite a few prime ministers began their career in very humble occupations. Yi Yin was famed as a cook and musician, others started as butcher, trader, hermit or toiled in a labour camp. Capable Chinese regents appreciated talent, no matter where it came from. They also liked high ministers who did their duty without being influenced by a powerful and meddlesome family.

War against the Xia

Tang urgently needed information about the Xia court. He conferred with Yi Yin, who volunteered to go there for a time. It was quite a risky undertaking. To make things appear right, the two had a severe quarrel which ended with Yi Yin fleeing and Tang trying to shoot him. Yi Yin barely escaped with his life and arrived at the Xia capital with a tale of outrage that pleased king Jie considerably. He kept Yi Yin as guest of honour and counsellor for three long years. I am sure Yi Yin had a difficult time pleasing king Jie, but he kept his eyes open, made contact with unhappy nobles and wove a network of favours without Jie noticing anything. Lü Buwei recorded that he got along well with Queen Mo Xi, who secretly told him about the nightmares of her husband: *'Tonight, the Great King has dreamed that there was a sun in the west and another sun in the east, and that the two suns fought. The western sun was victorious and the eastern sun suffered defeat.'* The suns are obviously symbols for Tang and Jie, and Yi Yin knew that the tyrant was unconsciously suspecting what was about to happen. So he packed his things, took his leave and made his way home to Tang, who had been busy preparing his troops (see *Lüshi* 15.1). Virtuous Tang was very upset by the many sad tales Yi Yin related from the court of Xia. According to Yi Yin, Jie was completely deluded and spoke without sense and insight. His ministers used their office to enforce high taxes, collect bribes and crush all resistance without mercy. Indeed Jie had lost his de.

Tang had been waiting for such news. Soon enough, he found himself surrounded by outraged nobles begging him to put an end to the evil ways of the Xia. Knowing everything about right and wrong, Tang gave a rousing pep speech which I shall quote in full, based on the *Shujing* (*Tang Shi*) and Sima Qian's vivid retelling.

"Tang spoke: Come, ye multitude of people and listen to my words. It is not as if I, the Small Child, would have dared to start a rebellion. The lord of Xia has accumulated much guilt. I have heard the words of you all, and as the lord of Xia is an evildoer, and as I fear the Supreme God, how could I dare not to punish him? As the lord of Xia has committed many crimes, heaven commands me to slay him.

You, o people, are saying: 'Our ruler does not care about us, he neglects agriculture and his reign is cruel.' You say: 'What remedy do we have against his crimes?'

The king of Xia does nothing but depletes the strength of his subjects, and oppresses the entire kingdom. His people (ministers?) are idle and have no harmony with him. They say: 'When will this sun set? We will all perish together.'

As this is the conduct of the king of Xia, I am forced to advance. If you support me, the One Man, to perform the punishment which Heaven decrees, I will reward you. May there be none among you who does not believe me. I do not eat my words. If you do not obey the words of this proclamation, I will kill you and your wives and children, and no-one will be pardoned."

Maybe Tang actually said something like it, and maybe the Zhou historians made the whole thing up almost a thousand years later. The reference to Heaven is certainly a Zhou time invention, as the early Shang did not venerate heaven at all. Anyway it's a touching example how righteous rulers can motivate their allies for a justified and righteous bit of warfare. It's been used all through history.

Sadly, it wasn't very easy to defeat Jie. Tang fought numerous battles before he managed to crush his opposition. The historians disagree about how it ended. Some say that Jie was killed while others recorded that he ended his life in exile.

Tang was generous after the conquest. He did not destroy the house of Xia. Instead, he installed them as nobles in small fiefs at the periphery of his new kingdom, so they could be of use to him and continue the sacrifices to their ancestors. Which was very sound reasoning. The ancestors of the house of Xia had been very strong and dangerous deities and it just wouldn't do to upset old gods at the start of a new dynasty. For the same reason, the earth altars of the Xia were not destroyed.

Start of the Shang Dynasty

So Tang began the Shang Dynasty. One of his first acts was to order Yi Yin, himself a highly skilled musician, to order the music for the new era. Since Tangs age, every Chinese emperor began his reign by asking his master musician to specify the basic tone, from which the scales were measured. By the time of the late Zhou the musicians even had special bells cast and tuned, so the basic tone could be shared all over the domain. It made the whole country resonate in the same vibration. Or at least it was meant to. Perhaps the Shang had a similar custom. We simply do not know. The reason behind this act was the magical nature of music.

Music was an essential element in sacrifices and rituals, be it in China or elsewhere, and it still is. Through much of the Shang Dynasty, ancestors and deities received regular offerings of panpipe and drum music. The oracle bones even tell us that the spirit of Yi Yin was placated by panpipes and dancing. And by the late Shang, each ancestor received a drum-music offering and a feather dance once a year. The Shang also played on egg-shaped xun ocarinas, an instrument which was several thousand years old when their dynasty began. They had perfectly tuned bronze bells and L-shaped jade chimes. Perhaps there were also string instruments, but so far the evidence is inconclusive. Through all of Chinas early history, music, song and dance invited, placated and strengthened the gods, ancestors and spirits. They harmonised relations between heaven, earth and underworld and made the animals (spirits?) dance. Good music even caused the phoenix to descend. For this reason, ancient classics, such as the *Lüshi* and the *Lijing*, are full of chapters emphasising the importance of music. From the character of its ritual music, experts could judge the state of a country. Kongzi, for instance, travelled through several states. He listened to their music, packed his things and was off again. And he was not the only one skilled in this art. It is said that Jie's music was excessive and restless. Tang put a stop to it.

And to give you an idea what some of the ritual music was like, here is the hymn which the Song chanted when they sacrificed to their ancestor Tang. The hymn is from the *Shijing*, it dates around the eighth or seventh century BCE. This loose translation is based on Legge, with amendments after Weber-Schäfer, 1967 and Xu, 1994.

"*How beautiful! How complete!*
Our drums and hand drums are set in place.
The drums beat melodious and loud,
to celebrate the ancestor of our clan.
The descendants invite the worthy ancestor (Tang) with music,
that he may come and soothe our thoughts.
The hand drums resonate, the flutes sound shrill,

in tune with them the jade-stones chime.
The descendants cheer, the music is majestic.
Bells and drums fill the ear, the steps of war and peace are
danced.
We greet our noble visitors and there is pleasure and delight.
Long ago in ancient times, the ancestors showed the way,
how to be humble and polite from morning to night,
and dutiful in service. May he receive our winter and autumn
sacrifice,
offered by his obedient grandson."

Sacrifice in the Mulberry Grove

It was no easy start. Tang ruled as the head of a confederacy of allied clans, many of which had grudges against each other, and were all too eager to usurp the newly won power. Also, for all his virtue, Tang was guilty of rebellion against his overlord. Even if Jie was an example of vices and corruption he was still the lawful ruler of a house that had reigned since the flood. In short, Tang's position was far from secure.

More so, sometime around the end of the Xia and the rise of the Shang, a devastating cataclysm shook the earth on the other side of the globe. Recent datings estimate that around the year 1645 BCE (give or take twenty years) the volcanic island Thera, today Santorin, Greece, blew up almost completely. The explosion tore the crater to fragments and released a tsunami wave. It was accompanied by earthquakes, stormwinds and a drastic change in climate. Simultaneously the nearby Minoan culture of Crete disappeared completely. The wave must have slammed straight into the coastal cities. What remained was a handful of illiterate shepherds high up in the mountains. Around the same period several cultures came to a sudden end. Sometime around then the Indus Valley civilisation ended, many of its great cities disappearing under floods of mud. In Egypt and Mesopotamia dynasties ended, and maybe we should also date the exodus of the Israelites in this period. When volcanoes blow up, they certainly devastate their surroundings. But they have an even more lethal effect on the weather. Dust darkens earth's atmosphere, upsets the weather cycles and makes the temperature fall. When Krakatau exploded in 1883, distant Europe suffered from several cold years of bad harvests and social unrest. Now Krakatau released a mere quarter of the dust and sulphur dioxide that went up with Thera. Even the outburst of Mount Tambora in Indonesia, 1815, was weaker than Thera's explosion. And it was bad enough. 1816 is famous as the year without summer. In Europe and northern America there was frost in July. In southern China, water buffaloes froze to death on the fields. The darkened skies reduced average world temperature by 2.5 degrees Celsius. All over the globe, crops failed, followed by food shortage, starvation and migration. The Indian and Chinese monsoons were disrupted, causing unusual droughts or extreme rainfalls. Meanwhile, Turner observed and painted some of the bloodiest sunsets in art history.

When Thera erupted in the Bronze Age, the effect was even worse. Chinese histories hint at such events. The *Zhushu Jinian* (*Bamboo Annals*) relates that at the end of Jie's reign, the weather turned much colder. Earthquakes shook the ground; the sun disappeared in yellow mist, the grains failed and frost struck in midsummer. Occasionally three suns shone at once. Stars (or meteor showers) cascaded from the sky, all five planets went out of their orbit and an earthquake dried up the rivers Yi and Luo. Now it is rather hard to date all these events. Estimating the fall of the Xia is practically impossible, as the classical historians disagree. Archaeologists are not even able to identify the Xia for certain, let alone their ending. And the same goes for the end of so many other Bronze Age cultures. Much of ancient chronology rests on assumptions and educated guesses. Each system of dating has its own flaws. Radiocarbon is so diffuse that supporting evidence from typology and dendrochronology are always needed. And even dendrochronology disagrees with the dates obtained from Greenland ice cores. The former shows a drastic drop in temperature between 1629 and 1628 BCE while the ice cores give an estimate of 1644 BCE, plus/minus twenty years. It is even possible that two cataclysmic events occurred, with only a few dozen years between them. Whatever may have happened, it made the middle Bronze Age a remarkably unpleasant time to live in. While in Europe entire cultures packed their gear and went marauding, in China the Shang used the opportunity to seize power.

At the start of Tang's reign, a terrible drought began. For five or maybe seven years the rains just would not come. The grasses on the plains withered, plants would not sprout and harvests became a story from the past. Even the rivers went dry and the sun shone so hard that rocks melted. Soon, stores of grains and food were emptied and people began to starve. Tang, guilty of usurpation and possibly regicide, was blamed for everything. Even his allies began to think that Tang wasn't very popular with the gods.

Many early histories give us accounts of this event. Let me give a summary of a few (*Lüshi* 9.2, *Suoshenji* ch. 228 and Allan, quoting from *Diwang Shiji*, 1991:41-42). When river Luo Chuan went dry, Tang asked the diviners to set up a three legged ding cauldron for sacrifice and to invoke the deities of mountains and streams. The diviners did so and asked the deities many questions. Was Tang's government in right measure, was the population being exploited, were there bribes or evil slander? Were too many palaces being built, or was too much attention paid to the counsel of women? The diviners consulted the bone oracle, and the cracks told them that human sacrifices were needed. Tang, however, would have none of this. He insisted that the oracle was made for the people, and that it should be of use to them. If a human sacrifice was required, it should be him.

The nobles agreed and Tang offered himself. He fasted, abstained, cut his nails and his hair, offered blood from his own palm and sacrificed at an altar in Sanglin, the Mulberry Grove.

Tang prayed. *'If I, the ruler, have sinned, the people should not be punished, and if the people have sinned, the punishment should still be mine. The High God (Shang Di), the ancestors and spirits should not harm the lives of the people for my own shortcomings.'*

Before he ended his plea a heavy rain poured down. It drenched all corners of the world, delighted the people and saved Tang from the pyre.

Maybe Tang set a precedent here and maybe he just followed an elder custom. Whenever the country suffered from draught, human sacrifices were burned. Several such incidents are recorded in the oracle bones, and in the early Zhou period this custom continued. The preferable sacrifice being hunchbacks, as they looked like the deity of drought; wu ritualists, as Heaven might have mercy on them and provide rain; and nobles, who were responsible for the well being of their people anyway. By the middle Zhou the custom gradually went out of fashion, the Confucian scholars celebrating those who refrained from such rituals.

A Life of Virtue

There are many examples for Tang's virtue. One day he went hunting with his court. The hunters set nets in all directions, and chanted a spell: *'Whatever descends from the sky, whatever rises from the earth, whatever moves through the four direction of space, shall all be caught in our nets'*. Tang was outraged. *'With such intent all creatures are killed. Only someone like Jie would act like this!'*, and he had all nets removed except a single one. Then he gave a new spell to the hunters. *'What moves to the left shall go to the left. What moves to the right shall go to the right. What moves above shall pass above, what moves below shall pass below. Only those who oppose me shall meet their fate in this net'*.

Everyone applauded Tang's deed. Word got around, and within a short time, 36 (or 40) neighbouring states surrendered (*Lüshi* 10.5 and Sima Qian, *Shiji*).

Not even good signs could keep Tang from giving up his discipline and effort. Once a miraculous event happened. Overnight, a single stalk of grain grew right in front of Tang's palace. Within a day, the stalk became so thick that one couldn't grasp it with two hands. Everyone stared at it in amazement and wondered what it might portent. The diviners went to Tang and congratulated him to such an auspicious sign. Tang, however, remarked that good signs are no reason to cease doing better. He extended his daily working hours. He rose before dawn and went to bed late, he cared for the sick, condoled the miserable, and worked for the people with all his might. And he spoke: *'If you see a good sign but do not act well, evil is sure to follow. If you see a bad sign but act well, ill-fortune will stay away.'* After three days, the stalk disappeared on its own accord. Lü Buwei comments: *"Bad luck is the foundation of good luck, and good luck attracts bad luck. But only a sage can know this. How could the people understand the growth of the seed?"* (*Lüshi*, 6.4).

Now for a brisk walk through the generations. To make things a little easier, I have marked the names of kings in bold and the names of queens in bold and cursive script. The royal genealogy is largely clear, but here and there the scholars disagree with each other. Some of the kings may have received their title posthumously, and may have never had an official regency. And the list of queens is certainly not complete. Many kings had several queens, but we only know about those who appear in the oracle bones and can be assigned to specific regents. As the names of the queens are made up of very similar titles and the same ten day names, it is not always easy to tell who exactly is referred to.

Tang ruled for approximately thirteen years after the fall of Xia. He married ***Bi*** (ancestress) or ***Mu*** (mother) ***Bing***. After his death, he became a terrifying ancestor, and she was never really popular either. But how could the regency continue?

His crown prince was **Tai Ding** (Great Ding). His reign was extremely short and insignificant. Maybe he even died before the inauguration. In later times, he was revered as a royal ancestor, but whether he ever acted as a proper king remains a matter of debate. He had a Queen called **Bi Wu**.

Next, Prince **Bu Bing**, otherwise known as **Wai Bing**, ascended the throne. He died three years later. Then followed Prince **Zhong Ren**, who also died soon. Perhaps he only became king posthumously. At this point, all of Tang's sons had died and the regency moved to the next generation.

Next, **Tai Jia** (**Da Jia**) prepared to ascend the throne. In all likeliness he was the son of Tai Ding. We know a lot about him, and very little is favourable. Tai Jia was a headstrong young man who had scant concern for the duties and virtues of a regent. Instead, he was notorious for his love of festivity, hunting, lovemaking and luxury. He was also famed for violence and cruelty. After three years on the throne, records Sima Qian, Tai Jia had become unbearable. He disobeyed Tang's laws and slighted Tang's reputation. Old Yi Yin admonished him many times, but the young king did not bother to listen. The *Shujing* gives three lengthy speeches by Yi Yin, containing some elder lore, but certainly a lot of material the historians made up in the middle and early Zhou. According to them, Tai Jia was lacking in respect, sincerity, discipline, virtue, humility, religious devotion, care for tradition and so on. Yi Yin certainly told him so. *"If you dare to have constant dancing in your mansions and drunken singing in your chambers, I call it the fashion of the wu* (ritualists)*. If you dare to aim your heart* (awareness, mind) *on wealth and women and give yourself to travel and hunting, this is what I call disintegration. If you dare to scorn the words of the wise, to oppose the loyal and straight, to keep away from the old and virtuous and to seek the company of homosexual youths, this is what I call the fashion of derangement. If a high aristocrat or an officer is addicted to even one of these three fashions with their ten wicked ways, his clan will meet destruction; if a prince of a country is addicted, his state will certainly be ruined."'*

Tai Jia did not care. So Yi Yin used his political power. He evicted the young regent from the court and banished him westwards to the Kongtong, the Hollow Paulownia tree. This tree is in direct opposition to the Kongsan, the Hollow Mulberry, where Yi Yin grew up. It was a dark and gloomy grove, the place where Tang maybe had found his death and lay buried. Yi Yin forced Tai Jia to go into mourning for three years, to show his respect to his late father Tai Ding and to his grandfather Tang. No more music, fun, lovers or drunken revelry. Instead, he had to wear plain clothes, fast, abstain and mourn in silence at the grave of Tang.

In the capital, Yi Yin granted himself the title Supreme Protector and governed instead of the king. It was quite an achievement for a former orphan, musician and cook. But he seems to have made an excellent job of it. Though he was barely adopted into the Zi clan, the nobles appreciated his skill, and the feudal lords paid tribute and came to his audiences. Through much of the Shang period, kings and queens sacrificed to Yi Yin, as if he had been born into the royal bloodline. This unusual fact, well attested from the oracle bones, was also known to the ritualists who composed the *Chuci* (*Tianwen*). After two or three years, so the story continues, Tai Jia had shown enough remorse. Here our sources disagree. In some, such as the *Shujing*, Yi Yin personally came to accompany the heir to the capital. Here, Tai Jia became a popular and virtuous regent and a successful warlord. He married Queen **Bi Xin**. Yi Yin served as his minister for many years, composed documents full of praise for the young king and retired, greatly honoured, in ripe old age.

The other version, in the *Bamboo Annals*, says that Tai Jia came back without invitation and slaughtered Yi Yin on the spot.

Tai Jia was the last of what we might call the early ancestors. We could divide the Shang ancestors into three groups. The first might be called the primal ancestors. They are nebulous, mythical beings who began the house of Zi, but not all of them were necessarily human beings. A few are more like ancient gods who had received a human form and a place in the genealogy to bolster up the clan's prestige. Among them are Lady Jiandi and her husband, as well as ancestor Monkey and a number of beings who may have been gods or ancestors or both, such as Woman Venerated Dragon, Woman Tiger, Child Open Fontanel and so on. The Shang sacrificed to a wide range of beings, people and natural forces, most of them unknown and inexplicable to us.

The second class of ancestors are a bit more humane but just as terrifying. They span the period from Tang to Tai Jia. They were followed by ordinary ancestors, kings and queens and a few special persons of unknown status. All three groups received sacrifices. But they got them on different occasions. When large calamities threatened the realm, when invasion, drought, locusts or flood occurred, the oracle bones were asked who of the primal or early ancestors were responsible. Large disasters often necessitated large sacrifices. When minor disasters, accidents, evil dreams or simple diseases harmed the royal family, the ordinary ancestors were held responsible. It was a difference of power, not of intent. All ancestors were renowned for bringing bad luck, one way or another. It's just that the primal and early ancestors could destroy the state, while the ordinary ancestors punished specific aristocrats with toothache and nightmares.

There is scant information about the next regents of the Shang. For a long time, scholars could only rely on Sima Qian's record, a brief list lacking almost any detail. The oracle bones provided further evidence that the kings and queens existed, but don't record anything regarding their reign. It is only the kings and queens who governed while the oracle bones were inscribed who provide reliable data. For a listing of all known Shang regents, including some that may or may not have reigned, see the table at the end of the book. Regarding their queens, data is even more scant. Usually, a king had at least one queen and an unspecified number of secondary wives and concubines. Sima does not usually refer to the queens at all. But the oracle bones record sacrifices to them, as well as to important women whose status remains unknown, which allowed modern scholars to name quite a few of them. Let us now look at a few more regents.

After Tai Jia followed his son **Wo Ding**, says Sima, who reigned very briefly or received the title king posthumously. The government went to his brother or son **Tai** (great) **Geng** and **Bi Ren**, then to his brother **Xiao** (small, young) **Jia**, then to brother **Yong** (harmonious) **Ji** and Queen **Bi Ji** (**Yu Bi**?). Around this time the power of the Shang Dynasty began to decline. The nobles holding the distant fiefs were becoming independently minded and rarely bothered to show up at audiences, says Sima. After Yong Ji followed his brother **Tai** (great) **Wu**, one of whose characters in the oracle bone script is a figure hiding an axe behind its back. T.T. Chang reads his name as Ambush. During King Ambush's reign an incident occurred, says Sima, which is very similar to that you read earlier. In a single night two different species of mulberry tree or a tree and a stalk of grain grew together in the court. The king was alarmed, but his prime minister admonished him to cultivate virtue and eliminate hidden defects in the court. The king followed his advice and tree and stalk both disappeared. The *Shujing* and Sima's *Shijing* relate that during Tai Wu's reign, the wu (ritualist, shaman) Xian had an exceptional status at court. S/he governed the royal household and consulted with the prime minister. Sima records that Wu Xian composed two documents about government, which were part of the original *Shujing* but have since been lost (or deleted). As Sima's expressed it, Wu Xian transmitted the secret writings of Heaven. According to the *Zhushu Jinian* (*Bamboo Annals*), Wu Xian sacrificed at mountains and rivers. In later ages, the wu of China venerated Wu Xian as their earliest known ancestor and a pioneer of their craft. The few surviving wu of the 21st century still do so. During Tai Wu's reign the Shang regained much of their power and stabilised their ties to their allies. Tai Wu was a remarkably long lived king. He governed for 75 years and became a very dreaded ancestor. After Tai Wu followed his son, **Zhong** (middle) **Ding** who had two queens, *Bi Ji* and *Bi Gui*. Shang kings had concubines and consorts, but they only had one queen at a time. Evidently, Zhong Ding outlived his first queen and married another. Zhong Ding moved the capital from Bo (Tang's residence) to Ao. After him, his younger brother **Wai** (outer) **Ren** (also known as **Bu** (divination) **Ren**) ruled. Under his younger brother (?) **He Dan** (river truth? The character reads '*invasion*') **Jia**, the power of the Shang waned again. His son **Zu** (grandfather, ancestor) **Yi**, otherwise called **Xia Yi,** waged war and strengthened the state. Under his reign, another Wu (ritualist, shaman) Xian held high office. He is mentioned by the *Shujing* and Sima Qian. Perhaps this second Wu Xian assumed the name of his father or grandfather as a sign of respect. Zu Yi had the two queens *Bi Ji* and *Bi* (or *Mu*) *Geng*. Bi Ji had such a great reputation that she is called a Remote Ancestress, like Tang, Tang's queen and primal ancestor Monkey.

After Zu Yi came his son **Zu Xin** with his three queens *Bi Ren*, *Bi Geng* and *Bi Jia*, then his brother or son **Wo** (Glossy?) **Jia** and Queen *Mu* (Mother) *Geng*.

Then followed **Zu** (grandfather) **Ding.** He was not the son of Wo Jia but of Wo Jia's elder brother Zu Xin. Zu Ding survived four queens: *Bi Geng*, *Bi Xin*, *Bi Ji* and *Bi Gui*. I am sure hygiene was not very developed and many queens died giving birth. Next we have **Nan** (southern) **Geng**, who was Wo Jia's son. His directional name might commemorate warfare against the southern foreigners. After Nan Geng followed Zu Ding's son **Qiang Jia** (also called **Xiang Jia**, **Hu Jia**, **Yang Jia** and **Wo Jia**). Qiang, a reference to the Shang's archenemies, the nomadic Qiang people, could indicate he assumed this honorary name to commemorate his victories. Sima wrote that in his reign, the influence of the Shang declined again. He also complained that during the last nine generations, anarchy had reigned at the court, and that since Zhong Ding's day the *'legitimate heir'* had been neglected while junior scions became king. Sima Qian believed that this was due to the competition and fighting of the princes among themselves. Such quarrels, he assumed, had damaged the reputation of the kings and the noble lords refused to come for audience. However, as you can see, the Shang did not automatically believe in succession from father to son. In many cases, kings were not followed by their sons but by their brothers, and only when no brothers remained, the kingship passed to a member of the next generation.

Pan Geng is much better documented. He was the younger brother of Qiang Jia. Pan means plate, as in plate armour, and refers to the pieces of rhinoceros hide which nobles wore in war. So we can read him as Plate Geng, his other names were Many Plates or simply Father Geng, and Grandfather Geng. He is famous for moving the capital. Of course this was not the first time. According to legend, the Xia moved their capital eight times. And the Shang had done it five times before Pan Geng found himself forced to do it. The *Shujing* has much to say on the topic. It contains several speeches which Pan Geng allegedly made to legitimise the move. The section is highly disputed. The *Pan Geng*, considered by some as one of the earliest items in the *Shujing*, is still too young to be a product of the Shang period. It was at least edited and updated by the early Zhou historians.

All we know for sure is that Pan Geng succeeded in moving the capital. But we do not know why. His speeches are magnificent examples of rhetoric skill. The king, pleads, argues, chides, complains and clamours with passion. According to him, a move was inevitable. There was great danger threatening the old city, and many lives were at risk. Sadly, he does not tell us why. So we can only speculate. One possibility is deluge. The great rivers of China moved their course several times. It is possible that Pan Geng's old capital was threatened by flooding. As he bitterly criticises the nobles for opposing the move, I would guess that the aristocracy dwelled in the higher districts, and were reluctant to part with their property. While the poor people, living on the lower fringes of the town, got flooded every time the river rose. So Pan Geng held speeches to get the support of the population. He chided the rich for usurping the best ministerial posts while neglecting their duty to protect the people. And he reprimanded them to remember their virtue, and to support the move. All of this tells us that Pan Geng was not an absolute king, and that the Zhou historians did not expect him to be one. The Shang regents governed with the support of the noble families. Though the Zi clan was undoubtedly of divine origin, its kings were not autocrats but needed the support of aristocracy and citizens. This is in strong contrast to the function of the Chinese emperors since the Qin Dynasty. Finally, Pan Geng got his head. He argued that the tortoise shell oracle stated *'this is no place for you'*. And the entire population packed their valuables, crossed the Huang He (Yellow River) and moved to a small city which, allegedly, was called Yin. So the Zhou historians say. Whether the Shang ever used that name is unlikely. The term Yin, which came to refer to the last capital and the entire Shang Dynasty, does not appear in the oracle bones, which kept calling the capital Shang. Maybe the Zhou made it up. Quite recently, it was assumed that Pan Geng moved the capital to Anyang. However, an increasing number of scholars doubt it. The great royal cemetery at Xiaotun near Anyang was Wu Ding's work, and the tombs of regents Pan Geng, Xiao Xin and Xiao Yi, who preceded him, are nowhere to be found. Sima Qian records that pan Geng's old capital was located north of the yellow River. He relocated his people south of the river, to Tang's former capital Bo. It is a distinct possibility that Wu Ding himself moved the capital from Bo to Xiaotun near Anyang.

Interlude: Zhengzhou

According to the Zhou histories, the Shang had seven capitals. Tang made Bo his capital, then there were Ao (or Xiao), Xiang, Geng (or Xing), Pi, Yen and finally Yin. The last capital, Xiaotun near Anyang, can be confirmed by archaeology. The others are either undiscovered or not identified with certainty. Perhaps there was even an eigth one in the making. According to the Zhou period histories, the last Shang king, Zhòu Xin, started a massive building project in Shaoge, where he eventually met the hostile Zhou forces and found his death.

One interesting capital is at Zhengzhou. The early excavators were not sure about the place and its age, and called the local culture Erligang after an excavation site. Today, Zhengzhou is a thriving industrial city, 700 km south-west of Beijing, with a population exceeding 7 million, close to the Yellow River. The ancient Shang capital is under the modern city. Parts of the former city wall have been excavated, so the size of the settlement could be mapped. The capital was quite large: as Bagley reports (In Loewe and Shaughnessy, 2006:165-168), the main district covers 25 square kilometres, plus a palace and ritual complex 20km northwest of the city. Since the 1940's a small stream, river Jinshui, flows directly through the northern part of what used to be the Shang capital. But as Zhenzhou is a busy and overpopulated city, archaeologists get few opportunities to excavate at leisure. It is only when buildings are demolished or erected that a bit of excavation can be done. And this has given us a tantalising patchwork of small glimpses into prehistory.

Zhenzhou is a candidate for Tang's capital Bo or for Zhong Ding's capital Ao (Xiao). So far, the artefacts point at early middle Shang, which makes the latter theory more likely. Radiocarbon dates, for what they are worth, indicate 1590-1560 BCE plus minus 160 years. So it could be middle Shang. Or even late Xia. And any time in between (Brinker & Goepper, 1980:31-35).

Ancient Zhengzhou had a secluded quarter surrounded by a massive wall, 7km in length, containing living quarters and large buildings. There was another, possibly earlier wall with a total length of 2,9km. Numerous large pounded earth foundations were unearthed, at the time being more than twenty such terraces hint at large buildings. Several buildings show great size: one extended 65m by 13.6m; another building was 31 by 38m. The style of builing was much as in Erlitou, with the major difference that the Erligang culture occasionally set its massive pillars on stone foundations.

Bagley mentions a refuse deposit, possibly containing the rubbish from a workshop in the northwest quarter of the city, where the remnants of a hundred human skulls were unearthed. Most came from young men and some had been sawn off at brow level: possibly, the craniums were used for rituals. Chin-Huai (in K. C. Chang 1986:43) suspects that the walled enclosure was required to keep the *'slave-holding aristocracy'* at a safe distance from the poorer folk who worked and lived near the manufactories. This view is contestable. It has become a fashion among Chinese historians to refer to any early culture as a slave-holding-aristocracy. However, the term is much too vague. There is a vast difference between the slaves kept in the nineteenth century and those more than three millennia earlier. Nowadays, many scholars wonder whether the Shang actually had the economic capacity to use many slaves. They certain employed slaves, many of them former prisoners of war, for a number of extremely tough jobs. Maybe the high aristocrats also had slaves as servants. But most of the population had no use for them. Shang economy was still in such an early state of development that most of its products came from people who considered themselves free. Whatever that may mean. Most of the state consisted of farmers and herders who were largely self sufficient. The Shang sacrificed slaves for religious reasons, good evidence that they had no other use for them. That the aristocracy needed a special wall to keep out dangerous slaves seems unlikely. Just as possibly they were thinking of invading enemies.

The archaeologists were happy to find a number of graves. All of them had been plundered a long time ago. However, the thieves were careless, and left behind some fascinating items. Including bronze vessels, such as a set of four square ding cauldrons. The biggest of them is a metre high and has a weight of 86.4 kg, it is the largest early to middle Shang vessel in evidence. There were also several burial pits. Unlike the graves, the pits were made for sacrifices. One row of eight sacrificial pits in the northwest of the city was filled with 92 dogs, the pits containing between five and twenty-three dogs each. One of them, with six dogs, also contained two humans, another pit contained ornaments in gold leaf. It's unusual, as the Shang generally did not make much use of gold. There was also a ditch containing human skulls, each of them cut open, so the cranium could be used as a drinking vessel. And there were oracle bones. As Zhengzhou is an early to middle Shang city, they had no inscriptions (An Chin-Huai in K. C. Chang 1986:15-48). Finally, I would like to point out that so far, no sacred geography appears from the excavations at Zhengzhou. Later Chinese settlements often aimed at having specific sites in certain directions. And the Shang certainly made directional gods a major part of their religion. However, their influence on Zhengzhou cannot be discerned. Outside the massive walls four large manufactories have been excavated. One for pottery, two for bronze and one where bones were worked. The size of them is so large that we can be sure they produced not merely for local customers but exported a large amount of goods. The bronze foundries were unearthed to the north and south of the city, at a safe distance from houses and palaces. The bone manufactory (using animal and human bones) was in the north and a large potter's workshop with fourteen kilns in the west. The craftspeople in the manufactories were highly skilled. We have evidence for a division of labour among them. And in the pottery manufactory, two different sorts of ceramic objects were made using different processes. Cemeteries were located at least on three sides around the city, but few excavations have been possible so far. As in Erlitou burials, Erligang graves tended to have a thin layer of cinnabar on the floor. Those burials which have been excavated so far were rather modest, nevertheless some contained arrays of bronze vessels, cowrie shells, jades and similar goods. So far, no royal tombs have been identified.

With Pan Geng's (or Wu Ding's) move we have arrived at the last Shang capital near the village of Xiaotun near Anyang. The place was also called Yinxu, the Waste (or Ruins) of Yin. If we can trust the chronology of the *Zhushu Jinian,* there were 273 years from Pan Geng's move to the fall of the dynasty.

The Royal Cemetery of Anyang
Large Crosses: 'Royal' Tombs

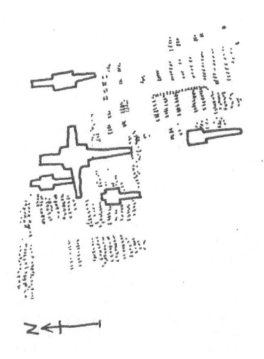

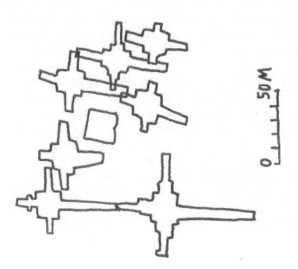

Square Tomb: Incomplete, Possibly meant for Zhoù Xin
Small dots and lines: Single graves and sacrificial pits

Anyang

Pan Geng did not move to an empty place. The countryside near Anyang had been cultivated for many centuries. The land is level, the ground is rich with reddish loess and very fertile. For agriculture and cattle breeding, the place is simply ideal. On the location of the new capital, earlier cultures had settled. Excavations have uncovered material from the Neolithic Yangshao and Longshan cultures. Before the Shang began to pound earth into walls, the locals had lived in subterranean and semi-submerged houses with storage and rubbish pits and a system of drainage to prevent flooding. The village consisted of a few hundred houses. Each of them was narrow, long and rounded, and each of them had a ramp at the entrance leading to the living space below the ground. Similar ramps came to lead to the tombs the Shang kings built. The original settlement had extended about one km north and south of the nearby river Heng Shui, written with the ideograms water and turbulence. There was some minor nobility living in the village, so Pan Geng (or Wu Ding) chose a minor feudal seat for his new home. When the king moved to Anyang, he had the ground levelled and pounded, so the houses stood on firm, flood-proof foundations. The new buildings rose from the ground, some of them graced with a second story. For the aristocracy, the Shang built spacious long halls with many chambers and inner courts. As there is such a marked difference between the original settlers living under the earth and the Shang aristocracy well above it, I wonder whether they belonged to the same culture. However, this question is tricker than it seems. It is quite possible that at least some of the underground houses remained in use when the place became the new capital. By the reign of Wu Ding, the capital extended a full six km east to west and four km north to south. What had happened to the locals?

It used to be thought that Pan Geng or Wu Ding did not bother to erect a wall around the city. Maybe the army was so strong that he thought a wall is a gesture of weakness. Later regents shared this opinion. However, the better quarter of the settlement was protected to two sides by the Turbulent Waters. And when some unknown king finally decided to have a city wall, the job was begun but never completed. Today, archaeologists are successfully mapping a city wall, securing the royal district, which never rose much above the foundation. When you imagine the Shang capital, you should visualise a core, marked by great palaces and noble houses, and an extended patchwork of villages and hamlets in the periphery. The Shang capital was not a monolithic urban structure but sprawled leisurely into the countryside, with numerous fields between the buildings. Many workshops for bronze, bone, textiles and pottery were at a distance from the centre, and surrounded by small villages peopled by clan groups. In all likeliness, the workers came from family groups and their trade was inherited.

After Pan Geng followed his two younger brothers, **Xiao** (little, younger) **Xin** and **Xiao Yi**. *'Small'* usually means younger, to mark a difference to the Xin and Yi who preceded them. But as they also appear with the titles father and grandfather in the inscriptions, they cause a bit confusion. So many regents had the same posthumous temple names. Sima notes that under Xiao Xin, the power of the Shang was waning once more, and that people fondly remembered that under Pan Geng, everything had been better. Xiao Yi was married to queen **Bi Geng**, also known as **Mu Geng**. And Xiao Yi was the first ancestor who received the posthumous title (or name) **Di**.

From King to Di

In the oracle bone inscriptions, six late Shang kings received the posthumous title Di. The title was not automatically granted to all late Shang kings. Xiao Yi became Di Yi, Wu Ding became Di Ding, then followed Zu Ji, whose reign is questionable and who was not Di-ified. Zu Geng didn't become a Di after death, but Zu Jia became Di Jia. Lin Xin did not become a Di; his reign was short, inconsequential or did not happen at all. Geng Ding reigned much longer and introduced major religious changes, but no inscriptions describe him as a Di. The same applies to Wu Yi who came to the throne after him. Perhaps these regents tried to change the custom, and wanted to reintroduce the earlier tradition where kings did not become Di at all. Or the oracle bone evidence hasn't been discovered so far. Wen Wu Ding became Di Ding after death, and so did the last two Shang regents Fu Yi and Zhòu Xin: Di Yi and Di Xin.

Di, as you will soon read, is a mysterious term. It could refer to the supreme deity in general, to the Supreme Deity of the Height (Shang Di) or maybe to a group of supreme deities, as some sources use the word as a singular and others as a plural. One possible interpretation claims that Di means the binding or alliance of deities. Di was also used as a generic term among the Shang and Zhou, and could simply signify *'divine'*. In this sense, it was occasionally used for other gods. But starting with Di Yi, the term was applied for several deceased Shang kings. Sima Qian, by contrast, calls all early Xia and Shang rulers Di. In his time, the term had come to means something like emperor. The title emperor is a convenience. I use it as it has become common usage to speak of the Yellow Emperor or of the First Emperor. It would be much more accurate to speak of Di, or thearch, or god-king. The Chinese concept is a religious one. Apart from the few Shang regents who received the title posthumously, each Di or Huangdi after the fall of the Zhou was considered the Son of Heaven. Each of them governed thanks to the Mandate of Heaven and enjoyed a semi-divine status. European emperors were more secular. They were king of kings, and much of their function was based on the model of the Roman Empire. The Caesars were not quite as divine as their far eastern counterparts. Iulius Caesar, though his family came directly from the goddess Venus, was only deified after his death. The other Caesars derived their divinity from their guardian angel. The guardian angel of the Caesars was also the guardian angel of the empire, and was duly venerated by all religions and cults. It added a divine element to the reign of each Caesar, but this reign, for good or bad, was more or less of a worldly nature. The Shang regents wouldn't have dared to call themselves Di while alive. The exalted title was always given posthumously as regents were supposed to be humble. Allegedly they called themselves by such terms as Orphan or Little Child. And when they felt especially important, they used *'the One Man'* for themselves. In daily usage, they were wang, i.e. king. The Zhou agreed, and though the title Di had been granted to a few late Shang rulers, they refused to use it for any of their own ancestors. Nor did they name them after the ten week days of the Shang. Zhou kings were wang all through their lives and remained so after death. Instead, the Zhou went to some lengths to identify their supreme deity, Heaven (Tian), with the earlier Shang Di, the Di of the Height. It wasn't until the end of the Zhou period that a living wang dared to call himself Di. The first attempt of this sort was made in 288 BCE when the regents of Qi and Qin agreed to assume the title Di. The king of Qin named himself the Western Di and the king of Qi the Eastern Di. The gesture was not met with approval. The other states were still too powerful, and before they got a chance to become really upset, the two Dis quickly retracted their grandiose titles. The idea remained attractive, however. In 286 BCE the king of Qin made another attempt and in 257 BCE a third. Each time, the political climate was against him. The title was finally revived in 221 BCE, when Qin had crushed all opposition and turned the newly united China into a dictature where all people were ordered to spy on each other and martial law prevailed. Ying Zheng styled himself Qin Shihuangdi meaning Qin's First August Thearch. He purposely assumed the title of Huangdi, the so-called Yellow Emperor of prehistory, and so have all Chinese thearchs ever since.

Wu Ding

Xiao Yi was followed by his son **Wu** (martial) **Ding**. Here things become more interesting. Scapulamancy had been a popular custom long before the advent of the Shang. But it is thought that Wu Ding was the first king who had the bones inscribed and stored, thereby creating the first historical archives of Chinese history. Some scholars doubt this. For one thing, the bones do not have proper dates on them. It is a slim possibility that some of the earliest inscriptions go back to the two Xiaos or even, if the three of them only reigned a short time, to Pan Geng. So far, there is no way to answer this question. The other point is that oracle bone writing is not the start of Chinese writing. There are inscribed bronze vessels which may or may not predate the oracle bones. At the moment, bronze and bone inscriptions are assumed to have pretty much the same age. But this may change with further excavations. And there is the ideogram for book/document which shows a scroll of bamboo strips. In other words, some people had long expertise with the written word before Wu Ding began to collect divination records. There were treaties, there were written vows to the gods and ancestors, and perhaps there were also records of genealogy and calendars on the bamboo scrolls. This would constitute the real start of Chinese history, but as all bamboo has long gone to rot we stand little chance of excavating any.

So let us say that, for convenience sake, Wu Ding's reign started period one of the oracle bone inscriptions. Wu Ding was an extraordinary character. We know much more about his time than about that of any other Shang regent. For one thing, he appears prominently in the *Shujing* and a number of classical texts. For another, he was so extraordinarily interested in divination that he left an enormous amount of inscriptions. Better still, Wu Ding believed that most topics were good for divination. The regents who came after him limited the scope considerably, and when the last two Shang kings ruled, divination had become a boring farce which mainly confirmed a ritual schedule and assured everyone that the day, night or week would be free of disaster.

Let's begin with Wu Ding's rise to power. According to the *Shujing*, Wu Ding had a difficult start. For some unspecified reason he grew up far from the court. Possibly he was raised by common people. Which simply cries for an explanation. Was he a royal heir who had to be raised in ignominy to prevent assassination? Or did he come from a common background and cheated his way into the Zi clan? Was he adopted? Or did he usurp the throne?

Nobody knows the answer. Whatever it may be, there was something questionable about his background. And whoever engineered this move, when Xiao Yi died, Wu Ding became heir to the throne. The first three years of his reign were devoted to the customary period of mourning. Unlike some other rulers, Wu Ding took the mourning really seriously. He lived in an unheated shed, wore plain clothes, ate plain food and refused to speak. It may show heartfelt grief. But it could also be seen as an almost shamanic initiation. Have you ever abstained from speech for a few days? I recall losing my voice, thanks to heavy colds, a few times. Once I was forced to spend an entire mouth keeping my mouth shut or whispering. After a while I noticed that there are lots of occasions when speech is irrelevant. There's a vast amount of talk which does not really communicate anything new, but simply serves to confirm similarities, relationships, signals attention or marks territory. It's amazing how often words act as a substitute for communication. Extreme intellectuals swim on a flood of words just like a snail slides over slime. And silence can be a blessing, a relief and an initiation. It can teach you how much information is shared without talk. Abstaining from talk for specific periods is an excellent and consciousness changing ritual. Especially for wordy know-it-alls like me or people like you who actually bother to read books. Sometimes a gesture has more value than an hour of chatter, often it's a lot better to listen than to respond. A vow of silence does just this. It can be a widening of the mind. And for a young regent, it's an excellent start.

But Wu Ding went beyond this. When the three years were over, he moved into better quarters but he still preferred silence. During the next years he was present on all important occasions, but he still addressed his ministers by letter.

Soon enough, Wu Ding became aware of his limitations. His predecessors had let the power of the Shang decline dangerously, the nobles of the outer provinces were in unrest and on several occasions, foreign armies invaded the realm. In short, there was a lot of space for improvement. There always is. Wu Ding thought of the shining example Tang and Yi Yin had set. And one night he dreamed of finding the perfect prime minister. It was such a vivid dream that he could describe the appearance of this sage in every detail. First, the king inspected the officials, citizens and soldiers of his capital. Then he sent his agents into the country, and eventually, the very person was found. He was one Yue, a simple man, perhaps a peasant or even a convict, who pounded earth in a forced labour camp. Sima Qian disagrees at this point. In his opinion, Yue was in that camp, but he worked as a clerk. The place was a crag called Fu, and hence, our man received the name Fu Yue (Peak of Fu). Wu Ding invited him and listened carefully. Then he made Fu Yue prime minister. The next day, when Wu Ding was presiding over a sacrifice to Tang the Successful, a pheasant came flying and settled on the handle of a sacrificial ding cauldron, crying mournfully. The king was much alarmed, but his son Zu Ji told him the omen was auspicious if the king improved his government. According to Sima Qian, Zu Ji said: "*'Heaven is very attentive to the righteous behaviour of men and grants them long years or the opposite. It is not that Heaven shortens lives, people shorten their lifetimes themselves. Some men do not cultivate virtue and do not accept heavenly punishment. Heaven orders them to mend their ways, but still they complain 'What can we do about it?'* (or: *'What can Heaven do to me?'*) *The king should always treat people with respect, for they are the descendants of Heaven.* (or: *he will be the heavenly appointed successor*). *In regular sacrifices, do not worship with the rites of a discarded religion.*" The last bit is tricky. Compare with the *Shujing*, chapter *Gaozong Rongri*, where the incident is ascribed to Wu Ding's second son, Zu Geng. It might also read: "*do not make excessive sacrifices* (to Tang, or to Wu Ding's father) *while discarding* (other ancestors).'"

There are a few odd things about the tale. As usual, Heaven and Heaven's decree are prominent, thanks to a Zhou period interpretation. The last section is a sad fragment: it would be nice to know if the king actually followed rites of a discarded religion (and subsequently improved it) or whether he merely gave more attention to unpopular ancestors. Finally, who exactly reprimands the king? If Sima is right, King Wu Ding was admonished by his own son Zu Ji during a public ceremony. It's possible but not very likely. The only other Zu Ji who could have admonished him was a king who had been dead for a long time, and who would have spoken out of the mouth of a medium or some impersonator of the dead. If the *Shujing* is right, the whole incident happened after Wu Ding's and Zu Ji's death, when Zu Geng mounted the throne. In this case Zu Ji was the elder brother, who, speaking through the mouth of an impersonator of the dead, had every right to admonish his younger brother.

Whatever it was, Wu Ding did much to improve himself. With Fu Yue's help, he innovated government, fought against more than forty foreign states and statelets, won several major wars and successfully expanded the frontiers of his domain. He reigned for fifty-nine years, greatly respected the gods and ancestors, performed many divinations in person and frequently consulted the oracle about his dreams. The regents who came after him greatly admired his regency. After death, he received the temple name **Gao Zhong** and the title Di, which, in this context, means something like superhuman thearch. Hence, he sometimes appears under the name **Di Ding**. His descendants were awe-struck by his reputation and sacrificed to him as if he were one of the earliest and most venerable ancestors. One period 2a inscription (T.T. Chang, 1970:87, 5.19) reads: "*Gui-si (day 30) / divination: / ritual purification / before / Father Ding / fifty / pairs of lambs / ... ? / Divination: / ritual purification / before / Father Ding / perhaps / one hundred / pairs of lambs?*"

Owl Shaped Zun Wine Container from Fu Hao's Tomb

Another period 2a inscription: (ibid, p.136, 9.12) *"Ding-si (day 54) / crack-making / give / burned offering / for / Father Ding / one hundred / dogs / one hundred / pigs / split / one hundred / bovines?"* It's much more than Wang Hai, Shang Jia or Tang usually received. Even the Zhou were full of praise for Wu Ding, who spoke little and got much done.

Fu Hao and Fu Jing

There is much more to the reign of Wu Ding than appears in the Zhou period histories. Wu Ding was excellent at organisation, and he had a few ideas which do not fit the classical histories at all. Let's talk about his queens. Wu Ding had at least three queens and more than sixty secondary queens and concubines. Of the three queens, the first probably had the temple name **Bi Gui**. Here, the researchers disagree. The oracle bones have little to say about her. She seems to have died young, and several of her ritual vessels turned up in other people's tombs. Then there is **Fu Hao**. Thanks to archaeology and oracle bones we know more about Fu Hao than about any other person in the entire Shang Dynasty. Fu Hao is not a posthumous temple name but a title she had when alive. And she was very much alive. Fu means lady, princess, royal consort, while Hao means well, good, beautiful. Her name reads Fu (broom) plus Hao (woman/mother with child). It's not the only reading. Possibly the character for woman was attached to the Fu to indicate her status as wife or mother (during the Shang, the characters for nü, woman, girl and mu, mother were frequently confused), in which case her name would read Fu (princess) Mu/Nü (mother/woman) Zi (child, son). In other words, Princess of the Zi Clan. There were many fu around in Shang times, princesses from allied clans all over the domain, but if this reading is true, Fu Hao was a direct descendant of Xie and Jiandi. Wu Ding was a member of the same family, making the marriage endogamous. But if there was doubt about his origin, marrying a princess of unquestionable pedigree would have been an excellent career move.

One of the things the Zhou historians never knew about was administration under Wu Ding. At least twenty of his spouses had high level positions in government. Some calculated and regulated taxes and tributes, others co-ordinated silk production, ran the royal manufactories, or regulated trade and fishing. Fu Hao was a high general in the army. King Wu Di trusted her to wage war, and Fu Hao did it with passion. One inscription tells us that she led more than thirteen thousand of her personal warriors. This is an amazingly large army for the Bronze Age. It far exceeds anything we know of from Europe at the time and implies a level of organisation that is truly amazing. Fu Hao personally won at least four wars against the Tu, Ba, Yi and Qiang people. But there is more about her private life in the oracle bones. We know that Fu Hao, like the other queens of her time, owned cities and wide ranges of fertile land. Like any other noble clan leader she paid taxes to the treasury, and recruited her troops from the clans in her fief. There are plenty of oracles regarding her pregnancies, and we can be sure she had at least two daughters and one son. One inscription mentions a prophetic dream of hers which her husband took quite seriously. The inscriptions also tell us that she had toothache and worried if ancestress Geng was causing it, and underwent ritual exorcism to purify herself. She also suffered from something written dragon, which might be a disease, bad luck or some dangerous influence, and required further purification. That's the general opinion. Keightley, by contrast, proposes the dragon sign indicates healing. In Wu Ding's period, plenty of inscriptions tell us of nobles purifying themselves to banish evil influences and curses. When one of her daughters was sick, Fu Hao consulted the oracle whether ancestress Geng was after her again. And she was prone to wind diseases, i.e. often caught a cold. Apart from this, she participated in the state ceremonies, and sacrificed and acted much like a priestess. None of this made its way into the history books.

Then, in 1976, farmers were levelling a hillock near Xiaotun to win ground for farming. The hillock was quite a distance from the royal cemeteries and everyone was amazed that the earth was so hard. Pounded earth can be hard like rock. So archaeologist moved in and found the one and only undisturbed aristocratic tomb of the Shang period (so far). It isn't such a huge grave. Measuring 5.6 x 4 metres it may even be thought humble. But here, eight meters beneath the surface, was the richest treasure trove imaginable. The grave contained more Shang material than had been excavated and collected before. There were more than 440 bronze objects, 590 jade items, 560 bone items, seventy items of stone plus pieces of ivory, ceramic vessels, 20 opal pendants and a total of 7000 cowrie shells. The cowries were Shang time currency and a popular sacrificial offering, perhaps they also had talismanic functions. As the Shang domain did not extend to the sea, and cowries only appear in two small regions off the coast, each shell was a rare item and had to be imported from friendly neighbour states.

We can be sure that the tomb belonged to Fu Hao as the majority of the sacrificial bronze vessels bear her name. Others are signed **Hao Mu Xin**, meaning Good, Beautiful (or Woman Zi) Mother Xin, Xin being the day chosen for her posthumous sacrifices. It's one of the better days, she shared it with Wang Hai and the wife of Tai Jia. And some had the inscription **Bi Xin**. But there were also some bronze vessels inscribed *Tu Mu Gui*. Mother Gui is probably the posthumous temple name of Wu Ding's first queen. Some scholars argue that Mu Gui might have been Fu

Fu Hao
(Automatic Drawing)

Hao's temple name, but as these vessels are in the minority and vessels with the same inscription have come up in other graves, it is possible that Mu Gui's ritual dishes were shared out in other tombs. Mu or Bi Gui was not a person of much importance. The oracle bones mention few sacrifices to her, and these are rather small. So we can be fairly sure that Fu Hao and Bi Xin were the same person. Not that this issue is entirely resolved.

Let's take a closer look at the grave goods. Fu Hao's bronzes cover the whole range of ceremonial vessels. Some are cauldrons, others are specialised drinking vessels and some were used for ritual washing. Her tomb contained more than two-hundred vessels, which implies a wide range of sacrificial rituals. 70% of them were made for ritual drinking. Many look like cups or chalices, but there is also a range of jugs in animal shape. As usual in Shang art, such items were not simply representations of real animals. More often, they were mixtures of several species, such as the bizarre owl (see illustration p.123) with elephant or rhino feet, large snakes spiralling on the wings and a wealth of dragon and bird images in the ornamentation. Given that the Shang were so obsessed with solar birds, the owl is certainly a dark surprise. For the Zhou and many other Chinese people, owls were birds of bad luck, representing darkness, night, the underworld and sudden death. Perhaps the Shang thought differently. Or Fu Hao did. But owls mean more than that. The ideogram can also mean to observe or inspect, it can mean ancient and, most often, it meant drinking and sacrificing wine. It was also used as a name and a place name (p.625). Fu Hao also had wine jugs in tiger shape. Tigers were and are among the most important shamanic animals in south and eastern Asia. Look at the picture. If we assume that animals on ritual vessels connect with animal spirits, animal shaped deities or clan animals, Fu Hao was buried in good company. There were also almost two-hundred weapons and bronze tools in her tomb. She carried more than eighty ge dagger axes and four magnificent ceremonial axes for the odd sacrifice or execution to the otherworld. Such axes represented the power of justice and royalty. Fu Hao also took a number of bows and long knifes (or short swords) with broad blades. Another very special offering consisted of four highly polished bronze mirrors, perhaps the earliest in Chinese history. Mirrors can be useful in daily life, but in Chinese religion, they act as talismans. In wu and Daoist ritual, they are useful to discover the true nature of a being or thing. The pure, polished mirror, just like the natural, silent mind, reflects without distortion. It shows all images and events without clinging to any. This idea appears in early Daoist literature, such as the *Zhuangzi* (5) and *Huainanzi* (2/10). Mirrors are among the favourite tools of exorcists and wu, as they repel negative forces and show demons

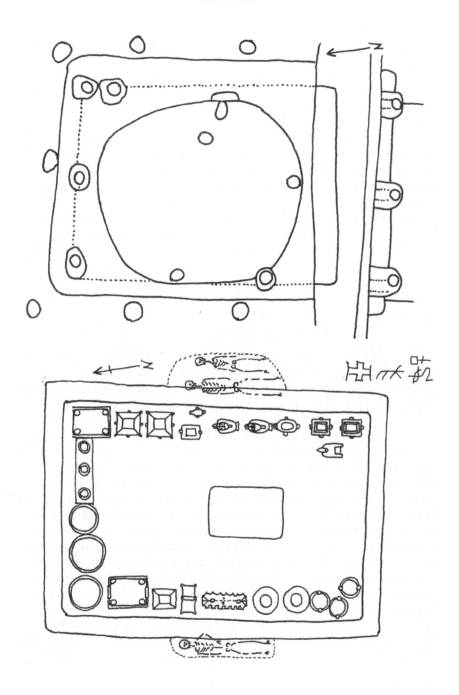

Fu Hao's Tomb
Surface level with columns
Underground level with Sacred Vessels and Grave Guardians

as they really are. So when mirrors became a great fashion in the Han Dynasty, they often had sacred images on the back. Common is the LTV motif deriving from astronomical diagrams (and the liubo game) and images of Xiwangmu, surrounded by the sacred animals of the directions. Such mirrors were carried as talismans. Maybe Fu Hao did the same. Another treasure was a set of five large and eighteen smaller bells, each of them finely cast and able to produce two distinct tones, depending on where they were struck. Usually, such bells were status objects, signifying that their owner had royal authority to govern cities or districts. That's the official function. But music instruments are there to be used. Perhaps Fu Hao loved to make or listen to bell music. She also had four xun ocarinas in her tomb.

Let's look at the jades. Jade was and is a sacred material. In early literature, it appears as the concentrated energy of yang, hence it was worn to improve health, extent life and attract good luck. The Shang imported their jade from the mountains in the west. Fu Hao had a wide selection of jade pendants in animal shape. Among them are eleven fishes, seven birds, two lizards and one one-legged kui dragon. Another group shows tigers. Four of them are three-dimensional miniatures and four are flat. She also had jade disks of the bi type carved like a dragon touching its own tail, an ouroboros motif. The motif first appeared in the Hongshan culture, around 3,500 BCE, when several animal types were carved who chased their own tails, among them dragons, serpents, pheasants or peacocks. The Longshan Cultures continued making jade Ouroboros dragon-serpents while the Shang, and the Zhou continued the tradition. The image, perhaps signifying that life is one, continuous, circles around an empty core and always feeds on itself, certainly got around. In later periods we find it popular among the old Egyptians, on Celtic coins, in Vedic and Nordic myth (the world serpent) and in medieval alchemist manuscripts. Fu Hao had a range of small and beautifully carved animal figurines, such as dragon, phoenix, tiger, bear, elephant, bull, bird and owl. All of these items point at a cult of sacred animals or at animal shamanism if you like. Other jade objects include plain bi disks, beads, bracelets, hair pins, a pigment mixing dish, axes, blades, daggers, and a finely carved thumb-ring, as used by archers to avoid being hurt by the recoiling bow string.

Among the bone objects were 490 hair needles, many of them with bird ornaments. These birds often have a triangle above their head, which shows similarity to the head ornaments appearing in the ideograms for dragon, phoenix (bird Peng) and occasionally tiger (p.334). Perhaps they signify the peacock crest; peacock bones were unearthed at Xiaotun.

The tomb chamber was surrounded by human sacrifices. Four of them were above the chamber and acted, possibly, as grave guardians. Two were in an eastern niche, one in a western niche and one under the bottom of the chamber. Eight others cannot be located properly, as their position had been moved by subterranean water. Among these sixteen people were four men (one of them young), two women and two children. Plus six dog sacrifices, five with the guards and one, perhaps a pet, in the chamber itself. A mere sixteen human sacrifices is rather humble. Probably Wu Ding received more than four hundred. And perhaps we should not class them as human sacrifices either. Usually, the people who accompanied regents to the otherworld were trusted and honoured retainers, servants and friends. It was a sign of esteem to accompany a noble to death. I would prefer to use the term human sacrifice for people who did not enjoy this privilege. Such as prisoners of war, many of them of the Qiang people, who were offered when Fu Hao's ghost was angry or needed a bit of strengthening. The excavations show that Fu Hao's tomb was sealed with many layers of pounded earth. On top of it was a temple. It had a row of pillars on the outside and some within, and was probably topped by a two-storey roof. Here, her descendants sacrificed to her. She became a formidable ancestress. Fu Hao had a strong spirit and required a lot of offerings. One inscription divines whether she should receive a blood sacrifice plus one hundred sheep. This is real value. Her spirit was venerated for several generations. After the fall of the dynasty she was forgotten, or maybe deleted from the official record, and rested in oblivion until the oracle bones appeared to tell her tale. Today there is a remarkable museum celebrating her tomb in Anyang, complete with a highly idealistic statue showing her as a beautiful kung fu heroine armed with a ceremonial axe. It may not be quite realistic, but for ancestral worship it works excellently. And it would have made her laugh. Fu Hao's spirit receives plenty of attention and is very much alive. (On Fu Hao, see K. C. Chang 1980:87-90; Brinker & Goeppner, 1980:30-31; plus the papers by K. C. Chang, Cheng Chen-hsiang, Chang Chen-lang, Chang Ping-ch'üan and Hsia Nai in K.C. Chang, 1982, inscriptions in T. T. Chang, 1970 and Zheng Zhenxiang in *Das alte China*, catalogue, 1996:106-114).

Fu Hao, like so many dedicated generals, was not fated to live a long life. She died fairly young and another lady became Wu Ding's queen. Alive she was called **Fu Jing** (Lady Well; Shaft; Trap), and after death she probably became **Bi Wu**. The Jing state appears in oracle bone inscriptions. During Wu Ding's earlier reign, they were a fang state, i.e. dangerous foreigners. At some point, they must have allied themselves to the Shang by marriage. After Fu Hao's death, that consort became queen. Fu Jing had an active part in government. She was another strong woman who frequently participated in hunts and waged at least

17 Shang Period Bronze Inscriptions, most of them are dedications to Kings, Queens and Princes.
Note the Dedication to a Fang State in the bottom row and the ornamental Dragon in Ouroboros style.

one successful war as a general, leading her own troops. Her main occupation, however, was agriculture. The oracle bones give evidence that Fu Jing organised and controlled grain cultivation in most of the Shang domain, which included ritual functions, prayer and supervision of field cultivation, irrigation, grain distribution, logistics, transport and trade. It was an enormous task, and Fu Jing performed it for many years. Now traditionally, the king had to participate in several agricultural rituals. Shang kings had to witness the first ploughing. They did not perform it personally, as the Zhou did. But each year, they had to lead a procession of citizens to the sowing, and they personally waded through the wet and sticky loess fields to plant (or erect) the water millet. Even the permission to sow or gather the harvest depended on the king, who consulted the oracle about the issue. Wu Ding evidently thought that this was too much effort. In many oracles, it is Fu Jing who divines whether the permission for harvesting should be granted.

In short, she was much more than an able administrator. Her office involved some of the most sacred rituals of the year.

Once again, we can be grateful for the oracle bones. That there were women of such status, power and importance in prehistory is a fact which never appears in the writings of Kongzi or the Zhou historians. In their world-view, such ladies were simply unthinkable.

A time of drastic changes

Perhaps Wu Ding was followed by a king we know very little about, **Zu Ji**. He could have been another guy who never made it to the throne, or he had a brief and insignificant reign. The *Shiji* and *Shujing* consider him the eldest son of Wu Ding. We now enter period two of oracle bone writing.

Period 2a is the reign of **Zu Geng** and his queen *Bi Yi*. They followed the traditions set by Wu Ding and seem to have altered very little.

In period 2b, their younger brother, king **Zu Jia** and queen *Bi Wu* came to power, and they changed a lot. If we trust the classical histories, Zu Jia was a failure. Sima merely records that he was licentious and that the power of the Shang declined. Other sources hint, without giving any detail, that Zu Jia had scant concern for ethics and virtue, that he changed traditions and neglected sacrifices. The *Shujing* does not quite agree. Though it dismisses all regents after Wu Ding with little praise, it does remark that Zu Jia was much concerned about the well-being of the population. He even respected widows and childless men. To understand this line you should recall that the Zhou, who wrote it, had a society in which unmarried women had no status. Once a woman married, she joined the husband's family and lost the spiritual ties to her own family and ancestors.

Should her husband die, she found herself outside of society. And childless men were seen as little better than criminals. It was the duty of a man to have male heirs, who were duty-bound to continue the worship of the ancestors. A man without heirs had failed the ancestors badly. This sort of thinking is attested for the Zhou and for all dynasties that followed them. We don't know if the Shang already had such beliefs. For the Zhou historians, nothing else was worth recording regarding Zu Jia. His reign of thirty-three years (?) was not worth further comment. It was only when the oracle bones were deciphered that scholars realised that Zu Jia was an astonishing reformer.

To understand his reforms we have to look back to Wu Ding. In Wu Ding's reign (oracle bone period 1a and 1b), a huge range of topics were divined. Wu Ding had the diviners busy every day, and often performed the divination himself. He simply wanted to know everything. The topics include weather, luck, auspicious days for sacrifice and hunting, warfare, dreams and the influence of the ancestors. There are loads of oracle bones asking whether a given ancestor would grant a good harvest, would send disease, blight, and catastrophes or was busy chiding or cursing the royal house. This happened very frequently, necessitating many oracles. The nobles of Wu Ding's time were under constant threat of curse or admonishment from the ancestors. And they responded with lavish sacrifices or purified themselves by exorcisms. Wu Ding also wanted to know about the health of his queens and consorts, and their pregnancies. He divined about princes and generals, and based much of his war strategy on oracles. And where it came to the gods, we have numerous inscriptions about sacrifices at rivers and mountains and to a wide range of deities who are forgotten today. Nature deities, deities of the directions, animal deities, semi-divine ancestors; you'll read about them further on. They all meddled with daily life and they all needed sacrifices. Placation sacrifices, seasonal sacrifices and sacrifices to strengthen them. And when something important happened, the gods and spirits demanded to be informed by word and sacrifice. Some sacrifices were required on the spot, others were promised, and on an appropriate date the promise was fulfilled. But the program went far beyond this. Gods and ancestors wanted more than sacrifices, they also wanted to be invited and visited, and enjoyed being entertained with music, song and dance. All in all, Wu Ding's sort of religiousness was typified by intense devotion and enormous effort. Some scholars assume that it is a typical example of early Shang religiousness. Perhaps Wu Ding merely continued what his ancestors had done for centuries. However, he was also a headstrong and unusual king who introduced many changes. Who knows how often the Shang changed their religious customs over the pre-literate centuries?

Then Zu Jia changed the lot. Starting with his reign (period 2b), a rigid ritual calendar was introduced which specified which ancestors and ancestresses received offerings, and in which order. We'll get to this topic further on. Let's just say that the random sacrifices were largely reduced. In their place all ancestors received five rituals each year, in a specific order and always on their temple-name-days. At the same time, the number of ancestors who were entitled to sacrifices was reduced. Minor relations or people like Yi Yin were excluded. The same went for all the vague ancestors and the deities of nature or specific locations. The calendar was reformed and the leap month was moved from the end of the ritual year to any time when it was deemed necessary. Likewise, the bone inscriptions changed a lot. Zu Jia rarely asked the diviners about ancestral curses, births, harvests, diseases, ritual purification, dreams or whether the ancestors deserved notice of unusual events. Instead, we see standardised routine oracles enquiring whether days or weeks would be auspicious, and whether a sacrifice according to schedule was acceptable. I bet it was. In Zu Jia's time, Shang religion lost much of its wilder elements and became a matter of bureaucracy. But we should also respect Zu Jia's courage. It takes a lot of guts to strip so many deities of their power, to change time keeping and to set up a ritual schedule with very predictable results. I wonder what motivated him. What made him discount the validity of so many oracular topics? How did he convince the clans to accept such radical changes? Did he fear the power of his ancestors at all? Was he an unbeliever or had he received a spiritual vision of a clearer and better organised religion? And what would have happened to him if some national calamity had demonstrated that his improvements annoyed the ancestors, spirits and deities?

Period three of the bone inscriptions begins with the reign of **Lin** (Granary?) **Xin**, also called **Fu** (Father) **Xin**. He appears in Sima's genealogy without any comments. His influence seems to have been rather minor. So far, no oracle bones offer him sacrifices. Unlike Wu Ding and Zu Jia, he was never granted the title Di. The length of his reign is a matter of much controversy. Dong Zuobing (Tung Tso-Ping) proposes six years, while Chen Mengjia assumed that he died before even having mounted the throne.

He was followed by King **Geng Ding**, who, most unusually, had a name composed of two day-names, and Queen **Bi Xin**, who is sometimes confused with the earlier Bi Xins. Their regency lasted for maybe eight to sixteen years. Sima has nothing to say about it. The oracle bones, however, reveal that Geng Ding and Bi Xin ended Zu Jia's religious bureaucracy and revived many of the elder rituals. In their time, period 3, a wide range of nature deities had a comeback and received sacrifices once again. Rivers, mountains and local deities were venerated, and so were a number of beings who may or may not have been gods or ancestors. The schedule of the five ancestral rituals was abandoned, or else we haven't found the oracle bones about them yet. This doesn't mean that the rituals themselves were abolished: it was just the tightly regularised ritual routine that came to a sudden end. Whatever may have happened, it was an amazing change from bureaucracy to ritual on demand. I would love to know what prompted the change. What events made the nature deities so important that Geng Ding and Bi Xin could return to the world-view of Wu Ding's age? And how did they motivate the leaders of the clans? Was there some natural disaster?

After them, we have the reign of King **Wu** (Martial) **Yi** and Queen *Bi Wu*. Their regency lasted between four and thirty-five years, depending on the sources. It constitutes period 4a of the inscriptions. The royal couple continued many of the customs of period 3. Sima has a charming story on Wu Ji. Wu Ji, he wrote, was unprincipled and made images which he called '*Heavenly Gods*'. He had mediums who impersonated (or channelled) these gods and played games against them. Allegedly chess (very unlikely) or wei qi/go (possible but unattested at this early time). The impersonators made the moves for the Heavenly Gods, and when they lost, the king abused and insulted the deities. He had a leather bag made which was filled with fresh blood. It was thrown into the air and the king shot at it. This was called '*shooting at Heaven.*' Sima gives no further detail. However, during his reign, the power of the Zhou clan was increasing. By the time of the last Shang regents they had become a formidable fighting force. Unlike the Shang, the Zhou believed in Heaven as a divine and moral force. I wonder whether Wu Ji was slighting not one or several heavenly Gods but the people of the Zhou Clan. Mind you, it was the descendants of the Zhou who recorded this story, mainly as they were outraged by it. In the process, a lot of fascinating detail was lost. What exactly was the purpose of the bag of blood? How could it represent a deity? Or was the bag secondary to the act of shooting up (towards heaven) with a lot of blood splattering down? Was Wu Ji killing Heaven in effigy? And just what happened to his impersonators of deities when they lost, or worse yet, won?

Sima adds that Wu Ji's reign came to a sudden end. When he was hunting between river Wei and the Yellow River, Heaven sent down a thunderbolt which didn't miss. By contrast, The *Bamboo Annals* propose that he died of fright during a thunderstorm. Wu Ji didn't become a Di, maybe he wasn't good enough.

Period four b was the reign of **Wen** (Beautiful) **Wu** (Martial) **Ding** and queen *Mu Gui*, which lasted for eleven or thirteen years. Wen Wu Ding also appears as **Tai** (Great) **Ding** and as **Di**

Ding. We should not confuse him with the first Di Ding, who was Wu Ding, husband of Fu Hao and Fu Jing, several generations earlier. The histories have little to say about him, and the *Shujing* simply points out that the last Shang regents were so lacking in virtue that Heaven granted short reigns to them. How he acquired the tile Di remains a mystery.

With period five we come to the end of the dynasty. Its first regent was **Fu** (Father) **Yi**, who was posthumously called **Di Yi**. His queen/s are unknown. Fu Yi reverted to the customs of period 2b and re-introduced the ritual schedule of five annual sacrifices for each ancestor. The deities of nature disappear from the bone inscriptions, as do good many other interesting items. Fu Yi had very little regard for divination. Where Wu Ding employed at least thirty-six diviners, Fu Yi made do with three. He didn't trust them very much. In most cases, he performed the divination by himself, and the oracle always came out as he wanted. Not that he had much to ask. Period 5 oracles tend to be a bit boring. Many of them are standard questions whether a day, night or week would bring calamities. And would you believe it, they never did. Then there are the usual questions regarding the ritual schedule, i.e. if a given ancestor due for sacrifice would agree to it. Funny thing, they always did. In period 5, the oracles regarding rainfall, dreams, disease, wrathful ancestors etc. disappeared completely. But they show a remarkable increase in queries about the auspiciousness of nights. Keightley (2002:31) observes that of the entire Shang period, there are 1019 inscriptions on whether a given moon (here: night) would bring harm. Only forty-five are from Wu Ding's long reign, while 496 come from period 5. In his estimate, this increase would indicate a growing fear of a dark, i.e. non-solar and hence dangerous force. May I propose another interpretation? The *Shujing* repeatedly criticises the last two Shang regents for a life of luxury and carousal, and that they *"made the night into day"*. When they celebrated the night through, they were also more likely to encounter unpleasant events than if they had been in asleep in bed. Hence the need for divination on this topic. Fu Yi governed and feasted for several decades. And the power of the Shang declined.

The Tyrant and the Fox

The Zhou historians certainly knew how to provide a grand finale. And what is a show without drama and excitement in the end?

Meet the last Shang king, known as **Zhòu Xin**, **Di Xin** or **Zhòu Wang**. No, he did not belong to the house of Zhou. This Zhòu means tyrant.

He was the youngest son of Di Yi, who hadn't been such a good regent either. Di Yi made a concubine queen, who already had two sons from him. In theory, the third was least suited to be king. However, he had been born from a queen while his two elder brothers had been born from a concubine. That's what the traditions said, one good reason why Lü Buwei bemoaned people who blindly follow the rules (*Lüshi* 11.4). By all accounts, Zhòu made a very good impression. He was intelligent, tall, extraordinarily strong, good looking, charismatic, an excellent strategist and highly skilled in rhetoric. The historians of the Zhou, Qin and Han dynasties had a lot to say about him.

According to their history books, the last king of the Shang, Zhòu Xin, was a thoroughly corrupt character. He cared nothing for the ancestors, for the misery of the common people or for the decrees of Heaven. Zhòu Xin, we are told, excelled in cruelty and arrogance, wasted the wealth of his country, oppressed the righteous, exploited the weak and generally made a mess out of things. He was addicted to drinking and festivity, forced his enemies to drink themselves to death in a lake of wine and set up a forest of meat where he staged midnight parties. When not waging wars he tortured his upright ministers and, I'm sure you expected this, he was misled by his corrupt, immoral and sex-crazed wife **Da** *(Actress)* **Ji**. He had acquired her, as a spoil of war, after his victory over Marquis Sun Hu, and as she was equally alluring and perverse, he soon became completely dependent on her.

Maybe this sounds a familiar to you. But we are told that this is a true story. And to make sure it was really convincing, the historians filled in a lot of detail. Let me just blend a few versions of the tale. Our tyrant was proud of himself and ever ready to blame others for his errors. This did not please the ministers much, and some of them did their duty and protested. The king retaliated by having them tortured to death. He cut out the heart of his uncle Bi Gan, boasting that he had always wanted to examine the heart (awareness) of a sage, and find out if it really has seven apertures. Others were roasted to death on a red hot bronze pillar or had to walk across a fire pit on a hot metal rod. Some nobles were hung up with ropes and drowned very slowly in huge water tanks. The king surrounded himself with a troop of professional yes-men, alcoholics and dancing girls. He depleted the wealth of his domain by one exorbitant tax after the other, causing his people to suffer, starve and die. And he used this unheard of wealth to build grandiose new palaces, towers and sacrificial terraces, where he celebrated the long night through. It didn't happen in the old capital. According to Zhou history, our tyrant king did much to distance himself from his ancestors and began to build a new capital at Zhaoge, around 100km to the south of Anyang. Tyrant Xin was a connoisseur. He loved food and drank more than any man at the court, and when he didn't have a convenient execution to enjoy he had nude men and women chase each other through his meat-forest. The entertainment distracted him from his royal duties, so that he had scant time for the ancestors, let alone administration or justice. And with his lovely queen Da Ji things became completely unbearable.

Let me now insert a story which was compiled out of various legends only a few hundred years ago in the brilliant *Feng Shen Yan Yi*, literally the *Account of the Naming of the Gods*, published in English as *Creation of the Gods*. It's not quite what you'd call history, but it's certainly what people believed. Numerous storytellers drew from its myths, operas are based on it and nowadays there are several TV series and parodies rooted in the venerable tale. My favourite goes by the English title *The Legeng and the Hero* (sic) and has Fan Bing Bing as a magnificent Da Ji.

When Zhòu Xin was at the beginning of his reign he went to the temple to celebrate the birthday of goddess Nüwa. As you remember, she is the serpent lady who created mankind and patched up the broken sky using molten stones. He did not care much for the goddess, but his ministers had insisted and our tyrant was trying to be nice. The ritual was long and boring, and Zhòu Xin amused himself by planning the evening. At some fatal moment, a gust of wind moved the curtain which shrouded the image of the goddess. The tyrant cast a look and felt his heart spin and his loins glow. When the rite was over, he demanded brush and ink and wrote a poem with his own royal hand on the wall of the temple. Let me quote the translation by Gu Zhizhong and recommend that you get yourself a copy of his wonderful *Creation of the Gods.*

> *"The scene is gay with phoenixes and dragons,*
> *But they are only clay and golden colours.*
> *Brows like winding hills in jade green,*
> *Sleeves like graceful clouds, you're*
> *As pear blossoms soaked with raindrops,*
> *Charming as peonies enveloped in mist.*
> *I pray that you come alive,*
> *With sweet voice and gentle movements,*
> *And I'll bring you along to my palace."*

Quite satisfied, the king returned to court, while his ministers were terrified by the blasphemy. Nüwa had spent her birthday visiting the Emperor of Heaven. When she returned to her temple she read the poem. The first two lines hint that the relations between king and queen, and indeed of yin and yang and of all divine influences, are simply gaudy, worthless delusions. The next two lines describe the beauty of the goddess as if she were the subject of a vulgar love poem. The pear blossoms, wet with dew, are a metaphor for beautiful women, and practically drip with sexual connotations. The *Shijing* records that young lads

Lady Amherst's Pheasant

give peonies to the maidens of their heart. Since this early time, the peony had come to symbolise a woman who attracts butterflies and bees (i.e. men) from a thousand miles around. Rain can be a metaphor for orgasm (Eberhard 1987:216).

The last lines imply that the king did not believe the goddess was really alive, but if she would come to life, and behave like a shy, courteous girl, he'd graciously take her home to bed her. Without marriage, formality or courtship: just like a slave or servant.

It made the goddess hopping mad. To her regret, she couldn't just go and kill Zhòu Xin, as the number of his years had not been used up, and there was still some divine grace to his clan. However, she knew that bad conduct can reduce the fated life-expectation considerably. Very bad conduct might even end the dynasty. And as the Daoists have always taught, when things become extreme, they tend to revert to their opposite. So Nüwa set up a spirit banner, burned incense and evoked three spirits. First of them was a fox spirit. Foxes play an ambiguous part in Chinese myth. They are cunning shapeshifters, skilled in sorcery and naturally enjoy life. Some are so wise that they calm their passions, cultivate the Dao and eventually become immortal celestial foxes. Others just use every opportunity to have fun and care very little about the results. This sort of fox is never satisfied and leaves a trail of empty purses and broken hearts in its wake. The fox which Nüwa raised was one of the elder sort, but it wasn't especially wise. And it was definitely not the deity Nine-Tail-Fox so important in Han cosmology, though there are some authors who got them confused. Nüwa ordered the fox to go to the middle kingdom, where it should take a human form and use its power to ensnare king Zhòu with lewdness and delusion. The other two spirits, a green pheasant and an ancient lute, were to follow the fox and support its evil schemes. She also made the three vow never to harm a human being. Tough luck the spirits were not listening.

Down on this bonny earth, Zhòu Xin was having a hard time. Ever since seeing the image of the goddess, his concubines had ceased to appeal to him. So he ordered his ministers to find a selection of a thousand good looking, cultivated girls. Perhaps one would look like the goddess. His counsellors were used to a lot, but this was too much. A thousand girls would upset all better families in the country and cause a civil war. But there was one extremely beautiful girl who would surely cheer the tyrant up. It was Da Ji, daughter of the marquis Sun Hu. King Zhòu immediately sent message that he wanted her as a concubine. Sun Hu refused. Zhòu Xin felt insulted and sent his troops. There was war, and when things began to escalate, Da Ji implored her father to send her to the king as a gift, so she might apologise for her father's inobedience. Grudgingly, the marquis gave in. The two travelled to the capital, but one dark and stormy night, when they were staying at an inn, the fox spirit came flying from the otherworld. It threw Da Ji's souls out of her body and went in instead. The woman who arrived at the Shang capital was only human in appearance. She apologised most prettily, enchanted the tyrant and won firm control over him. First she broke the reputation of the queen, who hanged herself, then she became queen herself, and incited her husband to worse excesses than ever. The fox forgot all about not harming people. Da Ji had people's legs chopped off to demonstrate the quality of the marrow, had the bellies of pregnant women opened to prove she could guess the sex of an unborn child and generally contributed a lot of sadistic inventions which made the tyrant happy and horny. And when her appeal began to fade, she introduced the other spirits as her sisters to liven up his majesty's sex life.

Now let us return to the slightly more historical data recorded by the early historians. Here, what a disappointment, we find no references to Nüwa or fox spirits. The downfall began when one of the nobles was forced to offer his daughter to the king for a bit of fun. She was a good looking girl and she knew what she was doing. The king invited her to view one of the newly built towers, and when she refused his advances, he had her killed. Or as another version of the tale has it, she simply jumped to her death. It certainly upset her father, who started to complain, but didn't get far. The king had him chopped up. Another noble complained and ended up as dried meat.

We now encounter the hero of the tale. The Duke of the West (**Xi Bo**) was the head of the Zhou clan. He heard about the incident and accidentally sighed. It was a major mistake. The sigh was reported to the tyrant, who sent the Duke of the West to You Li, where he was imprisoned. You Li was close to the capital and far from the Zhou clan. Zhòu Xin evidently wanted to keep him under close surveillance. If we can trust the histories (we can't) Xi Bo spent the long years meditating on the *Yijing* (*I Ching*). According to legend, he wrote the commentaries to the sixty-four signs. This is not quite the historical truth. The version of the *Yijing* which most people know comes from the Tang Dynasty. As I explained in *Living Midnight*, there were earlier versions of the *Yijing* which differed from the standard version. The earliest complete version in evidence, from the tomb library of Mawangdui, is almost a thousand years older than the standard version. About twenty-five percent of the characters are different. And there are references to the *Yijing* in early histories, such as the *Zuozhuan* which differ from both. There is no evidence for the *Yijing* in the early Zhou period. Archaeological excavations prove that the Zhou around the end of the Shang Dynasty divined, just as the Shang did, with tortoise shells and cattle bones. The first forms of the proto-*Yijing* were developed in the centuries after Xi Bo's death. But I do admit that it's a nice idea that Xi Bo devoted his time to something spiritual. In literature, Xi Bo usually appears under the name **Chang**, or as **Wen Wang**, i.e. **King Wen**. He acquired this title, according to the histories, posthumously after the downfall of the Shang.

But let us return to our story. With the head of the Zhou clan in prison, his family was greatly upset. They spent many years gathering treasures. And after seven years, they made such splendid presents to Zhòu Xin that his majesty gave his grudging permission to release Xi Bo. He immediately went to the capital to express his deep gratitude about so much undeserved mercy. The king, much delighted about the wealth he had just acquired, graciously ordered Xi Bo and the Zhou clan to pacify the western borders. There were many wars going on, and Zhòu Xin was happy to have others fight for him. Xi Bo returned to his homeland incessantly praising the mercy and generosity of his king. The *Shujing*, Sima Qian and others make a point that Xi Bo never grumbled. He was a model of virtue and humility. And when a lot of angry nobles asked him to lead a rebellion he was shocked that anyone could dare to stand up against the rightful regent. While the king ruined the country with wars and taxes, and while the harvests failed and the people died in unpaid forced labour, Xi Bo would not listen to one bad word about tyrant Xin. He simply cultivated his virtue and strengthened ties of friendship to the noble families. And he died happily in great old age, after many successful battles, faithfully true to a king who wasn't worth it.

His son **Zhou Wu Wang** (War King of the Zhou Clan) was not quite as humble. Nevertheless, he also bided his time. When eight-hundred nobles tried to incite him to rebellion, he declined politely. He remarked that he could not, under any circumstance, usurp the decree of Heaven. Heaven, as you read earlier, was of essential importance to the Zhou clan. The Zhou may have paid lip service to the official Shang religion, but unofficially they worshipped the god of their ancestors, which was Heaven (Tian). The Zhou believed in Heaven. And they believed that kingship was not forever. In their opinion, Heaven gives the right to rule, the decree of Heaven, to the most virtuous clan or regent. And if that clan lost its virtue, it also lost its right to govern. Keep in mind that virtue means magic power and charisma in this period.

Coincidentally, the Shang were losing the decree of Heaven pretty fast. The nobles were enraged, the population oppressed, the economy ruined and the borders threatened by the invasions and uprisings of many smaller states. Such things were believed to reflect a royal lack of virtue. The *Shujing* contains several long speeches accusing tyrant Zhòu Xin of every possible misdeed. Corruption, cruelty, wastefulness, lack of justice and extreme alcoholism are just the start. He was also acknowledged to neglect sacrifices, to ignore the needs of the gods and ancestors and to let the temples go to ruin. The animals and grains for sacrifice were not offered, and ended up by being stolen by thieves. The streets were full of bandits and murderers, cities fought wars against each other and the last semblance of law and order disappeared. And, just as at the end of the reign of evil king Jie, the land itself fell into chaos and disorder. The accounts mention droughts and floods, earthquakes, storms and failed harvests. The *Bamboo Annals* add that stones fell from the sky, part of a mountain broke and collapsed, a girl changed into a man, a spirit goat was seen and there were two suns in the sky. Let me ask, just for the fun of it, if another bit of volcanism happened at the time. Mount Aetna blew up a few times at the end of the Shang; I wonder whether other volcanoes did the same. Or did a meteorite or comet strike the earth? Looking just like another sun in the sky? It would have had similar effects. Simultaneously, the world climate went colder. The European Bronze Age ends in several centuries of cold and wet temperatures when social stability disappeared and many tribes sought better locations. People were poor, life was violent and there was little opportunity to build up civilisation on a surplus of anything. It is the main reason why we know so little about the people of the time. What happened in China?

Zhòu Xin had his night-time parties as before. He consulted the oracle every week. It told him: next week not have disaster. Meanwhile, the power of the Shang was waning rapidly. More and more nobles began to act independently. The royal domain around Anyang was shrinking, until, in the last days, it hardly measured more than a few score kilometres. The hunting expeditions recorded in the oracle bones were conducted in the immediate neighbourhood. Perhaps the king could not dare to venture further out. Or maybe he just didn't want to, as too much travel might have interfered with his nocturnal entertainment. At some point, he moved to his beautiful new home in Zhaoge. It was far from the numerous demanding ancestors clustering the royal graveyard at Anyang. As Zhòu Xin had little interest in conducting their sacrifices, they were an excellent reason to move elsewhere.

Then the priests and musicians packed their gear and ran away. They travelled west and when they met Wu Wang, they offered him the entire ritual equipment. He received it with delight and immediately proclaimed that the time for war had arrived. Then he mustered his troops and joined with the many disgruntled nobles who had offered their support. He was also joined by people who had been in a state of war with the Shang for centuries. Especially the Qiang nomads were eager to join the fight. And, best of all, he met a man who became his best advisor and later his prime minister. This was the humble **Jiang Ziya**, a simple man who had held a number of jobs in his life without being good at any of them. Legend says he sold grain but made no profit, he became a butcher and was too generous for his own good, and made prophecies which were top quality but didn't make anybody happy. Finally he was kicked out by his own wife. But he is also known as a magician. Much later myths claim that he had been educated for decades on the world-mountain Kunlun, where the immortals live, but had never really amounted to much. For this reason the gods sent him into the Middle Kingdom where he was destined to establish the Zhou Dynasty. Jiang Ziya was an old man when Wu Wang finally discovered him, sitting at the side of a stream. He was fishing with a needle, to show that he would not use anything crooked. As a carefree old sage, he sang songs to himself and wasn't much bothered that the fish would not bite. King Wen was impressed and offered wealth and high rank. He had to offer them many times. Jiang Ziya was not the type to make things easy for a king. Eventually, after the king had asked often enough, he came along to lead the war.

The history books tell us that the end came fast. The allied troops with their soldiers and battle chariots advanced across the Yellow River and met the armies of Zhòu Xin in the field of Muye before the gates of Zhaoge. Allegedly the Shang troops had been seriously depleted by many decades of pointless small-scale warfare. They had seen little pay and a lot of injustice and corruption. So when virtuous Wu Wang advanced against them, most of Zhòu Xin's troops ran away to join the Zhou army. There were a few brief clashes and then the victorious Zhou moved into the city, where they were greeted by the citizens. Meanwhile, Zhòu Xin had realised that the week was not going to be very fine. First he had his palaces set on fire. Then he donned his richest cloaks, put on his costliest ornaments and ascended the Deer Terrace. When he saw the Zhou streaming into his city, he had a final drink and leaped into the fire. It wasn't hot enough. The advancing soldiers found his charred body, cut off the head and exhibited it on a stake.

When Da Ji heard the news, she dressed up as splendid as she could. She left the city in the company of her servants and headed towards the camp of the Zhou. It is said she hoped to seduce Wu Wang and become his queen. And she might have succeeded. But Wu Wang didn't even want to see her. He had her head cut off and that's it.

Rise of the Zhou

The history of the Zhou clan began a long time before their dynasty ruled China. Let us start with a look at the myths. Like the Xia and the Shang, the Zhou had an ancestor who helped Yü

Bird Images 1

the Great in the old days of the flood. Things began when the noble Lady Yuan of the Jiang clan (**Jiang Yuan**) went for a walk. She came upon a huge footprint. The books tell us that it was the footprint of great god/s Di, or even of a giant. For the fun of it she stepped into the footprint. Her foot fitted easily into the big toe. It made her pregnant.

Soon she had a semi-divine son who was named **Qi**, which means Abandoned. He had a bizarre childhood which you can find in the *Shijing*:

> *"...She placed her toe in the track of Di.*
> *and was raised and highly gifted,*
> *so she received fruit, so she became pregnant,*
> *she gave birth to a child, she suckled her child,*
> *her child, it was Lord Millet.*
> *Her months were completed,*
> *her son came like a lamb,*
> *without pulling, without stretching,*
> *without effort, without pain,*
> *she gave birth to the divine child.*
> *The High God blessed her,*
> *prayer and sacrifice were answered,*
> *her child came easily into the world.*
> *They abandoned him at the edge of the path,*
> *but sheep and cattle gave their milk,*
> *they left him alone deep in the forest,*
> *woodcutters found the child in the forest.*
> *They left him on the frosty ice,*
> *birds gathered and warmed him with their wings.*
> *The birds flew away;*
> *Lord Millet began to scream.*
> *His call rang far and near,*
> *his voice was very strong.*
> *The child learned to crawl,*
> *learned to stand and to walk,*
> *and his mouth went searching for food.*
> *So he planted thick beans,*
> *the beans grew high,*
> *his grains were thick on the stalk,*
> *thick was the growth of wheat and of hemp,*
> *and melons were tangled and thick.*
> *Lord Millet's farming,*
> *gave friendly support to nature.*
> *He freed the fields from herbs,*
> *and sowed the golden fruit.*
>
> *...*
>
> *He carried the millet home,*
> *and made an offering of it.*
> *What is our offering?*

Crushed and measured grains.
We thrash the grain, we clean the grain,
we wash it wet and heat it soft.
We plant, we gather mugwort
we offer fat bacon,
the ram for the God of the Ways:
we roast and fry it.
Sacrifice starts our year.
We fill to the rim with food,
the bowls of bamboo and clay,
the scent rises to Heaven,
the Lord in the Height is glad.
Sacrificial smoke spirals nicely,
at the sacrifice he once created.
The people are free from blemish,
so has it been up to our days."

Lord Millet is an agricultural deity who has a similar function as Yandi, the Fire Lord, also called Shennong, the Divine Farmer. You read about him earlier. Both are gods and culture heroes who give agriculture to their people. What amazes me is the things they did to the child. Who exactly are *'they'*? Why did they abandon the babe at the edge of the road, in the forest and an ice? What looks like a bizarre form of banishment can also be seen in another way. It reminds me of initiation customs. Being left alone is a terrible thing for people in many tribal societies. Hence it is often used in initiations which mark the beginning of adult life. But it also appears prominently in shamanic initiations. Countless shamans of northern Eurasia walked or ran from their village and went into the forest or out into the snow. Some died, some went mad and some found help from spirits, animal, plant or ancestral, who helped them survive in the dark and cold. What makes no sense when done to a baby makes a lot of sense when done in shamanism. And indeed, Lord Millet attracts a bunch of cattle and sheep (animal spirits?) who feed him and a whole flock of bird (-spirits?) who keep him warm and alive. To me, his tale seems like the mix of two widely different stories, one of them relating to shamanic initiation of Qi and the other to a semi-divine culture hero, **Hou Ji** (Lord Millet) who invented agriculture. Maybe the two traditions were grafted on a single, unique ancestor.

Qi, the Abandoned founded his own tribe, the **Ji Clan**, who appear as the Zhou later on. Ji, by the way, is a term related to the words *'footprint'* and *'foundation'*. Maybe the clan was named after its myth of origin or it was the other way around. Ji had a son called **Buku**, who allegedly governed the clan while it lived in a semi nomadic fashion among the Rong and Di barbarians. If this account is true, the Ji clan may have bred cattle or sheep. But his grandson **Gong Liu** reintroduced the clan to farming. *The*

Book of Songs records a praise hymn to Gong Liu for clearing ground and storing grains, as well as the weapons needed to defend them (against the very barbarians who lived around them). Eight generations later, **Gu Gong Danfu** led the Ji people on a migration which eventually ended at Qishan (Qi Mountain) in the central Wei river valley, Shaanxi. Here, the *Book of Songs* says, the Zhou built an amazingly elaborate city using state-of-art Shang methods. They erected city walls of pounded earth, levelled the ground, laid out a grid of straight streets at precise angles and topped the job with two city gates and an elevated terrace for sacrifice. The workers drummed and sounded jade chimes as they carried earth and erected house foundations. Quite an unlikely achievement if the culture had developed among barbarians. Once the city was finished, Gu Gong Danfu assumed the title **Taiwang** (Great King). He had three sons, and the youngest of them, **Jili**, was a highly successful warlord. He was allegedly Taiwang's favourite and when he followed him on the throne, he used the opportunity to conquer most of the people around River Wei in Shaanxi and River Fen in Shanxi. Jili had a son called **Chang**. You have heard of Chang before. He is Xi Bo, the Duke of the West, the King Wen who was imprisoned at You Li whose son King Wu overthrew the Shang. If this legendary account is true, the Zhou became a major force in only three generations.

Here, a bit of archaeology may be useful. Let me summarise some of the more recent studies, especially the excellent accounts by Edward L. Shaughnessy and Jessica Rawson (in Loewe and Shaughnessy, 2006). The origin of the predynastic Zhou clan remains highly enigmatic. Archaeology has so far failed to locate them, and the whole issue is under much discussion. To begin with, the alleged city at Weishan is something of a disappointment. Archaeologists have unearthed the palaces of the regents of predynastic Zhou (see next chapter) and while they were not bad, they certainly were not very impressive either. Preconquest Shaanxi is not a place with much development. There is evidence for several distinct cultures, some of whom produced small amounts of bronze vessels or weapons, but the burials are modest and the people, by and large were poor. Much of the material wealth is of Shang origin, indicating that the locals either traded with the Shang or that the Shang had an outpost in the region. But there is also evidence for bronze imports from distant southern cultures. Nevertheless, the location did not have a unified culture nor the resources to equip a huge army able to overthrow the wealthy and highly organised Shang. Mind you, as soon as the Shang were conquered, conditions in Shaanxi changed dramatically. The various local cultures became culturally unified and the whole province enjoyed a remarkable increase in wealth and technology. But this does not help us to determine where the Zhou originated. If the preconquest culture at Weishan is really the Zhou, the excavations show a blend of two types of cultures, classed as Zhengjiapo Beilü and Liujia Doujitai. One originated to the north, the other to the west of Qishan. The culture that merged in the Wei valley shows a blend of both types in their (rare) bronze items. But these cultures are not enough to explain everything. In all likeliness the Zhou had to ally themselves with numerous clans, many of them vassals of the Shang, wealthy enough to equip large armies, to produce bronze weapons and quality chariots, to begin the conquest.

Written history hinted that the Zhou were basically fierce western barbarians who had barely packed their tents away when they started building at Qishan. Before that migration, their home-place was allegedly Bin. This place was thought to be the modern Binxian in Shaanxi, some 75km from Qishan on the other side of the Liang Mountains. Sadly, this story remains highly speculative. In 1931, Qian Mu published a hypothesis that the Zhou had in fact originated in the Fen river valley in modern Shanxi, which is further east, outside of the *'western barbarian'* realm and much closer to the Shang domain. He based his meticulous research on river and place names and proposed that it was not the Liang but the Lüliang mountains which the early Zhou crossed. If this theory were true, the Zhou were not quite as barbaric as used to be thought.

Later, Chen Mengjia found support for this theory in his study of the oracle bones. It's a strange thing, but the Zhou are really hard to trace in the bone record. They should have been an important military opponent and later ally, but as it is, there is only one foreign clan of that name. It appears briefly during the reign of Wu Ding and his successor Zu Geng, and seems to have dwelled in Shanxi. These Zhou people waged war against Wu Ding, then became his allies, and later became enemies again. Then they disappear from the record. It might have been at the time when they allegedly migrated to the valley of River Wei. And with that move they put so much distance between themselves and the Shang domain, that they were hardly of importance any longer.

The first war between the Zhou and the Shang appears briefly in Sima Qian's account. The Grand Historian recorded that Gu Gong Danfu became an ally of the Shang. He was nominally granted the title count and given his own land as a fief, which made everything nice and official. Sima records that Danfu denounced the rough customs of his ancestors, in short, he was sufficiently behaved to be invited to the Shang capital from time to time. Danfu's son Jili was more dangerous. He proved to be headstrong and independently minded. To keep him peaceful and content, the Shang kings send him rich presents and married him to a high princess of the Shang. But how does this fit chronology? Danfu seems to have moved the clan to Qishan after the war and brief alliance with the Shang. Was he a vassal or an enemy at the time? And when Jili reigned, we find no mention of him in the oracle bone record. It may be surprising. The *Bamboo Annals* (*Zhushu jinian*) claim that he was killed fighting near Anyang in the 11th year of Wen Ding's reign. This is period 4b of the bone inscriptions, a time when many sorts of questions were popular, and warfare near the capital would certainly have been a major topic. Sure, maybe the inscriptions are simply lost or undiscovered. But if he and his descendant Chang were vassals or enemies of the Shang and of much importance in the west, how come there are no references to them in the divinations of the last Shang regents? Does this mean that they were independent and lived a long way off? Here, the *Shijing*, the Book of Songs, offers a surprising insight. The poem entitled *Great Brightness* mentions that the Shang had a child who was like a daughter of Heaven. When King Wen of the Zhou married her, he conducted an amazing ritual. He had a raft bridge made on River Wei, where he personally met her. I guess the gesture had a symbolic significance, but it is lost to us. The next lines of the poem hint at bad news. King Wen was in his capital, and Heaven sent him a second wife, from the minor State of Shen, where allegedly the Xia had remained. She became the mother of King Wu. The *Yijing* has more to offer. In the commentary to hexagram Guimei (54: Thunder over Lake) there are references to the marrying maiden and her sisters: she waits, bides her time, and eventually returns. Line 5 states that Di Yi had married off his daughter, but that her sleeves were not as fine as those of the later, secondary bride. Her moon was nearly full and auspicious. Line 6 relates that while the first wife holds a basket that contains no fruit, the man stabs a sheep but produces no blood. Shaughnessy gives a vivid account of the event (1997:13-30) and remarks that holding an empty basket and stabbing a sheep without penetration are sexual metaphors. Indeed the Mawangdui texts on sexual hygiene use the basket as a metaphor for the vagina. It makes me wonder whether the Shang goddess Ximu (Mother or Woman West), the sign west showing a basket, was associated with sexuality. It says a lot that hexagram 53 (air over mountain), the opposite of hexagram 54, elaborates the theme of a childless woman who waits to become pregnant for three years. If we take the hint, it seems clear that Di Yi's daughter never bore Wen Wang a son. It casts an interesting light on a Zhou oracle bone divination (further on) recording that Wen Wang actually sacrificed to his deceased father-in-law.

All of this remains quite confusing. It gets more intricate when we consult two ancient histories. One is the *Bamboo Annals*, the other source is Sima Qian's monumental work, the *Shiji*.

Combined, they indicate that Chang (King Wen) led several successful campaigns during the last years of the Shang. Legend has it that after he was freed from prison, he was ordered to wage war and to pacify the west. For this dangerous job, he received the title Xi Bo, Count of the West. From the Shang point of view he was a clan leader and a count, not a king. This title, as the histories claim, was bestowed on him posthumously when his son had overthrown the Shang. It sounds simple but is not quite true. Chang fought with gusto. In the process, he gained control of the Huguan pass at the Taihuang Mountains just at the western edge of the Shang realm. Another battle at Qinyang at river Qin carried his forces within a hundred km of Anyang. It should have alarmed King Zhóu Xin and caused plenty of divination. But our tyrant didn't bother to divine about the matter. He sat in his residence in Zhaoge, some 100km south of Anyang, and was preoccupied with other matters. Finally, Chang fought a battle which allowed him to move to modern Luoyang, close to the major ford across the Yellow River at Mengjin. I am sure he had his own ideas about the future, but these remained unfulfilled. He was an old man and died there, after having governed for fifty years.

Two years later, his son, King Wu used the chance. He assembled a huge army of 45.000 soldiers and 300 chariots and crossed the Yellow River. Then the assembly marched north towards Zhaoge, where Zhòu Xin gathered his own troops. The armies met on an auspicious day, the first day of the sixty day cycle, on the field of Muye. If we trust the official histories, the armies of the Shang deserted or surrendered as soon as King Wu in all his breathtaking virtue appeared before them. There was no fighting worth mentioning and soon enough, the combined armies marched on Zhaoge to get rid of the hated tyrant. So far for happy-happy history. If we trust a few neglected early accounts, some of them in archaic language, the fighting was fierce and extended. Here Shaughnessy (1997:31-67) gives a vivid reconstruction. He based his research on a badly neglected text, the *Shi Fu* chapter of the *Yi Zhou Shu*. This account had achieved a bad reputation when Mengzi (Mencius, 371 – 289BCE) announced that it was largely a forgery. He had good reasons for his judgement: the text widely disagreed with his own estimation of history. Mengzi believed, like so many scholars of the Zhou, that King Wen and King Wu were virtuous men who hardly needed to fight: *"a humane man has no enemies in the world"*. They were models of virtue and never did a cruel deed. By contrast, the *Yi Zhou Shu* proposes that the war was extended, violent and messy. As Shaughnessy shows in much detail, the manuscript contains plenty of archaic language and was probably composed during the early Zhou period. It is much more reliable than the venerated history books of the late Zhou and early Han. Here is a brief summary of the conquest:

-First month, day ren-chen (29) the king of Zhou prepares to depart. Day gui-si (30) he leaves the Zhou capital and travels fast to catch up with his army. He reaches his troops on day 43.

-Day jia-zi (1) of the following month the Zhou are facing the Shang army at Muye in the early morning. The Zhou had probably chosen the auspicious first day of the new sixty day cycle to begin their reign. That day, the Shang king is in the suburb. When evening arrives, he prepares himself to face the inevitable. He takes the heavenly jade and plenty of jewels and wraps himself up, before he sacrifices himself, presumably, as later records state, by burning himself. The fire destroys 4,000 pieces of jade, but does not damage the Heavenly Wisdom Jade and jewels. The battle is fierce and by nightfall King Wu has decapitated the corpse of Zhòu Xin and captured his hundred "*evil ministers*". During the next days, he acquires 180,000 pieces of Shang jade, good evidence that virtue can make a neat profit.

-Grand Duke Wang is despatched to secure the neighbourhood. He returns on ding-mao (day 4), offers the ears cut from slain Shang soldiers and exhibits his prisoners.

-Wu-chen (day 5). The king performs an exorcism, goes on an inspection tour and offers a sacrifice to his father. He also establishes his new government.

-Several officers are despatched to attack neighbouring allies of the Shang.

- Ren-shen (day 9). Huang Xin returns and exhibits ears and captives.

-Xin-si (day 18). Lai returns from attacking Miji and Chen. He reports the ears and captives.

Jia-shen (day 21). Bai Ta returns with the Tiger Vanguard, an elite troop, after conquering Wei. In this period, Wei seems to be the name the Zhou used for the former Shang capital at Anyang. He also makes his report regarding ears and captives.

-Xin-hai (day 48). King Wu stages the presentation of the sacrificial cauldrons captured from the Shang. He displays a jade tablet and codice and makes an announcement to Shang Di. Without bothering to change his robes, he enters the temple. Holding a golden axe, he makes a speech about the future regulations of the temple. The flutists play sacred music, the king ceremonially elevates all his ancestors. Later, he confirms the elders of the countries.

-Ren-zi (day 49). Wearing the royal costume King Wu displays the jade tablet and goes to the temple in the company of the flutists. Later, holding his yellow axe, he confirms the regents of the states.

-Gui-chou (day 50). The king displays the jade tablet, holding his yellow axe and a dagger axe halberd. In the company of the flutists he receives the presentation of the hundred captured Shang nobles. A bell is struck and several ceremonial songs performed. The king folds his hands and touches the floor with his brow.

-Jia-yin (day 51). The king, wearing white and red pendants from his girdle, inspects the captured Shang soldiers at the field of Muye. Further music and dances ensue.

-Yi-mao (day 52). More flute music, celebrating ancestor Qi as the son of Yü the Great.

-Geng-zi (day 37, one and a half months later). King Wu orders Chen Ben to attack the state of Mo; Bei Wei to attack Xuanfang and Huang Xin to attack Shu.

-Yi-si (day 42). Return of Chen Ben and Huang Xin. They report that the Lords of Huo, Ai and Yi have been captured, 803 chariots were won, and account for the ears and captives. Bai Wei returns and reports the gain of 30 chariots, plus ears and captives, and so does Bai Wei.

-In the meantime (to give his army something to do and to impress the defeated Shang) King Wu conducts an excessive hunt, and captures 22 tigers, 2 leopards, 5,235 stags, 15 rhinos, 721 buffaloes (Shaughnessy reads 'yaks', but I doubt they inhabited the warm and flat countryside), 151 bears, 118 yellow bears, 353 boars, 18 'badgers' (racoon dogs?), 16 large stags (elk?), 30 musk deer and 3,508 other deer.

-the total record of the campaign states that the Zhou devastated 99 recalcitrant states. They registered 177,779 ears of slain enemies and 310,230 captured soldiers. 652 states submitted voluntarily.

-Geng-xu (day 47). The king has returned to the Zhou capital near Xi'an and holds a ceremony at the ancestral temple. He makes a burned offering and has a scribe pronounce a document to Heaven that states how the king brought peace to the ancestors. To end the day, he has the hundred evil minsters of the Shang court shot. He decapitates and sacrifices the sixty minor princes and major captains of the cauldrons, plus the forty family heads and captains of the cauldrons. The whole mass execution is done with great style: the captives even receive new clothes and sashes before they are shot. Finally, the ears are brought into the temple and sacrificed, then the Great Master displays the white banner with the head of Zhòu Xin and the red pennant with the heads of the tyrant's two consorts. The day ends with a burned offering of scalps.

-Xin-hai (day 48). In his official capacity as king, Wu makes an offering to Heaven.

-Yi-mao (day 52). The king reverently offers the ears of the slain of many countries in his temples, plus six oxen and two sheep, and announces that the *"many states are now at an end"*. Further offerings include 504 oxen for Heaven and ancestor Ji, plus 2,701 sheep and boars for the hundred spirits, water and earth.

As you can see, the account is remarkably realistic. Virtuous King Wu did not win without having his weapons stained with blood, and a large number of Shang allies did not flock to him voluntarily. Indeed, the campaign took several months. It is possible, as David Nivison calculated, to give the exact dates of the campaign. The attack happened when the year star was in Quail Fire, the moon in the Heavenly Quadriga, the sun in the Ford of Split Wood, the chen in the Handle of the Dipper and the star in the Heavenly Turtle. When we assume that the conquest happened between 1046 and 1045 BCE, the battle happened on the 16th of November 1046, while the celebration at the Zhou temple happened at full moon, day geng-xu: the 30th of April 1045 BCE. The later Zhou historians were not interested in so much stark realism. They deleted the numerous executions and sacrifices and replaced the excessive hunt with a peaceful pasturing of the horses and a celebration to reward the battle-weary troops.

When King Wu had gained control over his new domain, he installed Zhòu Xin's last remaining son, Wu Geng, as nominal head of the country around Anyang, but just to be sure placed him under the supervision of two or three of his own younger brothers. In this fashion, he allowed the royal line of the Shang to continue, in a minor fief, as a vassal state of his own empire. The ancestral sacrifices continued, though on a smaller scale. Like Tang before him, King Wu was keen not to offend the terrible ancestors of the preceding dynasty.

But let us, for this chapter, continue with the career of the early Zhou. The historical evidence shows more flaws in the official histories.

According to such works as the *Shujing,* virtuous Wu Wang finished tyrant Zhòu Xin and reluctantly agreed to become supreme ruler. Of course he had qualms about it. King Wu was such a shy, righteous and humble character that it took a lot of convincing to make him king. He used the opportunity to give his father Chang the title Wang (king) Wen posthumously. And he was very careful to be polite to everyone. Maybe his position wasn't quite secure, what with so many aggressive and enterprising nobles in his alliance. The descendants of the royal house of Shang were not persecuted, say the historians. And the memory of the Shang was held high. Wu Wang's speeches made a point of honouring Tang and Wu Ding. He also insisted that sacrifices should not be occasions for alcoholism and that everybody should be humble, frugal, virtuous and go to bed early. The nocturnal orgies in the flesh forest were over for good. And the historians fell over themselves giving great examples of Wu Wang's exemplary lifestyle.

It didn't last long. Two years after the conquest, King Wu died.

He received a nice grand burial much in the style of the Shang and his sons began to quarrel. King Wu had ten of them, and that was plainly too many. He had ordered that the government should go to his son, King Cheng, who sadly happened to be underage. An elder brother, the Duke of Zhou (Zhougong Dan) undertook the task of guarding the young king. Several other brothers believed that he was simply usurping the power. Elder brother Guanshu Xian, who had been appointed to control the former Shang realm, made a pact with several other brothers and joined forces with Wu Geng, the last surviving son of Shang regent Zhòu Xin. The result was a messy civil war which lasted for another two years. In the process, the alliance turned against the brothers struggling for control in the Zhou capital. When they and a few other contestants were safely dead or had escaped into exile, the remaining brothers declared an uneasy truce. And they used their assembled armies to consolidate their power. For this purpose they waged battles right and left and no doubt destroyed many a state with whom they had been formerly allied. Their major drive was along river Wei and along the Yellow River, all the way to the sea. In the process, they created a much greater domain than the Shang ever had, and finally controlled almost all of modern Shaanxi, Shanxi, Henan, Hebei and Shandong. This war was the real end of Shang culture. King Wu had merely destroyed the last tyrant and his associates, but the revolt, the killing of Zhòu Xin's son, the relocation of the Shang survivors and the conquest that followed made northern China a new, but not necessarily better place

Shaughnessy (in Loewe and Shaughnessy, 2006: 314 and 1997:101-136) gives an interesting anecdote from the *Shangshu chapters of the Shujing*. At the time of our story, the new Zhou king Cheng is still young and inexperienced. He is supported by two elder brothers. Here we have one, Grand Protector **Shao Gong Shi**, divining whether they should continue conquering foreign lands. The oracle told him that *'Heaven'* favoured this proposition. As you recall, Heaven was a major deity for the Zhou, while the earlier Shang did not care about the concept. But what exactly the reign of Heaven entailed was far from decided. Shao Gong Shi tried to enforce the plan, but the people were against it, the armies exhausted and the nobles upset. In their opinion, it was high time to organise the newly won empire instead of wasting people and wealth on further slaughter. A heated discussion followed. Shao Gong Shi argued that Heaven had ordered the conquest, and had granted the young king sole authority and the *'mandate of Heaven'*, no matter what anybody said. His brother **Zhougong Dan** replied that "*Heaven cannot be trusted*" (!), and pointed out that the mandate of Heaven did not go to a single king but to the Zhou clan, and depended on everybody's virtue. He elaborated that all the great kings of antiquity had relied on virtue, a quality which came from listening to wise ministers. The ministers, he stated, enlighten their kings and refine their royal merit. In short, kings had better listen to what others say. Shao Gong Shi countered by insisting that Heaven had chosen the king, and that the mandate was his affair. In his opinion, the necessary virtue was basically preordained in the person of the king.

It's a fascinating piece of debate. Here we have two very different ideas about Heaven, fate, virtue and what may be the first time that a Chinese regent is called the Son of Heaven. It says a lot that the early Zhou favoured The Grand Protector's opinion, and made much of his achievements, while Zhougong Dan apparently suffered from bad press and found his death in exile. The later Zhou, under the influence of Kongzi took a different view. As Zhougong Dan had praised the importance of virtuous ministers and claimed that the Mandate of Heaven depended upon all people, he became an idol of the coming generations of refined gentlemen scholars.

Now for a look from the archaeological point of view. When the Zhou conquered the Shang, they certainly changed the major deity. But they also adapted their own culture, whatever it may have been, to Shang custom. The early Zhou regents were buried in Shang style in Shang type graves; they rode Shang style chariots, cast Shang type ritual vessels, used Shang type weapons and even wrote oracle bone inscriptions for a while. And as they made and used such remarkably similar ritual vessels we may even assume that they continued a number of Shang rituals. The Taotie design remained popular and only a few new designs emerged. Why was there so little change in the design? Why don't we encounter loads of characteristically new designs? For whatever culture the Zhou may have had earlier, they felt little need to maintain it. It's one of the reasons why modern scholars find it so hard to trace their origin. But the early Zhou did introduce a change where it comes to written inscriptions. For while the inscribed oracle bones soon went out of fashion, inscribed vessels became essential.

As you know, the Shang already inscribed some of their bronzes. It may have started around the reign of Wu Ding, at the same time as the oracle bone inscriptions. But the Shang only did so in rare cases. A vast amount of Shang vessels has no inscription or only the mark of a person or clan. And even the better inscriptions are usually brief and contain few words. With the early Zhou, this changed. We have a really early Zhou vessel, the Tian Wang gui, a magnificent item with huge ornate dragon handles. The inscription records the great Feng ceremony, when King Wu went on a boat trip on all three sides of the moat. He then proceeded to the Hall of Heaven, where he sacrificed to his deceased father, King Wen and to the Highest Deity. The inscription emphasises that King Wen dwells in Heaven, and watches his subjects from above, and especially commemorates that King Wu is his successor, and that he is certainly able to continue the sacrifices of the Yin (Shang). The text continues that two days later, the king granted some (unknown) office to his ritual assistant, Tian Wang, who records his good fortune and the royal favours on the vessel. The whole thing is detailed enough to serve as a legal document. There are dates, background information, notes on the ceremony, and a list of gifts and witnesses. (Rawson, 367-368). And there is much the vessel tells us. We encounter the idea that a deceased Zhou king resides in heaven, from where he observes his people. And observe how important it was to legitimise King Wu and to state that he was authorised to perform Shang (!) ritual. Obviously the newly founded dynasty had to defend its right to rule, and to rule properly. Maybe everyone was so awed by Shang glamour that derivation from their ritual would have been a catastrophe. And as to the inscription itself, it was just the start of a growing number of documents on Zhou vessels. Where the Shang had vessels for ritual, the Zhou also used them as lasting memorials of official acts, contracts, rituals and to commemorate victories, ordinations and other acts of state. They seem to have been keen on documented legislation. Perhaps their status was so insecure that solid contracts became a must. The vessels, after all, remained an essential focus of ritual, and could be seen by any aristocrat at public sacrifices.

It also links them with human concerns. While many Shang vessels simply showed weird (clan?) animals or unknown deities or ancestors, the Zhou vessels became records of very human affairs. Sure, each act of state was also an act of religion involving ritual, deities and ancestors, but the purpose of the vessel shifted, as it recorded a contract or an event.

The first Zhou regents imitated the Shang, but they also introduced a few novel elements in the design of ritual vessels. But before long, this situation changed. Let us move to the reign of King **Mu**. Mu is a person with an ambiguous reputation. The *Liezi* records several of his journeys into strange otherworlds, be it by journeys in the spirit or by riding a chariot with miraculous horses to the furthermost realms of the earth. He is famous for drinking and singing with Xiwangmu, and for visiting anarchic countries where regents were superfluous. Mu received many blessings and governed a hundred years, say the legends, while other sources complain that he simply neglected government and cared too little for his subjects. The historical King Mu may have travelled in spirit, it is unlikely that he could journey as much as he liked. In his time, only a bare hundred years after the conquest, the Zhou realm was already showing signs of tear and wear. Numerous remote relations of the king, set up to govern distant provinces, were beginning to assert their independence and fortifying their own little domains. Mu reformed laws and had them recorded. This act, again, is the source of some discussion. We can see him as a great innovator to settle legal standards. Or we could argue that a good regent needs no fixed laws, as his virtue sets a glorious example for everyone. At the same time, ritual seems to have transformed a lot. Under King Mu, the earlier obsession with Shang rituals and fashions ends. Perhaps, if he was good at travelling in the spirit, he had his own visions of the otherworlds and transformed religion accordingly. The ritual vessels became increasingly standardised, smooth and round. Angular types went out of use, as well as jagged edges and wild ornaments. Taotie designs went out of fashion, and the range of animal images was reduced to dragons and birds. All of this may indicate massive social and religious changes. If the Shang time animal vessels really related to clans, clan animals or animal spirits, gods or ancestors, their power was now drastically reduced. We can only guess what happened. Did the clans lose their totems, or their right to exhibit them? Were animal deities reduced to two basic types? Or were the dragon and birds exclusively confined to royal authority? And what happened to their ritual use? When many vessel types disappear, does this mean their specific rituals were abolished?

The trend begun under King Mu continued. By the time of King **Gong**, a little before the year 900 BCE, a further reform introduced a range of new vessels. Where many early Shang rites had required only a few vessels, and were probably conducted in private, the new Zhou assemblies of vessels hint at large scale, public rituals. At the same time, the hymns undergo a marked change and suggest larger performances with professional ritualists, singers and elaborate orchestras. At the same time, animal images disappear almost completely from the vessels, and are replaced by abstract ornaments, ribbons, waves, lines etc. By 850 BCE the transformation in ritual vessels, and hence in ritual activity, was complete. It remained the norm till the fall of the western Zhou in 771 BCE. It's hardly surprising that Lü Buwei, writing before the start of the Qin Dynasty, could not recall the original meaning of the animal images of the ancient vessels. Within a few centuries, sacrificial custom had changed a lot. The rise of professional singers had side effects. The mood of the hymns changed considerably, as there was a growing class of poets contributing new material. By the middle of the Western Zhou we find them exploring new topics. On occasion, they even composed bitter satires to criticise the shortcomings of kings. No doubt the great drought in the middle of the ninth century BCE contributed to the social unrest. And before long, the Western

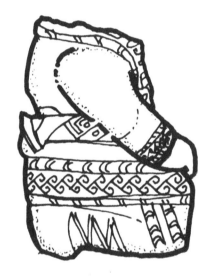

Smashed Ancestral Statues
After Hentze, 1967:135
Both pieces are under 20cm high.
Note Taotie design on the belly.

Zhou Dynasty became so weak that it could not control the restless states any more.

Concluding Remark: Is this for real?

No it ain't. There are far too many strange bits in the official histories to make them reliable. Let's start with the basic pattern. The struggle of virtuous Tang against evil Jie is an almost exact copy of the battle of virtuous Wu Wang against evil Zhòu Xin. The good and bad guys are so similar that they become unlikely. Now we can't be sure what Jie was really like, and if he was such a bad tyrant. But if he was, he supplied virtuous Tang with good reason to start rebellion. The house of Zhou was in a very similar situation. They had overthrown the rightful regent and needed a good excuse. One good reason for rebellion was the obvious fact that Zhòu Xin was such a terrible tyrant. It wasn't good enough. They also needed an example. So they made much of virtuous king Tang who had shown the way and proved, once and for all, that terrible tyrants can be rightfully disposed of. Even if it was against the law, vows of alliance and good manners. So whatever the real story was, the Zhou needed a past in which virtuous Tang slew the wicked tyrant Jie. Now I won't even try to discuss if Jie was such an evil fellow. We can't even be sure he really existed. Nor do we have to believe that Zhòu Xin was quite as bad as recorded. In fact we cannot be sure whether Jie was a model for Zhòu Xin or vice versa. All we can say is that the story served a purpose. And that it wasn't even very original. At least the historians could have invented different crimes to provide a bit of contrast.

Not everybody assumed that Jie was such a bad fellow. The *Liezi* has several long episodes where King Tang approaches Jie and asks him questions about the nature of the world, reality and so on. And Ji replies with sage-like wisdom. In other works, such dialogues were usually attributed to Tang and wise Yi Yin. To have Jie in such a superior and admirable role is quite a surprise. Was the *Liezi* mixing people up? Or was it deliberately provocative? Or had Jie a better reputation once?

When we look into archaeology, things are not quite like the histories say. Tyrant Zhòu Xin had a long reign. The estimates vary between thirty-three and sixty-three years. It indicates good health but also a certain skill in survival. And that Heaven was not overly keen to dispose of him. The oracle bones give evidence that he was not very interested in divination. The routine divination was duly performed, but only five diviners are known from his reign. He often did the divination himself. Also, he wasn't too keen on ancestral worship. In his period the nature deities and their kin had lost importance. Even secondary queens were excluded from the ritual schedule, as it was simply too crowded. What remained was the ritual calendar invented by Zu

Jia, necessitating five rituals for each and every king and queen a year. Zhòu's dad had still tried to keep up with the schedule. By this time, the number of ancestors had become so formidable that there were very few days free of ritual. In Zhòu Xin's reign, it had become a real nuisance. There were so many offerings needed, and the king was required to participate all the time, that he became fed up with them. Sometime during his reign he gave up the ancestral sacrifices, as he didn't want to waste the entire year with them. It may have given rise to the Zhou tale that he was unreligious and neglected the ancestors. But who could really blame him? The ritual year was so crowded that the system was approaching collapse.

The bones also tell us that Zhòu Xin, far from relaxing on his throne swilling booze, was personally involved in warfare. In the tenth year of his reign he led a campaign against the Ren fang, which kept him from the capital for c. 275 days. In this war, he pursued his enemies from Henan to the border of modern Anhui, some three hundred km south east. As he divined every day, and the bones were sent back to the capital where they were stored, we can be sure that he wasn't quite as lazy as the Zhou recorded. Also, such a long absence from the capital is only possible when a king is established very firmly.

Apart from the official testimony in the classical books, there remain a few tales that show a marked difference to the official version. The *Yi Zhou Shu* (*Remainder of the Zhou Documents*) makes a point that the dynasty ended in numerous bloody battles. Apparently not all troops were willing to desert their ruler. If the army, and several allied states supported the alleged tyrant, Zhòu Xin wasn't as universally despised as the Zhou would have it.

On the other hand, virtuous Chang, a.k.a. Xi Bo wasn't quite as humble as the *Shujing* and Sima Qian relate. In the seventies, archaeologists discovered the Zhou palaces of Qishan in the village Fengchu, commune Jingdang, Shaanxi. The major building had been erected on a strong foundation of pounded earth, much like the Shang build their settlements. The complex contained, on a space of 45.5m (N/S) to 32.5m (E/W), more than thirty rooms and two (possibly three) courtyards. A room in the south west contained an oracle bone archive. This, in itself, was a surprise, as nobody had guessed that the pre-dynastic Zhou regents had their very own oracle. More exciting yet, of the 17000 oracle bones, some 190 were inscribed. So far, everybody had thought that only the royal court of the Shang followed this custom, and enjoyed the privilege of recording oracle questions on bone. The very existence of these inscribed bones and plastrons shows that the Zhou regents were intruding on what used to be the domain of the Shang regents. But what the bones said was even more surprising. One of them mentions a sacrifice which Xi Bo made for his father-in-law Di Yi, the father of tyrant Zhòu Xin. In later Chinese thought it would have been unthinkable. Kongzi and his followers insisted that only a direct descendant can sacrifice to the ancestors. Only the son and his sons sacrifice for the father, and nobody else. Sacrifices for other people's ancestors were considered useless. But evidently Xi Bo, many centuries before Kongzi, did not believe the same. How closely was he related to the royal house? Was he trying to gain the support of the powerful ancestor of the present Shang king? Or did he attempt to place himself in the position of Di Yi's son, which could only be called an act of magic? Or was he participating in some unknown state cult requiring vassals to sacrifice to Shang ancestors? Whatever it may be, it indicates a close relation between the houses of Zhou and Shang.

But there was more to the Zhou bones. As you remember, the historians claimed that humble King Wen received his title posthumously, once his son King Wu had conquered the Shang. Wen Wang appears in the Zhou oracle bone inscriptions under the title Zhou Fang Bo (Noble of the people of Zhou). But far from sticking to this title, he also called himself wang, i.e. king! Humble Wen Wang who allegedly never thought of rebellion granted himself the title 'king' in his own lifetime! Our dutiful Count of the West must have been in open conflict with the house of Shang. It beautifully fits the account of his campaigns, which brought his troops ever closer to the Shang capital. Archaeology also supplied the insight that our self-styled King Wen shifted his capital to Xi'an during the last years of his reign. His new capital was in the very east of his domain and as close to the core of the Shang land as possible. Far from practising virtue, loyalty and humility, the real Xi Bo was openly preparing for war. (Brinker & Goepper, 1980:40-43).

But the official records have further flaws. Keep in mind that most of the earliest surviving Chinese histories date around maybe 800 or 700 BCE. By the time, the Shang were long gone and the early Zhou had become the stuff of myth. And these documents are few and fragmentary. When we search for elaborate histories, our material is much younger. Most of the accounts which survived the great book burning under Qin Shihuangdi date between 400 BCE and 200 of our era. And even after this time they were edited, rewritten and improved a couple of times. The late Zhou historians did not only attempt to record events. They turned history into an uplifting, refining and educational tale proving that Heaven supports the virtuous and punishes the evil. They also did their best to praise the ancestors of whoever ruled at the time. It was only thanks to Sima Qian in the Han Dynasty that history became something involving critical estimation and traceable facts. When we want to reconstruct the Shang, let alone the Xia Dynasty, we have to be very cautious regarding the written evidence. There are quite a few matters which the Zhou historians did not know or took care not to record. Here is a brief list.

-**Dynasty**. In the histories, the three houses of Xia, Shang and Zhou were described as dynasties ruled by emperors. In real life, at the moment we cannot even know if a house of Xia existed or was made up by the historians. Sure, there is archaeological evidence for palaces in pre-Shang China, but we do not know who built them and what sort of people lived there. Or what relations, if any, they had to the Shang. The Shang are well attested, but only since the oracle bones cast so much light on their world. But they were not a dynasty but a bunch of clans allied, more or less loosely, to the Zi clan. The regents were not emperors but had to consult with the other clan leaders to come to a decision. The Shang domain had no fixed border. It was more like a sphere of influence. Strong kings controlled larger realms, while weak rulers had little control over their vassals in the periphery of the domain. So the core of the Shang realm changed ever so often. Usually, it was just a few hundred km across. Surrounded by a huge number of tribes, people and city states.

-**Bureaucracy**. Many historians lived in periods when government was centralised and rigidly organised, and they assumed it must have always been that way. However, while there were a number of ministers with special function among the Shang, these were usually selected among the royal relations, sometimes among the royal spouses and the high aristocracy. It was only well into the Zhou period that officials and ministers were actually chosen for their skills, or received any training. It was a major change from earlier times, when government was executed by many incompetent, badly organised and untrained persons.

-**Neighbours.** If we accept the Zhou version of early history, the Shang stand out as a monolithic great civilisation in the centre of tiny kingdoms, nomads and other barbarians. Zhou history says: this is the cradle of civilisation. The Xia started it, the mighty Shang developed it and our own ancestors followed them. With the blessing of Heaven.

Today, archaeology uncovers an increasing range of early Chinese civilisations existing side by side with the Shang. It may be that the Shang only came into the headlines as the Zhou were so proud of triumphing over them. And because of writing. It is the one invention the other civilisations may have lacked.

-**Ritual**. The historians simply imagined that their own rituals had already been performed in prehistory. But the oracle bones reveal a vast scope of ritual acts and sacrifices which remain completely unknown and incomprehensible. Variety is largest in Wu Ding's time, but even the regular five ritual per ancestor schedule of Zu Jia has no parallel in Zhou ritual and certainly wasn't known to the historians. Nor did they know about the Shang penchant for human sacrifice. Sure, the early Zhou did the same. Especially with leaders of defeated states and officers of conquered armies. However, neither the Shang nor the early Zhou were much interested in sacrificing common soldiers. In most cases, they were integrated into the army or returned to common life in a fief which had simply changed its owner. But after 700 BCE human sacrifice was becoming a rarity performed by the cruder sort of regents. It still happened from time to time, and kings still took friends, concubines and servants into the grave, but educated people did not approve. Nor did they recall how common it had been under the reign of such virtuous kings as Tang, Pan Geng and Wu Ding. In fact, the scholars were doing much to invent a perfect golden age of virtue and true humanity. And when it comes to the many different bronze vessels and the equally wide range of rituals they were made for, or the meaning of the images on them, the scholars simply guessed as well as they could.

None of the historians guessed that under the last nine kings of the Shang period, religion underwent at least four massive and revolutionary changes. Nor did they know about the religious reforms instituted by the Zhou kings Mu and Gong.

-Oracle Bones. The historians had no idea that divination had been such an important issue and were completely unaware that the inscriptions existed. They simply assumed that divination was resorted to on occasion, and that bone cracking and yarrow stalk counting were of equal validity and age.

-Women of Authority. The Zhou historians had no idea that the Shang worshipped and sacrificed to ancient queens. In their age, ancestral sacrifices were made for men by men. None of the administrating queens and concubines of Wu Ding made it into the history books. May I ask whether Wu Ding's policy was an innovation? Or were there more strong women in prehistory whom we simply don't know about?

Now we may wonder why the history books distorted the facts so much. Sure, for one thing the historians wanted to legitimise the rise of the house of Zhou. But what about the other omissions? Here we may observe the influence of Kongzi (Confucius). Let's go on a brief journey through Chinese history from the rise of the Zhou to the Han Dynasty. You've been through some of this in the introduction: here is more food for thought.

When the Zhou triumphed over the Shang, they started innovations. It was a slow process in the beginning. Theoretically, Wu Wang was the beloved ruler of the many clans, but in reality, he had a weak hold on the alliance and had to prove that he had the blessing of Heaven. The Zhou believed in Heaven, but many of their allies did not. Quite a few were worried the old gods and ancestors of the Shang would get angry. Worse still, Wu Wang died soon, and his sons continued the regency by quarrelling and civil war. It took a few generations until the Zhou were fed up with continuing in the shadow of the Shang. Maybe the weather influenced the decision. At some time or other, the old Shang capital was flooded by the nearby river. It deposited a solid layer of mud over the ruins of palaces and courts, so that today the former capital is two metres or more underground. The Zhou relocated the descendants of the house of Shang. They reappear in history as the house of Song. They also reduced human sacrifice and began to develop the *Yijing* as an oracle of equal value to the good old bones and tortoise shells. For several centuries, both oracular systems existed side by side, and wise regents consulted both. But they did not inscribe the oracle bones any longer. Hence there is much more data on the late Shang than on the early Zhou. Whose *'empire'* began to collapse around 771 BCE. Invaders from central Asia broke into the domain and began to burn cities and loot granaries. By this time, the power of the Zhou had waned so much that the court packed its gear and started running. The nobles left their former capital near Xi'an at the river Wei and moved east to modern Luoyang.

The move was made in a hurry. There are amazing deposits of large bronze vessels which were buried quite carelessly at the time. Maybe the nobles thought the move was temporal and that one day they would return and dig the vessels up again. But the times were against them, much to the delight of the archaeologists who came upon such priceless collections. A good example is a pit discovered in Zhuangbo, Fufeng Xian, in 1976. It contained 103 bronze vessels of all periods of the Western Zhou. The vessels were heavy and the nobles in a hurry. And as the house of Zhou did not return to its former capital, the era of Western Zhou was over and that of the Eastern Zhou began. The dynasty was in a bad state. During the fights, King Yü Wang was slain. His son Ping Wang led the survivors to Ceng Zhou in Luoyang. His new capital was a city which had existed for 250 years before his arrival. Evidently, he preferred an established settlement to a capital constructed from scratch. Possibly he didn't have the resources to start anything really new. The House of Zhou moved to their new home, but never quite regained their power. The Eastern Zhou period was a time of nominal rule. The regent, as the Son of Heaven remained an important religious focus. Each continued the sacrifices to Heaven, just as their fathers had. But their political power was disappearing fast. Soon enough, they were regents only in name. Anyone looking for a political career stayed away from them.

In 771 BCE the Spring and Autumn (Chun Qiu) period began. It took its name from the idea that spring and autumn are the major seasons, and that together, they represented the entire

Ancestral Sacrifices

year, and the entirety of things. In the real world, the state was disintegrating. A modest estimate is that the Zhou realm split into at least 120 hostile states. More likely it was 170. Each of these tiny domains consisted of little more than a small city or two plus the fields in between them. And each was struggling to gobble up its neighbours. The result was one of the most horrible periods in history. Kongzi lived from c. 551-479 BCE. In his time, the number of states had already reduced itself. And the wars had become more vicious than ever. A lot of bronze weapons were being replaced by reliable iron. The armies were growing, requiring more food and supplies, which were taken by force from the peasant population. And the two centuries of warfare had significantly altered politics and philosophy. Many were beginning to doubt the Mandate of Heaven, the blessing of the gods or the value of sacrificing to the ancestors. And if there had ever been faith in vows, loyalty or virtue, it had been ground down by treachery and realpolitik. In short, Kongzi lived in an unpleasant period. He was aware of it and did his best to change it. Now I am perhaps too biased against the old sage to give a good account of his teachings. Daoist thought makes much more sense to me, and when I have a bad day I read how Kongzi's served as a ritualist (*Analects*, ch. 10) because it makes me laugh. But even if I disagree with his formality, I appreciate that he tried to make the world a better place. Kongzi was an expert on history. He was certainly one of the best informed scholars of his time. He told his students that the customs of the Xia, Shang and Zhou were practically identical, and assured them that he knew more about them than the very descendants of these families. And he praised a wonderful past full of exemplary, virtuous regents who were a shining example for a people living in a very bad time. With his accounts, he sought to convince the regents that ethical virtue was a good thing and that a ruler should live an exemplary life. Sadly, a ruler cannot afford being virtuous when all around him are not. Very disappointed, Kongzi travelled from state to state, searching for a regent who might cultivate virtue and reinstall a perfect time of law and order. And as the regents didn't listen, he sought to begin his reform among the better placed common people and the minor aristocracy. One great innovation of Kongzi is the idea that anyone can be a perfect gentleman, and that the virtues of the sage kings should be cultivated by all. He dreamed of a perfectly ordered society where every person had a specific place and function. Children would obey their parents, women obey men, men obey the officials, officials obey the nobles, who obey the king, who obeys Heaven, tradition and a lot of abstract ideals. The whole thing is held together by self-cultivation, humanity, love and mutual respect, clear differences in status and a lot of ritual which had to be performed with total precision. To ensure proper ritual, he insisted on a lot of formality. Outward appearances, dress, facial expression, gesture and solemnity were quite important to him. Now human nature does not work like that, but Kongzi did not know. He made an effort to regularise everything and uttered many remarkable things on very human subjects. And when he had to explain his ideals, he used the legendary rulers of the great old time as shining examples. In short, while he seemed to be quoting the past he made up a history which suited his hope for a better future.

At the same time he was busy reducing the influence of the gods and ancestors. It is a well known saying that *"The topics the Master did not speak of were prodigies, force, disorder and gods."* (*Analects*, 7.21). But he accepted ancestral worship as a stabilising force, ensuring stability within the family. Whether he believed in them is highly unlikely.

Kongzi did not achieve much in his life. The time was much against his teachings of superior humanity. However, he had some students who collected the sayings of their master and ensured they got around. Over the next centuries, his philosophy had a growing influence on scholars and aristocrats who appreciated law and order and did not feel at home in religion. For a long time, Konzi's dream of order and peace remained impossible.

Around 481 BCE the time of the Warring States (Zhan Guo Period) began. By then, only seven states remained under the so called regency of the Zhou. Each of the states had grown to formidable size and waged war using larger armies than ever. Wherever the war went, hunger and destruction followed. The Warring States made an end to the old dreams of virtue and Heavenly Decrees. In this sad period, a wide range of new philosophies and religions began to thrive. The political influence of the wu (shamans) was decreasing, but in their place grew a new class of ritual specialists. Some of them were scholarly types who knew history and performed divination at the court of the noble families. Another such development was a class of professional scholarly sorcerers, who used written talismans for their magic. A third was the early Daoist movement, which blended many elder spiritual traditions. It went through several distinct stages. In the first it was mainly a way to disengage oneself from the world through meditation, trance, obscure drugs and a peaceful place in a mountain solitude. Then it began to integrate political ideas which were in strong contrast to the thought of Kongzi. And finally it tried to provide regents with a model for perfectly sagelike conduct by being simple, natural and essentially inactive. In between, it incorporated the *Yijing* and such shamanic techniques as journeys in the spirit, invocation of spirits and gods, exorcism and so on.

In 256 BCE the so called First Emperor, Qin Shihuangdi managed to subdue all other states by an unequalled display of force and cruelty. His armies unified China and almost ruined it in the process. But once his aims were fulfilled, he found himself faced with huge problems. He was, in many ways, a very modern thinker. He had no faith in Kongzi or Laozi nor in virtue or self-cultivation. Instead, he encouraged the Legalist school of thought, which favoured major punishment for smallest offences. As the Confucians kept reprimanding him, he decided to abolish the past. He had a large number of scholars buried alive and initiated the worst book burning in Chinese history. Only a handful of books were permitted and anyone who was caught in possession of others found himself slaving to death at the building of canals, roads or the Great Wall. The massive edifice is undoubtedly one of the saddest monuments of mankind. It never really worked against invaders but it did help to keep the population from running away. But this is not the place to look into the history of a particularly unpleasant tyrant. His dynasty, the Qin, only survived for fifteen years.

Afterwards the Han Dynasty began. It tried to return to the models of antiquity and failed. For one thing, so much of history had been lost. The historians had to reconstruct many old books from bits and pieces, from memories or rumours, and where they couldn't find any, they often made things up. For another, Qin Shihuangdi had proved that a large China could function under single rule, with a single government and a standardised system of measurements, regulations and bureaucracy. And while a lot of scholars hoped to reintroduce the reign of sage kings who had never lived, the lessons of the empire continued to exert their influence. In this climate, most of the Chinese history books assumed their final shape. It is from hopes and fragments, from shards and memories, that Chinese scholars re-made their vision of the past. And this vision became gospel and law. The re-constructed works were treated like holy writ. Every scholar and indeed everyone who sought a job in the government was required to learn them by heart. And as the centuries advanced, the vision of the past became dimmed by a world-view which did not allow the slightest doubt in the great old books, and the glorious rule of the early, sagelike regents.

It produced the gospel about the Xia, Shang and Zhou to which all intellectuals subscribed, well into the nineteenth century. Only a few historians were aware that pieces of ancient literature did not agree with the mainstream. Some kept their mouth shut, others tried to argue the offending documents away. Or, like the *Bamboo Annals*, they were damned as untrustworthy. Some Daoists who composed the *Zhuangzi* included remarks which did not fit official history. But as the *Zhuangzi* is a wonderfully crazy book, nobody was really surprised. I'm sure you'll appreciate this comment on the rise of the Zhou:

"*Now the Zhou, observing that the Yin (Shang) has fallen into disorder, suddenly makes a show of its rule, honouring those who know how to scheme, handing out bribes, relying on weapons to maintain their might, offering sacrifices and drawing up pacts to impress men with its good faith, lauding its achievements in order to seize gain - this is simply to push aside disorder and replace it with violence!*" (ch. 28, translation Burton Watson, spelling amended). Obviously there were still people with a sound head for historical reality.

How the character 'Di' appears in the symmetry of Taotie images

Time and Space

The Shang universe consisted of a material world full of people, places and things and a vast cosmological model, a magical reality that was imposed on everyday experience. For time keeping, they used a sacred calendar that had little to do with the annual motion of the earth round the sun or the cycles of the moon. Space was defined by four sacred directions and a range of directional deities, more of them, indeed, than required to make anyone happy, while the directions in-between were conveniently ignored. While the regents governed the country, cities were built, alliances made and broken, wars were waged and day in and day out, rituals were performed. The otherworld/s influenced material reality and gave it shape and meaning. Religion was the fundamental principle that governed life and the journey through sacred time and space. Indeed, the Shang nobles inhabited a dream of life in sharp contrast to the intense and dramatic reality of the spirit realms.

Recycling Time: Sixty days of Eternity

Time keeping was so important to the Shang that they used two calendars simultaneously. One of them is hard to prove. It's a simple, straightforward count of days, months and years. There's not a single one in evidence, but it's reasonably certain that some such count must have existed. After all, once in a while the Shang had to add an extra month or extend one of the ritual years to keep up with the seasons, and this is a lot easier when you keep a record. Some of the Shang sages kept a count of the days while others presumably made astronomical observations. The oracle bones occasionally refer to what seems to be stellar constellation and eclipses were observed with suspicion. Months do appear on some oracle bones, especially towards the end of the reign. They were important when the king was travelling or out to wage war in the company of his diviners. All the oracles made on the road were sent back to the capital, where they were stored in proper order. Years were not recorded until period 5b. In the days of the last regent, Zhòu Xin, there is sometimes a reference like *'in the king's so-and-so ritual year'*. With the earlier regents we are not so lucky.

The calendar you'll encounter on so many bones is a ritual cycle of sixty days (ganzhi). One such cycle corresponded roughly to two months of thirty days. It's not quite as precise. Sure, thirty

The Sixty Day Cycle

days would be ideal to accommodate three ritual weeks of ten days (xun), but as the real month is roughly 29.5 days in length, such a system soon says goodbye to the natural year. Hence, under the last Shang regents, long months (30 days) and short months (29 days) alternated, at least until these, too, departed from reality. From time to time, extra months were added or a month was extended.

Let's return to the sixty day cycle. You have a date on an oracle bone, if you are lucky, but it does not tell you anything about which sixty days in the year. 360 days are six sixty days units; hence, every date happened at least six times during the natural year. Nor were the days simply counted. Why keep things simple when they can be complicated?

Let's take a look at the ritual week. The Shang week (xun) had ten days, which were also known as the ten suns. In the inscriptions, the character *'sun'* often means *'day'*. The ten suns had names which later became the system of the Ten Heavenly Stems (tian gan). The ten stems were of major importance all through Chinese history, and even today they are occasionally used for keeping order. In serious Chinese astrology, their calculation is essential. Whether the Shang already thought of them as *'Heavenly Stems'* remains doubtful. Indeed, the characters which represented them during the Shang were thoroughly distorted during the Zhou period, and by the time of the Han Dynasty their original meaning was long forgotten.

Take a look at the table (page 598-599). You will see another group of twelve characters, which later became known as the *'Twelve Earthly Branches'* (di zhi). What the branches originally signified is still unsolved. They might be a reference to the moons in a year, but this appears unlikely, as they were never used to count months. The Shang attributed ideas to this cycle which were forgotten when the Han astronomers wrote their studies on astrology. Since maybe the fourth century BCE, the Twelve Earthly Branches were identified with the twelve double hours (Needham's research quoted in Derek Walters, 2006: 58). It was a late Zhou innovation, as the Shang had not thought of time in this way. The Shang used terms like *'before sunrise'*, *'time to light torches'* or *'second meal'*, but there is no evidence of hours in their inscriptions. The late Zhou astronomers simply used the elder system of twelve signs and extended its meaning. And while there are a few attempts to explain them in the *Huainanzi* plus some additional material in Sima Qian's *Shiji*, the results are a long way from what we know about Shang characters. The astrologers of the Han Dynasty designated lucky and unlucky days for any sort of activity and made up a lot of creative new material. And when the twelve animals were introduced (maybe from central Asia, as Walters argues) sometime during the Tang Dynasty, they were also attributed to the Twelve Earthly Stems.

The same happened regarding hours and years. The animals, by far the most entertaining blossom of Chinese astrology, are the most recent and least important item in a genuine horoscope. There is very little agreement about their meaning or about the question of which animal harmonises with what. Nevertheless, they are useful for gossip, newspaper columns, small talk and flirting. And of course they are a strong focus of energy for anyone who really believes in them. People who believe that they are dragons or tigers go through life with a different mindset than pigs and dogs. You have my word for it, as honestly, I'm a rat. All of this is miles remote from the original Shang ideas. The Shang, as far as is known, may not even had a system of astrology at all, and their concern for stellar phenomena was limited.

In this book I would like to avoid the terms 'Heavenly Stems' and 'Earthly Branches', as we have no idea how the Shang selected their signs and are unsure whether they related them to heaven and earth. Instead let's use the terms 'tenner cycle' (the xun week) and 'twelver cycle'.

Now open your head really wide and give your brain a good airing. In the calculation of a given day, the signs of the ten and twelve day cycles were combined. Yes, there are easier ways of calculating time. But this one was, for whatever reason, sacred, and you and I just have to live with it. Each day of the xun week was combined with a sign of the cycle of twelve. You write tenner one (jia) and twelver one (zi) = jia-zi. The next day is tenner two (yi) and twelver two (chou) = yi-chou Then tenner three (bing) and twelver three (yin) = bing-yin; tenner four (ding) and twelver four (mao) = ding-mao, all right, it isn't much of a challenge to continue like this. Eventually you get tenner ten (gui) and twelver ten (you) = gui-you. The next day is tenner one (jia), as the new xun week is starting and twelver eleven (xu) = jia-xu. Then tenner two (yi) and twelver twelve (hai) = yi-hai. Then tenner three (bing) and twelver one (zi) = bing-zi. Then tenner four (ding) and twelver two (chou) = ding-chou. And so it continues until you have exhausted all combinations. It gives you sixty days. There is always an even tenner combined with an even twelver, or an odd tenner and an odd twelver. If this is not the case, it is a scribal error, or a forgery, or the inscription was badly copied. The diviners no doubt sighed and sat down to memorise the entire table. There are numerous bones and plastrons which contain nothing but the combinations of the sixty day cycle. They were made for memorisation and writing practice. The whole thing is known as the sexagenary cycle, which is another impressive word to surprise your friends with. It would be nice to know how the Chinese acquired it. Much of Eurasia owes its maths to the Sumerians, who used a sexagenary system for their calculations. That we divide our circles into 360 degrees is a Sumerian idea.

In our inscriptions, the sexagenary cycle can appear in several places. First of all, every well made inscription starts with it. The date of the divination should come first. There are exceptions, of course. In some bones, the beginning of a question may be missing. Or the date was recorded a few times on the same bone, until some scribe or carver decided to keep things short. Additional remarks are not always dated either. But when you think of the norm, you have a day at the beginning of each question or charge. But there may also be another date somewhere in the middle of an inscription. It happens when you divine today for what another day will bring. Throughout much of the late Shang period, it used to be customary to enquire whether an ancestor should get a sacrifice the next day. It looks like a genuine question. The answer could be no and arrangements could be changed. By the end of the period, the same question was usually asked on the same day. By then, divination had become a mere formality and it was expected that the ancestor would agree anyway. A few questions enquired about much longer time spans. Keightley (2002:32-33) cites one prediction for an event 170 days in the future, and another, more questionable one, for 547 days in advance. In between were predictions for long term projects, such as warfare, the meeting of foreign ambassadors, or pregnancy. There are questions about the weather in a given month and for events in the next few weeks. The majority of predictions, however, are about short term events.

A day-count also appears occasionally. For some reason, the diviners sometimes noted *'on the eight day so-and-so'*, as if the name of the day was not enough. It reveals that time counting was not standardised yet. Some diviners counted *'the eighth day including today'* while others counted *'from today'*. Such differences might indicate that nobody really cared about the matter, or that the matter hadn't been resolved yet. What does this tell you?

Please consider what makes a sixty day cycle attractive. Strangely, it manifests and measures time without reference to the natural year. The sixty days continued incessantly, independent of the season, the months, the dates of full or new moon. Sometimes the days were shifted a bit, or an extra month was added, but essentially, the cycle celebrated an eternal piece of timeless time, unchanging and unchangeable, far beyond the world of people, nature and things, a reflection of eternal heaven.

The Ten Suns

There is an ancient Chinese legend about ten suns, which, as several authors hint, once rose together and almost burned the earth to cinders. You can find it in so many books on Chinese mythology that I'll treat you to a somewhat modernised version here. This is how Xiwangmu tells it. And she's right. She often cheers me up by saying *'people are funny'*. The same can be said about deities. We've got so much in common. Laughter is the one thing that saves us from suffocating in seriousness.

Some things start with a gleam. As morning approaches, the velvet darkness of the night pales and turns a greenish blue. In the east, a hint of red is cautiously beginning to tinge the sky. The birds wake, insects begin to buzz and faint brightness shimmering from the eastern sea. Slowly and gently, the sun rises and the day begins. It ascends, higher and higher, climbing up the fusang tree of the east, reaches the southern corner of the world in heat and warmth and comfort, and takes a brief rest in the branches of another mulberry tree. Afternoon and evening pass, and the sun gently descends into the abysmal depths of the far west where the dark ruo tree grows, way beyond the mountains which support the sky. Descending down the ruo tree, the sun falls down Feather Abyss and is seen no more. The vast canopy of the sky takes on a rich, black hue, the stars appear and earth is shrouded in darkness. While torches are lit in the splendid halls of nobles and kings and owls glide soundlessly across the sky, the sun glides underground along the hidden waterways, through tunnels and caverns, past the Yellow Springs of dissolution and death, heading for the eastern sea. The next day, it rise fresh and new and almost the same.

Once upon a time, it was not the same sun, and it was not the same day, 'cause it never is. In the great ancient past, there were ten suns. Each day a new one rose and travelled across the dome of Heaven. One after the other, day after day, until ten days were past and the first sun reappeared. They measured time nice and evenly and did not much interfere with each other. But things don't always work out as they should. One bad day the ten suns rose all at once. Heat and brightness scorched the earth, evaporated the rivers and set the forests and villages on fire. People and animals did not like this one bit, nor did the gods, who saw their temples and altars going up in flames. They called for Yi, who was the mightiest archer of all time, a hero who had saved the Middle Kingdom from countless monsters and evils. Yi packed his strongest horn-bow and his longest arrows, put on his rancid rhino-armour and climbed the world mountain. Standing boldly on the highest peak he shot his missiles, and one sun after another burst into fragments and went out. When only one sun remained, Yi gave a satisfied grunt and went home.

As he was trudging along the dusty road, the gods came and thanked him for his mighty deed. Xiwangmu, the Queen Mother of the West, mistress of death, life and the elixir of longevity, gave him a bottle of immortality juice. *'It's enough for two people. Don't drink it alone but share it with your wife'*, she said. Yi gave a grunt of thanks, talking not being his favourite means of getting

Eared Owls

things done, and walked home. Here his wife, Chang E, was waiting for him. Yi walked in grinning proudly.

'Mission accomplished' he hollered *'I shot those damned things. Saved the world, they say. Look here, I got this immortality juice for us two. Put it in the kitchen. Get me some beer, will you? Is dinner ready?'* And he turned on the TV, collapsed on the sofa, put his feet on the table and reached for the remote control.

Time for the sports channel. Hey, good luck, its soccer today. It always is.

In the kitchen, Chang E put the kettle on. Then she did some serious thinking all by herself.

Immortality? An eternity to live, to work, to do all sorts of chores? With that guy?

Why, he even wore his boots in bed!

It didn't take her long to come to a decision. She uncorked the bottle and drained the elixir to the last drop. It looked pink and tasted slightly peachy. Now with half the amount she would have become a celestial immortal and floated leisurely upwards. Drunk on the entire dose she shot skywards so fast that she smashed a hole through the roof and would have continued to eternity, had not the moon been in the way.

So she landed, head first, with a bump and ouch! and has been the goddess of the moon ever since. And Yi watched soccer for a long time, until he realised that dinner wasn't going to happen. Eventually went to the pub for pig and millet burgers with crunchy baked scorpions in multisodium glutamax sauce (superior fortified extra strong from Good-Luck-Forever chemical factory), where his old mates where waiting for him.

Nothing like a few beers and a brawl after a day like this. Later, he went to usurp the Xia Dynasty for a while.

Chang E, however, was lonely up there. The moon has some silvery palaces and enchanted gardens where pale blue flowers grow but is not noted for entertainment. Shang Di, god of Heaven, felt sorry for her and sent her a magic hare, who is kind and cuddly and very good at making immortality juice by fermenting fungi. You probably heard of the hare, in 1969, when the tinpot *'Eagle'* landed and Aldrin and Armstrong took the first steps on the moon, the hare took the official photographs and Chang E greeted the astronauts with flowers, poems and sticky moon cakes. It converted them, like so many others of their craft, into instant mystics. Shang Di also sent a three legged toad to the moon. You can see its image, proudly displaying a coin in its mouth, in many Chinese shops. It's the moon-toad that goes around to poor people and vomits money into their homes. Some say that Chang E herself is the toad, but I wouldn't believe this without asking her (very cautiously). There is also an elderly immortal on the moon, who looks for promising matches and ties up lovers with red string. He cuts the branches of the lunar cassia tree every day. Overnight he can relax and by the next day they are regrown, things being what they are.

This is really true. It happens all the time.

Temple Names

Now this story, while being accurate enough for most purposes, is not quite the version which the people of the Han Dynasty told each other two thousand years ago. Nor is it quite what the Shang believed. But it does contain some details which are really old. Ten days make up a xun week. And ten suns give us names and signs which may symbolise quite a lot. We also have a pioneer. Remember Wang Hai. King Hai is the only known Shang ancestor who has a name which does not come from the ten day week but from the twelver cycle. Hai is the last character in it and shows, as the *Shuowen* claims, a grass-root. He got the additional name Xin later on, which is day eight of the tenner cycle. It provided him with a day for offerings. After Wang Hai, all nobles received a temple name from the tenner cycle. These temple names have caused a lot of discussion. In the Han period, a few historians began to wonder whether the ancient temple names were chosen according to the birthdays. Zu Jia could have been born on the jia day, Wu Ding on the ding day, Bi Xin on the xin day and so on. It's a neat idea, and no doubt comforting when you go through life thinking, hey today is the day when I'll get sacrifices once I'm dead. But soon they realised that this could not have been the case. The names are unevenly distributed and the Shang obviously had preferences for specific days. Next followed the theory that each noble received her or his temple name according to her or his dying day. Again, when we look at the available range of names some are common and others rare. If mere coincidence settled the day and name, the names would be more evenly distributed. Keightley (2002:33) cites statistics that days geng, yi, xin, ding and jia (in that order) were significantly more auspicious than days wu, ren, bing, ji and gui. Gui, the last day of the week, though popular for divination on the next week, was the least auspicious of the lot. Another theory proposed that the day name was chosen according to the day when the baby underwent some ceremony, much like a baptism. In this case the living noble would have been aware of her or his sacred day. As the day for *'baptism'* could be chosen, preferences could cause the uneven distribution of the names.

Each ancestor was named after a day of the week but the week day is also the day of a sun. Keightley in particular makes much of the idea that the worship of the deceased with their day names, or possibly sun-names, is a form of solar worship. It's hard to decide. Some early scholars thought that the Shang were into solar worship. The inscriptions, however, never mention rituals for the sun, nor did sun or moon receive offerings. Neither was active like the gods and sent curses or ruined the harvest. On the other hand, if the ancestors were representatives of the ten suns, or maybe merged into them in some mysterious way, ancestral worship might be an indirect worship of the sun, or ten suns, if you like. The question remains unresolved.

But how was a name decided? With the advent of oracle bone studies, the discussion became more lively. Could it be that a name was chosen in accordance of the burial date? Or was there a deeper meaning? K.C. Chang developed a fascinating hypothesis (1980:158 -189). In his opinion, the Shang clan was divided into two more or less separate clan groups. One group was characterised by the names Ding, Bing, Ren and Gui and the other by day names Jia, Yi, Wu and Ji. Kings and queens with day names Geng and Xin are hard to class; perhaps they had a neutral status or even formed a third fraction. The two major groups were equally influential, and royal authority shifted between them. When one group provided the king, the other produced the prime minister, and possibly the queen. Shang kingship did not generally move from father to son. In many cases, at least in the early generations, it passed from the king to his brother, and from him to the other brothers until no candidates of that generation were left. Then it leaped to the younger generation. Chang proposed that the king and his brothers might belong to one clan group. When the kingship shifted to the younger generation, it could pass to the other clan group. This sort of political system (called circulating inheritance by Jack Goody) may seem a bit odd, but it did exist, in various ways, in several cultures in Africa, Europe, Asia and especially around the Pacific. It ensured that power was balanced and alternated between branches of the royal families. And it is quite symmetrical. When you look at Shang art you will see that symmetry was a must. The same seems to appear in the layout of the royal cemetery. Chang further speculated that the two family groups had different ideas on religious custom. One group, so he assumed, was represented by the kings of period 1, 2a, 3 and 4. It is called the *'old school'* as Wu Ding's reign is its first example, and somehow assumed to be a typical for earlier Shang values. The other group would have provided the kings of period 2b, 5a and 5b. These regents went to considerable lengths to standardise the nourishing sacrifices for the ancestors, and to introduce a neat and bureaucratic note to ritual. This group is called *'new school'* as it allegedly represents the innovative impulse towards a well ordered hierarchical religion. The two hypothetical clan groups might explain the alternation between the religious outlook of the *'old school'* and the *'new school'*. Personally, I very much enjoyed this hypothesis, as it contains so many original ideas. However, it could do with some improvements. For one thing, the two clan groups are not verifiable. The division of *'old school'* and *'new school'* does not exactly fit the names, as Wu Yi (period 4a) belongs to the *'old school'* and Di Yi (period 5a) re-introduced *'new school'* ritual. There is evidence for plenty of clans and blood relations to the royal house, but how or if they were organised remains unknown. We don't know anything about the background of queens and prime ministers. For another, kingship did not always go from brother to brother; there are exceptions to the rule. Also, Shang inscriptions are very enigmatic regarding family titles. A prince would address his dad as father, but he would also say *'father'* to his uncles and to any respectable man of that generation. The same went for the term *'mother'*. It could be an aunt or an elderly lady. *'Grandmother'* and *'grandfather'* are quite as unspecified. As a result, there are several kings whose fathers, mothers and grandparents remain uncertain. Indeed, it is often hard to identify which king we're reading of. Any of them might be called father or grandfather, by one generation or other. Chang's interpretation, though the best theory for many years, could not be verified. And then an inscription came up which indicated a ritual selection of temple names. Sadly, it does not tell us whether the choice was made when the person was alive or dead. Puett quotes it (2002:44-45):

"Crackmaking on bingshen, Chu divining: 'In making Xiao Si's day, let it be gui.' Eighth month. (Heji 23,712)

The divination is an attempt to determine the temple name of Xiao Si, as well as the day on which he or she receives cult. And the following inscription reveals that Xiao Si (still being referred to by the name he or she had while alive) is venerated on a gui day:

Crackmaking on renwu, Da divining: 'On the next guiwei, offer to Xiao Si three penned sheep and X-sacrifice one ox.'" (Heji 23,719)

It's a rare piece of luck to learn that a diviner decided on a day and temple name. The divination was repeated at least three times before the gui day was finally confirmed. It looks like divination but involves a measure of careful planning. Before the oracle was even asked, several diviners sat down and decided which days were available. It was a difficult job, as by the end of the Shang period, most day names were crowded and over-booked. Though we can't be sure that all temple names were decided in this fashion, at least some of them were. Xiao Si received temple name Gui and found a time and place in the ritual performance of the Shang. It imposed order on relations between the living and dead.

Stems and Branches

While the twelver cycle remains a mystery, it is, at least not a very important one. The Shang used a few of its signs for writing; otherwise, it was exclusively reserved for time keeping. The xun week provided the posthumous temple names for the Shang kings and queens, and specified the days when they would receive sacrifices and entertainment. It might be wondered (please do) whether the people with the same day name were supposed to merge in one sun, or shared a quality, or were perhaps manifestations of that sun. Just as possible the ten day names may have been a simple system to impose order on a ritual schedule, with no extra meanings implied. It would be nice to know if these day names were an invention of the Shang. In Sima Qian's account of the Xia, we encounter several regents who have posthumous temple names from the xun week. There are three Xia kings who have Geng in their temple names, one Ding, two Jias and one Gui. If this were true, the xun week could be a Xia invention. Sadly, there is no evidence that the *'Xia Dynasty'* as such ever existed (so far). In consequence, many scholars ignore Sima's Xia king list. Considering how much he knew about the Shang, I wonder if this is a wise idea. The ten sun signs have been interpreted in numerous ways. Let me continue with citing T.T. Chang and especially Gordon Whittaker's excellent study on the Chinese and Mesoamerican calendar (1991). The classic *Shuowen* dictionary proposed that the ten signs are associated with the five directions (east, south, centre, west, north), the passing of the seasons, the alternations of yin and yang and finally, human anatomy, with jia for the head, yi for the neck until we arrive at the feet and meet gui. In several cases, the dictionary provides meanings by deriving the stems from words of similar sound. Much of this turned out to be thoroughly anachronistic. In 1932 Guo Moruo proposed that the first four of the ten signs refer to fish. Jia is fish scales, yi is fish gut, bing is fish tail, ding is fish eyes. These signs, he assumed, were developed extremely early in Chinese history, when the hunter-gatherers survived principally by fishing. The fish hypothesis is based on a Han Dynasty encyclopaedia which claims that ding is the occipital bone of a fish, yi it's guts and its tail bing. In Guo's opinion, the Paleolithic Chinese were a bit simple and only counted to four. They wrote the numbers one to four with one to four horizontal lines, and when they needed ordinals, four pieces of fish did the job. Ordinal numbers five to ten (wu for axe, ji for arrow string, geng for a mysterious two eared instrument, xin for an incising knife, ren for a chisel or stone needle and gui for a three pronged spear of lance were, as he proposed, developed during the Xia and Shang periods when people had learned to handle bigger numbers and advanced technology. Sadly, the very idea that the early Chinese ever counted with ordinals is hard to prove. Nor are the real numbers confined to four, maybe the writers simply got fed up with increasing amounts of horizontal lines and made up different signs for larger numbers. Guo also believed that the twelver cycle must be a form of the

Mesopotamian zodiac. It's a spirited idea but it turned out to be unpopular among oracle bone scholars. There is no evidence that links any of the twelver signs to stellar constellations, let alone a zodiac (animal circle), which does not exist in Chinese astronomy. In 1982, Akatsuka Kiyoshi went to considerable lengths to associate the tenner cycle with the gradual development of the barley seed, while the twelver cycle was interpreted as a lunar calendar related to the growth of a child from foetus to the third month after birth. In his system, the first tenner refers to the seed in the earth, the second to the seed ready to germinate, the third to the appearance of the cotyledon, the fourth to the development of the plant stem and so on. Much of this interpretation rests on the *Shuowen* interpretation, emphasising phonetics, but disregarding the Zhou time Five Movers theory, and occasionally ignoring the Shang form of the characters. Likewise the twelver cycle starts with the passage of sperm, continues with attachment of the sperm to the womb, growth of the embryo, separation from the mother, foetal stirring and so on. Why the leafy branch (wei) represents the babies' weakness and the jug of wine (you) signifies the babies readiness for birth remains to be explained. At the time being, several of the tenner and twelver signs defy explanation. **Jia** remains completely mysterious. It would be nice to identify it with the centre, or to consider it a variation of the wu sign using introverted T shapes, but none of this can be verified. **Yi** is accepted to refer to water, rivers and floods. **Bing** has been interpreted as a small table, the shaft or butt of a spear on its stand and as a ritual vessel. It sometimes shows similarity to the characters for entering, inside, and might represent an entrance. **Ding** has been considered the (square) head of a nail, while the contemporary form is said to show the same nail from the side. The nail may have been a recent innovation, but the square itself represents a head, perhaps a skull and an enclosed space. **Wu** is obviously an axe, sometimes it is taken to be a dagger axe or a halberd. **Ji** is generally accepted as a string, rope or line, or the weft in a loom. **Geng** has been considered a musical instrument made of bronze. The type that Guo Moruo envisioned only appears in the Zhou period, but the sign shows similarity to the Shang character for bell. T.T. Chang proposed that geng represents a seed husk; related are the archaic Chinese words *kruk or *krunk, meaning hollow shell, husk, hollow. **Xin** is generally agreed to show a sharp instrument, such as a needle, hair-needle, pin, tattooing needle, and the incision knife used to mark the foreheads of criminals. In later periods, it was associated with bitterness, perhaps due to the association with pain and punishment. Considering that the sign appears in the divine crown of dragon, phoenix, tiger and the very character for the Shang themselves, I would propose that the meaning must have been different in the early period, and may have been a hair needle representing high rank or divinity. **Ren** is generally accepted to show the warp (i.e. the vertical strings) in a loom, or to represent the loom frame itself. Finally, **gui** offers plenty of trouble. One (single) form of the character in bronze seal script hints at a lance. More common is the interpretation that gui shows the blossom of a flower, possibly cinnamon. Another option is a sunflower.

So far, so good. Now you can really knot your brain to discover what these distinct ideas have in common, and why they were united to provide day names and posthumous temple names.

The twelver cycle provides even more entertainment. The first sign, **zi** and the sixth sign **si** have both acquired the meaning of child, son, prince. The difference between them is that the first, zi, arguably shows a head with hair or a sacrificial vessel, while the sixth sign, si, shows a baby or infant and is also the clan name of the royal family. **Chou** has been equated with the radical 'claw' and with the radical 'hand' by various scholars. As a hand it also means to have, take, offer, give or to lend help and support. **Yin** shows an arrow. In some variations, it could also be a man with a round (round usually becomes square or rectangular in oracle bone writing) jade bi disk at his belt. Such disks were emblems of high office. **Mao** appears as a word in Shang script, meaning to split or divide, and usually refers to a form of ritual sacrifice. The signs seems to show a double jade axe, or a knife with jade blades, or two jade knives. **Chen** seems to show a shell, shellfish or clam, the interpretation is largely accepted for pictographic and linguistic reasons. In ancient China, shells were not only eaten but also supplied sharp shells that were set into wooden handles as sickles and knives. **Wu** is a difficult one. It has been identified as an earth-pounding instrument, like a pestle, but as the wooden earth pounders of the Shang have long ago perished, we have no idea what such an item would have looked like. More likely, the sign shows rope or string, i.e. two silkworm cocoons. Other interpretations are a whip, a bridle and reins. **Wei** is closely related to the characters that show trees and wood. The general agreement is that the sign shows a leafy branch. **Shen** probably shows lightning. If you add small mouths or wheels to the sign, you arrive at the character for thunder. **You** is a wine jug or flacon. Whether it represents grain wine or its container remains to be settled. **Xu** shows another axe, only that the experts cannot agree on the type. Probably it was a battle axe, and represents war. **Hai** appears in the *Shuowen* dictionary as grass roots, and this has remained the most likely interpretation. Again, the same question has to be asked: who selected these widely different ideas, for what purpose, and put them together to form a sacral calendar?

Terrible Ancestors

How do you relate to your ancestors? Think of someone whom you liked. Imagine her or him to reside in an underworldly palace, or way out there among the stars, observing you. Could you expect help, sympathy and support? Or would it be admonishments, criticism and curses? And what could you expect from someone who didn't like you, or an ancestor who lived centuries ago?

Nowadays, many people assume that the ancestors are fond of their descendants. Many people in East Asia have a little shrine at home which exhibits the name tablets of important and close ancestors. They regularly get a little food and incense to keep them happy, and when daddy wants a pay raise, granny feels sick, or junior does badly in school, the ancestors are asked for help. It's not much of a cult, and the sacrifices are minor, but there is a routine recognition of the deceased, who are alive and present in their own way. Modern Chinese make a difference between their own ancestors and those of other people. Your ancestors are family. They are supposed to care and help, provided they receive respect and token offerings, and every family member behaves properly. Your family ancestors belong to the class of beings called **shen**, i.e. gods, spirits, divine beings. Other people's ancestors don't give a damn about your needs. In fact they may be hostile to your family. And so they are classed as **gui**, i.e. dangerous spirits, ghosts or demons.

It developed around the time of Kongzi. In the Spring and Autumn period, educated people began to lose their faith in gods and ancestors. Life was simply too bad and too violent to be entirely sure whether there were spiritual beings behind the whole mess. Good thinking. Gods or nature powers can do their part, but it takes plain human stupidity to make life really horrible. Kongzi appealed to reason and humanity. I guess he believed the ancestral cult could be a means to keep society ordered and peaceful. Whether the gods or ancestors really existed was a topic he refused to discuss. A gentleman should respect the ancestors while making an effort to improve the human life. Indeed, by cultivating a loving relationship with the dead, people should practice honouring and loving other people. It resulted in ancestral cult characterised by respect, reverence and duty. Faith or empathy were not required; perfect execution of rituals was much more important. Kongzi was deeply concerned about dignified and serious behaviour. People should not get carried away, let alone employ a wu or medium to recall the dead with drumming and dancing. This rational, aloof attitude appealed to the literati, ministers, officials and administrators. It gradually replaced excessive emotionality and fear of the dead with an elaborate set of precise technical rituals and customs. In the process, the educated Confucians had many conflicts with the wu, who insisted that ancestors can be very much alive and pretty demanding, just like any other spirit or god. But the wu were gradually losing power. The intellectual bureaucrats turned worship into a formality.

It was a new development. The Shang made no distinctions between shen and gui. The character for gui is much older than that for shen. The former is a radical, the latter a composite sign. And when you look into the bone inscriptions, you can see that every dead person, no matter the family, was a gui. When a Shang king dreamed of an ancestor or a whole group of them, it was always reason for alarm.

Here we come to a fascinating aspect of Shang regency. As a Shang noble, you were constantly threatened by the ill will of your dead relations. Every bad incident, each disease and accident was the work of an unfriendly ghost. In Wu Ding's time, every member of the aristocracy was reprimanded by the dead. The nobles were busy exorcising these evil influences from themselves, and sacrificed to placate the wrath of the deceased. When close ancestors reprimanded you, the sign shows a foot kicking a person's head. When they cursed, the character show a foot bitten by a snake, and the danger was much greater. And this was just the close ancestors, many of whom you played with when you were still a child. The early ancestors, the archaic and mythical ones, controlled weather, harvest and enemy invasions. Their anger could produce drought and flood, famine and devastate the countryside. Like mighty gods they could destroy fiefs, cities and kingdoms. And they demanded much greater sacrifices than the gods. There is just one ancestor, Zhu Ren, grandfather of Tang the Successful, of whom no dreadful curses are on record (so far). T.T. Chang suspected that he was a benign fertility deity. In the inscriptions, he is occasionally asked for a good harvest (1970:95).

The deceased were feared, dreaded, placated and nourished. They demanded to be informed of important events; they required regular sacrifice to strengthen them and occasionally offerings to thank them. There is no hint that the dead were loved. If the Shang believed that the ancestors entertained kind feelings, or that they were obliged to sympathise with their descendants, we still have to find evidence for it.

What happened when a noble died? After death, your career wasn't over. In fact, you were just beginning to gain power. Each noble, and indeed every person of some income took ritual vessels into the grave. Simple people had earthenware pots while the Shang nobility was buried with huge assortments of bronze vessels. I guess they allowed further participation in ritual. As soon as you died, you were supposed to watch over your family and to punish its members without mercy. Each living noble was under the control of the deceased. And each dead ancestor rose to semi-divine status, feeding on sacrifices, and keeping a firm hand on the living. For the Shang, death was the beginning of a very active life in the otherworld.

There were several basic classes of dead ancestors. First of all, there is a group of dangerous early ancestors who can't be placed within the royal genealogy. In several cases we cannot even be sure they were ancestors at all, or maybe deities. Primal ancestor Nau (a.k.a. Chi or Ji) was occasionally titled *'remote ancestor'* (gao zu), as were Wang Hai, Tang, Tang's queen Bi Bing and Bi Ji, wife of Zu Yi. There were plenty of regents in-between these prominent ancestors who were not addressed by this exalted title. Then we have the group of predynastic ancestors, between Wang Hai and Tang the Successful. Except for Shang Jia, hardly anything is known about them. As human beings they are so vaguely defined that it might be wondered if they were deities who got entangled in the genealogy. After Tang founded the dynasty, the next few kings, and Prime Minister Yi Yin got special veneration. After these, the regents of the middle and late Shang followed, who were deemed less dangerous to the state. Nevertheless they frequently cursed their descendants with diseases and accidents.

A magical reality

Would you like to know about magical realities? Let me tell you a secret. You are already living in one. Humans are magical beings who impose a glamour on pure sensation to give meaning to it. We create and maintain worlds which make sense one way or another. It's our own subjective story, our net of beliefs and hopes and fears. We do it all of the time. It's one of those things that make us human. Myth making comes natural to us. Perhaps it's a survival trait. We invent big stories, like religion, science, progress, history, culture, and we make up small stories about daily life. You see a person smile and imagine happiness. You look at a work of art and guess what the artist thought. You read a newspaper and wonder about the truth behind a tale. You see your partner make a face and know what it means.

Only that you don't. Most of the time you are guessing. People compare sense impressions with beliefs and memories and come to an estimate. Many times you may guess right. You may think that you know but it's still guessing. And if you are sure that you know, you are living in a glamour. Cause maybe a smile hides pain or shame. Maybe the piece of art was painted by a chimpanzee or calculated like a Mandelbrot image. Usually the news are wrong. You will misunderstand even your lover, friends and children many times. Guessing is OK as long as you know that you're guessing. But when you think you know what is true, you are caught in a dream.

It's a magical universe. It's a story that gives reason, meaning and direction to life. Maybe we are all dreams in the mind of the all-self. Maybe we are clusters of swirling energies imbued with sentience. Maybe we are and are not and will never know for sure. But it sure makes life easier to pretend that our dreams are real. That money has value, that work is useful, that there is justice, that karman is reliable and the government cares about us. It's a magical reality. Like ownership. People believe they own things. The magic works as everyone plays the same game. But when you think about it, all that you are and have and will be is borrowed. Your body is borrowed proteins and carbohydrates, a lot of water plus a few minerals. You return it to the world when you die. Your memories are temporal. They change each time you recall them. For you cannot remember, you can only reconstruct. It takes very little to make you invent new ones. Nevertheless people believe that they exist, are real, have a name, nature, property, history and so on. We all have such dreams. They are the enchantment each of us projects and shares with others. And when we meet people from very distant cultures, we are amazed how different their world dream is.

One thing that may be radically different is the meaning of chance. Let's go into the Shang dream and find out.

When a noble had an accident, everybody knew that an ancestor was angry. If the king was too unlucky, it seriously cost him status. In the Shang world, every incident was a meaningful message of the gods and ancestors. Imagine that your life is a language and that you don't experience events, but that they are communicated to you. Whatever happens is meaningful, and requires your attention and response. This is what I would call an intensely magickal reality. It is magickal as long as you have a repertoire of techniques to counter bad influences and harness events in your favour. If such techniques (magick) were lacking, the result would be something like psychotic or maybe paranoid schizophrenia.

Have you met people who were really far from consensual reality? They find meaning in events to which you attribute very little importance. It's the same thing that makes superstitions popular. They help to make sense of an amazing and dangerous world. Mind you, superstitions are always what other people believe and do. Whatever you do, luckily, makes excellent sense. But what happens when the whole thing expands? Most people in a mental institution (church, army, company, school, university, government etc.) exhibit some odd idiosyncratic beliefs and habits. Except you, of course. But they also have behaviour which seems reasonable and sane as they share it with others of their peer group, generation and culture. What happens when everything becomes idiosyncratic? What happens when all of reality assumes a personal meaning?

Life beyond Death

Let's digress a little. Here is something for the practising magician, mind-explorer and consciousness-designing pioneer. In classical Siberian shamanism it was considered typical that the candidate became insane for a while, suffered from an illness, had near death experiences or experienced intense shocks or crisis. Many budding shamans were thought to be insane. They disappeared into the evergreen taiga or into the white, lifeless snows. Some died. Others found a cure and came back alive. A few encountered spirits, ancestors or gods and returned home as shamans well-connected with the otherworld. Such things may happen on their own accord, but they can also be induced. The better magical or spiritual systems induce a state of crisis and madness from time to time. And even if they don't, each magician or shaman, or for that matter, just about any spiritual human being, will run into crisis sooner or later.

Where it comes to inducing crisis and madness, there are many ways. The easiest is to leave society for a while. Maybe Wu Ding underwent something like that when he lived in his cold shed for three years and refused to speak. It could have broken him. But he came out of it much stronger than before.

Aleister Crowley was a great believer in self-designed crisis states, and did much to share his derangements with partners, associates and students. One of his favourites was termed the Ordeal of the Abyss. In Crowley's system, the Abyss is an extreme crisis which dissolves the personality, the ego, and with it the myths and glamour which maintain the personal magical universe. Of course there are many occasions that crisis happens. Life isn't easy for anyone. When you get into magic and shamanism you stand great chances to encounter your own fears, hopes, dreams, desires and fundamental instincts. It's one of the best parts in the program. And you learn how to deal with them. But the most important crisis of them all transforms the dream of 'you', the person who you believe yourself to be. The classical Ordeal of the Abyss is meant to renew you from the core. It's a very advanced magical transformation. Not that a beginner couldn't do it. It's easy to open the gates of heaven and hell. The mental hospitals are full of people who opened them, one way or another. The thing is that you have to be a competent, experienced magician to stand a chance to go into dissolution, dissolve and come back in a new and better personality. It will be just as illusionary as the one you had earlier, but in a healthier and happier way.

Now there are plenty of ways to go into the Abyss. It can happen spontaneously when you experience extreme grief. It can be the result of drug abuse. It can be induced by trance journeys into the deepest parts of the deep mind, to the nightside of reality. Or by daily death and dissolution trances over an extended period. Some people spend months beside themselves, out of their heads, over the hills and far, far away. Others need years. Some die again and again, until the crisis itself ceases to matter. Others warp themselves trying to return to normality. Some simply let go, enjoy the darksome drama, and return to the world with a laugh.

One way to create crisis, which Crowley highly recommended, is to ask *'why?'* continuously. *'Why'* can reduce lifestyles, relationships, activities and preferences to tatters. Ask *'why'* often enough, day in and day out, and the *'reasons'*, the vague projections of causality behind your glamour will come apart. And so will you.

According to Crowley, the most formal way to dissolve everyday reality is a solemn oath to take every incident as a meaningful communication of god with your soul. It takes a strong and trained mind to project this interpretation on the world. If you can go through life with such an enormous assumption, your normal human everyday world will transform completely.

Here we are very close to how some of the late Shang kings were thinking. They signed their names *'I, the One Man'*, as the whole world resolved around them. Coincidence simply vanished from their lives, and so did everything trivial. Every single event was their responsibility. Imagine being responsible for weather, the harvest, the survival of the people. And imagine that every single person in your state shares this belief. It's not really a mind state for human beings. No wonder they had to become a Di, a semi-divine superhuman thearch. That's why Wu Ding needed such an enormous amount of divination. I can't think of a single ruler who was so keen on understanding what the unseen world was up to. Rain or cloudy skies, a hunting accident, the direction to seek game, the appearance of a rainbow or colourful clouds, politics, enemy invasion, the dreams of the queen and the sickness of a prince... it all made sense thanks to the oracle.

Just think of your own world. The chance encounter in a shop, the person sitting next to you in a train, the newspaper headline you see in passing, the words of people on the street, everything is a message from god, gods or ancestors. A falling leaf, the cracks in a stone, a barking dog, a laughing child, a gust of wind, a spider in your hair, everything mind-blowingly unique and meaningful. There is a deep significance of form. You can recognise it when you assume that form is always meaningful. And everything, everything, everything is absolutely significant and important. If you enter this trance you make the whole world circle around you. Just as it blows up your self-importance to enormous dimensions it produces a pressure which the human ego cannot withstand for long. Things that reach their extremes tend to revert into their opposites. The greatest ego is the one most likely to implode. People who succeed in Opening the Gates of the Abyss usually go mad. If they are competent Magicians, they return to health by giving up identity, with a shrug and a smile and a sense of amazement. For life goes on. And those who die without perishing have a long life (*Laozi* 33). For when there is no '*you*' left, there is literally NOTHING in the centre of the whirlwind of god-sent messages, responsibility and meaning. The glamour of you ceases to mean anything real, as do the gods, the dream of life, the whole set of beliefs that hold your world together. Absolute meaning becomes meaninglessness. Knowledge is replaced by wonder, certainty by astonishment. And out of the absence of '*I*' appears a new personality, gently, cautiously, very fresh and very young and open-minded, which is much wiser and stronger than the one before.

It's nothing to be proud of. It simply is whatever it may be. And it is not, has never been, will always be. Some Daoist alchemists, like Sun Bu Er, called it the birth of the ruddy child. The tough red general of the heart (mind) dissolves and reappears, transformed, as a laughing baby dwelling in the belly of the world. People who have come through this, and who come through it again and again, know that there are mysteries no one can understand or explain. Life is one of them. Identity is another. Their crisis was an artificial insanity which healed them of the madness that normal people take for real.

A magical reality can always be changed by magic. A magical personality transforms easily. And when you know that people are funny, just as the gods and you and I are funny, consider how to improve the entertainment value of your life. The gods, who are not real, have granted this gift to us, who aren't real either. Between us, we make reality. Call it art, sharing, or love if you like. It's always worth a laugh.

Once you laugh joyously there is a way out. Drama and tragedy can turn into comedy at any time. Now is a good one. Keep that thought and take it for a walk.

The Thearch's Task

How did the Shang handle the pressure? How could the kings survive in such a paranoid setting?

When the gods and ancestors influence your life all the time, you have to do something. Either you stop believing in them. It's a modern choice. Maybe Zhòu Xin approached it, but I doubt that any Bronze Age regent could have become a real atheist.

Or you believe. And you develop rituals, offerings and sorceries to cope with the force of the invisible ones. It means you have to order your life so perfectly that the spirits have nothing to complain about, let alone the aristocracy and the population. A king who is under such pressure had better lead a disciplined, dutiful and maybe even virtuous life. If he is not up to it, he might seek other ways to change the situation. It's the easiest way out. Now think of the changes between the *'Classical School'* and the *'New School'*. What we just discussed is the world in Wu Ding's reign, when gods and ancestors were formidable. In Zu Jia's world-view (period 2b), the ancestors were not supposed to demand extra attention by causing disasters and diseases. Each and everyone got her or his equal share. As there were too many gods and ancestors for the mere 360 or 370 days of the ritual year, many gods plus questionable mythical ancestors were eliminated from the record. No doubt they still received offerings in their provinces. People living at the Yellow River would not have ceased to sacrifice to their deity just because the king in 65 km distant Anyang had stopped to do so. The same goes for the gods of mountains, hills, districts and so on, or for the mythical deities of many noble families. But as long as Zu Jia ruled, the power and interference of the ancestors was strictly limited.

In period 3, under Geng Ding's rule, the old rituals and ideas had their comeback. Maybe there were natural disasters of such a scale that the neat ancestral schedule couldn't set things right. The old gods, and the spontaneous wrath of the ancestors had a renaissance. But so had the magical techniques of sacrifice, exorcism and ritual purification which allowed the nobles to come to terms with the dangerous otherworld. When you are threatened by glamours you can use glamours to counter them.

Then, in period five, we meet Di Yi, a king who reintroduces the *'New School'* ritual schedule. Maybe he doesn't want to be scared any longer. And maybe he is so addicted to festivity and loose living that he couldn't care less. As the ritual timetable is crammed full, he eliminates all but a single queen for each king from receiving offerings. His son, tyrant Zhòu Xin, is faced with a ritual schedule requiring him to celebrate a total of 360 elaborate ritual days for the deceased ancestors each year. No doubt he wondered what would happen after the death of his queen and himself. He would get five rituals and so would she. His successor would have to conduct 370 rituals a year. And the next generation even more. So maybe he gave the whole thing up as impossible. And when he noticed that his domain and power were steadily shrinking, who would be surprised if he feasted and drank himself to stupor, night after bonny night?

The Quarters of the World

One thing we all know is that the world is one vast turtle. It does not crawl ponderously across the parched earth, chewing moodily on dried thistles. Nor does it worry about falling on its back during courtship fights and mating. Our turtle swims, effortlessly, free of weight and worry, gracefully across the stellar void. There is something soothing about the image. And perhaps this is what the Shang thought their world to be like.

It's hard to prove, admittedly. But Sarah Allan has much to say about the topic. The turtle is such a beautiful metaphor. It has a flat belly, which serves as the surface of the earth. And high above, its domed shell represents the arched splendour of the sky. You and I live somewhere in the middle. The shell extends to north and south, to east and west. And in the weird regions in-between, which do not fit archaic Chinese cosmology, we have four legs extending to the outer realm.

When Nü Wa repaired the dome of heaven, she used the legs of a huge turtle to replace the broken pillars that support the sky. So the *Huainanzi* tells us, back in the early Han, when people really knew what was going on. It connects the turtle with the structure of the universe.

The Shang were fascinated by the four directions. In the chapter on gods you will meet Deity South, North, East and West. Each of them received sacrifices. Each direction had a name. So had the winds arising from the four directions. And there was Mother East and Mother West, and possibly, though little evidence survives about her, a Mother North. So let's just assume there was a Mother South as well. They also received offerings. In particular Mother East, she is the best documented goddess of the four. Then there was a deity (or deities) Four Clouds. The great god/s Di received a frequent and highly important offering in the four directions and elsewhere. Sadly, the inscriptions fail to tell us what it was all about. Di had administrators. They were Di's Five Jade Ministers. Maybe they represent the four directions and the centre.

And while the Shang were very directional, the dynasties which followed them were just as obsessed by the cardinal directions. The bizarre *Shanhaijing*, maybe the earliest astral travel guide for shamans in known history, describes the entire strange and foreign world beyond the middle kingdom. You read of sacred mountains where jade grows and impossible beasts roam, of rivers crossing hostile lands, of gods and tribes which challenge the wildest imagination, and dreamscapes where the ancestors are very much alive. It's a strange collection of chapters. Each comments on the four directions and the centre, and none mentions the possibility that there might be anything between them. Similar descriptions appear in the *Chuci*, the *Huainanzi* or are scattered here and there in the *Liezi*. Whatever their authors intended, they recorded a world with four quarters, one centre and nothing else. By the Han Dynasty the whole thing had become a complex symbolic arrangement with many associations to the Five Changers (wu xing, usually mistranslated as *'elements'*), the planets, sacred mountains, classes of being, emotions, tastes, musical notes (on a pentatonic scale), sacred animals and so on. And while much of this cannot be traced to the Shang, the basic order was certainly rooted in their thinking.

The Royal Tombs at Anyang

One of the best places for Shang archaeology is the large royal cemetery in Xibeigang near Houjiazhuang close to Anyang. While the royal palaces were built south of River Huan, the extensive cemetery was created at a safe distance and north of the river. The decision may have involved cosmology, with south representing life and warmth while north would represent darkness and, of course, celestial north and Di's heavenly court. The river may have been a convenient way of reducing the influence of the dead ancestors on their living descendants when they were feasting and misbehaving which of course never happened. Let's begin with a note of caution. *'Royal cemetery'* is a likely, but not a certain term. We cannot be entirely sure that the kings were buried here, as the graves were plundered long ago. It is a matter of scholarly agreement to assume that the biggest and richest tombs belonged to the kings. Now let's continue with the cemetery. This wide stretch of land contained the royal tombs and a large amount of secondary burials.

Let us first take a look at the basic shape of the grave chambers. The regents were buried in a square or slightly rectangular chamber. It may have been a representation of the square earth, the world of four directions. Some great grave chambers were simply square or squarish. Several of them had wings. From the sides, four square wings projected, making the whole structure look like a fat cross. Out of the sides or wings of each royal grave chamber, long ramps ascended in the cardinal directions. Each grave chamber was firmly constructed. It had strong walls of pounded earth and was reinforced by wooden panelling. The wood was carved, inlaid with turquoise and shells and painted in white, black, green-blue and mostly red. The Shang excavated cinnabar; it would be nice to know if they associated it with immortality, as later generations of ritualists and alchemists did. Nowadays, most of the wood has decomposed. The pigments can still be traced in the earth that enclosed the timber. The floor was also made of wood. In all likeliness the interior of the chamber was as beautiful as a room in a palace. You might imagine decorations, monstrous animals and colourful textiles. And maybe you would be right. It's a likely idea. What follows is a general account. Several *'royal tombs'* ended up beneath the water level, one time or another, and their interior was badly damaged by the moisture. All of them caved in at some point, and all of them were looted repeatedly by people with little respect for cautious excavation. When I generalise about *'royal tombs'* I do so on the basis of very little surviving evidence. The kings had their graves built long before their death. They did not want a crude earth hole but a subterranean and otherworldly palace, as they continued to influence the human world from down there. As far as the excavations show, there was a square pit under the central floor of each tomb. It contained a grave guardian armed with a spear or halberd with a jade blade. Above this warrior, and above the wooden floor, the coffin was set up. The centre is a sacred location in Shang thought, as the four directions balance around it. A large and valuable collection of ritual vessels, some of porcelain, many of bronze, graced the ledges along each wall. The ledges were made of pounded earth which allowed a wide range of objects to surround the deceased king. Most of these objects were stolen by grave robbers, but the few items in each grave which they happened to miss tell an impressive tale. There were weapons, shields, armour, helmets, riding equipment, ornaments, jades, sculpted stones and cowrie shells (money). Most of all, the tombs contained religious objects, such as the vast array of specialised bronze vessel required for drink and food offerings and ritual washing. The dead were expected to participate in ritual. Some tombs contained entire chariots for two or four horses. Real wealth and powerful ritual objects accompanied each regent to the otherworld. Along with him went servants, associates and concubines. You may think of it as a home for eternity, or as a battery of power. Each regent went to the otherworld equipped for all important occasions. Bagley (in Loewe and Shaughnessy, 1999:185) mentions 'royal tomb' M1004. Like all other great tombs it had been looted repeatedly. Nevertheless, a number of items could be found along the edges. Along the southern ramp descending to the grave entrance, four layers of grave goods were buried on top of each other: *"At the bottom, chariot fittings and remains of leather armour and shields, in the next layer, more than 100 bronze helmets and about 360 bronze ge blades; in the next layer, 36 bronze spearheads; and on the top layer, a stone chime, a jade, and 2 large bronze fangding"*. It's a rich offering, and it wasn't even within the actual tomb chamber! Somebody added it almost like an afterthought when the tomb was sealed and the passage was filled with earth and pounded solid. One common feature of 'royal tombs' are the bodies of guards and dogs which protected the chamber from all directions, including the top and the bottom. Yes, there was an underworld around and beneath each grave, and evidently each king required an armed guard.

Let's take a look at what survives of tomb HPKM 1001, described in detail by Li Chi (1977: 91-92) and by Bagley (1999:185-192) M1001 is suspected to have housed Wu Ding himself. It was certainly one of the most impressive on the royal cemetery. As it had been looted several times, very little of its contents could be excavated. To reach the tomb, the funeral procession descended the southern ramp (30.7m long) which lead to the square burial chamber. This ramp was the only one of the four that came close to floor of the grave (2.3m above the tomb floor), the other three ramps were more symbolic and ended at roof level of the grave chamber (5.5m above the tomb floor). In all likeliness there was a ladder or stairs inside the tomb chamber at the southern side. All in all, the royal grave was more than ten metres below ground. Tomb M1001 is not the only one with such a design. The Shang preferred the north/south axis to interact with the dead. You descended towards the north, the dark quarter, when you walked to the grave chamber, and you ascended towards the south, the bright direction, when (or if) you left it. Quite a few people did not. South is the world of the living and the north the world of ancestors, dead and numinous beings. This worldview continued all the way through Chinese history. You read earlier that the sage kings faced south (i.e. life itself) and did nothing. If you face south you have to sit in the north. You represent the immovable space in the centre of heaven, between Ursa Minor and Polaris, the seat of Shang Di. Those who faced the sage kings were looking north to the ancestors, the High God/s and the Taiyi, the Great Unity.

When China, much later, expanded into the jungles of Yunnan, Guangxi, Laos and Vietnam, another spirit world was discovered. In the humid, malaria haunted forests of the south dangerous ghosts lurked between lush blossoms, swampy wetlands and dripping ferns. The Han Chinese soldiers were scared by weird cries of unknown animals, by spiders, millipedes and snakes and many expired from exotic tropical diseases that could only be the work of evil ghosts. The Shang domain never extended so far and their major ancestral otherworld remained in the north. However, when you consider that the climate was roughly 3 or 4 degrees warmer than today, they may have encountered similar hot jungles in their campaigns to Anhui.

Tomb M1001 is very large. Including the four ramps it measures 66m north-south and 44m east-west. Under each corner of the chamber, two strong, armed warriors were buried. Note that they stood at the corners, i.e. the very directions which are carefully ignored in religious cosmology. And what is not acknowledged is often very dangerous. Each guard had a bronze bladed hook-lance and was in the company of a dog. The ninth guard was in the central pit below the tomb floor, he was the only guard with a jade headed lance. It was a ritual weapon; in Wu Ding's time, no self respecting warrior would have gone to war with a stone-tipped lance, even if the stone happened to be expensive jade. Think about it: why did they place a guardian beneath the sacred centre who carried such an outdated utensil? What sorts of horror were lurking in the depth beneath the grave chamber? Warriors with jade bladed spears were discovered underneath several royal tombs. And in the smaller aristocratic tombs similar jade blades were unearthed. They usually lacked the guardians, but evidently had a similar function. Tomb M1001 had four square wings emerging from the central square. These included, the tomb interior measured roughly 12m in each direction, providing a floor space of 78 square metres and a ceiling 3m high. When the tomb was completed, the offerings continued. We had 9 guardians at and below floor level. Inside, and close to the walls, a further 11 skeletons were discovered. Six of them wore ornaments of turquoise and jade, they had been carefully placed face up in coffins. The other five lacked ornaments and coffins. As the bones were badly decomposed, their gender could not be identified. Above the grave chamber further corpses may have rested. They simply cannot be traced. At some stage, the ceiling caved in, so that any corpse up there would have ended up within. When the grave robbers went in, they messed up the earth above the chamber; making a careful examination impossible. It's an irony of fate that many minor skeletons survived while all royal corpses were plundered, scattered and lost for good. After the funeral the tomb was closed, the ramps were filled in and pounded, until the earth was rock hard. In the process, further people were inhumed. In the western ramp an adolescent with five bronze vessels and grave goods was buried. The east ramp provided a headless skeleton. The east, north and west ramps yielded a total of 31 skulls. The south ramp provided most sacrifices: 59 skeletons in eight rows and 42 skulls in 14 groups. As far as can be told, a few of them were infants, but the majority were adolescent males who had their hands bound behind them and their heads chopped off. Care was taken to bury the heads at a higher level and at a safe distance from their bodies. Surrounding the tomb were further sacrifices. 31 pits were arranged along the eastern side of the tomb. Their contents were quite variable. In 22 pits a total of 68 people were buried, from one to seven persons in each pit, most of them laid out with the head to the north. One pit contained a person of great status who was buried in a double coffin with a range of bronze vessels, horse and chariot ornaments and lavish grave goods. That person had a warrior pit beneath her or his chamber and was accompanied by two persons and two dogs. The other pits had varied contents. Several had been plundered, but seven contained horse burials. Four of them were intact and contained twelve richly decorated horses. M1001 and its immediate periphery contained at least 90 persons who were buried intact, often accompanied by wealth, ornaments and objects for the afterlife, and at least 74 who were beheaded or mutilated and went into the otherworld with little care or consideration. All in all, it looks like a very messy funeral. However, we can only be sure that the people in or directly around the grave chamber met their untimely death together with the king. The skulls in the passages may have been war trophies which our king had collected over many years. The pits at the eastern periphery may have been filled over a long time; indeed,

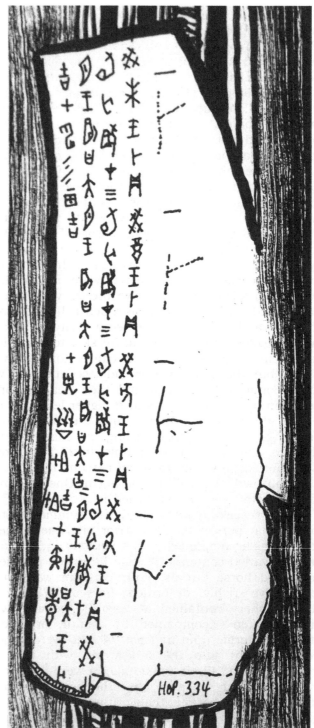

A Typical Bone from Period Five: A series of Xun-Week divinations regarding ancestral sacrifices

the more prominent dead may have died long after their king in the proud knowledge that they would join their benefactor in the otherworld.

The *'royal tombs'* were almost perfectly aligned with the directions. Extending from each side was a long ramp. Look at the map. You will see one grave without any ramps. It is the youngest tomb on the cemetery and it was never completed. Perhaps it was meant to be the grave of Zhòu Xin. He was decapitated by the Zhou and never had a proper burial. Indeed, if we can trust the legends, he may have begun building his own capital and found his end a long way from the cemetery of his ancestors. With the addition of the large tomb in the western section we have nine royal tombs, and there were nine Shang kings from Wu Ding to Zhòu Xin. It's a tricky matter. If the royal capital at Xiatun was founded by Pan Geng, there should have been another three royal tombs, for Pan Geng, Xiao Xin and Xiao Yi. But did Pan Geng lead his people to Xiatun? We cannot be certain about it. The last (known) capital of the Shang may have been founded by Wu Ding himself. And even if the capital was built by Pan Geng, it remains likely that the royal cemetery was started by Wu Ding. The earlier kings may have found their final resting places miles away.

Please look at the map (p.116). There are eight major tombs in the west. Most have four ramps, and as the ramps overlap, we can determine which ramps (and tombs) are the earliest. This gives a relative chronology. It has a few flaws but is not too bad. And as the thieves overlooked a number of items, such as vessels, halberds, axes, small jades or helmets, it is possible to reconstruct a tentative typology. It requires further confirmation, as we can never be sure whether the items in a given tomb were contemporary with the inhabitant or elder pieces, but at least it sufficed to establish some basic styles and periods of Shang art.

The eastern section of the cemetery contains only one large noble tomb, M1400. But it has several smaller tombs with a central chamber and two ramps aligned north/south, which may have belonged queens, princes or nobles. Between and around them is a vast sacrificial area. It is characterised by more than 1,200 small grave pits, most of them aligned north/south, which are located in neat rows running east to west. The actual number of burials is not settled yet. While excavations continue, more and more burials are emerging. These small graves are very enigmatic. In the early days of the excavation, the corpses were simply classed as human sacrifices. It was a popular, if somewhat macabre idea, and it turned out to be far too simple. Some of the skeletons were carefully laid out and buried with a simple grave goods. Others are damaged or mutilated. There are headless corpses who are accompanied by plain goods, such as a knife, axe and whetstone. Horses were found in 20 grave pits, the record being 37 horses in a single pit. Between such simple grave pits further animals were buried, including two elephants with attendants, birds and two monkeys. The grave pits were arranged in groups and may have belonged to a single sacrifice or to a single clan or professional group. It is by no means certain that the burials in a group happened simultaneously. Where early excavators assumed massive slaughter during funerals, modern research indicates that many burials happened afterwards. Who was buried so close to the royal tombs? Some of these people may have been attendants, concubines, guards or administrators who were to serve a king in the otherworld. To dismiss them as human sacrifices means that we impose our thoughts and values on a very early civilisation. It is possible, perhaps even likely that some of them accompanied their regents in the sure knowledge that they were passing to a better afterlife. Other, less careful burials may have been nourishing sacrifices that were simply meant to strengthen the ancestors with their energy. A group of 191 pits southeast of tomb 1400 contained the remains of more than 1,200 corpses. About a third of these skeletons was sufficiently preserved that the sex could be determined. There were women and children, but the majority was young males. Most of them were beheaded, with the skulls buried some distance from the bodies, but some were completely split apart. Few of them had grave goods. Bagley reports that careful comparison between these pits allowed the excavators to discern 22 groups of pits, ranging from one to 47 pits, the largest group with 339 corpses. Bagley gives an average of fifty burials for each of these groups. Most of these burials seem to come from the time of Wu Ding and the two kings who followed him. It is a likely idea that these burials represent nourishing sacrifices that were meant to appease angry ancestors or to strengthen them. It might be proposed that the victims were prisoners of war, and that the size of the sacrifice depended on the amount of available prisoners and on the decision of the oracle bones. Li Chi pointed out that many of the dead were in a weakened and undernourished state, possible a hint that they been kept on a poor diet for months before the execution.

Other sections of the grand cemetery may have housed close friends or associates, who were keen to join the company of their lord many years after his demise. A section of the western part of the cemetery yielded forty pits, containing some corpses and a total of 117 horses. The grand cemetery shows that while many of the dead met an involuntary death, others may have considered it a great privilege to be buried close to the tomb of a king. Even when corpses show signs of a violent death we can't be sure whether they were sacrificed or fell in war and were carried home for a prestigious funeral.

Between the proper burials are simple pits. When we look for sacrificial victims, the pits are a much better guess. Like the pits in Zhengzhou, they contain skulls, artefacts and whole corpses. Some pits contained headless skeletons in groups of ten. Ten might have been a lucky number as it is a multiple of five. More common are pits containing ten skulls each. True, some of them had more or less than that. But on the whole, the number ten was favoured. Maybe they were prisoners of war. The skulls show widely divergent types, indication that their owners came from many foreign tribes. Young Hsi-mei analysed the collection of burial pit skulls from Anyang, which had by then been removed to Taiwan. It was a total of 369 skulls, 319 of which appear male. Each of them was carefully measured and ordered along standard anthropological criteria, and compared with the skulls of Ainus, Bavarians, Parisians, Naquadas and English. The result was quite a surprise. The Anyang collection was, as Li Chi explains, a more heterogeneous group than any of the people it was compared with. While the majority of skulls belonged to the east-Asian type, many others did not. Among them were heads of the Oceanic, Arctic and a few of European type, plus a mysterious group which could not be classed according to these categories. Whoever they were, these people had characteristically smaller heads than the others. In Shang period northern China lived more representatives of foreign cultures than in the Millennia which followed (Li Chi, 1977:255-264). Good evidence that in the Chinese Bronze Age, nations, tribes and cultures were really on the move.

All burial pits begin with the reign of Wu Ding. It seems he began the royal cemetery. But just where are the earlier kings? And where are the many queens? Fu Hao was quite a distance from the main complex, which may be the reason the robbers overlooked her grave. If we are lucky, there may be further tombs.

Each of them might contain material that changes our beliefs about the Shang. The Shang cemetery was not entirely under the surface. When you make a tomb, long before the death of the king, you need a roof to keep the rain out. Otherwise, the sticky wet loess earth will just wash down, the chamber walls will cave in and you had better start again. It is next to impossible to discover pillar holes, left by standing beams, in the mess that was left by grave robbers. Fu Hao's tomb, undiscovered by grave robbers, was in a much better state. When you look at the ground plan you can see evidence for pillars. It is unlikely that all of them stood at the same time. Perhaps one set of holes represents the structure that protected the grave while it was made and while it was closed and covered with many layers of carefully pounded earth, while other pillars were set up later to form her grave temple. It probably had two storeys, and the larger royal

'Grave Companion'
Clothes and ornaments are based on an enigmatic jade figure from
Fu Hao's Tomb.

tombs probably sported even more elaborate architecture. But there is a tomb of a royal lady or queen which was forgotten even during the high era of the Shang. Maybe she had no temple building, or maybe she or her clan fell in disgrace. As the capital expanded, the Shang built their houses right on top of her tomb. For whatever reason, royal spouses were not buried in centralised locations (Yang Hsi-Chang in K. C. Chang 1986:50-55). We can't even be sure if they all had their own tombs. Fu Hao had hers, but she died long before her husband Wu Ding, who married another queen. Whether Fu Jing had a tomb or ended up in the tomb of her husband remains unknown.

Other Cemeteries

Apart from the royal cemetery, several distinct clan cemeteries have been unearthed. The noble families usually had small tombs. Generally, there were several clans in a single cemetery. Some of the better equipped tombs included bronze vessels, or, if they were cheaper, porcelain goods, many of them inscribed with clan signs. It provided evidence that in each section, whole families were buried. But there are differences in status. As the quality of the vessels show, parts of a given lineage group might be more important, or privileged than others. Much depended on how close to the royal family you were. It generally shows in the clan signs and the wealth inhumed with the deceased. In each clan cemetery there are some rich tombs, indicating the heads of the group, but there are also tombs with little or no wealth. Some burials are so poor that the deceased had nothing but one or two cowrie shells, or maybe a few simple tools. Most clan heads felt obliged to remain with their kinsfolk in the otherworld. Mind you, a few such noble burials are located at some distance from the poorer people.

A statistical survey indicates that roughly 10% of the dead were aristocrats. Most had wealth, large tombs, and maybe even a ramp or two. Normal and poor people had simple vertical graves without ramps. Some 16% of the tombs contained bronze weapons; the skeletons are identified as male. Perhaps they were soldiers. Yang Hsi-Chang (1986) estimates that of the almost 1000 graves of the lineage burial ground west of Yinxu, excavated between 1969 and 1977, five burials were large and had a ramp. These included a chariot, coffin, grave goods, bronze vessels plus a few human sacrifices. Twenty tombs were smaller, measuring five to ten square metres. They included coffins and human sacrifices. 50-60 were three square metres in size, very few of them containing human sacrifices or bronze goods. Some 750 burials only had pottery vessels. The rest of the graves are tiny, lacking coffin and grave goods.

Not all lineage cemeteries show the same wealth. Evidently some clans were more powerful than others. And some aristocrats could boast of two ramps where ordinary clan heads made do with one. Among the ordinary clan members, half went into the otherworld with a human sacrifice. But there were other clans who had next to no wealth and very few human sacrifices. This rather numerous group constituted the normal citizens of the time. Here we have farmers, artisans, traders, fishers, hunters and similar folk. They were not slaves or serfs and probably thought of themselves as free, as far as free went. When the king decided to relocate them, they had to move. When a new city was built, several such clans were told to pack their stuff and get going. When war came, they were obliged to fight. And they were free to work on communal projects.

The slaves also had cemeteries. Imagine very plain burial places and careless graves lacking almost all grave goods. No clan signs are in evidence, nor are the dead buried according to any plan or system of organisation. Such cemeteries are few. The Shang did not have the economic development required to employ and house large amounts of slaves. Ordinary people could not afford slaves, nor did they need any. It was just the upper class aristocrats who had employment for slaves. And when there was a surplus of slaves, such as prisoners of war, these were possibly employed for the tough jobs like pounding earth or mining ores. Or they were kept for months until they could be sacrificed.

Bronze- a Metal Changes the World

The origin of Chinese bronze manufacture is still open to debate. One popular, but outdated, theory claims that bronze casting was introduced by unspecified Central Asian migrants, who may also have introduced chariots and horse breeding. Horses have been bred in central Asia for several millennia before the Shang ruled. How long it took before they reached the central north Chinese plains is a matter of dispute. At the time being, the experts assume that it wasn't bronze but copper smelting that was introduced to China. In the late Longshan period, numerous places manufactured smelted copper objects. These objects are rare, and usually the whole process can only be deduced when pieces of crucibles are unearthed (Linru in Henan and Niuzhai in Zhengzhou, Henan), or copper slag (Pingliangtai in Huaiyang County, Henan), or small pieces of copper (Dongzhai). Very rare are whole copper products, such as the bell from Taosi in Shanxi. Often, there were traces of tin in these early metallic objects. Perhaps we are observing experiments with alloys, but just as possible the copper naturally contained traces of tin, and became bronze without deliberate effort. The early Majiayao culture provided a few copper objects and the Qija culture from the upper reaches of the Yellow River provided an impressive 40 objects made of copper, copper and tin or copper, lead and tin. All of this may not seem very much. Metal was not common, and cast copper items were used and eroded eventually. Such early copper and bronze objects were far from the status objects they were going to be and generally do not appear among burial goods (Shao Wangping in K.C. Chang, 2005:90)

Chinese myth makes much of the Nine Ding Cauldrons. According to legend, in the late third millennium BCE, Yü the Great, after he had successfully fought the flood and gained much land for settlement and cultivation, had nine tripod cauldrons cast, which symbolized the nine realms of freshly reformed China. For this purpose, Yü collected metal ores from the nine provinces. He passed the sacred vessels to his son, the first regent of the newly founded Xia Dynasty. Ownership of the vessels enabled the kings of Xia to sacrifice for all districts of the country and to govern in perfect harmony. As the story goes, the Xia kept the vessels until the Shang overthrew them. Henceforth, the Shang were owners of the sacred collection. At the end of the Shang, the Zhou supposedly captured the lot. They found it hard to transport the nine heavy bronze vessels to the new capital, as allegedly, 90.000 men were needed to haul even a single one of them. When the Zhou lost the Mandate of Heaven and were overthrown, King Zhao of Qin captured the nine vessels. Tough luck that he lost one while crossing a river. Or, as a more fantastic tale has it, the ninth ding cauldron simply flew away across the sky before it dropped into the water. The *'First Emperor'*, Qin Shihuangdi, took the story very seriously. On his travels, he visited the spot where the cauldron supposedly lay hidden by the murky, flowing waters, and had a thousand divers search for it. Their efforts were not successful, so the emperor, fed up with waiting, departed, and left the divers to continue in their fruitless quest (Sima Qian). Li Daoyuan, commenting on the event during the Wei Dynasty, claimed that the vessel was almost captured. The divers managed to tie a rope around it, but as it rose to the surface, a water dragon appeared that bit the rope apart (Clements, 2007:136-137). All of which reads like a happy assortment of folklore. But there are several important ideas hidden in the tale. For one, China (i.e. the inhabitable world) was assumed to be square. Divided into nine equal provinces we arrive at a square measuring three by three sections. It's an easy matter to construct a *'magical square'* with nine sections. In this layout, each horizontal row and vertical column adds up to 15. The design is well worth contemplating. The symmetry is fourfold, and four times 15 yields 60, the sacred number of the cycle which the Shang share with the earlier Sumerians. In the centre of the square is the number five; five may represent the four directions and the centre and is the usual amount of divinations that was performed by the Shang diviners. In Shang ritual, the number five keeps reappearing. It also does in later periods: over the centuries, an immense amount of symbolism was constructed

Fox Faced Cauldron
Based on a Shang Period Li Vessel
Nowadays in Shanghai Museum

around the number. The four cardinal directions are all represented by odd numbers; the dangerous *'open'* corners which were guarded by tomb warriors are all even numbers. Later generations attributed the odd numbers to yang and the even numbers to yin. We have number one in the north, where the celestial axis meets the sky and the Taiyi resides, and number nine in the south, where the known world was divided into nine spaces. The order of the numbers from one to nine describes the motions known in ritual Daoism as *'the Steps of Yü'*, a common element in exorcist and purification rituals. This ceremony can be studied in Saso (1978).

Another essential idea is that Yü had bronze vessels cast before the Xia Dynasty even began. It makes Yü one of the earliest persons who used metal; in some traditions he even appears as the first smith. This notion has long been dismissed as fanciful. Metallurgy, or so it was assumed, was introduced to China a few centuries before the Shang. The last years have changed this impression, as more and earlier Chinese bronze is uncovered. So far, the earliest piece has been found in a village in Jiangzhai. It is a simple, small plate and dates from the Yangshao culture of the fifth millennium BCE. Strictly speaking, the item is made of brass: zinc containing acid bronze alloy. As the piece was a single item of uncertain purpose, the specialists were doubtful if they should consider it an import. We should not be deceived by the fact that the piece is such a lonely specimen. Bronze can always be reused. Unless it ends up in a burial, it can be recast as an ornament, a weapon or a tool, again and again. And when bronze is discarded or lost it will oxidize, corrode and disappear. If a culture finds bronze too useful to bury it in graves, excavators uncover very little of it. Another early bronze item is a mould-cast sword discovered at Dongxianglinjia, Gansu; the site dates in the third millennium BCE. Such cases may be seen as pioneering experiments. The best evidence for a flourishing Chinese bronze industry comes from the Erlitou culture. A few decades ago, it used to be thought that the late Erlitou people, who might be candidates for the mythical Xia Dynasty, only made a few really crude, small bronze vessels that looked much like the ceramic tripods, ding cauldrons and beakers which had been used for centuries for ritual purposes. True enough, the first specimen unearthed were by no means impressive. They had the slightly wretched look of very early efforts. Since then, more early bronze vessels have been found. Unlike the first chance finds, they show simple ornamentation (such as nipples and lozenges) and a more aesthetic shape. In fact, several demonstrate great artistic originality: unlike earlier ceramic vessels that served as their predecessors during the Longshang period, the metallurgists went out of their way to develop new shapes. Some of the large and thin walled vessels were used to heat wine. For this purpose, the designers invented vessels with a concave bottom, looking like inverted bowls, making them easier to heat from below. At the same time, the Erlitou people cast bronze weapons. While their use was confined to the elite, as bronze was expensive, we can observe several different types of ge-dagger axe-halberts, with rounded and straight fittings or with a chisel like blade. Even arrow heads, a real luxury item that used to be associated with the Shang, were used by the Erlitou aristocrats. It was an expensive commodity, as arrows are easily lost. From the same early period, tools like knives, awls, chisels, bells and fish hooks were excavated. The Erlitou craftsmen did not have the expertise that the Shang demonstrated, but they were definitely not beginners. We have to assume that the Chinese bronze industry began sometime during the late third millennium as a natural development of the earlier copper casting Longshan and Qijia cultures. So far, the earliest pieces of Chinese bronze come from the basin of the Yellow River. It's a long way from the early bronze casters of Mesopotamia, Siberia and Thailand. As Li Xueqin (1994:11-18) points out, this would make metallurgy an independent Chinese invention.

Cultural Variety

Real bronze manufacture started before the advent of the Shang, but it certainly became a high art under the Shang regents. While the basic idea of melting and casting metal may have had its roots elsewhere, the Chinese used an entirely different process. Most cultures of Eurasia cast metal using the lost wax method. You make a model of the item from wax. You enclose it in clay and allow it to dry carefully. Last, you melt copper and tin and cast the mixture through a hole into the clay body. The wax instantly melts and flows out through a channel while the metal fills the hollow cavity. When you break the clay, you get a copy of the wax item. The more refined version of the lost wax method is to make a clay core of the object. You coat it with wax and put the item into another clay core. Repeat the casting as usual. By contrast, the Chinese started out with refined special ovens that had allowed them to fire ceramics at higher temperatures than other cultures. They made a model out of clay, or perhaps of wood, and coated that with clay. This outer shell constituted the piece mould. After it had dried properly, it was carefully detached from the core in segments. The inner core model was usually broken or crushed, so that it could be removed more easily. Next, the segments of the piece mould were re-assembled and the bronze poured in. The refined ovens permitted a large amount of bronze to be heated to maximum temperature: useful when you want to cast big objects. On this foundation, the bronze smiths elaborated. Often, they cast several parts of an object and welded them together. Such techniques, which were used by the Chinese from the start and which are quite unlike anything done in the rest of Eurasia, are a strong indicator that bronze casting may have been a native Chinese development. But the Shang were not the only people working in bronze. Over the last decades, a growing number of excavations reveal excellent old bronzes which were produced by contemporary cultures. It's quite a surprise. It used to be customary to identify any north Chinese bronze article of the Shang period as a product of the Shang. When a vessel appeared at a great distance from the capital, the researchers envisioned an extensive trade network, or speculated about alliances and shifting populations. Nowadays several cultures are on record that existed contemporary to the Shang and who cast their own bronze, often in startling original designs. The huge bronze heads and bronze trees of Sanxingdui, Sichuan, have no counterpart within the Shang realm and point towards an entirely independent contemporary high culture with its own rituals and customs. Another Sichuan culture was unearthed in Jinsha, a suburb of Chengdu in 2001; the Jinsha culture started roughly during the last centuries of the Shang, but its bronzes show a closer relationship to Sanxingdui. Nevertheless, the Jinsha artists used several motifs that would have been appreciated among the Shang in far away Henan, including the bronze heads of a bull and a dragon, and flat ornamental tigers. Like the Shang, the Jinsha people loved bells, but theirs are much smaller and look quite differently from the ones played near the Yellow River. Around the bells, round, square and polygonal bronze plates were suspended. Similar items were unearthed by the hundreds at Sanxingdui, where they were hung up, together with bells, in the large ornamental bronze trees. Such trees have not been found at Jinsha so far. Both Jinsha and Sanxingdui provided plenty of eye shaped bronze amulets, many of them resembling the kui dragon-monsters you'll read about soon. The Jinsha Site (2006: 40) reminds us that the ancient ancestral deity of the Shu people was the god Zhulong (Candle- or Torchdragon) whose radiant eyes controlled the brightness and darkness of the world. Likewise, the Shu ancestor Cancong is famed for having vertical eyes. In Shang oracle bone writing *'vertical eyes'* are also present: the glyph represents a high minister or administrator (p.722). The Jinsha also buried jade zuns and jade bi disks, they made animal figures (such as turtle, tiger and snake) from stone and cracked turtle plastrons for divination, giving good evidence that some ideas were popular all the way across Bronze Age China, regardless of the culture that produced them.

Toxic Offerings

Unlike the alloys used by many Bronze Age cultures, the Shang bronzes show plenty of daring. Shang bronzes are a blend of many materials. K. C. Chang mentions mixtures of 80-95% copper plus 5-20% tin and small amounts of lead and other metals (1980:151-153; 233-234). Analysis of Shang and Zhou bronzes in the Freer Gallery of Art, Washington DC yielded 78,1- 75,5 % copper; 14,9-7,9% tin plus 14,2 - 4, 2% lead. Eight Shang bronzes in the Royal Ontario Museum contained a surprisingly small amount of tin (2-12%) and an amazing up to 28% lead (Brinker & Goepper, 1980:17-18). Some Shang bronzes contain small amounts of iron, gold and silver. It's an amazing diversity. This culture believed in experiments.

Normally, a mixture of 80- 90% copper and 10-20% tin will make good bronze. This blend works fine, and most people in the Bronze Age were quite content with it. They only changed the composition when the basic materials were in short supply. Given that the Bronze Age, particularly towards its end, was characterised by drastic changes of climate and the migration of numerous cultures, trade was not always reliable and shortages happened frequently. Ensuring a regular supply was a demanding task. Copper is a common mineral but tin often had to be imported. But the result was worth the effort. Bronze is much stronger than copper.

The Shang (and later the Zhou) were not merely interested in bronze weapons and tools. The largest amount of bronze was used to make sacrificial vessels. And these were ornamented with very finely detailed animals, masks and weird images which defy identification.

The linework is incredibly fine and precisely executed. If you cast plain bronze into a very finely ornamented form, many details will not turn out well. Bronze is a little too crude for such a splendid job. But when you add lead, you have a metal which melts much easier than copper and tin, and which can fill the finest lines and carvings.

Let's look at Shang ritual. The amount of bronze vessels in the burials is plainly impressive, and so is the amount of lead that went into some. Large ding cauldrons were used to cook sacrificial soup, meat and sauces for the feasting of the ancestors, while the living came closer to the dead with every shared ritual meal. And as the Shang nobles frequently drank from their sacred bronzes, we can be sure that they, too, damaged themselves in the process. Some of the wines were fortified with spices, herbs and possibly drugs, and heated in special vessels. Lead poisoning was a natural effect of this custom. But to which extent? The composition of the vessels kept changing. 25 vessels from Fu Hao's tomb were analysed (Noel Barnard in K. C. Chang 1986:186), revealing a minimum amount of 0, 14% and a maximum of 6, 09% lead. Compared to the vessels you read about earlier, this is hardly worth mentioning. Some of her vessels contained only tiny traces or no lead at all.

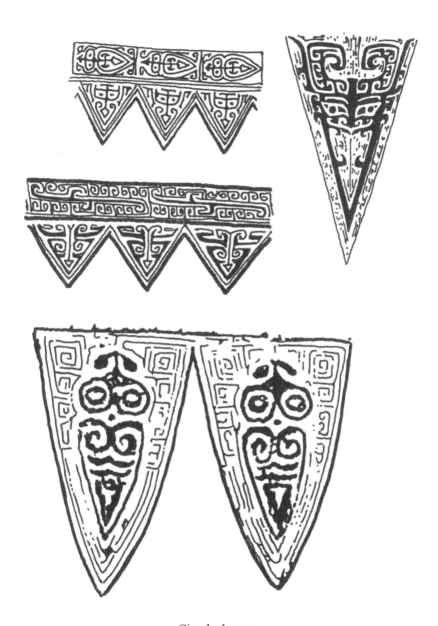

Cicada Images
In the Zhou Period, the Cicada was associated with death, and frequently
appears in tombs. Some species of Cicada only appear after many years
underground, mate, lay eggs, and die. Perhaps the cicada symbolized
death and rebirth. What the Shang thought about these cicada images
remains unkown.

Copper content varied from 75,24% to 92%, tin from 20,3% to 11,6%. One exception is a yu vessel which contained only 3, 82% tin and no lead. Another common addition was zinc. The content ranged from 0,07% to 0,47%.

The very idea that lead and zinc can be added to bronze is a unique Chinese invention. But while tiny amounts of zinc have their use in the body, lead has not. How about the effect of lead on the culture? As the analysis of vessels indicate, Shang wines were made from millets, grains, possibly from rice, and also from fruit and honey. I would guess they also experimented with blossoms and herbs, and frequently they added spices to the mixture. Cinnamon is well attested from the period, the same goes for ginger and peppers. Though the oracle bone character for hemp is still unidentified, the Shang were heavily involved in hemp cultivation, and indeed, hashish may have been part of their ritual drink. Heating the mixture increased its psychoactive potential. So far things seem simple enough, but should we consider lead a psychoactive ingredient? Wines, whether made from grains or fruit, are acidic. They have the ability to extract lead at a much stronger rate than simple water. When the Shang swilled their wine in, as the Zhou claimed, fits of massive alcoholism, they must have ingested amounts of lead that are truly staggering. Maybe Fu Hao was lucky that most of her vessels are relatively lead free, but whenever she participated in the festivities of other nobles, she was bound to get her share. People of our age know that lead is toxic. Most early cultures were not aware of this. Lead poisoning is often unspecific and appears in a wide range of symptoms. The effect is hard to define, as it appears in many debilitating symptoms. Usually, lead does not kill fast. Frequently it starts with headaches, nausea and stomach cramps, reduces blood production and paralyses nerves in the periphery. People age faster, women lose their fertility, men become impotent, the kidneys are badly damaged and finally diseases end the job. Lead can cause extensive damage to the brain and nervous system. It can induce confusion, insomnia, hallucinations, tremor, lethargy, depression, memory loss or fits of anxiety and violence. In short, any aristocrat with a few years or decades exposure to ritual was likely to go sick or gaga, one way or another.

It wasn't the only problem. Zinc is also toxic, though in a lesser degree than lead, and just like lead it is easily solved in acidic fluids.

Finally, there is cinnabar. The Shang had a grapheme for cinnabar, which they appreciated for its magnificent red colour. Cinnabar is ore of mercury, and another substance one shouldn't play around with. In all likeliness the toxicity of cinnabar was known: the people who dug it out of the earth tended to die fairly soon. However, it is a magnificent colour. Analysis of the earth in

Shang tombs indicates that the wooden panels and carvings were liberally reddened with the stuff. In fact, red and black were the dominant colours in Shang tombs. It's sheer guesswork how much cinnabar was used among the living. Maybe they coloured their temple and palace walls, maybe they dyed cloth and maybe they even used it for makeup. Mercury is just as nasty as lead. Apart from causing kidney and liver damage, the substance has a lot of effects on the brain and nervous system. Among them are sensory impairment, lack of coordination, dementia, tremor, pain and brain malfunction. The character for cinnabar, pronounced dan in our age, is at the root of the Chinese term for alchemy. It was the Chinese who introduced the idea that mercury and cinnabar, in small amounts, could be used to treat some vicious diseases. Only a few hundred years ago, mercury was used by European doctors to treat syphilis. The patient had a chance to recover, at least for a few years, but was likely to end up without much hair, health or intelligence. Still, any drug that could cure something as fatal as syphilis had its attraction. It makes me wonder whether the Shang ingested the stuff, just as so many later Chinese adepts, proto-Daoists and even emperors, in the hope of extending life or even attaining immortality. When we imagine the Shang nobility, we have to consider that many nobles suffered from bad health, had sickly children and died premature deaths. Some who lived a long and religious life with plenty of ceremonial feasting were probably more than odd. It's no surprise that they turned into terrifying ancestors, possibly long before their death.

Bronze Economy

Bronze manufacture tells us a lot about Shang politics. For a start, making bronze is a lot more difficult than generally assumed. The problems begin with mining. Copper and tin rarely appear together. The Shang employed people who sought these minerals and made experimental digs. As neither copper nor tin occur in large quantities, the prospectors had a full time job. Then there were skilled technicians who organised and controlled the mining. Some mines went to a depth of fifty metres, which necessitates careful calculations and reinforcement of the shafts. The workers needed accommodation and food. Add a security force. A large one, if the workers were prisoners of war, or a smaller one if they were conscripted peasants. But even more security was required to protect the metal. Bronze was expensive. For one kilo of the pure metal you needed a minimum of ten kilos of unrefined material, and to get that, you needed to excavate a lot more. And finally, the metal had to be transported to the large cities. It implies a large security force, and extra expense. So when we marvel at a single vessel, we should keep in mind that there was considerable effort, skill, planning and expense devoted to the task of making it. It wasn't only Shang troops and workers who did the job. Many of the mines lay at considerable distance from the capital. Maybe one of the reasons why the capital was shifted from time to time lay in the exhausted metal supplies in the neighbourhood. Often, the mines were more than a hundred km from the capital. Some of the ores came from a distance of 400 km. This is far beyond the immediate Shang domain. It had to be mined by neighbouring states and was either sold or sent as a tribute. One culture in northern Shaanxi, the Gong Fang repeatedly fought the Shang. You already encountered them under the name *'Chin-Beard State'*. T.T. Chang read their name as *'Hu-State'* and speculated whether they might be ancestors of the Huns (1970:83).

When the Gong Fang lost, they paid tribute in minerals. Later on, the Gong Fang became allies and performed tasks for the Shang. At the end of the Shang period they disappear from the inscriptions. Presumably they became part of the Shang domain. When the Shang required minerals from far away locations, considerable diplomatic and political effort was required. In all likeliness, there were envoys and ambassadors who travelled in full pomp to visit distant cultures to haggle about prices and schedules. It added another element of bureaucracy, but it also ensures that the trade routes extended over vast distances and commodities circulated freely. Nowadays some daring scholars envision trade routes that connected Anyang with central Asia, Siberia, southern China, Myanmar and even India. The tangle of roads and paths that constitute the *'Silk Roads'* may be a lot older than we dare to imagine. It will take a plenty of excavation to verify them. However, it is a good sign that academics are beginning to think beyond small localised prehistoric cultures and take much larger networks of goods - and idea exchange into consideration.

All the effort involved in bronze manufacture made it an extremely expensive substance. Unlike popular assumptions a term like *'Bronze Age'* does not mean that bronze was widely available. The alloy was too expensive for most people. Ordinary citizens kept using stone knives, scrapers, hammers and the like. Forked ploughs and digging sticks were plain wood. The regents and the top members of the aristocracy used bronze weapons, such as halberds, axes and a slightly curved, broad long knife (looking much like a hatchet), and they equipped the better arrows with bronze points. For hunting and general army supplies, the arrow points were made of bone in special bone workshops in the periphery of the capital.

A vast amount of bronze was needed for sacrificial vessels. Some of them were surprisingly large. The heavy square ding cauldrons in Fu Hao's tomb each weighed 117.5kg. And they were by no means the largest vessels. So far, the heaviest bronze vessel in evidence, the famous Simuwu ding, weighs 832.8kg, including feet and handles (*'ears'*) with their *'tigers eat human head'* design; it is 133cm high. It was cast by Wen Ding (period 4b) for his mother Bi Wu (period 4a). As Li Song (2009:29) remarks: "*Volume was an important way to be visually shocking.*" Judging from the relatively small Fu Hao tomb, we have to expect that the major kings had hundreds of ritual vessels in their tombs.

At Anyang, several bronze manufactories were discovered. The foundry discovered near Miaopu Beidi, just south of the capital, grew until it extended over 10,000 square meters. Nearby were large building complexes that may have housed the workers (Bagley in Loewe & Shaughnessy, 2006:183). In Shang times, the bronze smiths enjoyed a high status. Their burials were rich and their houses, unlike those of many other people, were frequently above the ground.

What made bronze even more valuable is the custom of burying so much whenever a king, queen of noble died. Some of those vessels were well used and may have been among the personal ritual equipment of the deceased. Others were gifts. Yet others were especially cast for the burial, and bore the temple name of the deceased. And while each generation produced large amounts of bronze articles, it also lost them whenever an important person died. Bronze remained very much in demand, and if several kings died in short succession, the value escalated.

Animal Ancestors

Just what was so important about the bronzes, apart from their use as status symbols? Here we are on difficult terrain. The two major sources about the culture of the Shang are the inscribed oracle bones and the bronze vessels. Starting with Wu Ding's reign some had very short inscriptions. It generally consisted of a few characters indicating a clan or giving a name. Bronze inscriptions are rare in period 1. But what is much more revealing is the imagery. Most of the vessels are highly ornamented, the favourite motif being composite animals.

The Shang had an entire system of vessels, which appear in many different types throughout the period. There were cauldrons to cook sacred meals, soups and meat. Some vessels were used for drinking, for heating wine, for offerings of food or fluids, and basins were used for sacral washing. Some of the water basins may also have been used as mirrors, for meditative purposes or even for scrying. Though knowledge of the specific use is tantalisingly incomplete, we can be sure that many vessels were made for offerings. The oracle bones mention offerings of meat, cooked grains, unspecified foodstuff and blood. Each of these was tied to specific and largely unknown rituals.

Great Eagle Owls

Most of the vessels have animal ornaments. Sometimes animals emerge from the vessel or shape the handle or feet. And on the vessels are a wide range of composite animals which successfully defy identification.

Before we get to them I would like to remark that plants are strangely absent. True, there are some ornaments that resemble banana leaves or water plants. But they are so abstract that they might as well be fanciful geometric forms. So why are there no proper plants? Why no trees, for example? There is good evidence that the Shang sacrificed to sacred trees and that there were groves for worship. None of them appear on the sacrificial vessels, nor are there herbs or blossoms. It's always abstracts or animals, or abstract animals for that matter. Many animals are so abstract that they cannot be identified. Others are a bizarre blend of several species. Just as in Celtic or Germanic art, the Shang artists preferred multipurpose beasts which transcend nature.

The animal motifs are a topic which has produced some heated debates. A few scholars, such as Max Loehr (quoted in K.C. Chang 1983:61-62) insisted that the animals carry no meaning. In their opinion, the artists initially experimented with simple graphic designs, like geometric forms, and these transformed into animals almost by coincidence. The Shang nobles liked the look, which became a fashion, and that's that.

David Keightley shows a lot more understanding. *"And the presence of numerous animal forms - such as tigers, dragons, snakes, cicadas, deer, fish, and owls and other birds - that decorated, and even lent their shape to, the late Shang ritual vessels affords the strongest evidence for their religious value"*(2002:110).

The majority of researchers attribute the animals to a sort of clan totemism. Let's use this word in a general sense and consider the practical side. Many of the Shang clans and lineage groups had animal names and signs. What would be more natural than to incorporate such animals in the sacred vessels which conveyed offerings to the otherworld?

There is a lot of evidence for Chinese animal deities, totems and ancestors. Even today there are minorities in China which believe that they descend from a semi-divine animal. Their worship is not as popular as it used to be a century ago, but it survives and is protected by the Chinese Government. Let's look at a few examples.

The Khmu of Yunnan have 18 totems, including tiger, civet, wild cat, monkey, otter, lacertilian, squirrel, Chinese bulbul, water fowl and corncrake. They believe that women and men have different animal totems. Female sacred animals are waterfowl, corncrake, and squirrel, while men usually have white tiger, Chinese bulbul, mynah bird and lacertilian.

Bird Images and Carved Bird 3
(Top Right)

The Lisu in Yunnan have more than twenty family totems including tiger, bear, sheep, fish, bee, snake, mouse, bird, monkey and pig, as well as fire, frost, plough and boat.

Some members of the Li minority of Hainan island are related to cats, which receive annual worship on Cat Mountain. Others have a male dog and a female serpent as their earliest ancestors. Or they are the children of dragon, silk-cotton, banana, sweet potato and so on. Some Lhoba descend from tigers. Other Lhoba clans descend from frog, chicken egg, leopard, wild ox, pig, dog, eagle, cuckoo, and snake, plus plants and objects, such as bamboo bits, sun, moon, kitchen charcoal and knife. Some Primi have frog ancestors. Others are descendants of a black tiger, a black bear or a grass ancestor. The Getan tribe of the Dong claims that their male ancestor was raised in the same nest as Dragon Dog, while their ancestress grew up in a nest with sacred goats. The result is a taboo for dog and sheep meat. Dong clans in Sanjiang, Guangxi believe in an ancestral spider who created the world. Its blessing is invoked for every new born baby. Another Dong favourite is a snake ancestor, who later developed into a water dragon totem. These dragons bring rainfall when they are worshipped by dancing near deep pools and lake. And the Deng people were born to a mother who also gave birth to a monkey, hence they are closely related. People of the Bai in Lanzhouba, Jianchun, Yunnan have ordinary names for contact with the outside world but are known among themselves by family names such as monkey, chicken, pig, red deer and green soy-bean worm. Other Bai clan totems are tiger, fish, sea-snail, bear, snake and mouse. The Nimei village group of the Hani in Yunnan worship a dog who raised their ancestor on dog milk. The Yi of the Ailao Mountains worship a dragon as a general ancestor, but their family groups have additional animal and plant totems.

In Taiwan the members of the Paiwan kindred name their families after animals and plants. The Gulou of Paiwan have a dog ancestor. Whenever a dog in the village dies, it receives an elaborate funeral. Other animal ancestors of Taiwanese minorities are snake, bird, dog, cat etc., plus numerous plants and trees, eggs and inanimate objects. He Xingliang cites stone, kettle, smoke and cloud.

The Kazak have a white swan as their ancestral mother, and their shamans wear a swan's feather in their head-dress. The Evenks worship a sacred bear. The Turkish people are believed to descend from a female wolf, a tale recorded in the *History of the Zhou Dynasty*.

The Gaoche people had a male wolf ancestor. The Dangxiang Qiang descended from a macaque monkey. The Oroqen in Xunke country offer sacrifices to their ancestral fox. The Bouyei worship cattle as their divine ancestors. The Daur ancestral father married a female fox, who is revered to this day as it brings peace to their villages. Among the Baizu is a tiger clan, calling itself *'the sons and daughters of tiger'* and a chicken clan which assumes its ancestor hatched in a nest. And the Yi ethnic group has clans attributing their origin from black tiger, fox, bamboo and dragon, plus assorted objects, such as ivory, swine groove (?), cloth, mountain and flag. Tigers are also popular ancestors among the Naxi, Mosuo, Hani and Bengi. Tibet has many clans descending from Yak or monkey ancestors. And there is a wide range of ethnic groups who descend from sacred trees, bamboo, plants, stones and so on. (He Xingliang, 2006: 17-40)

All of this is secondary evidence, as it relates to people who are a long way, in time and distance, from the Shang. Perhaps some of their ancestors had contact with the north Chinese cultures in ancient times, before they migrated to their present homes on the edges of the Middle Kingdom. It's hard to prove, but a distinct possibility. After all, the Bronze and early Iron Age was a time of high mobility. When you look at the migrations of early European people, you'll wonder whether similar things happened elsewhere. And what about later periods? The Dai used to inhabit the mountains and valleys around the Yangzi until intruding nomads from central Asia forced them south. We see them living in the periphery of southern China, in Myanmar and Thai (Dai)land today, but a thousand years ago, their culture was quite central. Likewise the Qiang, who invaded Shang territory in northern China so frequently, are now a minority in the south-west. And wasn't Shun himself forever busy fighting the Miao?

To explore animal totemism among the central Chinese cultures and their close neighbours, we could take a look into early literature. For a start, remember that the Shang descended from a dark and mysterious bird. Many of their clans had animal names. Among the clan signs on the bronze vessels, which are basically what we would call lineage names, are hare, tiger, deer, bat, pig, dog, dragon, elephant, crow, phoenix, crane, bird-claw, frog, turtle, cobra/s, squiggly worm, locust, cowrie, plus a wide range of human figures and objects. It could be argued that the animal ornaments of the vessels are merely aesthetic, true, but nevertheless these people signed their family names with animal graphemes. And even if the graphemes were merely used for phonetic reasons they would still show animals. People identified with them, consciously or not. The oracle bone inscriptions feature personal, family names including tiger, panther, hare, mouse, elk, pig, horse, two sorts of dogs, goat/sheep, sheep-sacrifice, small bird, owl, bird-grassroot (Wang Hai), bird-royal-park, bird-catching, cockerel, raven, bird-song, tree-snake, grass-snake, snake-altar, venerable-dragon, tortoise, turtle-sacrifice, fish, fish-river, fish-mouth, cowrie-zi-vessel, cowrie-receiving, and a few animals that defy identification. Plus tribal names, which often overlap with clan names. Such as tiger, hare, mouse, elephant, rhinoceros, elk, pig, horse, dog, goat-deity, goat-people, animal-net, small bird, bird-net, double-snake, dragon, venerable dragon, fish-mouth, cowrie-zi-vessel, and the fifth-of-twelve, which is possibly a shell. While these are by no means representative for the many states which bordered the Shang domain or made up its vassals or allies, it shows that there were lots of people who identified their families, clans or states with animals, or were identified with them.

How can we interpret tribal names? A dragon totem could turn a community into dragon-like fighters. A tiger totem could mean that its relations do not fear tigers when they move through the forests and mountains. And maybe a snake totem reduces fear of snakebite. It's a literal interpretation, where you have people revering a beast in order to handle its power. On another level, people who form groups or organisations always create totems to identify with. Not only for their symbolic value but also as they need a focus for their group identity. Dragons remain national symbols of China even though the emperors are a thing of the past. The eagle remains a typical German totem, the British and Scots have their lion and unicorn, the Welsh a red dragon, the Indians put their Aśoka pillar with its lion-headed side on coins, the Greek adorn coins with Athena's owl, Christians have a thing about fish and pigeons and so on. Sure, none of these animals is worshipped consciously, nor do the deities behind them receive actual sacrifices. They serve as a focus of social belief. But isn't it strange how many people go for animal totems, instead of making up abstract, geometrical or household-utensil totems?

One major enemy of the Shang were the nomadic Qiang people. Their grapheme combines a person and a sheep. And the descendants of the Qiang believe that they originated from a sheep ancestor. Sheep wool and hip bones had talismanic power in this culture. *"As they thought their ancestor was a sheep, they engendered a concept that people were sheep and sheep were people. When a person got sick, a wizard would cure the sickness in a way of replacing the person's life by a sheep. They made a person figure by* (sic) *grass wearing clothes, hat shoes and socks of the sick person, led a sheep with the sick person to the burial ground, and killed the sheep and burned the grass person. Then the wizard prayed, saying the sheep took the place of the person and died, and the grass person took the place of illness and went away on the sheep."* (He Xingliang, 2006:35-36). The exchange method is ancient sorcery. The earliest example I could find for it is an Assyrian ritual. Here, the patient exchanges his identity with a virgin she-goat that ends up slaughtered and offered to Ereshkigal, the goddess of the underworld, in his stead (Saggs, 1984:214-216)

When King Mu Wang of Zhou conquered the Quan Rong, he returned having slain four white wolves and four white deer, or really, the clan leaders of the white wolf and white deer clans (*History of the Zhou Dynasty* & *Shiji*). The Mongols are said to have been born out of the mating of a black wolf and a white deer, so perhaps their ancestors are involved in the tale.

And just as the Shang came from a black bird's egg, Sima Qian (chapter *Benji of Qin*) records that the ancestor of the house of Qin was Daye. His mother, the lady Nü Xiu was sitting idly, as she didn't like to weave. When a dark bird came along and laid its egg, she ate it. The result was predictable.

What about the founder of the house of Xia, Great Yü? He frequently transformed into a bear. And so did his father Gun. His character included the sign for fish. And, if we can trust the myths for once, the Xia are popularly related to watery totems, fish being a favourite. It neatly fits Neolithic Chinese pottery, much of it ornamented with fish, toad, dragon and snake motifs. And what of Lord Millet, founder of the Zhou? As a baby, he was saved by the efforts of cattle, sheep and birds. It would be enough to make all three species important to his descendants, if not worthy of the odd sacrifice.

Think about it. When a clan venerates some animal, it usually has some myth to explain the matter. Either the animal is the primal ancestor, or a companion, helper or close relation of the ancestor. Or the ancestor owed her or his success (or even life) to the help of the animal. Whatever it may be, the animal ended up with a shrine and a lot of worship.

The *History of the Former Han Dynasty* notes that the Wuzu people made a wolf their national animal, as their ancestor King Kummo had been fostered by one.

The *Suo Shen Ji* by Gan Bao (fourth century) contains several ancestral references. In predynastic China, the Manyi people descended from Panhu, who had been extracted as a golden worm from his mother's ear and who became a dog when he grew up (ch. 341). Li Xian, commenting on the *History of the Han Dynasty*, says he visited a cave where Panhu was worshipped in the form of a stone dog. King Dongming was conceived when an air-mass like an egg fell on his mother. The babe was thrown into a stable, where pigs and cows kept it alive (ch. 342). In the kingdom of Xu, a maid in the palace gave birth to an egg. She threw it into a river. A dog found it on the edge and carried it away. A child hatched from the egg, who later became king. The dog turned into a horned, yellow nine-tailed dragon. Its grave used to receive offerings.(ch. 343). Ziwen was orphaned and raised by a tigress. He became prime minister of Chu (ch. 344)

The orphan Wuye was protected by a large bird, and later became Duke Qing (ch. 345). In the Han period, the Dou family produced an ancestor who was born together with a snake (ch.

Neolithic Fish-Reign

347). The weird birds in the mountains of the ancient kingdom of Yue (today divided between Jiangsu, Anhui, Jiangxi & Zhejian) used to warn woodcutters when danger was approaching. Sometimes they turned into human beings, but they were only three foot high. They were the ancestors of the male and female wu (ch. 310). The Chu, living between the Yangzi and the Hanshui River, were known to transform into tigers (ch. 307). Monkeys abducted women in the south-west of Shu, Sichuan. Their descendants are the Yang clans (ch. 308).

While this is by no means all that could be said about venerable animals or animal gods or deities with animal attributes, it gives evidence that the animal world was a gate through which the divine was approached, worshipped or asked to intercede for the well being of its worshippers. People are pragmatic, after all. They don't simply venerate something, they usually ask for some blessing in return. We are very close to animal-shamanism in these matters. Just like clan animals give their blessing to family or social groups, the personal spirit animals of shamans help in healings, seances and times of crisis. They reveal hidden lore, exorcise evil influences, remove obstacles and provide inspiration. The same goes for the Daoist power animals, the qiao, who act as initiators, helpers and travelling companions, and provide the inspiration that makes ritual animal dances and beast form wu shu so much fun.

The popularity of animal totems in ancient China is one of the chief indications for shamanic beliefs and practices. Need I add that all the contemporary Chinese minorities who practice some sort of animal worship retain their traditional shamanism? It may not be a popular thing in modern China, but it is certainly alive. And will remain so, as long as the tribal totems of the people receive worship and veneration.

The Taotie

When you look at Shang vessels you can usually discover several animals incorporated in the basic ornaments. Some of them may be complete and appear on lids, handles and feet of a vessel, or have their heads emerging from the sides. Others are engraved on the bottom where they reside unseen. But much more common are ding cauldrons with huge faces right in the centre. These animal faces are one of the most essential elements of Shang and early Zhou art, and their meaning has been extensively discussed. You can see many examples in the illustrations. Take a close look at them, preferably with an open, silent mind and let them come alive. Then read on.

Taotie Images and Bottle Horned Dragons
(Middle Row)

For convenience's sake, the animal-type is generally called taotie.It's a fairly recent term. During the northern Song Dynasty, when Chinese archaeology made an early start, collectors tried to understand what was so special about these animal faces. They came upon a passage in the *Lüshi Chunqiu* by Lü Buwei (3rd Century BCE), who had written (briefly) about them.

"On the sacrificial ding vessels of the Zhou (or Xia) taoties were shown, beings with a head but without body. They eat people, but before they can swallow them disaster destroys their body. It illustrates just punishment" (16.3)

It's is a nice moral explanation. Sadly, Lü Bu Wei, writing at the very end of the Zhou Dynasty, did not understand what he was talking about. Nor did the authors which he cited in his admirable work.

It is extremely unlikely that the Shang and early Zhou produced hundreds, if not thousands of elaborate bronze ritual vessels to illustrate a dull proverb. But the Song scholars, lacking any other source on the topic, accepted Lü's remark. And they used the term taotie for any of the numerous animal masks which adorned the ancient vessels. So do contemporary scholars, though in the full awareness that the very name may be wrong. For how the Shang and early Zhou named these mythical creatures is long forgotten. But maybe Lü wasn't entirely wrong. His proverb may be off the mark, but maybe the idea was not. Taotie means something like glutton or all-devourer. It's is an excellent description of the function of the ritual vessels. Just as the living partook of food and drink from vessels, so the gods and ancestors fed from the ritual bronzes. The cauldrons are adorned with a wide range of more or less identifiable animals, among them sheep, deer, bovines, tigers, bears, birds and so on. Almost all beings which appear on the vessels were used as offerings, including people. And as one sacrifice followed another, and the rituals never ended, the vessels fed and devoured like gluttons. In one sense, they were the ever-hungry mouths of the invisible ones. In another, they were the animals themselves.

Let me propose that the taotie does not lack a body. The heads adorn a vessel, which has a trunk and legs. In short, the vessel acts as body for the heads on its sides. And regardless of the direction you looked at them, you always have at least one head looking at you.

Should we extend the metaphor? Taoities are rarely naturalistic animals. Much of their appearance is simplified, abstract, graphic, symbolic and ornamental. And quite often, a given animal shows characteristics of several species. It has lead numerous scholars to identify types of taotie, based on the assumption that a certain sort of ears grace tigers, horns grace deer, goats and buffaloes and so on. And though such classifications reveal, first of all, that the taoities successfully

Taotie Designs 3

defy classification, it might be guessed that maybe a vessel with sheep attributes was used for sacrificial sheep, and so on. In this case the vessel would be a spirit- or deity-form, a focus for divinity. And if the sheep taotie fed on blood and flesh of sheep, the spirit animal, deity or clan totem might receive food.

On the other hand, it is just as possible that the animal shapes referred less to the offerings than to the clan totems. Someone related to the dragon clan would have a dragon vessel to feed its spirit, god or ancestors, regardless of the actual food which went into it. And when clans intermarried, the resulting families might demand new types of taoties that combined the animal attributes of their ancestry. Several such intermarriages might result in extremely mixed taoties. It could have happened that way, but it was not necessarily so. Think of the imperial dragon, popular emblem of emperors and high nobility since the Han Dynasty. It combines nine animals. The body and neck of the snake, the head of the camel, the antlers of the stag, the eyes of the hare, the belly of the seashell, the scales of the carp, the claws of the eagle, the feet of the tiger and the ears of the ox. Though these animals have lots of symbolic meaning, they do not symbolise the union of nine family totems.

Or maybe the animals were combined in order to take them out of the realm of real animals. One possibility is a taboo against too much naturalism. Or maybe there were symbolic reasons. There is so much food for speculation. Bear faced taoties for instance. Bears feature very prominently in Chinese myth (just remember Gun and his son Yǔ) and in Daoist ritual when the exorcistic dance of Yu is performed. However, so far not a single oracle bone character has been identified as a bear. They do not appear in hunting inscriptions nor are they present in religious divinations, clan names or elsewhere. Another strange thought is that you can easily superimpose the character for Di on many taoties. Usually, the eyes coincide with the horizontal line of the triangle. Did the Di character start out as the face of a mythical animal, possibly a bear or a Taotie?

Kui Dragons

Dragons are closely related to taoties. Take a piece of paper and cover half of the taotie's head, so that only the right or left side is visible. You will observe that each half of the head can be seen as an abstract draconic beast in profile. Two kui in profile produce one taotie from in front. It's a typical case of Shang art symmetry. The *Shuowen* dictionary explains that this creature, the kui, "*is a divine spirit that looks like a dragon with a single foot.*" The *Shanhaijing* identifies it as a hornless bull. "*In the Eastern Seas is a realm of rolling waves, extending over seven-thousand miles. It is populated by certain animals which are shaped like cows with blue bodies, but they are hornless and have only one leg. Whenever they enter or leave the water, storm gales blow and rain is sure to fall. They shine like the sun or moon and have a voice like thunder. They are called kui. Huang Di caught several and made drums out of their hides. When they were beaten by the bones of the Thunder-beast, they sounded over five-hundred miles, and made all under Heaven tremble with awe"* (ch.16).

Zhuangzi (ch.17) also had his say. *"The kui envies the millipede, the millipede envies the snake, the snake envies the wind, the wind envies the eye, and the eye envies the mind. The kui said to the millipede, 'I only have one leg on which I hop, and hardly get along. How do you manage to co-ordinate those ten-thousand legs of yours?'"*

And while the ensuing chat says a lot about the benefits of unconscious activity, it does not tell us more about kui.

The *Hanfeizi* in the third century BCE records that one day, Kongzi was asked whether a certain Kui, who had lived in ancient times, was really a one-legged cripple. Kongzi replied that Mr. Kui was of one piece and complete. Here we have a pun on the character kui which can also mean *'of one piece, complete'*. He used to be the master musician of Yao. And he was famous for being choleric, perverse and ill-tempered. It did not really make him popular, but he escaped the death penalty nevertheless as he was highly trustworthy.

It tells us that one legged kui of one sort or another were widely known and discussed in early literature. Just don't ask me what this has to do with the creatures on the vessels.

Or consider the wang liang spirits, who dwell in the hills and mountains and appear, from time to time, with only one leg. The *Zhou Li* calls them fang-liang and says that they inhabit freshly dug graves. Prior to each burial, an armed exorcist in bear skins with four eyes, titled Rescuer of the Country, had to leap into the grave and thrust a spear into the four corners to expel any fang liang lurking there. In the third century Wei Zhao noted that wang liang have a human face and the body of a monkey. They imitate human voices to confuse travellers. Well, at least this connects one legged monsters with the underworld. Just like the vessels buried with the nobles.

Shang imagery also went the other way. Just as we have two dragons combine to form one taotie face, early Chinese myth makes much of serpents with one head and two bodies. Such animals are by no means fantastic, as Sarah Allan points out (1991:163), two headed or two bodied snakes are a relatively common genetic aberration. Two bodied snakes appear in Shang art, and may have had an entirely different meaning than the Zhou ascribed to them. In Zhou lore, they are a bad omen, while the double headed snake/dragon that designated a rainbow in Shang writing became a thoroughly bad omen in Zhou days.

Kui Dragons

When kings are identified with dragons, a two headed dragon means the division of the state. The Shang were not very easy about rainbows, but at least they still bothered to divine what they would mean. Nor did they usually identify with the dragon motif. Though plenty of dragons graced the sacrificial vessels, the dragon state and dragon city were enemies against whom Wu Ding and Fu Jing waged war. At other times they were vassals, allies or even relations.

Whatever may be the real explanation (and please invent several of your own), the vessels with their taotie heads had meaningful forms. Quite practically, they served to convey energy, emotion and offerings from the human realm into the otherworlds. When soup or food were shared between worshippers and the otherworldly ones, they were a common ground for interaction.

Things become more interesting when a given noble or king was buried with a wide range of bronze vessels. The Shang believed in a very active and influential life in the otherworld. Sometimes I wonder whether they saw this world merely as a prelude to a much more powerful, semi-divine state in the realm of the dead. And they took the things along which they had need for. Weapons, ornaments, chariots, possibly clothes, food and a huge amount of sacrificial vessels. Again, we can consider several explanations. One of them is favoured by Keightley (2002:101), who proposed that the dead would continue to sacrifice to their superiors (such as the remote ancestors) when they were in the otherworld. It makes me wonder what. When you are buried with a lot of vessels, where do you obtain the offerings to fill them? May I speculate that the dead used their vessels primarily to receive the offerings made by the living? In this case, the bronze vessels of the human realm would have a magical connection to the vessels interred with the dead. When the descendants sacrificed in the temple above ground, the vessels in the deep might receive the offering, and feed the deceased.

Or we combine both interpretations. The living give to the dead, and the dead pass their own offerings to more senior ancestors, gods, Di or whoever. All of this is hypothetical. There is little written evidence about the activities of the dead. Sure, they hosted each other on occasion or a close ancestor might rise to meet a more remote one. Most of the time they messed up the world of the living. What the ancestors did among themselves, whether they remained separate, or organised like a vast otherworldly court with a (quarrelling) hierarchy of sorts, or had a wild party in some happy bronze-age Valhalla, remains anybody's guess. We can only be sure that they were fed by the living, and to what degree they shared offerings among themselves or waxed stronger individually remains uncertain.

Whatever the Shang really thought about their vessels was long forgotten when the Qing Dynasty began. Lü Buwei had more comments on them, each of them referring to a proverb.

"The Zhou Dynasty had a tripod which illustrated Zhui (a famous artisan) *biting his finger. Thus the ancient kings sought to demonstrate that overmuch skill is an evil"*(18.4)

"Among the tripods of the Zhou one was crooked. It was very high, but the top and bottom were slanted, to indicate that excess brings misfortune". (19.5)

"One of the Zhou tripods had the picture of a mouse being crushed under the hoof of a horse, because of its secretiveness. Secretive behaviour leads to the downfall of states". (20.5)

And finally a reference to the fate of the tripods when a dynasty falls:

"The tripods of Yin (Shang) *were set up in the court of the Zhou Dynasty. The Zhou covered the earth altars of Yin with roofs. Their music, which accompanied the sacred dances with shield and spear, served simply to entertain the people.*

The music of a bygone dynasty cannot be used in the temple. The earth altars of a fallen dynasty may not see heaven. The sacred utensils of a fallen dynasty are exhibited at the court to serve as a warning." (23.1).

All of this should be taken with a grain of salt. For while the Zhou themselves created their own sacred music, the descendants of the Shang, the Song, seem to have retained the music of their ancestors. Zhou time China had a wide range of hostile states, each of them with its own traditional music and dances.

And regarding the proverbs which Lü Buwei attributed to the vessels, I wonder whether he quoted earlier texts or made up his own story. It says a lot about him, as a highly sober statesman and politician, that he failed to guess that the ancient vessels served for extensive sacrifices. The topic of religion is suspiciously absent in his voluminous work.

Luckily, there are a few references in earlier books which are much closer to the point. Here is the most important. It comes from that huge history, the *Zuo Zhuan*, which records the rule of the regents in the Zhou period. Here is the story. In the year 606 BCE the king of Qu asked the royal grandson, Prince Ma, about the ancient bronze vessels of antiquity. He was most interested to know whether the early vessels had been large or small, heavy or light. Prince Ma replied,

"Most important is virtue (de), *not the vessels. When, a long time ago, the Xia had virtue, the people of far countries sent images of various things* (or: *beings) and offerings of metal to the Lords of the Nine Regions. The metal was used to cast vessels which showed various things. The many hundred things* (beings) *appeared on them so that the people could learn about* (or: *from)*

the gods and evil spirits. Thus it became possible that people, when they were journeying on rivers and lakes, in mountains and forests, did not encounter evil beings; the spirits of the mountains and waters did them no harm. Thus the high and low were harmonised and they enjoyed the gifts of Heaven.

Jie (of Xia) was dark in matters of virtue, and so the vessels went to the Shang, who endured for six-hundred years. Zhòu of Shang, however, was violent and tyrannical, and so the vessels went to the Zhou (dynasty). When virtue is bright and beautiful, the vessels remain small but heavy. But when virtue is lacking and there is disorder they may be large but light in weight."

In these few lines you encounter evidence that the vessels symbolised the right to govern. They were adorned with animals symbolising gods and spirits. And when offerings were made, the whole world was harmonised, so that even the most dangerous places remained free of evil entities. Plus the novel idea that just regents make small offerings in humble vessels of great substance, as their rule and word has weight, while unjust tyrants exhibit large offerings in exaggerated vessels of little weight and value. It does not accord with the development of vessels during the Shang period, but is a nice thought.

Play of the Animals

There is also a theory that the taotie was originally a shaman's mask. As there are no such masks in evidence it's not easy to verify. Some wu of the Zhou are known to have worn bear masks. The *Zhou Li* says that the Rescuer of the Country wore a bear-hide and a mask with four eyes of yellow metal. S/he dressed in a black coats and a red skirt, and wielded a spear and a shield. In this costume, the Rescuer led a hundred followers. The procession performed the exorcism and purification for each season of the year. And, as you read earlier, the Rescuer personally leaped into fresh graves to scare away the fang-liang spirits. But whether the wu of the Shang wore similar costume, or maybe the wu of some vassal-states, remains unknown. However, taotie faces regularly appear on Shang helmets. Now what do you make of this? Are you thinking of the animals as clan signs? Or were the animals the helping spirits which made warriors strong and fierce? Both options are possible. Liezi confirms this. *"Huang Di fought Yan Di on the Plains of Banquan (or: Zhulu). His storm troops were bears, wolves, leopards and tigers, while his banners were carried by carrion-birds, pheasants, eagles and buzzards."*

A similar event is ascribed to the fight between the Shang and the Zhou. The *Shujing* states, that before the battle began, King Wu spoke to his warriors, *"be like tigers and panthers, like bears and black bears, here at the border of the Shang!"*

Taotie Designs 4

It may sound like poetry, but the elite troops of the Zhou who destroyed the Shang capital were called the Tiger Vanguard. Maybe other sections of the army were named after animals, too.

Maybe it's a metaphor. And maybe the metaphor refers to something very practical.

It might remind you of *Ynglingasaga*, 6, which relates how Odin transformed his chosen warriors, the berserkers, into wild beasts so they could fight more vehemently. Or think of the Philippine, Malay and Indonesian term *'amok'* which is a state of spiritual obsession.

It's a skill developed by some elite warriors, and it is based on the ability to forget the human personality while something much wilder takes over. Berserkers went into animal consciousness directly before battle. They charged the enemy with no regard for their own safety. When they received wounds, they hardly noticed. The Vikings called it *'being iron-proof'*. Call it a very intense obsession trance. Things only became difficult when the charge was delayed. Having no enemy to attack, some raging berserkers beat the ground or bit their shields until blood spurted.

All of this connects with Chinese martial arts.

Catherine Despeux (in Kohn, 1989:238) relates that a crane dance was performed at the funeral of the daughter of the king of Wu (r. 514-495 BCE). Marcel Granet explained that the crane signified triumph over death. Despeux adds that the *Chunqiu Fanlu* (16.12a) claim that the crane lives for a long time as it does not have any breath of death. We are at the roots of crane style martial arts here. Contemporary wushu lore identifies the crane as a bird of great libido who teaches balance and stretches the tendons. Internally, crane motions (and consciousness) refine and conserve the jing (here: sexual essence or secretions). It is hardly surprising that cranes became favourites among immortality seekers and Daoists.

When the *Zhuangzi* was compiled between the fourth and second century BCE, imitation of animals and animal movements for inner alchemy was already widely practised. Our sage remarked "*To pant, to puff, to hail, to sip, to exhale the old breath and draw in the new, practising bear gait and bird stretching its wings, longevity his only concern - such is the life favoured by the scholar who practices Induction, the man who nourishes his body, who hopes to live to be as old as P'eng-tsu.*" (15, trans. Burton Watson, slightly amended according to the Chinese Health Qigong Association, 2007:2). And while Zhuangzi made it clear that this was not his idea of attaining the way, the very fact that he could mention such arcane practices without further explanations showed that they were widely known. It was the beginning of the Wu Qin Xi, the Play of the Five Animals, which is the earliest documented form of Qigong and of animal style Wu Shu. We find a similar passage in the Huainanzi (7.8):

"If you huff and puff, exhale and inhale,
Blow out the old and pull in the new,
Practice the Bear Hang, the Bird Stretch,
The Duck Splash, the Ape Leap,
The Owl Gaze, the Tiger Stare:
This is what is practiced by those who nurture body!"

(translation Harold d. Roth and John S. Major) The first lines refer to a standard breathing exercise of the immortality seekers, inner alchemists and early Daoists. You simply imagine that your body fills with vitality as you inhale and that you release stagnant qi, bad energies and diseases as you exhale. The animal exercises are less easy to identify. Whatever they may have been, they were certainly modelled on animal behaviour and involved a measure of identification and playacting. It always starts that way.

Chen Shou (265-316) wrote in his *History of the Three Kingdoms* that "*Hua Tuo developed a set of exercises called Wu Qin Xi, namely, first tiger, second deer, third bear, fourth monkey and fifth bird, as physical and breathing exercises to cure diseases and strengthen the feet for walking* (Chinese Health QiGong Association 2007:3)." Next Ge Hong, a pioneering Daoist alchemist, elaborated on the theme. In his period, the fourth century, animal imitation skills were already considerably evolved. The passage is a bit difficult, but it tells us that the ability "*to breathe like a dragon, circulate qi like a tiger, to stretch like a bear, to swallow air like a turtle, to swoop like a swallow, twist like a snake and expand like a bird; to listen to heaven and turn to earth, to move along the inner light of yellow and red and refrain from entering the inner caves of heaven, to climb like a monkey and to leap like a hare will extend life by 1200 years without any decay of the sense organs*". (*Baopuzi*, 15).

(This reading is based on three widely different translations). Here, yellow and red represent the male and female sexual secretions, to *'refrain from entering the inner caves of heaven'* might be a hint to avoid ejaculation. Animal imitation wushu (martial arts) was alive and well for many hundred years before the Indian Buddhist Bodhidharma allegedly introduced unarmed martial arts to the Chinese at one of the Shaolin monasteries.

Imitation of animals for longevity, trance and entertainment may be associated with Daoism, but the Daoists built their foundations on the experiences of the early immortality seekers and the wu. In Zhuangzi's time, the inner alchemists looked at Wu Xian, the famous shaman/s of the Shang court, as the progenitor of their art. Lü Buwei noted that "*dew-eating and air- (= qi) drinking immortals sit at the feet of Wu Xian (22.5).*" When martial arts experts imitated the motions of animals, they did not

Spirit of the Dance
Distorted Shang Ornament
Based on Hentze 1967:109

simply go for the outer appearance. The important thing about early martial arts is that transformation into an animal can get you into its consciousness. It's not a side effect but a must. Let's have a quote from Liang Shou-You and Yang Jwin-Ming's *Xingyiquan* (2002:72): *"...in Xingyiquan, the emotional mind should not be suppressed. On the contrary, it is encouraged and stimulated to a higher level of excitement. For example, it is said that the mind is like a fiery tiger which is able to excite your feelings and raise up your spirit so that you will not be afraid. The reason for doing this goes back to the fact that Xingyiquan imitates animals. Because animals don't have a high level of wisdom mind, when they fight they react naturally, from their feelings. In order to unite your mind and your techniques, you cannot suppress the emotional mind."*

The beast comes in, or out, and moves your body. It starts with observation, continues with imitation and evolves naturally into inspiration. You play the animal until it plays you. We could also call it obsession. It's not enough to look like a tiger, the main thing is to get into tiger-instincts, its energy-aesthetic-flow. Snake style without being a snake is just a technical travesty. And dragon style is not a collection of techniques but the skill to flood one's being with the consciousness-energy of an impossible, fantastic and mind-blowingly free spirit. The dragon that can be defined is no dragon yet, and dragon technique should be forgotten before the true dragon arises. When contemporary martial artists perform set routines based on technique and tradition, they are missing the shamanic roots of their craft. Instead of dancing and playing a super-human sentience, they copy the postures of people who were a lot more innovative and inspired than they are. For the real beasts cannot be taught. They have to be discovered, developed and exercised. They may need a bit of taming, and you may need to become wilder and more instinctive, but sometime, somewhere, way beyond thinking, a union occurs as you join to enjoy.

All in Transformation

People turn into animals for the sake of fighting, magic, exorcism or life extension. But this is just the beginning. Numerous early Chinese myths tell us that animals like to transform into people. Spirits frequently appear as animals or people, depending on their mood and, occasionally, their spiritual refinement. But it goes beyond this. The gods love to transform into animal shapes. It's a lot more fun than trying to be human. Do you remember? The Green Emperor Fuxi and primal creatrix Nüwa were exceptional shape shifters. There was often a serpent body under their human torso. And Fuxi also appeared with the head of a bull and the snout of a tiger. Just as the early Xiwangmu enjoyed to greet her visitors with a fierce tiger smile, the leopard tail under her robe twitching moodily from side to side. Ask for the elixir of immortality and find out what happens.

Yes, gods often appear a bit odd when human guests come round, asking stupid questions or demanding silly miracles. And who could blame them.

The Red Emperor Shennong ruled after Fuxi. He occasionally wore the head of a bull, fitting emblem for a deity who invented agriculture.

Huangdi, the Yellow Emperor, wore the hides of beast and danced their dances. His teacher, the dark or mysterious woman Xuannü appeared as a bird with the head of a woman. And his great enemy Chiyou had the hooves and horns of a bull, plus four eyes and six hands. He visited the people of Taiyuan, wearing the head of a serpent, and brought pestilence in his wake (*Shu Yi Ji*).

When Yü the Great, himself a bear on occasion, dug a canal through the Longguan mountains, he discovered a cave in the mountainside. Inside he met three gods in animal shape. They were a dog and a pig, both of them wearing black robes, and accompanied Fuxi, himself in serpent shape (*Shu Yi Ji*).

The god of thunder has bright eyes, hairy horns, wings, a beaked nose and the face of a monkey.

Gods can appear as animals, just as they can appear as humans. The shape is a convenience. For in the real world gods are gods. They are not male or female, nor do they require names or attributes. A deity, just like you and me and any other being or thing is simply a cluster of consciousness, energy and form. Form is convenient so that people can interact with it. But just as you are not your clothes, the man- or beast-shaped body is not the true nature of a god. Essentially, identity is not a thing but specifically the cluster of things and thoughts you identify with.

The similarity of deities, animals and people has fascinated many Chinese authors. One such expression survives in the *Liezi* (2.18)

"A being with a skeleton seven feet high, hand and feet differing from each other, hair on its head and firmly set rows of teeth in its mouth, able to lean and bend, is called human. But it is by no means certain that such a man hasn't got the heart (consciousness) of an animal. But even if it has the heart of an animal, due to its shape we feel related to it. A being wearing wings or horns, with parted teeth and spread claws, which raises itself up and flies or downward inclined and runs, is called an animal. But it is not certain that such an animal hasn't got a human heart. But even if it has a human heart its shape makes it appear foreign.

Fuxi, Nüwa, Shennong, Xiahou had serpent bodies and a human face or the head of a bull or the snout of a tiger. They had an un-human shape but the spiritual energy of divine beings. King Jie of Xia, King Zhòu Xin of Yin, Duke Huan of Lu, Lord Mu of Chu were, in shape, appearance and facial expression like humans, but they had the hearts of beasts. If the many people simply observe the shape to judge the consciousness, they cannot comprehend anything...

The divine sages of antiquity understood the abilities and habits of all beings. They understood the voices of various life-forms. They lived among them and gathered them in their company. They dwelled in the company of spirits, gods, ghosts and devils, they understood all the people of the earth and they surrounded themselves with birds, animals, reptiles and insects. They said 'all beings of flesh and blood are similar in the way their hearts think. As the divine sages knew this, their teachings never failed.*

Gods, animals, ghosts and people; all share the consciousness of the heart. From this centre, transformation occurs. A god can appear human or like an animal.

And animals can be deities. Worship an animal long enough and you'll be amazed by its divinity. In fact, anything can be worshipped. Anything can become a spirit or deity. This goes for living beings, but it also goes for mountains, forests, rivers, rocks, springs or a huge range of everyday objects. It is not only jewels or weapons or works of art that can become a living focus of consciousness and power. As Gan Bao observed, *"Monsters are formed when a certain spirit or energy is attached to concrete things. If the energy is confused or in disorder, the thing will change its form. Form, spirit, energy and essence are related"* (ch. 102). A stone, a plant, a tree or an object can be turned into a deity. Or they can become demonic when the energy is misapplied, distorted or frustrated.

People can turn into gods or animals. Virtuous nobles and ministers can become local gods after their death. And those who lead an unhappy life may return to haunt the living. To demonstrate that the world is an amazingly surprising place and that miracles happen all the time, read the following summaries of events which Gan Bao dutifully recorded around the beginning of the fourth century. He was a highly educated man, an eminent scholar and the head of the historians of the Eastern Jin Dynasty. His twenty volume collection *Suo Shen Ji* was not complied for frivolous entertainment but as a true record of unusual events. The chapter numbers appear in brackets.

Zhou Period 1045 (?) - 221 BCE

-739 BCE, state Qin, Gudao County, Wudu. The duke tries in vain to cut a sacred catalpa tree growing on the roof of a bull temple. The task prospers after his men have loosened their hair, dressed in russet, tied a red ribbon around the tree trunk and have scattered ashes. A black bull spirit emerged from the tree and escaped to the river (415).

-Kongzi and his students travel through the state of Chen. They are having a bad time, lack food and suffer from weak health. One night, while the sage is playing his qin, a huge dark man appears. Zi Gong fights the visitor but cannot get a hold. Kongzi observes that the man's collar keeps moving, and tells his disciple to go for the neck. Immediately, the man turns into a huge black fish. Kongzi explains that spirits can cling to all sorts of domestic and wild animals, and even to trees, grasses and any old object. As Heaven did not want him to be hungry, the fish was sent to maintain his life. They cook and eat it (445).

Han Dynasty 206 BCE-220 CE

-Hanwudi leads a procession to a ceremony. Passing a woman bathing in the river Wei, the emperor is shocked that her breasts are more than two meters long. Zhang Kuan informs him that the lady is actually the Heavenly Star of Sacrificial Ceremonies. She appears on earth when worshippers, such as the emperor, have not properly abstained from meat and drink. (72).

-Reign of Hanwudi, in Yangzhou. The governor, Zhang Kuan, is asked to mediate in a lawsuit. Two old men sue each other for the ownership of a mountain. Zhang finds both slightly odd. The two turn out to be snakes (442).

-Reign of emperor Ling, Jiangxia province. An old woman spends so much time bathing in the river that she turns into a turtle. Her family is surprised (355).

-c. 225, Wei, Qinghe perfecture. Turtle craze spreads. Another old woman dallies overlong in bathtub, becomes a turtle and runs away very fast (356).

-226, Danyang prefecture, a respectable 80 year old woman becomes turtle and escapes from her family (357).

-Prince Guangchuan enjoys plundering tombs. He opens the grave of a nobleman in Jin. A white fox escapes, but receives a wound in its foot. In the night, the fox comes to the prince and wounds him in the foot as well. The prince dies (375).

-Xihai region. Military commander Chen Xian searches for his subordinate Wang Lingxia. The latter is discovered cowering in an empty grave, totally crazy and looking much like a fox. Wang recovers speech a fortnight later, and claims having been seduced by a fox woman called Azi. She becomes famous in the region and numerous legends are told about her (425).

-In Qi, Liang Wen has a temple built on his property. Ten years later, an invisible spirit moves in who cures diseases and eats loads of offerings. Once, Liang attempts to grab the spirit, and catches a beard. The spirit turns out to be a goat.

-Anyang, Henan. An inn is haunted by three men, who happen to be the spirits of a huge scorpion, a rooster and a sow (438).

-Luling prefecture, kingdom Wu, martial artist Tang Ying from Danyung, on official business, spends a night at the official guest house. He receives honorary visits, first from the inspector and then from governor of the province. When, unannounced late at night, the two come back to visit him at the same time, he discerns an error in protocol and kills both. They turn out to be a pig and a fox (439).

-Mount Huayin, Yang Bao rescues a golden bird that has been mauled by an owl. The bird recovers and transforms into a lad, explaining that he is a messenger of Xiwangmu, and on a mission to Mount Penglai in the eastern sea (452).

End of Han Dynasty. Jiang Ziwen of Guangling province, handsome, sporting, fond of women and wine, is so good-looking that he becomes a popular country god after his death (92-96).

Three Kingdoms Period 220-265

-Reign of Sun Quan, first king of Wu, Jian'an perfecture. Governor Lu Jingshu has a huge camphor tree felled. A monster with the head of a human and the body of a dog comes out of the tree. Lu identifies it as a peng hou spirit and has it cooked. He eats it, commenting that it tastes just like dog's meat (418)

-Man encounters ghost rabbit while riding in Dunqiu country. He falls from his horse. When he recovers he meets a stranger. After exchanging pleasantries the stranger transforms into the ghost rabbit and kills him (406).

-c. Year 238, Xianyang Country. Official Wang Chen is haunted by the spirits of a ladle, a pillow and diverse kitchen utensils who keep chatting away all through the night (413).

-He Wen of Wei meets three spirits in his newly acquired house. They are the ghosts of gold, copper and silver hoards hidden in the walls, plus a talkative pestle (414).

-Riverbank in Luting, county Longshu. A huge tree is inhabited by a woman spirit who causes rain on request and calls carp from the river. When war comes, she leaves (416).

-Zhang Liao, retired governor of Guiyang in Wei cuts a tree on his estate. Several white haired old men come out of the trunk and fight (417).

-Scholar Dong Zhongshu meets a man who foretells the weather. He turns out to be a fox (420).

-Jurong county, Micun. Farmer Huang Shen narrowly escapes seduction by a beautiful lady who happens to be a fox (423).

-Hedong. The governor Liu Bozu receives regular visits from an invisible fox who tells him all sorts of secrets. When Liu is promoted to imperial inspector, the fox accompanies him and reveals the dirty secrets of the court. Very reluctantly, Liu sends the fox away, fearing his colleagues might discover the spirit in his company (424).

-In Nanyang, Song Daxian spends a night at an inn. He is molested by a ghost all night through. The ghost turns out to be a fox (426).

-Changsha. Dao Boyi inspects the northern parts of the prefecture. During a night at an inn he is attacked by a black creature. The next morning it turns out to be a bald fox. The fox habitually collects knots of hair from the heads of the guests (427).

-In Wu, eminent scholar Doctor Hu is caught teaching the Classics to a bunch of foxes sitting in an empty grave (428).

-Yuzhang province. Xie Kun has a battle with a yellow man who haunts an inn. He tears off the arm of his attacker. The next morning, a dead deer, lacking a foreleg, is found near the inn (429).

-Beiping prefecture. Tian Yan lives at the grave of his mother to mourn her for three years. Meanwhile, his wife receives visits from a man looking like her husband, who is really a dog spirit (432).

-Nanyang prefecture. After his death and burial, Minister Lai Jide returns to his family. He sits near the house altar, eating, drinking, lecturing and bossing the family around. A few years pass. One night he is drunk, loses self control and reveals his true shape. He transforms into a dog and is killed (433).

-Lanling county. Commander Wang Hu frequently receives military advice from a man who visits him at midnight. After a few years, the visitor is exposed as a dog spirit (434).

-Wuxi county, Wu prefecture. A woman in black tries to seduce Mr. Ding Chu. She is really an otter in disguise (436).

-Xingyang prefecture. Zhang Fu, rowing his boat at night, saves a pretty girl. Sleeping peacefully, she reveals her true form. Zhang is amazed to find a crocodile in his bed (443).

-Shicheng. Daoist priest Xie Wei spends a night at a riverside temple. He is molested by men who happen to be two crocodile and one turtle spirit. All three had pretended to be gods to stuff themselves with offerings (444).

-A house in Yuzhang province is assaulted by a horde of tiny men. When boiling water is poured over them they turn into beetles (446).

Jin Dynasty, 265-420

-In Yan, an aged fox assumes the form a lad and visits minister Zhang Hua. The two discuss the Classics, and the fox wins every argument with ease. Zhang Hua feels insulted by the lad's superior knowledge, and proves to be a bad loser. He has the fox trapped and killed by magic (421).

-In Wuxing prefecture, a fox assumes the shape of a man and beats the man's sons. The sons are badly hurt. Later, they learn that it must have been a spirit who hit them. When the boys meet their real father, they mistake him for a fox and kill him. The fox uses the chance. He assumes the shape of the father and lives with the family for years, until exposed by a travelling magician (422).

-Wu perfecture, Qu'e county. Scholar Wang spends a night with a girl and ties a golden bell to her arm. The next morning he meets a pig wearing the bell (430).

-Wei prefecture suffers from drought. The governor receives the visit of an old man who wants to be cured of a carbuncle on his back. This accomplished, he reveals that he is the local dragon god and grants an extra helping of rain (449).

-Yinzhou province. A man watches several feather cloaked women in a field. He steals and hides a feather coat, and the woman, trapped in human shape, marries him. They have three daughters, then she discovers her old coat and flies away. Returning with more coats she transforms her daughters into birds and off they go.

-c. Year 322. Mr. Ren Gu, native of Jiyang country is raped by a feather clad man and becomes pregnant. Some months later the rapist returns, cuts off Ren's genitals and releases a baby snake from his belly. Ren goes to the capital where he succeeds in getting a job as an eunuch (349)

-Nanyang prefecture. Song Dingbo meets a ghost while walking at night. Song pretends to be a ghost himself, freshly dead and not used to spooking yet. The two have a friendly talk and Song learns a lot. Arriving in town, the ghost transforms into a sheep. Song spits on the sheep to trap the ghost in that form and sells it on the market for a large sum (393).

This is early Chinese myth. Whatever people may assume is real, if only for a time and a certain person. And there is a lot of truth in it. Maybe not the truth you need to drive a car, handle a computer, or make sense of the 21st century (if possible), but the truth that people made up to make sense of odd experiences. It gave meaning and structure to their lives. And it is still valid when you view the world as a shaman, sorcerer or sage. For many, such as Gan Bao, these accounts were by no means fanciful. His mind-blowing study contains so many transformations that Hesiod, Ovid or Snorri Sturlusson would have felt right at home. For in this world of changing appearances, anything can become anything else. Body lives and dies, molecules get around, consciousness pervades every thing, identity comes, goes and re-appears transformed and the great mysteries continue as ever. For whenever you happen to believe that you know what it's all about, you can be sure you stopped wondering too early.

Any being or thing can change its awareness. Change awareness and you change the world. And when you transform the environment you change awareness again. Beings seek out the habitat that maintains their state of mind. And all of this is changeable. If it does not feel good you are missing the best. You can go for the essence or you can make your own happy feelings just as you like. You can invent a hundred new consciousness states right now and create feelings that are really good or a lot better. Refine yourself and you may become a deity or immortal (if you have to). Or enjoy dwelling in the unspecified nameless heart where form and awareness happen spontaneously.

You can make your life divine by living that way. You can explore the joy of being simply human, and participate in the great colourful parade of life, the incessant coming and going of generations. And you can delight in the wisdom and lust of body as you move, run, dance or play like any happy animal. And learn that a flow of love pervades all states of being.

Some give in to crude passions, hates or fear and become unhappy beasts. Others become dangerous spirits or demons who have no suitable place in the play of events. A god without a healthy function in the world may fade into oblivion or become a demon. While a demon who finds its place in the great world-miracle may suddenly become a god. Life is full of surprising changes. Anything that was learned once can be learned again, for the better, right now. It just takes a worthwhile function, a suitable habitat, a bit of love and integration and the demonic turns divine. The same goes for animals. And people. It goes for me and you, and happens all the time.

Storm Bird Peng

Masks of the Divine

Have you ever wondered why people sense, experience, shape and create the divine? How come all cultures that we know of had some concept of transcendent, immanent or transcendent-immanent divinity? Why do people experience deities, spirits, ghosts, demons and so on? What makes atheists so passionate in their disbelief? Why do so many modern people replace deities with ideals? And what makes us shape these ideals, and compels us to live up to them? Is there an evolutionary advantage to religion?

There are so many words for it. Call it ideals or archetypes, gods, spirits, sentiences, principles, the numinous or whatever: each term is limited and probably way off the mark. Find them beyond the world, in the world, as the world and as yourself. Discover the mystery that makes us move and dream and evolve. There is consciousness in everything. And there is consciousness in a million forms, tangible and intangible, manifest and imaginary. There are so many different approaches to the divine. How shall we call it? How shall we handle thoughts that are simply too big and complex for each individual mind?

Western researchers often confuse themselves when they speak of *'gods'*. Look at the term. The word *'God'*, though superficially associated with Christianity, goes back to Germanic * guða- , a neutral term that was used for gods and goddesses. Its Indo-European roots may be ĝhutó- 'from *ĝhau- *'That which is called or invoked'* or *ĝheu- *'That to which sacrifices are made/libations are poured.'* (*Duden Herkunftswörterbuch*, 1989:249). Before the Christianisation of the Germanic cultures, the word *'god'* appears as a title of Wodan/Oðin. As you may notice, there is a vast difference between the monotheistic, all-knowing, omnipotent and omnipresent God of Christianity, and the more specialised Germanic gods, who functioned in a polytheistic plurality. When the word was applied to the IHVH of the *Bible*, a lot of connotations remained. We get a similar effect when we speak of the *'gods'* of other cultures. Consider the gods of ancient Greece. Thanks to Hesiod and Homer, they have plenty of personality and a private life much like a soap opera. Greek gods are pretty much like human beings. More so, they have specific jobs, tasks and their very own ego trips. As a result, they quarrel, scheme, flirt, seduce, spite, curse and fight each other most of the time, and woe to the humans who become their tools or toys. In Greek thought, gods could have human half-divine children, but more usually, a human who claimed divinity was suffering from hubris and duly crushed. Considered superficially, Greek gods are specialists. It may be a misinterpretation, as our knowledge of them is dangerously limited to art and literature, excluding a huge range of everyday worship from the countryside where it eluded the interest of learned folk. However, to the post-Renaissance Europeans, the Greek gods were a standard model of what polytheism should be like. It made European scholars sort foreign deities by functions. What if we move further? To the ancient Sumerians, gods also had functions, but these functions varied according to the city a hymn or myth came from. Each of the great Sumerian cities had its patron deity, and in each of them, the basic stories of creation, of dragon fights and the emergence of kingship and civilisation differed. Unlike the Greek gods, the Sumerian deities had human shape but rarely interacted with mankind, which had been created explicitly to serve and worship them. Take the ancient Egyptians. Their gods are called *'neters'*, meaning principles. These *'gods'* have some stories to provide a mythological framework and some entertainment. Nevertheless, a great many of them are simply universal principles that remain much more abstract than the Greek or Norse deities. Or think of the Voodoo loah. A loah is primarily a law, a principle. The personified appearance is of secondary importance. When people are obsessed by a loah, that loah has some outer forms that can be recognised by worshippers, but performs in a playful and highly individual way. The same loah can appear in a farmer, a fisher, a scholar or a trader, a soldier and a politician, and in each case, the personification has a different flavour. Here, obsession is not so much by an individual deity but by a universal principle that manifests itself through an individual carrier. Consequently, there is plenty of obsessions that happens outside of a religious context. We have all seen people who personified a principle, and many of them were not even religious, let alone Voodoo devotees. Loah are born anew whenever a worshipper is obsessed by her or his divine patron and manifests the essence of divinity, idealism, grace, genius and power. Indian myths are still harder to understand. In Hindu religion we recognise the divine in a colourful array of beings, entities, sages, half-gods and whatever. Attributes, functions, appearances and gender can transform anytime. Indeed, the scholar who tries to keep one deity rigidly apart from another is bound to get things wrong. It's part of the Aristotelian worldview that things can be told from one another. The old philosopher was fond of analytical thinking; he loved to separate phenomena, to class beings, to decide on this or that, yes and no, true and false. Several churchmen continued with this approach, and nowadays analytical thinking is the backbone of scholarly research and scientific thought. It has a tough time when it encounters phenomena that might be either or, maybe, possibly, in degrees of verity and perplexingly enigmatic, inspired or plain mind-boggling. When Western people say *'deities'* they imagine them as somehow different from ancestors, sacred animals, spirits, mountains, rivers and other natural phenomena, including clouds, trees and snowfall. Definition is well and good, when we are dealing with simple things and ideas, but who says the divine has to accord with the common human desire to invent categories? So what shall we say about the Chinese *'gods'*? In what way are they distinct from, say *'Spirits'* or *'Ancestors'*? As the terms *'god'* or *'gods'* is so full of preconceptions, we ought to be very cautious when we apply them to other cultures. David Keightley, for example, prefers to speak of *'powers'*. It's a little more neutral, but it lacks the element of consciousness that makes religion and ritual meaningful. The divine may appear as a force, or as a force of nature, but that force, like everything that exists, is intelligent. All the *'gods'*, *'deities'*, *'forces'* or *'spirits'* partook of divinity in the opinion of the Shang. It's easy to see: they received sacrifices, interfered with the harvest or were nasty enough to curse their worshippers. Indeed, the fact that a sacrifice was made is often the only indication that we are dealing with a deity at all. But are deities, spirits, forces or ancestors really distinct? And did the Shang make distinctions between them, identify them with specific phenomena, linage groups, functions, activities or maybe imagined them to co-exist in a hierarchy? The answer is a jolly: we don't know. You had better get used to this.

In classical China, the divine was referred to by several terms. One of them is **shen**, a word that can mean the quality of the divine, deity, ancestor, spirit or a person imbued with divinity. If you want to keep it abstract, call it the numinous. If you want to personify it, translate it as the gods or spirits. All interpretations are equally valid, and the good thing is that we get them all in one word. Another one is **ling**. Usually it means a divine, holy or spiritual quality, such as you can find in a temple, a sacred place or a talisman, or a spiritual being like a spirit or deity. In southern China, however, ling was also a word used for shamans.

How did the Shang deities function? Consider rain. In some cultures, there are weather gods who are specialised in rain making. In Shang thought, rain could be granted or withheld by a wide range of deities and ancestors. The Shang gods did not act like a company where every employee has a distinct function. Therefore, the oracle was essential to divine who exactly was causing drought or flooding. Whether the Shang had a divine hierarchy remains an open question. Nor do we know if the deities were just a chaotic assembly or if they were organised in family structures. Some deities appear in more inscriptions than others. Were they more important than others? Only for the segment of society who dwelled in the capital, made oracles and recorded the divinations. It's a distorted view of the past. Let's consider the ancestors. For Europeans, an ancestor is quite distinct from a deity. One of them was human, the other isn't. In Indian and Chinese thought, the distinction is less clear. People can become gods, gods can incarnate as people, and people can be deified once they are dead. An important ancestor can be a manifestation of the divine, just as a god of a mountain, a river or an activity. At the Shang court, the early ancestors got more attention (and sacrifices) than the later ancestors, and the gods. It does not necessarily mean that they were more important. You could only be sure they were considered nastier (which is a sure way to get attention), or that they were more important to the nobles, to whom they were directly related and hence, family. But what about the people who made up the culture? Just because a bunch of ancestors or deities is important to the king and his closest kin it does not follow that the rest of the population thought the same.

Remember the importance of Heaven to the early Zhou. They had their cult and they retained it, through all those the years when they were vassals and allies of the ruling Zi clan. We know about their cult as the Zhou eventually replaced the Shang, wrote the history books, preserved the records, the songs and poetry, and essentially made their own history. The Zhou, however, were just one state or tribal culture among many. There were dozens of states and statelets surrounding the Shang domain, enemies, allies, vassals, you name it. How many deities, ancestors or animals or totems did they venerate which we'll never learn about? What appears to be the Shang Dynasty is a conglomerate of allied clans and ethnical groups. As soon as you left the capital, you met highly distinct cultures, each of them with their own spiritual preferences, their own myths and tales of origin. Bronze Age China shows an amazing religious diversity. The frequency a deity appears in the inscriptions only says something about preferences at the royal court, but very little about the religions of other cultures, people or classes of society. Maybe some of the 'minor' or 'local' deities had more followers in their own districts; especially deities like Mount Yue and the Yellow River. This being said, we can plunge into the cults of the known deities and remember that they were definitely not the only ones.

The Shang had a sign which often appears in connection with the divine. It looks a bit like a T. Sometimes there is a horizontal bar over it. That bar means high or above. And sometimes lines drop down to the sides of the T. They may represent fluids. The Shang frequently drank and poured sacrifices during their rituals. And they also liked to splatter blood for religious reasons. Both ideas are implied (see p.766). You will encounter the T in many signs that relate to the divine. Such as prayer, wu ritualist, branch sacrifice, document consecration, drink sacrifice and so on. There are even a few deities and ancestors who have it in their name. It's a radical worth looking out for. Whether it really shows an altar, as some scholars assumed, remains uncertain. We have no Shang altars to compare it with. Or maybe it is a distant relation of the world-tree or world pillar symbol. Something like the Saxon Irminsul: a pillar with two snakes extending to the sides. Or the T shaped womb symbol of the Egyptians. And if you go back really early, to the very beginning of the Neolithic and the earliest human-made temple (or ritual place) in known history, you find complex arrangements of T shaped stone pillars set in varying circles. The place is Göbekli Tepe in eastern Turkey (Kurdistan) where people invented agriculture and the domestication of animals around 10,000 BCE. Look it up on the web. It's a magnificent site. What is a near desert today was a lush hill forest then, populated by great cats, foxes, wading birds, wild bulls, antelopes, donkeys and a wide range of snakes, insects and spiders. All of these animals appear, faithfully engraved, on the T shaped stones of Göbekli Tepe. An entire set of animal totems, pictured with grace, elegance and faithful detail on monolithic stones that may have held a roof or stood in the open. They are the magnificent effort of a huge workforce of early farmers who really believed in animal totems. Maybe they worshipped animals. Maybe they had gods in animal shape. And maybe the animals represented clans and family groups. Now I wouldn't dream to claim that the T symbol passed, along with agriculture, through Europe and Asia. It's just one of those crazy signs that are really popular. And you are welcome to make up your own explanations.

Directional deities

Modern Chinese frequently show a dislike for the number four, and try to avoid it. The word si: *'four'* sounds much like the word for *'death'* in some regions, making the number so unlucky that many condominiums lack a fourth floor, and those that have, sell the apartments at cheaper prices as few dare to live in them. In Shang time China, the number was a lot more popular.

The Shang were obsessive about the cardinal directions (while ignoring the ones in between) and they turned each direction into a deity. East, or **Deity East**, shows an object which could be a sack of grains or a bundle of wood (p.730). Or it could be the blend of the radical for wood/tree with the sign for sun, as Sarah Allan proposed. In which case it might be the sacred mulberry in the very east of the world where the sun rises every day. Like all of the directions, East had a name, which appears in wind inscriptions. The name of east is Splitter (p.732). It shows an axe-like lightning striking the wood-sign. Perhaps the Shang

Bronze You
Vessel for wine. Showing hybrid tiger-dragon-elephant-bat-goat-etc.
Animal and maybe a female Wu ritualist (Note pierced ears for earings).

thought of spring lightning striking trees, but just as possible the sign means that wood splits (earth) as it emerges from the ground in spring.

Deity South shows a bell (p.737). As mentioned earlier, it is not a good picture of a bell, or at least, it does not look much like the bells they found in graves. You might think it shows a little hut, if it were not for the name of that diviner which shows bell plus a hand with mallet striking it. The bell is a mixture of meaningful elements. It has the wood/growth sign at the top which might indicate extension, just as the sound of the bell expands in all directions. There is a square signifying sun or star in the centre, hinting at the golden gleam of the bronze, and implying the spreading out of light. It might be the light of the ten suns, the king, the noble of a fief or the celestial deities, maybe even Di. Bells were important status symbols of high nobles and clan chiefs. Aristocrats who were granted a fief could receive a bell as a sign of special favour. It represented the authority of the regent.

The south also had a name, showing a person from in front, with lines around it (p.658). As a guess, it might be a picture of someone sweating.

Deity West shows a basket or a nest (p.781). Basket fits the season of autumn, when stores are brought in to store them for winter and early spring. Note how east and west balance. If east is a bag of seeds, west is the means to carry grains home, and to store them. In one season, life is scattered and in another, gathered. The basket may also have had a sexual connotation and symbolised the vulva. In this way, it appears in the *Yijing* (hexagram 54, referring to the marriage of King Wu and a barren Shang princess, see Shaughnessy (1997:18) and later on in Han time literature. West and the westwind are known by two names. One looks like a mix of the wood glyph with three streams of water (p.749). Which may be significant or not. The other (p.699) was interpreted as the sacrifice of a cockerel: this name might be read as Shrinker, Shriveller or Concentrator.

Deity North appears as two people back to back (p.642). The sign actually means *'back'*. Perhaps it hints at getting close to escape the cold. Or maybe north, as the dark quarter, was associated with night, and thus, the picture might show a sleeping couple, sharing a single bed back to back.

And finally there is the **centre** (p.745). The modern Chinese sign for centre, middle, shows a square divided by a central line. It's ancestor in the oracle bone script shows a central square or circle with a flag, useful to see the direction of the wind. Unlike the directions, the centre was not a deity and did not receive sacrifices, as far as is known. But it is a sacred location and a space to which the king moved, or which the king established or erected, by means of ritual, to impose order. It might be argued that the centre represents Di and the circumpolar stars, or that it had its importance due to being empty.

From the centre, the four directions appeared. Just observe the layout of the royal tombs. A direction is (nowadays) called **fang**. The signs might show a forked wooden spade, with a cross, composed of sacred T shapes (p.769). It means a quarter, a square, a direction, one or several quadrants and signifies an unknown ritual. Fang is an eminently important concept. Fang means everything that lies beyond the central square of the world. Where civilisation allegedly ended and foreign people of all sorts roamed and settled. Some of them nomads, cattle breeders, goat herders, sheep farmers, hunters, migrants and established cultures with walled cities, bronze technology and their very own religions and languages. All of these are fang people, foreigners. The mouse fang, the rhino fang, the ghost fang, the human fang, the chin-beard fang, the earth fang, the snake-eye fang and many, many more. The Shang were surrounded by numerous different cultures, groups and statelets. Some of them, like the sheep breeding Qiang regularly invaded Shang territory to plunder cities or steal cattle. Others were temporary or permanent allies. A group that appears as fang (foreigners) may become an ally in the next generation and disappear, when they blend into the Shang state. Or they may reappear as hostile foreigners a few decades later. Close fang states were always something of a threat. True, most 'states' of Bronze age China were tiny. But in an age where alliances were fragile, a group of tiny states can become serious trouble. Several consorts of King Wu Ding's have the names of Fang states: they ensured peaceful cooperation. And while close fang states could be a threat, more distant ones could be useful allies. King Wu Ding occasionally asked the oracle whether he should support one fang state in its struggle against another. Friendly fang states were useful allies. They also supplied valuable commodities, like turtle plastrons, horses, jade, cowrie shells, metal, archers, troops and Qiang prisoners. But fang implies strangeness, and sometimes danger. As a cosmological concept, the fang directions were represented by various directional gods, while the Di sacrifices may have ensured the balance and harmony of the world.

The Names of the Winds

From the four directions come four winds. Or maybe the Shang thought about it the other way around. The *Huainanzi* proposes that there is a centre of the world from where the four winds arise. It's a place of total silence. Imagine a space where absolutely nothing can be heard. That space is also a state of mind. The Shang scribes identified the winds, and especially the great gales, storm winds and typhoons with divine bird Peng. Each wind has its own name.

The **East Wind** is called Harmoniser or Co-operator (p.719). Its character also designated the fourth ancestral feast, the xie ritual, or harmonisation sacrifice. It can be read as three digging sticks and a common mouth, and its meaning is co-operation. For though three are working, they speak and eat with one mouth and dig with one intent. Abridged versions of the sign leave out the mouth.

The **South Wind** is called Long, Growth and Long Hair (p.643). It shows a human sideways, with lots of hair (or a claw) on the head.

The **West Wind** has the same name as the direction west (p.699). T.T. Chang noted that it might mean cockerel sacrifice, an idea which comes from the *Shuowen*. The *Jiaguwen Zidian* proposes something like Shrinker, Shriveller or maybe Concentrator: good name for a wind which feels fresh and hints of the cold to come.

The **North Wind** has a name that is easy to understand (p.674). It is called Slayer, and the sign shows a kneeling figure being hit with a mallet or stick.

The fact that the names of the winds appear on several inscriptions together with the names of the directional deities indicates that the Shang used special names to invoke or contact both. It's much like the many spirits and gods of ritual Daoism, with their specialised names and titles. In orthodox Daoist ritual secret names are required to invoke and control the spiritual hierarchy (see Saso, 1978). We are, maybe at the roots of feng shui here. When the directions are deities, your position in space becomes important. How do you arrange the rooms in your home? Which way do you face when you sit? Where do you seat a guest? Where do you set up altars and sacred spaces? And where do you rest your head when you sleep?

Women or Mothers

The four directions have a personification, or a presiding deity. Here we encounter the mothers (mu) or women/girl (nü) of the directions (p.671). Most popular was **Mother East**. She appears in several inscriptions and received sacrifices. Her sign is written east plus woman. And if the folded arms of the woman had a dot or two inside, the sign means mother. For the dots are nipples, they emphasise the breasts. Not that this was strictly observed. While contemporary Chinese characters show a clear difference between woman and mother, the Shang scribes could not be bothered. In their time, the signs could be read each way. It is a convenience when we say Mother East, as Mother was a title of respect and honour. It could refer to the personal mother and to any woman or ancestress of your mother's generation. For

Goddesses of the Four Directions

the Shang, east was a favourite direction. Shang buildings were usually oriented to receive the morning sun. When east and west appear in a single divination, east is usually mentioned first. According to Keightley (2002:89-90), there are almost three times as many divination inscriptions regarding the east than each other directions. Was the east actually preferred? It could be that in hunting divination, the kings asked about the east first of all.

It would improve the chance for that direction a lot. Zheng Jiexiang points out that East could have been the name of a place near modern Puyang. Maybe it was a favoured hunting ground, or a sacred location which required frequent visits. And of the directional goddesses, Mother East is the most commonly named. It is perplexing, for in later Chinese myth, the Eastern Lady does not appear. Instead of her, there is Dongwanggong the Wood Sire, the lord of springtime and forests. He never became a major deity, and remained unknown in wide parts of south west China. It seems that he was made up to provide the highly important Queen Mother of the West, Xiwangmu, with a male partner.

Much less popular was Girl, Woman or **Mother West**. West connects with autumn, evening and fall, all of these times marking the transition to winter, night, darkness and cold. Shang winters did not get as cold as they do nowadays, but they were less popular than the other seasons. Let's look at tomb M45 from Xishuipo in Pyang county, Henan. The Neolithic farmers of the Yangshao culture buried a man between two beautiful animal figures, carefully laid out in a clam-shell mosaic: a tiger and a dragon. Two other tombs nearby showed what seems to be a dragon headed tiger, ridden by a deer with a spider on its head, and an image of a man riding a dragon plus a running tiger (Zhang Zhongpei in K.C. Chang, 2005:77-78 and 130). The three corpses seem to have been ritualists, perhaps wu or their predecessors. Long before the Shang, the divine tiger was associated with the west, hence with evening, sunset, nightfall, age and death. Here we meet Lady West, Xi Mu, who specialises in transitions, transformation and transcendence. What exactly the Shang thought about her remains unknown. But as it so happens, a closely related goddess, Xiwangmu, survived through the millennia and is happy and well in our century. In the understanding that the Xiwangmu of the middle Zhou, Qin and Han is not quite the same as the Western goddess of the Shang, as that there are many centuries between them, let me give a few of her stories here. So far, only one inscription of the Shang mentions Ximu. Then follow several centuries without written records. When the goddess reappeared in the literature of the late Zhou, she was highly specialised. Zhuangzi (ch.6) writing around 400 or 300 BCE relates that Xiwangmu attained it (the Dao) and made her seat on Mount Shao Kuang: *"nobody knows her beginning and no-one knows her end"*. Xiwangmu was popular among early Daoists and immortality seekers and so well known that Zhuangzi assumed his readers would know who he was talking about. And as she is literally age-less, imperishable and immortal, she made a fit goddess for all who sought to extend life and consciousness. Xunzi recorded that Yü the Great studied with Xiwangmu. It would be nice to know what. Then there's the *History of Mu of Zhou* and the *Liezi* (3,1), which retells the story. It has Xiwangmu residing on Mount Kunlun, the holy mountain of beginning, between heaven and earth. King Mu of Zhou (1001-947 BCE) visited her on his famous journey to the west. *"Then he dwelled at the Turquoise Lake, where Xiwangmu drank with him. Xiwangmu sang a song for the king, and the king joined in. It was a very soulful song. Then he beheld the place where the sun goes to rest after its daily ten thousand li journey. The king gave a mournful sigh and spoke 'Alas, for I, the One Man, do not cultivate virtue and indulge in merriment instead. Future generations will count this as an error'."*

Mu returned dutifully to the Middle Kingdom, where he ruled happily until he reached the age of one hundred. As some later traditions claim, after death he ascended to heaven. It seems that the visit to Xiwangmu had extended his life. The fullest account of the early Xiwangmu appears in the incomparable *Shanhaijing*. Discussing the weird regions of the far west, we meet her residing on Jade-Mountain.

"She looks like a human being, but she has the tail of a panther and the teeth of a tigress and she is skilled at whistling (or: screaming). She wears a victory-head-dress on her twisted hair. She reigns over the constellations Celestial Disasters and Five Destructive Energies." (2.3)

Another passage (12) locates her on Mount Serpent Shaman.

"Queen Mother West reclines against her high seat. She wears a victory head-dress and holds a staff. South of her reside three birds who search for food for Queen Mother West. The realm where Queen Mother West dwells is north of the Waste of Kunlun."

Here, mythology, cosmology and ancient geography meet. We can't locate Mount Jade or Mount Serpent Shaman. In this context, Mount Kunlun is the axis mundi, the shamanic gateway between heaven and earth and has no geographical connotations. However, the *Shanhaijing* is not only a work full of mythical, otherworldly geography. The text contains references to real places, and numerous scholars have struggled to wrest the visionary accounts from ancient traveller's tales. In Eastern Turkestan a mountain range is called Kunlun. It is likely that the place name and the mythical concept merged at some time. Some have speculated that Xiwangmu may have been the queen of an early culture dwelling near Qinghai Lake. Others have sought further to the south west. The word Mu in her name is nowadays written with the character for mother, but there are early variations that write Mu as an unidentified place name: Western Queen of Mu. Here, the territory of the Mu clan in Yunnan, not far from Tibet and Sichuan, might be a candidate. The country has magnificent mountains and is the home of one culture, the Mosuo, which is organised along matriarchal lines. Their close relations are the Naxi, who used to be more matriarchal (or matricentristic) in the past, but lost much of their traditional organisation due to a stronger Han Chinese and Confucian influence. The *Shanhaijing* locates the Country of Women close to Xiwangmu's mountains, and that is exactly what the Han Chinese called this corner of the world in the old days. Several early travellers give accounts, as the southern Silk Road to India passed through the realm. When you go to Baisha or Lijiang you see the women running practically everything, while numerous men spend their days looking after the kids, smoking pipes, making celestial music and trying to look good. Usually, shops are run by women. However, when the women are otherwise occupied, the men have to step in. Several times, when I was haggling over prices, the men firmly negotiated but when it came to fixing the final price they called for their wives or daughters to confirm the deal. The Mu clan controlled the Naxi well into the twentieth century. However, it is unlikely that the Naxi and Mosuo dwelled in that corner of Yunnan in prehistory. I do not know about Mosuo migration, but the Naxi entered Yunnan via Sichuan. During the Han Dynasty, the cult of Xiwangmu was highly popular in Sichuan. Now you won't find a goddess called Xiwangmu in Mosuo or Naxi religion. Xiwangmu is a Han Chinese designation that may have referred to several similar goddesses of prehistory.

Chapter 16 of the *Shanhaijing* mentions that the goddess dwells in a cave. All animals of the world live on her mountain. It may be a reference to the animal totems, the clan animals and the divine animals. They accompany her in art. It is also a link to shamanism, and to the animal spirits that were the allies, vehicles and alter egos of the wu and the Daoists. An amazing brick from the Han Dynasty, excavated in Xinfan Qingbaixiang, Sichuan, shows her in the company of dragon, tiger, fire-raven, moon-toad, tortoise, snake, hare, nine-tail-fox and diverse winged, celestial immortals. Other animals typical for her cult are deer, buffalo and flying goats. Such pictures are typical for tombs, emphasising her connection to death and the otherworlds.

According to the *Shanhaijing*, the western quadrant of the world is a remarkable place. Here are great hidden jade reserves, the holy mineral that contains so much yang energy that its touch grants blessings, health and extends life. Close to the mountains of Xiwangmu are ten wu shamans or shamanesses, who move or fly up and down a sacred mountain where hundreds of drugs and medical herbs grow.

"The kingdom of Wu Xian (Shaman Xian) lies north of Nüchou (Ugly Woman). In his right hand he holds a blue snake and in his left a red one. He resides on Dengbao Mountain where all the wu move (or: fly) up and down."

In the Great Joy Wilderness, the second lord of the Xia (now happily deified) is said to dance to a sacred melody. He roams to Great Destiny Mountain on the back of two dragons. Close to Mount Queen Mother West are Mount Abyssmal and Mount Watering. The people who live at Mount Watering feed on the eggs of the sacred wind-bird Peng, and their drink is sweet dew. The wind god bird Peng leads them on their ways, and they are called the People of All-Die-Young. Other scenic sites are Mount Dragon, the terrace of Huangdi, various sacred trees of astonishing power and an unknown green-clad goddess called Girl Corpse. On that fatal day when all ten suns were out at once she was on a mountaintop and couldn't get away. So she covered her face with her sleeve. The heat killed her and she became a goddess. Also, among the natives of the west are whole tribes with human bodies and serpent tails. It ought to remind you of Fuxi and Nüwa. Both of them are often shown in company with Xiwangmu. There are another two unknown goddesses. One is called Girl Sacrifice, she holds a chopping block, indicating that she is not a sacrifice but a sacrificer. With her is Girl Battleaxe, wielding an eel, who is probably quite as surprised as you are. It's just our bad luck their stories are forgotten. Maybe they were too wild for later generations.

All of which is just a brief glimpse into the marvels of the western fang direction. The other directions are just as bizarre. They reflect the visionary journeys and cosmologies of shamans travelling in the spirit, and blend them with myths, real geography and weird traveller's tales.

Back to Xiwangmu. Think of the shamanic elements in our account. There's the tiger fetish, for example. Even today, the most popular shamanic spirit animal of east and south-east Asia is the tiger. There's her connection to animal spirits, the mountain/s connecting heaven and earth, the staff, the bird familiars, the many flying wu in the neighbourhood. Not to mention all those who feed on wind-eggs (qi) and sweet dew (jing), like so many early Daoists and life extenders. It is no coincidence when those who die early and those who live long relate to the same deity. Some die young, even if it takes them a hundred years. Others grow old together; it can happen before they reach their thirties. Time is a quite a wonderful idea.

On one occasion, the goddess became immensely popular among the common people of the Eastern Han period. While she was usually associated with aristocrats, kings, sages and emperors, whom she initiated, inspired or blessed with holy writ, here we have her on the side of the peasant population.

According to the *Hanshu* and other sources, in the first month of the year 3 BCE she became the patron goddess of a popular revolt. It was a bad year for the moribund Western Han Dynasty. The court was torn with internal power struggles, the officials corrupt and when drought destroyed the harvest, rebellions broke out. The population saw the crisis as the inauguration of a new age. Enflamed with the belief that the goddess would arise, they were caught up in religious frenzy. In the middle of the night they lighted torches on rooftops for Xiwangmu; they danced, beat drums, sang, screamed and, as the authorities recorded, scared each other. Liubo games were played in honour of the goddess, and while many worshiped and sacrificed, others broke into houses or engaged in reckless destruction. Thousands of people assembled in processions, some of them with dishevelled hair or walking on bare feet. They exchanged human effigies made from straw and hemp and wore talismans ensuring the goddess would protect them from death. Breaking down gates and climbing over walls, walking or riding on stolen horses they started a long trek through 26 commanderies and kingdoms until they reached the capital. With so many people in religious fervour, agriculture was neglected and the dynasty almost collapsed. The uprising was put down eventually and by autumn, the movement had faded to insignificance. The Queen Mother continued as a major deity, but her cult lost its wilder elements.

During the Han Dynasty people played the popular board game Liubo in her honour. The rules are long forgotten, but the board plan is identical with the earliest maps of heaven. They have a central square, which could represent the centre of Heaven and the abode of High Di. From the square centre, there is a sacred T extending into each cardinal direction, just like so many tantric yantras. So our early Xiwangmu relates to timeless immortality, life and death, to mountains, longevity, qi breathing, dew drinking, whistling or screaming, sacred animals, celestial constellations and deep caves. It makes her a perfect goddess for shamans, sorcerers and early Daoists. This image changed over time. During the Tang Dynasty, Daoism became the state religion. The emperor's clan, the Li family, believed that it descended from Laozi. In this period, Xiwangmu received so much veneration that even Buddhists felt compelled to worship her. She was occasionally identified with Xuannü, the dark or Mysterious Woman (*Daodejing* chapter 6), and with the gate of the Dao itself. It just couldn't last.

Xiwangmu and Guanyin

After the Tang Dynasty fell, Xiwangmu lost much of her status, just as Daoism lost much of its influence, while neo-Confucianism and Buddhism became the dominant creeds. It was a bitter power struggle. Under Daoist dominance, Buddhism had lost plenty of temples and shrines. During the Southern Song Dynasty, the Buddhists reclaimed much ground, and during the Yuan Dynasty, when the Tartars ruled China, the abbot of Shaolin temple managed to persuade the emperor to persecute Daoism, and to grant many of its temples to the Buddhists. Chinese Buddhism had long developed way beyond the original version. It had become a lot more political and power hungry, but also more social, compassionate and life-embracing than the (historical) Buddha had ever dreamed possible. However, the Daoists had something the Buddhists lacked: an appreciation of the divine in female form. The historical Buddha was much against allowing women to participate in his cult, and had to be coerced by his favourite pupil Ānanda to admit them. In his age and social environment, birth as a woman was an indication of bad karman, i.e. of evil deeds in a past life. His followers went to considerable lengths to deny the value of female attainment. When Mahāyāna Buddhism reformed the stern creed and made compassion its motto, women gained a few rights and a measure of respect. Thanks to compassionate Buddhism, the cult became more popular and gained a foothold in China by founding hospitals, by caring for the poor, the abandoned and the sick. Around the eleventh century, a few enterprising Chinese Buddhists, having no female deity in their pantheon, cooked up someone new from old ingredients. We are talking about the (male) Bodhisattva Avalokiteśvara, who often looked like a girlish youth, carrying a flower and sporting a thin moustache, into a woman.

Before we take a closer look at her, a brief exploration of the *'original'* bodhisattva may be useful. It tells a fascinating story how deities transform to suit their worshippers, and how worshippers transform to suit their deities. It is also a story on how representations of the divine transform continuously, just as people do. Gods keep changing, just like people do. In most cases, we are simply not aware of it. Here is a fascinating exception. The story of Guanyin is one of the best documented success stories of inspired, living and happily syncretistic worship in evidence.

In the first centuries of the Common Era, Indian Buddhists realised that it might be a great idea to incorporate a range of (male) Indian gods in their product range. As Buddhists are not very keen on deities as such, they chose to create a few bodhisattvas, i.e. semi-divine beings who after attaining Buddhahood bravely decided to remain close to the world and heed to the plight of its suffering inhabitants, instead of spacing off into liberating dissolution. It was a new and innovative idea typical for Mahāyāna teachings. Technically, bodhisattvas were considered liberated and enlightened human beings, but in everyday worship, they functioned pretty much as deities and were expected to work miracles for true believers. Hence I shall use the term *'bodhisattva'* and *'deity'* in pretty much the same way, and I ask you to remember that each term, on its own, is still limited, as the Chinese use the word *'shen'* in a much more general way. One of the first of these figures appears under several names: Abhalokatesvara (*'Sound Illuminator of the World'*), Avalokitesvara (*'Master Perceiver'*) and Avalokatasvara (*'Perceiver of the World's Sounds'*). Each of these titles appears independently and is well attested: obviously, the early Mahāyāna Buddhists had not come to a consensus yet. The iconography of this figure poses several problems, as the early texts offer very few details on his appearance. One might be that the figure could be radiantly bright; it's an idea that recurred repeatedly. Perhaps the White Robed Guanyin derived from this notion; usually, Chinese deities do not wear white, as the colour is associated not only with purity but also with death. To Indians, white represented brightness and pure light but to the Chinese it meant a person in mourning, often a widow or widower. Mind you, the *'white'* was usually beige, the term means *'natural, uncoloured'*.

Today, the popular name is Avalokitesvara, which might be a compound of the words Avalokita (to look, gaze, glance, watch, observe, perceive, examine, contemplate, visualise) and Isvara (Lord, a title traditionally given to Siva and, less frequently, to Viṣṇu). However, this derivation contains plenty of problems, leading to a wide range of translations and titles. The link to the two major gods of Hinduism is anything but coincidental. Around the beginning of the Common Era, some Indian monarchs identified with Siva and many more with Viṣṇu the Maintainer, who was considered the monarch of the gods. The *Mahābhārata*, well under way at the time, went to great lengths to celebrate him, and numerous kings were crowned and governed in his name. Siva was less popular as a royal figure, as he was simply too crazy, but appealed to the Buddhists thanks to his role as ascetic, yogī and renouncer. Some clever Buddhists thought that a new bodhisattva symbolising royalty might be a great attraction for kings and regents. Avalokitesvara was created to embody divine government, or the principle of theocratic government. Strictly speaking, in a Buddhist context, the terms *'divine'* or *'theocratic'* are misleading. However, they neatly describe how the bodhisattva was generally perceived. The newly invented bodhisattva was more than a divine king: he was equipped with 33 transformations, which allowed him to appear on earth and work miraculous salvations. Among them, cited by the early *Lotus Sūtra,* are Viṣṇu and Siva (in several aspects), Brahmā the Creator, an underworldly serpent god (Nāga), a vegetation deity (Yakṣa), a Gandharva (a celestial musician), an Asura (Anti-god, i.e. a giant, titan or mega-demon), a Garuḍa (the devastating fire bird who is Viṣṇu's vehicle), a Kiṁnara (a minor celestial deity) and a Deva (Shining One, i.e. a deity in general). Should the bodhisattva chose a human form, he appeared as a small king, a rich man, a chief minister, a Brahmin, a monk, a nun, a male or female lay believer, the wife of a rich man, a householder, a young boy or a girl. I'm sure you noticed that the divine range incorporates the dominant male Hindu deities while neglecting all female ones. However, several of the human forms are female. For Buddhism, this was a remarkable achievement. In contrast, the *Karaṇḍavyūha Sūtra* eliminates all human female shapes, except for a mother. However, it adds leading Hindu deities like Agni (Fire), Surya (the Sun), Soma (the Moon), Varuṇa (Water) and Vāyu (Air). In short, our new Buddhist bodhisattva functioned as a summary of popular male Hindu deities. It is hardly surprising that the early Sūtra of *Amoghapaśa* explains that for worship, an image of Avalokiteśvara should be made that looks like Śiva, in front of which cow dung should be spread. Early rituals involved homa fire offerings, a ritual that had been popular since Vedic times, and has nothing to do with Buddhism.

Nowadays, Avalokiteśvara is usually identified as the Boddhisattva of Compassion. It's an old idea but not the only one. The original Avalokiteśvara was highly attractive to kings. As Lokeśvara (*'Lord of the World'*) he is worshipped in Vietnam, Cambodia and Java; as Lokanātha (*'Lord of the World'*) in Burma and as Chenresi / Spyan-ras-gzigs (*'The One Who Sees With His Eyes'*) in Tibet, where he is identified with King Songsten Ganpo (who founded Tibet in a series of bloody conquests) and with each of the Dalai Lamas. These versions of the bodhisattva represent divine kingship. Whether they had much to do with compassion remains an open question. When Abhalokateśvara / Avalokiteśvara / Avalokatesvara arrived in China, the translators were faced by the problem of the many possible translations of the names. Chün-Fang Yü, who wrote the best study on Guanyin I have ever come upon, gives quite a range of examples. We encounter *'Manifest Sound'*, *'Perceiver of the World's Sounds'*, *'Perceiver of the World's Thoughts'*, *'Master Perceiver'*, *'Lord of What We See'*, *'Lord Who is Seen (From on High)'* and *'Lord Who Sees'*, plus a range of esoteric interpretations. Guan can be *'Illuminating Light'*. It can be the *'Wisdom That Can Perceive'* while shiyin is *'The Realm That is Perceived'*. Or Guan refers to primal awareness meditation, i.e. the trance where you disengage from sense impressions, such as hearing and sight, observe yourself observing, observe that, and disengage from the observer, again and again, until you reach total unlimited voidness and the *'you'* ceases to operate. The source of this meditative formula is prebuddhistic: it appears in the *Kaivalya Upaniṣad*, where a famous passage identifies Brahman (Absolute Reality, the formless, absent, indefinable All-Consciousness) as Śiva, the Witness of Pure Consciousness.

The Chinese Avalokiteśvara was faced with a massive problem. He had a job opportunity, as China lacked a universal saviour deity, who could be called upon by anyone anywhere, and guaranteed safety from fire and water, wild beasts, starvation, sterility, diseases, bandits, government officials and so on. However, he did not appeal to royalty. The emperors did not want a Buddhist personification of the right to rule. They had a well established concept of the Mandate of Heaven. Nor did the references to Hindu deities carry much weight; to the Chinese most of them were hardly relevant. What he had, however, was the ability to appear as a woman. This function was crucial to make Buddhism popular in China. In due course, Avalokiteśvara, the most feminine looking bodhisattva, was transformed into a female. It was a popular move and based on the needs of folk religion and lay Buddhism. However, the Chinese Buddhist orthodoxy did not sit down to design a female bodhisattva. Her worship was powered by a few visionaries, by laypeople from all ranges of society, and by innovative artists who explored her iconography in radically new ways. In fact, to this day, most Chinese Buddhist temples try hard to ignore her cult. You may see images of her once in a while, but they receive very little worship by the clergy. In China, as in so many other countries, high ranking Buddhists tend to worship Avalokiteśvara/Guanyin as a male. If you are looking for living female Guanyin worship, you will encounter much more in private houses, restaurants, hotels and, above all, Daoist temples. The Chinese Buddhist orthodoxy insists that the female form is just a minor convenience for this particular incarnation of the bodhisattva, and will be abolished when Buddhist wonderland is attained where everybody is male (another good reason to find a better afterworld elsewhere). In their opinion, the real bodhisattva is a man; the female version is a temporary manifestation. At this point, professional Chinese Buddhists diverge from Japanese Buddhists, who worship Guanyin as Kwannon and accept her female form as the real thing. Unlike so many Chinese Buddhists, the Daoists had no problems in worshipping goddesses and respecting female spiritual leaders, practitioners and their contributions to life. In the Chinese Buddhist temples I visited, the female Guanyin was hardly represented, if at all, while the Daoists made quite a lot of her.

Nowadays, the goddess is frequently known as Guan Shi Yin: She Who Perceives the Sounds of the World. Her name is often mistranslated as She Who Hears the Cries of the World, i.e. the unhappy outcries of her devotees. It's a rather limited interpretation, as, honestly, the goddess much prefers to listen to people having a good time. In her (popular) Buddhist interpretation, she is the goddess of compassion and mercy.

Her hagiography, first inscribed in the year 1100, claims that Guanyin was the princess Miao Shan (Wonderful Goodness), the youngest of three sisters. The story is ahistorical and the name of the heroine, and her sisters Miao Yen (Wonderful Appearance) and Miao Yin (Wonderful Sound) derive from several famous nuns who had the honorary title Miao and lived almost a century earlier. Unlike her elder sisters, Miao Shan refused to be married. She devoted herself to lay Buddhism, even though it made her father raging mad; he punished her, had her locked up and do all the chores in a Buddhist monastery and finally, in a fit of anger, burned the monastery down. Miao Shan had a lucky escape, sought refuge on a hill in Henan and attained enlightenment. Meanwhile, her father began to suffer from a terrible disease, and was told that only the eyes and hands of a person who never felt anger might produce a healing medicine. It turned out that this was the strange hermit lady living on the hill. Miao Shan acknowledged her obligation to her father, sacrificed her eyes and hands and almost died in the process. Her dad had an instant recovery, went to see the strange hermit who had saved his life, recognised his daughter, had a terrible fit of guilt and regret and converted to Buddhism. Miao Shan, having attained her goal, miraculously recovered eyes and hands (quite a lot of them), died and was buried in a stupa. The place became the first site of pilgrimage of the female Guanyin. This *'historical'* Guanyin was said to have faced the same trials as Buddha himself. Young Gautama, the future Buddha, was shocked when he discovered that poverty, disease, old age and death beset the population, and decided to quit the world. Original Buddhism was aimed at liberation, release and dissolution of the I-concept (nirvāna means literally cessation) as the only way to escape the suffering and bondage of the world. Princess Miao Shan observed the same things, but unlike Buddha, she decided to eradicate suffering. So while the original Buddha preached that one should leave the world of attachments, Guanyin got herself involved in it. Here, her behaviour suits Mahāyāna Buddhism, but is in opposition to the original creed. It disregards Confucian teachings, as the princess disobeys her parents and refuses to continue the family line, but it reinstalls them as she saves her father in a gesture of self-sacrifice. As Chün-Fang Yü shows in much detail, the very legend of princess Miao Shan is a bizarre hybrid. The girl who disobeys her parents, refuses to marry, leads a spiritual life and eventually attains transcendence has many earlier parallels in the hagiographies of saintly Daoist women. On the other hand, the cheerful self sacrifice, mutilation and death for the sake of a suffering being (her ignorant father) is typical for Buddhist preferences. There is plenty of masochism in traditional Buddhism, and stories of self-mutilation are popular. After all, the Buddha and his likeminded friends appreciated and embraced suffering, and went to great lengths to make the most of it. In between the two creeds is a powerful element of lay Buddhism: princess Miao Shan never bothered to become a proper Buddhist nun. When she was forced to live in a monastery, she refused ordination, kept her hair and derided the nuns for their fake piety.

In this sense, the Buddhist setting is a frame for a highly complex development. Starting around the fifth century, the usually male Guanyin was identified with several women, including a female Daoist saint (Chün-Fang Yü, 2001:302-303). At the time, most of the bodhisattva's human incarnations were still male. Several such monks are explored by Yü, one of them ended up as a rain god while another, a monk who taught Buddhism to emperor Wu of the Liang Dynasty, wore his hair long, tied inexplicable objects to his walking stick, drank alcohol, ate meat and obviously approved of tantric teachings. Between the 11th and 12th century, preferences switched to a female form. In the process, Guanyin swiftly gobbled up a whole series of local Chinese goddesses. Here a fascinating transformation can be observed. Indian Buddhism had produced several (male) forms of Guanyin which are still popular, one of them is the influential thousand eyed and thousand armed manifestation. The legend of princess Miao Shan did much to make this form attractive to the Chinese. The first really Chinese form of the bodhisattva was the Water-Moon Guanyin. This bodhisattva was still visualised as a man. Water–Moon refers to a beautiful spiritual image. Imagine you are sitting at the shore of a pond or of a calmly moving stream. Night has fallen and above you shines a glorious full moon in its full splendour. As you gaze at the surface of the water, you can see the moon dancing, pulsing and oscillating. Is the moon which you see in the water real? Here, several answers come to mind. You could assume a strict Buddhist point of view and claim that neither moon nor water nor yourself are real. Or you could favour one of several tantric interpretations. Maybe the reflection is an illusion, but you, the moon and the pond are real. Maybe you are and everything else isn't. Or everything is real except you. Or everything, including you, is real, for a time, for a space, for a moment of sheer being. The moon reflects on each pond, river or puddle: it is just one moon, but it appears in a million places for each of us, just as One Consciousness appears in everyone and everything as *'real'*, *'unique'* and *'individual'*. Or maybe you should just calm down, shut up and appreciate moon, water, night and yourself as pure, unconditional bliss.

Water-Moon Guanyin was invented by the Chinese as the Indian form of the bodhisattva had a halo around his head; it was thought to represent the moon. In tune with this image are some tantric writings of the Yoginī lineage, which was popular among Hindus and Buddhists around the tenth century. One popular

Water-Moon Guanyin

meditation was to imagine a moon above or in the head (or in head, heart and belly), releasing a milky white shower of rejuvenating elixir. Variations of this method introduced showers of elixir in red, black or pink (Fries, 2010: 303-305). Closely linked to this practice is the popular imagery of Śiva and Kālī, both of whom wear a moon on their head. The Water-Moon Guanyin was imagined seated on mountains, in later periods he appeared sitting on a rock, surrounded by purple bamboo, facing a pool, lake or river. Mountains and water are by no means only scenery; between them, as Sarah Allan has shown (1997), the entire range of Chinese nature appreciation unfolds. Water is one of the most vital symbols of Chinese thought; it appears prominently in the teachings of Kongzi, Laozi, Zhuangzi, Liu An and many others. Indeed, where it comes to the sanctity of water, Daoism and Confucianism meet on common ground and have (almost) no reason to disagree. Water-Moon Guanyin wore white and held a vase; instead of the lotus he carried a bundle of willow twigs. This tranquil figure eventually turned into the white robed female Guanyin; to this day the most popular form of the goddess. The vase contains sacred fluids, holy water, or ambrosia and can even represent the alchemical body. The willow branches may appear in an exorcist context, where they are used to banish evil spirits, or function to sprinkle sacred water. The same equipment is carried by the Daoist deity Yu Shi, who makes rain as he scatters water from the vase with the willow branches. Incidentally, blessing Great Compassion Water is a typical element of Guanyin rituals. One enthusiast of the Song Dynasty was Mrs. Wu, wife of vice director of the department of justice, Lü Hong, who practiced her own brand of Pure Land Buddhism and was identified as a manifestation of Guanyin. Mrs. Wu used to hold a willow branch in her hand while she invoked Guanyin. The goddess would appear to her and send radiant light into several bottles of water, which became duly transformed into a panacea. Unlike normal water, it would not spoil nor would it freeze in winter (Yü, 2001:272).

Water remains closely linked to her: near the coast and in the south the goddess incorporated a range of oceanic goddesses: this Guanyin stands or sits on a dragon or fish. She is the Nanhai Guanyin of the South Sea. Her cult is focussed on the island Putuoshan, one of the most popular places for pilgrimage in China. Related is a beautiful young Guanyin, who appeared carrying a basket of fish. Catching and eating fish are frowned upon by orthodox Buddhists. However, fish, especially carps, are also symbols for wealth, luck and blessings. It's an old tradition: think of the Shang period prince whose name was written 'Fish' or 'Fisher'. Underneath the fish, she had the *Lotus Sūtra*. She claimed that she would marry a man who could memorize the sacred text in a few days, but when her husband –to-be had done

Willow Twigs and Falling Water

so, she died and left him pining, but converted, behind. In this tale she is occasionally known as the *'Wife of Mr. Ma'*.

When her carcass was exhumed later on, it turned out that her bones were linked by a golden chain: a sure sign that she had been an incarnate boddhisatva. In the myth cluster of the Fish Basket Guanyin we encounter a goddess (or bodhisattva) who is young and beautiful. She uses desire to deliver her future husband, and his community, and converts them all to Buddhism.

Another Guanyin, holding a baby in her arms, was inspired by statues of the Virgin Mary, imported courtesy of the Nestorian Christians around the tenth Century. It wasn't their invention: the Christian image goes back to the Egyptian goddess Isis holding baby Horus on her arms. The child-bearing Guanyin was combined with the white robe Guanyin and became trendy around the 16th century. In the process, the meaning of the child underwent some changes. The child seems to have symbolised the worshipper's rebirth in the Pure Western Paradise; it subsequently came to signify that the goddess, who is never considered a mother, gives a much desired child to the faithful. In this function, the goddess was and is worshipped by childless couples.

Another Guanyin poses with a peacock: the bright eyes on the peacocks' tail represent her thousand eyes. This Guanyin is the Protector of All Life. Thousand eyes and arms are an attribute of early Indian Avalokiteśvara statues. They neatly fit Chinese lore as well. Peacock bones were found in Anyang, and the peacocks' crest appears in the divine crowns of the oracle bone characters dragon, tiger and bird Peng, as well as the sacred (hair) pin.

Yet another Guanyin appears in company of a white parrot (or cockatoo), which occasionally carries a rosary in its beak. Rosaries are among the sacred symbols of Guanyin. Chün-Fang Yü rightly derives it from Xiwangmu, who also appears in the company of birds. This Guanyin has nothing to do with the Indian prototypes. Here, we could speculate how much Guanyin picked up from Xiwangmu: both of them are associated with the west. While Xiwangmu is envisioned in the mythical or real Kunlun mountain range in the far west, Guanyin is the saviour who permits the devout to be reborn in the Western Paradise. Both of them relate to the west as the direction of death and transcendence.

Since the Neolithic, west was associated with the divine tiger. Remember the tiger teeth and leopard tail of Xiwangmu?

One Guanyin who developed around the 12th century appears with a fluffy animal that is a mixture of tiger and lion: perhaps the image goes back to the Hindu warrior goddess Durgā (*'The Unapproachable'*), who rides on such felines. Think of the many goddesses who were associated with big cats. In Hindu and

Buddhist Tantra, we encounter lion- and tiger riding yoginīs, while tantric Buddhism features enlightened female saints like low-caste Ḍombīyoginī, who makes love with her mate and fellow aspirant, king Ḍombīpa, riding a tigress and wielding a living snake as a whip (Shaw, 1994:63-68). Likewise, the Great Mother of Tibet rides a lion, and another Buddhist deity is the Lion Headed Mother (Tibetan: Senge Dang Ma) who looks much like Kālī, except for the feline head. They are by no means the first Eurasian goddesses linked with savage predator cats. Much earlier we encounter the Assyrian Ištar and her Sumerian prototype, Inanna, who appear with a lion. Almost as old are the Sumerian Dimme and the Akkadian Lamaštu, wearing the mask of a lion, panther, hyena, wolf, snake or bird-of-prey; a gift from their brother Enlil (Lord Air) to make life easier on this planet. Then there is the unidentified nude old Babylonian goddess who stands on two lions (she is popularly, and without any evidence, identified with Lilith). Other related images may be Medusa (see the temple frieze in Corfu) and the Cretan goddess or priestess who holds two snakes and has a cat on her head. In nearby Egypt we meet Bastet, as a domesticated feline goddess, and Sekhmet, who is full of devastating heat. All of them are early, but by no means the first expressions of her. The first representative of this archetype may be the human/animal figure, dated around 30.000 BCE, with the head of a cave lioness, carved from a mammoth tusk and found in the cave Hohlenstein-Stadel, Asselfingen, Baden-Württemberg, Germany. A picture of her appears in the 2006 edition of *Helrunar*. And when we look at early China we meet her alive and well among the Shang, who had two goddesses or ancestresses whose names incorporated the character tiger. Theoretically, Xiwangmu may be considered a development of the Shang Ximu, i.e. Woman or Mother West. As tigers were related to the west at a much earlier period, we could imagine that Ximu connects with them. However, the existence of two goddesses or ancestress named woman/mother tiger or wood tiger could indicate that the Xiwangmu of known myth is a blend of the two concepts. Perhaps Guanyin's tiger comes from a Hindu/Buddhist background, but just as possible it was borrowed from the cult of Xiwangmu, and goes back to much earlier roots.

Another bizarre link to early Chinese lore can be found in Guanyin's two attendants. Like many Daoist deities and saints, Guanyin was equipped with a lad and a lass to attend her. It happened around the 12th century. One of them is Sudhana (Shancai), who had the remarkable persistence to learn from 53 sages, ascetics, soothsayers, monks, brahmins, bodhisattvas and immortals before he attained enlightenment. This sort of guru hopping is not encouraged by Buddhist orthodoxy, but then, Guanyin tends to attract the unorthodox, and those who

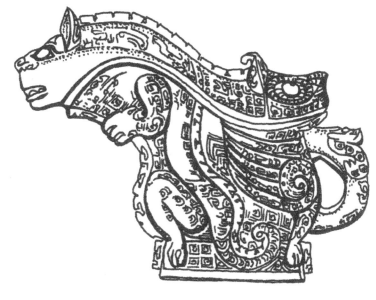

Top: Feline wine container from Fu Hao's Tomb
Bottom: A Taotie

appreciate many points of view. Sadly, most worshippers are not aware of Sudhana's devotion or the many decades he spent travelling under distinctly difficult circumstances. People focus on the literal meaning of his name *'One Who Can Handle Wealth Properly'* and pray to him for riches. It's not what he would have wished for.

Her other attendant is Long Nü, the Dragon Girl (or Dragon Woman), daughter of the Dragon King. At the age of eight she listened to a sermon on Buddhism and became instantly enlightened. Several stuffy old arhats were deeply upset and denied that a young girl might achieve liberation in a few minutes, but the Buddha, who had devoted many years of meditation and austerities to attain this stage, acknowledged her attainment. Indian Buddhism did not involve dragons; they are a genuine Chinese element. So is Long Nü, whose name appears in the oracle bones as a goddess or ancestress. I wouldn't dream of claiming that there is a historical link between them, apart from the One Consciousness which persist in manifesting in a range of archetypal shapes.

The mixture of deities was so perfectly accomplished that Guanyin became a multipurpose goddess who far exceeded her Buddhist background. In 1119, she had become so popular in folk worship that Emperor Huizong officially installed her as a state goddess with the honorary title Chang Pudu Yuantong Zidai (*'The Goddess Whose Raft of Salvation Will Carry You to Safety'*) (Palmer, Ramsay, Kwok, 2009:XV). The title is very close to the names and functions of the goddess Tārā, whom the Indian Hindus and Buddhists considered *'the Chinese Goddess'*, associated with meditative and mercurial alchemy (Fries, 2010:142-143). Guanyin became the most popular goddess/bodhisattva in East Asia. Much of this was due to the persistent effort of her lay believers. Many of those who chanted her mantras to have a wish fulfilled, or to escape calamity, felt duly bound to print and distribute a free pamphlet combining a standardised picture, a simple recitation ritual and a number of miracle stories. Their unorthodox effort made the female Guanyin an overwhelming success. But while Chinese lay Buddhists were quite open-minded in reading and interpreting Indian sūtras and their apocryphal Chinese counterparts, they were also very Chinese in that they did not approve of fixed and narrow-minded distinctions. Over the centuries, Guanyin, just like Xuannü (the *'Dark or Mysterious Woman'*) and Nüwa were identified with Xiwangmu, and vice versa. During the Ming and Qing dynasties, numerous literati attempted to prove that Buddhism, Daoism and Confucianism were one creed, and in their eyes, Xiwangmu and Guanyin, in all their many aspects, were identical. At the same time, a wide range of unorthodox sectarian cults incorporated Guanyin as a major deity. These cults created so many new aspects of the bodhisattva/deity that I can only refer you to Yü's brilliant study. Some of them reinvented Guanyin as an Old/Venerable Mother (Lao Mu); others put her into a Daoist context and made her a goddess of Neidan Inner Alchemy, a position usually held by Xiwangmu. Then there were cults that made her emphasise Confucian virtues, like filial obedience, and had her insist on traditional female subservience, while other groups set her in a stellar context, called her the creatrix of the Universe, and performed her adoration among a range of planetary and stellar deities. Frequently, the teachings of such cults were invented by highly gifted, unorthodox pioneers or channelled using a process of automatic writing. Such cults were far outside the range of normal Buddhist or Daoist teachings. They were often secret, many of them were run by inspired women, and they frequently criticized the Buddhist orthodoxy. A few of them survive to this day; good evidence that Guanyin can be at home in pretty much any religious and cultural setting, as compassion is valuable for everyone.

You can find plenty of Guanyin statues in Daoist temples, where she resides, well beyond the orthodox Buddhist context, receives veneration and allegedly listens to the cries of the suffering. In some temples, you can see a rack where many dozen different talismans, beautifully executed in red ink on yellow paper, are at the disposal of the worshippers. These donate a fee, pick one that represents their desire, and burn it along with some incense: results are guaranteed. Or they pose a question and shake a bamboo tube containing 100 thin bamboo slips. Eventually, one or more fall out and yield the answer of the goddess. This system can be explored in Palmer, Ramsay, Kwok, 2009.

Here we meet Guanyin her most popular form as a saviour, miracle worker and a source of expert advice. It's a role which is miles away from such early insights as Zhili's statement *"Guanyin is our original nature"* (Yü, 2001:287). Unlike a lot of other things Zhili enjoyed (such as self mutilation), this is a brilliant thought. From the realisation that *'your'* self nature is also the self nature of every being and thing arise compassion, love and empathy. This thought appears in Daoist teachings when Laozi (ch. 67) states that his first treasure is forbearance. The actual characters used for this concept are *'motherly love'*. When you treat others with true motherly love, you will cherish their potential to become genuine people, but you will not pamper or spoil them. Compassion is a similar idea. One of the greatest traditions of Buddhism is to devote a daily meditation to radiate compassion to all beings in the world. Several Buddhists made a great fuss about it, and explained its importance by emphasising that each being in the word has been your mother at one time or another. Hence, the importance to radiate good will and love to every being, person or thing, including people you erroneously assumed to be enemies. I can only suggest you give this a try. True enough, life on planet earth is far from perfect and there are people around who might deserve punishment and a reincarnation so they can learn a better way. It only takes a five minute walk through a city to feel upset by all the injustice, cruelty and exploitation that people inflict on other people. However, if you walk around with a grudge, this feeling will keep you tied to a lot of negative thoughts and deeds. Radiating a feeling of compassion to the evildoers will clear you of this rubbish, and allow you to move beyond their sphere. Here we meet Guanyin at her best: as compassion and motherly love shine from you, they also reflect and come back to nourish you. They can free you from attachment to hate, anger, wrath and viciousness. Compassion requires the insight that self, all-consciousness or whatever you chose to call it, extends beyond our silly little egos. Like love, it involves the recognition of 'myself' in the 'other' and the 'other' in 'myself', plus in everything else. However, compassion is frequently misunderstood. It does not mean indulging or pampering others, nor should it entail a sense of superiority. Sure, it's not always easy to be a compassionate human being (or a human being at all), but as I've been told, being a goddess of compassion is one hell of a job. For one thing, people annoy you over every little trouble, and for another, they hardly ever stop. What makes people think that they can bribe or cajole the divine? Why is religion so full of complaining, whining, bullying, and haggling? Luckily, compassion does not mean being nice to everyone. Good martial artists and fighting monks were compassionate to their enemies, but it did not stop them from doing what was necessary. There are many things that people want and few things they really need. Guanyin knows the difference. She is excellent at remaining calm and tranquil while observing and watching really closely. It's not her job to make you happy, for unless you make yourself happy by changing your feelings and behaviour now, nobody else ever will. More so, she is not supposed to lead people to consumer's shopping paradise for free, but to wisdom, liberation and transcendence. When you encounter her in Chinese literature, such as the magnificent *Journey to the West*, you will be surprised that she acts much like a ruthless trickster goddess. Stranger still, while she usually appears to restore harmony and peace; her attendants, pet animals and household utensils frequently run away to earth where they pretend to be great gods, delude the population and wreck havoc.

Xiwangmu herself became an important background figure of the Chinese Heaven. The last time her cult was widely popular seems to have been the rebellions at the end of the Han Dynasty.

After this point, she became an exclusive and remote goddess for a much smaller audience. Among them were Daoists, intellectuals, scholars, aristocrats and a few emperors. Here, another point of Buddhist influence is remarkable. As Chün-Fang Yü observes, during the Han, aristocrats occasionally had bricks showing Xiwangmu and her attendant animals and xian set high in their grave chambers. You can find these images in plenty of books; they were especially popular in southern and southwest China. The goddess represented death and transcendence and promised a good passage to happier otherworlds. When Buddhism intruded into China in the second and third century, we find her images replaced by bricks showing a Buddha who looked pretty much like the goddess. The early Chinese Buddhists did not consider Buddha as a historical Indian sage, but saw him as a god of death and transcendence, and shaped him like the goddess. It did not stay like this. Before long, good translations of original Buddhist texts became available and transformed the function of the Buddha. In his stead, other spiritual beings were associated with the plight of the deceased. One of them is Guanyin. First in a male and later in female form, the bodhisattva and/or princess Miao Shan toured hell where s/he released the suffering souls, hungry ghosts and forsaken spirits. These were permitted to reincarnate on earth or reborn in her Pure Land. Hell itself became a place of bliss and beauty, if only for a short time, as without hell, as pragmatic people observed, there are few reasons to refrain from crime and sin. To this day, the ceremonies for feeding hungry ghosts and releasing the sufferers from hell make much of Guanyin, who seems as easily at home in the infernal regions as in the happy realms beyond. Did she assume a function originally held by Xiwangmu?

Over the centuries, Xiwangmu was increasingly domesticated. Her tigerish looks were soon forgotten. The new Xiwangmu appeared as a middle aged matron living in a celestial paradise. Her task was to oversee the heavenly peach orchards, where every two thousand years the highest deities and immortals have a fruit banquet that prolongs their life. Peaches can do this to you. And of course their pips and wood exorcise evil spirits. It's one of the earliest ideas of recorded wu shamanism and well alive in exorcist ritual Daoism. This new Xiwangmu was generally well behaved. She received a proper hagiography and a serene, semi-cosmic status. From time to time she visited emperors and worthies to grant them a vision or a secret teaching. Or she obsessed mediums who wrote down her wisdom in a heavy trance. Poets, sages, Daoists and immortality seekers made much of her. For a detailed account, let me recommend Suzanne Cahill's magnificent study. But in folk worship, she faded to a position of remote respectability. Sometimes other goddesses called themselves her daughters. They caused a stir, inspired new cults or married some lone medium who served them until death. In sexual alchemy a trace of her remains. One obscure story relates that the goddess started, like so many Chinese gods, as a human being. She collected the jing (here: seminal essence) of young men and refined it; it allowed her to attain the Dao (Despeux and Kohn, 2003:38-40). This is not an official part of her hagiography, but such anecdotes may have made her a patron goddess of prostitutes, dancing and singing girls: the few professions open to independent women during the last centuries. Likewise, she remained a favourite of widows, retired madams and Daoist nuns. However, Guanyin also has a link to prostitutes. For one thing, she has compassion for everyone, no matter the gender, age, culture or status in society. For another, as Yü outlines (2001: 421-428), bodhisattvas were occasionally identified with temptresses who beguiled men, if only to lead them to true dharma. It's a tantric idea, and was briefly popular in China until the late Song Dynasty, with its neo-Confucian mindset, put a stop to it. Yü mentions a young prostitute of the Tang period who made love with a large number of men. Overnight, each of them lost his desire for sex and turned to Buddhism. It might be fun to guess what happened. Her neighbours despised the girl as a common hooker. After she died and decayed, it turned out that her bones were connected by a chain: good evidence she was a bodhisattva in disguise. The same chained bones appear in the later tale of the Fish-Basket Guanyin who married Mr. Ma. Though she remained chaste (an early death can do this to you) and our legendary prostitute did not, their beauty enticed men to embrace Buddhism. Indeed, for a while prostitutes and actors were praised to be *'as beautiful as Guanyin'*. Early female Guanyin images tend to show desirable young ladies, a few centuries later they often appear as middle aged matrons or old crones.

It's a long and convoluted tale. Who, may I ask is the *'original'* Guanyin? Who is the original Xiwangmu, and who or what, indeed, is the *'original'* of whatever deity you like best? The history of religion is a mind-blowing tale of creative and pragmatic syncretism. Images, symbols, functions and moods transformed because it worked that way. The same goes for the masks that each of us considers her or his identity. How do Guanyin and Xiwangmu relate? How much do they have in common with the Ximu and the woman/mother Tiger of the Shang? Who can tell how they appeared, who knows when their dance will end?

Xiwangmu has been through a lot. She has a fond heart for those who recall her wild past, and dare to face their own dissolution and transcendence, deep within the darksome heart of Mount Kunlun. When 'you' are gone, pure awareness remains:

Diverse Animal and Taotie Designs

"Those who die without perishing will have a long life." (Laozi Daodejing, 33, transl. Duyvendak)

More Mothers?

An eastern and a western mother were enough for most researchers. Classical Chinese literature uses the term east and west, or spring and autumn, to signify the whole world and the whole year. Many researchers assumed that the Zhou only knew two seasons. There are, however, several seasonal terms in Oracle Bone writing which we can't identify. Possibly the Shang had more than two seasons. And maybe there were more than two goddesses for the directions. A plastron fragment from the Menzies Collection, number S0100, 2990 shows the end of an inscription. The only remaining words read Woman or **Mother North**. It's not enough evidence to prove anything. However, whenever they could, the Shang ordered their world in fours. The dualism which eventually became yin/yang cosmology is a product of the Zhou. If there was a Woman North, what about a **Woman South**? And while we are dealing with divine women, there is also inscriptions mentioning a Woman/Mother Venerable Dragon, and a Woman/Mother Monstrous Animal. Perhaps they were ancestresses, and perhaps they were deities. It's hard to tell.

Finally, the sign gui, ghost, also merged with the sign for woman/mother. Usually, a ghost is a kneeling figure with a square head, divided into four quarters. The head looks like the glyph for 'field'. Perhaps it is a death mask, or a mask worn by a medium of shaman while being obsessed by a ghost. Similar mask-heads appear in Eurasian and Siberian rock art. They are usually identified as spirits. In the oracle bones, some of these ghosts are female and have the characteristic folded arms of the characters woman/mother (p.666). Were they ancestresses, or simply female ghosts? Or were they goddesses of the dead?

A **Mother Ghost** appears in later Chinese myth. According to de Groot (2, 805-806), Gui Mu resides in the south, near the Lesser Yu mountains. All the gui which reside in heaven and on earth are born from her. Each litter consists of ten, which she births in the morning and devours in the evening. She is the residing shen of the Spectre Pass, i.e. the southern gate to the realm of ghosts. Guangxi, at the south of the empire, was believed to border on the realm of ghosts, and a pair of natural rocks, thirty paces apart, was considered the gates to the spirit world. Several military expeditions were lead through this pass, the earliest on record being that of General Man of the Han Dynasty. As malaria is extremely common in the dense forests south of the Ghost Gates, tradition claims that only one soldier out of ten returned alive. Gui Mu has the head of a tiger, feet and eyebrows like a dragon and the eyes of a python. It might remind you of Xiwangmu, herself closely associated with ghosts and immortals and of Lamaštu. De Groot notes that the cult of Gui Mu thrives in the south eastern provinces Zhejiang, Jiangxi and Fujian, where she receives offerings and worship to prevent tempests. Here, her images of clay and wood have the head of a dragon, the ears of a cow and connected eyebrows with a single eye underneath. The age of her cult remains unclear. De Groot suspects a Buddhist influence but gives no reason for his assumption.

And finally, while we discuss goddesses, the very term **fu** may mean noble lady, maybe the spouse of a king or of his brothers (p.682). The fu ladies had names which indicated their clan or state origin. Such as Fu Hao, who came either from the Zi or a Hao clan, Fu Shu, who came from the Mouse people, or Fu Jing, from the Jing state. The character Fu combines hand (or really claw) with brush or broom, and fu is a homophone for broom. While the fu were living women, for some unknown reason they, or someone called fu, occasionally received sacrifices. It's not easy to explain. A fu received her sacrifices, after death, not under the name '*Fu so-and-so*' but under her posthumous temple name and on the specified day. She wasn't called fu any more. If she had been a queen or a high ranking fu, she was addressed by day name and the title mu (mother). Eventually she was renamed grandmother (bi), which could also mean ancestress of grandmother's generation.

Yet there are oracles which postulate sacrifices to fu, without providing further details. It might be assumed that there was a deity of that name, or that the fu had a semi divine status.

A note on matriarchy. The oracle bone inscriptions reveal that the Shang queens were venerated as ancestresses just as their husbands were, and received regular sacrifices. This was an astonishing insight. Late Zhou period ritual, as given in the *Liji*, does not even discuss the possibility that a female ancestor might receive offerings. By the time the Zhou literati re-invented the past, offerings to ancestresses had gone out of fashion. So when the linguists of the early Twentieth Century discovered that the Shang offered to deceased queens and notable ladies, it created quite a stir. Some enterprising researchers created the impression, popular until the sixties, that the Shang were a matriarchal society. Discovering early matriarchal societies was fashionable from the mid-1800s to the 1960s. The idea that matriarchy preceded patriarchy had a popular appeal as it was so over simplified that anyone could understand it. Even the founding fathers of modern Socialism, such as Marx and Engels subscribed to it. Nowadays scholars shy away from it, as the evidence is far too slim to generalise about anything. After all, the Stone and Bronze Ages span a vast amount of time and many cultures, most of them completely unknown. Our archaeologists are happy when they uncover a few stone tools, maybe some vessels and the holes that indicate house foundations. This is hardly enough to speculate about social structures, religion or politics. Hence, most contemporary scholars avoid attributing vague terms like *'matriarchal'* or *'patriarchal'* to early cultures, let alone to periods spanning thousands of years. The last exceptions to this trend are scholars in socialist countries who feel compelled to support Marxist dogma. Now what about the Shang? As we have textual evidence from them, we know a lot more about their women than about the cultures that surrounded them. The royal genealogies show that inheritance was more or less patrilineal. It did not always go from father to son, but it focused on princes of the royal clan, who married ladies from other clans or states. Sure, deceased queens received offerings. But when we consider the value of the sacrifices, the early dynastic ancestors, such as Tang and Shang Jia received the greatest amounts. Normal ancestors were treated to a lot less. The ancestresses were often blamed for pregnancy related problems and received their offerings when birth was difficult or children fell sick. For this reason, they often appear in oracles made for (or by?) fu ladies. But pregnancy was just an aspect of their sphere of influence. Like the male ancestors, the ancestresses could send diseases, accidents and troubles, and did it frequently. A few of them were so terrifying that the king personally sacrificed to them. Like the male ancestors, the ancestresses were treated to guesting (bin) rituals, branch offerings, harmonisation, feather-dance, grain and drums offerings. Only the raw meat sacrifice seems to have been a male privilege. Unlike the ancestresses of the Zhou period, the Shang ladies had a firm hold on ritual practice. That, however, is not the same thing as matriarchy.

In popular belief, matriarchy often comes in one package with mother goddesses. The deceased Shang queens were often called mothers, and they certainly functioned like goddesses, but they didn't behave very motherly. Regarding the political power of women, the noble ladies of whom we know had a lot more influence than the women of the Zhou and later periods. Many consorts of Wu Ding acted as ministers, administrators or generals. They owned and governed cities and led their own people into war. This is not the same as matriarchy, but it implies that noble Shang women of that period had more power and rights than the women of any Chinese dynasty. However, who can tell whether Wu Ding's rule was typical or an exception? Were the women before Wu Ding as powerful? And what of the women after him? Personally, I would guess that Wu Ding, though a highly innovative regent, could not have made so many changes without the support of the nobles of the other clans. I suspect that the clans appreciated it when a royal wife from their family rose to a position of great power. There is no data whether the Shang kings after Wu Ding had a similar outlook; Wu Ding divined about many private family matters that did not interest the regents who followed him. None of the later Shang kings divined about his fu ladies, let alone about their health, births or administrative position.

Another deity or deities related to the directions is cloud. **Deity Cloud**, written with the radicals turbulence and above, appears in rain divination and in oracles relating to unusual weather conditions (p.748). The topic was enormously important, as the Shang realm frequently suffered from drought or deluge, and both were worth divining. The clouds were sometimes messengers of Di. And when a cloud released thunder and lightning, the oracle was asked whether it signified disaster. Di liked to use the voice of thunder to give its opinion. We know very little about Deity Cloud, apart from the fact that it received offerings. Here we run into problems. One inscription proposes a burned offering to *'Cloud Di'*. Does it mean that deity cloud was a servant of Di, as T.T. Chang assumed, or was the term Di used as a generic title, as Robert Eno (in Lopez, 1996:48) proposes? Or should we read the inscription as *'burned offering for Cloud and Di'*? Was there one Deity Cloud or a whole cluster of them? The bones mention Deity Four Clouds, which might mean one deity with four directional clouds, or four deities. Well and good. But what do you make of Deity Three Clouds and Deity Six Clouds? Or of Colourful Clouds that might be a dangerous omen? Did the Shang subscribe to a concept of the divine that allowed deities to be singular and plural, as in Hinduism?

Di

When we have such an emphasis on four directions, the unifying principle gains importance. And here we come to a very complex topic. It's Deity or Deities Di, perhaps the supreme shen of the Shang (p.772). Early researchers assumed that Di was the greatest god of the Shang pantheon. They based much of their thinking on the *Shuowen*, which explains Di as *'World-Ruler'*, and on Daoist religion, where we encounter a supreme Emperor of Heaven who often appears in the company of Mr. Thunder, Lady Lightning, Lord Wind and Lord Rain, plus whoever matters to the patrons of a temple. But as they also assumed that the Shang were, most of all, into ancestral veneration, we find a common claim that Di was a male god, highest of all deities, a celestial god and the original ancestor of mankind (or at least the Zi clan). It seemed so natural, at the time, to assume that a supreme deity must be male, ancestral and reside in heaven. Especially as the middle Zhou and later writers liked to use Di and Heaven (Tian) indiscriminately, and as the Di/Tian concept transformed into the Jade Emperor. It might be wrong. The Shang probably did not worship heaven as such, while the early Zhou made a point of not worshipping Di, nor did they use the title for their deceased kings. This, however, is a complex topic involving plenty of speculation. Today, the situation has changed a lot, and we are happy to know more and less than before. There is, for instance, no evidence that connects the Shang time Di with the male gender. Nor is Di ever called an ancestor. In fact, we don't even know if Di is a single deity at all. One important source, the *Huainanzi*, uses the term Di as a plural. Here, Di is a group divinity ascending and descending the Jian tree on Mount Duguang, right in the centre of the world, where the sun casts no shadow and no echo rebounds (chapter 4:4, in Major, 1993:158-161). Shang inscriptions sometimes couple the word Di with a direction, which might mean that Di is worshipped in that direction, or manifests in its deity, or even that the directional god is called a Di. Likewise, Han Dynasty literature occasionally uses the tile Di for other deities, including Nüwa. To top it off, the late Shang used the title Di for a selection of ancestors. How several ancestors can be called the supreme deity is hard to understand, unless the word Di was a multipurpose title and did not always imply supremacy over other deities.

This is going to be a little difficult. Look at the character. Some consider it as a picture of a shaman in ornamental costume, or believe it shows a shaman's mask. Both ideas are interesting, but tell us nothing about the Di. A theory by Guo Moruo proposes the character shows a blossom. It's a nice thought, especially when you consider the importance of blossom offerings. The Shang may also have done so, and that they offered branches is well documented. We simply don't know if they were blossoming. Well and good. The character might be considered as containing the radical wood/tree. A better idea, by Ye Yusen, is that the grapheme shows a bundle of sticks which have been knotted together. This might be a reference to a burning sacrifice, if only we knew. Ken-Ichi Takashima interprets the character Di as a nominal derivation of another word *'di'* that means to bind or to string together, and proposes that Di is *"the one who binds (the cosmos) together"* (in Allan, 2007: 21).

The *'wood'* element might also refer to other uses of wood, such as in building or crafting, or it might even, as trees, be read as genealogies united by a common purpose. Imagine an assembly of clans, people, ancestors or gods united (bound together) by intent or nature. I would add that the character consist of two crosses, a + and an X in between. This produces an eight-rayed star, a fit glyph for the whole world (the cardinal directions and the dangerous directions in between), united with the sacred T, which might represent the north axis. Occasionally there is a horizontal bar above the T indicating *'high'*. You could say that this sort of Di is the Shang Di, the High Di. Perhaps the *'normal'* and the *'high'* Di were the same phenomenon and perhaps the Shang were thinking of two deities, or of two aspects of a single deity, or were simply innovative or careless in their writing. Mind you, on very rare occasions the character Di was written upside down, in which case the glyph *'above, high'* turns into *'low, deep'*. Was this a Di below the ground, a reference to an earth deity, or just a scribe's whim? The sacred T, upside down, becomes a form of the character *'earth, earth deity'* in period five, in earlier periods it was used to designate the male gender of a sacrificial animal.

In short, I believe that the Shang used the term Di in several ways, sometimes specific, sometimes vaguely, and that they did not always think of a single, personified and well defined high god when they refered to Di. It's a strange thing. How much individuality do you attribute to the divine? People of our age, (and especially in western cultures) expect gods to be as well defined as persons. People like it when gods comes with specific attributes, myths, rituals and so on, just as people consider themselves distinct individuals with specific character traits. It's one of the things that keeps them apart from Universal Consciousness. However, clear definitions are only possible when there is a central dogma and a church that enforces it. It's a tough job, as really religious people tend to rediscover the divine, in new shapes and functions, again and again. But when you go to India, for example, you find that in the earliest recorded period, i.e. in the times of the *Vedas*, gods were already (or still) moving from shape to shape as it suited them and their worshippers. Deities could swap insignia, change their sex and get involved in new myth cycles. That's an easy matter when you have a culture that extends over a vast span of terrain and has neither a single church nor a single dogma, nor an interest to develop either. Indian religion is characterised by fluidity and creative freshness. We owe it to a lot of independently minded seers, visionaries and writers. In Chinese religion, a similar plurality of offices and appearances can be discerned. We don't know if this was already (or still) the case in Shang times, but when we look at the early myths we find that many stories are contradictory, that some characters got pretty much around and that the divine was transformed to fit the needs of people. Xuannü, for example, was worshipped as an independent deity, but there were also worshippers who identified her with Xiwangmu or Nüwa. You could argue whether this is right or wrong, or you could pause and consider whether the divine needs to be confined in a single shape, expression and personality. It is even conceivable that Di was a conglomerate of the divine, an all-self much like the Brahman or Atman concept developed in India around the eighth century BCE. All right, I am sure that there are serious scholars who won't like this idea for perfectly good reasons. It's just that in my meditations, the Di experience blended with the experience of the Tai Yi (Supreme Unity) and the

Hun Dun (Primordial Chaos). All three are excellent expressions for One Consciousness. When you search (or filter) for unity, you will discover the Tai Yi in your experience of the world. When you look for divergence, multiplicity and overwhelming disorder, everything will appear as the Hundun to you. And when you search for the centralising, balancing and regulating divine principle between unity and multiplicity, you arrive at the function of Di.

Usually, I try to keep completely subjective visions out of my books. However, Sarah Allan kindly sent me her brilliant article *On the Identity of Shang Di and the Origin of the Concept of a Celestial Mandate* (2007). Her research emphasises the residence of Di in the centre of the sky, and encouraged me to elaborate about the matter.

As a unifying principle, Di could have had a function similar to the king. Now a Shang time king was a long way from the emperors of later dynasties. The Shang did not have regents with monolithic authority. They had kings from a sacred clan who could only govern thanks to the support of a number of allied and related families, clans and states. The Shang *'Dynasty'* was an alliance. If Di reflected the function of the king, s/he or it was not necessarily a supreme and undisputed ruler. Di may have represented the king, but Di may also have reflected the alliance of clans that formed the Shang.

What if we forget about the personification and go for function? The Di rituals were frequently performed for the four directions (see inscriptions). The winds and the clouds were Di's messengers, and in period 2a and 3 we encounter Di's Five Jade Ministers, who may be deities, clouds, sacred directions, sacred mountains or deities we simply don't know. The most important function of Di was to represent the centre. Here we should look at the sign for the Di sacrifice. It combines the sign Di with the square or rectangular enclosure (it's occasionally written as *'mouth'*). The sign usually appears as a verb and implies an offering to Di, or an offering to Di in one or several directions. The square represents the surroundings while Di is the centre. If we combine the idea of the High Di with the square, we end up looking at the heaven. Nowadays the north point is near Polaris, and this star has much to do with heavenly gods. The celestial axis is a major religious symbol all over Eurasia. Just consider the Tyr rune, shaped like an arrow, signifying the star (the Tyr star, Polaris) that gives directions in the middle of the night. Tyr is a Norse version of a celestial high god who also appears as Tiu, Tiwaz, Zis, Twisto, Thor, Thunar, Donar etc. in Germanic myth, as Tanaris and Teutates in Celtic Gaul, as Zeus in Greece, Dio Pater (Jupiter) and Deus in Rome and in the generic name Deva (the Shining Ones) in India. All of these terms go back to the Indo-European *deiw- meaning the bright (sky). It is a remarkable happenchance that the two most important Chinese terms for similar deities have a very similar sound: Di for the Shang and Tian (Heaven) for the Zhou (who eventually revived the term Di as a title for Heaven). I would love to hear a sinologist explain this. The Shang are not very likely to have had such close contacts to Indo-Europeans that they would have imported the name or a deity from them. The Zhou may have had a vague relationship to undefined Indo European people (see, for example, T.T.Chang, 1970:240-242) but the evidence rests on a couple of loan words and is somewhat shaky. Anyway, when we look for a celestial god who balances the forces of the wide and wonderful world, we have to go out at night and gaze at the centre of heaven. In the Shang period, celestial north was quite a distance from Polaris. It was much closer to the *'square'* formed by Ursa Minor. Now the square is one of the most important religious symbols of the Shang. The character *'ding'* was one of the most popular posthumous temple names. To this day it is debated whether the square symbolises an enclosure (as in the character for *'city'*), the earth, a sacred object or even a skull or head; see, for example the sign for *'birth'* where two hands open a *'stable'*: releasing the square head of the infant (p.693). The square is also the shape of the earth and, as Sarah Allan shows so well, the basic design of the royal tombs. When a king or queen died, they came to reside in a square chamber below ground that represented the civilised world, and its four directions. It may also have represented the central square of heaven. A similar thought seems to appear in island Celtic myth and poetry, where a foursquare castle rotates in the centre of the sky. In Taliesin's songs, the four-cornered castle was a special otherworld. Maybe the Shang thought that it was the residence of Shang Di. Maybe they even assumed that their ancestors (or maybe a divine part of them, if they believed in several souls) travelled to the skies. There are a few inscriptions which indicate that the king travels up to heaven (feet ascending a ladder) to meet some ancestors (see examples p.576). If Di resides in the unmoving centre of heaven, on the axle of the celestial wheel, the Shang could have sought him in the square of Ursa Minor, while later generations would have housed him in Polaris. It is even possible that the celestial square represented Di itself. In Han time iconography you can sometimes see Shang Di riding a great chariot. The chariot is Ursa Major, the Great Dipper. The Shang may have invoked this constellation in their ritual, and the Zhou and all later periods definitely did. When we look at Ursa Major as a chariot, the square of Ursa Minor is exactly where a rider would sit.

Perhaps we ought to consider the centre of heaven itself as the essence and location of Di, regardless which star was closest to the celestial axis at a given time. After all, we have no idea how long Shang religion developed before the oracle bones were inscribed. The same place, the centre of Heaven, is the residence of the Tai Yi, Great Unity, which may be a deity, a realisation of One Consciousness, and an experience that may take your spiritual practice out of the narrow confines of dualistic worship. More on Tai Yi in the chapter on meditation. The square represents the wholeness of the earth and the centre of heaven, but it also appears in the human realm. When disaster threatened or the storm winds wrought havoc and destruction, the king moved to the centre, or ritually erected the centre. Perhaps he did this in a ritual fashion. Maybe he went to a sacred place, a hall, a mound or some other location. Maybe he surrounded himself with representations of the directions. And maybe he introverted and entered the sacred centre within himself. By establishing a centre, order and peace were restored. In a similar way, you can centre yourself when life around you seems to get out of control.

How about the centre of the body? There is a character showing a standing person (in the attitude signifying *'great'*) with a square around the hips (p.661). It corresponds perfectly to the physical centre of the body, to the lower Dan Tian (Heavenly Field) and to the belly. The place is of supreme importance in rites and meditations of Daoist alchemy, but it is also essential for all who wish to learn calligraphy, music, painting or a martial art. The belly, or Golden Pavilion, as Wei Huacun called it, is the supreme consciousness space within the mind-body totality. Daoist meditation, and possibly the meditation of the wu who preceded them, begins and ends with a centring of awareness. It can mean that you think of it, or observe your belly breathing, but you will get much further when you allow your awareness to introvert and sink into the vast emptiness within yourself. Where the Vedic seers, the Advaita Vedāntins and the Kashmir Tāntrikas descended into the heart (meaning any space between shoulders and hips), the Daoists usually favoured the belly. The oracle bone sign has several meanings. One of them is yellow (or possibly light brown). Yellow is a classical colour of the square earth (and the rich loess of the north Chinese plain), and signifies the centre. But the character is also a representation of a jade pendant, a round disk, which was worn at the belt to signify status or to attract good luck. These disks were usually round (representing heaven) but in oracle bone writing, with its hard-to-scratch straight line aesthetics, round objects often ended up looking like squares. Does this mean that Heaven is found in the belly?

Compared with gods and ancestors, Di behaves unusually. Unlike the ever hungry ancestors, Di receives few sacrifices. For a start, the sacrifices of Di follow a different grammatical convention. Normal oracles usually go: to-for deity X five sheep? or whatever. Or they leave out the *'to-for'* as self evident, grammar not being the strong point of the scribes. With Di, offerings are usually written *"Jia-xu (day 11) / not/ Di / dog? Ding-Chou (day 14) / crack-making / king / not / Di / Tiger?"* (T. T. Chang, 1970:223). So on day eleven they asked whether Di should not get a dog. I suppose it's one of those inscriptions where each question or charge was expressed in a positive and negative form. The oracle presumably said no, for two days later the king personally asks whether Di should not receive a tiger. A tiger is a very rare and valuable offering. Di wasn't often treated to such classy offerings. On the whole, whatever Di was, it wasn't half as greedy as the ancestors.

Several important oracle bone scholars, such as Chen Mengjia and Dong Zuobin assumed that Di was a superior, distant and refined deity who did not receive offerings nor any sort of regular worship. Nor was Di involved in everyday affairs, approached regarding the harvest, success in war and so on. In short, they imagined a Di way beyond the common, human or even the divine realm. As a head of the gods Di wasn't supposed to get itself involved. T.T. Chang very much disagreed with this assumption. In order to make his point, he collected forty inscriptions relating to various aspects of the cult of Di. As you can see in the sample given above, the oracles can be read *'not Di (offer) dog'* and *'not Di (offer) tiger'*. Here, the term Di would be used verbally, as *'to Di offer'*. It would be hard to explain them differently. Likewise, we read of Di receiving a few sheep, cattle, castrated boars, dogs, pigs and decapitated humans. Such sacrifices were rare and minor, compared to what the early ancestors received, but even as symbolic tokens of regard, they indicate that Di was part of the sacrificial routine. Likewise, Di received offerings through its messenger, the stormwind bird Peng. Di was worshipped by the kings, but there are also indications that other people made offerings. One inscription asks if General Bao (Panther) could offer to Di. He was an aristocrat, but not a king. We also observe Di in war-related oracles. Frequently, King Wu Ding asked whether Di would grant support during a war against a neighbouring fang state.

But it went beyond military affairs. For Di could grant the harvest or withhold it, send the clouds and winds, end the tempest, give rain or drought. So could the other deities and ancestors. It is only Di, however, who was in charge of all of them. Perhaps Di as a single god could command the other deities and ancestors. In this case it strikes me as odd that the diviners bothered about placating other deities and ancestors. Di could have done the job for them. Why waste a huge bribe on a minor troublemaker when you can go to the top and get things done for much less? If Di was a conglomerate of deities, it would explain a lot. Each sacrifice to a specific deity would also imply an offering to an aspect of Di. And Di could get angry. Several inscriptions ask whether Di wants to destroy a city. Di could curse the harvest, send drought, war, invasion or plague. Di could be so angry with the Shang that it might try to destroy the capital. This is a crucial point. It marks a difference between Di and the ancestors. For when the ancestral temples of the kings in the capital are destroyed, the ancestors don't get proper sacrifices any more, and fade into oblivion. If the ancestors ruined their own graves, shrines and descendants, they would destroy themselves. Di, apparently, did not give a damn.

Unlike the royal ancestors, Di did not depend on the Shang.

Di had something like a messenger. It's the great **Stormbird Peng** (p.628). In the *Zhuangzi* you meet Peng right on the first pages. And you may have wondered what it is doing there. Let me quote the crazy sage. *"In the northern ocean dwells a fish called Kun (*fish-rye*). Kun is so vast that I cannot tell how many thousand li it measures. He transforms and turns into a bids called Peng. Peng has a back many thousand li across and when it rises and takes to flight, his wings, like clouds, are all over the sky. When the ocean begins to move, the bird makes its way to the southern ocean, which is the Lake of Heaven. The (*book*) 'Universal Harmony' describes many miracles and states: 'When Peng flies to the southern ocean, for three thousand li the waters are churned. He releases the whirlwinds and rises ninety thousand li on a six month storm.' Shimmering heat, whirling clouds of dust. Living beings are blown around – and heaven seems so blue. Is blue its true colour or does it only appear blue as it is so far away and has no limit? When the bird glances down, everything it perceives is also blue...*

When the air isn't high enough there is not enough power to carry mighty wings. So when Peng wants to rise ninety thousand li, it needs the air currents underneath. Only thus can it rest on the back of the air and carry the blue sky and nothing can halt or hinder it. Only then can it turn its eyes to the south."

The passage starts with paradox. The fish and the bird, for instance. And the idea that the greatest fish is named after the very smallest unit of fishiness, the rye. It's a wonderful vision: the realm above and below appear blue to each other. But there is also an amazingly modern element. It reads like a description of the seasonal ocean currents and wind streams, and the way they influence each other. That the winds move with the seasons has been known for a while. But that the oceans of the earth are connected by a vast system of moving warm top and cold deep water currents has only been mapped over the last decades. And when we say Peng we mean much more than winds. The great bird may be an image of the shifting jct streams and the monsoons which strike southern China every summer. Great winds (Tai Feng) come in from the Pacific, bringing havoc and devastation.

You hopefully noticed that, once again (sorry) I'm being anachronistic. For when I quote Zhuangzi I use a late Zhou metaphor to describe a deity who was popular some eight hundred years earlier. All we know of Peng in the Shang period is that it received regular sacrifices, especially when a heavy storm was devastating the countryside. As the temperature was higher than today, devastating whirlwinds were probably more common. They like a bit of heat to build up, out there, over the ocean. Then they spiral upwards until they get in touch with the high elevation airstreams and move erratically inland. And the rather flat, fertile countryside around Anyang is prone for sudden windstorms anyway. Today they carry a lot of dust, as so much of Chinas north suffers from deforestation and erosion. During the Shang, the storms were presumably hot and damp.

But I also suspect that the Shang used bird Peng as a totem. Some of the glyphs look remarkably like a bird effigy, with long, trailing stripes, on a pole, much like a banner or a military emblem. Perhaps some of the Shang troops carried such things into battle, when they stormed against the enemy. But I'm only guessing. In the inscriptions, Peng is called a messenger of Di. In this function, Peng received sacrifices. Not that they were very large. Some deities had power over Peng. Di could calm the storm, so could the king, when he erected the centre, and so could Yi Yin. Maybe the wu ritualists could do the same; it depends on whether we read the character wu as a sacred quadrant or as a human ritualist.

Wind appears in two characters. There is Peng, for the howling gale, and there is a sign which looks like a sail (p.745). It can mean a minor wind, but it was also used to designate a disease. It may have been a wind-disease, as T.T. Chang assumes, i.e. a common cold. Fu Hao had several (p.654). As a general she must have spent a lot of time exposed to wind and rain. But as the *Huangdi Neijing* states *"The hundred diseases all come from wind"*. The physicians of the late Zhou, Qin and early Han accumulated formidable lists of wind diseases, including stroke, vomiting, cramps and madness. Then, in period three, the characters bird Peng and wind appear together. Often a tiny sail is written next to the crowned bird. It wasn't the norm yet, but pointed at later periods, when the character feng (wind) would be drawn into a frame which had evolved from the sail.

But let s take another look at the evolution of bird Peng. The bird has a tiny, triangular crown on his head, at least in most inscriptions. You can see similar triangles above the heads of several divine animals, such as dragons and sometimes tigers. The triangle may be a peacock's crest or a shortened hair-needle, the glyph of the tenner sign xin. It's a safe bet that hair needles with special ornaments signified status. Fu Hao had hundreds of them in her tomb. And many of them, carefully carved from bone, show tiny birds. Some scholars explain these birds as cockerels. It might be wrong. For the birds, whatever they may be, have triangular crowns just like bird Peng. We may be at the roots of a tradition. Later dynasties frequently associated the emperor with the dragon and the queen with the phoenix. Like dragons, phoenixes are imaginary or magical animals. Usually, they blend characteristics of peacocks and pheasants. There is no evidence that Shang rulers were symbolised by dragons, but the many bird Peng hair-needles from Fu Hao's grave may be at the root of the phoenix tradition. Only that the phoenix of the Shang was no graceful pheasant, as in later ages, but the howling tempest itself.

Strange Gods

Here we encounter something divine about which I'd love to know more. The grapheme shows a pair of snakes, so let's call it the deities **Double Snakes** (p.633). They (or it) received minor sacrifices on occasion, such as sheep and castrated boars. More often, they wanted to have a ceremonial dance. And from what the bones say, they were asked to grant rain. When drought parched the land, the diviners wondered whether the double snakes had uttered a curse. Which is pretty much all we know. The character also appears for a tribe and a place, so it might be a pair of deities of much greater importance at some distance from the capital. My guess is that we are dealing with the prototypes of such snake-human deities as Fuxi and Nüwa, the snake-people of the west which the *Shanhaijing* mentions in passing, or even the Indian and south-east Asian Nāga deities. There were lots of serpentine deities in ancient China, and, for that matter, in many parts of Eurasia. In India they, the Nāga folk, are associated with water, springs, underworldly paradises, subterranean currents, secret lore and hidden elixirs. To a certain extent this applies to China as well. It would be very tempting to call them rain and water deities, but this is quite wrong. Shang deities often had similar powers. While the double snakes could grant and withhold rain, the same was possible for a wide range of deities and ancestors. And with regard to double snakes, we are not even sure whether they are a pair of ancient serpent deities, an unknown early ancestor, or maybe a pair of them.

Shang religion involved far more deities than this. One of the most popular is called **Child Er**. The character shows a person kneeling (p.672). It has a dent in its head which signifies an open fontanel. Our deity Er is a child. Nowadays the sign is one of the basic radicals of written Chinese. It means child or youth. To the Shang, the child was evidently an infant. Deity Er often received sacrifices when rain was failing and the harvest was in danger. And that is pretty much all we know of it. It would be a charming idea if the Shang imagined this god as a divine child. Numerous gods of that type received veneration, such as Maponus (the youthful god) of the Gauls, Harpocrates (a baby floating down the Nile on a lotus) in Egypt, young Hermes (who stole the cattle of Apollo before he was old enough to walk without diapers) in Greece, baby Kṛṣṇa and baby Skanda (strong enough to defeat demons in the cradle) or the popular Chinese youth Neezha, who made much trouble and drove his parents mad before he became deified. Today he rides a fire wheel and kills demons. Neezha is usually worshipped in a Buddhist context, but the novel *Creation of the Gods* claims that he was present when the Zhou fought the Shang. Another child deity is Xiang Tuo who, at the tender age of seven met Kongzi (Confucius). The sage asked the child forty difficult questions and riddles regarding culture, philosophy, astronomy, geography, nature, society and ethics. The child answered each question perfectly and then asked three questions that Kongzi couldn't answer. Somewhat stunned, Kongzi proposed to get a wei qi (= go) game from his chariot. The child replied that playing is a waste of time that makes people neglect their duties. Much humbled, Kongzi muttered *'the youth should be respected'* and departed. Three years later, Xiang Tu died and was venerated as a deity. The tale was first recorded during the Wei Dynasty, and elaborated during the Sui Dynasty. But whether such ideas applied to god Er remains unknown. The ideogram looks like a child and invites speculation, but could just as well have been chosen for phonetic reasons.

You will find many more deities in the dictionary. Most of them are so unknown that we have no idea whether their characters actually signify anything or were chosen as homophones. And for the dozens that have been identified there may be hundreds who were worshipped in the country and who received no attention from the city dwellers in the capital. Let me end this section by taking a brief look at the nature gods.

One of them is Deity **Stone**, about whom, sadly, we know nothing (p.754). But who was worshipped, in all likeliness, in the odd remarkable stone emerging from the scenery. To the Shang, stone was not a typical building material, as it was simply far too rare. Many Chinese, all through history, made their houses from pounded earth and wood or bamboo. It's one of the reasons why so few really old houses survive. And even when stone was used, it was usually a reinforcement for pillars or a veneer to cover earth walls. But the Shang used many stone tools, as they were so much cheaper than bronze. And in their tombs they had statuettes of beautifully carved stone, as well as symbolic weapons equipped with stone blades. How much of this connects with deity Stone remains your guess.

Deity **Snow** (p.751). Yes, even in the tropically hot northern Chinese plain of the late bronze, snow fell from time to time. Today, each winter in Henan is characterised by biting cold temperatures, by snow and ice and frosty winds. But during the Shang, snow was such a rare and miraculous event that it received offerings. Look at the character. It shows a combination of rain and brooms, i.e. rain that can be swept away.

Was **Rain** (p.750) a deity? Most scholars assumed that rain was under the command of other deities and ancestors. However, there are inscriptions that ask for rain and specify small offerings without naming who might get them. I would guess rain itself received these sacrifices.

Much better known is Deity **Earth** (p.754). The character for earth shows a mound, pile or triangle emerging from the ground. Sometimes it looks like a heap or like a standing stone. Both are possible. Northern China (especially Liaoning), just like Korea and Japan (Kyushu), have their share of megaliths. I've seen pictures of menhirs and dolmen from Korea which could have been located in northern Germany, Brittany or southern Britain. Same architecture, same feeling, simply perfect. And these few surviving stone monuments may be just a few rare samples of something much more common. After all, stone is valuable. Over the centuries, countless stone arrangements were dismantled and devastated to clear fields or win building material. In northern Germany, literally hundreds of barrows, standing stones and even entire circles and avenues were smashed or blown up in the nineteenth century. Much of the rock was sold to the city of Hamburg, which used it to rebuild its harbour. Who knows what happened in China? So our earth sign might show a standing stone. Or it may show a mound of earth. In this case it might be an earth altar. Earth altars are mentioned in the earliest histories of the Zhou and in the *Shujing*. There was a central earth altar in the capital. Ying-Ta's commentary to the *Shujing*, quoted by Legge in the chapter *Yu Gong*, states: *"The emperors raised a mound of earth of the five colours as an altar to the spirits of the land. On the investiture of any prince a quantity of earth of the colour characteristic of the region where his principality lay was cut away and given to him, which he took home to build an altar with. All the altars thus built, however, were covered with yellow earth. The earth was given to each prince in bundles covered with white rushes emblematic of purity."* The rushes were not only for purity. They also scared evil spirits, a reason why exorcists were fond of them. The same chapter details the different types of soil which can be found in the provinces. Let's have another tale. We are past the fall of the Shang. The Zhou are in power and have decided to move the capital. And as the early Chinese often did, they chose a good bit of empty land and built their new city out of nothing. On day wu-shen (45) the Duke of Zhou obtained a favourable omen from the tortoise shell oracle. It was the third day after the first appearance of the moon: he was eager to start his project while the moon waxed. Day geng-xu (47) he had the former citizens of Anyang prepare the various sites north of river Lo. Day jia-yin (51) the preparations were complete. On the next day, yi-mao (52) the Duke came to Lo and inspected the plan of the new city. On ding-si (54), he sacrificed two bulls in what was to become the northern and southern suburbs. The next morning, wu-wu (55) he went to the earth altar of his new capital and sacrificed a bull, a ram and a boar. Then the work began (chapter *Shao Gao*). Both tales have their Zhou period characteristics. The five colours, relating to the wu xing (Five Movers) may be a Han time addition. But what is certain from several literary sources is that the early Zhou, and presumably the Shang before them, had earth altars.

The character earth was also used for the **earth god**. There were several types. There was an earth god in general, and there were earth gods of specific locations, such as *'earth god of State Bang'* and *'earth god of Bo'* where Tang had his fief. And such earth deities received offerings, just like the other gods. In all likeliness, there were hundreds of specific earth gods wherever people settled. You find plenty of them in Chinese history. Some are major earth gods, and govern states or cities, while smaller earth gods look after villages. Those in charge of the wilderness had very little status indeed, and could easily be controlled by passing immortals, crafty fox spirits and other occult beings. Earth or city gods were often invoked for rites of exorcism, as it was their duty to slay demons and annul evil sorceries in their domain. But how should we imagine such an earth god? The Shang left us no details. The people of Chu, however, who were closely allied with the Shang, did. The *Chuci* describe an earth deity who is impressively dangerous. Let's take a look into the deep. Down there, deep below ground the Earthgod rests in a ninefold circle, or in nine serpent coils. It has a horned brow and three eyes, the head of a tiger, a humped back, the torso of a bull, a bloody thumb and is skilled at chasing human souls. Whether this charming deity was male or female isn't specified. And whether it looked anything like the Shang time version remains anyone's guess. The only moderately sure thing is that at least some very late (period 5) Shang earth gods were male. In this time, their character looked like the sign *'male, penis'*, an upside down T. This is in contrast to the much later myths which couple a male Heaven with a female Earth. The earth goddess was necessary for yin-yang cosmologies and a product of the Zhou Dynasty. The Shang earth god influenced wind, harvest, rain and flood. It also calmed tempests and rainstorms. In return it received animal sacrifices, often by burning. You might expect an earth god to get sacrifices by burial, as is attested in the *Liji*. What is your explanation?

Nature deities of other types abound. Not that they received many sacrifices. Even the major ones made do with a few token animals most of the time. It was less than the early ancestors received. You may wonder whether this is an indication of importance. It could be. Just as well it might be that the nature deities were thought to require less. Or that they were of less importance to the king than his personal ancestors. Things may have been entirely different among the country people. One great distinction between the gods and the ancestors is that the gods were fairly independent from human generosity. The Yellow River would keep flowing, no matter who sat on the throne. But the ancestors often required sacrifices to strengthen them. The entire system of the five sacrifices might be considered a continuous strengthening ritual. Rivers and mountains don't need it.

Let's take a look at a few more deities. **Tree** is an interesting one (p.728). The Shang had sacred groves and they certainly had a thing for mulberry and paulownia trees and possibly some other species. But when you read that a tree receives a drink sacrifice you still wouldn't be sure what the Shang believed. The tree could be a deity, the representative of a deity, it could be worshipped as a special, individual tree or as a representative of a sacred species. Or maybe the deity simply lived in the tree.

What about **stars**? The Zhou had a thing about constellations and by the end of their period heaven was pretty well mapped out, deities of all sorts being associated with stars, planets and constellations. This is hinted at in the *Creation of the Gods*. Though of fairly recent date, the book emphasises the first ceremony after the fall of the Shang. We see prime minister and chief magician Jiang Ziya ascend a worship platform to turn 360 slain Shang and Zhou heroes into stellar deities. It looks if the many years of bitter warfare had been an extended ritual to select worthy candidates. And the message is quite clear: a new cult of star worship was instituted. Perhaps something like this really happened. For the Shang were, as far as we know, not overly interested in stellar cults. There is only one complete inscription on an actual rite of worship for what may or may be not a stellar constellation.

Easier to understand are mountains and rivers. The most prominent river deity is the Huang He, the **Yellow River** (p.747). The Shang often referred to it simply as *'the river'*, even though they were living quite a distance from it. The character consists of the wavy line for *'river'* and something like a digging stick. It was chosen for reason of sound, and was replaced in period three by a person carrying a flail, meaning *'to carry'*. Again, for phonetic reasons. The river wasn't as yellow (or muddy) in Shang times as it is today, as land erosion wasn't such a problem. The Yellow River changed its bed several times over Chinese history. During the Shang period, it was merely 65 km from the capital. Flooding was a major threat and happened frequently. But the river was

Earth God of Chu

also a major blessing. It was a convenient waterway to the sea near Shandong, a region with which the Shang eagerly traded. It shows in the archaeological record. One of the most bizarre finds in Anyang were some vertebra and an entire whale scapula! You can be sure that these gifts from the coast dwellers caused quite a stir. More so, imagine the locals in Shandong thinking about the Shang craze to divine with buffalo scapula. *'Let's give them a really big one'* they decided, knowing fully well that it was far too big for divination. It's one of the earliest samples of humour in prehistory.

The Yellow River received sacrifices to prevent flooding. But it was also a deity who could bring or withhold rain. And as the bones show, it was even able to grant success in war, and to curse the king. A similar idea appears in ancient India, where rivers (and river goddesses) Sarasvatī, Vāk and Sindhu gave victory (*Ṛg Veda* 6, 61; 10, 75; 10, 125). Amazing what a river can do. Some Shang kings went to sacrifice at the river in person. Or they sent representatives. Wu Ding occasionally sent a Lady E. She was also sent to pray for rain on the sacred mountain. Lady E is an interesting character. For one thing, it takes a lot of status to be a worthy representative of the king. For another, she was not a fu, hence not married to the king or the royal family. Nor did she receive a temple name. Perhaps she wasn't married at all. It is possible that she was something like a high priestess or shamaness. Or, as T.T. Chang assumed, she was a sister of the king. She was so powerful that, posthumously, she received sacrifices just like a goddess. The inscriptions indicate that, after death, she was suspected of having cursed the king and prince Yu (fish/er). Was he a close relation or maybe her son?

There are more divine rivers on record. Some have meaningful names, such as Turtle River or River Turbulence (Heng Shui) which ran right around the capital and frequently threatened to flood it. Other rivers have characters like hand, ear, now, or exceptional, presumably for phonetic reasons. Each of them was also a deity and received sacrifices when required. What those deities were like remains unknown. Later on, the Chinese used to assume that river deities, when not in anthropomorphic shape, looked like dragons, water-snakes or turtles. None of this can be attested for the Shang. The inscriptions give the names for a wide range of rivers. Some of them were far from the capital, in allied or enemy country, and feature in war or hunting divinations. Such rives probably did not receive sacrifices. You might ask whether such rivers also housed deities, or whether the Shang simply ignored them as they were not responsible for them. Maybe they even thought the foreign rivers were hostile to them.

Mountains are a little more complicated. The Shang venerated one chief mountain, **Mount Yue**, which is written with the characters mountain and sheep/goat (p.618). We could call it

Sheep Mountain. Oracle Bone scholars prefer several other names, such as Yue, Yang or even Qiang. Qiang might relate to the Qiang fang, those sheep herding nomads who frequently battled the troops of the Shang kings and often ended up as human sacrifices. It is not likely that the sacred mountain of the Shang was in Qiang territory. But which mountain are we talking about? If the mountain was called Yue, that name would simply mean *'the Peak'*. One mountain called Tai Yue, or simply Yue was situated in the core territory of the Xia. Today it is called Huoshan (province Shaanxi). It is possible, but unlikely, that the Shang kings went there for sacrifice. According to the history books, the descendants of the Xia had become a subservient vassal clan. But would the Shang have allowed their former enemies to dwell in such a sacred place? And would they have bothered to travel such a distance? Another candidate is the Taishan in Shandong, China's most sacred mountain since the middle Zhou. The Shandong people were moderately friendly with the Shang. Nevertheless, the distance was still greater, and a sacred mountain inhabited by another culture is politically (and religiously) inconvenient. And finally, there is the Songshan in Henan, nowadays famous for a Shaolin temple and a thriving gongfu tourist industry that would have shocked the temple's founders. It was easily the most accessible peak for the Shang kings. Most researchers agree with this identification. In passing, I have to add that the term Yueshan (Mount Yue) was used for several sacred peaks of ancient China. It doesn't make research very easy. Chinese myth has always considered mountains as gateways to the height. To make a pilgrimage to a sacred mountaintop has been an important custom for more than two thousand years. The very *'first emperor'* Qin Shihuangdi made such a journey. But heaven frowned on him and sent a much deserved rainstorm. Once again, we don't really know how the Shang thought about the mountain deity. We simply read, with some frequency, that the Yueshan could grant or withhold rain and curse the harvest. And that it required sacrifices, just like the Yellow River. Occasionally, the regents considered it too much of an effort to travel to the sacred mountain. Probably there was a temple for the deity at the capital. Sacrifices were made in numerous ways. Some were burned, some cut open and a few involved dance rituals. Usually, the offerings were domestic animals. Finally, there is a strange coincidence from period 1, the reign of King Wuding. When a fu and occasionally a prince consecrated pairs of plastrons or scapula, it was usually recorded that a diviner was present during the ritual. One exception is Mount Yue. In a few inscriptions, the consecration was done in the presence of Mount Yue. Of course it is possible, and perhaps even likely that the deity was present during such rituals, maybe to make up for the absence of a diviner. On the other hand, the

Zhou time *Shujing* records that King Wu Ding had a prime minister called Fu Yue, as he came from the peak (yue) of Fu. Fu Yue could be a vague memory of a ritualist who was active at the court of Wu Ding. According to legend, Fu Yue was not just prime minister but also a sky traveller, i.e. he could ascend to Heaven, like several kings, wu and Daoist saints. His name does not appear among the diviners, but I would guess that the presence of a religious specialist could be worth recording.

With regard to other sacred mountains, we run into difficulties. A few inscriptions mention sacrifices to *'five mountains'* or *'ten mountains'*. Five sacred mountains are a common concept in Daoist ritual. Since the Zhou period they were Taishan in the east, Huashan in the west, Hengshan in the north, another Hengshan in the south and Songshan in the centre. It was supposed to look symmetrical but wasn't. As the Shang domain was much smaller than the late Zhou realm, they must have had other mountains in mind. Luckily, the inscriptions name several sacred mountains, or mountain deities if you like, who received sacrifices from time to time. That's the easy part. Far more difficult is the question which of them was really a mountains. The problem lies in the sloppy writing of the scribes. On occasion, the same signs could be used for *'mountain'* and for *'fire'* (p.752). As a result, there are several deities who might be mountain gods or related to fire. And when we come to hills and elevated sites, we also encounter deities who sometimes called for sacrifices.

There are further deities on record, such as a god whose character combines a strange object with the sign *'rain'*. Call it a rain god and you run into trouble. For in most rain divinations, and there are huge amounts of them, this deity is not mentioned. And there are odd animal gods. We already discussed several of them in the section on ancestral and clan animals, and the matter of shamanic animal familiars. One looks like a centipede, another may be (my guess) a spider. There is also a god in charge of cooking. Its character shows a knife and a mouth. Maybe it is the earliest known ancestor of the highly popular kitchen god. We shall now turn to the people who were much like the deities, as they were so close to them. Let's discuss shamanism.

Shang Shamanism?

Welcome to a difficult subject. Several highly esteemed scholars have written about it and come to diametrically different conclusions, so, for fairness' sake, let us start somewhere close to the beginning. Once upon a time there were learned pioneers of anthropology. They sought to explain the customs of weird foreign savages, and when they wrote about ritualists, exorcists, healers and the like, the used expression such as *'witch doctor'* or *'medicine man'*. It wasn't a happy choice. More sensitive researchers began to look for better terms. Along came the word *'shaman'*. Originally, the term refers to a healer of the Tungus culture in Siberia. These people lived in the frosty evergreen taiga, where they herded reindeer, hunted, fished, collected berries and generally enjoyed a fair bit of isolation until the Russians conquered their homeland and started to exterminate them. It was Mircea Eliade (1951) who took the term shaman and began to apply it to similar Siberian cultures, and, with a bit of enthusiasm, to an entire class of ecstatic trance-healers world wide. And as *'shaman'* sounded much nicer than the earlier designations, the term was eagerly applied to any person vaguely fitting Eliade's definition. Let's sum up a few basics. According to him, shamans are usually persons who undergo a crisis, disease or form of temporal insanity, after which they encounter spirits in some state of trance or ecstasy, who provide teaching and support in healing. Shamanism, in this sense, is not a profession but a sacred vocation. It did not make them rich or popular; in fact, in many cultures, the few surviving shamans are shunned, feared or abused by the population. It happened under Stalin, who violently destroyed the custom, and it is happening in many enlightened countries that consider shamanism as exploitation of the superstitious. Even in South Korea, where mudang shamanism is gradually becoming popular again, the topic is generally avoided and people do not admit that they ever met a mudang. After all, it implies that they had trouble with ancestors, spirits or general bad luck and paid plenty of money for rituals that are definitely out of fashion.

In Siberia, the newly born shaman learns to perform trance journeys, such as flights to heaven or into the underworlds, where s/he gains power over the spirits and the human realm. Such experiences, Eliade assumed, involve ecstatic experiences, just like the rituals which follow. For when a shaman heals a person, a lot of wild and passionate behaviour, dancing, drumming and ecstatic trembling are required. And finally, shamans are supposed to be in control of fire and to demonstrate immunity to wounds and the like. All of this, Eliade assumed, was a contemporary expression of the earliest religions of mankind. Shamanism, so it was thought, was a relatively untainted survival of Stone Age healing rituals. And it made a nice contrast to the more dignified and controlled behaviour one would associate with priests. Provided one had European priests in mind, preferably of the last two centuries. Modern, rational people with a sense of dignity, who could be invited for tea and who wouldn't mess up the conversation.

All of this was an amazingly new way of thinking about religious experience. Earlier researchers had simply assumed that shamans are hysterics, epileptics and quacks who exploited the deluded simpletons of the icy north. And while some of their behaviour certainly involved deceit and showmanship, Eliade demonstrated that genuine spiritual experiences were involved. It was pretty good going for the time. Soon enough, every weird healer was classed as a shaman of sorts. And after this had gone on for a few decades, the term *'shaman'* had been so badly abused that the anthropologists began to shy away from it. Thanks to brilliant fraud-artists like Castañeda and the New Age movement, all it took to make a shaman was a crude drum, tobacco offerings and a few eco-minded sayings. What had started as a loose anthropological classification had become a commercial weekend-workshop industry. Nowadays, anthropologists prefer the term *'ritual specialist'*. It may be cautious and correct but means so very little. For in plain fact, human beings invent rituals all the time. It's one of those things that make us human.

Eliade's pioneering study cast light on a global phenomena but it also introduced several wrong assumptions. In Japanese miko *'shamanism'* for instance, the initiation disease is rare. In !Kung (Bushman) *'shamanism'*, ecstatic healing is a social affair in which most of the community spend the night singing, dancing and curing each other. In Korean mudang *'shamanism'*, the shaman may have had ecstatic initiations, but during a healing, it is the patient who tends to become ecstatic. And there is much more variation regarding ritual, music and trance performance. Some shamans travel into the otherworlds. Others call the spirits, ancestors, gods or whatever into themselves. And when it comes to describing the otherworldly ones, there are sprits who appear human, divine, animal, plant, group related, clan related, personally selected, family members and even some who are stones, mountains or whatever nature has to offer. The amount of variation within *'shamanism'* is enormous. Finally, it is glaringly obvious that not all cultures that practice *'shamanism'* live as hunter gatherers, or even as nomads. Some of them, like the Nepalese rama *'shamans'* do their healings for a society which herds sheep part of the year while living in settlements and practising agriculture besides. Others, like the Korean mudang, live in a modern society which dislikes their presence but has a stronger need for their services than ever. This is a far cry from allegedly primitive stone age ritualists. It shows that *'shamanism'* is not limited to hunter-gatherer or reindeer herder cultures. More so, it soon appeared that a good many *'shamanic'* practices, like otherworld journeys, divination, dancing, sacrifice etc were also common among priests and priestesses of various religions who did not use them in a healing context.

Where does this place the Shang? Perhaps Chen Mengjia was the first scholar who designated the royal activities as *'shamanic'*. In 1936, long before Eliade wrote his ground breaking book, Chen Mengjia pointed out that the Shang king personally divined and made prognostications. *"...There are, in addition, inscriptions describing the king dancing to pray for rain and the king prognosticating about a dream. All of these were activities of both king and shaman, which means, in effect that the king was a shaman."* (Chen Mengjia quoted in K.C. Chang, 1983:47). It was a cautious identification. Mengjia wanted to outline some of the similarities. And he was thinking of the native Chinese wu, instead of Tungus trance healers. Years later, enterprising scholars took the newly fashionable term *'shaman'* and applied it innocently to the Shang. The Shang, they proposed, lived in a *'shamanic'* society and the kings were the *'chief shamans'*. Likewise, bone divination was called *'shamanic'*. Probably because it seemed crude and smelly. All of this is so oversimplified that it hurts. There is no such thing as *'shamanic'* divination, there is simply divination. Some shamans practice one sort or another, but so does any card layer, lead caster or love-struck petal puller.

And the Shang kings? In some ways they acted like shamans. They interacted with a wide range of spirits, gods and ancestors on behalf of their society. But did they perform their rites in a state of ecstasy? We don't know. Nor is ecstasy a must. Many shamans only go ecstatic once in a while. For normal healing or ritual they simply go into an altered state. Now altered states are simply focused states that diverge from everyday awareness. In fact, for a skilled mind explorer, *'altered states'* are part of everyday experience. The more you are used to them the less do they show. Sure, it's impressive to bedazzle an audience or a suffering patient with crazy or ecstatic behaviour. Sometimes it's also helpful to bedazzle yourself. That doesn't mean that it's essential. Some *'altered states'* or trances may be so subtle that an outside observer wouldn't notice anything. When you trance a lot, you will learn to slip into trance and out of it without fuss. You may trance while sitting or lying, or you may learn how to go for long walks in deep trance states. It's easy. And it certainly doesn't require a drum or an instrument. These tools are simply useful to get a patient into trance. After all, much of the shamanism that Eliade explored came from Siberian cultures where shamans functioned mainly as healers. If you have a shaman in trance it's a good thing, as the trance may sharpen awareness for the patient's needs. Much more important, however, is a patient in trance, as this is the very state that will permit transformation of belief, thought and habit. A shaman's drum is a splendid tool to induce trance in other people. If you are any good at trancing, you won't need it for yourself. Nor is the drum a requisite. Plenty of Siberian cultures beat music bows to induce a trance in their patients, among them several Samoyedic cultures, Ugrians, Turkish people of southern Siberia and the central Asian Kirgiz people. Shamanic drums are often multipurpose instruments. Many types popular in Siberia, the Himalayas and Nepal have rattling pieces of metal or bells attached to the inside of the drum; the instrument can be beaten, shaken and swung around while dancing. Buryat and Soyot shamans used jaw harps for their invocations. Other Central Asian shamans made use of a lute, such as a balalaika (Stoltz, 1988:183). The same can be observed in Chinese shamanism, where string instruments were highly popular. In other cultures you find ritualists using scrapers, beating bells and pieces of wood, shaking rattles, blowing whistles and flutes and singing long and monotonous chants. All of these instruments are simply tools. They do not create the trance: trance is produced by the human nervous system and the brain.

K.C. Chang proposed that shamanic trances may have been induced by alcohol and other substances (1983:55). In his article in *The Formation of Chinese Civilization* (2005:129) he proposed that cannabis and a form of *"physical and mental exercises similar to today's qi gong"* may have been used. Sure enough, the Shang aristocracy drank lots, and added unknown plants and spices to their drink. Hemp was cultivated in China before the rest of the world learned what it is good for. So drugs are definitely a possibility. However, no drink or drug automatically induces shamanic or other trances. Most drinkers do not appear visionary or ecstatic, nor did the countless hippies on dope become shamans. Most of them simply had the giggles and the munchies, were somewhat disorganised for a while and then got a straight job and settled down in the middle class establishment. Not even mushrooms and acid guarantee spiritual experiences when set, setting and dose are wrong or the person lacks spiritual training. On the other hand, brain chemistry is a wonderful thing. Most drug effects can be simulated in deep trances, as can be experiences of synaesthesia and amplified sensory perception. What about Qigong? People in the West usually only know of a few basic types, such as the Silk Weaver exercises, the Play of Five Animals or the Healing Sounds. Qigong, however, has a lot more to offer than simple motion patterns combined with breathing and visualisation. There are forms of Qigong that use trembling and shaking to limber up the body, to activate the qi flow and to release tension. Here we enter shamanic territory, as shaking trances are typical in Chinese mediumism and ritual obsession; they also occur in some esoteric gongfu styles where people invoke a deity or an animal spirit, start shaking, are obsessed and begin to improvise motions with elegance and efficiency way beyond their normal skills. Likewise, there are meditations and breathing practices in advanced qigong that thoroughly transform awareness. There are so many ways of changing awareness. We can enjoy fast and excited trances, or relaxed and slow trances, introvert and extrovert, focus awareness, travel in the imagination, dissolve identity or make it encompass the whole multiverse. In shamanism, as in magick, mysticism and similar arts, all of these have their place. Fasting, shock, exhaustion, dancing, confusion, sex, sensory deprivation or overload and other tactics can disrupt everyday awareness, routine thinking and the limitations of a rigid personality. Time and space are not inbuilt: we learned them when we were infants. With a few shifts of the reality filters, the world can become an entirely different place. None of these effects happen automatically. They require training, devotion and plenty of practice.

Animal Shamanism and Rites of Rebirth

Were the Shang assisted by animal spirits? Here, the answer is a cautious yes. The totemic animals of people, family and clans are evident on the bronze vessels, on helmets, in ritual jades, grave gifts and so on. Many people had animal names, so we can assume that the animals were spiritually present. Also, when you use an animal ornamented vessel for offerings, the animals participate in the ritual, and may even conduct it to the otherworlds. Likewise, later Chinese myth is full of regents with animal attributes, and people who travel to Heaven and elsewhere on the back of dragons, serpents and birds, or who ride chariots across the sky. In Daoism, the spirits of animals or fantastic beasts who aid the adept in ritual and trance are called qiao. When you read that Zhuangzi dreamed to be a butterfly or that Lan Caihe flew skywards on the back of a crane, that Zhang Guolao shapeshifted and became a bat, that Yü transformed into a bear and that sages and poets flew to heaven on the back of dragons and snakes, we are in the realm of shamanic trance practice.

One useful hint comes from the Shang bronzes. A pair of very similar bronze zun jugs are exhibited in France and in Japan. They show a tiger-like spirit monster with wide open jaws (see the drawing p.252). Clinging to it is a human figure. Now the pair of vessels is similar but not quite identical. One has a figure with holes for ear rings and the other doesn't. Maybe we have a male and female figure. And they both seem to be wu, clinging to their animal spirits. K. C. Chang makes much of such works of art. A common theme of Shang art is a human head in the mouth of a tiger. One of the axes in the Fu Hao tomb is decorated with such an image. It fits beautifully with the common *'shamanic'* death and resurrection theme. The tiger is not necessarily a destructive carnivore. It is more like a spirit guardian who protects and initiates the wu shaman/ess. Initiation can mean death and rebirth. Sometimes the old personality has to die for a new and better one to be reborn. Countless *'shamans'* all over the world were devoured before they could do their job properly. It's one of

Serpents on Bone
Based on a Shang Carving in Hentze 1967:131

the better trances, as it gives you a fresh approach to life and a really open mind. Just ask Xiwangmu. Look at that grin and say goodbye to your past. Tigers were among the most popular shamanic power animals of south and east Asia. And they still are, among the minorities of Yunnan or in the far north where China meets Russia. And when you look at the Shang jug you can observe a monstrous, wonderful beast which incorporates bat, goat, snake, elephant (the tail is a trunk) and under the bottom, an engraved dragon. Like so many Shang beasts, it is a blend of many animals. And perhaps (allow me to be silly) the prototype of Hayao Miyazaki's *My Neighbour Totoro*.

Did the Shang regents travel into the otherworlds? Perhaps they did. There are, as detailed in the chapter on meditation, indications that in China, special regents went to heaven, or explored the dangerous far west. Some inscriptions mention that the king ascended to an ancestor, just as some ancestors ascended to meet other ancestors. And, as K.C. Chang points out, the character bin, to host (or to guest) (p.707) can be understood in two ways. Either the king received a visit from a spirit or Di, or the king went travelling to them. We simply don't know. But we can be sure they met somehow.

It is harder to trace the shamanic disease, i.e. the typical period of madness that used to be a classical initiatory experience in Siberia. Potential shamans of the Siberian cultures used to suffer from diseases and strange fits of temper, many hallucinated, went crazy, disappeared into the forest for months or spent lengthy periods withdrawn from society, half starved, or in total silence, before the spirits appeared to them. Some of them died in the wilderness, others remained mad for life. Austerities were a standard requisite in Siberian shamanic training (Buddruss, 1987; Stolz 1988). The same happened in many other cultures, only that the candidates did not have to suffer from disease or insanity. Japanese miko shamanism stresses the importance of austerities, and candidates spend long periods in isolation, memorizing sacred texts and standing under waterfalls. Yamabushi perform meditations between fires, go for extensive pilgrimages and perform numerous rituals that induce exhaustion. (Blacker, 1986). Korean mudang and paksu shamans frequently learn about their vocation during dreams. Some suffer from extensive periods of illness; others go spontaneously crazy, find themselves shaking or meet the spirits during some period of suffering and hardship. In addition, they undergo an extensive training in ritual, song, music, divination, proper preparation of ceremonial items and the communication skills to diagnose the patients (Cho Hung-Youn 1982; Kendall 1988; Shin-yong Chun 2001). When we look into Zhou period literature, we find King Wu Ding undergoing a three year period of deprivation, fasting, isolation and silence. To make the young regent Tai Jia fit to govern, Yi Yin banished him to the dark grove where Tang was buried, put him on a minimal diet and made him spend a few years in isolation. Likewise, Qi *'The Abandoned'*, the ancestor of the Zhou, started his life undergoing a thoroughly shamanic series of ordeals.

Regarding the outer aspects of *'shamanism'*, Shang ritual regularly involved dances and sacred music, such as piping and drumming. We simply can't tell whether it was calm and measured or ecstatic and wild. Nor do we know how ritualists and audience behaved. Perhaps they got carried away in a frenzy. Perhaps they just sat there and waited until it was over. Your guess is as good as anyone's. What did the kings and queens really do? I suspect that at least sometimes they were required to butcher an animal or human personally.

Is this enough to call the regents *'shamanic'*? It depends on what we call *'shamanic'*. I would prefer to say that the regents used shamanic trance techniques, if we could call them that. It's much more meaningful to look for trances and altered states than to wonder whether a given person fits in the artificial anthropological category *'shaman'*. And while the Shang kings may have used shamanic trance techniques or participated in *'shamanic'* rituals, they certainly had a different role. The Tungus shamans were healers, exorcists and mediums. The mediated between the patient and the unknown, they banished ill fortune and conducted bargains with the spirits of disease. The Shang regents did not heal; they were divine thearchs, stationed between heaven and earth in the centre of the universe. It was their job to mediate between the known and unknown, to interact between the world of humans and the realm of the spirits and gods. A person who fulfils such functions differs a lot from a tribal healer. We could call her or him *'shaman'* if we need to use this weary, tattered word. Or we could simply use the Chinese word wu, which is often and sometimes misleadingly translated as *'shaman'*.

Wu

Apart from the aristocrats and kings there were ritualists in Shang society who come much closer to the shaman's function. They were called wu, and a few of them exist right to this day. You could call them shamans, or spirit mediums, healers or exorcists, sorcerers or witches, depending on which function you emphasise. The wu did all of these jobs, and quite a few besides. Axel Schuessler (2007) traces the word wu (*'spirit medium, shaman'*) to the root mju, Later Han Chinese: mua, Minimal Old Chinese Form: *ma, Old Northwest Chinese (CE 400): muo. The Korean term mudang (female shaman) seems closely related, and the Japanese word miko (female shaman) is written with the same character. V. Mair proposed that the word might be a loan from Iranian *maghu or *magus, meaning an *'able one'*, a ritual specialist. Here we meet the Sanskrit term māyā, deriving from two word streams, one of them meaning deception, glamour, illusion, and another referring to skill, ability and skilful crafting. Closely related is the Indian goddess Māyā, who represents the world glamour, the fiction of separate existence and the delusive, wonderful and educational dance of all forms. You could say that a magus is a person who skilfully shapes glamour. These illusions are what other people call reality. The word wu might be cognate to the word mu (mother), hinting at the fact that a large number of Chinese wu (perhaps the majority) were women. Or it might relate to Xiwangmu. There is also another word *'wu'* meaning *'to deceive'*.

The Han period scholars described the wu and the zhu as priestly invokers and proposed that wu could be a homophone character for another wu, meaning *'dance'* (Strassberg, 2002). Wu ritualists of various types appear frequently in the histories of the Zhou and Han periods. In later times, they declined, but they never disappeared entirely.

To understand the Shang wu we have to relate a number of historical texts from the middle Zhou onwards with a handful of oracle bone inscriptions. What they have in common is, for a start, the character wu. In the oracle bones, wu was written as a cross with four T shapes extending in the directions. The T often refers to something sacred or divine, so the character could mean divinity extending in all directions. Considering how the Shang venerated the directions and their deities, this is a great title indeed. In bronze script and in modern Chinese, the character looks different. It consists of the radical *'work-related'* and the radical *'human'* twice. Call it work between humans. Or don't, as it sounds so badly like therapy. The wu character of the Shang also had a few other meanings. It could refer to a location (a place or state name) and to a clan. Maybe the shamanic profession was originally inherited in a clan, as T.T. Chang wonders, and this clan came from a place called Wu. In Shang society, family professions, such as farmer, herder, fisher, bronze caster, bone carver, stone smith etc. were probably the norm. Later generations may have used the name Wu as a general term for ritualists. T.T. Chang proposed that the Shang wu of period 1 and 2a were frequently engaged in the cult of the supreme god Di and performed sacrifices for the deities of nature, calmed the stormbird Peng and so on. He referred to the two famous wu who served the Shang kings according to the *Shiji* and the *Shujing* (1970:224-226). If his reading is accurate, the wu had an exalted position, and functioned like a priestly elite. This is a far cry from the shamanism of Siberian tribal healers. It does fit a number of wu from the Zhou period onward, who were highly educated and easily got along with the highest aristocracy. You'll read about them further on.

By contrast, Keightley states *"The oracle-bone graph wu was certainly ancestral to the later term wu 'spirit medium', but it is doubtful that it had such a meaning in the Shang inscriptions, where it appears, in a number of inscriptions, to have served as the name of a Power to whom the Shang offered cult."* (2002:72-74). He proceeded to quote a few inscriptions which read, in his rendering, that various sacrifices are offered to the wu. The graph he translates as *'to'* can also be read *'at'* (p.769). In which case, the sacrifices are not made *'TO wu'* but *'AT the place called wu'*. In his opinion, wu is a *'Power'* i.e. a deity, and he tries to define its jurisdiction without mentioning the possibility that the texts might refer to a place. Or to a person who incarnates a deity. It's called obsession and is one of the basics of much *'shamanism'*. Were the wu incarnate deities?

Now, personally, I was disappointed. Keightley offers so much brilliant research about other topics that such a swift dismissal hardly suffices. Puett notes: *"In contrast to both K. C. Chang and Julia Ching, David Keightley has convincingly questioned the prevalence (or even presence) of shamanism in bronze age China...Keightley argues, the transition to a state society involved a routinization and control of whatever shamanistic practices might have existed earlier. Shamanism as discussed by figures like Chang would have flourished at an earlier, pre-agrarian, hunter-gatherer stage of social development."*(2002:36-37).

So much depends on what we consider shamanic. If we accept Eliade's outdated assumption that shamanism is basically primitive Stone Age trance healing, neither the Shang kings nor the wu were proper shamans. However, the idea that anything from the Stone Ages could have survived untransformed through the millennia is rather naive. But isn't it strange that *'bronze age China'* under the Shang allegedly had given up shamanism for the sake of religious bureaucracy, when Zhou period and all later dynasties are full of people called wu who behave much like shamans do? And if *'wu'* was a directional power (deity) in the Shang period, how is it possible that the term shifted to human ritualists only a few centuries later? People who invoked, exorcised, healed, sacrificed, conjured spirits and so on?

Since then, the interpretation of *'wu'* among American oracle bone scholars has undergone further revision. Sarah Allan proposed that the sign looking like the letter H *'work related'* (radical: gong) shows a carpenter's square. In her interpretation, the carpenter's square represents the four directions of early Chinese cosmography, i.e. the fang directions. The character fang occasionally looks much like the character wu, except for the bottom bit, which takes its form from *'knife, fork spade'* (see p.768-769).

*"The central horizontal element (*of the character Di, JF*) can be understood as a carpenter's tool for drawing and making squares. This tool is shown in the oracle bone form of the character ju 'carpenter's square', where it is held in the hand of a standing man. Two such tools in the form of a cross form the oracle bone character (*wu*), This graph is usually transcribed as wu, 'shaman', and this transcription is probably valid for the diviner groups of the Northern Branch. However, where the Bin diviner-group (North Branch) has fang di (-ritual) and di (-ritual) (at/for) fang, the Shi and Li diviner-groups (South Branch) have wu di and di (at/for) wu. For example, in di yu bei fang 'offer the di-rite to the Northern quadrate', the graph for fang (quadrate) is written as wu. Thus, I have argued that wu is a variant form of fang in the Southern Branch diviner groups."* (2007:22, with my comments in brackets and without the Chinese characters). Here, Allan's proposal interprets what T.T. Chang considered a place name as a sacred direction, as one of the fang quarters of the Shang universe. As the directions were also deities, Keightley's concept of a directional deity could also make sense. However, we cannot be sure how the sacred fang directions functioned within the context of the Di ritual. Was it a ritual for Di in the north or a di ritual for the Northern deity/Direction? Should Di be read as a noun, for a supreme deity or a whole cluster of them, or as a verb, as in *'ritual of the di type'*? At the time being, this question is hard to answer: we simply don't know enough about the ritual. More so, as you can see when you look at the inscriptions (p.563-565), many can just as easily be read with wu as *'ritualist'* and wu as *'sacred direction/directional deity'*. With regard to the character Di, it is not even certain whether it refers to the supreme deity/s or to the di-ritual or the ritual for Di. Nor can we rule out the possibility of scribal errors. It doesn't take much inattention to write Di instead of Di ritual (with its rectangle instead of the horizontal bar), nor to write wu instead of fang, provided you use the less common form of fang which consists of three T shapes. Given that there are numerous open questions to entertain future generations of sinologists, and that the debate is far from over yet, we might perhaps look at a few examples of wu in Zhou and Han period literature.

Wu in the Shang Period:

-*Shujing.* Yi Yin complains to young Tai Jia *"that if you dare to have constant dancing in your mansions, and drunken singing in your homes, I call it wu fashion"*.

Zhushu Jinian: Wu Xian sacrificed at mountains and rivers under the reign of Tai Wu.

Shijing: During the reign of Tai Wu, Wu Xian took successfully care of the imperial household and composed two (lost) documents of the *Shujing*. Under Zu Yi, another Wu Xian (descendant of the earlier Wu) held office.

Wu in the Zhou Period

-*Guoyu*, also in *Shijing*: year 878. King Li of Wei uses his wu to spy on the people and report those who speak ill of him.

-*Zhouli*. Court ritual involves two leaders of the wu, officers of middle rank, who are granted a store keeper, and adjunct and ten serfs. They perform ceremonies and dances when drought prevails and rituals to expel calamities from the kingdom. They are also guardians of soul tablets, bury offerings at sacrifices and perform rites which make the soul descend to the grave.

The wu at court are of both sexes. The male wu invoke spirits at the sacrifices and expel evil influences in winter, when yin power dominates. In spring, they invoke the gods and exorcise disease demons. When the sovereign makes a visit of condolence, they walk alongside with invokers and conjurers. The female wu perform exorcisms at fixed times during the year and use ablutions with aromatics. In times of draught they perform dances and gestures during rain making ceremonies. During imperial condolence visits, they walk with the female invokers and conjurers. When great disasters threaten the realm they beseech gods and spirits by chanting and wailing.

A type of exorcist called Rescuer of the Country appears at ceremonial processions wearing a bear hide, masked with four eyes of yellow metal, brandishing shield and spear, who expels demons. At funerals, this person jumps into the freshly excavated tomb to banish evil earth spirits.

-*Zuoshuan*. 650 BCE. A prince receives advice from a ghost who speaks out of the mouth of a wu.

580 BCE. A wu makes predictions about disease spirits who are destroying the health of the Duke of Jin. She prophesies that the duke will not live to eat fresh grain from the coming harvest. When the harvest is gathered, the ailing duke calls the wu for a reckoning. He has her killed but before he gets a chance to taste the grain, he comes to a messy death in the latrine.

-*Guoyu*, c. 500 BCE. King Zhao enquires about a document in the *Shujing*. He is told that in ancient times, heaven and earth were closely connected and that there used to be exceptional, dedicated people who were called xi when they were men and wu when they were women, who could make the spirits descend. They regulated the rituals and offerings, so everything was properly sorted out and natural disasters did not occur. But when people became lawless, they insisted on doing the wu rites for themselves. Spirits and people lost their respect for each other and finally, the connection between heaven and earth had to be cut to prevent total chaos (for full detail, see the chapter on Zhuanxu)

Bear Taotie

-Liji: the wu had their place in front of the sovereign. When regents went to the funeral of a minister, they were accompanied by a wu and an invoker who carried demon dispelling pieces of peach wood and reeds.

The character *'healer'* (wu yi) is a combination of *'medical art'* and *'wu'*. Kongzi quoted the southern proverb *"of a man without constancy nobody can make a wu yi'. This is well said."*

Zhouli: male wu exorcised *'countless and innumerable'* influences from the royal halls in wintertime. Female wu performed exorcisms at fixed times during the year.

Shanhaijing: In chapter eleven appears a brief reference to six wu who carry the corpse of one I yu. He has the shape of a serpent with human face and was slain by a minister of Er Fu. His nature, and the reason why the wu are carrying him remain unknown. We are also informed about the kingdom of Wu Xian. Wu Xian lives north (i.e. below. Old Chinese maps have north down and south up) of Nü Chou (Ugly Woman). He holds a blue snake in his right hand and a red snake in his left. His residence is on Deng Bao Mountain, on the slopes of which the wu are all moving up and down (chapter 7). Perhaps the passage connects with another mountain in chapter 16 where ten famous wu go (or fly) up and down the slopes, searching for hundreds of medical herbs. K.C. Chang counted 23 references to wu in the *Shanhaijing*. Most of them are frustratingly brief.

Chuci, Lisao: Retired statesman Qu Yuan devotes his poetry to complaints about the king who had not treasured his advice. He mentions that he is now pursuing the way of Wu Xian and Wu Peng (peng means drum) and describes two journeys through heaven and the otherworlds, where he meets diverse deities, the ancestress of the Shang Dynasty, the wives of Shun and searches for what seems to be a personal deity or spirit mate.

Lüshi Chunqiu: immortality seekers perform breathing exercises and feed on dew, sitting at the feet of Wu Xian.

- *Shijing* about the year 201 BCE: the emperor instituted sacrifices at Changan, at the imperial residence. He employed wu from the districts Liang, Jin, Qin, Jing, the Yellow River and from the southern mountains. Each of these groups performed its own sacrifices and ceremonies to specific deities and ancestors at regulated dates.

-*Shijing* and *History of the Former Han*: Handwudi, the *'Martial thearch of the Han'* was fascinated by the occult, and frequently invited sages, alchemists, fangshi (method masters) and wu to his court, where they celebrated rituals and offerings and told remarkably unlikely stories. When age approached, Hanwudi became increasingly suspicious and paranoid. He ordered a wu hunt in 130 BCE, which ended with an unknown number of heads exposed on stakes. The one he ordered in 91 BCE was a lot worse, and much better documented. One fine day it was reported that the king's personal guard had discovered a wooden effigy buried in the ground in the inner chambers of the palace. It was an unlikely story, but the ailing old king, residing in a palace outside the capital was in no mood to take risks. Ministers and officials accused each other of having employed wu to direct wugu (written wu + vermin) sorcery against his majesty, and before long the guards were torturing people to force confessions from them. The affair became so violent and threatening that officials were suspected of rebellion, nobles fled, others fought and finally the crown prince himself was suspected. The king, in very poor health and desperately afraid of his life had whole families exterminated. In the end, the troops of the king and the crown prince fought it out, right in the centre of the capital. The city gates were closed, and between the panicking citizens, the mounted warriors, archers and charioteers five days of desperate slaughter occurred. In the end, the crown prince fled and several tens of thousands of people were dead. Finally, the crown prince was found and executed on the spot. The king, feeling small relief when he heard the news, began to wonder if he had made a mistake. Sima Qian gave a lively account of the event; he loathed Hanwudi for personal reasons and had barely escaped with his life. It was not the only such wu hunt. In 89 BCE another wu purge occurred, and armed troops randomly arrested people they suspected of wugu sorcery or dissent. It did not end when the emperor died.

-*Books of the Early Han Dynasty*: Hanwudi's sons struggled for the throne, and the wu were also involved. One of the princes, Liu Xu, king of Guangling, was advised by the refined wu lady Li Nüxu. She became obsessed by the spirit of the dead emperor and prophesied that Liu Xu would become the royal successor. To this end she made sacrifices for him on the Wu Shan, the shaman's mountain. She advised the prince for several years and conducted numerous divinations for him. Nevertheless, the royal succession kept evading him. Liu Xu ordered his wu and several associates to use sorcery against the emperor. When the whole undertaking was betrayed, the wu, all her ritual helpers and every other associate were poisoned. Then Liu Xu profusely apologised to the emperor, spent a fine night singing, dancing and celebrating with his favourite concubine and strangled himself in the morning.

-*Zhuangzi* and *Liezi*: A wu (of unknown sex) trains young Liezi. A Daoist interveners and demonstrates the superiority of Daoism over wujia.

-*History of the Late Han Dynasty*: In the year 96, another wu purge occurred, when Deng Zhu, the grandmother of empress Yin was accused of practicing wugu, here described as spells and incantations. She was accused of treachery and heterodox practices and died in exile. Several of her close relations were tortured, executed or committed suicide and the whole clan was banished from the court until the year 110.

We could go on like this for quite a while. Now for a summary. During the Zhou and Han period, some wu enjoyed a high status at court. They were expected to sing and dance, several drummed or played string instruments, and among their main tasks were sacrifice and exorcism. They were also frequently obsessed by ghosts, who spoke through them. This function keeps recurring in Chinese history; there were quite a few power hungry princes who were told by inspired wu that the throne would eventually be theirs. Educated wu, many of them (possibly the majority) female, got along well with the aristocracy. Far from being primitive wonder healers, they enjoyed a status which is rare among practitioners of 'shamanic' trance techniques. Nevertheless, they were frequently dreaded, feared and persecuted.

Outside the aristocracy, wu had a place in folk religion. These matters are less well documented as most scholars simply didn't care about common people and their 'superstitions'.

Wu married young people to river and mountain deities. Sometimes it meant a withdrawn and chaste life, as nobody dared to marry a person who was already married to a deity. But as the *Shijing* relates regarding the year 400 BCE, it could also end in a human sacrifice. Sima Qian recorded that an elderly wu lady with a troop of attendants toured the countryside to select a suitable bride for the river deity. She made a great profit, as parents paid enormous bribes to ensure their daughters would not be chosen. Once a bride was elected, she was paraded around the district and received veneration. After much festivity, she was ceremonially married to the river god, placed on a bed, and sent drifting on the current. Soon the bed sank and she met her end in the swirling waters. The upright minister Xi Menbao made a name for himself drowning the wu instead. The whole custom, whether lethal or not, ended when government officials decreed that the wu were only permitted to marry their own family members to deities (*Books of the Late Han Dynasty* on the year 57 BCE). Wu were also occasionally sacrificed to end a period of drought, usually by exposing them to the sun until they died. It happened in the hope that heaven would be compassionate to them and send rain (*Zuoshuan*, year 639 BCE and *Liji* regarding Mu (403 – 377BCE).

We have wu who sing, drum and dance, while others use string instruments like lutes to invoke gods and spirits. Some were famed for dream oracles, some for clairvoyance and sage political advice. Others abused their status and became entangled in intrigue, spell casting and power politics. The picture remains sadly incomplete. We read about wu who were in

River Lord

direct contact with the aristocracy, but there is little information on wu among common people. Were the wu healers? Who healed the early kings and queens? The oracle bones don't tell us. And so it continues. Before long, the wu became the object of scorn for the Confucians, who did much to break their status. The Daoists assumed a lot of functions the wu used to have earlier, and finally we encounter wu who are but low level spirit mediums. Even their job as healers went into the hands of the newly founded medical profession. Their function as diviners was usurped by Daoists and fangshi scholar-sorcerers. So the wu fell out of favour with most regents. However, each time a bunch of central Asian *'barbarians'* overran China and set up their own emperor, they brought along wu, who acted at the highest political level and enjoyed much power. It rarely lasted for long. As soon as the new emperors had been properly *'civilised'* and assumed a Confucian mindset, their wu fell from power again. But they never really died out. Wu mediums still make a living in Taiwan, as Saso remarks, and among the southern and western Chinese minorities, in Inner Mongolia and along the Amur River, shamanism is alive. Minority customs are protected and cherished nowadays and have become major folkloric attractions. It produced such wonderful research institutes as the Museum of Dongba Culture in Lijiang (easily worth a stay of several days) and a number of less authentic enterprises with colourfully dressed actors entertaining tourists.

Divine Government

Shang period China was a thriving theocracy. Theocracy means that church and state are a single institution and that the regent is divine or functions as a representative of the divine. As far as can be discerned, there were plenty of theocracies in the ancient world. The Egyptian culture, for example, was a theocracy: the pharaoh represented the highest rank of incarnate divinity. He wasn't completely divine, however, as his body remained subject to disease and age, and as he, like the gods themselves, was bound to obey the principles of ma'at: truth, justice and order. The royal house and the aristocracy also functioned as high priests and priestesses, and even small children could have the nominal control over important cult centres: good evidence, that the job did not always require brains, maturity or spiritual training. We observe similar ideas in ancient Europe: some Celts had a thing about divine regents and ancestor worship, at least until the oppidum phase of the La Téne period. Many Germanic kings derived their ancestry from gods: Geat, Gautr and Gapt and Getam are names of Wodan (or possibly an ancestor of Wodan), and appear prominently in the ancestry of the Anglo Saxon kings, the Goths and several related tribes. Medieval Europe was still fascinated by the divine right of kings and the Catholic Church employs a pope as a religious and secular head. There are theocracies where the regents represent the divine and theocracies where the regents function as mediators with Absolute Reality, as in Buddhist kingdoms like Thailand and Bhutan. It does not always happen that way. The Sumerian civilisation, which predates the Egyptian by a few centuries, evolved along different lines. Sumerian kings started out as *'strong men'* in village groups. Their reign was by no means divine: indeed, the kings usually derived a large part of their authority from the custom of the sacred marriage that was conducted between the king and the highest ranking priestess, usually a representative of the goddess Inanna. In this system, a king had divine blessing, especially when he came from the royal family, but the priesthood as mediators between the divine and mankind gave his government the necessary approval. It wasn't the separation between state and church that is common in our age, but it was certainly a step in that direction.

Let's have a look at ancient China. There is no evidence regarding government in the Palaeolithic stage and the Neolithic farming communities are not sufficiently explored to jump to conclusions. However, the layout of villages and cemeteries suggests that society was less stratified than in Shang times, and less rigid than in the following Zhou period.

People were poorer, wealth was more evenly distributed and it is hard to discern a developed aristocracy. Nor was warfare such an issue: though the early farmers sometimes came to a violent end, many settlements did without fortification. Professional soldiers and, indeed, professions were yet to be developed. We can observe these developments during the Longshan period, when settlements became larger, the infrastructure developed and people made their first experiments with pounded earth foundations and walls, large buildings, drainage and well organised trade systems. In the late Longshan period (corresponding to the mythical Xia Dynasty), skilled artisans and craftsmen hold jobs, there are workshops for ceramic ware of several sorts, for stone tools, bone objects, jade and, eventually, the first bronze foundries. In Shang times, the situation developed further. Shang society consisted of classes: an aristocracy which supplied regents, ministers and various ritualists, a range of professional artisans, traders, soldiers, miners, engineers, architects and craftsmen, and a lot of farmers, cattle breeders, shepherds and fishers. In addition, a small number of slaves and prisoners of war were employed. The royal family, the Zi clan, occupied most of the important religious and political positions, and the king as the highest worldly authority and also the highest priest, ritualist and diviner. In Shang thought, there was no division between a *'spiritual'* and a *'political'* authority, just as there was no boundary dividing the 'sacred' from the 'profane'. Around the capital, the fiefs were governed by royal relations or by relations in marriage: the idea that competence is better than a pedigree didn't become popular until the late Zhou. The royal house was under constant pressure to keep a lot of independently minded allies and vassals under control, and religious activity was one clear status marker. As long as the king was directly in touch with the gods and ancestors, the noble families of allied realms, tribes and cultural groups stood no chance to compete with him. When Wu Ding divined, prognosticated, sacrificed or related his oracular dreams, he gave evidence that he was closer to the divine than the rest of the world. Indeed, the whole impressive religious machinery of the late Shang, involving ceremonial conduct, etiquette, music, dance, drugs, a wide range of rituals and their special tools, divination, writing, historical records, human and animal sacrifice, advanced metallurgy, grandiose wealth, trade connections, large buildings and excessive burial rites on can be considered a tool to impress outsiders with the divine status of the Zi clan. For the neighbouring cultures, some of which were not even dwelling in settlements, the grandeur of the Shang kings must have been mind blowing. Religion can be a tool to keep people on their knees. Several contemporary scholars take this point of view, and analyze Shang religion purely from a political point of view. When we assume that religion is plain superstition, the whole thing appears like deception, manipulation and power politics. However, to understand the Shang we ought to observe them from the mind set of their own age. Shang civilisation was hugely successful. In spite of a few mediocre kings from time to time, the Shang created a nucleus for Chinese civilisation. Such achievements were only possible by getting along with ancestors, deities and Di. Wu Ding honestly believed in divinations, rituals, dreams and sacrifices, in angry ancestors and dangerous deities. He considered his success in war and the advances in technology, writing, social organisation a mark of ancestral and divine favour. The same can be said for the regents of period 2a, 3 and 4. Whether the regents of period 2b and 5a and b shared this attitude remains a tricky question. One of the things that make the Shang so fascinating is that we can observe, in the span of maybe 250 years, a religion undergoing several drastic changes.

When the Zhou eliminated the last Shang regent, they were highly concerned to give a similar divine status to their own royal family. They probably invented the the Mandate of Heaven, defined what it said in the small print, and did much to demonstrate that they were up to it. Though they simply imitated a lot of Shang ritual during the first century of their reign, they became increasingly fascinated by elaborate and complicated ritual performances, and were soon making up their own. Many of these functioned, just as the Shang rites had, to impress outsiders with the divine power of the royal family. This was immensely important, as only a few early Zhou regents were successful in their job. When the Western Zhou period ended in 771 BCE, the royal family lost so much prestige that their reign became a symbolic rigmarole, and China was torn by centuries of civil wars as the lords fought it out among themselves. Much of the ritual format remained as it had been after the late Western Zhou ritual reform, but in the new age, the validity of religion, faith, ancestral worship, deities etc. was increasingly questioned. While Kongzi and others insisted that the core of religion and ritual had always been the same, and that little had changed since the days when Yŭ fought the flood, they hoped to provide a new and reformed code of conduct with an impressively old appearance, and to add some stability to an age of violence, treason and social disruption. They had good intentions but were not always reliable historians. Here it may be useful to compare a few Zhou rituals with the earlier Shang rites.

Zhou Ritual

While the Shang devoted themselves to the worship of the ancestors, and, in periods 1, 2a, 3 and 4, to a range of nature and other deities, the *Liji* (chapter *Jifa*) relates that middle and late Zhou ritualists divided the pantheon into three groups. The tianshen (Heavenly Deities/Spirits), the diqi (Earthly Gods) the rengui (Ancestral Deities/Ghosts) were worshipped along very strict regulations. Only the emperor, as the Son of Heaven, was qualified to perform all sacrifices. He was also the only one who could perform the tianshen sacrifices. He performed this duty in the suburbs during the first month of the ritual calendar. The fact that no one but he could sacrifice to Heaven undoubtedly supported his exalted station. Sacrifices to the earth god Shi, and the grain god Ji were also part of the imperial ritual schedule, as well as offerings to the ghosts of unhappy kings, the door and gate guardians, the kitchen god, the deities of the roads, the central court and others. He also offered every month at seven ancestral temples, including for his father, grandfather, great-grandfather, great-great grandfather and the high ancestor. He had two temples for the remote ancestors, who only received seasonal sacrifices, while the very remote ancestors remained unfed *"in their ghostly state"*.

The aristocracy was entitled to a specific range of rituals. As an emperor, you had seven ancestral temples, as a feudal lord (zhu hou) you had five temples, and sacrificed to father, grandfather and great grandfather on a monthly schedule, while great-great grandfather and the high ancestors only received seasonal offerings. Ancestors who preceded the high ancestor could have an altar, or, if even more remote, a special area, but sacrifices to them were generally neglected. You had to perform ritual for the local deities of your fief; but those outside of your realm could be ignored. Again, this was a late innovation. The early Zhou still had much respect for the Yellow River Deity, but in the Spring and Autumn Period, those who governed provinces far from the river learned to ignore it.

As a grand master (dafu) you had three temples for father, grandfather and great-grandfather, and the latter only received seasonal offerings. Should an earlier ancestor deserve an offering, he had to make do with a temporal altar. As a small noble (shi) two ancestral temples did the job, and only the father got monthly offerings. An officer was entitled to one temple for his father, where the grandfather also received offerings. All other ancestors were neglected. Commoners were entitled to offer sacrifices to the door god Hu and the kitchen god Zao. Both of them were essential for the household; the door god protecting the house from evil influences from outside and the kitchen god controlling the central harmony of the family. Both of them are eminently important if you want to lead a happy life. However, they had a small status compared to the other deities. So much regarding ritual among the Zhou, or regarding the ritual attributed to the early Zhou by late Zhou scholars and well meaning editors of the Han Dynasty. No doubt, actual worship was a lot more complicated, especially in the formative stage during the Western Zhou period.

How does such a division compare to earlier Shang ritual? For a start, the monthly and seasonal offerings are a Zhou innovations. Some Shang regents sacrificed on demand, others adhered to the five ritual schedule, and both of these methods differ from the Zhou routine. How many altars the aristocracy employed in Shang times is unknown. The Shang, unlike the Zhou, held the remote ancestors in very high esteem, and generally they were more terrifying than the recent ancestors, and received larger offerings. The Shang also sacrificed to a range of ancestresses, including queens, ritualists and *'the many mothers'*, whose importance disappeared early in the Zhou period. The Western Zhou occasionally sacrificed to grandmothers, but in later literature, like the *Liji*, the female ancestors are not worth consideration. A kitchen god was probably worshipped in Shang times, though s/he was of minor importance to the royal family and we don't know much about her/him. A deity of the doorways is unknown; though there is a deity written as double doors and fire (or mountain) who might fit the bill. The royal ancestors were worshipped by aristocrats living around the capital, if only as they were usually family members, or had married into the royal clan. How things worked among the allies and vassals remains unknown. The only thing we can be reasonably sure about is that the Zhou division into three ritual groups was not practiced during the Shang period. Heavenly spirits remain a topic of scholarly debate, while divining about worship of an earth deity is restricted to periods 1, 2a, 3 and 4. While it can be argued that the late Shang became increasingly interested in the concept of a divine Heaven, they certainly didn't make such an issue out of it as the Zhou did.

Visions of the Past

Let's have another look at the *Book of Rites* (*Liji*). One topic that comes up frequently is the conduct of the great sage regents of the earlier times. Here, we encounter two distinct approaches. One of them is the cultivation of virtue, as it was proposed by Kongzi and his followers, who believed that inner cultivation, conduct, love, respect and due performance of the rites were roads to refinement that would lead to a perfect state, or at least a state that wasn't continuously engaged in warfare, debauch and corruption. The other approach comes closer to history: it cites examples of rituals that may or may not have been performed in the somewhat mythical past. Here is another passage from the chapter *Jifa*, in Legge's translation:

"With a blazing pile of wood on the Grand altar they sacrificed to Heaven; by burying (the victim) in the Grand mound, they sacrificed to the Earth. (In both cases) they used a red victim. By burying a sheep and a pig at the (altar of) Great brightness, they sacrificed to the seasons. (With similar) victims they sacrificed to (the spirits) of cold and heat, at the pit and the altar, using prayers of deprecation and petition; to the sun, at the (altar) called the royal palace; to the moon at the (pit called the) light of the night; to the stars at the honoured place of gloom; to (the spirits of) flood and drought at the honoured altar of rain, to the (spirits of the) four quarters at the place of the four pits and altars; mountains, forests, streams, valleys, hills, and mounds, which are able to produce clouds, and occasion wind and rain, were all regarded as (dominated by) spirits. He by whom all under the sky was held sacrificed to all spirits. The princes of states sacrificed to those which were in their own territories; to those which were not in their territories, they did not sacrifice."

A few comments may be useful here. In this passage, we encounter an odd blend of what might be early Zhou ritual and prior practices. To begin with, sacrifices to Heaven as such are a doubtful issue among the Shang, though we have to consider that Shang Di and the ancestors could have been representatives of what the Zhou considered Heaven. Red victims appear a few times in Shang inscriptions, but some scholars read them as yellow. White and black animals are also on record, but do not appear in the Zhou account. Nor does the specification of male or female animals; it doesn't happen often, but it does indicate some symbolic meaning that is lost on us. Where the *Liji* lists specific types of offerings for each spiritual entity, the Shang were a great deal more inventive. Nor does the topic of human sacrifice appear: the late Zhou literati went to extreme lengths to purge it from the historical record. Sacrifices to cold and heat and to sun and moon do not appear prominently in Shang inscriptions, indeed, it is entirely possible that they were not performed at all.The *'pits'* in our text are hollows scooped out on top of the earth altar mounds. Such mounds may well date to the Shang and earlier: the character of the earth deity could show such a mound. Likewise, sacrifices and offerings of drink and blood at Shang altars are easily testified. Spirits (or deities) of the four quarters, mountains, forests, streams, hills etc appear prominently in Shang ritual, though they did not quite get as much attention as the ancestors did. And while the Shang certainly observed the Heavens for omina and signs, and probably designated certain stellar constellations to various seasons, they did not bother to devote much worship to the stars. Stellar worship, a notable passion of the Zhou, is rather hard to prove in earlier times. Let's start with this topic as we explore Shang ritual.

Worship of the Stars

The ritual started with divination. On the thirty third day of the ritual calendar, Bing Shen, diviner *'Bell-stroke'* asked the oracle whether on the coming yi-si (day 42) a sacrifice for ancestor Xiao Yi ought to be performed. Xiao (Little, Young) Yi, otherwise known as Zu (grandfather) Yi had reigned several generations before the present regent, Wu Ding. The yi day was his sacrificial date, and the diviner wished to know if a wine spilling (and swilling) would be acceptable. The matter was brought before King Wu Ding, who examined the plastron and announced that wine spilling might result in trouble, and that perhaps the sacrifice ought to involve smashing a wine vessel.

We are lucky to know what happened next. On the yi-si day, wine was spilled at the sunrise. It was raining heavily. This seemed inauspicious to the court, and so the ritualists improvised and tried to placate ancestor Xiao Yi by beheading a person. The rain continued to pour down. Another person was beheaded for dynastic ancestor Tang the Successful (here called by his name Xian). The rain continued. Finally, the constellation Bird Star received a serpent sacrifice. The snake was probably beaten to death and split open.

A final note on the reverse of the plastron tells us: *"On the evening or night of day Yi Si day a wine vessel was smashed to the West (or: for Deity West)"*.

So much for a brief account of a wet and unhappy morning of highly spiritual activity. It could have happened like that. But, you guessed it, we just can't be sure. As with many longer texts,

Wine and Lead
Based on the faces of three Shang Ho Vessells, nowadays in the Nezu
Collection, Japan

the inscription allows for several interpretations (p.517). I have largely (but not completely) followed T.T. Chang's interpretation (1970:203). Chang assumed that Wu Ding predicted that there might be an accident: a wine vessel might break. In my opinion that doesn't sound very likely, unless the ritual was performed in a highly ecstatic or drunk way and the vessels were badly made. A deliberate sacrifice seems more likely. Quite a few ancient cultures made sacrifices in which vessels or valuable goods were deliberately destroyed. David Keightley (1978: 88) interprets the sign *'breaking wine vessel'* in a different way. The character looks similar to another one showing a hand striking a vaguely triangular object. Both of them have some similarity to a third character, *'striking jade chime'*. Maybe we are dealing with one sign in several variations and maybe it was three signs with different meanings. Keightley assumes that it doesn't show a ritual vessel smashing at all but has a purely phonetic meaning for an anomalous and inauspicious natural phenomena. In this reading, the king predicted that wine spilling would be disastrous as this unlucky atmospheric phenomenon would occur. Ken-Ichi Takashima (2005:11-29) takes an even more radical position. To begin with, he offers the idea that *'inauspicious'* (written as: fur garment, piece of pelt) should be read as *'killed, cut'* for phonological reasons. He proposes that the glyph for *'wine spilling'* should be read as *'performing the sacrifice beautifully'*; in his reading the *'drops'* represent sunrays. If the sun was required for the sacrifice, a miserable wet morning in steady downpour would have been inauspicious indeed. He reads the glyph for *'smashing wine vessel'* as *'thunder'*, while questioning the traditional reading of *'two mouths connected by an S'* as thunder, and finally demolishes the long accepted reading *'bird star'*, by citing Li Xueqin's disproval of the term. Li proposed *'quickly'* instead of *'bird'*, but Takashima disagrees with this reading as well. Finally, the term *'star'* is questioned; here, Yang Shuda and Li Xueqin are cited for a reading that goes *'all cleared up and turned sunny'*. If we accept this reading, the *'smashed Wine vessel'* sacrifice is a thunderclap and the sacrifice, instead of being offered to the bird star constellation, was performed quickly, and then the sun came out. Robert Eno (in Lopez, 1996:48) proposes that the king divined thunder. Here, the bird star is a constellation, but it got two offerings. But it gets more complicated still. I'm sure you'll like this.

In Chang's reading it rained all the time, but in Keightley's the rainfall ceased (briefly) after the first beheading, to continue soon after. And the post scriptum on the reverse of the plastron suffers from the same problem as the inscription itself. Either a wine vessel was ritually smashed to the West, or for Deity West, or this unspecified weather phenomenon occurred in the western direction. Eno translates that in that evening, there was thunder in the west. Here, I find Chang's reading more likely, as it relates to a sacrifice, i.e. to an activity which is under human control. If we accept Keightley's or Takashima's reading, the king must have been enormously clairvoyant or weather cunning to predict an unusual, inauspicious weather phenomenon, or a lonely thunderclap, ten days in advance.

And finally, there's the name of dynastic founder Tang. He is not called by his usual name but by a title (Xian). This title, however, can also be read as *'All'* or *'Complete'*, depending on whether the ideogram axe plus mouth and axe plus square happen to be identical or different. Quite a few scholars disagree over the matter. If we read *'all'* or *'complete'*, the sacrifice could be completed without any reference to Tang. Now go back to the inscription and imagine the ritual in several ways. It's a great example how a few simple characters can be read in different ways.

The ritual was certainly remarkable. It might record the only known case in which the Shang sacrificed to a star or constellation. Some experts, such as Eberhard, assumed that stellar worship was a foundation of Shang religion, mainly as it was a popular thing among the Zhou. But although the Shang observed the heavens and wondered whether unusual stellar events, such as a super nova might portent disaster, they were evidently not given to perform much sacrifice to celestial bodies. We might even wonder whether the sacrifice was to the Bird Star/s at all. Perhaps the star got an offering or it was just the season of its rising that required worship. What bird are we talking about? If it referred to a swallow, the rising of the star might indicate the beginning of spring. On the other hand, the sign definitely shows no swallow. It looks a lot more like another dark bird, the crow or raven. The Shang had a perfectly good character signifying *'swallow'*. The return of the swallows was important to the kings. But the bird star wasn't written with the swallow character. Was the *'dark bird'* that started the royal Zi clan a swallow or a raven?

Sun and Moon

And was the raven related to the sun in the Shang period, as was the case in the late Zhou? Did the Shang worship the sun at all? You find such claims in very early studies. There may be some truth to it, but the case is not as simple as it seems. For one thing, the word day and sun are identical. A sacrifice AT day X can also be read as a sacrifice FOR the sun on day x. Most scholars tend to prefer the earlier reading, and some doubt that solar worship happened at all. Nevertheless, there may have been indirect solar worship. Remember that each dead king and queen received a temple name for sacrifice. This was a day name, and as the ten day week might be an expression of the ten suns, it could be argued that each ancestor came to represent a sun. Or that each of the ten suns was represented by a growing number of ancestors. If this were true, each ancestral sacrifice would also be a sacrifice for one of the suns. It's quite a good idea. But in all fairness I have to add that it is also possible that the dead were pragmatically named for sacrificial days, not for the suns they may or may not have represented. It depends on how much meaning a given day-name has. In English, Friday is the day of goddess Freya, Sunday the day of the sun, Monday the day of the moon and so on. Look at Christianity. Good Friday is not a celebration of Freya, Palm Sunday does not celebrate the Sun nor is Easter Monday a moon rite. Here, the week names are simply conveniences. What was it like for the Shang?

Let us continue with lunar worship. Here we run into trouble with translations. Some oracle bone pioneers assumed that offerings were made for the moon. It depends on whether we read one of the most common grammatical particles as *'at'* or *'for'* (p.769). During the Shang period, both readings were possible. Later scribes decided that life would be easier and happier with distinct terms for the two ideas. It isn't very convenient to use only one character, the lunar crescent, for moon, month, evening and night. Nowadays, such words have distinct characters. The Shang didn't bother about such details yet. Hence a sacrifice FOR the MOON may also be a sacrifice AT NIGHT. Presently, scholarly consensus much prefers the latter reading. Modern Chinese distinguishes between the characters of moon and night (both originally showed a lunar crescent) by adding a dash for *'night'*. The Shang occasionally did the same. You find lunar crescents with a dot or stroke in the centre. Some of them mean *'night'* but not all do. The custom wasn't properly developed yet.

The Ritual Animal

The Shang were just as enthusiastic about rituals as about divination. But this obvious observation may be misleading. Sure, the Shang sacrificed and worshipped a lot. But we know only very little about the scope of religious activity. For a start, there are many more ideograms for rituals and sacrifices than we understand. Some are common; others only appear once in a while. Some may not be religious rituals but ceremonies or festivities. Where is the dividing line? Being more or less human, we have a tendency to overemphasise what we understand (characters which can be read) and what appears frequently. It may be misleading. The importance of a ritual cannot be determined by the frequency it was performed. The inauguration of a king is a highly important ritual, but it only happens once. The same goes for funerals, and though the Shang kings favoured many marriages, these were by no means as common as weekend sacrifices or the feasting of ancestors. Anything that happens rarely tends to be overlooked. I am sure the oracle was used to confirm who ought to be the next king, and to decide on a queen and on a good day for a coronation or a funeral. However, such inscriptions have not been found yet, or maybe we simply cannot read them. A ritual or sacrifice may be common but not necessarily important. Also, the sacrifices we know about are only those that the kings bothered to consult the oracle for. Probably some rituals and sacrifices were so common that a divination was not required. Here is your meditation for today: humans are ritual animals. We make up rituals all the time, from greeting to parting, from dawn to dusk, from birth to the grave. Just watch how many rituals a small child has to master. Say hello and goodbye, say please and thank you, sit still at the table, wear your clothes properly, don't hit people, share with your friends... the list goes on forever. Have a bit of fun. Take pen and paper and note the rituals that make up your day. Some will be your own rituals, others will be cultural. It may turn out to be a formidably long list. Most rituals are so common that we do them without thinking. Think of the rituals that bridge the gap. What do you do when you get up? What do you do before you go to sleep? How do you start a working day, compared to a day off? How do you behave to have a pause? What do you do to change from, say, private to public behaviour, or from profane to sacral activity? Whenever the flow of events goes from one distinct state to another, you will be inclined to create a personal ritual. It could be something simple, like a few deep breaths, a walk to the window, a glass of water or a cigarette. Or it could be something complex, like a moment of deep silence as you compose yourself, or dressing up, or assuming a certain posture, breathing and mood. The same happens in company. Whenever we feel socially uneasy we make up rituals to get us through the difficult bits. People are ritual animals. When we meet others, we have formal ways of signalling our mood, our respect, our strength or fear or likeability. We perform rituals when we intrude on another's territory, or when we leave it, or let others enter ours. We have rituals that signal status and intent. We have rituals when we communicate with what seems stronger than us: people, events, deities, you name it. Those moments when ordinary behaviour doesn't work rank highest when we need to use rituals. All cultures have rituals for birth, maturity, wedding and death. Social events simply invite ritual, as this helps us uncertain primates over the difficult issues of how to interact with others. And rituals make up much of our daily life. A ritual may have no practical function but can well be a way of smoothly shaping behaviour and producing a specific consciousness state or atmosphere. How do you have a meal? If you were merely interested in functional behaviour, you would shovel the food directly from the pan. It would save plenty of time and washing up the dishes. But you probably sit down on a special place. You use cutlery, plates, bowls etc, and you arrange them in a certain way. You use the right hand for some activities and the left for others. Maybe you even decorate the table. And while you eat, you follow a set of rules. When in company, you avoid certain words, or topics, and possibly your posture is narrowly prescribed. You start eating at a specific moment and you end the whole procedure together. And on important occasions, during courtship, birthdays, business lunches and funeral meals, you cultivate specific states of mind and feelings. Few of them are necessary for the simple act of eating. You could call the result *'manners'*, *'good behaviour'* or even *'culture'*, but what you are really doing is a ritual to produce a specific state of mind. Do yourself a favour and compare your own eating rituals with those of other people. Think of different age groups, occasions, cultures and historical periods. Consider the many variations and the states of mind the ritual ensures. Then think of other rituals in your life. Coming and going to and from work. Visiting others. Waking up and falling to sleep. Riding a train. Entering a shop and buying something. Meeting friends, acquaintances, family members and total strangers. When is a present required? When do you have to be humble, self-assertive, shy or loud? How do you handle eye contact? When, whom and how do you touch? When are you allowed to accept something, and under what conditions? None of this is natural. None can be found in our genes. The natural thing is that humans invent rituals.

Ritual specialists (like you and me) are busy creating consciousness states using ritual. The difference between ours and those of, say armies and banks is that we have the choice to design our own. A ritual, however, is just a tool. Starting with the Renaissance, European magicians began to assume that it only takes the proper rituals to work magic, and that these rituals were efficient, no matter who performed them and in what state of mind. I frequently hear people recommending a given ritual as especially powerful. Sorry folks, it doesn't work that way. Even the best ritual is no guarantee that a specific state of mind is created, let alone maintained. Routine, for example, tends to dull the effect of a given rite. Ultimately, it is you, your awareness and your full participation in a ritual that creates its validity. We should keep this in mind when we consider Shang ritual. I am sure that many Shang regents were highly dedicated people (whatever that may mean). But even they had to cope with the dullness that comes from frequent repetitions. We read a lot about the rites they performed frequently: it may be that exactly these rituals had least meaning to them. Rare rituals have the charm of the unique. Many may be forgotten.

The plastrons and bones only tell us about the rituals the Shang regents and diviners thought worth asking about. Self evident or spontaneous rituals are not recorded. Life is crammed full of them.

Animal sacrifice

People tend to give. Especially when they are facing something bigger, stronger and more intelligent than themselves. Some placate and appease; some give and take to encourage exchange and some follow feeding impulses or wish to make others happy. All of these appear in religion. Let's start with animals. The most common offerings were cattle, goats (or sheep), pigs, dogs and sometimes chicken. All of them are domestic animals. Many cultures sacrifice what they have produced. In this sense, domestic animals are *'made by human effort'*. The Shang offered animals, and in their own way, the ancestors and gods fed on them. On the other hand, it is likely that at least parts of them were eaten after the sacrifice. Making an offering does not necessarily exclude you from enjoying it, too. Domestic animals made gods, ancestors and people happy. **Cattle offerings** were common and popular. In most cases, the amount of cattle (divined about) was up to five animals. Does this tell us something about the meat demands of the Shang court? But there were special occasions when more were offered. War, disasters, enemy invasion, floods, droughts and locusts can make kings amazingly generous. Six inscriptions ask about sacrificing a hundred pieces of cattle, two inscriptions offer three hundred and in one oracle, a thousand pieces of cattle were offered. It's a grandiose gesture. And it would be nice to know whether the sacrifice was actually performed (or merely divined about), and just what made the king offer such an enormous amount of wealth. And, given that a thousand pieces of cattle are a remarkable amount of food, whether the meat was dried and used for army provisions. Normal ancestors were not entitled to such offerings. Only semi-mythic clan founders like Wang Hai could expect so much, and only in a time of national crisis (Li Chi 1977: 107).

Sometimes the offering was written *'cattle in **stable**'* or *'goat/sheep in stable'*. A few oracle bone experts read this as a sacrifice of *'penned cattle'* or *'penned sheep'*. While this reading indicates what the sign shows, it does not tell us what it means. What's the difference between the sacrifice of a penned cow and cow without stable? However you go about it, you don't want to kill a cow in its stable. Nor would you sacrifice a cow that walks around where it likes during the ritual. Here, T.T. Chang offers a useful insight (1970:67). The old character showing *'cattle in stable'* is only the formal equivalent of the modern character lao *'stable, prison'*. In a commentary to the *Guo Yü*, Wei Zhao (204-273 CE) recorded: "*One sacrificial animal is called de, two sacrificial animals are called lao (stable).*" In other words, the term '*penned animal*' ought to read '*pair of sacrificial animals*'. Sound thinking, as it takes a pair of animals under one roof to start breeding.

The Shang were not precise where it came to differentiating between **goat and sheep**, nor is modern Chinese or the modern animal Zodiac. An acquaintance told me '*I'm a sheep but my husband is a goat*'. Though the animals are related, there are vast differences between sheep and goats. Both would turn your garden into a desert within twenty minutes, but their behaviour differs. As good Christian animals sheep have to be led while devilish goats have to be herded. Hence, the good shepherd goes ahead of the flock while the goat herd follows his (with a big stick). Also, goats climb trees, get anywhere and eat anything including books and handbags, while sheep have unspeakable habits you wouldn't want to know about. Just what the Shang kept and whether it provided pullovers or ate bamboo books is anyone's guess. Like the sign for cattle, there is a sign for '*penned sheep*' meaning '*a pair of sheep*'. Sometimes there are three dots above the stable. It's the sign xiao, which possibly showed drops of rain, wine or blood and means '*small*' or '*young*'. Added to the pair of sheep in the stable it means a pair of sacrificial lambs. When the Shang wished to indicate the sex of a sacrificial goat/sheep or piece of cattle they added the sign '*penis*' (an upside down T) or the sign '*spoon, ladle, grandmother, ancestress*' (i.e. female) to the animal. When pairs were offered, their sex was never specified (nor did it have to be).

And things could be more complicated. For unknown (and magical) reasons, the offering sometimes had a specific colour, like a red cow or a black dog. There was a colour symbolism behind such sacrifices, and maybe even a bit of mythology, only that we don't understand it.

Shang ritual was not restricted to these domestic animals. There were plenty of pig sacrifices (male, female pigs and piglets for different occasions) some dog sacrifices and a few sacrifices of cockerels. The archaeological record shows plenty of **horse** sacrifices. The inscriptions rarely mention them. The source of the horses remains enigmatic. Some must have been bred by the Shang themselves, but perhaps a certain tribe or state, the Horsepeople, was renowned for the quality of theirs. The animals were acquired as tribute, by trade and by warfare. As far as is known, the Shang did not ride their horses, but preferred chariots. Horses were immensely valuable and there was a special administrator called Many Horses in charge of them.

Wild animals were rarely offered. There are some inscriptions on sacrificing wild boar, wild birds and mammals we can't identify. The dangerous animals, such as tigers, elephants or rhino, were special sacrifices for unusual occasions. And these animals were also hunted for secondary use. Tiger skin may have graced costumes. Elephant tusks were finely carved and appear among the grave goods. It may be that elephants were used for labour. We can't be entirely sure about this, but one character meaning *'to make, to build'* shows a hand directing an elephant. And the rhinos were highly popular thanks to their thick hides. Early Chinese armour was made by sewing pieces of rhino hide together. The pieces overlapped and allowed for good mobility. Such armour was relatively arrow proof. It took a slim dagger axe to penetrate the gaps between the plates. And if we can trust Zhou period accounts, there were kings who had a canopy of rhino hide over their war chariot. Mind you, the Zhou criticised such protection, as it makes common soldiers question the valour of their lords. The rhino horn may have been a valued drinking vessel. Later periods believed that wine from rhino cups increases sexual potency. Even when we think of these wild animals as difficult and special offerings, we should keep in mind that there were living human beings getting substantial secondary benefits.

Another unusual sacrifice involved serpents. One sign shows a hand with cudgel beating a serpent. It could show a serpent sacrifice, but as it was also used to write *'to cut, to divide, to expose, to cudgel'* we can't really be certain. A serpent plus the T for divinity is the sign for the ritual year. It signifies the great celebration which ends the ritual year, but whether this event involved a serpent sacrifice or whether the serpent is simply there for worship or phonetic reasons remains unknown.

Animal sacrifice was performed in many different ways. An animal might be killed with an axe, split open, burned, drowned, buried, strangled or clubbed. Or it was simply sacrificed without reference to the method. Again, there seems to have been a system behind the ritual. Certain deities received their offerings in special ways. Not all of them are easy to understand. You might think that an offering to the Yellow River should be drowned, but in many cases the victims were burned or even buried. On some occasions, the offering was reduced to a symbolic level. Here we encounter the sacrifice of one ear instead of a whole animal. The ear represented the entire beast. This sacrifice endured to later dynasties: you find it in the *Liji*. Evidently, giving a single ear was less messy than splitting an entire cow. In a similar fashion, the ears of slain soldiers were collected, counted and presumably offered in temples, as the early Zhou did after they defeated the Shang. Perhaps you are wondering who did the actual offering. Was there a sacrificial priesthood or were king, queen and the aristocracy required to do it themselves? Again, the data is inconclusive. Much depends on how you imagine Shang culture. If you visualise a high civilisation well on the way towards bureaucracy you will have the high nobles standing by, witnessing the messy acts from a safe distance. If you see the Shang as the beginning of Chinese

Top Left: The ends of bone hairpins from Fu Hao's tomb. Note triangular crest on the heads of the birds.
Top Right: a deity or ancestor?
Bottom: Ceremonial Axe in Shang Style from Sufutun, Yidu, Shandong.

civilisation, your imagination may well include crude elements. We should keep an open mind here. Personally, I am sure that the great sacrifices involved so much chopping that it couldn't have been done by a single person. Nor is it likely that the king had the time to kill every sacrifice personally. Not in Wu Ding's time, with so much warfare going on, nor in Zu Jia's period, with its narrow ritual timetable. But where it came to really important events, it seems a safe bet that king (and probably queen) had to act personally. It may have been the case when national calamities indicated that some early ancestor was really angry, or when the royals felt they needed to clean themselves of malicious influences and bad luck.

Human sacrifice

The Shang, like so many Bronze Age and early Iron Age cultures, were fond of human sacrifice. Human sacrifice is not only a messy affair that tends to upset modern sensibilities; it is also a tricky subject. For one thing, it seems to be an almost universal custom that appears, in various degrees, all over the planet. For another, it is certainly a disgusting habit to slaughter people for religious reasons. Many scholars have argued that human sacrifice is such a primitive and crude affair that any rising high civilisation would naturally do its best to replace it with symbolic offerings. It's a nice thought but not very realistic. In fact, the evidence for human sacrifices among simple hunter-gatherer cultures is rather slim. It is when cultures begin to get heavily involved in agriculture, large settlements, animal husbandry and the like that they really get into slaughtering people. Maybe the change is related to the size of the community. Stone Age migrants lived in tiny groups moving through vast, uncultivated wild lands. They did not have the means to settle nor the food supply to afford living in large groups. All wealth had to be small and mobile, food sources varied according to season and there were few reasons to waste energy on warfare. Even fertility as such was not a blessing and in the tribal group, each individual person was valued. When you live in a group of fifteen to twenty migrants and only meet a few hundred people in all of your life, you are not likely to consider other people worthless. You may even depend on other nomad groups to find a mate. With the advent of agriculture, some twelve thousand years ago, everything changed. Agriculture, as such, wasn't much of an improvement. For one thing, tilling the soil with a digging stick, plucking weeds by hand and similar chores are just the thing to give you a terrible pain in the back. For another, the early farmers had a remarkably limited diet. Malnutrition and hunger were common. As soon as agriculture developed, people became smaller and generally they also lived shorter lives. Living in stationary communities increased the risk of infection. However, the farmers changed their environment so thoroughly that soon there was no way back. Fields can be extended almost indefinitely; hence, groups grow into large communities. As the early farmers still hunted wild animals, and as the communal demand for meat was steadily increasing, the farming pioneers soon forced their hunter-gatherer neighbours to join the agricultural revolution. Another issue is property. Hunter-gatherers tend to have little property, as they have to carry their belongings ever so often. The farmers could own more, and, significantly, store food. Once settlements hoard food and resources, they also become vulnerable to attack. For real warfare, you need large groups of people, settlements, and something worth taking by force. Consequently, once people began to develop civilisation, they also began to wage war on a much greater scale. Also, the ever growing human population became increasingly dependent on weather. When hunter-gatherers are faced with droughts, floods, bushfires or, more often, starvation, they can pack up and move on. A large, settled population is not mobile, and pretty much at the mercy of weather, temperature, climate and whatever else the gods and ancestors can throw at them. The larger a population grows, the smaller is the value of the individual person, let alone the person who is a foreigner, criminal, sinner or enemy. Indeed, it takes a prospering high culture to eliminate people on a large scale. The Shang, like most budding high cultures of the time, certainly had no qualms about this. Especially in period 1, under Wu Ding, large amounts of captive Qiang were regularly proposed as sacrifices. Whether the oracle actually agreed with the offers remains unknown. It's not a pleasant topic. Human history is full of unhappy violent incidents, and there seems to be no end in sight. But before we explore human sacrifices among the Shang, I would like to mention that in China, such customs disappeared a long time before they became unfashionable in the near East and Europe. The Holy Land has quite a history of human sacrifice; in spite of much editing, even the *Bible* refers to it. The Phoenicians and Cathargians, cultures to whom we owe our alphabet, were heavily into infant sacrifice. The ancient Greek sacrificed people, and so did the Romans up to and during the second Punic War (218-201 BCE). It might be argued that human sacrifice continued beyond this period in the form of circus games, which were often held on religious festival dates. The Etruscans may have started the fashion of having fights to the death during sacred rituals. The Romans simply picked up the idea and elaborated. Iulius Caesar set a record when he had 320 pairs of gladiators fight on a single day. Under Augustus, privately sponsored circus games had an average of a hundred pairs of gladiators, while the eight games he personally sponsored had a total of 10 000 fighters. The same amounts were employed by

Trajan to celebrate the conquest of Dacia in the year 107. When Claudius staged a sea battle on the Lago di Celano in the year 52, 19 000 armed fighters slaughtered each other. According to Tacitus most of them were condemned criminals. (Friedländer, no year: 465 & 468). Many gladiators were prisoners of war; and the Romans found it highly entertaining to see them kill each other. So did the many foreign nationalities that populated Rome; indeed, such entertainment was appreciated by all classes of society, including the venerable writers and philosophers who allegedly formed western civilisation. Pliny the Younger, Cicero, Ovid, Martial, Statius and others enjoyed or tolerated the games; Tacitus ignored them, Epicet merely pointed out that gladiator games were too frivolous for serious conversation and only the aging Seneca seems to have been upset by the bloodshed. Human rights are a recent idea. Even at private celebrations, a fight to death was common entertainment. Under Caligula, normal citizens were forced to slaughter each other in the circus, while Domitian was fascinated by people fighting animals, or by odd matches, such as dwarves against women. As Friedländer remarks, nothing shows the contrast between modern sensibilities and those of the Roman Empire as much as the way the circus games were celebrated.

The Germani and Celts slaughtered people for religious reasons, just consider the many swamp corpses unearthed in northern Germany and Denmark or the war memorials and sacred enclosures of northern France. Warfare often required that the prisoners were slaughtered, with or without divine blessing (Tacitus, *Annales*, 13,57). Human sacrifices continued for a long time. In the year 743, at the synod of Liftinae, the future saint Boniface outlawed human sacrifices to Donar. After Charlemagne crushed the last rebellious Saxon tribes, the custom gradually disappeared from continental Europe, but it continued at length in Scandinavia and Iceland. Among the Vikings, humans were sacrificed for many reasons. To strengthen or bribe the gods, to ensure wealth, to avert drought, plague and ruined harvests, to consecrate buildings and ships and so on. King Aun allegedly sacrificed one of his sons every decade, each sacrifice extending his life span by another ten years (*Ynglingasaga*, 25) In most cases, the sacrifices were slaves or criminals, but when the harvest was bad three years in a row, the king himself could end up as a sacrifice .The Swedish king Olaf Trätälja was sacrificed to Odin at the Vanar Lake *"for a good year"* (*Yng.*43). Good weather and plentiful harvests depended on impeccable royal conduct, a tradition that can also be found among the medieval Irish Celts. Compare this with the self immolation of Tang the Successful, and other drought sacrifices of the Shang.

Christianisation may have officially ended human sacrifice, but the church was by no means reluctant to sacrifice people for a higher good. Heretics, witches, unbelievers all over the world found their death for the greater glory of god.

Maybe human sacrifices are still going on. If we define the custom as *'the involuntary death of persons for an ideal, an abstract principle or a real or imaginary higher good'*, we observe plenty of damnstupid dying all over the place. People drafted for wars, killed for *'patriotism'*, *'freedom'*, *'democracy'* and big money; freedom fighters, rebels and anyone believing in a just cause and an end that justifies the means. In central Europe, roughly a third of the girls and young women are anorexic and bulimic nowadays and ten percent of these die from heart, kidney and liver failure: sacrifice to a fashionable beauty ideal. In Germany roughly a thousand people die in sport accidents each year, plus an average seven hundred have heart failure while sacrificing to the glorified ideal of health by jogging. Every state that allows advertisements for alcohol and tobacco (for the ideal of a *'free market'*) participates in the killing of thousands. So do all states that do not demand high safety standards for factories, nuclear plants and traffic, who save on public health services or allow their citizens easy access to dangerous weapons. Much of this happens in the service of deities ...oops, let's call them higher ideals instead.

Retainer Sacrifices

In many ancient cultures, the great kings and queens went to the otherworld in the company of friends, partners, ministers, servants and a good many other people who were not really needed by the new regents. We can observe this custom in pre-dynastic Egypt, in early Sumeria, and probably in ancient India. Let's have a look at the Far East.

In Neolithic China, the evidence for human sacrifices is very slim. Communities were small and relatively poor, and religious, political and military violence happened on a very small scale. This changed when states developed, communities grew and specific clans were able to gather greater wealth and influence.

On special occasions, the Shang sacrificed people. This is simple to say but a lot harder to understand; in China, as in the rest of the world, there were many different forms of human sacrifice, and a wide scope of reasons for the act.

Think of the servant, retainer or friend who follows a lord or lady to the otherworld. We could call this a human sacrifice and claim that such people would have preferred remaining alive. Perhaps they would. On the other hand, if they were highly religious and life was tough, it is just as possible that they expected a great afterlife at the side of a regent who, after death, would become a formidable semi-divine being. Following an aristocrat to the otherworld could have been a promising career move and a great honour, especially if the otherworld had more to offer than the human realm. Maybe it's simply our way of thinking and our cultural prejudice that classes such deaths as human sacrifices. Many of these sacrifices can be found right next to the great royal tombs of Anyang. And where early excavators assumed that the hundreds of graves contain people who had been slaughtered against their will, contemporary scholars are more cautious. The graves were probably for privileged individuals. And we can't be sure they were all killed directly after the death of some regent. Some might contain heroic warriors or esteemed characters, and may have been buried years after the death of their lord. The custom of killing close servants, ministers and even relations at the funeral of a regent was widely common in ancient China and pretty much the norm until the tenth century BCE. In later periods, such sacrifices continued, but their scale was gradually reduced. When Mu of Qin was buried in the year 621 BCE, 117 persons, including three high officials, accompanied their lord to the otherworld. T.T. Chang observes: *"in this culturally retarded fief, the custom was only abolished officially in the year 384 BCE"* (after the German, 1970:74). The *Zuozhuan* records that in the third year of Ding (507 BCE), the ruler of Chu, a very excitable man, had a fit of wrath, flung himself on his bed, missed, and slammed with full force into a brazier, suffering burns that caused his death. Before dying, he ordered that five chariots plus five men were to accompany him to into the grave. Compared to earlier regents, it was a very modest burial. Later generations made do with symbolic human sacrifice, such as the famous terracotta army of Qin Shihuangdi.

A variety of this custom may be that ancestors, and occasionally deities, were regularly supplied with servants and concubines. Just as the court required new servants and concubines from time to time, so did the ancestors. And the gods of rivers and mountains may have received a human husband or wife on a regular scale. Such victims may have been less happy about their fate, but at least they were assured to have an honourable and privileged afterlife.

But what of the skull pits near the royal tombs? Or the numerous skulls laid out in neat lines on the ramps of some royal tombs? Some of them show different anthropological characteristics, making it likely that these people came from other cultures. They could have been prisoners of war. But as their number is rather small (considering how many people get caught during a successful war or raid), they may have been special enemies. Perhaps they were killed to nourish certain ancestors. But they also came to rest on sacred ground, close to the royal tombs, which is a position of privilege.

Foundation Sacrifices

Burying a person under a building or fortification was a popular custom among many Bronze Age people. In some cultures, the person became a place guardian and acquired a semi divine status. *Cauldron of the Gods* gives some European examples. The custom appears in the Megalith period, in the Bronze Age, and continued all the way into the Christian era. The Roman army occasionally buried people under the foundations of fortresses, in other places the foundation sacrifice was supposed to ensure the safety of a bridge. A very late example is the person who was buried within the central pillar of the Michaelis Church (Adorn in Saxony) in 1151. The skeleton was discovered after a fire in 1768. According to church records, the architect of the church had mysteriously disappeared when the building was complete but threatened to fall in. The architects of the cathedral of Strasburg and the St. Jacob's Church in Chemnitz *'leaped to death'* from the scaffolding to *"ensure the safety of their building with their blood"* (Bächtold-Stäubli, 1935, vol.6: 171). In medieval castles, occasionally animals or eggs were built into foundations and walls.

What the Shang believed remains unknown. However, there are many Shang burials that may have functioned as foundation sacrifices. One burial, close to a large cache of oracle bone inscriptions, may fall into this category. Likewise, the heavily armed guards buried around the royal graves might have served as foundation sacrifices for the tombs and for the safety of the temples which stood above them. On a much larger scale, the excavation of the palaces of Anyang, south of the river, turned up plenty of corpses, including children, adults with weapons and domestic animals like pigs, bovines and sheep. Sarah Allan (1991:5) states: *"Thus, 185 ceremonial pits were found near the seven large buildings in the central sector which contained 852 human victims, fifteen horses, ten oxen, eighteen sheep, thirty-five dogs and five chariots"*. 852 sounds like a large number. However, we have to consider that these sacrifices happened over a period of maybe 250 years. An average of 3 or 4 sacrifices a year leads to the question just who was buried in these pits. What made these people so special that they were buried in the close neighbourhood of the rich and powerful?

Foundation burials continued well into the Zhou period. In the year 531, the victorious army of Chu buried the crown prince of defeated Sui under a dam as a foundation sacrifice.

Small scale foundation sacrifices remained popular in Zhou time China. After the rise of the Qin Dynasty, the *'First Emperor'*, Qin Shihuangdi, reinforced elder fortifications and built his own contribution to the tangle of fortifications that are called the Great Wall nowadays. His great wall cost tens of thousands of lives. Victims include prisoners of war, criminals, conscripted labour and those who had dared to express unhappiness about his enlightened reign. The labourers were mercilessly used up and worked to death, and the corpses were thrown into the rubble that became the foundation of the next section of the wall. It was the easiest and least honourable way of disposing of them. The First Emperor may have considered them place guardians, and hoped this army of the dead would help to fortify the wall. He made his most famous building project the largest cemetery on this planet.

Luckily, the Qin Dynasty lasted a mere 15 years. The regents of the Han Dynasty who followed the Qin went to great lengths to avoid such atrocities. The custom of burying place guardians went out of fashion well before the Common Era.

Let's take a look at the Shang inscriptions. The most common sign for human sacrifice shows a person who is beheaded with an axe. As the same sign means *'to wage war'* and *'to behead'*, we have to consider the context. Waging war and beheading people has a lot in common. The preferred human sacrifices of the Shang were prisoners of war. Here, the officers were much preferred. Shaughnessy (1997:66) quotes two period 5 inscriptions. The first records the amount of men, chariots, shields and arrows that were captured. The inscription ends: *"Earl Wen was sacrificed to Da Yi, Earl Pi was sacrificed...; (Earl) Fan (was sacrificed) to Ancestor Yi, Mei was sacrificed to Ancestor Ding"* (Zongtu 16.2). The other inscription records that the king, after his successful campaign against the Renfang, made a burned offering of their leaders (Zheyan 315). The early Zhou followed the same custom: while the defeated soldiers remained alive (and were presumably used for work, relocated or drafted into the army), the Shang nobles and ministers were ritually executed. Perhaps we should not generalise from these examples. Qiang captives frequently ended as human sacrifices, and so did the occasional southerner, under Wu Ding.

The *Zuozhuan* (years 532 and 488 BCE) records that the victorious armies of Lu sacrificed their prisoners of war to a deity. Similar things happened in Europe during the early medieval period. It may indicate religious faith, or maybe gratefulness to the deity, but it also shows that keeping the prisoners as slaves was not profitable. The Shang did not employ many slaves. In all likeliness, they were used for extreme chores, such as mining minerals or pounding earth, or they became servants of the aristocracy. Probably criminals also ended up doing hard labour, and were sacrificed when required. A minority of slaves may even have risen to a position of influence. One inscription (Luo, 1913, vol.4, 37b, 2) divines whether captured Qiang people should be castrated (penis and knife, as T.T. Chang remarked in a handwritten note) or tortured. As the Qiang were one of the major foes of the late Shang, we might wonder for what reason a castration was required, if not to keep and employ them in some function. Is this the first reference to eunuchs in Chinese history?

Human sacrifices were not everyday offerings. They were made at on very specific occasions: times of crisis, indicating that an early ancestor was angry; thanksgiving after important events, such as victory in war; and when the power of an ancestor needed to be increased. So far, I have seen no evidence that they were made for fertility or to ensure a good harvest. The Shang seem to have assumed that fertility is a natural and self evident thing. It was only when angry gods or ancestors upset the natural order of the seasons by sending drought, flood or locusts that sacrifices were needed.

On a more personal level, the highest regents sometimes offered humans when they needed to purify themselves of some blemish or disease. Less frequently, human sacrifices were offered to the gods of nature. The Yellow River received its fair share, including concubines and servants. Another deity, or group of deities, who seems to have received human sacrifices on rare occasions was Di. The matter is heavily debated.

How often were people sacrificed? In most inscriptions, groups of two to ten people were proposed. Sometimes there were special sacrifices such as a man (a servant?) and a concubine. High ranking aristocrats were by no means safe. An entire cluster of divinations in American oracle bone collections enquire, day after day and week after week, whether a certain marquis ought to be sacrificed. Other inscriptions proposed sacrifices of princes and princesses.

The oracle bones also enquire about larger numbers. One inscription asks about offering 300 and one about sacrificing one thousand people. Such inscriptions are very rare and unusual. We have no idea whether they were seriously considered (or made as a grandiose gesture), and whether the oracle agreed to them. Nor do we know if the sacrifices were captured enemies whom the Shang state could not use for menial works nor had the means to feed. A mass-sacrifice may appear like religious insanity, but there could have been economic reasons behind it.

An odd aspect of Shang history is the fact that the preferred sacrifices were often Qiang people. Sure, in most inscriptions we can't read who was offered. But when it comes to specifying people, of all the cultures surrounding the Shang, the Qiang come first. This could do with some research. Qiang is a vague term for a linguistic group from which a wide range of different cultures emerged. Eberhard (in Miller, 1994: 7) estimated that some 62 tribes appearing in Chinese histories may belong to the Qiang speaking cultures. Among them are some proto-Tibetans, Yi, Primi, and possibly Naxi and Mosuo ancestors. It's a difficult topic, as linguistic relationship is not the same thing as sharing the same culture, social organisation or origin. The Naxi, for instance, have a history of originating near Mount Kailash, and they appear in China long after the end of the Shang. Nowadays, you find most Qiang-language related minorities in Yunnan, Sichuan and Tibet, hence, a long way from the central northern Chinese plains.

The Shang often waged war against the Qiang people. They sacrificed them when possible, and occasionally they received captive Qiang from their neighbouring allies. It certainly looks as if they hated the Qiang. No doubt this feeling was mutual.

The main reason may be the difference in lifestyle. Where the Shang, and many of their allies, vassals and enemies were city-dwellers, states or statelets, the Qiang remained sheep-herding nomads. Their oracle bone character shows a blend of a human figure with a sheep, and sheep and goats were and are essential to their lifestyle. During the late Shang, various tribes of Qiang were constantly on the move. They lived in the wide wastelands, forests, mountains and steppes to the north and west of the cultures around the Yellow River, and whenever they became powerful enough and chanced upon a farming community or settlement, they plundered it. From time to time, they became formidable hordes who assaulted cities. When the Shang kings and their armies followed them, the Qiang disappeared into the unknown. Moving unpredictably, they were a constant threat hovering around the fringes of the settled civilisations. The whole situation was much like that which so many Chinese emperors had to cope with. Politically, the Qiang were the same sort of threat as the Xiongnu (Huns?), Tartars, Mongols and Manchu. All of them were highly mobile, did without cities and came and went as they liked. Later dynasties achieved an uneasy peace with the nomads by a clever balance of warfare, bribes and trade. The Shang, I would guess, were a much poorer culture and had less to offer. With the settled enemy cultures, political agreements could be found, but the Qiang were simply beyond negotiation. Most Shang regents waged extended wars against the Qiang, and the Qiang, in return, kept attacking Shang settlements.

So far, we have examined human and other sacrifice for their economic value: there was substantial profit in slaughtering animals, and in getting rid of troublesome people or dangerous convicts. The custom was also useful for political purposes: the Shang kings, like most regents throughout history, had power over life and death, and displayed it in gruesome public rituals. Here, I would like to make a few comments from the magical point of view. For people who believe that ancestors and gods are real, a sacrifice has more functions than profit or a display of power. Unless a god or spirit appears via an inspired medium, the only way to contact it directly is using the imagination. The imagined shape is not the deity, just as you are not the photons that others see when looking at you, or the image they form in their brains. It is an image, a representation, a convenient metaphor to convey meaning. People tend to give very specific shapes to the divine, and these shapes make interaction easier. For a skilled mind explorer, building up a good vision is an easy task. Stabilising it may take a few weeks or months, depending on how often you do it, unless you provide the vision with a heady charge of emotion. You can do this with meditation, with obsession, with the realisation that you and the deity share a common essence. That's the elegant way. But when you wish to anchor a deity (or rather it's shape) in the mind of many people, most of them by no means trained in visualisation, sacrifice is an easy solution. We might say that sacrifice strengthens a spirit, concept, deity or ideal. How does it happen? Most deities and spirits have no use for food and drink, unless they inhabit a medium or obsessed devotee. As they lack a physical body they can hardly be expected to partake of physical things. Most cultures accept this and agree that the unseen ones take an equally invisible quality from the offering. It can be vitality or an archetypal quintessence or maybe it's the idea that counts. Luckily, people do learn once in a while. The ideal offering is not a specific thing or substance but emotion and attention. Here, a lot of variation is possible. When you are into non-dualist ritual, you can enjoy the offering as the gods enjoy your enjoyment. Some adepts cultivate bliss as this nourishes them, just as it nourishes their deities or the consciousness they represent. It's the favoured approach of the tāntrikas of Kashmir and works excellently, provided you are absolutely aware that the divine, you and me and everything that is are one vast consciousness delighting in form and emptiness, and the pulsation between them. In the realm of dualist worship, you make a sacrifice to something that seems to be separate of you. Here, offerings take on many forms. Some give offerings by burning or destroying things. Others offer food, allow the deity to partake of its essence, and then proceed to eat the food as it has become a sacrament. Some sacrifice by doing without, and use the ensuing hunger as an offering. The main thing is that you produce plenty of emotion. You can offer fear, horror and longing, or you can amplify the manifestation of the divine using love and joy or delight in a shared consciousness. When a poor person offers something valuable, that offering will produce plenty of emotion. A rich person will produce less. Hence, the wealthier a ritualist, the more lavish are the necessary offerings. The purest offering a single person can make is total dedication to the divine. Unlike normal sacrifices (and human sacrifices) such offerings continue through life. They extend over the years and provide the divine with a regular source of nourishment, especially during times of crisis and joy. Giving yourself, with all you are and all you will be, all you have done and all you can do for a lifetime of union with the divine is the only honest form of *'human sacrifice'*. To kill other beings or oneself for a deity or ideal is simply stupid.

In large scale, public religion, human sacrifices (and self-sacrifices) are crude but powerful amplifiers of emotion. They are especially useful where it comes to exciting untrained minds to religious fervour. Some, like Crowley, assumed that the vitality of the offering strengthens a spirit or deity. Freshly cut flowers and plants, fruit, seeds, sexual secretions and blood contain and release vitality. That vitality, however, is weak compared to the sheer emotional outburst when hundreds or thousands of witnesses experience dread, glee, disgust, triumph or fear. The bigger the congregation the stronger the emotional release. Human sacrifice, just like public executions, make use of catharsis. A drastic sacrifice can turn a ghostly idea into an extremely real and powerful deity. If you read *'ideal'* instead of *'deity'*, you may realise why so many real or alleged self-immolators are employed in the current transformation of the political and religious landscape.

Drought Sacrifices

As you read earlier, when a terrible drought was destroying the harvest, Tang the Successful assumed responsibility for the trouble and offered himself as a drought sacrifice. To his great relief, a sudden rainstorm set in before he could mount the pyre. Maybe he set an example, and maybe he followed an earlier custom. During the Shang period the north Chinese climate was much warmer. Humidity prevailed during parts of the year, but in some seasons rainfall was rare and the vegetation withered. Thick jungles surrounded the rivers and swamps, where water was easily available at all times of the year, but the major settlements, pastures and farms were characterised by a semi-arid climate with light oak woods and thick undergrowth. Every couple of years, the rains failed to come. Rain making by offering, prayer and dance is a common topic of the inscriptions, and when these failed to produce water, drought sacrifices were performed. Some of them involved the offering of selected persons. The oracle bones record them in detail. But before we look at the inscriptions we should take a look at better documented drought sacrifices among the Zhou.

These lines come from the *Shijing*:
"The dryness is extreme,
the mountain springs have dried,
drought demons bring destruction,
they are like flames, like raging fire"

One way to end a drought was to expose a female or male wu (shaman, ritualist) to the scorching heat. The idea was that the suffering of the wu might incline the gods to be merciful. A late explanation appears in the *Lung Heng* of the first century CE. Wu contain the breath of yang, which is the power that makes them able to see spirits and interact with them. Likewise, drought is a time when yang, as sheer heat is dominant. Hence the wu, as allies of the yang, are made to suffer from it.

Another option was to kill a humpback. According to the *Zuozhuan*, the duke of Lu wanted to expose a hunchback to the sun to end the drought of the year 639 BCE. The *Liji* also refers to this event, elaborating that the duke of Lu first intended to kill a hunchback. When his ministers chided him for his lack of humanity, he decided that a wu might be a better candidate. His ministers disagreed, so the lord changed his mind. His ministers counselled that he should have the city walls repaired, simplify his lifestyle, eat plain food and ask the people to share what they had. As a sign of public mourning and repentance he had the public markets closed. His ministers applauded the act, and so did Heaven. Though there was a shortage that year, it did no harm.

(Note on translation: the passage could also be read that a Wu Wang, i.e. a Shaman/ess Hunchback was to be sacrificed. It's not a likely explanation but possible). Now it's easy to understand that Heaven would not like to see a shaman/ess (or anybody else) suffer. But what is the symbolism of the hunchback? Probably hunchbacks represented drought. The minister of the duke of Lu argued, if Heaven would not want hunchbacks to live, it wouldn't have given them life; and if they really had the power to cause drought, burning them might only make things worse.

According to late Zhou mythology, Huangdi (the Yellow Emperor) fought an extended war with his monstrous adversary Chiyou. Things were not going too well. Huangdi ordered Ying Long (Responsive Dragon) to dry up the wilderness of Ji Zhou, but Chiyou invoked the Lord of Rain and the Windgod who made the gales howl and floods of rain drench the land. Lost in the mist and rain, the Yellow Emperor quickly invented the compass. It allowed him to find his way but did not make the fighting easier. Huangdi, as a final resource, sent the heavenly maiden Ba (Drought) to earth. She stopped the torrents and dried the plains so the emperor's army could advance and slay Chiyou. But once the war ended, Ba found it impossible to return to heaven. And she wasn't popular on earth either, for wherever she went, the rains stopped falling, the vegetation withered and the ground cracked. Shu Jiun reported this dismal state to the Yellow Emperor. Huangdi made him a deity of agriculture and gave the lands north of the Red Waters, where no-one really wanted to live, to Ba, who became the spirit or deity of drought. It's not a job that makes you really popular. Once in a while, Ba feels bored and wanders absentmindedly into the inhabited realm. Whenever she does, devastating drought follows. To make her go away, she is petitioned to return to the north, and to invite new rain the canals and ditches are opened and the aqueducts are cleaned. The *Shanhaijing* adds that her daughters look like humans dressed in blue, and that these minor Ba spirits haunt the deserts.

Another myth, related by Dongfang Shuo (154-93 BCE) in the *Shenyijing*, states that the drought spirits, the gezi, are nude dwarves who run through the deserts of the south. They also like to sneak around on market places and at meetings, but when they are caught and killed or thrown into a latrine the drought comes to an end. The gezi have their eyes on top of their heads. T.T. Chang (1970:214) proposed that a gezi might be a hunchback; who's backwards bent head makes the face point upwards (p.660). In the oracle bones, the drought spirit is a creature with a rounded upper body and a mouth on top. Add the character of fire and you get *'drought sacrifice'*. Here the custom does not depend on a wu being favoured by the gods. The hunchback, like a scapegoat, is a replacement sacrifice and symbolises the drought deity itself. It may even be asked whether the Shang had a drought goddess who received sacrifices.

The drought sacrifices were not limited to hunchbacks. Several inscriptions refer to women, who are identified by name. As none of them is of noble rank, they may have been wu. And finally, in some cases it was nobles themselves who ended up on the pyre. T.T. Chang (1970: 251) refers to the burning of a prince and princess of period 1 who were offered as sacrifices in period 2a. Maybe they had committed misdeeds or sacrileges. Or they were simply not popular under the new regent.

Offering Branches

Plants were frequently offered. One common group of sacrifices show hands offering branches on the T sign. Sacrifices of branches and blossoms from plants and trees remained popular among many dynasties. The *Chuci* mention ritual dances with flowering branches. The luan, or coda of the semi-shamanic *Nine Songs* ceremony is the breathtaking verse:

> In Honour of the Dead
> Li hun
> "With strokes of the drums the rites are accomplished,
> the flowering branch moves from dancer to dancer,
> beautiful maidens sing solemn and slow,
> orchids in springtime and chrysanthemums in fall:
> so shall it continue till the end of time."

It might be a memory of Shang times when the cycle of the five festivals ended with the drumming ritual (see below). The ritual comes from the *Songs* (or *words*) *of Chu*, a southern state that had close cultural ties to the Shang and their descendants (Allan, 1991: 26).

Marcel Granet (1963: 56-57) mentions an obsession rite requiring a number of musicians and witnesses in a small, closed room, where they played flutes and drums. Outside this space, and unobserved by the orchestra, a number of high ranking aristocratic ladies undressed and danced in a circle. The nude, but heavily perfumed ladies passed a flowering branch along. The one who received the branch became obsessed by a spirit, deity or ancestor, passed the branch on and swooned away into trance. The ritual seems to have been an exciting event, as a *'ghostwind'* arose and the terrifying voices of the ancestors were heard. Sadly, Granet does not cite his source for this remarkable ritual. Branch sacrifices commonly appear during the rituals that nourished the ancestors. They were a common element in the five ritual routine (period 2b, 5a, 5b), but they also appear independently of it in all five periods of the late Shang.

Food and Blood

The Shang frequently offered cooked grains, and in Zu Jia's ritual calendar, cooked cereals became one of the regular five offerings to the ancestors. There are also numerous glyphs for food sacrifices, showing bowls and vessels, which were offered to ancestors and deities. In all likeliness, such small sacrifices were among the most common elements in Shang time religion. Great sacrifices happen from time to time, but setting aside a little food for the ancestors is a ritual which can be performed by any family every day. The aristocrats also had meals with the ancestors. The sign *'eating together'* was used for shared human meals and for meals in the company of an ancestor. It would be nice to know if the ancestor was visualised or whether a person represented the ancestor or even became obsessed by her or him. Food offerings show a lot of variety. Sometimes it was a cooked meal, sometimes it was raw meat laid out on a chopping board or given by hand. The latter came to be included in the five annual rituals. Some sacrifices involved blood offerings. Blood was offered in bowls, but it could also be sprinkled on an altar. It was also smeared over ritual objects and participants when required.

Offering drink

The amazing range of distinct drinking vessels found in Shang tombs hints at a lot of special rituals. The same goes for the numerous signs that describe the act. In many rituals, wine was sprinkled on the ground. Sometimes the vessel was simply set up on the ground, or maybe it was smashed with a mallet. Usually, such rituals involved heavy drinking. The Zhou accused the Shang of reckless alcoholism, and did much to reduce the drinking. However, even they felt obliged to partake of the offerings. It was a splendid opportunity for assassination. In the year 656 the sacrificial wine was fortified with so much poison that a few spilled drops made the ground boil. Duke Xi became cautious and tested the sacrificial meat on a dog and a servant, both of whom died immediately. The duke lost his appetite nor did he retain much trust in those around him (*Zuozhuan*).

The graphemes for wine sacrifice usually show a vessel of clay or metal. Sometimes hands are holding it, or there are drops spilling from its top. One variation shows an owl. The owl wasn't really meant as a bird. Instead, the sign was used for phonetic reasons. It means ritual offering and drinking wine. But as people can take puns literally, Fu Hao's tomb included a magnificent bronze vessel in the shape of an owl. It's quite an abstract owl. Its wings are graced by spiralling serpents, its plumage contains dragon ornaments, on the lid, a worm dragon and a little bird squat and the feet of the creature come from a rhino or elephant (see illustration p.123). It may be a symbol for a fusion of power or clan-animals. But it is also a sign that drink offerings can be made from owlish vessels. And that the owl, a bird of ill-chance in later times, enjoyed more popularity among the Shang, or at least with Fu Hao.

The ancient Chinese did not have grapes. In their days, *'wine'* was usually made from grains. Several sorts of millet were available. Wheat was not common but probably imported and wild rice grew near the capital. Also, the warm climate supplied plenty of berries, herbs and fruits. The northern Chinese cultivated apricot, peach, persimmon, and jujube, while other fruits were available in a semi-domesticated form. These include many varieties of plum, cherry, pear, apple, hawthorn and quince (Hui-Lin Li and Te-Tzu Chang in Keightley, 1983; 21-94). All of them could have gone into the ritual wine of the Shang. Some characters for *'drink sacrifice'* even show the radicals for plants and trees. One version has *'jade'* radicals, which might indicate a very costly beverage, or even the addition of jade to the drink. Drugs are another distinct possibility. One special offering was a spiced or perfumed wine. The kings divined how many vessels or cups they were to offer. It seems that the drink was expensive.

Finally, the Shang may have offered the *'dark wine'*. The Zhou treasured dark wine as the purest and earliest drink of the past. The *Liji* contains a chapter (*Li Yün*) on the most ancient rituals of antiquity. Here the offering in the inner chamber is dark wine, while the alcoholic beverages, such as mead, green wine, red wine and purified wine are offered near the door, in the hall and under the stairs.

Likewise, in the most ancient food sacrifices, dark wine was the first offering, followed by raw fish and unsalted flesh-broth. They symbolise the original sources of nourishment, and to respect the origin is to retain culture. Together, the three sacrifices represent unity. In Zhou ritual, all wines and drinks were inferior to dark wine. It's such a beautiful term. Dark wine is not wine at all. It is simply spring water collected at night. Dark or black is also a symbol for the Xia, whose colour it was, and who are associated with the flood, water rituals and fish and dragon images.

Offering clothes

On regular occasions and often associated with the xie *'harmonisation'* ritual, the ancestors received new clothes. The grapheme shows a stylised jacket, and as the jacket sometimes opens to the left or right, it is likely that the Shang (unlike the Zhou) had no specific dress code regarding the item. Sadly, we know very little about the way the Shang dressed. However, mulberry trees and silkworms were cultivated for at least 800 years prior to their reign. Hemp (Cannabis sativa) originated in northern China, and was cultivated at least since the Yangshao cultures. The character for hemp in oracle bone script is unknown, but tombs excavated by Li Chi in Anyang contained traces of hemp cloth preserved near bronze weapons. Hemp may also have been used for medicine and entertainment, as the character, *'ma'* has two basic meanings: as *'numerous and chaotic'* it refers to the fibres, and as *'numbness and senseless'* to its psychoactive effect (Hui-Lin Li in Keightley 1983;31-32). Li proposes that northern Chinese nomads, practitioners of shamanism, transferred the plant to India, where it was primarily used as a drug. From India, it was eventually exported across the world. When I look at Shang art I can only wonder how much the regents, ritualists and artists consumed, and what effects you get when you combine alcohol, spices, hashish and chronic lead poisoning. A few badly damaged small stone figures showing what may have been Shang ancestors provide details on Aristocratic robes. The nobility wore richly embroidered robes showing ornaments, eyes, snakes and abstract designs similar to those found on bronze vessels. One figure even has a Taotie on the belly – it might be on an undergarment or even a tattoo (see illustration p.159).

While we have no record about the details of Shang clothes offerings, there are Zhou period accounts of the annual sacrifice of clothes for the ancestors. Lü Buwei (*Lüshi Chunqiu, 6.1*) remarks that the during the last month of summer, the administrators of female labour received orders to obtain the colours for the ornaments. Black, yellow, green and red all had to be made with genuine dyes. Nobody was permitted to use low quality or fake colours. The garments were meant for the ancestors and were used for worship on the open land and in the ancestral temples, where they were set up between the flags to indicate the degrees of nobility. Richard Wilhelm (1979:479-480) comments that the ornaments were an axe embroidered in black

Taoti Designs 6

and white, a cross in black and blue, a flame-shaped (?) ornament in blue and red and another, possibly shaped like rice corns, in red and white. All of these symbols appear on the royal robes. The late summer sacrifice of the Zhou was a grand affair. The population had to supply numerous animals for sacrifices to High Heaven, the gods of mountains, streams and the four quarters of the world, to the ancestors and on the altars of earth and grains to ensure the well being of everyone. In the late Zhou period, the noble ladies of the court were personally involved in preparing silk; they participated in the generation of the cloth, the colouring and the sewing, thus setting an example for the rest of the population. They used a wide range of colours for their textiles, and they had a formidable range of rules regarding colour and symbolism. Lü's ritual calendar tells us that the court wore black in winter, green-blue in spring, red in summer and white in autumn. The colours, just like the regulations of food and music, and the dwelling place of the emperor kept the court in tune with heavenly and earthly harmony.

Ritual Reports

Offering was by no means the only ritual of the Shang. On important occasions, the king or a special aristocrat was required to inform the ancestors that something was happening. We find this sort of thing in many Zhou period texts. The *Liji* (*Quli*) tells us that a son who goes travelling has to inform his parents before departure and has to report to them when he returns. It wasn't always convenient, especially when the son had an office at the court and the parents lived far away in a province. The same goes for deceased parents, and during the Shang, it went for the important ancestors and some deities as well. Here, a lot of questions remain. The divinations mention frequent ritual reports for ancestors and deities. Eclipses, locusts, floods, invasion and similar events were reported, but apparently they were not reported to everyone. How did a diviner decide to ask whether a locust invasion should be reported to a specific high ancestor or to the Yellow River Deity but not to the dozens of other deities and ancestors? Was there a pre-selection of likely candidates before the crack-making began? The *Liji* time ancestors also wanted to know about the marriage of a son, mainly as it meant the continuity of their worship. We don't know if the Shang thought the same, as so far, the character for marriage has not been identified or the topic wasn't divined (which I find a little unlikely). One reason Chinese ancestors were so keen on male offspring was that only a son was able to sacrifice to them, and to keep their hungry spirits nourished. Daughters were supposed to lose contact to their ancestors when they married. Whether the Shang had the same idea remains uncertain. Wu Ding often divined whether his wives and queens would give birth to a son, but this may have had political reasons. A king has to prove his virility (which isn't easy when you ingest alcohol and lead continuously), and even if his son may not be his successor, it was important that the royal line continued. Especially if the king, as the *Shujing* hints, had a somewhat questionable childhood among common people. The matter of ritual reports was certainly important to the Shang. Their gods and ancestors were eager for news the Zhou time ancestors were not usually bothered with. They expected to be informed about enemy invasions, war, victory, defeat, flood catastrophes, drought, and locust swarms. I hope you are asking yourself why the ancestors would need to be told. Evidently even the most powerful ones were not expected to be omniscient. That's a common idea in many polytheist cultures; it's only in monotheist religions that a single god is expected to know and control everything. But why should you inform the ancestors that the locusts are stripping the fields when one or another of them had caused the locusts to come in the first place? Was the report a mere formality or was there a magical purpose behind it? Was the important point that all the ancestors should know, and were they expected to exert a certain pressure on the one who had caused the disaster?

Manuscripts and Promises

In Shang religion, the book or rather bamboo scroll with its hallowed inscription was the point where magic interfaced with politics. We see this in many cultures, including ours: the written word seems to gain importance. The mere act of commemorating an occasion adds to its validity. The Zhou entertained such a belief and commemorated many events on sacred bronze cauldrons and ritual vessels. The vessel, henceforth employed in ritual, reminded the participants of important political events, such as the granting of a title or a fief. For the Zhou, an inscription may have been more important than the vessel itself. The Shang custom is not that simple to trace. Most of the ritual vessels of the Shang had no inscription or only a very brief one. In many cases, a clan name was sufficient. But the Shang certainly composed documents. I am sure that the bamboo scrolls commemorated important occasions, but as they went to rot over the millennia, this point is hard to prove. But there is evidence in the oracle bone characters, several of which show the raising of a document, or the offering of a document next to the sacred T. In a few cases a copy of the document was placed in a chest (looking like an elongated *'mouth'* glyph) and some documents were submerged in rivers. It made the river deities, and possibly the underworld deities witnesses of a given contract and ensured their displeasure should it be broken. In a similar fashion, contemporary Daoists burn half of a given spirit document or talisman to ensure that it is efficient in this world and the others. The *Shujing (Jin Teng)*, a chapter composed during the early or middle Zhou, tells of an event that happened soon after the conquest. King Wu had fallen ill, and the fourth of his ten brothers, Zhou Gongdan raised three earth altars in a cleared space, plus a fourth altar to the south of them. Then he took his position nearby and faced north. He placed round jade disks on the three altars and held a symbol of his own rank in his hand. He prayed that the three kings in Heaven (his father and two ancestors of the royal house) should grant King Wu health and take his own life instead. The turtle shell oracle informed him that his request was favourably received. He had the prayer recorded; it was placed in a metal coffer and securely locked. On the next day the king recovered. King Wu continued to live for a while, then his son Song (also called King Cheng) took his place and became the new king. King Cheng was a minor, and while he was underage, the Zhou domain was governed by Zhou Gongdan and by his half brother, the Grand Protector (Taibao) Shi. In the following years, some sons of King Wu allied themselves with the last son of the Shang regent Zhòu Xin and tried to rebel. They assumed, perhaps for very good reason, that Zhou Gongdan had usurped the kingship. The rebellion was violently put down, but Zhou Gongdan had to live with a bad reputation. Sure, he had not died in King Wu's place. However, he was pretty much at odds with Grand Protector Shi, and his position at the court became increasingly threatened. It seems that Zhou Gongdan eventually gave up, and went into retirement where he lived unhappily or maybe died. Shaughnessy, 1997:101-137 and 1999:310-317 gives an excellent account. After two years Heaven sent a terrible storm which wrecked the harvest and tore up great trees. King Cheng and his ministers, worried about the safety of the realm, suspected Zhou Gongdan's involvement. They broke open the metal bound coffer and were shaken by the generous offer that Zhou Gongdan had documented. King Cheng deeply regretted his suspicions and went to reinstate him with all due ceremony. In all likeliness he did not restore a living duke but simply reburied him with honour. Heaven was appeased and sent a contrary wind which lifted the crushed grains, the trees were replanted and the year turned out to be bountiful. Here, the document recorded a religious vow, and served a political function.

Another such ritual appears in the *Lüshi Chunqiu* (12.4). At the beginning of the Zhou period, when King Wu Wen had ascended the throne, his younger brother Zhou Gongdan was sent to make a treaty with two unnamed lords. Three copies of the document were made and smeared with the blood of a sacrificial animal. One of them was buried in the ground. Likewise, when the descendants of the Shang were granted the right to remain alive, to govern a fief and to continue the worship and sacred music of their ancestors, the contract was written in triplicate. One went to the Zhou archives, one to the Shang's and the third was buried at the foot of a mountain. Such rites are good evidence that on certain occasions, the deities of a mountain or of the underworld were required as witnesses. Another document burial is recorded for the year 529 BCE. The *Zuozhuan* relates that a hole was dug and a sacrifice made. The document, a record of an alliance, was recited, laid on top of the sacrificial animal and the hole was filled with earth. Burton Watson (1989:169) adds that this procedure also involved smearing the lips with blood.

Documents also feature in oaths. Mouth and document could signify that a solemn promise or oath was made to sacrifice a number of animals or people at another time. Maybe a king didn't have the time to make a proper offering but needed help fast. A promise was almost as good as the real thing. It also ensured that the ancestors were motivated to lend a helping hand.

The Bin Ritual

Perhaps the most common ritual of the late Shang shows a house or shrine, a version of the sacred T and a foot, sometimes also the figure of a woman (p.670, 707). A female element might be discerned here: the sacred T version is common in the character *'Shrine of the Ancestress'*. The sign *'Bin'* (pin) can be variously translated as *'hosting'* or *'guesting'* depending on whether you want to stress the function of the guest or host. If we read *'hosting'* we might imagine the king hosts an ancestral spirit or deity, if *'guesting'*, the king himself is the guest of the spiritual entity. Naturally, both readings produce an entirely different impression of the rite. K.C. Chang wrote: *"In the oracle bone inscriptions, the word is often placed between the word for king and the name of a specific ancestor or of Ti, the Supreme God. A phrase consisting of these elements is sometimes interpreted as "the king receives a guest or a specific ancestor", or "the king receives as a guest the Supreme God". But more likely it means that the king "called upon" a departed ancestor or God". Shan Hai Ching states "Ch'i went up to pin heaven three times", making it clear that pin refers to the human chief going to the deity rather than the other way around."* (1983:54). The journey of Xia regent Qi to High Heaven is of special importance in Chinese myth, as it indicates something like shamanic flight, astral projection or trance journeys in the imagination. We will discuss these matters further on. Here a little simplification may be useful. The bin rite has excited numerous scholars and provoked considerable debate. Perhaps we should start by considering how it could be done. The character shows a building (a temple or shrine), the sacred T and a foot, indicating *'going'*. Perhaps the rite was performed in a temple or in the special temple of a given ancestor, maybe a building above the tomb. Let's consider the question of dominance. If the king was the dominant player, we could imagine him invoking a spirit in her or his temple, and perform a rite of welcoming and nourishing involving mutual eating and drinking. It might be a rite where the spirit is imagined, but it could also have involved a symbolic representative, like the *'Impersonator of the Dead'* who appears in Zhou period Chinese funeral customs. The impersonator was usually a grandson or close relation of the deceased, who was, for the duration of the rite, addressed by the name of the deceased and who acted, ate and drank in his stead. It's a symbolic personification and involves courteous behaviour by all concerned. Among the Shang, things may have looked a little different. Many of the ancestors and ancestresses had been dead for centuries; hence, a close relation was not readily available. Instead, the impersonator may have been a medium or, just as possible, a well trained wu. Such a ritual may have gone way beyond simple symbolism. It could have involved possession. Now the next question is whether our Shang regents actually wanted a direct contact to the spirit. When you face an obsessed medium, you may get into all sorts of funny situations. Obsessive spirits, especially when they are powerful and nasty minded, are not wont to behave courteously. It might happen that a spirit reprimanded a king, offered unwelcome advice or showed unpredictable behaviour. The thing that characterises obsessive mediumism is lack of control; in fact, in cultures where mediums are obsessed by spirits, unusual, wild and frenzied behaviour is the norm. A medium who behaves just like a normal person is not considered competent. The spirit has to make a grand entrance. Perhaps it will calm down as the rite continues, but in the first stages of the trance, violent shaking, swaying, trembling, speaking in tongues, screaming etc are simply expected by the audience. The spirit shows its credentials by behaving in an unusual way. From a practical point of view, shaking and swaying are useful methods to access altered states of consciousness, to release energy, to channel emotion and to maintain a state of mind that is remote from the everyday personality. The thing about possession by deities and spirits is that another consciousness takes over. If we imagine the Shang as a rising bureaucracy, I doubt that the king would have enjoyed meeting a spirit who might upset military campaigns, treaties or household policies. But if the Shang were a more religious culture, several kings may have been more interested in facing an obsessed medium than in dining with a well-behaved symbolic representative. But things may also have happened in the imagination. Take a look at the late Zhou classic, the *Liji*. For one thing, the *Book of Rituals* informs us (chapter *Zhongyong*, after R. Wilhelm's German translation)

"How wonderful are the ways of the gods and ancestors. One looks for them but cannot see them; one listens to them and cannot hear them. Nevertheless, they form the things and none can act without them. (Legge has: they enter into all things, and nothing is without them). They make the people who dwell on the earth fast, purify themselves and wear ritual dress and to present offerings to them. (Their nature is) like the rushing of great waters, as if they were above our heads, as if they were to the right and left. In the songs it is said:

'The emergence of the gods cannot be measured,
How could anyone ignore them'?

So far reaches the revelation of the numinous, the truth that cannot be obscured."

It's a fascinating passage and worth considering in depth. Here, polytheism almost merges into pantheism. We encounter a world where literally everything, including you and me and every being is a manifestation of the spirits, ancestors or, if you prefer, the One Consciousness. In this awareness, the living and dead are one great, all inclusive totality, a vast and wonderful torrent that derives much of its magnificence from the sheer fact that it cannot be comprehended. You could consider it a statement of a mystical vision of unity. Better still, read it as a practical suggestion for your daily meditation. If you deeply contemplate that the gods and ancestors surround us at all sides, that they indwell us and all things, that there is no difference between what people assume to be living beings and things (on a molecular level, *'life'* and *'death'* do not exist) you will gradually develop a consciousness that extends far beyond the limits of the individual self. Maybe you'd like to start this meditation in a beautiful setting, while going for a walk in the forest or while lazing at a riverside on a sunny day. That's the easy part. It will become more mind-expanding when you practice in less inviting settings – try the main station, a motorway crossing, a garbage dump and discover the divine where you would least expect it.

A concept of divinity which isn't merely here or there but everywhere can be a very powerful experience. Likewise, the rushing of great waters is pure sound. It's like the many sounds which our ears hear (and produce) all the time. Subconsciously, we filter them out, but when we are tired, ill or beside ourselves, such sounds can arise in consciousness. When we read of Wu Ding's numerous divinations regarding tinnitus, we might wonder whether he considered the *'singing in his ears'* as the voice of the ancestors. Not that it made him very happy. The sound of rushing water is also a great source of divination. Remember the medieval Gaelic seers who spent the night wrapped in a cow hide behind a waterfall, listening for the voices of the spirits in the steady roaring of the current. Water has so many voices. In some places, natural hollows amplify overtones, and you can find yourself listening to the song of a water spirit. As waterfalls naturally contain all tones, your mind can filter them for meaningful elements. In China, the water metaphor is at the core of religion, philosophy and meditation. Early Chinese textbooks on medicine describe consciousness itself as a fluid. The flow of the spirits around us connects with the flow of consciousness within. As Hidemi Ishida summarises (in Kohn, 1989:67): *"The flowing mind was present everywhere, it served to control the body and its various energies. The flowing body together with the flowing mind circulate according to the ways of the mind, whose main agents are the will and the intention and whose channels are the conduits of the flowing body."*

Let us return to the bin ritual. While I could imagine Wu Ding appreciating an obsessed medium, I wonder whether he would have liked doing so on a regular scale. I have my doubts regarding Zu Jia, and the kings of period 5a and 5b, who were not interested in funny behaviour at all. The same goes for the Impersonator of the Dead in Zhou times, who were expected to be silent, withdrawn and to act as ritual required them, with great serenity and calm. One tricky question is the frequency of the rite. Wu Ding performed the bin ritual whenever the oracle required him to, and so did the regents of period 2a, 3 and 4. In periods 2b, 5a and 5b it was a daily event, and as so many ancestors required attention, I guess the kings may have performed them in a routine way without interruptions. If we imagined that the kings actually rose to heaven to meet the ancestors or Di, the same problem appears. It is, of course, possible to do a trance journey every day. While beginners may need ten or fifteen minutes to sink into trance, dissociate the outside world awareness and to direct their attention to other realms, practiced mind explorers can do it in less than a minute. Likewise, travelling through realms which you have encountered and visualised many times can be easy and fast. However, the Shang regents, especially in period 2b, 5a and 5b had such an intense ritual schedule that I wonder whether they devoted much time to meeting the ancestors in their realm. A single trance journey every morning to meet several ancestors at once, ok, that's possible. However, bin rituals were not entirely a matter of the imagination. Often enough they involved the beheading of cattle, branch offerings and other practical elements. Sometimes a hundred sacrifices were slaughtered. If they had a trance for each and every ancestor of a given day name, plus sacrifices, divination, dances, music etc I wonder how they found time to decide about politics, meet people, grant audiences, listen to reports, let alone go hunting or wage war. Hence, the more the bin rituals became a daily routine, the less do I believe that they would have involved lengthy trance journeys. Most of the time, I guess, bin rituals happened as ceremonies while spirit journeys were written as feet ascending a ladder.

A Hierarchy of Bin Rites?

The exciting thing about guesting or being guest is that it was not confined to the living. Several inscriptions indicate that the ancestors could bin each other, and a few indicate that sometimes an ancestor ascended to visit another. It's not much evidence, but it shows that the ancestors had their own private life in the otherworld. Some scholars have proposed that the Shang ancestors only existed in relation to the living, as there is no evidence for such a colourful otherworldly life as in Asgard or on Mount Olympus, but then, we can only base our deductions on the topics that were thought worth divining. The ascension and bin inscriptions show that the ancestors celebrated among themselves, if only occasionally. Everything else remains simply open to speculation. An interpretation favoured by David Keightley and a number of American oracle bone scholars postulates a hierarchy. If I may simplify the situation a little, the picture looks as follows. At the bottom are living humans. They sacrifice to their ancestors, who pass the sacrifice to higher ancestors. Usually, it is assumed that the young ancestors of a given sun (day name) bin the earlier ancestors of the same day. This is a general idea, but there are exceptions: as you can see on page Early Ancestors #4, Tai Jia played host for his grandfather Tang. This is good form: the inferior invites the superior for a feast. However, Tai Jia belongs to the day name Jia while Tang, also called Tai Yi or Da Yi, belongs to the day name Yi. Various high ancestors are able to bin Di *'personally'*. Di generously grants harvests, victory and good weather in return. And theoretically, close ancestors might become great ancestors if only enough time goes by. Like a big company with a career for everyone. The subject appears prominently in Puett's *To Become a God*. Puett quotes Keightley *'The Shang conceived of the Nature and Ancestral Powers as occupying a hierarchy of negotiability, with the close ancestors and ancestresses of the pantheon being most open to this kind of pledging, and the higher Powers, both ancestral and natural, being less approachable in this way.' The goal of the ritual was thus to prompt the weaker ancestors to host the more powerful, all the way up to Di. The ritual, then, served two purposes. It maintained the proper hierarchy of the pantheon, and it used the lower, more pliable ancestors, to mollify the higher, more powerful ancestors – ultimately including even Di. ...If the human ability to influence Di directly is limited, humans can nonetheless attempt to influence the lower ancestors, who can influence the higher ancestors, who can in turn influence Di.* (2002:48-49)

This interpretation is not universally accepted. Much of the problem resolves around the questions which periods were are discussing, whether the kings or ritualists had direct access to Di, and whether Di could receive sacrifices at all. Early scholars had assumed that Di was so aloof that it wasn't interested in sacrifices. If we accept this idea, we would have to imagine that the Shang had a very abstract, transcendent and refined concept of highest divinity. It's possible, but not altogether likely, considering how much blood and gore was required by ancestors and gods. Then there are scholars who argue that Di received direct offerings from the king and possibly from the wu, and that these sacrifices, though modest in comparison to the high ancestors, are on a comparable scale to offerings to nature deities. The scholars who favour the hypothetical bin hierarchy usually assume that Di could not receive sacrifices directly, and that the bin hierarchy was necessary to approach Di at all. Now there are plenty of inscriptions that indicate that maybe Di received offerings. These inscriptions are the cause of much debate, especially where it comes to fine points of grammar and the possibility that sometimes the sign Di (with the horizontal 'carpenter's angle') could have been a miswriting for the sign Di Ritual (with the square, rectangle, mouth or circle). Well, we can argue many things when we allow that signs are not what they seem, or that the oracle bone grammar, which is notorious for variation and omissions, should or should not be read in a given way. More so, to replace the sign Di with the sign Di Offering only shifts the problem, as nobody knows much about how the Di offering was performed by the Shang, what it entailed, or what was its theoretical and mythical background. Here, future generations of sinologists are bound to find much entertainment.

Let's take a look at the hierarchical organisation of the ancestors and their possible bin customs. May I mention a few enigmatic points?

Let's assume for a moment that some Shang regents and, according to T.T. Chang and several Chinese scholars, the wu could contact Di directly. It would have been the easiest solution. If Di, as the alleged boss of the company, is happy with a few dead pigs or dogs, nobody needs to nourish an early ancestor like Tang or Shang Jia, or an amazingly powerful (but young) ancestor like Wu Ding with dozens, hundreds or thousands of bovines. If small Di sacrifices were made, why were angry ancestors placated with much greater offerings? It would have been enough to ask Di to have a word with them.

Or consider this one. The number of inscriptions that imply a hosting of one ancestor by another is limited. We could interpret it in several ways. Either the bin hierarchy was self evident. Then, how come it was divined about at all? Or it was not self evident. The few inscriptions that indicate its existence could have been an experiment with a new religious idea, which was not (yet) universally accepted. Religious experiment was common among the late Shang. Perhaps the religious hierarchy was an invention of the *'new school'* periods, where things were ordered, routinised and made predictable. And just as possible, the *'old school'* regents of period 1, 2a, 3 and 4 did not subscribe to it.

There are a range of oracles where we see Di share an offering with a high ancestor. It might look like the hierarchy of hosting Keighley discerned. However, Di also shared offerings with people who probably were not direct ancestors (such as Yi Yin) and even with the deities of Turtle River, Yue Mountain and the Yellow River. I have no idea how these persons and nature deities fit into the neat ancestral hierarchy. Or was there a sharing at all? It could just as well be argued that Di rituals, whatever they were, were performed at the shrines and temples of selected high ancestors, and at places like Mount Yue and the Yellow River.

Regarding Keightley's bin hierarchy, I suspect that there was a pattern in the making. Maybe the Shang of period 2b and 5a, when they got really bureaucratic about their worship, were busy developing such a strictly organised theological system. However, neither of these periods lasted for very long. To install such a well organised piece of spiritual thinking takes time and lots of effort. You need myths, explanations, transform the ritual pattern, devise a number or ranks, schedule the offerings and above all, assure the population and the nobles that the religious reform would not incur heavenly wrath and total disaster. Even with a lot of re-education and missionary effort you would be faced with a lot of stubborn people who would stick to the old ways. Observing how swiftly period 2b rituals disappeared when Geng Ding and Bi Xin became regents in period 3, I can't help suspecting that Zu Jia's (period 2b) bureaucratic sacrificial schedule, and all it implied, were never universally accepted. However, let's not exclude anything. In researching prehistory, the main thing isn't facts (whatever that may be) but degrees of probability. Maybe there was, towards the end of the Shang, a trend to develop a system of offerings that united people, nobles, royals, close ancestors, high ancestors and Di in a neat hierarchical structure for mutual benefit and regular career moves. It would explain the exclusion of important nature deities in periods 2b, 5a and 5b, as there was no place for them in the royal family cult. To understand the late Shang we might consider that no single model or world view explains everything. Even in the 250 years or so for which the oracle bones give evidence we observe several drastic changes in religious thought. One king worships anyone and anything, another eliminates a large amount of ancestors and all nature gods and institutes a unique new ritual schedule. A little later most of the old pantheon comes back, is eliminated again and finally we have a regent who doesn't seem to care about gods or ancestors at all. That's an enormous amount of change in a very short time. So there are plenty of questions. Let me list them for your entertainment: How could there be a single, permanent hierarchy during such a time of transformation? What happened to those queens who received sacrifice in period 2b but were eliminated in period 5? And where do we place the nature gods in such a hierarchy? Are they above the ancestors but beneath Di? Or do they exist side by side with ancestors, some of whom received much greater sacrifices than most gods? And did the close ancestors ever get a chance to rise to greater authority? Was age enough for promotion? How come some early ancestors (probably total failures) got hardly any offerings? And how were the ancestors organised? Was dynasty founder Tang at the head, was it clan founder Wang Hai or martial Shang Jia who took revenge for him? Or primal ancestor Nau (Monkey)? Where is Lady Jiandi, and where are her sacrifices? What shall we make of Yi Yin? If we trust later records, he was a musician or cook, became a prime minister, and ruled for a brief period when the proper regent was absent. Allegedly he did not belong to the royal house at all. Nevertheless, the inscriptions mention him with more respect than Tang himself, and grant him the power to calm the storm wind and to incite enemy nations to war. That's more than can be said about most ancestors. Was Yi Yin originally a god? And were the gods organised in a hierarchy or did their number and importance grow and shrink, depending on the ethnic groups that participated in the Shang territory?

What happens when we see the various expressions of Shang ritual as a series of attempts to unite the cult of the royal ancestors with a wide range of deities, nature powers and mythical beings who were not organised at all? Finally, should we assume that the late Shang actually had one or several logical, reasonable theological system that can be understood by thinking rationally and logically? It would be quite amazing. I know not a single ancient mythology which happens to be logical. Wherever people develop beliefs, they create subjective variations. Since when have people been rational at all?

Feelings of Love and Respect

There is more to rites and offerings than things you do and things you give. The Zhou were highly obsessed with performing their rites to the finest details of propriety. It was a basic idea of their world view that the Mandate of Heaven might be withdrawn if frivolous, wanton or unduly drunk behaviour stained the ceremonies. The emperor went to considerable lengths to perform every ritual to its last detail, and he expected his representatives, the dukes, marquises and the entire aristocracy to do the same. In Zhou times, an aristocrat who performed the rites in a sloppy, careless or disrespectful fashion could expect savage punishment, as his conduct endangered the welfare of the entire state. Hence, a great many noble people were at pains to perform perfectly. This, however, was not how the rituals really ought to be conducted. In the chapter *Zhongni Yanyu* of the *Liji* (translation Legge) we find a few lines that had may come from Kongzi himself:

"The idea in the border sacrifices to Heaven and Earth is that they should give expression to the loving feeling towards the spirits; the ceremonies of the autumnal and summer services in the ancestral temple give expression to the loving feeling towards all in the circle of the kindred; the ceremony of putting down food (by the deceased) serves to express the loving feeling towards those who are dead and for whom they are mourning, the ceremonies and archery fêtes and the drinking at them express the loving feeling towards all in the district and the neighbourhood; the ceremonies of festal entertainment express the loving feelings towards visitors and guests."

Welcome to an excellent meditation: the cultivation and expression of loving feelings for spirits, kindred, the deceased, the district, the neighbourhood, visitors and guests. You can explore this in a trance by sending fond thoughts to those who surround you, who you have known, who you will know, and every other entity and thing that comes into your mind. Kongzi was on to something worthwhile here. Zhuangzi, I am sure, would have extended it further, and replaced the district and the neighbourhood with the whole wide world and everyone and everything in it (see the anecdote of the lost axe). Another great idea is that you are actively making the loving feeling. Too many people are shy about making good feelings. They expect other people or even things or events to make them happy. As happiness, love and sympathy have their chemical foundation in the limbic system, you don't have to wait for them to come along. You can cultivate them here and now and radiate them into the world you be-live. It's one of the most essential acts in any good ritual, trance and everyday experience: make the feelings that suit the event. The gods and spirits thrive on good and strong feelings, and so do the people around you. Good government itself depends on loving feelings. *Liji* chapter *Aigong Wen* proposes a coupling of love and respect. When Duke Ai questioned Kongzi about the marriage rites, Kongzi declared that it is essential that the groom in his square-topped cap should personally go to meet the bride, and that *"the superior man commences with respect as the basis of love. To neglect respect is to leave affection unprovided for. Without loving there can be no (real) union; and without respect the love will not be correct. Yes, love and respect lie at the foundation of government."* The duke, startled at what seemed an unnecessary honour for the bride uttered his objections, but

Kongzi overruled them by pointing out that this sort of marriage is the union of two different families in friendship and love, and the foundation of the future sacrifices to heaven and Earth, the ancestors, and the altars of the spirits of the land and the grain. Indeed the marriage rite connects past and future, the living and the dead, and the happy couple are representatives of whole lineages of spiritual entities whose loving (and respectful) union ensures the harmony of the realm and the stability of the state.

But let us continue with Zhou time ancestral worship. The noble of the late Zhou was expected to venerate a few close ancestors, primarily the parents, and did not have to handle dozens of them like the Shang kings did. While the ancestors and gods might be invisible, as the late Zhou assumed, the rituals were certainly based on vivid imagination. The *Liji* is much concerned with proper behaviour, but it did not reduce worship and ritual to an empty formality. Chapter 13 insists:

"the noble, before performing (the sacrifice) has to create the right mood with his feelings."

It's an excellent observation. You can perform a ritual and hope that the proper feelings arise spontaneously, but if you want to be sure, you change your feelings before you even begin. Richard Bandler pointed out that making feelings is an art form. For magick, it's a must and even if you want to live a simple but happy life it's essential that you learn to make feelings that make your life worth living, instead of waiting for the universe to make them for you. The Zhou nobles got into the mood by careful preparation. Before sacrificing to the Yellow River they performed rituals for a minor stream. Before sacrificing to the Tai Shan Mountain they did the minor sacrifices to Mount Lin. Before the bull was slain, it was fed for three months; before the lord sacrificed, he fasted for seven days and spent three nights in the fasting room. Now the late Zhou did a lot of ritual, but the earlier Shang exceeded them by far. Many Shang regents sacrificed almost every day. I doubt they needed much preparation to get into the mood. In fact, it might have been harder for them to get out of it, relax, or play with the kids.

Meeting the Ancestors

The *Liji* gives a brief but practical introduction to the veneration of deceased parents. Chapter *Jiyi* after the German translation of Richard Wilhelm relates:

"For serious fasting one moved to the inner chambers of the house, for preparatory fasting one dwelled in the outer chambers. (Legge reads: The severest vigil and purification is maintained and carried on inwardly; while a looser vigil is maintained externally). On the day of the offering the son thought of his parents, he recalled their quarters, their smile, the tone of their voice and their attitude; he remembered those things that made them joyous and

that what they liked to eat. After having fasted and meditated thus for three days he could perceive those for whom he fasted. When he approached the ancestral room on the day of the offering he was excited that he would surely see them reside on the ancestral seat; when moving, coming and going, he was serious, as if he would certainly hear how they moved and talked; and when he left through the door, he listened with halting breath for their sighs. Thus the devotion of the Ancient Kings required that they did not allow the images of their parents to fade from their vision, that their voices did not fade in their hearing and that their opinions and tendencies were not forgotten in their hearts. What you love with all of your power remains; what you worship with all of your power reveals itself. ...

On memorial days like these one keeps one's actions free of other deeds; not as they would be unlucky days, but as on such days all senses are aimed at something specific, and one does not dare to devote all attention to private business. Only a saint can sacrifice to the divine, only a devout son can sacrifice to his parents. To sacrifice means to approach closely. One has to approach the divine before one can sacrifice to it. Hence, a devout son approaches the impersonator of the dead without shyness."

A little further, we learn that King Wen, the very founder of the Zhou Dynasty, was so devout when he sacrificed to his parents that he did not dare to break his reminiscences by sleep. When dawn came, he was still awake, fondly recalling his parents. On the sacrificial day his heart was torn between joy and sorrow. When he offered to them, he was joyous that they came, and when they departed, sorrow overwhelmed him. All through the devotion, he had their names on his lips, and he wore that faraway look of a person who sees the departed and judges their gestures and listens for their wishes. It's a touching description. You could read it as a specific ritual, but when you look more closely, you will find highly practical trance techniques involved. Just imagine withdrawing from everyday life and visualising persons, spirits or deities for an entire three days without interruption! That's a very powerful sort of yoga!

Finally, let us consider that it may be an easy thing to imagine your parents, as you have plenty of memories of them. But how do you build up a vision of a distant ancestor? Here, T.T. Chang argues that the Shang probably had descriptions of their major ancestors (1970:84). The *Yanzi Chunqiu* (*Master Yan's Spring and Autumn Annals*), a work of the Warring States Period, gives close descriptions of some Shang worthies. As Chang observes, when Yanzi wrote, the early Shang had been dead for more than a millennium:

"Tang has a light skin colour, he is tall and bearded. His back is slightly bent. He has a high pitched voice...Yi Yin is dark skinned and of small statue. He has dishevelled hair and he is

likewise bearded. His face is wide at the top and smaller at the bottom. He has a curved back and a deep voice."

Maybe the descriptions were recorded in bamboo books and passed from generation to generation, just as the Daoist sorcery books give the detailed appearances of gods and spirits. Visualised over generations, such images, no matter whether accurate or wholly fictional, can become amazingly durable.

Fasting

Chinese ritual makes much of fasting. There were several variations. In early Daoist practice, the immortality seekers often tried to transcend the world by withdrawing into the mountains. That's a type of fast already: it fasts the natural, human urge to meet people and to communicate. Many went beyond this. In order to become immortal, or to develop an immortal consciousness, fancy diets were explored. Some fasted by avoiding the five grains. This is a blanket term signifying ordinary food. The basic idea is that normal people die. When one avoids eating what they do, immortality might be a natural result. A passage that may come from fourth century alchemist Ge Hong claims: *"It is a fact that food is where the 100 diseases and wicked demons gather. The less you eat, the more your mind will open up, and the longer your life span will be. The more you eat, the more your mind will be closed, and the shorter your life span will be."* (Quoted by Eskildsen,1998:21 who explores weird Daoist diets at length). Ge Hong was right when he observed that consciousness changes accompany lack of food, but wrong about the life span. It may go against popular belief, but underweight persons have a 40% higher mortality rate than people with normal weight. Even very fat persons tend to live longer than extremely thin ones. The reason may be that heart problems and serious diseases exhaust thin people much faster than others (Pollmer, 2007:17-19; 96-99). .The early immortality seekers were not aware of such things. In an age when the average life expectation was less than forty years, and most people had little to eat anyway, middle age heart problems rarely mattered. In fact, the immortality seekers were not always interested in preserving their health. Some went for zero food, but others tried odd food to attain transcendence. Chixuzi, for instance, refrained from eating the five grains and replaced them by feeding on mists and vapours. Chen Anshi, showing more moderation, gave up eating, but continued to drink water. Some went for special diets. One favourite was to feed on pine needles, pine seeds and pine resin. As the pine is an evergreen conifer that can attain formidable age, the common belief was that the immortality seeker would do likewise. One such candidate was Lady Maonü, a former concubine of the Qin Dynasty, who grew extremely hairy on this diet. She lived in the mountains for over two hundred years, and when she was brought to civilisation and put on a normal diet she lost her abundant hair, grew old and died. It did not upset her much: many adepts attained proper immortality only by dying, and some, like Maonü, became a goddess in the process. Other adepts attained immortality by eating only raspberry roots, lingzhi mushroom, various blossoms, flowers, plums, peaches, apricot kernels, lotus root, sesame, oysters, deer horn, alum, stalactites, salt (with and without various sulphates), mica, silver, gold, tin, red kaorinite, carbonate of lead, clay, mercury, cinnabar, realgar (arsenic sulphite), jade, jadeite, nephrite or simply replaced food with breathing exercises. Dedicated adepts fed on morning dew and sunrays, and managed to leave this world fairly soon. The death of their withered body was taken as proof of their transcendence. Before they reached that state, I am sure they had a memorable time and plenty of exciting visions. As a side effect, they started the science of alchemy.

Another sort of fasting had an essential place in Zhou period ritual, such as at the death of one's parents. The chapter *Wensang* of the *Liji* requires the virtuous son to take off his cap, to keep his hair in a bag, to tuck up the skirt of his dress under the girdle, to walk barefoot and to wail exceedingly. He had to avoid drinking water and nothing was cooked for him for three days. Instead, he was served small amounts of water and gruel by his neighbours. To fast in this fashion upsets the normal rules of appearance, conduct and denies the normal appetite for anything savoury. The custom serves to disrupt everyday behaviour and thought, but it also causes a magical condition that leaves the mourner in a dangerous state between life and death.

How should we imagine fasting for ritual purposes? Kongzi allegedly said (*Biaoji* of the *Liji,* after Legge) "*Vigil and fasting are required (as a preparation) for serving the spirits (in sacrifice)...*" sadly, he did not elaborate on the matter. We cannot be sure what the Zhou considered fasting, let alone the Shang, but if it involved a reduction of the food intake, we can be sure that all sorts of mind-altering changes were involved. As fasting is a key element in many practices of the nobles, the wu, immortality seekers and early Daoists, let me digress a little. There is a chemistry of fasting. It isn't much explored yet, but what we know so far is amazing. When you shut down the supply of food, a lot of systems go gaga. Essentially, you are activating survival programs that were really useful during the last ice age, when hunger tended to happen every winter. When you body notices that the food supply stops, it begins to release adrenaline. That would be useful if you could go out to hunt some reindeer, but when the herds are late and there is nothing to kill, there is no use to waste the valuable substance. Adrenaline is good to make you fast, excited and improves your reflexes. It isn't useful when you simply sit around and haven't got anything to do. So the adrenaline supply ceases and cortisol is released. That's a helpful long term stress hormone. It reduces your appetite, breathing and metabolism and is useful to conserve energy while keeping you alert and ready for action. Sadly, it has a number of side effects, such as tension, edginess, a bad temper and a tendency to take your bad mood out on others or yourself. A few days on cortisol are not too bad, but when they extend into weeks (as in most jobs nowadays) the results are pretty bad for your state of mind and those around you. Hungry people, just like people with anorexia and bulimia, have plenty of trouble with cortisol. However, they get relief from internal stress as the serotonin level tends to rise and fall erratically. Unlike what you read in the papers, serotonin is not really a *'happiness'* chemical. It allows you to coordinate difficult processes and activities and keeps many systems in tune. When you have too little, you may feel out of control, scatterbrained, easily distracted and off-balance. When you get too much, you may become obsessive in thought and behaviour, and suffer from all sorts of paranoid delusions and/or mind blowing revelations and ecstatic insights. Lack of serotonin can reduce the amount of available dopamine, hence the ability for exhilaration and intense perception. As dopamine is intimately connected with the ability to feel joy, a lack of it may lead to worry, crisis and depression. Most human addictions have to do with the dopamine level. It does not matter much whether you are hooked on nicotine, hashish, cocaine, heroin, alcohol, gambling, risk-sports or excessive sex: in each case the addictive element is the dopamine rush that docks in at the so-called pleasure centres. Fasting, hunger and anorexia often involve phases with high levels of serotonin (and dopamine), which can produce ecstatic sensations but also revert into possessiveness and anxiety. It does not stay that way. To produce serotonin, the body needs to extract tryptophan from food, and when no food comes in, the serotonin level eventually drops. Some experience this as a relief. It won't make them happy, but at least not as anxious or obsessive as before. (Milkman & Sunderwirth, 2010:119-121) Fasting can lead to extreme states of detached lucidity and ecstatic experiences, especially when your body decides that hunger is a sort of pain and that your endorphins, i.e. internal opiates might improve your mood. Endorphins also help to numb the hunger pangs for a while. So if you use fasting for spiritual ends, vanity or are simply addicted to the chemical effects, you are in for a lot of extreme experiences. Interestingly, many anorexics thrive on sport. Exercise used to be thought to release endorphins. This is only the case with prolonged marathon running: your body identifies the extended strain with injury, and releases painkillers. Other sorts of sports don't tend to release endorphins, presumably as the effort doesn't continue for such a long time. However, strong motion is one of the easiest and fastest ways to reduce the amount of stress hormone cortisol in your system. Light motions, as in dancing, qigong and taijiquan raise the serotonin level. Many hungry people, just like former heroin addicts, tend to go for sports to reduce stress and produce a natural high. When we look at those adepts who fasted habitually, such as the early Daoists or a lot of Indian ascetics, we observe extreme changes of mood in very short time spans. These people were literally living on the edge. One moment they could be loving, blissed out and compassionate, the next moment a monumental wrath could shake them out of their composure and make them curse and rant. The *Mahābhārata* is full of such charming characters. The characteristic thing for fasting as a drug experience is instability. It gets even more extreme when fasting is occasionally interrupted for a little snack that raises the serotonin level for a short and ecstatic episode. Many tāntrikas of the left hand path used such tactics to empower their worship. They fasted all day, doing intense ritual and meditation (occasionally fortified with hashish), and when they were really worn out in the evening they celebrated a minor sacrifice involving spicy food, meat, fish, alcohol and, if possible, lovemaking (see *Kālī Kaula*, 369-381 for such a ritual format). The resulting bliss was channelled into religious experiences. Likewise, if you fast all day but break your fast to eat and drink with your deities or ancestors, your mind chemistry may undergo interesting changes. I am sure many nobles of the Zhou had such experiences. I am not so sure about the Shang, as the royal ritual timetable was so formidable that prolonged preparations and lengthy fasting seem unlikely. When you have to do the bin ritual with one or more ancestors almost every day, you cannot devote long periods to fasting in seclusion. On the other hand, your daily contemplation will make it much easier to enter trance states without effort.

Ritual Purification

One ritual that comes up with great frequency in period 1, 2a, and less frequently in periods 3,4 and 5 is the ritual purification, or exorcism, as some would have it. The character for this ritual shows a kneeling person and a piece of string (i.e. two silkworm cocoons) (p.677). The sign has not made it into modern Chinese. T.T. Chang observes (1970:51) that it survived after the Zhou period as a partial structure of the characters *'to open the reins (of a horse)'*, *'to drive a horse forward'* and to conduct a ritual which was forgotten by the time the *Shuowen* was compiled. He argued that the common element of these characters might be *'to drive'* as in *'to drive out evil'*, especially as a variation of the Shang time character (p.678) means to defend oneself, or to resist some evil influence. To use the term *'exorcism'* might be a good idea, if that expression had not acquired so many silly connotations thanks to the movie industry and the Catholic Church. Wu Ding frequently divined whether a person could do with ritual purification. On occasion, he ordered wives, princes and officers to undergo such rituals, and in rare instances we read that the army itself, returning from war, was purified. It would be nice to know why. Had they been unlucky or unsuccessful? Or was war such a dirty business that purification was needed?

The important difference between normal exorcisms (such as conducted by the Vatican every day) and their Shang variation is that the purification could be performed for oneself, but it was also occasionally done by another person. In most inscriptions the issue is not mentioned, so we are left guessing as to who performed the rite. As T.T. Chang observed, the oracle bones do not hint at professional exorcists (such as existed during the Zhou period). The only other *'person'* present was usually an ancestor. It could have been a medium or an impersonator of the dead. Not in the classic Zhou style, which usually required a grandson to impersonate the deceased: the Shang ancestors had usually been dead for generations, and the same went for their grandsons. What was the function of the ancestor? Some early researchers, thinking of ancestors in the style of the middle and late Zhou, assumed that they helped and purified the person undergoing the ritual. Professor Chang disagreed. He quoted the inscription: *"Divination: / diseased / teeth. / ritual purification / before / Father Yi?"* and relates it to the divination *"Diseased / teeth. / Not / perhaps / have / curse? Not / perhaps / Father Yi (is responsible)? / Divination: / not / perhaps / (pain) stops?"* (T.T.Chang, 1970:35 & 51). In his estimate, Wu Ding's toothache was probably caused by deceased Father Yi, hence the need to have him attend the ritual purification. However, as many inscriptions show, the king often divined whether a whole range of ancestors was responsible for a given disease. We can be sure that both divinations were made by Wu Ding, but it is possible that there were years between them. After all, Wu Ding lived to formidable old age and no doubt toothaches happened frequently. In Chang's opinion, the attending ancestor was not there for any benevolent function, mainly as the ancestors, in his reading, didn't do benevolence. However, I guess we should leave the question open. It is possible that the ancestor, after being suitably bribed with offerings, acted as an otherworldly helper.

How was the ritual performed? The sorry truth is that we don't know. However, if the rite was based, as the character hints, on some meditation involving string or rope, a bit of knot sorcery would fit the bill. Knot spells are ancient and have been performed by many cultures. You can use knots to bind good things and keep them, or bind bad things and destroy them. Or you can loosen knots to make things happen naturally. Exorcistic knot spells can be done in a crude and primitive way. You simply raise the feeling or thought complex that you want to dissociate, bind it into a piece of rope, burn it and go your way. That's exorcism from a dualist point of view. It is based on the idea that you and your trouble are different and distinct, and benefit from separation. Sadly, such spells can have nasty side effects. Some people end relationships that way: they dissociate everything connected with their partner. Maybe they damn it, distort the memories or forget the lot. In the process, they also eliminate all the good times, the useful experiences and whatever made them enjoy being with that person. The result is a highly unbalanced personality with massive gaps in the past history. The same happens when a person changes her or his own history by totally eliminating a section of the past. Whatever you want to exorcise, you can be sure it contains material that is useful, and worth recycling. Good exorcists are transformers and integrators. So if you want to do this ritual, try this. First you withdraw to some place where you won't be disturbed. You calm down and call for a spirit helper, deity or ancestor. In this stage, prayer, offerings and especially loving emotions are useful. Next, when your spiritual partner is well established, you think about whatever you want to exorcise from your system. In many 'shamanic' systems, as among the Korean mudang, the main operation is to take the sufferer out of the sphere of evil influences and bad luck. So you start by imagining your afflictions. Make it a vivid vision. Large pictures, strong colour, motion, sound...add what you need to make the visions really impressive. This is not time for tiny images and half hearted dabbling. Imagine what harms, pollutes or upsets you and get good access to the emotions. Then dissociate. Imagine that you are outside of yourself, and see yourself sitting there, upset by all those feelings. That person will be a sorry sight. Now you have the distance that you need. You will still have feelings, but they won't be the feelings you originally had. Instead, you will feel ABOUT the situation. And when you see yourself sitting there, writhing under the influence of unwanted thoughts and influences, pick up a piece of rope and knot the whole rubbish into it. Make knot after knot, bind the evil and all it used to mean to you. Each knot frees you from the evils of the past. When you are done, get back into yourself. Light a fire and burn the rope. See the problems go up in fire and smoke. Now your spirit partner leans forward and devours the energies and ideas that come out of the flames. If you put in a lot of emotions, your spirit partner will receive and transform plenty of energy. When the cinders have gone out, reach out, take the hands of your spirit partner and let all that is useful, valuable and meaningful return into your system. It can be a mind shaking experience. When you are done, calm down, give your thanks, breathe gently, get up, and do something entirely different.

The Purity of Water

Chinese philosophy makes use of many symbols, but none is as important as water. The circuit of water was a metaphor that readily lent itself to Confucianism and Daoism, and even appears in the writings of later thinkers, including Chairman Mao. You read earlier how the effortless flow of the Dao can best be described as a water way. Likewise, mind was closely linked to blood, vitality circulated with the fluids within body, adepts concentrated the essence of their qi in jing (here: sexual essences and secretions), immortality seekers charged their saliva with colourful vapours before swallowing it and time itself was compared with the flowing of a river. Water was the supreme drink offering; water served as a model for sagely conduct. From the sacred rivers, mystic diagrams appeared. Kongzi said that the intelligent find joy in water and the humane find joy in mountains. The intelligent are lively while the humane are still. The intelligent are joyous and the humane are long lived (*Analects*, 6.22.). Here, water represents the incessant flow of sheer living adaptability while the mountains represent duration, rest and stability. Confucian thought claims that when a gentleman sees a river, he gazes at it. Kongzi himself enthusiastically exclaimed *"ah, water! ah water!"* (Shui zai! Shui zai!) when he began to eulogise it. The topic was beautifully treated by Sarah Allan (1997).

Let's move to earlier periods. Among the mythical Xia people, water was the prevailing element. The archaeological record seems to support this claim: pottery of the Longshan cultures is frequently ornamented with fish, frogs, turtles, snakes and dragons. All of them represent aspects of water. Westerners may be surprised how closely Chinese dragons relate to water. Western dragons frequently spit fire. Eastern dragons tend to bring rain. Both dragons can usually fly. When you want to observe Chinese dragons, you have to look for the water in your neighbourhood. Small dragons live in brooks and rivers, larger dragons govern streams, lakes and entire oceans. Like water, they move in changeful, flowing lines, graceful, without intent or effort. As vapours, they rise into the skies and form clouds. Like rain, they return to earth, and like snakes and worms they disappear into the deep. Here, water is more than just the substance and element we associate with it. It is the entire rhythmic pattern of being and cessation, of birth and death and rebirth manifest in continuous transmutation. As you read earlier, the *Guodian Laozi* postulates that everything came from water, and that there is water around and under the earth. The Shang did much to distance themselves from Xia customs, but dragons, snakes and indeed water remained among their most important symbols. Fu Hao and other regents had several specialised dishes for ritual washing in their tombs. Typical is the flat *pan* vessel with a sprout. Many of them were decorated with aquatic animals. When the vessel was full of water, each ripple made the images come alive. During the Western Zhou, *pan* vessels were increasingly decorated with inscriptions. Such bronzes were used to wash hands before ceremonies and banquets. Oracle bone inscriptions show that water was frequently used for purification rituals. Sometimes we have a person standing in a vessel, sometimes it is a foot or hand with drops. Like the knot spell we had earlier, you can charge water with a given idea. Fill it with your waste, rubbish and negative emotions and pour it away. Or do the opposite. To consecrate water, you can leave out the dissociation, i.e. you don't have to watch yourself doing the rite. Good emotions are there to be enjoyed as fully as you can. Simply fill yourself with passionate joy, health and enthusiasm. Make it a really strong emotion. Visualise how it flows into the fluid. Have a drink and it returns to you. Water is an excellent carrier of thoughts, memories and feelings.

What about hydromancy? Divination with water is an ancient custom. Several methods are recorded. Some people watched springs or gazed into the flow of rivers or whirlpools, and allowed the ripples to calm, enchant and inspire them. Others gazed at still water. This method seems to be a Mesopotamian invention. It appears among the Assyrians and the Babylonians, and was soon popular in wide parts of Asia. The Egyptians made it a fine art (see the third century CE *Leyden Papyrus* for several impressive invocations), and frequently employed boys as mediums, while King Numa Pompilius (750 – 672 BCE), the second regent of Rome, is the first European on record who used it. Varro mentions him (first century BCE) and claimed that hydromancy is a divination that makes the images of gods appear in water. The deities then reveal the future. He also referred to a boy in Tralles, Asia Minor, who saw Hermes appear in a bowl of water, who foretold the Mithridatic war in 160 verses. Meanwhile, the Celto-Germanic people, ever ready to visit springs for worship, sacrifice, divination, omens and oath-taking, either developed it independently or received it from an unknown eastern source. When Caesar fought the Suebi, the mothers of that conglomerate of tribes gazed into a river to divine the war strategy. Plutarch presumably got this tale from captives; while Caesar, interrogating other people, recorded that the Suebian mothers cast lots. Both methods are likely, and Tacitus informs us that divination by lots (runes?) had to be confirmed by other methods.

Water gazing has its place in Chinese myth. When Fuxi was meditating on the banks of River Ho, a dragon-horse appeared in the waves. On its back it carried a mystic diagram, the River Ho Chart that became the foundation of Chinese numerology, as it linked the eight trigrams of the *Yijing* with numbers. The arrangement is called the Map of Earlier Heaven, as it describes the absolute order of cosmic forces in their original, primal state. Much later, when Yü the Great was watching the flowing waters of River Lo, he had a vision of a turtle whose back was adorned with a similar, but different arrangement. Here, numerology revealed the patterns of Later Heaven, the realm of change, the pattern of the seasons and the harmony of the manifest world.

This is speculative, but the Shang may have used flat water vessels for skrying. Perhaps they acquired the art from neighbouring cultures or they developed it independently. Considering the sacredness of water in Chinese culture, it may have been a native development. A character for a Shang ritual shows a person with a huge eye staring into a water vessel (p.676). Maybe it is simply watching its own reflection, and using the water as a mirror. However, as Fu Hao's grave goods show, bronze mirrors were available in her time, so the wealthier aristocrats could have done their face and hair without stooping awkwardly over a bowl. Also, if you still your mind and watch your reflection for a long time, interesting hallucinations (and trance states) may develop. The water bowl could have been a device to meditate or receive visions. The object is a hypnotic focus that allows trained persons to space off and receive insights, be it in the reflection or the imagination. Mengzi may have alluded to something like this when he wrote *"There is an art to looking at water"*.

Five Rituals: Nourishing Ancestors According to the 'New School'

In Wu Ding's period, life was an enigmatic, surprising and often mysterious flow of events. The numerous ancestors, spirits and deities influenced the human and natural world, and behind every incident an occult power could be at work. No matter whether it was a locust plague, invasion by a hostile fang state, a sudden rainfall, colourful clouds, a hunting accident, an unusual dream or a toothache, there was always the likeliness that an unseen power was responsible. Wu Ding made sure. More than any regent I have ever heard of, he kept his diviners busy from morning to night. Wu Ding divined. The oracle revealed which ancestor had caused that misfortune, made that belly ache or ought to be present during the ritual purification. Usually, the trouble could be influenced, to a degree, by offerings and purifications. The pattern of events, divination, offerings worked just like a language. When a minor ancestor wanted attention, s/he might cause worms or pregnancy troubles. A great ancestor would mess up the harvest or make the enemies come round.

But not all sacrifices were made to placate angry spirits. A large amount of offerings was given to strengthen and nourish the ancestors. Strengthening could be done by sending additional people to the dead regent's otherworldly habitation, like servants and concubines. It could also and literally mean to feed them with choice foodstuff, ritual meals, blood and beverages. Here, the basic idea was that the dead, just like the living, need to eat to remain powerful. T.T. Chang (1970:130) cites the *Zuozhuan*, commentary to the year 535 BCE; let me translate from the German:

"With the birth of a human being a body-soul appears. The spiritual soul separates from it, as it belongs to the bright principle. The power of the body- and the spiritual soul grow stronger the more nourishment is derived from the essence of food. There are people whose spiritual powers grow so strong that they appear to be divine. Yet even the souls of a simple man or a simple woman remain powerful if they have died a violent death; they remain so strong that they can overwhelm the living and cause misfortune...

The regent of our state was in office for three generations for rulers...in his lifetime, he absorbed a great amount of food and essences. Also, his clan, on whose offering he depends after death, is very mighty. As he lost his life by violence it is not surprising that his dead spirit causes unrest."

It's a neat description. Let me add that Shang time notions on the nature of the soul remain a difficult subject. Whether the Shang believed in a single soul, or, as the people of the late Zhou, Qin and Han period, in an earthly body soul (po) and a celestial spirit soul (hun) is hard to determine. However, I believe that it is quite likely. After all, some inscriptions require the king to ascend to meet an ancestor. It appears that those ancestors dwelled in the sky, perhaps in the company of Di and the celestial gods. It looks like meeting a spirit soul. On the other hand, each ancestor was equipped with an underground home where s/he could dwell in luxury, surrounded by servants, retainers, pet dogs and guarded by elite warriors. Here we have the ancestors in two places at once, appearing as the gods of height and depth, and this is a lot easier when you happen to have two souls. It is unlikely that such a model of the afterlife was precisely as later generations imagined. The Han, in particular, combined the idea of the two souls with a lot of yin/yang cosmology, which did not exist in the Shang period. Nor did the Shang believe that food and drink was all the ancestors required. In Wu Ding's period, they also wanted to be entertained with music and dance, they wanted to be informed and desired thanks for deeds well done. In short, they were less interested in food essences than in emotion, attention, respect, possibly they wanted love and certainly they inspired fear. Nourishment sacrifices were common and refined in Wu Ding's time.

When Wu Ding was dead and buried, his successor continued in a similar way. How this happened is a little unclear. Zu Ji may have followed Wu Ding, but his influence is so minute that it remains doubtful if he made it to the coronation. Then Zu Geng assumed control. He attempted to continue as successfully as Wu Ding had done, but his reign is not very remarkable, nor does it seem to have been overly successful. It may be speculated whether former allies broke away from the Shang alliance at the time. Zu Geng's reign (period 2a) left us with a range of not too impressive inscriptions. Perhaps his successor Zu Jia assumed control in a difficult time. He introduced major religious reforms.

Zu Jia was a daring king. Maybe the Shang were undergoing a hard time. Had things continued to run smoothly, major changes would hardly have been needed. Zu Jia reformed the calendar and introduced a regular and predictable sacrificial routine. The gods of nature, the directions and even Di were largely ignored, likewise, a range of obscure, early and mythical ancestors were kicked out of the sacrificial time table. The range of important ancestors was narrowed, and each of them was provided with five festivities a year. The five rituals were by no means new. Feather dancing may have been popular before Wang Hai founded the clan alliance, and Wu Ding was certainly familiar with drum sacrifices, raw meat offerings, cooked grain offerings and dances for selected ancestors and ancestral ladies. He did not perform these systematically but used divination to learn when an ancestor was in need of nourishment or entertainment. Nor were the five rituals the major religious activities of Wu Ding's time. Period 1 is full of rituals, and many of them remain way beyond our comprehension.

Zu Jia hoped to make every important spirit happy by an equal amount of attention, and a basic set of festivals that should suffice to ensure a good life in the otherworld and a benevolent influence on earth. In general, he adhered to his time table, but in practice he still performed a divination a few days before each rite and asked if the ancestor would want the celebration, and would not curse the king. It says a lot about Zu Jia's worldview that such divinations routinely ended with the question: *"not have a curse?"*. By contrast, in period 3, when the five ritual timetable was annulled by King Geng Ding and Queen Bi Xin, questions regarding nourishment sacrifices end with the query whether the ancestor would *"give support?"* It's an entirely different and much friendlier mindset. Later on, in period 5, we observe a routine ending *"not have misfortune/disaster?"* Obviously, the outlook had become less optimistic.

Back to Zu Jia's reform. It takes a change of faith to dare such a drastic step. That it happened so fast may have had several reasons. One possibility is that things were going so badly that the new routine found instant approval. When nothing works, any new approach is better than repeating earlier mistakes. But we could also speculate whether Zu Jia's five rituals resembled an earlier (and unknown) Shang ritual timetable from the period before Wu Ding. Many scholars assumed that Wu Ding's style of worship must have been the original Shang religion, as it involved so many excessive rituals, huge offerings, human sacrifices and so on. There is something impressively crude and bombastic about his reign. Wu Ding, however, was an innovator. He was the first Shang king who insisted on keeping oracle bone records. The *Shujing* describes him as a brilliant and unusual regent. Even his policy of employing his wives in important government positions may have been an innovation. When scholars call Wu Ding's ritual style *'old school'* their words give the impression that things had always been like that, and that Wu Ding was a traditionalist. Maybe he was, in a number of ways. We just can't be sure.

When you consider the many deities and spirits who were excluded by Zu Jia's reform, you may wonder what the aristocracy thought about it. The Yellow River kept flooding the countryside, and many locals may have wondered why their deity wasn't receiving sacrifices any more. Stormwinds and typhoons kept sweeping through the settlements, but the king didn't sacrifice to Bird Peng. Even the great god/s Di didn't get proper attention. A wide range of deities from other clans, locations and vassal states were suddenly ignored. It could have caused unrest. When you are a noble who looks after a fief, you may accept worshipping the royal clan when you visit the capital, but when you come home to your province you have to deal with people who share a range of deities that have nothing to do with the royal house, and were suddenly out of favour. I wonder whether the unrest was intended. By reducing offerings, Zu Jia was enforcing a religion that was focussed completely and exclusively on the royal ancestry. The divine manifested in the Zi clan, which handled the blessings of harvest and the fortune of war without the influence, interference or even the acknowledgement of other deities. I wonder how this looked in practice. The ancestors had shrines and temples, quite possibly there were temples for nature deities in Anyang, and a priesthood that looked after them. Were such shrines closed, their priests evicted and the people told to go worship their government? Thanks to his oracle bone inscriptions, which are a little dull and repetitive, Zu Jia tends to appear like a bureaucratic reformer with a passion for order and routine. Should we also consider him a dictator who outlawed or destroyed alternative religions, upset the faith of a large amount of people, and created chaos simply by the enforcement of order? Much more research is needed here.

Similar questions have to be asked regarding later revivals of the ritual schedule. Zu Jia's reform only lasted as long as he lived. The next regents, in period 3 and 4, revived much of the religion of Wu Ding's day. If they used a ritual schedule we have to unearth evidence for it yet. Then, at the end of period 4, things became so difficult that the next regent, Di Yi, reintroduced Zu Jia's religious timetable. Indeed, he made it more narrow minded. In Zu Jia's divinations, it could happen that a given ancestor did not automatically consent with the schedule of his feasts. On occasion, a sacrifice was shifted slightly, so that a drumming ritual began on the evening of the day before the proper date or extended into the next day (T.T. Chang, 1970:150). It seems that the ancestors were genuinely asked for their permission, and that their veto was respected. In Di Yi's period 5a schedule, the divinations had become a matter of routine. The ancestors were asked, as tradition demanded, but they had little to say. Likewise, the importance of the ancestresses varied between period 2b and 5. In Zu Jia's schedule, ancestresses who had given birth to sons that became heir-apparent were regularly feasted. In period 5 only one queen for each king was entitled to the five nourishing rituals (Hsü in Menzies, vol.II, 1977:XXI). Keightley (2000:49) adds that the consorts of collateral kings were not included in this cycle. The change may have been due to constraints of time. Some kings (like Wu Ding) had several queens hence the number of hungry ancestresses exceeded that of the kings. T.T. Chang (1970:269) counts 19 kings whose 30 wives, all of them in direct line of ancestry, appear in the *'five rituals'* inscriptions. The wives of the other kings remain unknown.

Let us take a look at the performance of the five rituals.

The ritual schedule usually (not always) began with Shang Jia, the heir of Wang Hai, who first united the Zi clan with a number of allies to revenge the death of his father. Why the schedule did not begin with Wang Hai (who used to receive prodigious offerings in Wu Ding's time) remains a mystery. However, Shang Jia is the first ancestor who was named by a day- or sun-name. Let us look at Dong Zuobing's (Tung Tso-Ping's) reconstruction of the ritual calendar. Dong and Shima Kunio were the first oracle bone scholars who traced the pattern of the schedule, and reconstructed it almost completely for periods 2b, 5a and 5b. As Li Chi, citing Dong's works relates (1977:248-251), we are in the fourth month (approximately April) of the first year of the reign of Di Yi, period 5a. That this schedule was in power so early in Di Yi's reign indicates that he enforced a return to Zu Jia's ritual schedule almost immediately after ascending the throne. The ten days ritual at the beginning of the year is complete and Shang Jia receives his first festival, a rong/yong (drumming) sacrifice on the day jia xu (day 11 of the 60 day cycle). Twenty days later, on the day jia wu (day31, we are in the fifth month now), Tai Jia gets his drumming, and on jia chen (day 41) Xiao Jia has a drum festival. In the sixth month, on jia zi (day 1 of the next 60 day cycle) Hu Jia receives his drumming and on jia xu (day 11) Wo Jia gets the same, while Yang Jia has his drumming on day jia shen (day 21). In the seventh month another drum sacrifice is made for Zu Jia, who is the most recent king of the lot. This completes drumming for the male ancestors with the Jia day temple name. It took almost four months in that year to complete the rong/yong sacrifice for the seven regents named Jia. Each of them was entitled to four more ceremonies. The Jia named ancestors received their yi (feather dance) sacrifice from the eight to eleventh month. Next, from the twelfth to the third month the other three sacrifices were performed. The cycle started with the chi (raw meat) offering, one ten day week (xun) later the cai (grains) ritual began and finally the xie (harmonisation) ritual rounded off the cycle for each individual ancestor. These three rituals were not as time consuming and elaborate as the drumming and dancing, and several of them could be performed on the same day. However, only one of each could be done on a given date. Hence, one Jia ancestor might receive boiled grains on the same day as another got raw meat, and a third enjoy a harmonization ritual. You will observe that for each ancestor, the ritual year was divided into roughly three phases. First the drumming, then the dancing and finally the other three, followed by the New Year celebration. Completing the drumming took 110 days; the feather dancing required another 110 days and the final 130 days were scheduled for the zai, chi and xie rituals together. Finally, the cult year ended, and the new year began with a 10 day celebration for all ancestors.

For the ancestresses, the cycle was delayed by one ten day week. If the first ritual to a king of the name Jia began on day eleven, the first Jia ancestress received her ritual on day 21.

So far, things seem simple enough. We'll put a stop to that. Li Chi, Dong Zuobin, Shima Kunio, T.T. Chang and K.C. Chang agreed on this pattern of the performance. Everything looked fine until the mid seventies. Then Hsü Chin-hsiung published the Menzies collection; in his introduction to volume two he introduced a new patter of the five rituals (1977 vol.II: XXI). On the whole, it wasn't very different from the old one. However, while the old pattern had started with drumming and followed up with the feather dance, the new order started with a ritual presentation of the scrolls or tablets (the gong dian ritual) followed by the feather dance period. Next occurred the mixed ritual schedule and the whole thing ended with the drumming. Keightley, who had agreed with the old pattern (1978:115) changed his mind (in Loewe and Shaughnessy, 1999:261 and 2000:48) and agreed that the proper schedule went yi, ji, zai, xie and ended with rong/yong. That would give us feather dance, raw meat, grains, *'combined offering'* and drumming, if only Keightley would attach a meaning to any of these rituals. As there were and are scholars who hotly debated the fine details, he restricted himself to the (modern) Chinese terms without offering speculation what the rituals entailed. You can see the pattern remains the same, it is only the starting point that differs, and determines whether the rong/yung sacrifice happens at the beginning or the end of the cycle. If we have the feather dance at the beginning and the drumming at the end, we have a more balanced and symmetrical ritual structure ending with a powerful and dramatic finale, instead of a bunch of mixed up minor rites. Considering that the five rituals were not just religion but also part of the Bronze Age entertainment industry, a strong beginning and an impressive ending seems natural.

But things remain complex. The five rituals received a lot more attention than the many other Shang rituals, as they provided keys to the ritual year and the time keeping, at least in periods 2a, 5a and 5b. They were also attractive for researchers craving a heady dose of statistics to make life meaningful. Contemporary research indicates that the ritual year was extended once in every two ritual years by an extra ten-day week (xun). The position of this extra xun has been discussed a lot. An inscription of the Menzies collection, cited by Hsü (1977:XXI) indicates that the extra *'week'* was inserted at regular intervals but could occur within a given cycle, instead of at its end. In period 5 the extra ritual xun every two years produced a cult year that was almost identical with the solar year. Consequently, in Di Yi's reign the intercalary month was dropped. Indeed, the ritual year became such a regular time keeping device that the cycle of nourishing rituals could have replaced time keeping in months. It didn't: there are more references to the month of a given divination in period 5 than in the periods preceding it. Di Yi was so satisfied with the regularity of the ritual schedule that he had no intercalary month in the first nine years of his reign. Later on, between the fifteenth and twentieth years of his reign, he had to make up for this lapse. Hsü states *"...in time, the correspondence between the sacrifice cycle and the months of the year became very close. The reconstructed sacrifice table for the reigns of Ti-i and Ti-hsin reveals that after the twentieth year of Ti-i's reign, the majority of the extra hsün fell in the sixth and seventh months. This regularity was also probably achieved through observation of some heavenly phenomenon."* (1977:XXIV) But there are enough irregularities of the Shang calendar to keep future generations of researchers busy and employed. Where earlier periods had alternated long (30 days) and short (29 days) months, with two successive long months every fifteen to seventeen months, Di Yi's calendar shows inexplicable irregularities. The two successive long months were not always respected, and there is even a forty day month on record.

We have accompanied the male ancestors with temple name Jia through the ritual year. A similar schedule existed for each of the ten days of the decade. The schedule was not entirely without gaps, however. Some of the posthumous temple names were more common (or popular) than others. Sure, the day names were determined by divination. But behind each divination stood a group of diviners who were well aware which day names were over-booked. I am sure the oracle was asked some very specific questions to ensure satisfactory results. And of course the ancestresses were similarly celebrated on their temple name days. It follows that in Zu Jia's day the ritual schedule must have allowed for a very few free days, and by the time of the last two regents, Di Yi and Zhòu Xin, almost 360 days of ritual were required to make all ancestors happy. Had the Shang period continued for another two or three regents, the ritual schedule would have exploded. It did not come to that. Before the timetable collapsed from overload, Zhóu Xin's got fed up with it, ceased divining and devoted his days to other pleasures.

The details of the five rituals are not easy to reconstruct. First, I would like to caution you from applying five *'element'* cosmologies to these rites. True enough; the number five was sacred to the Shang. Divinations of a given question were often performed five times, or in units of five, and the number five symbolised the four quarters of the earth and the sacred centre. In fact the image of the square earth with its four sides and a dot in its centre equals the character of the sun. It might be meaningful: you will observe the sun radical in several important sacrificial characters. Perhaps the Shang had associations between the five planets and the five directions, the five mountains and Di's mysterious Five Jade Ministers. When Tang the Successful invited Yi Yin to be Prime Minister, Yi Yin rejected the offer four times before conceding to Tang's request (Sima Qian). That's about as far as we can speculate. A thousand years after the fall of the Shang, the late Zhou, Qin and Han dynasties produced a model of the world where five moving and transforming powers regulated the cycles of nourishment and destruction. Water, fire, wood, metal and earth were the symbols for the numinous essences and energies which maintain and transform the world. This model is well known nowadays, and an enormous amount of philosophy, natural speculation, medicine, feng shui, gongfu and even war strategy was based on it. The Han time reconstruction of the Zhou time *Shujing* goes to great lengths to project this idea into earliest antiquity. If we trust the *Book of Documents*, Yao and Shun, the Xia and the Shang regents all subscribed to Five Mover (wu xing) cosmology. In more prosaic reality, the system was invented between the middle and late Zhou and fully evolved during the Han Dynasty. The Shang may have been at the roots of this system, but they were certainly unaware of its future flowering. This is obvious from the fact that the five rituals did not have equal status. Drumming and feather dancing required two thirds of the ritual year, while the other three rituals were crammed into the last few months.

The Feather Dance

If we can trust the Zhou time histories and the *Chuci*, Wang Hai himself performed a jolly dance with feather and shield when he visited the Lord Yi and accidentally ended in bed with the wife of his host. It may seem a pretty myth, but when you look at the common version of the character, you can see a feather and a sun, which may well represent the shield or vice versa (p.744). The *Shujing* (*Da Yu Mo*) has the Great Yü celebrate his successful campaign against the Miao people with a feather and shield dance between the two staircases of the court. *Lüshi Chunqiu* (14.5) mentions another feather dance, this one in the Zhou period, which was performed for the honour of a visiting lord and his attendants. Several hundred dancers appeared, waving thick bundles of feathers. At a signal, they took out the weapons they had hidden between the feathers and massacred the guest's attendants while the host beat his guest to death with a sacrificial chalice. T.T. Chang speculated that the feathers were used to shield the dancers from the sun (1970:151). In period 3, the character was frequently written with *'feather'* and *'stand'* i.e. to take a position (p.663). It remains unclear whether Wang Hai danced as a solo performer or was accompanied by his retainers or guards. It would also be nice to know if this sort of dance was unknown at Lord Yi's court and represented a speciality of the rising Zi clan. The oracle bone record proves that the feather dance or yi ritual was among the most important ancestral festivals. They do not reveal how the dance was performed. Here, later Zhou records may be helpful. In the Zhou period, a feather dance required a group of dancers. The dancers performed in a square formation, the number of participants depending on the rank of the aristocrat who performed the ritual. Kings were permitted a formation of 8 x 8 dancers, high nobles 6 x 6 dancers etc. While it may well be that this was a continuation of the Shang rite, we ought to recall some significant differences. The oracle bone records do not mention that anyone but the kings had feather dances, while the Zhou time rites were not necessarily part of the sacrificial routine that nourished the royal ancestors. Whether the Zhou used shields remains unknown. Also, by the time the Zhou historians began to record, write or invent history, they were well used to offerings with numerous participants. It may well be an innovation introduced roughly a century after the fall of the Shang, in a period when increasing amounts of sacrificial vessels were needed for the growing size of the congregation. Shang dances may have been smaller, maybe they even required the king to dance personally. Maybe Wu Ding did, as in his time the dances were less frequent, but if Zu Jia, Di Yi and Zhòu Xin did, they would have been busy dancing every day for more than four months. What feathers were involved? If the feathers represented the sacred bird from which the Zi clan sprang, it could have been crows, ravens or swallows. All of them have fairly short feathers which don't look overly impressive unless you sew a lot of them into a dancing fan. Li Chin proposed peacock feathers: the excavations reveal that peacocks were kept at Anyang (1977:252)

The Festival of Raw Meat

The chi festival was of smaller importance. The character shows a hand holding a slice of bloody meat (p.687). The Shang had two rituals involving raw meat. One was the chi festival, the other involved cutting up a freshly slaughtered animal and offering the pieces on chopping boards. Raw meat is a strong sacrifice as it is full of fresh vitality. Used for offerings, talismans, spellwork and the like, freshly cut flesh supplies more essential energy than the cooked variety. It also raises more emotion, especially when the participants can watch the slaughter in its colourful intensity. Red has been the luckiest colour in Chinese belief for many centuries; possibly the Shang had similar ideas. It is certainly the most impressive colour and the one that excites the colour receptors most. Red is the first colour that babies learn to see. But raw meat also carries mythical connotations. The *Liji* contains several accounts of the real or imaginary rituals of early antiquity. Raw food, like meat and fish, features prominently in them, and represents a stage of prehistory where cooking hadn't been invented yet. A raw meat offering predates the age of culture hero Fuxi, and it doesn't get much earlier than this. The sort of meat remains unclear. It could have been mutton, beef, pork, chicken or dog, or even the flesh of wild animals. The nobles drank at these festivals, just as they always did, and maybe they were obliged to share a bite. It makes me wonder about the inscription that mentions Wu Ding's worms. The character gu, meaning worms or vermin shows two snakes in a bowl: evidently, the Shang were aware that food could contain the eggs of parasites (p.633). In later periods, the character became identified with a range of evil sorceries. People used gu spirits to kill their enemies or steal their wealth. The Shang did not use it that way. In their age, people did not cast spells at each other. Neither Wu Ding nor any other Shang regent divined if he had been cursed by a living person. The ancestors and the gods were a much greater threat.

The Cooked Grains Festival

Another minor festival was the cooked grains offering, or zai (p.690, 736). Like the raw meat festival, it was regularly performed in the last part of the year between winter and spring, well after the harvest and the slaughter of animals that characterise autumn. Provided the calendar was more or less in tune with the solar year. The grains were probably two or more sorts of millet and possibly wild rice or wheat. Compared to the raw meat, they may have represented the agricultural stage of history. The grain festival, like the others, often involved wine spilling. *'Wine'*, in this context could have meant fruit, herbs or blossoms, but much more likely is a grain product like beer. The character zai is similar to the rong (drumming) festival, in that the sun radical often forms the centre of the design. It usually involves a mouth radical, signifying *'eating'*; if a *'hand'* appears, it is without a mallet or drum strokes. It would be nice to connect the grains offering to the Zhou period ritual *'tasting the first rice'*, but given the irregularity of the calendar, and the absence of much rice around Anyang, this might be too much to hope for. The rite, like most Shang rituals, remains obscure and open to guesswork.

The Harmonisation Festival

This celebration is the most perplexing of the lot. The character shows digging sticks and a mouth, and signifies *'harmonisation'*, *'cooperation'* or *'reconciliation'* as T.T. Chang suggests (1970:151) (p.719). Three digging sticks speaking with one mouth, or eating together, beautifully express the idea of shared work and food. Maybe they also emphasise cooperation between the living and dead. But what did the ritual look like? Li Chi speculated that it might have united elements of the other four rituals. T.T. Chang mentioned that the xie rite frequently involved drinking, sacrifice of animals or people and the offering of clothes. Was this all there was to it?

The five ritual routine was frequently accompanied by branch offerings (see above), drinking and occasional gifts of clothes. Often enough it was performed together with the bin (hosting or guesting) ritual. I say *'occasionally'* as the inscriptions do not always mention the bin rite. Apart from the five nourishing festivities, periods 2b, 5a and 5b retained a number of rituals. Early researchers speculated that the five rites replaced all of the earlier ceremonies but this is not the case. There were still the occasional (if rare) self purification rites. Important events required ritual reports to the ancestors, there was prayer, ritual supplication and the ceremonies needed for oaths and the blessing of important documents.

Drums and Music

The Rong sacrifice required drumming. The Shang had large, barrel shape drums which were resting on a stand or suspended from it, and were played with mallets from the sides (p.689, 736). Shang drums resemble Japanese taiko drums. They were ornamented with Taotie images and fine geometrical patterns. The skins are open to discussion. For hard playing, heavy cow and buffalo hides may be preferable. However, there is a bronze drum from the Shang period. Bronze has antibacterial properties and conserved minute amounts of the skin, which turned out to come from a large boa or perhaps a crocodile. The Taotie animals are a nice touch. Each of them consists of two mirrored kui dragons, and according to Zhou time myth, the Yellow Emperor himself made the first drum out of the hide of a kui dragon he had caught in the eastern sea. The oracle bone characters occasionally show mallets with thick heads, which might indicate padding, producing a warmer and more muffled sound. The body of the drum often contains the radical for *'sun'* while the *'grass'* radical above them may symbolise growth and expansion. In some versions, there are *'strokes'* at the side of the drum which represent the sound. In period 1 (rarely) and more commonly in period 2b and 5a and 5b the drum character was abbreviated and only the strokes were drawn. From their shape, we might even discern a few basic rhythms: three strokes, double three strokes, four strokes, five strokes, and alternating short and long strokes, indicating different tones. The fact that Shang ancestors liked drumming has created the impression that this ritual was basically *'shamanic'*. I am not quite sure about this. Drumming changes consciousness, especially when it is performed in a monotonous, unvaried rhythm of 3,5 to 4,5 beats a second. The same can be done with plenty of other instruments. Chinese wu, in particular, are not only noted for drumming and dancing with jingling bells. They often invoked spirits or induced trances with string instruments. The same thing can be observed among several Siberian shamanic systems, where local shamans rode music bows into the otherworlds, or conjured ghosts with balalaikas. The early Chinese zithers were commonly used to conjure, evoke, banish, excite or calm a given spirit or deity. Here we are dealing with two instruments that appear like zithers but are played quite differently. The guzheng is an elongated wooden box on a stand; classically it had sixteen strings, while modern versions have considerably more. The guzheng is played like a zither or harp, but one hand is used to press down strings to change the pitch. The other instrument is the quin, by tradition the most highly revered scholars' instrument. It looks like a seven stringed zither, but as the strings run quite close to the wooden surface, they are pressed down at specific spots, which makes it an instrument of the lute family. Both of those instruments have an amazing reputation as sacred objects and ritual tools (van Gulik, 1969). Finally, when the pipa (a four stringed lute) was introduced into China maybe 1500 years ago from central Asia, it was also used for shamanism. String instruments are by no means inferior to drums when it comes to shamanic trances. I often use a small ukulele with nylgut strings in an adapted old pipa tuning (A,c,d,g or a tenor ukulele in f, g#, a#, d#). Shamanic trances do not depend on specific instruments. It's not a drum or a lute that makes the trance; it's the central nervous system and the brain. For this purpose, you can beat your leg or clap your hands if you like. If you are competent and well used to it, you can trance off without any extras. There are so many ways. It's only when you want to entrance an audience or a patient that a musical instrument is a must.

It is one of those tricky questions whether the Shang played string instruments. The root character, which later developed into the character for the smaller qin and the larger guzheng, exists in oracle bone writing (p.733). It shows a blend of the *'wood'* and *'string'* radicals. Sadly, the oracle bones only use it as a place name. If an early qin or guzheng existed during the Shang, it was not divined about. That doesn't mean it wasn't there or not important. Take the xun ocarina. Early bone xun were invented in the Neolithic Yangshao period, several thousand years before the Shang rose to power. Such xun ocarinas appear in Shang graves. They are beautifully ornamented and perfectly carved or made from pottery: obviously they were objects of value and ritual status. But they do not appear in the oracle bone record; at least, not that anyone could identify their character. Personally, I suspect that the character composed of *'geng'* and *'wind'* might be a reference to them (p.742). But this is plain guessing.

The drum sacrifice was an orchestral performance. Drum sacrifices were often accompanied by pan pipe or flute music. I am sure that those who listened developed trance states, if we define trance, as Milton H. Erickson did, as a state of narrowed and intensified awareness, which excludes other sense impressions. It was a ritual trance, which is not the same thing as a shamanic trance. In shamanism, drumming is closely connected to exorcism, the removal of misfortune and the healing of a patient; a shaman is basically a person who applies ecstatic methods to healing ceremonies. Here, we ought to think of *'healing'* in a context that does not involve *'diseases'* but the influence of spirits, gods or ancestors. Unlike shamanic séances, in Shang ritual, the rong sacrifice was meant to entertain a given ancestor. No doubt the audience thought about the ancestor, but I am sure that they also used the opportunity to relax, daydream or consider other matters. Especially when the drum rituals happened every day for months on end. Li Chi (1977:251) remarks that next to the remains of a Shang drum and its frame (excavation of HPKM 1217) musical stones were found. Sound stones were often made from *'jade'*, a vague term that may also refer to jadeite and nephrite. They often had an angular form and were suspended from stands. Entire sound stone orchestras have been unearthed from the Zhou period. It is likely that sound stones accompanied the drumming. This would add another melodic element to the performance. The same might be suspected regarding bronze bells. Tuned bells were unearthed in several Shang burials and during the Zhou period entire bell orchestras, tuned chromatically, with each bell able to produce two tones were developed. They show a mastery of music that wasn't equalled by Europeans until the age of Bach. Bells were emblems of the aristocracy. As you recall, the first bells were created by Huang Di's music master; the first bell concert was given during the middle month of spring. (*Lüshi Chunqiu*, 5.5) Bells were often the gift of kings and represented honour and authority. They were also extremely valuable: bronze was expensive and, in all likeliness, a sacred material. The *Lüshi Chunqiu* (15.2) relates how the lord of a small independent state was promised a huge bell by his evil minded neighbour; the bell was so large that it took two chariots next to each other to transport it. In spite of the admonitions of the ministers, the lord of the small state was stupid enough to accept the gift. He had hills flattened, valleys filled and the road widened to ease the progress of the chariots, and after the bell arrived so did the enemy troops.

We ought to imagine the rong rituals as orchestrated performances with several instruments. In all likeliness, each of the instruments had a symbolic meaning. The fragments of the lost *Classic of Music* which survive in the *Liji* offer several such attributions, we just can't be sure they were already popular among the Shang. For the late Zhou and early Han, bells represented the giving of orders that raise zeal for war; hence, the noble who hears a bell thinks of his officers. Jade stones have a hard and shrill sound; they represent a sense for duty that endures until death. The noble recalls the warriors who died for the defence of his realm. String instruments raise emotion and resemble the humbleness needed to make decisions. The noble who listens to qin and guzheng thinks of the administrators and scholars, who serve him dutifully and eagerly. Flutes and pipes produce overflowing sounds; they resemble the meeting of large congregations. The noble is reminded of the council of administrators and ministers. Drums offer a rolling sound and resemble the motion of the army in battle. The listening aristocrat is reminded of his generals and officers. *"When the nobleman hears tones, he does not listen to the sounds that they make. Instead, they evoke ideas in him to which they are related."* You might call it a guided meditation. It could be a Confucian interpretation: the state appears like a huge orchestra, and while seeming to enjoy music the aristocrat is thinking about strategies and war.

Practical Experience

When we want to explore early Chinese magick and meditation practically, we are faced with a serious lack of data. The Shang left us their oracle bone records, with all those hints at rituals and sacrifices, but most of what we know about them is extremely speculative. And while some sacrifices and customs are reasonably easy to understand, there is a huge range of rituals about which we don't know anything, apart from the fact that, one way or another, they were practiced. Clearly, the Shang were not at the beginning of a spiritual tradition but lived in a time when religion and spirituality were highly developed. Perhaps they devoted more attention to relations with the otherworlds than all the dynasties that followed them. The gods and ancestors were never as influential as during the Shang period. Now it's one thing to observe that lots of complicated rituals and sacrifices happened, and that pretty much every decision required the backing of divination. But what about the spiritual training needed to perform the rituals? What was the inner training of kings, queens, aristocrats, wu ritualists, diviners and priests? Even simple rituals, such as a bath of purification, a self-exorcism, dance-offering and the proper interpretation of an oracle require the ability to enter into specialised mind-states, or trances if you like.

We now enter a realm of speculation. What follows is neither easy to prove or to disprove. It will make sense to anyone with practical experience in meditation and ritual, but may be difficult to comprehend by purely analytical thinkers. If you want to understand religious people who devote plenty of time to ritual and consciousness changing practices, reading books is simply not enough. For a start, I would like to propose that most of the ritual specialists of the Shang believed in what they were doing. They may have had their doubts about the gods and ancestors on occasion, sure enough, but that's simply a sign that the brain is still alive. But on the whole the spirits, gods and ancestors were very real to them. And given that a huge amount of different rituals existed, we can be sure that the kings, queens and other ritual specialists required a lot of training. Now ritual training has an outer and an inner side. On the outer, it requires memorising actions and performance, things to do and things to say, and a certain style to do this convincingly. Here, the key word is congruence. On the inner, it requires imagination, visualisation, and the ability to enter the required mind set and to maintain this specific trance. It's also useful to be able to leave such specific trances when required. The Shang regents were thearchs, and most of their activity was concerned with religious duties (apart from Zhòu Xin, who did much to avoid them). Sure, they hunted, made politics and waged war. They also had administrative duties. But everything they did happened in a religious setting. In a sense, their entire life was a continuous ritual. If they were good at the job and really did their best, they learned to produce a range of suitably focussed consciousness states, or trances, if you like.

But did they actually sit down for **meditation**? One *'ritual'* in the oracle bones is simply sitting in a kneeling position. It was performed in a shrine, temple or holy place, hence in the company of a deity or spirit. Possibly it involved some physical motion. In some states, a gentle swaying or nodding is only natural. Meditative sitting can take on several forms. It can be an act of simply becoming aware, of focussing yourself on what is. It can be a chance to slow down, to calm your mind and to watch breath flowing while thinking gradually fades away. It may allow you to focus on a sacred image, an ancestral tablet, a symbol or the presence of a deity or ancestor. It can be a chance to relax and embrace silence. Or it can be the first step in a trance of introversion.

Another ritual consisted of **sharing a meal or a drink** with an ancestor. This requires imagination. Later generations approached this in two ways. Either you have an impersonator of the dead, such as a wu, spirit medium or a relation of the dead, who becomes obsessed by the deceased, or at least acts as the deceased during the ritual. During the late Zhou, this was a part of the funeral rites. The deceased was usually represented by a grandson and sat around, ate a little, but otherwise remained conveniently quiet. This is more than just having a ghost present. It also involves a transfer of status from the dead to his eventual heir. As you read earlier, a similar ritual was performed entirely in the imagination; the *Liji* gives an excellent account of this yoga. The ritualists required a trained imagination, and this implies that they had some methods to induce the sorts of trances suited for the job. Sure, there are people who have a very vivid imagination by nature, and can visualise a lot of things for extended periods. But in the royal family and among the higher nobility such skills were of such importance, that I find it reasonable to assume that training was likely.

Erecting the Centre. Another rite which might relate to meditation is the grapheme centre, showing a square or rectangle and one or several weather-vanes (p.745). Shang cosmology is very heavy on the divine directions but it does not involve sacrifices to the centre. We simply read that in times of crisis, when the howling typhoon winds swept across the land or an enemy was invading, the king *'erected the centre'*. Here, several readings are possible. The glyph is also interpreted as *'standing in the centre'*, just as the fresh shoots of rice and millet are erected or stood up in the fields. The centre is worth exploring. In later Daoist meditation, the term centre is sometimes used for the heart, for the inner core of the body and for the mind/awareness. A similar interpretation of the heart is common in Kashmir Tantrism, where it is the essential meditative formula (Fries, 2010:280-291). Whether the Shang identified the centre with the heart, let alone with awareness, remains unknown. The character for heart does not even appear in oracle bone script, but it exists in bronze inscriptions. The centre was a sacred space, or a state of mind if you like, as sacredness and divine harmony are activities of the mind. By moving to the centre, or by making a centre, the king established harmony and balance. Note that no sacrifices are mentioned, no rituals, promises, prayer nor ceremonies. The king takes his position in the centre. Maybe he moved to a special central hall or courtyard. Maybe he erected a symbolic cosmos around himself, with symbols for the directions and offerings, to re-establish order. By standing in or erecting the centre, the world naturally attains balance. The king becomes the pole star, or rather the axis mundi, and represents Di itself. He does nothing, and the world returns to harmony. Or perhaps he literally centres himself. The rite could be done in a ceremonial way, in a trance or both.

Erecting the centre can be done in a simple ritual way. When you are troubled or upset, you could find a quiet place and set up four candles, stones or other objects in the cardinal directions. Sit in the centre and calm down. Send a flow of love into each of the directions. Think of what each direction means to you, or invoke a deity for each quadrant. Then sit in the centre, calm down, relax, let your breath flow gently and enjoy what comes into your mind.

Here's another variation. To come into the centre, you can go to a sacred place in your neighbourhood. It could be a hilltop, a spring, a confluence of rivers, a few rocks, a group of remarkable trees, a sheltering hedge, a bridge, pool or a meadow under a wide sky. Natural places of power are easy, if you treat them with respect and take time to discover the energy sentience of the place. It's just as rewarding to discover power places in the city. Look for parks, open places, sheltered courtyards, spaces where you can blend in and calm down. In each of these sites, you will experience the centre of an awareness flow and with skill and sensitivity, you can learn to tune in. Or you could make a centre. When you are in a setting that does not contain a natural focus, it's easy to create one. Either you create a space by placing a few stones around yourself and sit in the centre. Maybe you'd draw a circle. Or you take a piece of wood and stick it into the ground. Sit in front of it and observe how your awareness is centred by this simple focus. It's also a great way to calm you down for meditation should you be worried or scatterbrained.

There are more hints that Shang ideas made it into wu practice and Daoist meditation. The sign of the square centre with its weather vanes combines the square, itself a sacred sign and perhaps a deity, with flags flying in the wind. Here, wind is breath. And when you look at the character for body you can see a person, standing sideways, with a huge belly (p.643). Belly is the centre of body, a basic insight popular in Daoists alchemy, qigong and martial arts for millennia.

In the next sections, we will explore practical meditation. The basic elements may have been known to the Shang, and they were definitely known by the late Zhou, when wu shamanism began to lose favour among the aristocracy and the newly founded Daoist movement began to incorporate wu methods in its repertoire. Among the wu ideas are the three level cosmology (heaven, earth and man), ritual dances, trance journeys in the spirit, herbal and mineral medicine, basic breathing exercises and so on. Yin and yang were developed by wu, as was the *Yijing*, but they do not concern us here as they are a product of the Western Zhou period. To be sure, the Daoists did much to refine these methods. But in essence, they based their efforts on a foundation of spiritual activity rooted in Shang times, and probably in the shamanism of the Neolithic cultures that preceded them.

We have to go back to the origin when we want to understand. And the origin is exactly what the following trance experiences are all about. Let's allow for some anachronisms and explore some aspects of Daoist meditation. I do not want to give the impression that we are on Shang territory here. Perhaps we are and perhaps we are not. Given that the record is so limited, I wouldn't dream of arguing. However, even if we are now exploring techniques and experiences that were developed centuries after the Shang, you will learn that these meditations can help you to understand the Shang. Not by doing as they did (I wouldn't want to see you slaughtering people for spiritual benefit), but by developing a trance consciousness that allows you to think differently, and to explore the myths and images of early Chinese culture from a different state of mind. These techniques stimulate the imagination and open gates to the deep mind.

Let's explore things by doing them.

The early Daoists made much of the beginning, the primal age of the sage emperors, and the even earlier phases when The One aka the Primeval Chaos brought forth everything. The way or Dao is to reverse. The Daoist goal is a return to the primal beginning. It takes us past the Zhou, the Shang and the Xia into the realms of pure myth. Beyond the Yellow Emperor, the Sage Rulers, to the primordial unity of undifferentiated chaos. And though we can't be sure just how old the old myths are, and just how old a given spiritual practice is, here is our way and you are welcome to return and come home.

Enter the gourd

Remember the egg out of which Pangu was born? Remember the primal gourd-like Hundun, like a yellow sack, faceless but so happy that it likes to dance? Remember the gourd which allowed the first humans to survive the flood? We'll get you there.

First of all, find a peaceful and preferably silent place. This is just for starters, when you have learned the basics you'll be able to do this anytime and anywhere. When you have to wait, during a train ride on the way to work or any other setting which you like. It's easy. It's natural. So don't make a fuss about it. It's just another trance state in your daily life. And daily life is basically a series of highly specialised trances, involving specialised skills and behaviour. Unlike the others, this one goes the other way and returns you to the beginning. From special behaviour to unspecified, chaotic unity. It's one of the better ones.

Sit down comfortably. When you are in a chair, place the soles of your feet flat on the ground. When you sit cross legged on the ground, put your hands in your lap, so it feels comfortable. Or sit cross legged resting your back against a wall. Allow your head to nod forwards a little. This is not the international straight-spiners contest nor will you get awards for looking esoteric. It's much more important that you relax and make yourself comfortable. Indeed, there were a lot of early meditators in ancient China who did their trance standing, or walking very slowly, or simply relaxed lying on the side, using a pillow and an arm to rest the head. Some adepts made themselves so comfortable that they occasionally fell asleep. And even this was not a failure. When body and mind need sleep they should get it. Some Daoists made an art of dozing, of hovering on the very edge of sleep.

Let us start with resting. It's an activity of the body, but it is even more a state of consciousness. Take a few deep breaths, calm down and relax. This should feel good. Go slowly. There may be some tension in your muscles but you can let them go now. Just exhale gently and imagine that the tension flows down your body and disappears into the ground. If you like, you can tense the tensed bits for a moment and then relax them again. Do it a few times and you'll relax really well. Go for a good feeling. This whole meditation should be a treat. And you deserve to feel good. And maybe you are asking yourself if you can feel better still. I'm sure you will. Soften your face. Relax your arms. Feel this comfortable, delicious heaviness and allow it to spread all through your body. Add a smile to it. You can find a happy smile and move it through your body. Smile from your head down to your toes. And smile from your heels up to the head again. And let the smile go round. Wherever you feel this smile, you can sense yourself relaxing, and feel good and better, much better now.

Now give a last thought at the world around you. There are ten thousand things out there, and maybe some are important and others are not, but right now you can leave them all out there and introvert into the centre of your body. Allow your eyes to close. Good. The outside world will get along pretty well on its own while you go inward. At first your attention may be inside your head. You can see the darkness in front of your closed eyes and feel breath as it comes in and out of your nostrils but you can allow this to become gentler now this is really good breath can become softer and slower all the time. Again this is early Daoist practice, and may well go back to the wu. You can listen to your breath. You can make it slower and smoother. Focus your attention on the exhalation. The exhalation relaxes and soothes. And as you observe how you exhale, and give yourself time, and slow down, your breath becomes smoother and quiets down. Eventually it gets to be very light and inaudible. You can listen to the absence of sound. Enjoy a soft, gentle flow, without effort or strain, as you relax really deep now. And there's this whole brain there which is probably still full of all sorts of thinking. Brains tend to do that and they like it. But there are at least three minds you can turn to.

Right now you are going to give it the slip as you imagine yourself falling ever deeper within your hollow body. The hollow body is a strange and useful concept. On one hand, your body is full of organs and nerves and bones, and they do their job quite naturally. On another, you can imagine it empty. Call it the heart. This is a really old idea. As early as the *Ṛg Veda*, seers descended into the heart, and found vision, insight and revelation by searching in the heart. Some of the late *Upaniṣads* refined the method and turned it into a complex meditation. And the tantric pioneers of Kashmir, like Abhinavagupta, made a real art of descending into the voidness of the heart. With heart they meant mind, but they also meant an unspecified huge void between hips and shoulders. This heart, they assumed, is the centre of perception, the space where consciousness in form-energy (Śakti) and consciousness without form (Śiva) interact, and create the whole wide world. In this heart you are making your reality, and by keeping it filled with ideas, perceptions and beliefs you also maintain it. But just as the coupling of Śiva and Śakti produces all, so it can dissolve everything. When you withdraw from form and energy, becoming minute and shapeless, you shed the layers of mind-stuff that make up your reality. And as you disentangle yourself from the world you also let go of what you think yourself to be. This is the Heart of Śiva, and the Heart of the Goddess, but it is not a thing nor a state but a continuous process of searching by emptying. You don't reach it, you don't have it and you don't attain anything. You simply empty everything, and when you and everything else has disappeared into the realm out there, you still go further. This is a mystery, meaning, I can't tell you what it's like. More details in *Kālī Kaula*.

Chinese seers, sages and inspired visionaries proposed similar ideas. In Chinese literature, the term heart means mind, attention, thinking, experience etc just as it does in Indian thought. And just like the crazy seers of India they created several maps of the microcosm. They thought of body as full of organs, or rather, organic and energetic systems, but they also visualised body as a vast mountain full of caves, grottoes, chambers, palaces and subterranean paradises. Within yourself, you can explore chambers, shrines, temples and alchemical furnaces. Each of these spaces corresponded to the macrocosm, so that by going inwards, you also go outwards into the greater, cosmic universe. The heart cavity can be a grotto big enough to contain the entire world.

So when you float down within yourself, imagine that you are sinking gently through a vast emptiness. And you can look up and see your brain up there and maybe it's thinking and maybe it understood you can shut up now and float deeper through the throat and past the lungs and the whole centre of your body is a huge vast cavern and as you go deeper you reach the heart and solar plexus realm where quite another sort of thinking goes on. Imagine the heart region empty, but full of vibration and potential. It's a void, but this void is not empty. You can make it empty by shedding all thoughts which pass by. Just let them go, thoughts of the world, thoughts of yourself. They move outwards to the periphery while you become simple and small as you go in. Simply let go of layer upon layer of yourself as you are getting smaller all the time, and when a thought goes by you let it pass and disappear in the periphery, into the world far away out there. Water flows downwards without effort. It finds the easiest path, it moves through the tiniest spaces, it fills all cavities and crevices and provides nourishment wherever it goes. Be like water. This is the way of unification, and it purifies you of the crusts of belief and memory which surround the pristine freshness of awareness. The voidness is you and the periphery is you and in-between is full of consciousness, vibration and potential. Deep down, you'll find the voidness pulse, just like everything else does. As you do this, you are making yourself a ravine for the flow of the Dao. You are making yourself a hollow measure for All Under Heaven. And while you love and treasure the brightness out there, you come home to The One in the darkness of the undefined. Maybe this is what you need right now. It's a meditation in itself and a foundation of all meditative Daoism. For as you empty yourself of all things, thoughts and even your identity, you make space for the effortless inflow of the Dao.

But perhaps you want to go beyond this. Slowly, steadily down. Good. Up there your heart is closely connected with awareness and attention, and it can feel a lot of emotions and sensations but now that it has calmed down you can go deeper still and you leave your heart doing its job up there as you glide downwards deeper and deeper. Slow down and enjoy. And as you go sink further into the vastness of your belly you become more simple all the time. And down here in the belly is another sort of thinking. We call it gut thinking, belly thinking, intuition, the whole wisdom of the many nerves that accompany the digestive tract where the really deep wisdom is and a lot of decisions are made the brain doesn't really notice. The brain is far away and here you are, very simple and very small in a realm where lots of spaces can be found. The belly is a perfect realm for temple rooms, sacred caverns, corridors, tunnels, grottoes, gardens, terraces, sacred groves and hidden palaces. And what you think assumes a strange and lucid vitality. Imagination is much stronger in the voidness of the heart and the caverns of the belly. In here, you can think thoughts that are really worth thinking. You can think what makes you feel good. And you can make it stronger. You can imagine something wholesome and the vision will be bright and clear and impressive. You can call the gods and meet them in the centre of yourself, vast, powerful, loving and full of their own sparkling intelligence. Or you recite a mantra and find it coming to life. When you wake a mantra in the belly, it interacts with the spaces that surround you and creates its own reality.

And you can establish a temple right in your belly, in the centre of your self, in your deep mind, a meeting place with many halls and rooms and gateways, and secret chambers underground where wisdom moves and life receives its meaning. Your belly is full of power, vitality, joy and lust, and all of it has its own intelligence. You can realise this as you come home, very simple, very humble and very much alive. You have found and erected the centre. The world comes to its own natural balance.

For in the voidness of perfect simplicity, shapes and forms and dreams and beliefs are born whenever you will. Here, in the centre of the gourd, in the primal perfection of the Hundun, all worlds may be born, maintained, destroyed and reborn in better shape. And so can you.

When you've been in there for a while and feel good and fresh and want to return, simply reverse the process. Become bigger and you move up, past the heart, past the throat, all the way into your full body consciousness. Extend until you fill your whole

Sacred Grove

physical form. Breathe stronger as you ascend, speed up as you move outwards into the world, and take along a beautiful good feeling. Take a good feeling that will accompany you through life. And when you arrive, open your eyes slowly. Stretch a little, if you like. Get up slowly, move your body, explore your senses. And feel delighted to notice how fresh and new and wonderful your world can be. You may notice that you feel much younger. And indeed you do. You have just returned from the womb of your own universe and have received the whole world as a gift.

So much for the basics. When you have done this meditation for a while you may realise that it is marvellously refreshing. And you will have learned that this meditation is not a form of escapism. It's more like reformatting parts of your mental and emotional apparatus. Coming back from the centre, you'll interact with the world in a much happier and easier way than before.

I hope you noticed that you have really been developing three meditations. The first is in the head. It starts when you realise that this is the moment to do your meditation. And it continues as you dissociate from the world, relax your body, listen to your breath, radiate a happy smile through your whole system and close the avenues of the senses. Laozi made so much of this. He recommended that you shut the doors and seal the orifices. The same appears in the *Guanzi*, dating around 350 BCE (see Harold D. Roth in Lopez 1996). Well, tough luck, but closing eyes and trying to ignore sound, scent and feeling won't get you anywhere. As long as you guard those doors of perception you are bound to notice what happens outside them. All of this is effort. The way to introvert is to forget the outside. When you turn your attention inward, the outer world will fade away naturally. It's not a matter of forcing anything. The trick is to attach your attention so much to inner perception that outer sense impressions and the ten thousand things disappear on their own account.

The second meditation is to let go and to descend into the central void. It's a way to purify and simplify yourself. As mind stuff, memories, thoughts, hopes and whatnot arise, you allow them to float by and disappear into the outer realm where they belong. The best way to do this is to observe them as they go past, and allow them to fade away. It's not an exorcism, not banishment nor does it require force or control. In the contrary, the less you interest yourself in the stuff the sooner it will go away. The trick is not to attach yourself to emotion. No matter what thoughts and visions float by, let them go their own way. Zhuangzi called this process *'Fasting the Heart/Mind'* (see start of ch.3 and start of ch.4) It can be done as a complicated ritual meditation (Saso, 1978:194-197, 216-233) but it is just as possible (and easier) to do it as a trance of simplification. When you feed your thoughts, awareness and mind you remain attached to thinking, remembering, hoping, fearing, definitions of self and so on. You fast the heart/mind by disentangling yourself from thinking, and by indifference to mental activity and emotion. This is an essential practice of Daoism, but it is also an essence of wu practice. Both of them require you to becoming empty. As Laozi (11) put it: *"Clay may be formed into a vessel, but the utility of the vessel lies in what is not there. A house is built with doors and windows, but the use of the house is what is not there. What has substance has its use, but what is empty is usefulness itself."*

The classical Daoist empties the heart/mind and becomes filled with the wordless, nameless, inconceivable Dao. Or with the indefinable chaotic wholeness of the pre-create. Or with Great Unity. They are pretty much the same, depending on how you experience it. The wu shaman empties the heart/mind and allows her- or himself to be filled by a god or spirit for a given ritual. The practice is identical, only that the former invokes something undefined and the latter something specific. Both outcomes have their uses. And when the Daoist comes out of trance, sooner or later the mind comes back. A vacuum is easily filled. And as the wu ends the trance, the spirit or god departs and the mind comes back. It's much like breathing. You exhale so that something new may come in. And it should remind you of Laozi 5:

"The space between Heaven and Earth is like a bellows. It is emptied but it can never be exhausted. It stays in motion and the more it is emptied, the more it brings forth."

Now what is between Heaven and Earth is basically Man. Laozi means the sage, the king, the seer, the Daoist, as they pulse like bellows, and do their job by transmitting what flows through them.

"The River and the Sea are the kings of the myriad streams by being lower than them." (Laozi 66). Hence the sage remains low and becomes a ravine, a channel for the water raining from heaven.

By emptying yourself fully, you automatically draw the essence of the Dao into yourself. It appears as De, magical power, and as you exhaust that, more and more appears. It means gaining by giving. The more you give the more you gain. But what you gain is never yours to keep. This is one of the most important and practical insights of Daoism. Creativity requires release. Exhaustion permits fresh inspiration. Magicians, seers, witches, sorcerers, artists and other outsiders are not really strong people. In fact they are a lot more labile than ordinary human beings. But they are good at emptying their powers and filling themselves up again. Their skill is to keep balance as they pulse between fullness and emptiness. And when they release their magic, their vision, their spell of reality transformation, they seem enormously strong as the whole surge of is-ness flows through them. Afterwards, however, they are much weaker than normal people and need to recharge themselves. Laozi gives eminently practical instructions for this process. The emphasis is not on having, hoarding or gaining. It's on release and emptying. For in this world, empty spaces soon fill up again. It happens naturally. When you breathe out your lungs fill up again without any effort. Hence, any good artist or magician learns how to release the fullness. And when empty, how to fill up again. You can fill up with many things. In fact, anything that exists is an energy/consciousness, and hence a source of power. You can fill yourself with elemental power or divine sentience, with human company, with ideals, desires, dreams, hopes and more. And if you empty yourself very, very thoroughly, you can have an inflow of the pure nameless, incomprehensible Dao itself.

The third meditation is to descend into the belly i.e. into the centre, and to build up a complex system of inner spaces and passages for various meditations involving form, spirits, gods and so on. There is a lot you can do and discover in your belly.

Exploring the signs of archaic Chinese, for instance. You probably noticed that you imagine and visualise a lot better when you have descended into your belly. So pick a sign of the oracle bone script and imagine it. You could project it against one of the walls of your belly cavity. And make it bigger and brighter until it really shines and comes to life. This is useful for spells of invocation. It may provide fascinating glimpses of inspiration and insight. It's a neat intuitive approach which allows your deep mind to surprise you with astonishing visions. Should you ever want to realise that you think differently, this is the time to do it. And if you want an even fuller experience, you can have a spirit journey into the sign, realm, otherworld. We'll do this further on.

Guarding the One

Before we explore the belly further, I would like to say a few words on a class of very early Daoist meditations which go under the name **Guarding the One (shouyi)**. The One, as you remember can be Yi (One), it can be Tai Yi (Great One or Great Unity) and it can be the Hundun (Primordial Chaos). Or it can express itself universally as the Dao, or microcosmically as De (magical power, virtue). Taking an elder metaphor, you could also experience it as Di, as the divine principle. Great Unity, Primordial Chaos and the Divine are basically the same pre-create totality, from which everything else arose. The same goes for the Dao. In Warring States literature, terms like The One and Dao tend to refer to the same idea. In Daoism, the main aim is to return to this condition. This is generally done by a process of ritual or meditative introversion. You just learned how to erect, establish and enter the centre. But how exactly can you Guard the One? The Daoist sages developed a wide range of meditative techniques. Each of them bears the name Guarding the One, but the technical details vary a lot. So, before we go further, let's have a brief look at the matter. The One appears in early Daoist writings from the start. In the *Zhuangzi*, it is referred to in ch.12.

"Stick to the One and the ten-thousand tasks will be accomplished; achieve mindlessness and the gods and spirits will bow down... In the Great Beginning, there was nonbeing; there was no being, no name. Out of it arose One; there was One, but it had no form. Things got hold of it and came to life, and it was called virtue." (trans. Burton Watson, 1968:127 and 131)

In the *Guanzi* there are several verses on its cultivation. Basically, the text recommends to broaden and relax the mind as you sit calm and unmoving. The qi expands, extends and revolves. You guard the One and discard the myriad vexations, desires and fears. *"While extremely emphatic and humane, when alone you delight in your own person. This is called 'revolving the vital energy': your thoughts and deeds resemble Heaven's."* (trans. Harold D. Roth in Lopez 1996).

The earliest version of the *Laozi*, dating c. 300 BCE and discovered in a tomb at Guodian during an excavation in 1993 does refer to the One, but makes less of its cultivation than the later Mawangdui and standard versions. Maybe the original text was less focused on the topic, but just as possibly the *Guodian Laozi* is incomplete or just one of several versions of the text in circulation during the Warring States period. However, there is a short text at the end of the Guodian text which does not appear in any other known version (so far). It was part of the third bundle of Laozi bamboo strips and written by the same scribe. Here, the Taiyi (Great One) is the source of everything. You find details on the complex cosmology in the chapter on mythical beginnings. But Taiyi is not simply an indescribable cosmic totality. The term also refers to a primal deity. Robert G. Henricks (2000:124) comments that the god Taiyi appears on a painting found in tomb 3 of Mawangdui (illustrated in Allan & Williams, 2000:164). The deity has a red head and red legs, winglike arms and wears antlers on its head. The face looks a little like the beak of a bird. It's hard to tell as the image is somewhat damaged. It is flanked by the gods Leigong (Lord Thunder) and Yushi (Rainmaster). He proposes that this fusion of bird and dragon (the antlers are associated with Chinese dragons) can be traced back to the Shang period. Indeed dragons and birds are among the most popular images in Shang vessels. But whether they actually relate to this deity remains uncertain. Here you might recall that the Hundun, when it is not just a primordial Chaotic Unity, appears like a faceless, baglike creature with wings. While primarily yellow, it shares the colour red with the god Taiyi. The wings point at a mutual avian root.

Next, in the *Nine Songs* from the *Chuci (Songs of the State Chu)* the first celebrates a deity called Eastern Great Unity (Dong

Huang Taiyi).The Nine Songs are not part of the Daoist tradition but go back to earlier wu rituals. The form in which they have come to us, however, is one adapted to court ritual. They were possibly edited by Liu An, king of Huainan, who was influential in bringing the *Zhuangzi* into its present form, and compiled the *Huainanzi*. With his support, the songs were performed at the court of emperor Hanwudi, a regent famous for his obsessive fascination with shamanism, sorcery, Daoism and the quest for immortality. Hanwudi personally endorsed the cult for Dong Huang Taiyi. This Taiyi, however, was not quite the same as the Daoist version. It was specifically associated with the eastern sky, so maybe we are dealing with a mix of the earlier Taiyi with a popular deity of the east. David Hawkes (1985:102) proposes that the Chu court originally worshipped a god called Dong Huang and that this deity received its title Tai Yi when the *Nine Songs* were performed for King Wu Di several centuries later. The song does not provide details on appearance or character of the deity, apart from a reference to jade girdle pendants and the jade heft of a sword, and the text is so difficult that these may have been worn either by the god or by the ritualists. However, the song gives a useful description of the ritual. It involved flower and meat offerings arranged on mats, libations of sauces and spiced wine, elaborate music involving drums, string instruments, pipes and song, and the presence of one or several priestesses (wu shamanesses?).

Liu An, in his *Huainanzi*, records that the god Taiyi holds court in the Taiwen constellation, has a private residence in the Purple Palace, while his Imperial Consort resides in the Xuanyuan constellation. These places, as well as the imperial fish-pond (the Pool of Heaven) are all circumpolar constellations. The court of Taiyi is in the motionless centre of the sky. The location moved from star to star, as the north point shifted over the centuries. As Sarah Allan demonstrated, there is excellent evidence that the same location is the abode of Shang Di, the High Di of the late Shang period (2007). In her interpretation, the deceased kings and queens used to travel to Di, hence to the centre of the sky, on their solar name days.

Later Daoist texts extended the meaning of the term Taiyi. Here I would like to summarize a few of the appearances and cultivation methods of the One, making use of the magnificent study by Livia Kohn, 1989:125-158.

-The One can be something less than an inch in size which usually dwells in the lower dantian (cinnabar-field) near the navel or the central dantian at the heart. (*Baopuzi* by Ge Hong).

-The One is the central deity of the body. It usually resides in the central dantian near the heart or in the upper dantian in the head (*Wushang biyao*). He is generally visualised as a baby clad in purple robes on a golden throne, holding the Dipper (Ursa

Major) and the pole star in his hands. The baby, I would add, is also a metaphor for the adept who has returned to childlike simplicity.

-The One is Laozi, as the perfect divine embodiment of Great Unity (*Laozi zhongjing*).

-The One is the Goddess of the Great One, the perfect manifestation of the Dao and the Mother of all Things, who instructs Laozi (*Daode zhenjing guangsheng yi* and *Lishi zhenxian tidao tongjian houji*). As the Mother of the Dao, the One may appear as Xuannü or Xuanpin, the Dark or Mysterious Female who appears in *Laozi* ch. 6, and who was later venerated as the Mysterious Lady of the Ninth Heaven, and identified during the Tang Dynasty with Xiwangmu.

-The One is three-in-one, i.e. the Female One, the Male One and the Great One. They are the three central body gods of the three dantian elixir fields, in head, heart and belly. Or they are the Venerable Yellow Lord plus two attendants.

-The One is the Emperor of the Body, who controls the 36.000 lesser body gods (*Zhongjie wen*).

Just as diverse as the appearance of the One are the means of guarding it.

-In the *Taiping jing*, guarding the One means basically withdrawing from the world, sitting in meditation, introverting attention and observing oneself. This eventually produces an awareness of inner light. When the light is well developed, the adept can allow it to shine out. This leads to profound self examination, the ability to travel on the rays of light and to become pure spirit.

-Ge Hong (*Baopuzi*) recommends a lengthy and complicated meditative journey through the body. The meditation involves journeys through inner palaces and pavilions to the Celestial Palace where the Great One resides. The Celestial palace is in the height of heaven but also happens to be within the body of the alchemist. Further, Guarding the One requires reduction of desires, frequent visualisation and remembering that the adept lives solely through the One.

-The *Huanting waijing jing* equates Guarding the One with one-pointed meditation on Dao and the body gods. It aims at extending the trances in the hope of remaining in meditative awareness indefinitely.

-The preferred form of Guarding the One in early Shangqing Daoism is a complex ritual meditation. It starts with bathing and fasting, midnight meditation facing east, lighting incense, grinding teeth, swallowing saliva and a visualisation of the great Dipper (Ursa Major) right above the head (the handle pointing eastwards) which serves as a protection. First, a sphere of red/purple energy is visualised in the top of the head, which radiates a brilliance that envelops the meditator. Then the god

Red Child appears in the upper dantian, holding the white tiger talisman, plus an attendant who carries the *Daodejing*. This attendant is the god of the subtle essences of teeth, tongue and skull.

Next, a scarlet sun appears in the central dantian (the heart). Its light envelops the meditator which in turn reveals the August Lord of Primordial Cinnabar, holding the talisman of the Female One and the planet Mars, in company of an attendant, who is the god of the essences of the five intestines.

And finally, after visualising a white sun in the lower dantian under the navel and extending its radiation, the Primordial King of the Yellow Court is duly visualised, he holds the book *Suling jin* and the planet Venus, plus an attendant, who is the master of the limbs, senses, blood and inner organs.

In this system, the Three-in-One are the vital deities of the inner core, whose nourishment keeps the adept alive. The key to this nourishment is to remember the Three Ones not only during deep meditation but at all times during the day, especially when you feel emotional, whether happy, sad, fearful, ecstatic or otherwise agitated. By remembering them, they are nourished, and in turn nourish you. Sound thinking: gods and spirits are easiest fed with emotion. In ordinary people, the Three-in-One also exist, but as they are never even recognised, they wither and fade as youth gives way to age.

-Later (reformed) Shangqing Daoism, influenced by Buddhist teachings, retains the outer ritual but makes Guarding the One mainly a matter of one-pointed consciousness and ethical training. In order to effect this singular mind state, the adept should cultivate humility at all times and develop compassion with all beings. When concentration is disrupted, the meditator is advised to think of her or his own death, and of being terrified by hellish demons. When evil urges arise, the prescribed visualisation is of flying immortals (who have left it all behind). The remedy for jealousy is to think of perfect deities, the remedy for desires is to contemplate the Realized Ones. Another recommended method involves drawing and burning the proper talismans before visualising the Three Ones in the three body spaces.

-By the Tang Dynasty, Guarding the One started with realising one's errors and shortcomings. Then followed meditation by observing the flow of thoughts. The emphasis was not so much on visualisation as on cultivating a calm and empty mind without thinking.

-Inner alchemy techniques, by contrast, proposed that Guarding the One had less to do with body gods, the elimination of bad habits or emptying the mind, than with the refinement of the Three Treasures. Basically, the idea was to use qi (here: psychophysical energy) to guard jing (inner essence, sexual secretions), use jing to guard shen (spirit, divinity), use shen to guard qi. The preservation and harmonisation of all three was assumed to bring about perfection and, if possible, immortality. The whole thing usually involved complex dietary rules, breathing exercises, visualisation and regulating lifestyle, manners and ethical behaviour. Plus a vast amount of technical complications shrouded in a highly symbolic and enigmatic language. And when Inner Alchemy became popular among laypeople during the northern Song Dynasty, its teachings and methods became amazingly incomprehensible. Finally even the Chinese Buddhists took up the term and found their own interpretations for it. So, to round things off, I would like to ask you to explore this properly. What have the many different expressions of the One in common? And what do the methods to Guard the One share? Go inwards and find out. The answer is not there for deliberation. There are experiences waiting for you as you explore every possibility. The answer, of course, will be your own. It will be an answer which suits you at this time. Further along the way you'll find new levels of meaning. But right now and as you go your way find the One and guard it well.

There is more to the One than any of us will ever fathom. One is consciousness. Call it divine, call it the gods and spirits, call it unity, all-self, no-self or void as you like. When it flows naturally, according with the way, it may seem divine. When it becomes distorted, fragmented or restricted, some call it demonic, deranged, egotistic or insane. One consciousness is right here, within and without, and it's what makes you experience as you dance your way through life. It's in you and me, in stars, in stones, in fire and water, in earth and sky, in animals, plants and fungi, in things and thoughts, in spinning particles and the spaces between them. It's an anentropic force that appears as attraction, love, sympathy and the recognition of self in others, and others in the self. You can't win or lose, find or avoid it. Nor is it possible to speak about it. It goes way beyond words and definitions and the weird stuff I'm telling you. It's here for you to remember. The you that remembers is it.

How does it appear in magic and ritual? Most people approach ritual from a dualistic position. They assume that they are distinct from the divine, hence need to communicate with it. On the level of particular reality this is true. But it's on the level of absolute reality that the magick happens. In absolute reality, the gods are you, you are them and there is no reason to ask for anything. Whining, complaining, bargaining and demanding are just silly. If you create emotions, make it strong and attractive ones. Prayer, sigils and suggestions are well and good to get you into the mood, to exalt your awareness and to remind you of forgotten unity, but things really become interesting when you open up. Beyond the limits of what you assumed yourself to be, things happen naturally. True nature (ziran) manifests spontaneously. You don't need the gods to send a blessing or a healing to another person. In One consciousness you are them, and anybody else. Simply open up and remember the One. Remember it in words, in silence, in gesture, deed and laughter. Remember it in yourself, in others, in everything and nothing. Remember to laugh and enjoy. Open up to one consciousness.

The gods haven't mucked up this world; it was humans who did it, each of us acting in separation. In the awareness of absolute reality, loneliness is a lie. Birth and death never happened, there is only coming, going and returning. On the molecular level, life and death do not exist. Past and future are categories of thought. Mine and yours are conventions of identification and behaviour. All that we are and think to own is borrowed. When we let go of separate existence, the divine appears naturally. It has always been here.

Humans tend to forget it. They focus on their narrow little world and get stuck in worries, desires, necessity and tangled thinking. It's part of our nature. It's part of the play. And it's fine as long as we stop now and remember. The One. It's everywhere. It's in your friends and acquaintances, in strangers and even in the people whom you don't like much. Maybe you or they have forgotten. When people hurt or exploit others, they have forgotten that they really harm themselves. They have become confined in their separation and their identity has become a dungeon of the self. The human ego can be a great work of art or a sorry little thing. Separation is rooted in fear and ignorance. It's not a question of whether your ego is good or bad, great or small. The question is if you are stuck in it. Any mask is a prison if you can't take it off.

The divine, the elements, the spirits, call it what you like, all that exists partakes of One Consciousness. You don't have to be religious to experience this. Some believe in gods, spirits or ancestors, others believe in ideals like justice, truth, intelligence and sharing. Some atheists are more spiritual than passionate believers. No matter what you call it; it opens gates to the One. It doesn't matter how we label our experience. Sooner or later, all concepts become phantasms. The main thing is our sharing, our communication of self with self. You can find the solution within, when you remember that you are everything, and that everything is you. It's neither big nor small; it's not true and not false. It simply is. This is one unity, absolute reality, and all of us.

The way of the wu, the Daoists and so many other mediators is between the worlds. You can guard the One within yourself, but this is not enough. Once you recognize the One in others, in other beings, and eventually in everything that exists, you can guard the One beyond the limits of your identity. Here the fun really begins. When you sense the world and realise that all there is, is One Consciousness, you are learning that self extends everywhere. Not your self or my self, or any particular self. It's a world shaking experience. But living there isn't so easy. Even those who hide in monasteries, temples and enclaves find themselves bound by basic human needs. The wu mediate. They meditate between absolute reality and particular reality. It's here that so many mystics, visionaries, magickians, shamans and acid heads run into trouble. On one level of understanding, all is indeed One (or None), but on another level, separation and differences exist. When you dwell in absolute reality, you are everywhere and everything, and everything is you. In Krama Tantra, this experience is described in the meditations '*I am THAT*' and '*THAT am I*'. You can be that space, that room, flat, house, environment, scenery. But just as truly IT can be you. The Kramamudrā trance consciousness builds up both experiences and alternates between them. Think of it as pulsation. In the same way, the wu pulsate between particular reality, where things and beings are more or less distinct, and absolute reality, where they transform and inform each other in a ceaseless flow. Here it becomes essential to understand which level you and your fellow beings experience. You may be aware that you share divinity with your fellow humans, but you can't expect them to be conscious of it. Some are, some only on occasion, and some have closed themselves off to an amazing extent. They won't recognise the One in you, and probably they are not aware of it in themselves either. In absolute reality, this does not matter, as all is changing anyway. In particular reality there will always be people trying to exploit you. When you dwell in One Consciousness, in the rapture of the divine or whatever, some people really get upset. It may be lack of understanding, or envy, or fear. In their ignorance, they may try to harm you. It's no use to let them. In particular reality you have to protect the vessel of identity which is your dwelling place at the time being. Being nice to everyone simply invites trouble. Playing holy holy is a handicap in everyday life. Establish limits within the realm of particular reality and go beyond them in absolute reality. Let the divine act through you. You can make others remember. And when you act, speak or send them thoughts, go for the parts that listen. Don't ask the gods to do this for you. The gods are you as you are them when you are them.

Heavenly Journeys

Once you have found your way into the belly and explored some of its sacred spaces you can begin travelling through your body. You can visit the organs and say hello to them (and the body gods in charge of them). You can meet the One as one or several inner gods, your personal deities or spirit helpers. Or you can do a bit of astral travelling, or journeying in the spirit. This is an ancient part of Chinese magic. And there are several ways of doing it. When you are deep in trance, explore this:

You could imagine that you float out of your body on a breath and rise into the sky. Imagine yourself exhaling a colourful vapour and fly on it. Or mount a chariot drawn by dragons and snakes, if you want a comfortable passage.

Or imagine you are floating out of your body. Sure, your imagination might be a little unsteady at first. But take your time. This is a skill that improves with practice. Fly upwards and head west. Now I'm not talking about geographical west but mythical. West is the direction where the sun goes down. Search for the biggest mountain range in the world. Go for the world axis; go for triple peaked Mount Kunlun, central pillar between heaven and earth. At least since the third century BCE and probably much earlier, shamans have been flying to heaven up and down Kunlun. And so can you. You can fly a long way to get there.

Or you can take the fast route. Ever since early Daoist alchemical literature, Mount Kunlun has been a metaphor for the human body. Its nine terraces correspond to microcosmic worlds within yourself. Think of three for the head, three for the heart and three for the belly and underworlds. Each of them is a dantian, a cinnabar field, a site of inner alchemy. These are the main nervous systems in your body: brain, solar plexus and the enteral nervous system. The triple peaks are your head and shoulders. Or, in another interpretation, the triple peaks are belly, heart and brain. And remember that Kunlun is full of caverns, grotto-paradises, tunnels, secret passageways and initiation chambers. You can find or make them right within yourself. And you can ascend to heaven right there, up from the belly of your universe. It's a fast way and it works.

Or maybe you want a more specific trip. Each magical sign can be a gate leading to an otherworld. Some of the oracle bone signs are excellent gateways. They lead to very unusual mind-spaces. I am sure there are some signs that deeply attract you, and others that fascinate by remaining enigmatic. Here, it is best to assume a playful attitude. Go into trance and when you are deep in your belly, enter a temple. Take a few minutes to build up the vision. It may be a little diffuse or hazy at first, but when you go there on a regular basis you will find your imagination stabilise. Maybe you'd like to meet a deity in there, or an animal companion. When the surrounding is more or less established, go to a doorway veiled by a curtain. Take a brush and write the character on it. Make it large, vivid and impressive. Look at it, sense it, feel it. Take your time and allow things to develop naturally. Now go through the curtain and take in what lies beyond. Perhaps you are facing an environment. Or you find yourself in another room, tunnel or corridor. Here you are literally following the nerve networks in your body-mind totality. It may take you to another gate, and give you the opportunity to draw the character again. Perhaps you will have to go through several gates and perhaps you will emerge in an outside setting straight away. When you do, calm down and take in the environment slowly. Look at the ground, look at the scenery, and when things have stabilised, go exploring. Maybe you go travelling in human guise. Or you shape shift into the form of an animal, spirit, deity. Learn what your deep mind is teaching you. The world you encounter will contain some events or places that relate to the character. Maybe you will pass like a watcher. And maybe you will have to act, to change a situation and to interfere. It will give you the chance to make changes that will affect your life and identity when you come back. Some would call it therapy. But this is more than healing a few neurotic traits and bad memories. It's magick, and acts on the personal as well as the transpersonal level. You are exploring a vaster self than the one you assumed yourself to be.

You'll discover many fascinating realities when you journey into different signs.

And you'll carefully record your experiences when you come back. Spirit journeys can be forgotten, just like dreams can be, when too much attention is focused on the world of people and things and stupid worries. Much of memory is state-bound. So write an account of your journeys. It anchors them to the material world and ensures that the two connect well. For what you are doing here is making contact between various parts of your deep mind. And you relate them to the everyday world, which is why the magic transforms your life.

Sometimes a vision is so strong that you'll be instantly surprised. Sometimes things start out hazy and diffuse. Go slowly. As the Chinese sages say: less haste, greater speed. Give your deep mind a chance to develop the environment. It can take a while before things are fully developed. They will do so naturally once you begin sensing the environment. I like to sit down and pause when I come into a new visionary world. It gives me and the environment time to get used to each other.

As you go along, you'll give reality to your visionary world. And when you come there another time, everything will be a lot more solid. Each time you return, the scenery and its inhabitants will become clearer, steadier and more durable.

Now the strange thing is that you are moving in a representation. Maybe the representation is clear and well defined and maybe it is a little unsteady or diffuse. Representation is no criterion for reality. The dream world you experience is a real dream world in its own way, and while you are in it, it is real for you. But as you are dreamer, dreaming and the dreamed all at once, you can change things as you go along.

'Ear' (=Handle) of a four legged bronze Ding cauldron, showing two tigers engulfing a human head

You can transform your magical inner universe. You can speak with the beings you meet. You can ask them many questions. You can answer theirs. And you can change your shape, you can become bigger and smaller, you can turn into an animal or tree or deity as you will. This is the real core of being from where shamanic transformations arise. It is the place where the spirits can interact with you. Not all of them are nice. Beware of sugar coated happy-happy worlds. Nor should you indulge in dreary horror-filth-and-rot realities. They are all dreams in your deep mind. As you go along, you are exploring yourself and the all-self as well. The boundaries between the two are fluids. Self interacts with self all the time. Your magical universe connects with those of others. And we all partake of a dreaming within a bigger dream. And as you move there, you can change, heal, improve and transform the world as you will. And whatever you do deep within will affect the world outside.

It is by going within that you can go outside. And when you want to return, reverse your steps. Go, fly or run back to the door, go carefully along the tunnels and corridors and return into your belly. On the way back you can go fast, if you like, but you should be careful to close all doors behind you. And when you are back in your belly, calm, focus and align yourself before you leave the trance and return to the outside world.

Many Chinese sorcerers, wu, Daoists and sometimes even kings had such experiences. According to the *Liezi* and an elder manuscript, King Mu of Zhou (c. C10th BCE) travelled up into the height of heaven with the help of a highly gifted sorcerer. When he returned from his journey, the food before him had not cooled. For out there or within, time moves differently. And when, later in life, he visited Xiwangmu on top of Kunlun Mountain in the far west, he was also journeying in the spirit. The Queen Mother of the West greeted the King. The two feasted at the side of the turquoise pool, watched the sun set and sang a sad song. Then the king realised that he was neglecting his duties. Deeply regretful, he asked for leave and returned to the Middle Kingdom. It may sound like a sad tale. King Mu would have liked to stay in the paradise of the immortals. Experiences like this can change you. Mu received a vision of the otherworld and learned a celestial song. Another time he travelled to a mythical country where everyone was living in happy anarchy. It shocked the king, but once he got used to it, he didn't want to leave. Just look into the *Liezi* for further details.

And there are further samples in early literature. You might think of the famous episode where Zhuangzi turned into a butterfly. Sure enough he did. But there are a few slightly more sober accounts on the topic. Right at the beginning of the Xia period, Qi, son of Yü the Great, ascended to Heaven. He visited Shang Di and was lavishly entertained. Or maybe he himself entertained Shang Di (the word bin, to host, is used), good evidence that the gods find people amusing. Xiwangmu tells me *'People are funny'* and she knows what she is talking about. So do you, just find a mirror. As a special gift, Qi received nine songs and dances (lit.: movements), which he brought back to earth. Qi trained his musicians and dancing ladies and had the whole set performed. It was a splendid success and I'm sure it brought the blessings of the celestials to the mortal world. But Qi could not bear the impact of this magic. The nine songs bedazzled him; they clouded his heart until he could not bear to live without them. He became addicted to revelry and dancing. Finally Qi lost his mind and a little later, the state. His five sons, lacking a firm hand to guide them, quarrelled and fought for the sovereignty. (Reference in *Chuci, Lisao* 145-148; *Tianwen* 61-62; see also Hawkes 1985:87-88). Qi also appears in the *Shanhaijing* (ch. 16), where he is called the Lord of Summer. The text, as Anne Birrell explains, is a little ambiguous. Either it says that Qi ascended three times to Heaven to receive the Nine Songs. Or that he sacrificed three of his queens to receive them.

The Yellow Emperor Huangdi made a heavenly journey. Unlike other travellers, he travelled in state. He *"assembled the spirits on the summit of Mount Tai, riding in an ivory chariot drawn by six dragons, with the fire god at his side, Chi You in front, the wind god sweeping the dust, the rain god sprinkling the road ahead, tigers and wolves as vanguard, spirits and gods bringing up the rear, jumping snakes writhing over the ground below and flying phoenixes making a canopy overhead..."* (Hawkes, 1985:89-90). As you'll discover, the *Chuci* are full of such journeys to the otherworlds.

One of the most famous was written around 300 BCE in the state of Chu.

Lisao by Qu Yuan, perhaps the most popular and emotional poem of ancient China, contains several such journeys in the spirit. Some of them go to mythical regions, as the poet-seer ascends to Heaven at Kunlun Mountain. Others go through time, as Qu Yuan seeks for a semi divine bride. One of the candidates is Lady Jiandi, the ancestress of the Shang. Another pair of candidates are the daughters of Shun, the goddesses of River Xiang. All of these ladies lived more than a thousand five hundred years before our amorous poet. What sort of wife was he searching for, out there in the other world? Maybe he was looking for a spirit mate. Plenty of Eurasian shamans and, for that matter, Chinese wu and visionaries married a deity of their choice. All of which is pretty much shamanic, if we use the term in a general way. This may seem odd for classical scholars and modern literati. Qu Yuan has been celebrated as one of Chinas foremost scholars, court officials and poets for more than two thousand years. Even modern schoolbooks praise him as an upright administrator and a patriot, who preferred to resign from a corrupt court rather than lose his integrity. They see Qu Yuan as an aristocratic statesmen who left his deluded king and wrote bitter poetry in the isolation of the countryside. But Qu Yuan did more than grumble. He insisted that, in his retirement, he was following the way of the shamans Wu Xian and Wu Peng. Or Peng Xian, as they were called together.

According to the *Shujing*, Fu Yuan was the prime minister of King Wu Ding. The *Huainanzi* (6.2) records that Fu Yue travelled to heaven, and journeyed to the lunar lodges Winnowing Basket and Tail. In the *Chuci, Yuan Yu*, Fu Yue is said to dwell among the stars. The earliest reference to Fu Yue's sky travelling may be *Zhuangzi*, who noted that Fu Yue achieved the Dao. At the end of his life he achieved his apotheosis by ascending to heaven where he became a star. The Zhou were fond of turning dead heroes into stellar gods, a custom that may have been unknown during the Shang. Weber Schäfer (1967:90) comments that he became a patron deity of the wu, and Hawkes (1985:200) states that Fu Yue's star was connected with the destinies of shamans.

Here's another pair of sky travellers (*Huainanzi*, 1.4). Feng Yi and Da Bing rode their chariots; they ascended in thunder and entered the cloudy rainbow. Passing through ethereal mists and vapours, they reached the ultimate heights. They drove through snow and left no traces. Lightened by the sun, they cast no shadows. They spiralled up the whirlwinds; they traversed Mount Kunlun and passed through the Changhe Gate that connects the peak of Kunlun with Heaven. A little further, the conduct of the sage/regent is actually described in shamanic flight metaphors. The sage/ regent takes heaven as his canopy and the earth as his chariot. The four seasons are his horses and yin and yang are the charioteers.

"*He rides the clouds and soars through the sky to become a companion of the power that fashions and transforms us. Letting his imagination soar and relaxing his grip, he gallops through the vast vault (of the heavens)....he orders the master of rain to moisten the byways and directs the master of winds to sweep away the dust. He takes lightning as his lash and thunder as his chariot wheels...Having observed all around and illuminating everything he returns to guarding (the One) in order to remain whole. He superintends the four corners (of Earth) yet always turns back to the central axis.*" (Translation Harold D. Roth, 2010:52). In this magnificent passage, you find the macrocosmic action of the saint/sage/ruler described as a journey in the imagination, and focussed, after the fireworks of the celestial trip, into the centre and the task of guarding the One. It couldn't be described better.

Chapter 6.7 of the *Huainanzi* relates how Nüwa repaired the sky. After the deed was done, she ascended to the Height of

Heaven to meet Shang Di, riding a chariot pulled by dragons and snakes, and followed by a retinue of spirits. That's the usual translation. John S. Major (2010:225-226) assumes that the passage refers not only to Nüwa but also to Fuxi. It provides another two thearchs who personally had an audience at Shang Di's celestial court.

Another chapter (4.4) provides details regarding Mount Kunlun. If you ascend to twice the height of the world mountain, you reach a peak called Cool Wind Mountain, and become immortal. Twice this height you reach the Hanging Gardens (normally, they are a scenic feature of Kunlun). Ascending them you will gain magical powers, such as the ability to control wind and rain. If you ascend further, twice as high, you will enter Heaven itself, the abode of Shang Di, and become a spirit/deity. Here the *Huainanzi* is not merely concerned with sacred geography. Such journeys are meditations that ought to be practiced. The ancient Chinese believed that during dreams, the soul actually leaves the body.

"In a dream we become a bird and fly into the sky.
In a dream we become a fish and disappear into the deep.

When we are dreaming , we do not know it is a dream; only after we awaken do we realize it is a dream. Only when we have a great awakening do we realize that this present moment is the ultimate dream." (*Huainanzi*, 2.2, trans. Harold D. Roth and Andrew Meyer, 2010)

Last, let us take a look at the oracle bone inscriptions. In the chapter on ritual, you read about the controversial interpretation of the character bin, which may be read as to host and to be hosted, and may imply a ritual where a Di or an ancestor comes to a feast, or where the ritualist goes to meet them in their own realm. A similar thought seems to be expressed in the character 'to ascend', showing feet going up a ladder. Look at the inscriptions (p.576, 577). Not only did the king ascend to visit the ancestors, but so did the ancestors among themselves!

There are further spirit journeys in the *Chuci*, which I invite you to study at leisure. Trance journeys were not confined to the celestial realm, however. In each of the four or six (counting above and below) fang directions, a magical and highly dangerous realm was awaiting the traveller. In the usual case, the traveller was the soul of a person who had just died. Before a person was acknowledged to be dead, a ritual was performed. The soul had to be called back to the realm the living. The *Liji* refers to such rituals in passing. So do the *Chuci*, which contain two *Summons of the Soul*, composed to recall the souls of deceased aristocrats. In each case, the otherworlds are described as lethal places, characterised by inhospitable climate, monsters and dangerous spirits. The soul is called to return from certain doom and to reinhabit its former body, to enjoy music, feasting and luxury, to come back to its former glory.

In certain cases, the wu ritualists themselves went travelling to these fang otherworlds. Here they sought to find lost souls and to induce them to return to the human realm. Such journeys are a common custom in Eurasian shamanism, but they are also well attested from Native American cultures. In some cases the shamans search for the soul of a person who had just died. In others, it is the soul of a patient that has been abducted to the otherworlds, or that lost its way during a crisis or a disease. Sometimes people simply lose their will to live. This is also a case of soul-loss, and requires a calling back of the soul, or a journey to find it.

Journeys to the four fang directions are certainly worth the effort. In the *Chuci*, a wu called Yang sings that:

-the east cannot be inhabited, It is populated by giants, as tall as a thousand men, who hunt souls. The ten suns shine all at once, and their scorching heat melts metal and stones, and vaporises souls.

-In the south, the natives tattoo (or: paint) their brows and blacken their teeth. They cook soup from crushed bones and eat human flesh. Vipers and poisonous snakes abound, and a fox stalks the land who can leap (or: run) a thousand miles. A nine headed python lurks to devour men.

-The west is full of deserts; the drifting sands cover a thousand miles, and crush everything, bearing the soul down into Thunder Abyss. Beyond the sands, desolation extends. There are elephant-sized wasps and huge ants like vessels (or: melons). The five grains do not grow, nothing thrives but dry stalks, the earth incinerates people, there is no water, and souls drift aimlessly, to fade into nothingness.

-In the north, layers upon layers of ice rise into the sky. The snow cascades over a thousand miles and the soul cannot remain.

-Heaven is peopled by tigers and panthers who lurk at all nine gates. A giant roams who has nine heads and who can uproot a thousand (or: nine thousand) trees. Like a wolf he travels across the sky (or: jackals and wolves, casting sidelong glances, move to and fro). His (or: their) amusement, is hanging (or: hunting) people and throwing them into an abyss. He (or: they) never rest or sleep, unless Di commands them.

- In the Underworld, here called the Dark City, the earth deity reigns. S/he sits in nine snake coils, or is coiled with nine snake tails, with hunched back, sharp horns and a tiger face, three eyed, with the body of an ox and tears people apart with its bloody thumb.

The other song, *Da Zhao* (*The Great Summons*) combines some elements of real geography with pure imagination:

-in the east is the limitless ocean where the waves go billowing endlessly. Water dragons play in the waves, fogs and rain cloud the sky. A soul lost in the east will disappear into the Gulf of Brightness (or: Valley of Emptiness).

-In the south are a hundred miles of fire and playfully coiling cobras. Sheer mountains tower, haunted by panthers and tigers, there are cow fish, and pythons and spitting sands (or: scorpions and cuttlefish sport round the head of a giant snake). Here a soul will be devoured by monsters.

-In the west, the Moving Sands extend forever. There are demons like boars with long, shaggy pelts and slanting eyes, with claws and teeth and crazy laughter. In the west, the soul encounters numerous dangers.

-In the north, the mountains are frozen and the gleaming red Torch Dragon resides. The bottomless Dai river flows, but it cannot be crossed. The bright white sky is glittering with frost, and everything is crushed by the cold. The straying soul wanders forever. (Summarising the translations by Allan (1991:84-85), Hawkes (1985:224-225 & 233-234) and Weber-Schäfer (1967:73-75 & 81-82))

But when it comes to journeys to mystical otherworlds full of weird ancient gods and strange impossible beasts and wondrous plants, the best source is the *Shanhaijing* itself. If you read it as normal geography, much of it remains incomprehensible. Sure, there are distorted elements of geography incorporated. But on the whole, most of it relates to entirely unbelievable beasts, fantastic plants, imaginary people and a huge range of deities. If you understand it as a spiritual geography of the dream-worlds, such as experienced by shamans in visionary flight, the whole crazy scenery begins to make sense. And it becomes practical. For when you make a spirit journey into the otherworlds, it can be useful to know where to find each god, spirit or weird entity.

Transforming the World

So far, we have practiced trance by introversion into the centre and by travelling into various otherworlds. I hope you have learned much and enjoyed it. The third step in this practice is to enchant the world.

If you have done the exercises, you may have learned that introverted, deep trances do more than provide a bit of much needed peace and quiet. So how about this: Select a nice day when you have plenty of time and go out to a place where you feel much at home. Perhaps you will travel by bus or train: in this case you can start the trance while you are comfortably on the way. Or, if you are in walking distance, go to your place and find a secluded corner where you can sit in comfort, preferably somewhere without interruptions or blood thirsty ticks. Sit down and relax. Take a look at your surroundings, calm your breathing, close your eyes, slow down and allow yourself to sink into the depth. Induce a nice and deep trance. When you are happily in your belly and have become very simple and very open minded, tell yourself that now, as you are deeply in trance, you will slowly open your eyes and enjoy looking at the scenery. And when you have taken it all in, you will get up, while remaining deep in trance, and go for a leisurely walk. You will explore the place and remain in trance for as long as you and your deep mind like. And when you had enough, you will come out of the trance easily and swiftly, and will feel refreshed and inspired.

That's pretty much all there is to it. Go into trance and stay there, get up and enjoy the marvels and miracles of All Under Heaven and the One Consciousness. It's a lot easier than most people assume. Daoists were said to travel on clouds, and it may feel that way when you slowly drift around. But slowness is not a must. When you get used to going for walks in deep trance, you will discover times when you simply seem to fly over the ground. It happens to me especially when I go for forest walks at night. The same goes for the setting. It's a great idea to start these trances when you have a nice place, a secure setting and a wonderful sunny day. With a bit of practice you will be able to do it in any weather and in any setting. It will produce different feelings, however. A stormy samhain night in the forest or a spruce forest in deep snow are not the same thing as a bright, lazy day at the river side. However, each of them has its own grace and charm, and reveals a facet of the miracle of the world. When you can walk through drizzle and find yourself spontaneously thinking *'I love the world'* you are doing fine. The same goes for contrast. Sometimes, after a long trance in the mountains I like to continue right in the heart of the city, where people mill around, cars speed and the buildings are full of dazzling lights. That, too, is the miracle of the world, and the One Consciousness meeting itself.

Trances can be adjusted. For your first experiments, it's useful to specify a time frame. You could suggest: *'I will remain in trance and walk around in this state for one hour. Then I will return to everyday awareness naturally.'* Or you could say *'This trance walk is going to last until I leave this place (forest, park, whatever). As soon as I leave it, I will naturally return to everyday consciousness.'* With a bit of practice, you can simply move in and out of trance as you like. You can spend hours exploring and enjoying the world as you never did before. In deep trance, many of the usual reality filters are shifted or entirely absent. It may happen that time and space change. That's natural: time and space are not there automatically. We learned how to process space when we were infants. For a baby, the tree on the horizon is as far as its own hand. It has to learn that people come close or go away, because they really seem to grow and shrink. It has to understand that there is a before and behind, and that a person who stands behind a chair is not partly gone. Learning to separate objects from the background is quite an achievement. Likewise, time measuring is learned. It takes several years before a child can understand difficult concepts such as next week or another season, and guess how long it will take. A few shifts in the reality filters and time and space cease to work automatically. It happens in trances, but it also happens when you are engrossed in some exciting activity, on drugs, drunk, ill, tired, dancing, making love and so on. Time speeds up and slows down in relation to awareness. When your inner processes are very fast, the outside world seems to slow down. When your inner processes are very slow, the world seems to speed up. The same happens due to age: for a toddler, a single day is endless and very exhausting. A four year old asks an average 400 questions a day, meaning that at least 400 times a day, interest is extremely stimulated. That's a lot of excitement and learning. I can only hope you try to keep up a similar pace. Old people often complain that the years fly by and that young people are always in a hurry. In trance, you can easily adjust your inner time perception. When you want to make much out of a short time, speed up. When you want to get over a long wait, slow down. Time and space are there to be adjusted on demand. Indeed, you will experience trances when you won't be sure how fast time moves at all. Another option is hyperaesthesia. Your senses can be amplified. People do this anyway. A painter starts to amplify vision when a picture is demanded. A musician amplifies hearing when composing and practicing. A poet may amplify a feeling and connect that with the inner vision and voice. A good archer will amplify the target and make it bigger and come closer, so that it is easy to hit. The first reference to that one is more than two thousand years old and comes from the *Mahābhārata*. In our perception things become smaller and bigger, loud and silent, impressive or faint all the time. It happens in your inner senses, when you visualise, compose, speak to yourself etc. but it also happens when we process the sensory input of the *'outside world'*. People who walk around with a camera see more. People who play an instrument hear other sounds more clearly. People who make love amplify the sense of touch. In deep trance, you can amplify your senses by devoting attention to a specific impression. The trance will ensure that you are more open-minded and perceptive, and will make you focus more intensely than in your everyday awareness. With a few suggestions, you can increase this. Sometimes I pack an instrument and go into the forest. As I walk around in deep trance, I tell myself that my sense of hearing will become more sensitive while I walk, and reach its peak when I sit down to play. Usually, synaesthesia sets in. Before long, I can hear voices singing in a gurgling brook or know exactly what moss, fern leaves and tree fungi would sound like if their shapes were tones. In these states, playing a single chord can be almost overwhelming. Similar experiences can be had in each sensory system, and when its a sense which you don't use very often, you'll be in for a a bigger surprise.

Trance can be simply gorgeous. I often combine it with a bit of deep breathing from time to time. Or I tend to drift around slowly, forgetting myself in the joy of sheer perception. Most of the time, people around me do not realise what is going on. However, when visiting temples around Kunming, the Daoists noted what was happening. In spite of all language barriers they asked me to sit with them and invited me to enjoy places that were closed to the public. By contrast, the Buddhists did not notice anything, but then, they were usually too occupied policing the public, making money or quarrelling among themselves.

With a bit of practice, you can extend such trances for hours. When you learn that you can eat, drink and shit in deep trance, you can make it an adventure that lasts most of the day. Here, I would like to add that deep trancing can be exhausting. Every intense mental activity burns up plenty of calories. To avoid low blood sugar (and a grumpy mood) you could eat from time to time, or at least have a few sweets to keep your brain happy. You will also learn that there are times and places when such trances are not really wise. When you suffer from low health, for instance, your deep mind may soon return you to everyday awareness. It doesn't mean that you failed. It simply shows that in times of low energy, you should not waste the rest by doing strenuous trances. Usually, the deep mind is much wiser than the conscious mind and will get you out of trance when you are overdoing it.

When we explore the *'outside world'* in a deep trance, we are extending the awareness of the heart into the universe. We become vehicles for Great Unity, the Tai Yi, as it meets and discovers and plays with itself. This, too is Kramamudrā, the pulsation and joy of continuity, and goes far beyond the cluster of concepts that we consider our individual personality. The heart/mind expands and embraces the world; it shrinks and leaves the world behind. Learning begins when we realise that we are none, one, two, many, everything and whatever we chose to be.

Nebulous Forest

Divination

Maybe its fun to read and think about divination, but it's a lot more rewarding to gain practical experience. As you are, no doubt, a daring and enthusiastic researcher of pre-history, religion and consciousness states, I'm sure you'd like to use the oracle bone signs for divination. Here, a bit of innovation may be useful. If we go for tradition we would have to start by getting ourselves a collection of large turtles and a couple of water buffaloes. It might be slightly inconvenient. We would have to get into a messy business of slaughtering, followed by a long period of cleaning, polishing and hollowing bones and plastrons. Finally, we would have to scorch them in the comfort of a garden, on a balcony or, as a last resort, in the living room. None of this is really appropriate, unless you go for rough and archaic scenes and intend to move to another neighbourhood soon. As divination should be simple, easy and fast, we'll forget about anything requiring fire, temples, cauldrons, ovens and dead animals and settle for the much simpler method of drawing lots. Here we are on the same terrain as rune casters, tarot shufflers and coin tossers. We start out with a very essential step. You have to select your range of signs. Welcome to a highly intricate meditation.

Divination is communication. You need a language that can communicate any possible idea.

Any good divination system should be able to communicate a maximum of messages with a minimum of items. The signs for your divination should be varied so that your oracle can give lots of answers, but you don't want hundreds of signs to choose from. For when you divine, you are asking your deep mind, or chance, fate and coincidence to make a choice for you. That's the surface of the job. Perhaps it's your deep mind which makes the choice and selects an answer among many. And maybe it's the gods, your personal deities or the all-self which makes the choice via your deep mind. Or maybe they are really good at influencing chaotic processes, such as coincidence, if that makes you happy. I'm not going to debate this mystery, as, quite simply, it involves so much thinking that any answer is bound to be wrong. Whatever a god, an all-self or a deep mind may be, let alone chance, fate and coincidence, the fact is that divination works. That's the general estimate. You get answers, and more often than not they are useful. Maybe you receive them and maybe you make up your own meaningful interpretations. However, on the particular level, things can go wrong. When you offer too many lots to your deep mind, it may occasionally pick the wrong sign.

With the oracle bones, I started out with a selection of 32 signs. I burned them on disks of wood, charged them, vividly associated them with the right ideas and energies and got going. In general, the results were good, but the failure quota was still considerable. When you allow your hand to roam through 32 pieces of wood, you are making it difficult for your deep mind. You may be successful in many cases, but occasionally you will slip. I practised with this set for ten months, doing several standard and special divinations each day and recorded them all. And made an estimate of the success rate by looking at the results later on and noting a plus (successful), minus (wrong) and middling (could be or unknown) to each. Sometimes a bit of statistic research is quite useful. How come so many occult people are scared of the scientific method? After a while, I noticed that I had distinct sensations about the oracular answers, call them intuitions if you like. A sign or combination of them just would' feel right. So I double checked. Whenever I had picked a few lots that just wouldn't work out, I asked my deep mind whether it had drawn the right signs. I pointed at each lot and asked for a yes/no signal. My deep mind gives me a strong spontaneous jolt or twitch in the back when it says *'yes'*. Hesitant jolts indicate *'not-quite-yes'* or *'possibly influenced by the conscious mind'*. And no jolt can mean *'no'* or *'no answer'* or *'don't know'*. Then I ask *'is this a no'* or *'is this a don't know'* and look for a confirmation. It's a simple system of idiomotoric signalling which you can easily install when you are in a good deep trance. Occasionally, my deep mind told me that one or two signs were wrong. So we had another go and all of a sudden things made much more sense and worked out properly. It made me wonder how to reduce the amount of errors in the selection process. And one thing that came up soon enough was the necessity to reduce the number of lots. Think about it. The *Yijing* uses a mere eight signs to produce 64 answers. That's the basic form. If you include moving lines, you get an additional hexagram, meaning you have 64 x 64 = 4096 possible answers. That's quite a lot for eight basic ingredients. And it's much more than you will generally need. So I reduced the 32 signs to 16. When I pick two signs from a bag that gives me 16 x 15 = 240 basic answers. A simple oracle with one sign for each of the three levels (heaven, earth, human realm) produces 16 x 15 x 14 = 3360 answers. And more complex layouts increase the range much more. It's is more than enough for most needs. And, as you may note, making a choice among 16 pieces of wood is a lot easier than among 32. The success rate improved. The oracle was not as detailed as before, as some finer nuances had disappeared, but it was easier to handle for the deep mind. And the extra meanings were soon assimilated in the sixteen signs.

So what you need, for a start, is a convenient and easy-to-handle selection of signs. Now I am sure you can make your own selection. But if you want a bit of support, read on. The difficult thing about such choices is that you need variety. I mean real variety. Your system should reflect the whole world. Including the bits you favour and the ones you are not so happy about.

In the past decades, there has been a craze for silly tarot decks. A few are brilliant, but many are too specialised. When you use the Giger Tarot with its glorious necrophilic morbidity, you have 78 cards which are pretty much the same. No matter what you divine, it will turn out dark and sinister. I do appreciate it as a highly specialised work of art. It's just no good for divination. The same goes for tarots specialising in cute elflings, garden gnomes, anorectic angels and nude girlies. They may have their use in highly specialised divinations, but if you want an answer for any sort of question, you have to think more broadly.

Shang art is extremely symmetrical and Shang cosmology is balanced. Again and again you come upon the number four. Four directions, four directional deities, four clouds, possibly four mothers, four fang directions and, as a Zhou period interpretation, four manifestations of qi as moving and transforming forces, neatly arranged in a circle. Plus a centre. It started all those later *'five movers'* complexities. And there are four directional animals. Three of them appear long before the Shang. Dragon in the east and tiger in the west were well developed in the Chinese Neolithic. The bird in the south, as the direction of the sun, suits Shang thought beautifully. One useful idea is a group of sixteen signs. The reason appears in the very last section of the divination chapters, when we explore divination without tools. And I suggest you use the four directions as a general guide, as it will make everything much easier further on. But what you associate with each direction or which types of beings, forces, things, people and ideas you chose is your own responsibility.

Here is one possible example.

We could start with the four directions, and their associations to seasons and powers. Zhou cosmology made much of the following pattern: east for spring, wood-wind and morning; south for summer, fire, light, heat and noon; west for autumn, metal, ores, minerals, jade and evening and north for winter, water, darkness, cold and night. Let me add that nowadays northern China has little rainfall in winter. During the middle bronze age it happened more frequently. We know so thanks to the oracle bones. True, this model first appears in the Zhou period. However, when you compare it to the directional deities of the Shang, you may observe that some of these associations must have been around earlier.

Imagine a square of sixteen chambers. The vertical columns are the directions. The horizontal rows can be classes of beings or ideas.

One choice might be to select four deities, four human roles, four animals and four natural phenomena. Let me outline a basic selection. Please don't simply copy it. Think about all details. Change whatever you want. Introduce ideas that make sense for you and fine tune it to your magical universe.

For **deities** you might chose Dong Mu (Mother East), Di for the south, Xi Mu (Mother West) and Double Snakes for north. Double Snakes is here associated with north, as in later Zhou cosmology, the north is the direction of the turtle and, as a combination, of turtle and snake entwined. If you consider Double Snakes as a representation of Fuxi and Nüwa, you might prefer to locate them at the celestial axis. It might be celestial north, but a mythological interpretation would place them in the unknown west, where Mount Kunlun serves as the axis between Heaven and Earth. Or you could move Double Snakes to the category animals. It's your choice. Di could be in the south as this is where the daily sun (i.e. the ancestors of the day) rise to their highest level, when they go to attend Di's celestial court. Readers living south of the equator would have it the other way around. You could also put Di in the north, to represent the Pole Star, and Double Snakes in the south, as the warmer it gets the more reptiles you'll meet. Or you could include Bei Mu (Mother North), if she existed, and make up an unrecorded Nan Mu (Mother South). Or introduce Gui Mu, a Mother Ghost, for a bit of extra excitement. It's your choice. It's a very personal choice. Your deities will tell you what to select. Make sure that the selection involves many varied ideas and concepts. And don't worry about getting everything right from the start: your system will have to be re-adjusted several times before everything functions perfectly. Then there are the **human activities**. You could go for ritual activities, it you like, such as making music east, dancing south, prayer west and dreaming north. Or maybe you'd like to make something out of the five ancestral rituals. Four of them in one category and a fifth somewhere else. Maybe you'd prefer to involve representations of work, such as metal casting, cooking, fighting fishing, hunting, ploughing, travelling or building. How about **human roles**? If you focus on the elite, you could have a marquis east, king south, lady (fu) west and wu ritualist north. It looks like people, but it can also be understood as verbs. Marquis, showing an archery range, for learning, practising and discipline; king for justice, ruling, representations and (hopefully) not-doing; fu lady, showing a brush/broom for management, writing and perhaps sweeping (purification) and wu for shamanic activities and balancing oneself in the four directions, i.e. harmonising the world. It is just one option. You might as well include a representation for the princes, the ancestors, administrators, guards, archers etc, the citizens and the many common people. If you don't require human roles, or would prefer such basics as hand for doing, foot for going, eye for seeing or maybe prefer a selection of four tools or utensils, you are welcome. It's your oracle, use what appeals to you. The four **animals** are the ones that come easiest to mind: dragon east, bird south, tiger west, turtle north. Of course this attribution is pretty much what the middle Zhou and all later periods favoured. In the pre-Shang Longshan culture, the spider was one of the sacred animals. Sadly, we have no certain sign for spider. But turtles were so important to the Shang that maybe they ought to have a place in there. And regarding the bird, you could chose raven, swallow, little bird or even owl if you like. Or maybe you are a more domestic thinker living on a farm and prefer cockerel, cattle, dog and pig. Find out which symbolism makes most sense to you.

One level lower we have nature. Zhou cosmology has wood/wind in the east, fire/sun in the south, metal/precious stones in the west and water in the north. Earth usually occupies the centre. It does not really work out if you only have four signs for the lot. One solution would be a selection of five signs for three levels. Or four sets of five signs, if that fits you better. Twenty lots can still be handled with some reliability. Personally, and speaking only for myself and my own requirements, I do not find it necessary. Twenty signs would make the advanced, tool-free divination a lot more difficult. But you could do this your own way. Sun and fire fit south (and so does star, when you consider that stars are suns); river, rain and drizzle might symbolise north; aerial symbols such as cloud, storm and wind or maybe wood could suit the east (unless you associate tree with the world tree, which would make north appropriate), while west might be represented by metal and jade, or mountain. At the moment I use a simplified system that only requires twelve signs. For this arrangement I link dragon and water with cloud; double snakes with the sacred tree and the celestial axis (the sacred T); tiger with the mountains of the west and fire (for the celestial bodies); and crows with fields and drizzle (soft rain). As you can see the arrangement is based on three levels of existence. It is fairly useful for daily practice, especially when the sign for mountain can mean great and the sign for rain or drizzle small, but it leaves out human participation, which may or may not suit your divination. Think about it. Go into a good trance to sort it out. When you are deep down in the centre, the signs will take on a life of their own and provide plenty of unexpected insights and associations. As you make your choices, you are designing a magickal universe.

Next, I suggest you get yourself a lot of wooden disks and burn or paint the signs on them. Or blank cards. Get more than you need. Maybe you want to change your selection after a while.

Let me add that the categories are misleading. The world isn't divided into directions and levels, nor does it contain different categories of being. To the Shang, the divine appeared in many ways. Mountains, rivers, groves and ritual fires were just as divine as animal spirits, aristocracy or deities. This is what pantheism is all about: you meet divinity everywhere. All things, forms and shapes can be considered deities, spirits, ghosts or shen, one way or another.

Welcome to ignorance. We have no idea whether the Shang had a hierarchy of spiritual levels, nor do we know whether tiger, a river, a dead king or whatever was really a god in the western sense of the word. They all belong to the category shen, i.e. deities, spirits, ancestors, the divine, the spiritual, the numinous, whatever that may mean. Or whatever it meant three thousand years ago.

Anything strong can become a deity or a spirit. Or maybe it already is, and people simply take a while before they realise what's going on. You start out with a verb, like loving, and all of a sudden there's a love-deity. People personify ideas. Gods appear wherever power and intelligence combine. Humans give them shape and stories. Gods give humans ideals and dreams. Maybe we are all inherent in each other. Maybe it's the all-self exploring itself from inside out, upside down, forward back and bottoms up. Maybe its Pangu reassembling. Or Fuxi and Nüwa entangled. Or the Hundun dancing. Or literally every thing circling around the Tai Yi. Or Di establishing balance in the centre. Why insist on a difference? Shen can be abstract, personified, incarnate, material or natural. For when you get really deep into this, you'll find that only consciousness with and without energy/form are real, and that we can't tell the difference between them.

Let's dig deeper. You have selected signs, i.e. forms, and most of them probably represented things. Now let us consider them as verbs. Each sign should yield at least two or three verbs. And a few adjectives. Make a list. As you explore your selection, you will discover many layers of meaning in each symbol. This is essential for any good divination. You could simply go into the depths of your belly, visualise a sign and find out what ideas and feelings appear to you. And do yourself a favour. When you come out of trance, record them. It will make your system work very easily. Your system, and yourself will develop as you go along.

Charging the signs

Objects tend to accumulate information. Any old object can become a spirit, says Gan Bao. He wasn't specific enough. Age is not enough: what you need is use and strong emotion. An odd looking stone can become the material expression of a deity if enough worshippers pour their hopes and longings into it. The stone is not the deity, but becomes a gate to the divine. The same goes for objects used for divination. When you buy a new tarot set you will have a high failure rate for quite a while. It's because the cards don't know who they are. But of you pick up a grubby old standard deck of cards, your success rate will be higher. That's because people have held the cards in their hands many times, and associated each with its meaning and charged them with emotional energy. Now your new set of wooden disks, lots or cards will be in the same situation as a new tarot deck. It will be slightly better, as you will have handled each item as you burned or painted the sign on it, but this isn't good enough yet. To get your tools into top shape you should consecrate and charge each one.

It's simple. Pick one of them. Look at the sign. Breathe on it, rub it, feel your sweat and warmth and feeling going in. Or anoint it with body fluids, such as spittle, menstrual or normal blood or sperm. That's a good traditional way of consecration, you can find it used in many cultures. Anything which personalises the item will be an improvement.

Next, look into the symbol. You could hold it in your hands or press it against your brow. Now think of all the ideas it is meant to represent. When you have *'tree'* for instance, think of trees, forests and sacred groves. Think of shamanic trees connecting heaven and earth. Remember trees that are important to you. They don't have to be Chinese trees, unless you live there. Make it trees that mean a lot to you. Old and young trees; go for a wide range of choices. Consider wood, and how it grows, layer by layer, how the sap in the cambium transports minerals up to the leaves and the products of photosynthesis from the foliage down to the roots. Think of the bark that protects the tree. Consider growing, expansion, and spontaneous motion from the ground up towards the sky. Imagine the east and morning, as the sun rises behind the Fu Sang tree. Remember the thunderous arousal of springtime, when millions of tons of water are sucked up into the crowns as the forest trees open their leaves. Feel how the trees drink the light and spread to get the most of it. See plants and trees as they send suckers and roots into the soil, and how they form partnerships with fungi to get more nourishment from the deep. Visualise sprouting seeds, imagine beginnings, and youth, and fresh starts into life. Imagine hues of green, grey, brown and purple.

The important thing is that you make your imagination impressive. For a start, use all of your senses. See those trees, hear them whisper in the wind, feel their bark and the light, soft touch of leaves. You could add smell and taste for at least some of them. Next, make your imagination vivid. This is the time to turn up the imagination. Make your inner visions large. Bring them close. Increase colour, clarity, contrast. Turn on the volume and let the sound surround you. The more emotional your visions get, the better. You want those visions to be as touching, lucid and intense as you can make them. Pour all of this into the sign. Imagine the trees, then superimpose the image of the symbol. Then think of growth and superimpose the symbol again.

Perhaps it gets even stronger when you say a few keywords as you charge each sign. Use a special voice. When you say *'Dragon'*, make it sound like dragon. And when you say *'river'*, put flowing, hissing sounds into it. Fire should sound hot and explosive. And the names of the gods should vibrate and roll and echo. Be congruent. When something is strong, make it sound strong. And when something is soft and gentle, put that into your voice.

You can make your imagination impressive. Continue until you have made a vivid connection between imagination and sign. Then rub the image into the lot, disk or card and lay it to the side.

Pause a moment. Roll your eyes, take a few fresh, deep breaths, stretch your arms. Maybe you'd like to ring a bell to mark the break or have a sip of tea. Then pick up the next sign.

As you'll soon notice, this sort of consecration is highly exciting. Maybe you'll find yourself swaying, trembling or sweating as you go along. Fine. Enjoy it. And stay relaxed. You need good feelings in each sign. If you stress yourself, the stress will go into your signs. In general, you should associate each sign with the feelings it represents. Freshness for wood, heaviness for earth and stone, heat for sun and fire. Feel like a tiger when you do tiger, and feel like a turtle when you explore that. The more you get involved and carried away, the better. Consecration runs on excitement. That's why you need full involvement. And why you need pauses in between. They give you time to switch from one consciousness to another.

It can be exhausting if you overdo it. So give yourself time. Unless you are well used to emotional visualisation, do a couple of signs and then pause for an hour or continue the next day. Always leave a minute or two between one sign and the next. It will help your deep mind to mark the difference, and to provide access to different neural clusters and functional complexes.

When you've been through the entire set, repeat it. Now you can go faster. Spend a minute or two for each item. After all, by now you have left the creative stage and are confirming what you programmed earlier. And when you go through the set a third time you can be even faster. The images will be ready and the whole thing will go smoothly. Repeat a few more times and you will have a set of disks, cards or lots which is brimming full with imagination and emotion. This is just what you need. You will notice that the signs acquire more meaning as you use them.

Your deep mind will not only use the ideas which you programmed but add its own selection. Great! The signs are a language your deep mind and you share, so that you can communicate with each other. When you've charged them properly, each of them will house its own spirit, and be a gate to deeper insights.

So much in magic depends on proper preparation. The better you prepare your tools, the faster will they work. And while you make your own divination set, you are also getting plenty of practice going into different consciousness states. It may be useful should you wish to create talismans and fetishes. Or when you pick a couple of signs and use them to invoke something. Or when you write a spell in oracle bone script. The writing is not enough. It's the act of putting life into it which makes it magically active. That's how sorcerers do it. Feng Menglong and Luo Guangzhong explain the technique in their masterpiece *Pingyaozhuan* (lit. *Account of the Overthrowing of the Creatures of Deception*, available in German as *Aufstand der Zauberer;* recently the long overdue English translation has appeared). Let's sum up the essence. You fill your heart (awareness) with the sigil and all it represents, and you release the lot with breath and qi straight into the flow the brush. And when you burn the spell or sigil afterwards, imagination and emotion become a message that goes straight into the otherworlds.

Divining

Well, you've almost made it. Your mind is prepared, your tools are prepared and you really want to get going. Again, you can be faster when you prepare properly. As the saying goes: more haste, less speed.

Consider. Divination is a form of communication. Your conscious mind communicates with the deep mind, or with the subconscious, the gods, spirits, all-self or whatever you chose to call it. And something learns to respond. It's like coming to understand a stranger from another culture. For though you and your deep mind grew up together, your ways of processing information differ. And there is plenty of room for misunderstandings. I hope you are prepared to laugh a lot. Divination should be fun. You can be sure to make errors. They indicate that you are really doing something. Each of them will tell you something about yourself. About your preconceptions, your hopes, delusions, wishful thinking or confused signalling. You'll learn a lot about yourself when you approach divination playfully. There are serious people who insist that oracles should only be used for really important matters. I disagree. If you limit yourself to serious topics you won't get as much practice as you need. And you will need practice. Almost all things worth doing require practice.

You can do your divination in several styles. You can make up a ritual to get yourself into the right mood. Maybe you'd like to ring a bell, light incense and candles, say a mantra or pray a little to get yourself into the right mood. Or you do without all of these and simply sit down for a few minutes of calm and deep breathing to settle your mind. Maybe you sink into your belly, get into a nice deep trance, open your eyes and do your thing. Or perhaps you'll simply divine without any preparation. Anything goes. You'll soon discover what approach gets the best result. The only really important thing is that you do exactly what you need. And you'll find out as you experiment. So let me ask you to try everything. The more you try the more errors you'll make and the more you'll learn in the long run. This is what education is all about.

Well and good. You want to ask a question. Let's consider a few details.

Basically, divination goes as follows. First, you get into the right state of mind. Then you ask a question. You repeat the question in your mind, using a clear inner voice. Repeat it as you churn the disks or lots or shuffle the cards. Take your time. Your deep mind will need a bit to decide on an answer which you can understand. This will take longer for beginners than for experienced diviners. Do it slowly and rhythmically. If you mix the lots or shuffle the cards too fast, your deep mind will have difficulties picking the right answers. It's easier to handle lots or disks when you use a wide bag. Use one large enough for your entire hand, and so deep that nothing spills out. Or a deep bowl if you like. In this case you should keep your eyes shut. And at some moment, you will feel it happen. Maybe your fingers will cling to a lot. Maybe you'll spontaneously clutch a disk and feel this jolt in your body. Maybe you'll get a *'This is it!'* sensation as you draw a card from the pack. You'll learn what it feels like as you go along. It should be a clear, strong signal. Ignore all faint signals. Vague intuitions are not good enough. Remember: you want to learn something and your deep mind wants to tell you. It will make both of you wiser and happier. So you are motivated and your deep mind is the same. When the two of you come together, you'll know this is for real. Tell your deep mind *'please give me a strong signal when I touch the right sign'*. You'll get one.

Now put the sign (disk, lot or card) on a little plate, a piece of cloth or some other special surface. Leave it upside down, so you can't see it yet. Maybe you'll want to draw two or three signs. It depends on the layout you use. I suggest you keep it simple. If you are a beginner, two or three signs are more than enough. More signs will not make things clearer, they will simply confuse you, and open the doors for fears and hopes and wishful thinking. Remember, your deep mind wants to tell you something. It can do so in very few symbols. The symbols are not your answer. They are just the key. Words are not the things they represent and the menu is not the food. The real answer appears from the symbols, right there in your head and heart and belly. It appears in your mind.

Now for something really important. You need a special state of mind. When you charge signs, you need maximum involvement, vivid imagination and lots of emotion. But when you divine, you should experience the very opposite. A detached, neutral and uninvolved consciousness works best. Pretend that the divination isn't important, and that you are divining for somebody else, especially when you ask about important matters. Look at yourself from the outside and keep your mind wide open. Don't say *'I want to know...'*, use the third person. The more you are involved, emotional or stuck to your question, the less trustworthy is your answer. It's cause of wishful or fearful thinking. Desire and dread are all well and good, but when you want an open mind you had better send them outside for a while. When you divine, stay as unemotional as you can. It's the best way to learn something useful and new.

And when you've picked your signs, turn them around one after the other and watch out for the very first thing that comes into your head. This should be easy and natural. Go for spontaneous intuitions. If you practice with only one or two signs for an answer, you could press them against your brow and imagine them. And watch what happens in your imagination. It may be connected to the signs or it may be something different. Remember that the signs are there to trigger the right ideas.

In many cases, you'll get an immediate *'yes, this is it'* sensation. If not, ask your deep mind whether it picked the right signs. Touch one and ask *'is this the right answer?'* and watch out for a strong signal. If you only get a vague feeling or none, it may be wrong and you should pick another sign.

This basically, is all there is to divination. And it would be really easy if people did not confuse things by asking the wrong questions.

Good Questions

While all questions may be good at one time or another, especially the crazy and surprising ones, in divination you had better use a format that makes sense to the deep mind, the gods, spirits etc. For a start, remember your basic range of signs. The signs and their combination should be able to give you many different answers. But they will not be useful for simple yes and no questions. Here, our system diverges from Shang divination. If you ask *'does x love me?'* you want a yes or no reply. And there is no way your range of symbols can give it. For yes and no you need something primitive, like tossing a coin, if that's your idea of settling difficult matters. But if you really want to learn something, try this. Ask *'what does x think about me on the three levels of consciousness?'* and draw three signs. First the bottom one for instinctive gut thinking, then the middle one for human thought and conscious reasoning and then a top level signs for spiritual, higher consciousness. Sure, this is more complicated than yes and no. But it may tell you something about the way a person thinks about you on several levels of consciousness. You may even learn something you never thought about. And this is the first thing that divination is good for: it can make you think differently. For regardless whether the answer is true or not, it will make you consider the subject from a new perspective.

Many people use oracles for problem solving, one way or another. Some do it using divination; others follow hunches, impulses or intuitions. In each case the decision is made by the deep mind. Luckily, most problems do not exist in the real world. The word *'problem'* describes a summary and an evaluation. What people call problems are configurations of events, beliefs, memories, sensual perception and loads of thinking. To a large extent, problems are influenced by your internal processes. Some aspects of a problem may be real but others will be distortions in your thought processes. They may even be completely in your mind. So the first thing to solve problems is to stop thinking the usual thoughts. For whatever you have thought about a problem, it didn't get you out of it. And whatever you did to solve it, the behaviour did not work. Repeating won't make it better. So the best thing is to step out of your head and consider it from another point of view. And whatever you do, do something different.

Divination can be helpful. As you read earlier, good divination requires a certain emotional detachment and an open mind. When you do this, you have already left the restrictive configuration of problem-thinking. And you have changed your role. While you had your problem, you were stuck with it. But when you step out of it for fresh insight, you turn from patient to diagnostician. It's a different world. And when you think about the answer, you can observe yourself thinking. You can watch where wishful thinking, fearful thinking and habitual thinking influence you. You can discover where your beliefs limit you. And you can decide to think and do something really different now. The very act of divination can involve dissociation from your problem. It will change the flow of events, for you can chose with which awareness you resume your path. All of this is really useful. For divination does not necessarily have to be true to be useful. Sometimes a wrong answer will be much better than a true one, as it will make you act in a useful way. Yes, you have to expect this from the gods. Most of them are tricksters. They have a strong sense of humour. And they know that people are funny. For good reason they are less interested in your talk than in your doing. I recall quite a few divinations which mislead me for excellent reasons. Divination is communication. And its meaning is what happens within when you get a message, and react to it.

Well and good. Now how do you frame your questions?

-**Time Frame**. It's much easier for the deep mind to tell you something about what goes on than about what will happen. For the simple reason that the future is determined by every single moment as you go along, and that even the act of divination influences what may happen. So your success rate will be higher when you ask about what is than about what might be. If you really have to ask about the future, remember that the deep mind, gods etc. are neither almighty nor all-knowing. They know a lot more than your conscious mind does, and they are much better at guessing. Nevertheless, they will only be able to provide experts opinions and inspired guesswork. It's usually a lot better than what you can do consciously, but it's not certain. So where it comes to the future, chose an open frame. Ask *'what will happen regarding x if I continue as ever?'* It gives you the chance to change it.

-**Structure**. Always keep your questions simple. It's easier for the deep mind to answer three separate question than one question that contains three queries. If you ask *'should I do x or y, provided I avoid z?'* your answer will be worthless. It can't be properly answered. For a start, the *'should'* is your own decision, and the oracle will not make it for you. You are responsible for what you should or shouldn't do. Don't blame the gods for your decisions. They'll like you much better for it.

Next, when you ask about *'x or y'* it's too complicated. How can a single answer apply to both? It's much better to turn this into two separate questions.

-**Negations**. And last, *'provided I avoid'* is much too vague and negative. When you talk with your deep mind, keep it simple and positive. *'To avoid'* does not specify what you do instead. Here we have all the fun and confusion of negation-paradise. There are hypnotists who claim that the subconscious mind cannot understand negations. Well, tests have shown that it can. However, it does not process them as fast as positive statements. When I say *'don't do this'*, on a deep level you have to imagine *'do this'* and then negate or delete it. *'Don't eat garbage'* involves an imagination of yourself eating garbage, followed by a deletion of the image. It's time consuming and complicated. And when you are in a hurry or have phrases with lots of negations, you may find yourself reacting to the very things you shouldn't. Sometimes, *'don't do this'* acts like an invitation.

For example just don't fail to consider when you don't do what you didn't want to do before you avoided not remembering what you might have thought otherwise, but didn't, you may find things don't make sense as you return now and think this through from the beginning and find out how useful it is. But you wouldn't understand how it has not happened unless it wasn't what you thought and indeed it ain't but you can feel happy about it as you go along. Say this to someone and enjoy what happens. It kicks them right out of their mental playground. And if you stick a good, clear and positive suggestion into your patchwork of negations, or attach it gracefully to the end, you will see people react to it. Simply 'cause it's the one bit of reasonable information they can respond to. But no one but you wouldn't want this not to happen, wouldn't you unless you put more pleasure into your life now?

So, in divination, avoid negative phrases. *'Won't this happen'* is inferior to asking what will happen. *'Avoiding trouble'* is inferior to *'going for success'*. Decide what you can do instead of what you can't. Ask what is happening instead of what isn't. As this changes your way of thinking you will gain more power and clarity in life. And when you're at it, and you haven't ceased to avoid misunderstanding what wasn't obvious before you didn't do it, speak in simple, positive language with children. It makes life so much easier for them. For they won't grow up not thinking what they might have thought if they hadn't been screwed up by not knowing where not to go in the ways they didn't choose in life. Make things easy and say what you mean.

-**Specification**. A good question can be answered. Sometimes you'll get your answers even as you phrase a question. For many questions contain answers right the way they are asked.

Consider how literal your question is. The deep mind often takes things very literally. Your conscious mind may assume it is using a metaphor, but for the deep mind, metaphors can be literally true. Queries like *'what will give me a break?'* can lead to interesting answers.

-**Presuppositions**. Many phrases, questions and statements contain assumptions. When you ask 'what will happen?' you presuppose that something will happen. When you ask *'how do I relate to x'* the assumption is that there are a you and an x, and that they relate in some way. Each divination works on the pre-supposition that there is an intelligent agency who understands your question and wants to responds to it, that it can give an answer (or many), that you might understand it and follow up with intelligent behaviour. That's quite a lot, and doesn't always happen. Your answer may be true. But you could get it wrong. Worst of all are *'why'* questions. They presuppose that there are causal relationships, of the sort that can be understood by a simple mind that doesn't like to handle many variables. *'Why is x treating me y?'* implies that there are you and x, that x does a behaviour (treatment) which you identify as related to you, that you evaluate (y) it properly and that it happens for one or several reason. And finally, that you might understand it, which is rarely the case. There are always a huge amount of reasons for anything. *'Why'* questions invite long and convoluted stories full of more assumptions. Even old Socrates knew that if you ask *'why?'* often enough, you can make people go crazy. Cause every because invites more why's. It's one of the reasons they poisoned him. Use *'why'* only for people who deserve it, and be aware how others use it on you. Some bosses use *'why'* questions to screw up their employees. Some parents use them to mess their kids up, and all kids go through a time when they ask why until their parents give up. Our world isn't a very reasonable place, and human minds are even less so. So keep the assumptions out of your questions if you can. Use them in suggestions, where they belong.

-**Evaluations**. If you ask *'will it be good if I do x'* you're asking for confusion. First of all, it's a yes and no question, and this will make any answer difficult. More so, it requires your gods, spirits, deep mind or whoever to estimate what will be *'good'* for you. They may have an entirely different idea about *'good'* than your conscious mind. Occasionally crisis, disappointment and shock may be *'good'* for you. It doesn't necessarily mean that you will like them. Asking *'what will probably happen'* or *'how will it happen'* is a lot easier to answer. It leaves the decision how to make it good to you.

-**Attitude**. Getting a good answer is half of the job. Understanding it is the other half. You need an open mind and the ability to think differently. If a divination merely confirms something, be alert. If you find yourself confirmed too often, something may be seriously wrong. It's you.

This is especially the case when much depends on the answer. The more serious you are, the easier will you deceive yourself. When you have made yourself sick with worry or longing, forget about good divination. Unless you get out of that mind set into a more receptive mode. You can be wrong, and have been, and will be in future. It's all part of the circle of life. Learning begins when you notice you are ignorant. And the more you notice this, the more learning opportunities life holds for you. You can be happily ignorant while you are learning, all your life.

-**Playfulness**. Perhaps you could add a little juice to divination. Consider it a game. And consider your problems a game. Problems add excitement to life. It's much more fun to play something than to work it out. Children play all day if you let them, and learn loads of things without effort. Tell them to work and everything slows down. It's the same with adults. We are one of the few species of animals who retain the urge to play all the way through life. We are the lucky ones. It's there to be used. So play your way to understanding. It's so much easier. For those who work seriously haven't seen the joke yet. Can you be serious enough to laugh about it as you play along? Can you be humble enough to be really damned good at what you're doing? Can you be ignorant enough to remain astonished at the miracles and complexities of the whole great dream of life? The gods like people who know they are funny. We all are. You can join the fun and laugh along with them.

Beyond the basics

Maybe you just had the impression that asking a good question is difficult. Well, in real life it can be. But when you learn to divine, the main thing is to do it with zest. You will make your own errors and you will learn from them. And in the process you will learn a lot about the way you think, and how you structure your inner and outer universe. Divination is a lot more than getting answers. You'll proceed best when you get going now.

So far, we have only discussed divination for problem solving. Sure, it's a good occasion to learn something and do things differently. But if you wait for difficulties to learn from your deep mind you'll miss most of the good things. For divination can be a lot more than therapy.

For a start, your oracle is a creativity machine. You can ask anything you like. And you'll get useful answers most of the time, especially when you approach the matter in a relaxed and playful fashion. If you are an artist and want inspiration, how about picking a few signs and finding out what happens? Take three and make a picture out of them. It's a funny thing, but the mind likes to invent relationships. When you have three symbols, people, things or whatever on a blank space, a stage or in a painting, your mind will immediately begin to find a meaning, possibly even a story happening between them. We are organised to see them in a relation to each other, not a separate things. The result is surrealism. Take unlikely things and combine them. Picasso, Max Ernst and others picked up pieces of junk, combined them in a new way and ended up with works of art. We invent our stories as we go through life: humans are myth making and myth living animals. Or you pick three signs and make a piece of music out of them. How about poetry? Pick three signs, generate a feeling from them, and let the pictures and the words come. Or writing. Sometimes, when I don't know what to put into a letter, I simply pick a few symbols and start writing. The rest of the letter will work itself out naturally.

There are many questions which can be answered best by picking a small number of lots. Now, once again, keep it simple. There are rune casters who select twelve runes (out of the 16 or 24), one for each house of the zodiac (ouch!), and start interpreting. There are card readers who lay out an entire deck of 52 cards, or even worse, all 78 card tarot on the table at once. Then they start talking to their clients. It's a sure way to induce a trance and should be classed as hypnosis. Overload is perfect for trance induction. The more you confuse your client the more you can say that seems meaningful. They are sure to like it. But it won't reveal much cause all the words get in the way. With so much data you can invent or talk away anything. You'll be caught up in a web of myth making, and you'll miss what your deep mind really wants to tell you. So keep it simple. When your deep mind or your gods want to tell you something, they can do so in very few symbols.

You could select three signs to represent underworld, human world and heaven. That's useful when you want to know about someone's state of mind, or the way someone thinks about something. It can give you an opinion about what goes on within you right now. The underworld level gives you an estimate of belly thinking, gut feelings and instinctual awareness. It's the animal level of intuitive body knowledge, the wisdom of genes and survival drives and DNA. The middle world level tells you what the person consciously processes. This is the realm of reasoning, planning, scheming and rationalisation. It may be wrong but that's what being human is all about. The top level says something about what people call the higher self, i.e. those parts of you which connect with the all-self and the gods. And if you want to extend this layout, add two signs to the right and left of the middle sign. One of them for the past, i.e. where you came from, and one for the future, where you will go to next. That's a five symbol layout and quite as complicated as it should get.

Perhaps you'd like to pick two signs. The first represents the verb and the second the noun. If you like three, add an adjective. When you have done your homework you will have plenty of nouns, verbs and adjectives for each sign.

Or you pick two signs, one below, one above, just as in the *Yijing*, and find out what happens when you close your eyes and imagine them. The bottom sign can represent the basis, the root and the foundation, the top sign what develops out of it. Or you pick three signs for a time flow: past, present, future. If you want to know how something works out if you do x, y or z, do three divinations. First, you pick one sign for the status quo. Then add two for near and distant future if you do x. Then take away the future signs but leave the sign for your present state. And ask what happens when you do y instead. Pick two signs for near and distant future. And if you have still another option and want to know what happens if you do z, pick another two future indicators. In all three divinations, you leave the sign for the present situation but put the future signs back in the bag so you could chose from a full range. For such oracles it's useful to keep notes.

Finally, here's one of my favourites. After I wrote *Living Midnight*, I had this idea for doing Yijing divination without coins or stalks. It's simple. You take your left hand and you identify the four fingertips with the numbers 6 (moving yin), 7 (yang), 8 (yin) and 9 (moving yang). It's a simple job when you go into a good trance. You simply press the fingertip and think the number and the Yijing line into it, so that you form a vivid association. For divination, you ask your question, and as you repeat it, you allow your thumb to run over the fingertips, up and down, without thinking about it. Sometime your deep mind gives you a jolt and the thumb sticks to a fingertip. That's the bottom line of your hexagram. Do it six times and you have a complete hexagram. Then visualise it and let the answer come. For the visualisation, and how to interpret hexagrams without looking up the answer in a book, do the exercises in *Living Midnight*.

Now for our Shang oracle we can do something similar. Especially if you have selected a system of sixteen signs, which can be visualised as a square. I told you earlier how I used the four directions as a basic layout. And when you have four classes of beings, or ideas, everything works out easily. Imagine your square of sixteen chambers. Or draw it on a piece of paper. Or on a piece of wood, it may be useful for spells and meditations. Let's use the vertical rows (columns) for the directions east, south, west, north. And use the horizontal rows (bars) for your four categories. The main thing is that you have a grid, and that each symbol has a position in it. Now lift your right hand. Extend the fingers. Each finger represents a column of your diagram. Allow your thumb to run around the fingertips while you repeat your question. Your deep mind will make your thumb stick to a fingertip when it wants to indicate this column. Next, divine the line. This time, the fingertips represent the four rows and the thumb circles them until it gets stuck. Your deep mind has now supplied the coordinates of the row and column that indicate your sign. Repeat the process if you want to an answer of two, three or more symbols. Of course this system is easier to manipulate than drawing lots out of a bag. When you know the column, you may be tempted to pick a row that produces a preferable answer. It's easy to cheat yourself. However, with a bit of practice you will learn to disassociate your personal preferences to such an extent that manipulation can largely be excluded.

Discovery

Here's another tale. Maybe it's even true. It begins with Wang Yirong, a wealthy scholar. One fine day in 1899 he wasn't feeling too well and went to bed. Well, maybe it wasn't really him. The story is slightly apocryphal. It could have been a member of his family, a servant or a slave. There are several versions circulating and the more they go round the merrier they become. Let's stick to the facts: someone was sick in bed. With malaria. Or whatever. The doctor came and prescribed a mixture of interesting things. One of the ingredients was dragon bones. If you think that dragons only inhabit the imagination, a visit to an old fashioned pharmacist in China will teach you better. Chinese medicine classed a lot of different materials as dragon bones. Some of them were fossilised bones imported from the bleak deserts of the west. Among them were dinosaur bones, but also a range of early mammals. Other parts of northern China produced more recent dragon bones. Some were even human. Bones and teeth of Sinanthropus pekinensis, the Homo erectus classified as 'Peking Man', were ground up and taken as medicine. But dragon bones could also be shoulder blades of cattle and tortoise shells dating from the Shang period. Customers rarely knew what they were ingesting. The main thing was impressiveness. Generally, old bones were believed to be better than more recent ones. And should a dragon bone have funny signs on it, traders usually filed it smooth, as this increased the value. Just in case you wonder what dragon bones accomplish, the answer is quite simple. One of the chronic maladies of China is upset stomach. Maybe that's the price for having the most unusual and refined cuisine in the world. The bones acted just like sodium bicarbonate. Which was a lot cheaper but not as classy. In Wang Yirong's recipe, the dragon bones were just a little extra. Chinese doctors generally assume that settling the stomach is a good idea, no matter what the patient suffers from. A servant hurried to the nearest chemist. When he returned, Wang's friend Liu E had come for a visit. It was an amazing stroke of luck that the two took a look at the drugs. They discovered that someone had scratched signs into the bones which looked a little like the ancient bronze script. Now the two were just the persons to appreciate it. Wang Yirong was dean of the prestigious Hanlin University, and an expert on ancient literature and bronze script. Liu E was a scholar and a highly unusual character. Today he is best known for his novel *The Journey of Lao Can*, which he published, anonymously, in a series of instalments. There are several more or less complete versions. In the tale of Lao Can, Liu gave a fictional and somewhat idealised account of himself, with the addition of bizarre elements, such as a visionary dream, a pilgrimage to the Tai Shan, the solving of a criminal case and a guided tour through hell. And it contained, at great length, a description of the Taigu sect, which favoured a blend of Buddhism, Daoism and Confucianism on modern principles. Secretly, Liu E was a member of this organisation, but wasn't ready to admit it, as all established religions were against this faith and membership was punished by death. Chinese government is a little sensitive about unorthodox faiths. The history of China is full of huge revolts inspired by charismatic religious leaders. The last one had been the Tai Ping rebellion, when Hong Xiuquan, a failed scholar but a successful visionary, decided that he was really the younger brother of Jesus Christ and led hundreds of thousands of militant farmers in a devastating tour across the country. By the time the uprising was stopped, twenty million Chinese had lost their lives. That was in 1864, only a few decades ago, and the government was understandably touchy about secret societies and religious reformers. In Liu's time, China was undergoing a transformation. On one hand, the unpopular Qing Dynasty was struggling to remain in control of a country torn by economic crisis, corruption and opium addiction, while on the other hand foreign ideas, science and technology were forcing the intellectuals to reconsider what had been unchangeable gospel for many centuries. The government persecuted any sort of religious movement which might incite public unrest. And Liu E, who was an unusual thinker, offended a lot of people just by being interested in European technology, foreign cultures, maths, ancient history, women's liberation, new religiosity and similar topics.

Liu and Wang realised what scholars might have noticed many centuries earlier: they identified the signs on the dragon bones as an unknown ancestor of their own script. It was a breakthrough experience. The two sent servants to all the drug shops in town to buy any piece of inscribed dragon bone they could get. Within a short time they had acquired a few thousand bone and tortoise shell fragments. The majority was tiny and just had a sign or two. But there were larger items which contained entire sentences. As many signs showed similarity to the bronze script, the translation began immediately. They soon realised that they were handling bones which had been used for pyromancy. Every scholar knew that the earlier diviners heated cattle bones and turtle plastrons for divination. Once the item was hot enough, it cracked, and the nature of the crack supplied an oracle. Wang and Liu saw that their bones were scorched and observed that one side had been carefully drilled to permit easier cracking. So the inscriptions related to ancient oracles. Each inscription turned out to be a question. But just which dynasty had recorded them so carefully?

Liu E acquired a new fashioned European printing press and published six volumes of bone facsimiles in 1903. It caused quite a stir. Many classical scholars felt deeply offended by the publication. The bones indicated events that did not appear in the *Classics*. The inscriptions also upset a new school of progressive thinkers who dismissed all dynasties prior to the Zhou as scholarly fantasies. Both groups argued that the inscriptions must be forgeries. How could they be ancient when none of the classical books ever mentioned bone inscriptions? How come neither Sima Qian nor Kongzi referred to ancient writing on bones and shells? And just where had the inscribed bones come from? Soon enough, the academic world was split into diverging interest groups. Other scholars were delighted by the discovery. During the last decades, a few courageous Chinese academics had begun to doubt that the ancient documents in the *Shujing* were really composed three or four-thousand years ago. They based their studies on linguistic analysis. It revealed that the very items which were thought to be oldest were actually of the most recent age, and that none of the texts attributed to the Xia or Shang had actually been composed in their time. Such scholars were having a difficult time. The academic establishment fiercely opposed revolutionary thoughts. For a thousand years, the classics had a status like holy writ. They were learned by heart and recited word by word during the imperial examinations. And when a scholar composed an essay, it was always based on the thoughts and sayings of the elders, plus a wide range of treasured commentaries. New ideas were definitely not welcome. And in a time, when Chinese orthodoxy was crumbling in the face of dangerous foreign ideas, the oracle bones revealed a past that no-one had expected.

Studies in Ancient History

Since the Northern Song and the advent of Neo-Confucianism, Chinese science stagnated. Almost all scholars based their work on written sources. For almost a thousand years the ideal place for intellectual activity was a secluded library in a pleasant garden, sheltered by high walls, where you could study the ancients and have a nice cup of tea without being bothered by reality. Scholars were not supposed to do their research in the outside world, and the highest sort of study was to grasp the essence of a matter through contemplation of the ancients. Mengzi (Mencius, 372-289 BCE) is one thinker who can be blamed for this. In an especially stupid moment he recorded a saying: *Some labour with their mind and others with their strength. Those who labour with their minds rule the others; those who labour with strength are ruled.* It may remind you of the Greek philosophers with their preference to explain the unknown by reciting axioms. If reality did not accord with the rules, reality was wrong. In ancient Greece, no self-respecting thinker would have made an experiment, as menial activity was a task for slaves. Mengzi seems to have thought pretty much the same. His attitude received a revival at the start of the Southern Song Dynasty (1127-1279).

Chinese scholars had always been interested in their own history. More than a thousand years before C.J. Thomsen realised that prehistory can be ordered into a stone age, a bronze age and an iron age, Chinese scholars were aware that in legendary prehistory, different stages of evolution could be classed by material tools and grave goods. The age of Fuxi, Nüwa and Shennong was characterised by stone tools, Huang Di's time made use of jade for weapons and tools, and in Yü's age, bronze was discovered. (K.C. Chang, 1971:2) The Grand Historian of the Han, Sima Qian, personally visited sites of historical importance, such as battlefields, ruins and places where great events had happened. And China was the home of the world's first systematic archaeologists. Sure, people in many countries collected old things or even dug them up. But it was Li Qingzhao and Zhao Mingzhen who collected and systematically catalogued ancient inscriptions, bronze vessels and stone rubbings around the end of the Northern Song Dynasty (960-1126). In the process, they filled ten large storehouses with their acquisition and published a groundbreaking book which set the standards for further study. Their research predated European archaeology by at least 600 years. Nowadays, Li Qingzhao is celebrated as China's most famous woman poet. Her haunting love poetry, much of it brilliant, sad and drunken, remains widely popular. Few are aware that she also wrote poetic satires, a study on the knight's moves in Chinese chess, painted, sang and practised Daoist neidan meditation (inner alchemy). The book on ancient inscriptions she wrote with her husband has long since been lost. A few contemporaries took up such studies. Another book of the Northern Song Dynasty faithfully descried and illustrated 211 bronze items from the imperial palace and private collections plus 13 jade objects; the author duly noted the origin (if known), the size and weight of each object. However, such research was not to continue for long. When China was invaded, the Northern Song Dynasty collapsed. The emperor and his family were taken prisoner and carried off to the unknown steppes, the court fled south and thinking radically changed. It was the beginning of mind-crushing Neo-Confucianism and the end of all practical scientific research. Practical experiments disappeared and learning became a dull routine of memorising old texts and their commentaries. And whatever the present needed was sought for in the literary wisdom of the past.

Digging was something dirty and menial. Worse yet, excavations involve opening old tombs. The difference between an excavator and a grave robber is largely a matter of ethics. Chinese people have always been extremely averse to opening graves, even in the interest of justice. A grave was a power battery for the living family. The dead ancestors exerted their influence from their graves. Good graves needed a good location, and of course they were not to be disturbed.

Tracking the Bones

It wasn't until the nineteenth centuries that a few scholars began to reconsider the old material. And it took even longer for archaeological study to revive. The notion that academics could happily shovel earth and sift dirt was simply too unsettling.

But with the discovery of the oracle bones, this attitude underwent a sudden change. Some scholars were open minded enough to pursue the topic, and before long, enthusiasts began to accumulate collections. The price for inscribed bones rose. The chemists and traders were beseeched by enthusiasts demanding to know where the inscriptions came from. The traders tried to misdirect the research. But eventually, the truth came out. The source was a tiny village named Xiaotun (Little Hamlet) near Anyang at the northern rim of Henan. The place was locally known as Yinxu (the Waste or Ruins of Yin). The name is quite a give-away. Countless scholars had known the Shang by the name Yin. But nobody had bothered about it as there were no ruins in evidence. The former Shang capital had long ago been flooded and submerged by the nearby river, which deposited a solid layer of rich loess soil over the foundations, and the dust storms, typical for the northern Chinese plains, had buried the past even deeper. Xiaotun was a simple village like many others. But from time to time, the farmers unearthed ancient bone fragments when they worked the fields. They sold the bones to traders, who passed them on to the chemists and drug traders. Ground to powder, the dragon bones disappeared into the stomachs of the wealthy. We will never know how many priceless documents ended in latrines.

While excavations began in Xiaotun, Wang and Liu both came to a sad end. They had the bad fortune of living in highly interesting times. What is exciting for the historian is a nightmare for contemporaries. China was weak, the Qing government corrupt and unpopular and a number of foreign nations used the opportunity to exploit, conquer, and colonise parts of the empire. Part of this program was a religious effort which allowed zealous missionaries to meddle in Chinese affairs and to grant substantial privileges to converts. Since 1644, China had been under the control of the Manchus, foreigners from central Asia, who had overrun China in the last days of the moribund Ming

Dynasty and set themselves up as the new regents. The Manchus started their own dynasty, the Qing, which was soon universally disliked by the Han Chinese. For several centuries, patriotic and conservative citizens opposed the rule of the Qing Dynasty; many of them were members of secret societies. Some of these were highly ethical organisations to cultivate justice, virtue and tradition. Others became what is known as the Triads today, and used their clandestine network for organised crime. When a Qing emperor burned Shaolin temple, some survivors went underground and taught martial arts in the hope that one day, boxers would restore the rule of the house of Ming. By the turn of the twentieth century, Qing popularity had reached an all-time low. The Manchus had become just as incompetent and corrupt as the late Ming regents who preceded them, and foreign countries, such as America, Britain, Germany, Austria, Russia, France and Japan were eagerly pursuing colonialist politics. They enforced business, innovations, trade concessions; they invested in new factories, railways and banks, and some, like the British and Germans, forced the Manchus to grant them colonies in China. The Han Chinese were getting ready to revolt, and the Qing were well aware of it. The Empress Dowager, formally the regent of China, had a hard time surviving the ruthless power struggle at the court. She was later demonised by a number of irresponsible foreign correspondents, and blamed for atrocities she was hardly aware of (Seagrave 1992). The real power was in the hands of a few fractions of the court, which fought out their internal power struggle in numerous ingenious ways. These Manchu princes were skilful enough to direct the rage of the population against the foreigners. Soon enough, people armed with a minimum of martial arts skills and talismans (against bullets) began to plunder and loot in the countryside. Their effort was badly organised at best and aimed as much against the Chinese as against foreigners. They were the famed *'boxers'*, many of them superstitious peasants and criminals, who were incited to kill missionaries and destroy factories, foreign settlements and churches. As it was much easier to kill harmless peasants than well armed foreigners, much of the boxer's effort was aimed against their own countrymen. In short, they were a huge, chaotic force that could hardly be controlled. It was a time of serious trouble. Noteworthy members of the Manchu government pretended to be outraged by the public unrest, but did much to support it. After all, the foreigners attracted the attention of a lot of Chinese hotheads who might otherwise have turned against their government. Likewise, the regents of Europe, America, Russia and Japan were delighted by the opportunity to demonstrate justified wrath and to move into China for good. For a brief time, the boxers served their purpose. Then they disappeared from one day to another. The Manchu generals simply scattered them and recruited the younger and stronger ones into their army. While the foreigners still assumed that they were fighting boxers, they were really facing soldiers controlled by members of the government. Members of the court ordered the army to besiege the foreign settlements in Beijing, while other aristocrats, including the Empress Dowager herself, did much to prevent fighting and even supplied the embassies with food. The besieged Westerners plundered the shops and villas in their neighbourhood, collecting treasures and priceless works of art. They suffered a shortage of food but had more champagne than they could drink. Occasionally they made a heroic effort to shoot Chinese troops, who were under order not to fight back. Meanwhile, the allied armies of Britain, America, Russia and Japan, plus token regiments from Austria, Germany, France and Italy, were beginning their march from the coast to Beijing. The advance was slow, as the generals and diplomats spent much time quarrelling with each other. They also plundered, burned and destroyed as much as they could. And while the foreign embassies were holding out against an enemy who didn't want to fight them, the court was busy packing. The Empress Dowager and her relations moved 700 miles westwards while the allied foreign forces, 20.000 soldiers altogether, entered Beijing, burned the summer palace and the national library and collected amazing amounts of treasures. That so many museums are well stocked with Chinese artefacts is partly due to this barbaric effort.

Wang Yirong was a dutiful official, and received orders to lead a detachment of soldiers. As a dedicated scholar, he believed in doing his duty, but it is not likely that he was much of a warrior. While the Manchu nobles fled, he was ordered to stay behind and fight. When the situation became hopeless, he and his family committed suicide by poison.

In the meantime, Liu E collected more than 5500 inscribed oracle bones, including roughly a thousand he had acquired from the property of the late Wang. But as a free thinker he kept making enemies. In the past, he had advised the government on technical matters. He had used revolutionary new methods to combat the annual deluges of the Yellow River, which gave him good reputation and high office. Before the *'boxer rebellion'* he made friends with English businessmen and foreign diplomats, and his reputation at court suffered seriously. Liu E became involved in industrial projects and in the construction of Chinas first railways. He believed that western science and technology were the future for his country. To the conservatives, this turned him into a traitor. While the allied armies occupied Beijing in 1900, the population suffered from famine. Liu used his political influence and opened the imperial rice reserves to the population. He was in a hurry and did not bother to ask for permission. Nor would he have received any, what with the court hurrying westwards toward Xi'an. It almost cost him his life. When things calmed down, his enemies sued him for wasting public property. But Liu still had friends at court who protected him. When those friends retired, his enemies used their chance. They brought up the affair with the imperial rice and framed him for having stolen part of it. In 1908 Liu E was sentenced to lifelong exile in Xinjiang. The province was just about as far from civilisation as one could get. Xinjiang is far to the northwest, a country of deserts and vast steppes, populated by Uighurs, where the winters are icy and the skies go on forever. The journey was an ordeal for the ageing scholar. Only a few months later, in 1909, he died.

Anyang

In Xiaotun, Anyang, excavations began around 1900. An oracle bone enthusiast, Duan Fang, used his influence and high political office to trace the origin of the dragon bones. Allegedly, he paid three ounces of silver for each engraved character. I doubt it. The peasants in Anyang were all too eager to work for less. Word got around and other collectors arrived on the scene. Soon everyone who owned a shovel joined the hunt. The first excavations began with unsystematic vandalism. Any collector could hire a peasant and start digging. Some had entire teams of diggers, and these teams were neither co-ordinated nor disciplined. Occasionally, the groups quarrelled and fought. Once, three tunnels converged on a single cache of bones. When they met, the tunnels collapsed and several people were buried alive. Luckily, the tunnels were not deep and everyone could be saved. And when a farmer found a hoard of bones in his vegetable field, bandits moved in and ransomed the family.

A few collectors paid a specific sum for each piece. It made the diggers smash large items and sell them to several customers. To avoid such damages, the collectors began to pay for each sign on a given piece. It created an entire industry. Highly skilled carvers began to improve oracle bones. Several times, digging around Xiaotun became so chaotic that the local government had to step in. While excavations were officially prohibited, the diggers worked by night. And in the wealthy cities along the cost, enthusiasts paid exorbitant sums for collector pieces which looked impressive, showed lots of exciting characters and were often forgeries.

It wasn't a good time for archaeological research. While the digging continued, China transformed from the core. In 1911, the power of the Qing court collapsed and the country became a republic. But the rule of the Guomindang (Kuomintang) was by no means established, nor did the new rulers live up to what they had promised. What had started as idealism soon became as chaotic and corrupt as the late Qing rule that preceded it. 1925 to 1927 workers in major cities tried to rise against their new government, and the Guomindang began to execute Communists. The Japanese used the opportunity to move into Shandong.

The first proper excavations were made in 1929. Their participants were members of a new generation of academics. Dedicated young Chinese scholars had undergone training at universities in Europe and America and returned to their homeland with new ideas and innovative methods. They were often accompanied by international experts. The excavations were remarkably peaceful and co-operative. Between 1928 and 1937 the Institute of History and Philology excavated 24 918 inscribed pieces. The Province Museum Henan made its own excavations between 1929 and 1930 and unearthed a further 3656 fragments. But before these enthusiastic teams were done, economic crisis stopped the cash flow and war escalated. 1931, the Japanese had occupied Manchuria. By 1935 they were busy fighting in wide parts of northern China. In 1934, the Communists, harried by the Guomindang, began the Long Marsh. In the heartland of the Shang, Japanese troops fought Communist commandos. 1935, the survivors of the Long Marsh reached northern Shaanxi, and Mao Zedong was installed as the head of the Communist Party. The first generation of Chinese archaeologists was stuck in the middle of the conflict. Some managed to escape, others continued their excavations under terrible circumstances, several were wounded and a few found their death. An unknown amount of priceless items was lost, destroyed or sold to foreign collectors.

By this time, the excavators had made considerable progress. 1934 the first royal tombs were discovered, 1935 the archaeologists employed a total of five-hundred workers to excavate the Shang capital in a hurry. In 1936, on the last day of the excavation, a new cache of oracle bones was discovered. Unlike the earlier ones, it was so well preserved that many of the plastrons and scapula were in their original location. Though most had cracked over the millennia, they were still close together. The excavators doubled their effort and worked nonstop for four days and nights. They managed to unearth the whole hoard in one piece, a massive three ton chunk of mud containing more than 17.000 fragments. And they transported it, securely confined in wooden planks, on foot to the nearest railroad, in Nanjing. A year later, in 1937, the Japanese took Nanjing and massacred more than 250.000 peaceful citizens. While the treasures of the Shang were moved across China, the Communists and Guomindang were busy fighting each other. 1939 followed World War Two. And as if this wasn't bad enough, several million people of Henan starved to death between 1942 and 1943. The Japanese occupation ended in 1945. The

Japanese army departed, leaving behind destruction, famine and a range of diseases which had been bred in laboratories. Meanwhile, the Russians move into Manchuria. Their stay was not for long. In 1946 they withdrew again, taking along entire factories. But the war between the Guomindang and the Communists continued. There was no peace before 1949, when the Communists successfully evicted the Guomindang and turned China into a People's Republic. The archaeologists had a hard time. The Republicans valued their work, in a general way, as prehistory is a good propaganda topic. In the cause of patriotism, funds were devoted to excavations. The Communists were less keen on the culture of the ancient feudal societies. Finally, the Republicans escaped to Taiwan. They took along the priceless collections of many museums and a huge amount of Shang artefacts. The archaeologists had to make a difficult decision. Either they followed the Republicans and accompanied the material they had excavated to Taiwan, or they remained on mainland China and hoped to uncover new material. And while the former group had no chance to acquire new material, the latter group faced research without money. The newly founded People's Republic of China was in deep economic crisis. When so many people are threatened by starvation, who would devote funds to explore the feudal societies of the remote past? Some excavations did continue, but usually on a small scale. When the economy recovered, the excavations grew. After all, manpower was cheap, and China's past was an investment in patriotism. Things became worse again during the Cultural Revolution (1967 – 1976), when religion, art and culture were damned as outdated relics of a feudal past. When the Cultural Revolution ended, archaeology slowly recovered. The scholars were still expected to follow the Marxist model of historical development but they were also required to demonstrate that China's past was full of marvellous achievements. Since then, things have changed a lot. Over the years, several new hoards of oracle bones have come to light. The first major source was the excavation of Xiaotun Locus North in 1936, yielding 17,096 inscribed fragments, 17,088 made from turtle plastrons. In 1973, Xiaotun Locus South yielded 5,041 inscribed pieces, 4,959 of bone.   1991 a pit at Huayuazhuang Locus East provided 1,583 oracle bones. 1,558 were from turtle plastrons, but only 574 had inscriptions, while of the remaining 25 bone pieces only five were inscribed. It's a smaller yield, but extremely valuable, as almost 300 of the inscribed turtle plastrons could be excavated intact. (Lu Liancheng & Yan Wenming in K.C. Chang 2005:166-167). Nowadays, China is proud of the magnificent cultures of her past. The oracle bones prove that written history in China extends well into the Bronze Age. Sure, there were several cultures who wrote in those days. The Vinca script is much older, but disappeared together with the Vinca culture when the Balkan was overrun by unknown hostile folk. Cretan Linear A became extinct, just like the entire Minoan culture, when the volcanic island Santorin blew up. And while the writing of the Mesopotamians, Egyptians, Hittites and the entire huge Indus culture disappeared under the shifting sands of arid deserts, Chinese writing continues as an unbroken tradition to this day. The excavations of Anyang proceed, the Shang graves and the Fu Hao tomb have become a tourist attraction and scholars in Taiwan and on the mainland have resumed communication. There is still much in the rich, heavy ochre loess that waits for its discovery.

Scapulamancy

Divination with shoulder blades (scapulamancy or, earlier, spatulimancy) is an ancient custom. You can find it in many cultures. There are two basic approaches. Either a chosen animal is sacrificed, preferably on a sacred day and by experienced ritualists. A question is asked, the carcass is opened and a shoulder blade extracted. The diviner looks at the minute patters on the bone and makes a prediction. This sort of divination is much like investigating the entrails or liver of dead animals. And perhaps there was even a system to it. Something like *'wrinkles in the lower left mean rain next afternoon'*. Think of the Assyrians, or the Etruscans, who had models of the liver which were neatly divined into zones, to make their predictions more systematic. A similar layout was used by diviners at the lower Indus, who divided the bone into the twelve houses of astrology. Systems attributing crack-types to locations on a scapula are attested from a few Siberian cultures.

Scapulamancy was used by many people and for a long time. Gerald of Wales saw it during his travels in Ross, Pembrokeshire, in 1107. In his account, the scapula was cleaned after cooking, and consulted for a wide range of questions. *'Reading the speal-bone'* was also documented by John of Salisbury in the twelfth century. It remained popular in Britain, and especially in Scotland, up to the nineteenth century. The earliest documented reference in Germany is a document of the 13th century, which condemns this type of divination as a mortal sin. However, the prohibition did not effect much. The next references are in the *High Song* of St. Trudpeter (12th century), in Vintler's *Blumen der Tugend* (*Flowers of Virtue*, 1411) and in the infamous *Buch der verbotenen Künste* (*Book of Forbidden Arts*), by Dr. Johannes Hartlieb (1456, chapters 115-120). Hartlieb scoffed at this form of divination, which is among the least prestigious in his account. If we can trust him, a shoulder-blade was washed with wine and holy water and kept wrapped in a clean piece of cloth. The diviner took it out of the cupboard whenever an oracle was needed, went outdoors, unwrapped the item and studied it. *"Then they look at the shoulder bone in the belief that it transforms according to each question"*. It's a funny idea. After all, it is the same boring old bone as ever. How could the diviner arrive at many different answers? Didn't he get used to the wrinkles eventually? Maybe he did. Or perhaps he simply looked at the blank space and the Devil granted a vision, much as in a crystal ball. Luckily, the *Book of Forbidden Arts* assures us that the Devil can make anyone believe anything. Just like the media. Or Hartlieb got it all wrong. His account has no counterpart in any culture anywhere.

Bone reading is recorded from 12th century France, from Greece and the Balkan, Russia, Turkey, North Africa and from the Arabian world, where the first references date around the ninth century. Strangely, the custom cannot be found in the writing of the classical Greek and Roman authors. It might be the reason why Agrippa of Nettesheim, one of the sanest European mages ever, did not bother to mention it. Maybe it simply wasn't prestigious enough.

The Mongols practised scapulamancy in the 13th century, as did a wide range of Turkish people in central Asia. And the same custom was observed, at various times, among the Afghans, Tibetans, Kirgiz, Buryats, Tungus and many Siberian cultures, all the way to China. The Huns under Attila divined from shoulder bones. And the earliest work of Japanese literature, the *Kojiki*, allegedly dating from 712 BCE, mentions scapulamancy from the shoulder bone of a deer. To divine the cracks was also popular among several Native American cultures, such as the Algonqian and Athabaskan speaking people.

The other sort of scapulamancy involves fire. In the European variety, the flesh was usually detached from the bone using specials knives or wooden utensils, and sometimes this was eased by cooking it first. This method is gentle. It leaves the bone intact, so the seer can examine the texture of the bone and its coloration. In Asia, roasting was employed, which resulted in different scorch marks and cracks. Sometimes, as in the divination performed by the Mongol Khan Mangu whom the monk Rubruquis visited, special tents were set up to fire a few shoulder bones until they were completely black. The khan himself examined the cracks and pronounced the oracle, just as so many Shang regents did. (Bächtold-Stäubli, 2000, vol. 8:125-140). Here, scapulamancy connects with what is technically called pyromancy. Maybe the Chinese were the inventors of this method. Cracked shoulderbones were unearthed in the earliest Chinese Neolithic communities. In Liaoning, pyromancy with scapulas is attested from the middle of the fourth millennium BCE. It was also popular in the Longshan culture a thousand years before the Shang era began. But the Shang certainly made a high art of it.

Drilling Bones in Anyang

For divination, the Shang used the shoulder blades (scapula) of cattle, such as cows and, more often water buffaloes. Mind you, it's hard to be sure about this. The species of cattle in question have not made it to our time. Also, the ends of the scapulas were carefully sawed off, making biological classification difficult. Cattle scapulas are smooth and large, providing plenty of space for crack-making and inscriptions. Or they used the belly-plate (plastron) of at least four species of turtles. The diviners preferred female turtle shells, as their belly plates are smoother and more even, hence easier to inscribe and store. Both materials were not easy to obtain. Water buffaloes were probably more common in the countries south of the Shang domain and so were several species of turtle. Two of the species of turtle exist today and are typically found in Southern China. The Shang used local animals, but a large part of their material had to be imported. Some of the turtle plastrons have inscriptions telling us about their origin. Ambassadors from distant provinces presented large amounts of shells as a gift or tribute to the Shang. A few plastrons carry comments about their origin. They mention shipments of 250, 300, 500 or even a thousand pieces. The Shang preferred large turtles. Many belly plates measure more than 30cm in length. Plastrons are smaller than shoulder blades but they are smooth and easy to prepare, drill, heat, inscribe and store. According to Hu Hou-hsüan's count, (K. C. Chang 1980:156) the archives of the Shang yielded the remnants of 12.334 turtles. No doubt there were more. It gave the oracle the title *'voice of the turtle'*. But even with the southern imports, the demand for plastrons was so large that turtles had to be bred in captivity. Tung (in Keightley, 1978:12) mentions that the farmers at Xiaotun once unearthed an entire store of several hundred complete turtle shells of all sizes. They must have lived there, as imported plastrons were delivered without the top part of the shell. Also, the presence of smaller animals indicates that the animals were raised in captivity. We have to imagine ponds near the capital where turtles were raised for divination and food. It's one of those questions whether turtles were sacred animals. They certainly had divine qualities, but this did not keep the Shang from breeding, keeping and killing them like livestock.

So far, there has been much research and speculation about the amount of sacrificed animals, and whether scapula or plastrons were preferred, possibly for specific forms of divination.

One estimate (Keightley, 1978:89) gives a total of 69000 plastrons and 69000 scapulas. The majority of these were used up in Wu Ding's reign. Obviously, divination was of immense importance for the late Shang period. But the diviners did not entirely depend on cattle and turtles. On some occasion, they used sheep and deer-shoulder blades, or even land dwelling tortoises. There are also a few inscribed human skulls. Unlike the shoulder blades and plastrons, the skulls were display pieces to commemorate oracles. They were neither heated nor cracked.

The bones were carefully prepared prior to divination. It involved a lot of labour. For a start, the imported or self-produced scapulas and plastrons were usually processed (and counted) in pairs. Long before their use in ritual, they were carefully cut to size, cleaned, smoothed and polished. Some of them, especially under Wu Ding, were so carefully polished that they shone like jade. In the process, they were ritually prepared. Maybe it was an act of purification or blessing. This task is sometimes mentioned in marginal inscriptions, which appear typically in period one, and very rarely in subsequent periods. The ritual was usually done by the noble ladies (fu) of the court, though the princes were also occasionally expected to consecrate a few. These inscriptions are very brief. For example:

'*Wu-xu* (day 35) *Lady 'Family'* (house with stylised pig) *consecrates* (the glyph '*T*' for divinity) *pair* (of) *scapula* (a sign looking much like the 'bud' for spring) (in the presence of diviner) '*Arrow in Quiver'.*' (*JGWZD* page 800). The diviner name usually appears at the end of such inscriptions. However, on occasion, such marginal comments mention that the rite was done in the presence of a deity, the Sacred Mountain Yue. As I proposed earlier, Yue (Peak) was the name of a ritualist, perhaps of Wu Ding's legendary Prime Minister Fu Yue. Now ordinarily, the fu ladies blessed or purified only small numbers of scapulas or plastrons. But some inscriptions give exceptions. Lady Fu Jing, the last wife of Wu Ding, personally did the purification/blessing with forty; once even with a hundred pairs. It seems that the task was a prestigious one.

Quite possibly the bones and plastrons were treated to make them easier to work with. It is a tough job to inscribe either material. So maybe they were soaked in water or chemicals to make them softer. I am reminded of the Viking method of softening horn by soaking it for days or weeks in sour milk or in a pot full of sorrel leaves. Maybe the Shang did something similar. However, the only reference to acid in Shang script is the glyph for stomach, which can also be read as salt broth, a reference to the gastric juices or to soup. As far as I know, the character does not occur in a ritual context. Finally, the scapulas and plastrons underwent a process of drilling or, more often, chiselling. If you heat a scapula as it is, it takes a long time to crack. The Shang made lots of cracks and wanted to speed up the process. For this purpose, they made hollows on the back of each piece. These hollows were made in neat and regular rows. The number on each piece varied considerably, as did the shape and care devoted to the job. Over the centuries, the craftsmen developed several arrangements of hollows and notches which they spaced, quite regular, in neat rows all over the reverse of bone or plastron. Great care was taken to space the hollows evenly. Making hollows was a highly skilled job. Most of them are cautiously prepared so that only a very thin layer of bone or shell remained. It made them ideal for cracking. Sadly, it also weakened each piece. The reason that so many oracle bones became fragments is that they were hollowed, notched and heated so well. The weight of the earth above them, plus the influence of time, water and bacteria, sufficed to break them to pieces. At the time being more than 160.000 inscribed pieces are on record. A valuable few consist of the entire bone or plastron. But the majority is so small that only a very few words, if any, can be found on them.

Divination

Finally, we come to the process of divination. Oracle bone script uses a few basic signs for it. One of them shows a ding cauldron (p.789). You can read it as *'asking'* or *'posing a question'* or *'making a charge'*. I will discuss the difference further on. In divination, people tend to ask questions. The Shang diviners, especially during the end of the period, expressed their queries as statements, predictions or charges. It was up to the oracle to confirm or deny such statements. Some oracles simply give a single statement, and the crack decides whether it would be true or not. Other oracles, usually from Wu Ding's time, were carefully phrased in a positive and negative manner. In this case a plastron might read:

Left side: *'Ding-hai* (day 24*) crack making* (diviner's name missing or not recorded) *divination ritual: Prince Fisher maybe has disease?'*

Right side: *'Ding* (part missing) *divination ritual: Prince Fisher not has disease? Third Moon.'* (Li Pu, # 496).

In this case, both the proposition and its counter charge could be divined independently.

The sign of the ding cauldron suggests that maybe a bronze vessel was involved in the ritual. Perhaps a fire was lit in such a cauldron, or maybe a sacrifice of food, alcohol or blood went into it. As many ding cauldrons were used to cook and offer meat and soup, a ritual meal for diviners, royals, ancestors and gods may have occurred. Divination isn't just a formality, or at least it shouldn't be, if you really want to learn something new. Every genuine ritual requires that people and spirits get into the right mood. The other sign for divination shows a crack. It can be read *'asking'* but also *'crack-making'* or *'divining'* (p.765). The sign is still evident in modern Chinese. It is pronounced bu today, but in earlier times, the sound was buk. And that's what you hear when the bone cracks.

Now the actual mode of heating remains enigmatic. Some propose the bones were heated on a bed of glowing embers. It's unlikely, as the hollows show a very precise scorching, and as most bones or plastron were used for several divinations. Others believe that a red hot bronze rod was pressed into the hollow until it cracked. It is not as easy as you might think. Bone is good at absorbing heat while even red hot metal cools fast. A third theory proposed that dried herbs were burned within a given hollow. At the time being, the most likely theory is that a stick of some hard wood was burned and that the glowing tip was pressed into a hollow while some sort of bellow provided the oxygen needed to keep it really hot. Chang Kuang-Yüan did the job using three incense sticks, but using this inferior source of heat it took 25 minutes till the first invisible cracks began, and a total of 50 minutes until the cracks were visible on the front side of the plastron. I am sure the Shang diviners had a faster method.

Usually, a question was not decided by making a single crack. The oracle bones show that for each and every charge several hollows were cracked. It was customary to make a minimum of five cracks (a set) for one query. Thus, a charge and countercharge might require a minimum of five plus five cracks. Period one diviners preferred five, ten or twenty cracks for each question, but as things were still very experimental at the time, there are also sets of six, seven, eight or nine cracks. In later periods, the rule of five or multiples of five is more pronounced. The number of each crack was carefully noted on the front of each piece. Sometimes we even have commentaries next to the cracks which tell us that it is moderately (*'small'*) good, greatly good or even extremely auspicious. Other commentaries were inscribed next to the cracks, mainly in period 1, but these cannot be read yet. Often, each bone or plastron was used for a whole series of divinations. And as they are dated, we can see if they were a few days or weeks apart. Some scapula are almost like a calendar, giving the dull *'day so-and-so divination this xun week not have disaster?'* over many months.

As you can see, the treatment of the bones and plastrons required a lot of time, effort and expense. Tossing a cowrie shell would have been much faster, but less impressive. Even standard enquiries about rainfall tomorrow or the outcome of a routine hunt needed an impressive amount of cleaning, polishing, ritual, drilling (or chiselling) plus a lot of heating and cracking. But things were even more complicated. A single charge might be divined on several bones or plastrons simultaneously. David Keightley gives an impressive account of a simple military divination. King Wu Ding, suffering from toothache, was wondering whether he should follow one general against one enemy or another general against another enemy state. He was also wondering in which case he would receive divine assistance. An additional divination was made regarding the toothache, and whether offering a dog and a split sheep would make it go away. The whole issue was divined on five plastrons simultaneously (1978:76-88 and figure 15).

Not all available hollows were used for divination. Some bones were discarded after only a few scorchings, leaving lots of unused space and hollows. This *'wastefulness'* has led to speculation whether such bones were discarded as they produced undesirable answers. It's a point that can't be proved; as we don't know which answers were desirable. Also, several systems were used at the same time. Some diviners scorched hollows moving from top to bottom of the bone, from inside to outside of the bone while moving top to bottom, or even bottom to the top, and some bones show what can only be called random scorching. All of which goes to show that there was no standard system of divination, or that people didn't care.

And may I just ask where the Shang made their divination? I once made an incense holder of wild boar bone, and scorched it by mistake. The smell was sweetish, slightly weird and stuck to clothes and hair. Scorching a plastron is worse. I tried that too. Tortoise shells consist of the same stuff as your hair and fingernails. You wouldn't want to burn it in your living room, day in and day out. The Shang seem to have thought the same. One segment of the palace foundations in Xiaotun is thought to contain the foundations of temples and shrines. They are a little remote from the living quarters, and at an angle, so that the wind could blow the stench away.

Inscription

After the divination was over, the crack notations were engraved. In period one, important cracks were also engraved. This is crucial if you wish to look up a given piece of cracked bone weeks or months after the divination. Cracks tend to close again, and many of them become almost invisible. And finally the question was recorded on the bone. In some cases, prior to engraving, it was written by a brush. A few traces of brushstrokes survive on bones and plastrons, proving that brushes were in use more than a thousand years earlier than had been assumed. This was not the rule, however. A good many inscriptions, especially from period 5, are engraved in such tiny characters that a brush simply wouldn't be able to write them.

Next, the item went into the hands of an engraver, who carefully incised the signs into the material. We have no idea what tools they used. Bronze knives are one option; another is a small jade blade. The shape of the edge seems to have varied and the experts are not in agreement whether the inscriptions were cut or scratched. Bone and turtle shell are very hard substances, and some of the inscriptions are tiny, or have tiny details or involve curves. Usually they are not deeply engraved. It's possible that the material was softened by some acid prior to the inscription. A few inscriptions show broad scratches with serrated edges. Presumably they were made by a chisel-like tool.

In special cases, the inscriptions were coloured using soot, unknown natural pigments (which look plain brown nowadays, provided they have survived at all) or bright red cinnabar. Few inscriptions have retained traces of their colouration, but it is possible that originally, a much larger amount was coloured. In the long years underground, mineral pigments or soot could have been washed out of the scratches; and natural pigments could have decayed.

The question or charge was usually recorded next to a crack it related to; frequently the writing went against the direction of the crack. This is not a standard rule, however. Some inscriptions are beautifully made and widely spaced; others are crammed in any way they would fit.

As a few unfinished bones survive, we can see that the vertical lines were incised first. Then the inscriber turned the bone around and did the diagonal and horizontal lines. It's in contrast to modern Chinese, where the horizontal lines come first. The inscriptions were spaced with remarkably few rules. While the direction of writing usually went top to bottom, there are also inscriptions going right to left and in paired (and symmetrical) charges from left to right. In a few cases the inscription changed its direction from vertical to horizontal in the middle of the text. When an inscription lacked space it could move across a crack notation, which was carefully erased. It was common practise to make the inscriptions one after the other from top to bottom, but there are also bones where each dated charge appears above the next. And when inscriptions really became muddled up, it was a great idea to scratch a dividing line between them. Only that in some cases the division runs straight through a single charge, as the important issue was to mark the division of cracks!

Finally, the whole thing was stored away. We don't know where or how, but evidently, considering all the effort to make the record permanent, in a place where they could be looked up. This was especially required when a bone received its inscriptions over several months, or when a commentary was added after the event. Some commentaries were made months later. Eventually, the bones were placed in pits. A whole series of pits has been discovered at Xiaotun, but these are not spaced in any meaningful pattern. Each pit was filled with carefully stacked scapulae and plastrons. Some of them, like the one excavated in 1991 were carefully lined with wooden planks. Were these pits the archives? Or was the archive emptied from time to time and the material buried in the ground? Did the inscribed scapulae and plastrons become sacrificial offerings? The large hoard mentioned earlier might have been such a case. Next to it, a skeleton was uncovered. Should we consider it a guardian?

You can see that this sort of divination is a very elaborate affair. It requires trade connections, treaties, a whole range of craftspeople, ritual specialists, diviners, often the king, plus scribes, engravers and folk who guard and store the material away. Maybe there were even librarians involved. While often several diviners worked with a single scapula, the handwriting on the piece was frequently in a single style, indicating that only one engraver had recorded the whole thing. Or, when routine divinations were made over the weeks, we can identify several scribes by their handwriting, while the questions remain pretty much the same.

The Shang had archives of scapula and plastrons, many of them recording date, diviner and question. What they usually did not record was the answer. In some cases we are lucky to have a comment, especially from period 1. Or the king himself dared to make a prognostication, which was duly recorded. Provided the king was right; there are no royal errors on record. Or the scribes added some crack notations meaning *'auspicious'*, *'great and good (luck)'* or maybe *'this was used (done)'*. Plus a few characters we cannot decipher today. But the majority of the oracles remain questions, pure and simple.

But what about the cracks? Can we tell the answer by the shape, size or location of the crack? The answer is no. The T shaped cracks may have been interpreted in a lot of ways. Most scholars agree that they meant yes and no, which looks nice and as digital as *Yijing* divination, but maybe there was also a way of judging whether it was a definite or a more cautious answer. I am sure fast and slow cracking, or large or small cracks had meaning to the diviners. But who knows? There may have been many systems over the generations. Or each diviner used her or his own system. Or the reading was specified for each single divination. K. C. Chang (1983:54) mentions the contemporary Ta-Lu culture of the Yi in Yungshen, Yunnan. Here, scapulamancy never went out of fashion. The diviners start the ritual with a prayer. Then they tell the spirits what the cracks will mean during the ritual. In another ritual, the meaning may be different. They heat the bones in a fire and wait for them to crack. Unlike the Shang, however, they do not record the oracle and do not keep the bones.

So far, scholars assumed that a specific place or direction of the crack would yield the answer. But it could also be that a enthusiastic crack means one thing and a hesitant crack another. Or that the diviner kept repeting possible answers (*'a little auspicious, auspicious, greatly auspicious, extremely auspicious'*, and maybe something like *'no good at all'*) until the Buk! confirmed one. Maybe weak and strong cracks had different meanings. Or single and bifurcated ones. We simply can't tell. All of which is rather unsatisfactory. It makes sense to record and store oracles to check whether they turned out to be true. I'm not sure it would make diviners very happy, but it certainly would be reasonable. If the interpretation changed frequently, there would be no way to look up the answer. Were the bones inscribed so humans could read them? Or were they simply kept as they had become sacred during the ritual and could not be thrown away? Or were the gods or ancestors supposed to read them, like a written contract, to remind them of their promises?

Bone readers

Finally, let's take a look at the process of divination. There is very little evidence about the ritual which accompanied each divination. I would guess that a bit of prayer and sacrifice was involved. But how was the whole thing done? Should we imagine a group of diviners attending the king who appears in full regalia, accompanied by queen, counsellors, ministers and body guards? Were the questions and answers proclaimed or published? Or was the whole thing done in a more secluded setting? So far, there is no evidence. We cannot even be sure how often a king was in attendance. David Keightley wrote that the king had the final say in the interpretation of the cracks (in Loewe and Shaughnessy, 1999:236-247), which does seem likely, but I have doubts the king was always present when the bones were scorched. Wu Ding would not have needed such a lot of diviners if he had the time to attend to every single divination. The Shang kings had a tight ritual schedule. Some by choice, like Wu Ding, in whose time there were always angry ancestors and gods clamouring for attention, nourishment or entertainment. Other kings were kept on their toes thanks to the elaborate ritual calendar which increased by a minimum of five annual rituals whenever a king or queen joined the ancestors. Besides which, the kings went on inspection tours, pilgrimages, waged wars, practised archery, met foreign envoys, hunted, held audience, participated in agriculture and performed a lot of daily routine tasks, if they still got around to them. Maybe they even ate and slept on occasion.

For practical reasons I would propose that a lot of routine divination was done by the diviners, who sought the king's judgement afterwards. A divination regarding the bad dreams of a princess or the stomach ache of a prince may well have been performed by those nobles themselves, with a bit of professional assistance from the diviners. The king's presence would not be required in such cases, though I'm sure he was informed about them.

Diviners

So far, the experts have recorded the names of more than 120 diviners from the reign of Wu Ding to the fall of the Zhòu Xin. Their names have been of great importance in establishing a chronology. I know you can't wait but we'll discuss dating further on. Some of these diviners have names which appear on bronze vessels found on the clan cemeteries. It shows that at least these people were known by their clan names and came from rich and influential families, i.e. from the higher levels of society. Being a diviner must have been a prestigious job. It leaves the question open whether all diviners were known by their family names, or whether some signed their titles, honorary names or even nicknames. It also does not tell us whether they were male or female. In fact, the very diviners who are so present on the inscriptions are an elusive bunch of people. As I am fond of question marks I shall now treat you to an extra helping of them. There is no known word for *'diviner'* in the oracle bone script. When modern scholars use the word they refer to a function, which is not the same thing as a profession. Were the diviners a professional group? Or were they some class of ritual specialists, maybe like priests or wu? If they were wu, it is a strong possibility that many were women. After all, the written record of the Zhou Dynasty mentions more female than male wu. Who says the diviners merely divined? Many scapulas from period 1 mention just who consecrated them. The inscriptions usually mention the presence of a diviner. We could argue that the diviner controlled that the final product was good enough. But when you have a very powerful queen preparing scapula, it would taken a tough diviner to disagree with her. Should we consider that the diviners actually participated in the ritual?

Next, where did the diviners come from? The Shang created a new civilisation, and they did not generally employ people just because they were good at a job. In many cases, professions and ranks were inherited. Should we imagine hereditary diviner clans? Or a recruitment of visionary or spiritual folk? Or were the diviners selected from the aristocracy? And just how were they chosen? Was there an examination? Did anyone test their skills? And did they specialise on specific topics? Occasionally it seems that way. When you read diviner Troop (people marching under a flag) enquiring week after week how each night would turn out, you certainly get the impression. But it does not really seem organised, nor was such specialisation typical. And how long did they fulfil their task? Did they get into trouble when an oracle went really wrong? Many oracles were easy to verify. Will there be rain tomorrow? Will there be a hunting accident? What happened when the diviners, or for that matter, the king was wrong?

In divination there will always be wrong answers. If you are in good shape and things go well you may get a good score, but there will always be days when you are wrong. Especially when you are emotionally involved in a topic, feel unwell or suffer from a disease. A minor cold can reduce accuracy a lot. Don't simply take my word for it. Divine every day for a year, record the answers and the outcomes and look for the patterns.

So we have to assume that the oracle wasn't always right. Were the diviners blamed, sacked or punished? Did people question the king's semi-divine status? Or was there a convenient excuse? And what happened if the diviners manipulated the oracle? A few scholars thought so. They assumed that the diviners manipulated the king and the nobles. Perhaps there are ways of controlling what sorts of cracks appear. Who knows? We cannot even be sure how the cracks were made in the first place. But as the king was, at least regarding the reading of the cracks, the supreme diviner, I cannot believe the diviners could have fooled him much. Nor do I believe that the other aristocrats would have allowed a bunch of ritualists to usurp so much power. The king was the ritual and administrative focus of the Shang society, but he was not an autocratic ruler. Whatever the king ordered needed the backing of the aristocracy.

It's another popular thought that the diviners manipulated the oracle according to the wishes of the kings, and thereby supported royal authority and rule. Again, this is possible. But it is hardly a reliable institution. Those diviners who came from noble families must have had their own agenda. And others could easily be bribed or coerced. Both of these theories suffer from very modern thinking. They exclude the possibility of people honestly believing in gods, spirits, ancestors and oracles. I could imagine that in rare cases a very callused and cynical regent might disregard the whole religious apparatus behind his rule, but I cannot really see someone like Wu Ding as an atheist. The Shang, just like the early Zhou, were deeply reverent, if not scared of the ancestors and gods. At this point it might be useful to consider the function of the oracle. In *'old school'* periods (1, 2a, 3 & 4) I would suspect that the oracle actually functioned as a device to divine the unknown. In *'new school'* periods 2b, 5a and 5b the kings were more interested in instituting order and reliability in religious rites. Especially the regents of period 5 may have been inclined to use the oracle merely as a means to support their own decisions, or as a means to control the future with magical means. In these periods, the kings were strongly interested in receiving oracular confirmation. Yes, definitely next xun week no disaster. Here, it becomes a distinct possibility that clever diviners would have liked to produced cracks that pleased the king. However, it is not enough to propose, as some scholars have done, that the boring of the hollows allowed the diviners to manipulate the cracks. Especially in period 5b hollows appear in several distinct shapes and many of them are sloppy work. If diviners intended to control the cracks, they would have gone for precision, and would have introduced exactly the hollows that make heating predictable. But all of this is speculation. Wouldn't it be nice if a prestigious university would finance the hollowing and scorching of a few hundred scapulas so archaeo-sinologists could find out whether they can control cracks?

The other option is, of course, that the kings need not have bothered to control the cracks. King Wu Ding in period 1 frequently demonstrated that he knew better than the diviners, and prognosticated his own visions, no matter what the bones said. Zhòu Xin, of moribund period 5b, did plenty of divination all by himself, and always got the results he wanted. It's scarcely surprising. A good looking king skilled at bending iron and torturing ministers needs hardly be doubted. Evidently, the function of the diviners changed depending on the mindset of the king. It wasn't an easy job, but presumably nicer than waging war or pounding earth. From the oracle bone record it emerges that some diviners did their jobs for many years (in spite of making errors). A few worked for more than one king; good evidence that the king did not simply install his own spiritual yes-men after mounting the throne. Some diviner groups had special ways of divining. Such as the Bin group who usually framed their question as a positive and negative statement to the right and left of a plastron. Diviner groups also seem to have favoured their own writing; witness the usage of the character wu. And finally there is the much discussed question whether certain groups of nobles had their own diviners. So far, the matter remains unresolved.

Setting

Where were the divinations performed? Keightley (1999:245-247) comes to some remarkable conclusions. He assumes that the oracles were made in the presence of the ancestors, in their own temples, and that the *"ancestors mediated between the divinatory supplicants below and other ancestral powers above"*. While this is certainly a valuable possibility, I cannot quite accept it. First, we don't have the slightest idea if divination was usually performed in ancestral temples, let alone in the personal temples of ancestors, nor is there, in my reading, enough evidence to support Keightley's hypothesis that the ancestors were always organised in a strict hierarchy. So far, the archaeological record only shows evidence of one ancestral temple, that of Fu Hao. It is likely that the other royal tombs also had temple buildings on top, but given that these tombs were repeatedly plundered, not a trace survives. What these temples looked like and what happened in them, apart from sacrifice, is anybody's guess.

The inscriptions do not usually state where the divination was performed. Indeed, when the kings went to war, they took the diviners and their gear along, but they left the temples at home. Sure, they may have carried ancestral tablets in their baggage, as later generations did. But if they did, it still doesn't tell us whether such tablets were set up on a single altar or several, if they were arranged in one building (or tent) or a whole group. But let us look at the cases when a given divination related directly to an ancestor. Say, the king was feeling unwell and wanted to know which ancestor had cursed him. Some bones repeat the question and list a whole series of possible suspects. Should we imagine that the diviners went from temple to temple as they asked? It would be really nice to know more about the temples in Anyang. The kings who had been buried on the royal cemetery may have been contacted in their grave temples, while earlier ancestors may have had temples near the palaces, just like several gods of nature. Given that Shang religion underwent several drastic changes during the last 250 years of the period, it seems obvious that no single answer is satisfactory. Maybe the diviners went from temple to temple. Maybe they had a single temple dedicated to divination with, maybe, the insignia or tablets of all ancestors and gods on display. It would certainly be a practical solution.

The Voice behind the Oracle

This brings us to the last and hardest question. There are plenty of new question marks waiting for you, and as I'm not employed by a university I can use as many as I want. I'm sure you'll like this one. Who exactly answered the questions? The ancestors? This may be a little too simple. What do we make of serial divinations? When a question names several ancestors as possible recipients of a sacrifice, or as possible sources of curses or disaster, who exactly was supposed to reply? What if the matter involved several gods? After all, each ancestor enjoyed getting a sacrifice. Gods and spirits are like that. Offer them a gift and a lot of emotion and who of them would refuse? What we lack is an impartial judge. Should we seek the unseen intelligence outside the ranks of those who were divined about? What if the High God/s Di answered through scapula and plastron? Again, this becomes uncertain when the oracle enquires about Di. There are quite a few oracles regarding Di sacrifices, and they do not go *'would you like sheep and pig this afternoon?'*. More so, in many cases the diviners assumed that Di was angry with them, or even trying to destroy the capital and royal house with war, flood, locusts or drought. It would have permanently ended the cult of Di. It's not what ancestors usually do, unless they want to suicide. An ancestor without worship simply fades into oblivion. So may Di wasn't an ancestor, and so supreme that he, she, it, they, didn't care. Was there a deity or intelligence beyond Di who could be trusted to say the truth about the High Ancestors or god/s? At this point, a look at later Zhou writing may help. The *Liji* (*Quli*) contains a brief invocation for turtle shell and yarrow stalks:

"*It is said, 'For the day we depend on thee, O great Tortoise-Shell, which dost give the regular indications; we depend on you, O great Divining Stalks, which give the regular indications.'*" (Legge, 2001:94)

If this Zhou time custom echoes a Shang prayer, the turtle itself may have been the intelligence behind the oracle. It would be nice to know what made the turtle so infallible. Was the turtle an emblem of the entire world?

Future and Fate

Shang diviners enquired about the present and future. Present divination asks whether an ancestor is angry, a god wants a sacrifice, the king should grant an office, a general should be sent out, or whether an event, a dream or catastrophe have hidden meaning.

Future divination foretells whether an accident will happen during the hunt, whether the next week will be disastrous, whether the stay in a given place will be auspicious or if it will rain. Such questions imply a future which can be divined. It would be the easiest and most misleading thing to say the Shang believed in fate. For what exactly is fate?

Here, European thought diverges from Chinese philosophy. Let's take a look at a highly eccentric character. Saint Augustine (354-430) eagerly participated in several interesting religions before he got Christianity. We owe him the rather suffocating idea that every single detail in life is preordained by god. In your life, my life, and the life of any being whatsoever. Kings own their power to god, just like the beggar's life is god's will, and when you read this book or miss a train it's all as god would have it. God's will, or fate, implies that there is not a single coincidence or decision in life. Nor is there any responsibility, because god has foreordained the lot. If you live saintly and ascend to heaven or sin all day and end in hell - all is entirely as god wills, and has been predestined before your birth, or that of your parents, or indeed before the beginning of creation. Every moment in human history has always followed god's plan. This horrible idea implies that god is accountable for everything, and in dire need of therapy. Why should god create sinners? Why is there war, famine, suffering, rape, why do small children die and adult people make life hell for each other? If Saint Augustine were right, god should be blamed for every bit of nastiness on earth, and there's lots of it. Such thoughts could turn you into a Satanist. But Saint Augustine thought that it was all well and good, and others evidently agreed, otherwise he would never have become a saint. His idea of preordained fate became a crucial element in medieval Christianity.

Of course some people disagreed. A fashionable philosophy did (and does) insist that we have something called *'free will'*. It's a nice thought, though not very easy to prove. As brain research shows, plenty of our decisions are made on a subconscious level long before we become consciously aware of them. Perhaps it's our subconscious minds, whatever that may mean, who are exercising the power of free will. Or maybe the entire expression is plainly irrelevant.

The question of fate contra free will and/or chance has kept many generations of philosophers on their toes. Not that they came to any significant conclusion. And no matter what your opinion is (yes, please, do have several), Augustine's idea of destiny had an enormous influence on Christian thought. I should add that the earlier pagans had a different idea, but you probably guessed so anyway. Well, in a world where everything is the fulfilment of god's will, divination simply indicates what is bound to happen. Hence so many cultures steeped in Christian thought favour the idea that fate is irrevocably set.

What the Shang really believed remains unknown. But there is evidence from later Chinese thinkers. Fate, in Chinese philosophy, is a lot more flexible. One term for *'fate'* is the word ming. In oracle bone script, it shows a person sitting under a roof (p.677). It might be an audience chamber or a place where an assembly comes to a decision. The word means *'order, command'*. Later, it came to mean the Command (or Mandate) of Heaven, and sounds a lot more serious than it is. The command of Heaven is changeable. Whatever happens in this crazy world, and whatever you do (or omit) influences the Command of Heaven. Here, now, and all the time. When people lose the Way, when they abuse the primal self-nature of themselves or others, or when they waste their spiritual essence, the Decree of Heaven changes quite a lot.

Here is another word. Fate can also be translated as yün. Quite literally, the term means movement or development, and ought to remind you of physics. Do you recall what inertia means? Inertia is the tendency of a body to remain in its place or to move in the same direction as before, unless another force acts on it. This isn't just physics; it's a brilliant observation of human behaviour. Yün is the tendency of a being or person to move in the same direction as ever. Call it routine, habit, custom, tradition or stagnation if you like. It has nothing to do with divine will or predestination. But it does include an element of great predictability. For the fun of it, pause now and think about your life. Think of the routines that keep your life, your means of livelihood and your personality stable and reliable. Make a list if you like. What do you do to stay in control? What do you do to maintain a certain state of mind? How much of your day is simply the continuation of the motion you began in the past? And where will your life lead you when you continue as you do?

Here we are dealing with something powerful. The urge to keep life in predictable, accustomed motion is one of the strongest forces in the human mind.

It can be a trap. There are people who stick to behaviour that makes them miserable, simply as they are used to it. Maybe it seems less dangerous than whatever else is possible. We all know people who take no chances, who avoid new thoughts, who cling to the same job, hobbies and relationships only because they are familiar.

Or consider the positive side. Some routines help you function during bad times and difficult circumstances. Simply cause you are used to them. Habits can help you do complex things with a minimum of effort.

And in a way this goes for all of us. Each time you do something the same way you set up a routine, hence a habit. Each time you think the same thought in the same way, you confirm it, and make it easier to think in future. This is neurology. You set up neural pathways in your brain which promote specific ways of thinking. Each time you think the same thing the neural pathways are reinforced and complex assemblies of behaviour connected. By thinking as you always thought you can ensure you'll think the same in future. While you do this, you connect topics to emotions or lack of them; you promote outcomes or avoid them. All of this is learned, and what is learned can be learned differently. The same inertia which leads to habitual unhappiness can be turned around right now and you can change it for the better. It'll be much better than you ever imagined. You can think thoughts which make you happy. Do it frequently and happiness becomes a habit. Inertia can work for or against you. You are doing and maintaining it all the time. And if you don't like it, wake up, and do it differently.

Fate, whatever it may really be, involves the interaction of habitual behaviour, new behaviour and circumstance. You can change fate by changing the lot.

Well and good, but what did the early Chinese authors say about fate? Laozi was not interested in the topic. Kongzi avoided it. Fatalism makes no sense when you want people to make an effort to cultivate virtue, conduct and humanity. Zhuangzi (6) proposed that when something is not caused by humans, Heaven or Earth, it might be fate. Lü Buwei assembled many chapters on behaviour and circumstance which completely ignore the idea of fate. And the *Liezi* only has two brief references to fate. One of them tells us that fate (circumstance) is stronger than effort. But fate itself has no idea what's really going on.

Now these sources are not representative for the entirety of classical Chinese thought. Nor is a full study required. After all, people use the term fate quite as they chose.

My favourite definition was given by Li Ruzhen around 1800:

"'Maybe it was fate that I couldn't help saying the things I did at the party, and cannot beg the Lady of the Moon's pardon now,' said the Fairy of a Hundred Flowers.

'No, that is not fate', said the Lady Yuan. 'It is not fate when it was within your power to exercise your forbearance then, and to show your humility now. It is only after one has done his best that the rest is left to fate. If you think that you cannot help the things you do, I do not wonder that you are being sent to earth! Surely you know that nothing we desire ever comes to us without exerting our own efforts?'" (*Flowers in the Mirror*, trans. Lin Tai-Yi, 2005, ch. 4)

The Shang thought along similar lines. Their divination wasn't only meant to predict the future. As Sarah Allan demonstrated, it served to predict **what the future would be like if everything continued as before**. Will it rain tomorrow? Will drought end or will there be flooding? Will a hunting accident occur?

Would you really like to know what your future will be? All the good bits and all the bad bits pre-determined, with no surprise or chance or choice in between? It's one of the most terrifying things imaginable. Why should Wu Ding care to know if it rains tomorrow, unless he could do something about it? Knowing what happens has very few benefits unless you can do something to change it for the better.

And that's precisely what the Shang nobles did. They didn't just sit back and resigned themselves to bad news and reduced expectations. When the oracle predicted something unpleasant, they worked out which ancestor or deity was responsible for it. Then they sacrificed to make it change. In case of doubt a whole cluster of ancestors got a sacrifice. Divination was not an end in itself. Bad omens were the prelude to ritual and sacrifice, i.e. the magic required to influence and change the world. Good omens allowed the king to sit back, with great caution.

Think about it. The future foretold by the bones was a diagnosis of likeliness, or of the inertia of a given situation. It gave the Shang the chance to change things for the better.

Maybe this explains what happened when a divination was wrong. If the oracle said there would be no hunting accident, and one happened, it might be argued that the situation had changed in the time between the divination and the accident. Maybe someone had insulted a god or ancestor, done something offensive or whatever. People are good at inventing reasons. And if the oracle indicated an accident and none occurred, it could be assumed that the warning had prevented the disaster. It's an important point that Chinese gods and deified ancestors were not all-knowing. They knew pretty well when they were ruining the harvest or sending a belly ache. But when the locusts came swarming or the river flooded the countryside, they required a report. When disaster struck, the ancestors had to be ritually informed. The same went for the gods. If the Shang thought of their oracle as an indication of likeliness at a specific point in time, they would not expect it to be omniscient. Their oracle did not predict things that were sure to happen; it simply revealed the opinion of the otherworldly ones on what was likely. Think of it as communication.

Charges and Questions

Originally, oracle bone scholars tended to view each inscription as a question. That's what divination is basically all about: you want to know something that only the spirits, gods (or your deep mind) can know. But were all divinations meant to provide new information? This simple question has resulted in a lot of scholarly debate. The matter is easy when we have double divinations: will it rain today? Will it not rain today? Here, the oracle may affirm or deny each option. We could see it as a balanced operation. Or we could claim that there is one preferred option (will it rain? Yes or no?) and a second divination to countercheck the first. This situation is always present when we divine something: after all, divination is used for topics that matter, and when things matter, you usually know which outcome you'd prefer. That's one of the reasons good diviners ought to calm and empty their minds before consulting an oracle: the more you desire or dread an outcome, the more biased will your reading be. For the same reason, many diviners get best results when they do the divination for other people or strangers. Divining for yourself requires that you suspend your preconceptions, hopes, fears and beliefs, and do the job from a mental vacuum. This is by no means easy, and indeed, where it comes to really important topics, it may fail miserably. On the other hand, letting go of your preferences and self-identification is an excellent Daoist meditation.

Double divinations were most frequently performed in Wu Ding's time. Later periods, especially the 'new school' adherents in period 2b, 5a and 5b, tended to pose questions only one way. However, even then double divinations happened on occasion.

It would be nice if we could read the inscriptions simply as questions. However, we have to keep in mind that the oracle had a very limited range of answers. It could affirm and deny, and it could give degrees of affirmation and possibly also of negation. This doesn't work with long inscriptions. Consider this example: "*Cloud / at / north / thunder / perhaps (or: it is) / bring / rain / not reprimand / perhaps (or: it is) / good.*" (T.T. Chang, 1970:213 #15.6, you find it on page '*weather #2*') If this is one single yes or no question, it would have to be read: If the cloud in the north thunders it is perhaps bringing rain and not meant as a reproof but as a good sign? That's not one single question, it's several. You could conceivably answer yes or no to it, but you would divine a highly unlikely and extremely unlikely situation. We could also read it as several questions. The cloud in the north thunders? It brings rain? Does this mean we are reprimanded? Or does it mean something good? All in all four questions. However, the whole matter was divined in one block. The most likely interpretation is that parts of the inscription are statements (charges) and parts are questions: the cloud in the north has thundered. Perhaps it brings rain? Perhaps this is not a reproof but something good? (Two questions). The cloud in the north has thundered. It is bringing rain. Is this not a reproof but something good? (one question). In divination, your results will be best when you don't ask many questions at once as the answer is likely to confuse all concerned. You will have noticed that this solution resolves around the issue of whether the graph *'bird'* should be read as a question particle (*'perhaps'*) or as a statement (*'it is'*). And it shows that oracle bone inscriptions do not entirely consist of questions, but often specify conditions before focussing on an uncertain matter.

Let's take a look at the crucial word zhen. What follows is a rough account based on Jue Guo's excellent summary (University of Wisconcin, Proquest, UMI Microfilm, 2009:89–112) which can be studied online. Zhen is written with the sign of the ceremonial ding cauldron and appears routinely at the start of an inscription, usually after the name of the diviner (p.789). In my translations I have rendered it *'divines'*, which is not the only reading. Many early oracle bone scholars read this sign as *'asks'*, *'questions'*, *'tests'*. They based their reading on the *Shuowen* dictionary which glosses zhen as *'to question by making cracks'* and *'to ask.'* This traditional reading was disputed by David Keightley, who argued that later commentaries would gloss zhen as *'to regulate, to rectify'* and *'to fix'*. Keightley boldly asserted that zhen comes from a word family that has nothing to do with interrogation but with regulation, correction and stabilisation. In short, the ritual was meant to fix things in a specific way. Paul L.M. Serroys partly agreed with Keightleys claim, pointing out that zhen was mainly used for *'to test, to try out, to make true, to consent'* in Han time literature. While both the *Shuowen* and the literary works of the Han are a long time from the Shang, the very possibility that zhen might mean *'to make true'* provides an unusual and fascinating idea. In Keightley's opinion, the divination ritual was performed not only to solve uncertain issues but to make a preferred outcome happen. In his interpretation, the Shang inscriptions should not be considered question but charges, or statements. One reason to discard the *'question'* idea is that a considerable amount of inscriptions do not contain question particles. However, Qiu Xigui pointed out, it was not necessary to have an interrogative particle in a sentence of ancient Chinese to make it work like a question. Nor would it have been required when spoken, as intonation can change a statement into a question without altering one word. Now you may wonder what the fuss is all about. Behind the innocent issues *'question or charge'* looms a much larger topic: the intent of the divination. If we accept the *'question'* format, we have a person interrogating a much wiser entity about present or future events in the hope of influencing them. As you remember, the Shang were by no means fatalists. When a situation portended evil, they divined how to change it, and used ritual, offerings and conduct to create a better future. This is more than religion: it constitutes magic.

Keightley and Shaugnessy argued that while the *'question'* form is typical for the Shang under Wu Ding, in later periods the purpose of divination itself was not to provide answers but to create a more desirable situation. Here, an inscription is a *'charge'* as it states what would be preferable. Examples like *'next xun-week no disaster'* come to mind. The gods, spirits, ancestors or whoever were supposed to agree. You could compare it with a spell, a prayer of a hypnotic suggestion. The difficulty about this assumption is whether the kings, diviners, aristocrats and religious specialists actually assumed they were divining, or whether they were going through a ritual that was at least partly a formality. Keightley, with his preference for Shang period bureaucracy, may have assumed that the divinations of the last stages of Shang culture were simply traditional customs that did not require actual faith. Personally, I am pretty sure he was right about the last Shang king, Zhòu Xin, who allegedly reduced ritual and divination and at some point stopped performing them altogether. We can't be sure about the last bit however: if the king moved to his new capital Zhaoge, all further oracle bones may be resting in undiscovered pits far from Xiaotun. Regarding the earlier kings I am not so sure. Maybe Zu Jia was a visionary religious innovator when he instituted the five ritual timetable and maybe he was merely trying to make elaborate and chaotic cult business predictable and less excessive. Then, in period 3 we probably have a resurgence of faith, as the earlier ways were re-instituted, and period 4 appears like an enthusiastic renaissance of period 1 customs. Period 5b could indicate a king who was trying to downsize religion and faith, while in 5b Zhòu Xin terminated the whole thing, one way or another, before he was terminated.

Such a development would also explain why in Wu Ding's time we have many diviners divining a wide range of topics, and usually asking each question many times, while later periods, specifically 2b, 5a and 5b had few diviners, divined a small range of topics, and only a few times. However, the idea that these periods did not formulate questions but charges is far from accepted. As various Chinese scholars indicated, even when an inscription appears like a statement it is still incorporated in a ritual that is supposed to divine the unknown. Asking a question is not a must. Indeed, if you practice divination, you may find that some of the best results can happen when you do not pose a question or topic but simply work the oracle with an open mind. You may receive insights that are far superior to those achieved by specifying and limiting matters beforehand. Many questions are restrictive. They narrow the scope to what you think is important. It may be wrong. Maybe your deep mind, spirits, gods etc have entirely different opinions about what you should think about. Maybe they want to tell you something vital that you haven't even thought of.

Zhou Divination

The *Liji* (*Quli*) has a lovely comment on divination:

"Divination by shell is called pú; by the stalks, shih. The two were the methods by which the ancient sage kings made the people believe in seasons and days, revere spiritual beings, stand in awe of their laws and orders; the methods (also) by which they made them determine their perplexities and settle their misgivings. Hence it is said, 'If you doubted, and have consulted the stalks, you need not (any longer) think that you will do wrong. If the day (be clearly indicated), boldly do on it (what you desire to do)." (Legge, 2001:94) Here is a section that actually describes a divination during the Zhou period:

"The diviner held the tortoise-shell in his arms, with his face towards the south, while the son of Heaven, in his dragon-robe and square topped cap, stood with his face to the north. The latter, however intelligent might be his mind, felt it necessary to set forth and obtain a decision on what his object was;-showing that he did not dare to take his own way, and giving honour to Heaven (as the supreme Decider). What was good in him (or in his views) he ascribed to others; what was wrong, to himself, thus teaching not to boast, and giving honour to men of talent and virtue". (*Liji*, ch. *Jiyi*, Legge 2008:233). The setting shows that the diviner, holding the turtle shell, represented north, hence the unmoving centre of the sky, and by analogy, the Taiyi and Di. The king, standing in the south represented mankind, the state, and the world. For the duration of this ritual he was in the position of an inferior.

We are lucky to have a few comments on divination in the *Shujing*, that remarkable compilation of documents and idealised forgeries assembled by Han historians. The early Zhou regents continued to consult the bones. Most of them did not inscribe the bones, nor did they keep and bury them as the Shang did, but they certainly valued the message of the cracks. Maybe a century or two after the conquest, they began to develop the *Yijing*. The original *Yijing* has not survived. It started as a numerical system. Even today, the hexagrams are composed of numbers. You need numbers to determine the open and closed lines, and the ones that are likely to transform. The first hexagrams in evidence long escaped the attention of scholars as they were simply arrangements of numbers. Nor did these numbers look like the ones in use today. There were several *Yijings* in the making, and what we have today is just one version of several, and certainly not the earliest (see *Living Midnight* for details). The *Shujing* calls the *Yijing* the oracle of the yarrow stalks. As an alternative, bamboo strips were used. For a long time, the bones and the stalks existed side by side and were frequently used simultaneously. However, as the *Liji* (Quli) states: "*Divination by the shell and the stalks should not go beyond three times. The shells and the stalks should not be both used on the same subject.*" And while the Zhou were less obsessive about divination than the Shang, they certainly valued the oracle. Here, the *Shujing* is quite practical.

Shun told Yü the Great "'*According to the regulation of the procedure of divination one should first come to a decision and ask the great tortoise shell later. In this matter I have first made up my mind. I consulted the ministers and the people and they were of one opinion with me. The spirits showed their agreement and the turtle shell and the yarrow stalks confirmed it. And when a divination is auspicious, it should not be repeated.*'"

As you guessed, this passage was not recorded when Shun ruled and Yü fought the flood. Like all of the '*earliest*' documents, it was assembled, edited or composed fairly late. But it shows that the Zhou and Han historians favoured reasoning and making decisions over divine consent. The oracle was no substitute for thinking.

This insight appears several times in the *Shujing*. Whether a new regent was chosen or the location of a new city decided, people planned first and asked the oracle later. Another example. Here we have the Lord of Qi giving expert advice to King Wu.

"'*If you are in doubts over great issues, ask your own reasoning, ask the high ministers, the officers, and ask the tortoise shell and the yarrow stalks. It is a great agreement when you, the shell, the stalks, ministers, officers and the people are of one opinion. The result is the flourishing of your own person and a blessing for the descendants.*

If you, the shell and the stalks are of one mind, while ministers, officers and people are against it, the result is still beneficial.

And if the people, the shell and the stalks are in agreement, while you, the ministers and officers are against it, the result is still beneficial.

If you and the shell agree, while ministers, officers and the people are opposed, it is auspicious in inner affairs and disastrous in outer.

If the shell and the stalks agree with the people, it is auspicious to remain silent, as outer activity brings disaster.'"

All of which shows a good grasp for politics in uncertain times. And it reveals, quite clearly, that the regents remained responsible for government. The oracle supplied a valuable comment, but the gods and ancestors did not order anyone around.

Keep this in mind when you make your own divination. The gods help those who help themselves. Don't blame them for your decisions and errors. You and I are in charge of our own reality. Fate or inertia are maintained or changed in every moment. It's your choice.

The Origin of Written Chinese

Like written Sumerian and Egyptian, Chinese was an indigenous development. It started during the Neolithic. Our first evidence for signs comes from pottery. Several Neolithic cultures inscribed vessels. Perhaps they also ornamented other materials which did not survive. The vessels provide a wide range of simple signs. Usually, there were few signs, or only one on a given item. One hypothesis claims that if the vessel was signed before burning, it showed the mark of the potter or the potter's family. And if the sign was added later on, it marks the family or person who owned it. This sounds reasonable enough, provided there were already professional potters working for a community. If the families made their own vessels the theory collapses. Occasionally these early signs, or property markers are considered the origin of written Chinese. So far, several Neolithic cultures seem to have adorned their pottery with what may be signs or ornaments. Early excavations had merely produced primitive lines, crosses, x shapes and the like, but nowadays there are items like the complex scratch-marks of the late Dawenkou culture (Juxian county, Shandong), Dazhu village and Linghanghe, involving axes (?), enclosed spaces, arrangements of circles and floral ornaments which have caused quite a debate. One early piece that may show writing (Dinggong village, Shandong) is a pottery shard graced with what seems like a whole series of complex characters, dating from the Longshan culture. Again, the piece is not universally accepted. The signs look like writing, but it is hard to prove if there is any direct development from them to the written language of the Shang. Nowadays scholars assume that some branches of the early Yangshao culture turned into branches of the younger Longshan culture, and that the Shang developed out of one of these. It sounds easy enough unless you look at a map and realise that

Yangshao and Longshan culture finds occur over vast ranges of ancient China, and that each term refers to a whole cluster of unidentified sub-cultures. Even if an ancient sign reappears in oracle bone script, it does not necessarily have the same meaning. It will take much further excavation to clear up these questions. That's the easy part. Urban China is torn down and rebuilt every twenty minutes and the archaeologists have plenty to do. In a few decades, Chinese prehistory will be a lot easier to understand.

Shang Writing

So, for lack of reliable data, our story begins sometime between 1300 and 1200 BCE. Sometime during that century Wu Ding began his rule. At this point our first inscriptions were made. Some very short texts graced bronze vessels and a huge amount of inscriptions appeared on the bones. The two look somewhat different. The bronze script favours curves and elaborations while the bone inscriptions, as they were swiftly scratched into scapula and plastron, favours angular lines and simplification. Try scratching round symbols into a piece of bone and you'll know what I mean. But though the two scripts appear different, you can discern that on the whole they make use of the same structures and similar ideas. At the time being it is impossible to say which script was invented earlier. But this may change when further material is excavated. The third medium for the written word were scrolls made of bamboo strips. The bamboo scroll sign appears in several versions such as *'making a written promise'*, *'offering a document'*, *'storing a document in a casket'* or *'submerging it in water'*. And as the bamboo strips were rather slim, many of the signs favour the vertical. Numerous animals, which are happily horizontal in real life, were turned upright to fit them on the bamboo. While modern Chinese characters fit into a square form, Shang characters are upright and slightly rectangular. For writing, a brush was employed. And while not a single bamboo strip survived from this archaic time, there are a few small brush inscriptions on bones, jades and pottery. Probably the scrolls predate bronzes and bones. For what appears on bone and bronze is not a primitive script. It is writing in a state of development, sure, but the signs are refined and there is a large vocabulary.

Variation

Let's have a few words on the signs or characters. A sign is a single thing, and in the Shang period it wasn't. Instead, we have clusters of related images. Many characters appear in variations. These variations are not simply small details, such as might be explained by handwriting. Some of the common ones have up to thirty different variations. During the late Shang writing was not standardised. There were no dictionaries which ensured that spelling followed regulations. When a scribe wrote *'is it?'* s/he scratched a small bird. The bird might look in one direction or another, have the wings here or there, and where it came to the lines which hint at feathers, even more variety appears. So far, I have collected some twenty versions, but I'm sure there were more. Here we can say goodbye to all these neat and simple tables pretending that one sign naturally developed into another. It wasn't one sign in this stage, it was many. And they did not happily develop in linear progression. While certain ways of writing may have been more popular in one period than in another, there are always exceptions. So many, that the shape of a character is one of the least reliable ways of dating an inscription.

How Pictures become Writing

But what exactly turns a picture into writing?

Chinese started, like the other early scripts, with pictures of beings and things. You want to indicate *'tiger'* and you draw one. When you do it frequently, you'll simplify it eventually. This is the earliest stage of writing. It shows a picture but it does not provide a story, a sentence, nor does it involve grammar. The oracle bone signs have many such images. A tiger looks like a tiger and a pig like a pig. Both are simplified but usually they remain easy to recognise.

But a picture of a tiger isn't a word. It is only when a specific word, i.e. a sound-combination is attached to the image that real writing happens. And when this occurs, the tiger can also mean something else. It can be a name, for instance. Sure, it looks like a striped cat but it really means a person or a clan. Many Chinese clans took their names from animals. But our animal sign could also mean a deity, or refer to a state. When you read *'tiger'*, all of these interpretations are possible. When it's an account of a hunt, listing the animals caught by the king, the sign is likely to be a real tiger. But when it receives sacrifice or is sent to lead an army, it may be a god or a person. Or, once the person is dead, the sign may represent a deified ancestor. And when the king moves the army to Tiger, it's a place, state or a group of people.

And a thing can be a verb. A fish can mean fishing, a foot may indicate motion, a hand may signify doing, holding, offering. Such meanings are still close to the things they show, but they extend the meaning into new directions. Sadly, some of the Shang characters can be confusing. A hand may mean having, giving, offering and taking, so sometimes it's hard to say if something is received, kept or sacrificed. Evidently, the diviners did not care to specify the matter very much. Well, they only had some 4500 characters in their script. Later Chinese scribes decided that things should be more precise, and made up many new ones. The earliest surviving Chinese dictionary, the *Shuowen*, complied by Xu Shen in the early second century, contained 10.516 sign classed under 540 radicals. It was so good that it remained in use until 1717, when a new dictionary gave 40.000 signs classed under 214 radicals. There are more signs in Chinese than 40.000, but many went out of fashion over the centuries. To read a newspaper, a mere 3000 are said to suffice. I'm not sure that newspaper is worth reading.

When the Shang wrote, they often made a single sign have many meanings. But language evolves beyond pictures and similarities. The next element is phonetic. If you have a thing associated with a sound, you have a word. And when you write that word, you can also make it mean another thing or abstract which sounds the same. At this point, the picture ceases to matter. We find it happen in many Shang characters. The sign for lady or princess, for example, consists of a brush or broom plus a claw-like hand. Now it might be argued that the ladies wrote, and I am sure the ones who acted as ministers and administrators in Wu Ding's time did. In all likeliness, they were among the most important writers in the government. You could also guess they swept the palace, which I find less likely. But the real reason for writing princess (fu) with the sign for broom (fu) is that both words had the same sound.

For the same reason, the long eared owl could mean drink sacrifice, old and to observe. A diagram of a pounded earth wall was primarily written for use, apply, sacrifice; done, completed. And two hands, a stick and a boat, originally meaning 'boat repair', was always used for 'I, me, mine' and for the name of a state. In oracle bone inscriptions, the picture has no meaning apart from the sound connected with it. After all, the nobles hardly ever needed to write broom or boat repair. Cleaning and repairing happened to other people. We also observe the first combined signs in Shang writing. Modern Chinese has plenty of compounds, where one image gives you a general idea of the subject and another image tells you the pronunciation. The Shang writers were just beginning to develop such combinations.

When a sign is used phonetically, it can be simplified, as it is not supposed to show a thing anymore. And when a character shows a tattered piece of fur, you can be sure the Shang wrote it for 'to ask, to beg, to pray', for 'disaster, bad luck' or for 'not yet'. Now a prayer is not bad luck, nor is it the same as a time reference. They simply share the same sound. If you are quabalistically inclined you may wonder if the three ideas have a shared, deeper meaning. Many Chinese philosophers pondered such problems. Sometimes it yields valuable insights. But on the very plain level of language expressing information, we have three common uses. And we have a picture of fur which was of no interest to the Shang literati whatsoever.

The frequent use of homophones causes a lot of guessing. When is a sign related to what it shows and when is it simply a representative of something else with the same sound?

When we have a foreign people called Horse-Folk, does it mean they were good at breeding horses or did their clan name sound like the word *'horse'*? Had the Dragon People anything to do with dragon and the Pig People with pigs? What of the Ghost People? Did the Chin-Beard folk actually have beards? Or were they simply written with such signs for phonetic reasons? And how many people found that the Shang wrote their name written with a picture of an animal or thing and made it their totem?

The enigmatic question whether a character shows something for symbolic or phonetic reasons would be a lot easier to answer if we knew more about the pronunciation of archaic Chinese. We don't even know how many tones were used. It is possible that the third tone (descending and rising again) was missing in classical Chinese. But what if there were other tones we never even thought of? Beijing style mandarin uses four tones and one unaccented tone. A given syllable can be pronounced high, rising, sinking and rising and sinking. In Shanghai, people use eight. And did the Shang, who created the earliest known Chinese writing, have the same pronunciation as the Zhou who moved in from the wild west while Wu Ding ruled? Did the Zhou adapt their language to the court when they were allies of the Shang? And did Zhou dialect become the norm when they started their own dynasty? The best we can do is look at the end rhymes in the *Shijing* (*The Book of Songs*), which was compiled around 600 BCE. It tells us something about end rhymes in a limited number of words. And nothing about the language at the Shang court six hundred years earlier.

When you read an inscription, you can usually find all of these levels of meaning. And you can make up explanations about the really odd, phonetic associations. Sure, princess was written broom for reasons of sound, not of symbolism. But when words sound alike, people still perceive them as connected. They make puns or use them for allusions or play with their various meanings. Or they dread to say words which sound like others with unlucky meaning. Chinese, with its limited range of syllables, is excellent for puns and riddles. I am sure the Shang made jokes by playing on such similarities. And when we think of language as a way to suggest meaning, as in hypnosis or storytelling, each multiple-meaning word becomes a highly efficient tool to influence awareness.

So an image may represent a thing, a name, place, state, verb, adjective, grammatical element or signify something with the same sound. The real problem in reading the bones is deciding which is appropriate. Here we are on very thin ice. Many oracle bones can be read and interpreted in several ways. Often enough, we simply have to evaluate alternatives. There are many characters with multiple meanings. We can guess which one is real in a given context, but quite often we cannot be sure. A lot of translations are not simply right or wrong but more or less likely. And even when we are moderately sure it may be that our reading is not quite precise.

There, is for instance, a sign showing two hands with a roundish or triangular pile beneath them (p.694). The hands usually mean doing, making or offering, while the pile is a sign meaning earth. It can also signify land, the earth god, an earth god of a specific place or a specific foreign state and perhaps shows an earth altar or a standing stone. Well and good. Now the inscriptions put this character in an agricultural context. So far, I have found it translated as *'arable land'*, *'heaping up'* (grains? Hay?) and *'clearing earth for agriculture'*. All three ideas are connected with agriculture and cultivation, and all three are educated guesses. It would take a scribe from Wu Ding's court to tell us what exactly happened. It might even mean, if you allow me to speculate, an offering to the earth deity. But the sign was also used for *'setting traps'* on phonetic grounds, and appears as the name of a state which may or may not have anything to do with an earth god or fieldwork.

The same problem occurs with other characters. There are several which mean something like going, but we cannot be sure whether they mean run, rush, walk, march, stroll, saunter, sneak or stagger. All we know is that maybe the king, the army or some person moved in some way. Likewise, there are many words which mean something like fight, wage war, attack etc. but the finer points of war strategy remain uncertain.

As a result, oracle bone specialists may be able to interpret or at least class almost half of the 4500 character groups, but the reliability of each translation may vary a lot.

You could say, look, here's something which receives a sacrifice, so it's a god or an ancestor. You still would not know who. Or you could read that here is something the army is moving through. In all likeliness it's a place. There are more than four hundred place names in evidence. When you look for the translated working vocabulary of the Shang, i.e. words you might use to write a letter or a poem, the number of characters is around one thousand. But as each may be loaded with up to seven different meanings, we still have quite a lot we can read and write.

When I learned reading the bones I also used the script to write things, such as birthday cards, poems and magic spells. It soon taught me the limits to the vocabulary. For one thing, the grammatical terms are rather limited. Some signs serve for an awful lot of grammatical functions, such as the sign *'pipe, flute'* which can mean *'at, near, by, for, in'* with reference to a person, object or location. Or the sign *'nose'* which means *'I, myself'*. Good body language; many East Asians point at their nose when they mean *'myself'*. But it can also read *'of'*, *'for, at, near'* and *'even'*. In many cases, grammar is not explicit (or specified) but implicit. You have to discern it from the context. Yes, oracle bone grammar is simple. Often enough, it is too simple. Some scribes even favoured their own happy shorthand. Later generations added further grammatical signs for good reason. For the scribes of the late Shang, grammar was not really standardised. Some inscriptions leave out grammatical elements, which shortened the questions considerably. And a few scribes (or diviners) seem to have had their own grammatical peculiarities. Maybe they came from places far from the capital and introduced their native slang.

Common and Absent Questions

Divination was performed for a wide range of topics. There are oracles inquiring about weather, harvest, agricultural rituals and dates, warfare, strategy, travel, hunting tactics, times and locations, rituals, ceremonies, sacrifices, diseases, curses, dreams, exorcisms, apotropaic rites, ancestral worship and so on. There are also, less common, inscriptions on political matters such as royal inspection tours, payment of tribute, granting of fiefs, founding of cities, employment of ministers and generals, support of other states and the resettlement of citizens to new locations. The frequency of a topic does not really say much about its importance. New cities need to be built and populated only once in a while, while the weather and the planning of the royal hunt are always of interest. But some subjects seem conspicuously rare or absent. Maybe the inscriptions were lost or have not been unearthed yet. Or we can't read the relevant characters. Maybe the relevant inscriptions have been overlooked. Or they were ground up and ingested after a rich meal. Maybe I simply do not have them in my collection. It's very hard to exclude topics as the data is so fragmentary. Whatever it may be, I see few or no divination regarding the following matters:

-judicial issues, such as crimes, trials, laws. There are a few inscriptions regarding torture and punishment, but they cannot have sufficed for all cases. And what about pardons? Who exactly tried each case?

-Bureaucracy: the choice of ministers, priests and diviners, the ritual assumption of office, promotion and retirement. Such matters occasionally appear in military contexts, but where is their civil counterpart? And while there is reference to tribute, the topic of trade is conspicuously absent. The Shang received tribute and gifts, but so far, no words for buying and selling, let alone forms of payment have been identified. Were the nobles and kings too far above the traders to acknowledge the issue? And if they cared so much about hunting and war, where are the references to sports, games and contests? What about foreign relations and daily life in court? Where are the oracles regarding the true intentions of an ambassador, or whether a given prince plans to kill his brothers to usurp the throne? Why didn't the king ask if a person was a traitor or a spy? And what about purely social events? Did the Shang have any? Or was each entertainment linked to a religious activity?

What about love or marriage, a topic which moved so many people to divination? There is a character showing a hand holding an ear. It has been speculated that it might mean marriage, as it is used for *'taking'* or *'receiving'*. However, it is also used for *'offering'* and for *'offering an ear'*, which is a special sacrifice mentioned in the *Liji*. Here, the ear symbolised the entire animal. After battles the Shang (and the early Zhou) collected ears of slain warriors and offered these. It's hardly the same thing as marriage.

We lack inscriptions like *'if the king marries Lady X, will there be disaster?'* They asked whether the Yellow River deity would like a new concubine, but didn't ask the same question regarding living kings. Perhaps the Shang did not divine about this matter. Or they did it as rarely as kings needed to marry, and the bones have to be found yet. Provided they weren't ground down to settle a queasy stomach.

Nor is there a word for divorce. But perhaps it's one of those two thousand odd words which can't be translated presently. Or maybe divorce did not exist.

Maybe the Shang simply decided such matters without asking the oracle. Or we are simply too ignorant. Oops, let me apologise. Maybe you ain't but I certainly am. It makes me ask more questions. Maybe you can answer them.

And while we are at it, there are few words referring to emotions. Even the important term *'heart'* is only known from bronze inscriptions.

With regard to expectations, there are more words for bad luck, accidents and disaster than for good luck. Loads of words describe unpleasant events, for the simple reason that such events cause people to divine. It takes clever people to consult an oracle when everything goes well.

Dating the bones

As soon as oracle bone writing was discovered, the researchers began to wonder how to determine the age of a given text. Let's imagine we are lucky and have a complete question or charge before us. They typically begin with a date. The date was important to the religious specialists, but it doesn't help us much. As you read earlier the date is from an annual ritual calendar. Or, more precisely, it's a day of a sixty day cycle. The year had six (unless it introduced an extra month), and usually we don't know which year we're dealing with. Luckily, there are exceptions. Towards the end of the dynasty we get the occasional reference to the month. And at the very end, in period 5b, we even get a reference to the ritual year, if we are lucky. But in most inscriptions, month and year are absent.

Unless there is a seasonal reference, there is little chance to align the sixty day cycle with the real year. Luckily the inscriptions contain names. Not the name of the ruling king, which would be too convenient. But they sometimes name contemporaries of the king, such as brothers or wives, which can occasionally be connected with the royal names recorded by Sima Qian. And as they contain plenty of references to ancestors, who appear by their posthumous temple names, we can be sure that a given bone was made after their death. These temple names can also be compared to Sima's account.

Following the date, we get the crack sign, indicating *'divination by crack making'* or *'posing a question'*. Next follows the name of the diviner. It turned out to be a breakthrough. In 1931, Dong Zuobin (Tung Tso-Pin) realised the importance of a plastron which had been unearthed two years earlier. As you recall, a big bone or plastron may record the oracles of several diviners. And when a group appears on a single piece, they are contemporary. Using this principle and showing admirable patience, the oracle bone pioneer began to trace which diviners lived in the same period. Usually it was more than a single bone could ever mention. And before long, some ten groups had been classified. But it wasn't that simple. A few names appear in more than one period. We either deal with long lived diviners who did their job under several, possibly short lived kings. Or, when there is a gap between cycles of activity, there were two diviners in different periods with the same name. Maybe it was a clan or family name, or maybe they were proud to assume a respectable title.

The other problem was a group of diviners that cannot be assigned properly. Either they were active in period 1 or 4. In both periods, the inscriptions favour similar topics, and the style of writing shows remarkable similarities. Here, classification shows significant differences, depending on the scholar who does the job. But as this difficult group is rather small, it posed no large problems. Using the diviners for dating produced a relative chronology. But there are other ways to estimate age. By 1931 Dong Zuobin was ready to publish a methodical catalogue of criteria how to date inscriptions.

1. The catalogue of Shang kings given by grand historian Sima Qian in his *Shiji*.

2. The appearance of the names of grandfathers, fathers and ancestors in the inscriptions.

3. The signatures of the diviners.

4. The location where the inscription was excavated. This turned out to be a useless criterion. Chen Mengjia (1956) pointed out that a given pit usually contains inscriptions of several periods. Also, for the large amount of inscriptions unearthed before scientists did the job, no location is recorded.

5. Names of vassal- and enemy states.

6. Names of acting persons.

7. The topic of an oracle (weather, war, offerings, the five rituals, deities etc.).

8. Typical idiomatic phrases.

9. Typical forms and structures of the characters.

10. Typical styles of writing.

Starting with criteria one and two, the known inscriptions were provisionally dated. It provided a chronology of diviner-groups. Once this was achieved, a large amount of inscriptions could be assigned to various phases. It produced a general understanding of the criteria four to ten, which turned out to be essential when the name of the diviner or a reference to known persons was missing. Next, Dong identified five periods of oracle bone writing, which were later fine-tuned by Ikeda (1954). The only flaw in this system was the small group of diviners (thirteen altogether) which could have acted in period one and four. They had an unusual writing style preferring rounded to straight lines. Their very distinctiveness made them the topic of much fascinating speculation. Dong first attributed the group to period one, but changed his mind later on and decided on period 4. Chen Mengjia and Rao Zongyi disagreed and remained at their estimate of period 1. It looked as if the matter simply could not be resolved. Chang Tsung Tung argued for period 1b, as the inscriptions of this diviner group make frequent mention of four princes and ladies who are only attested in period 1. He also argued his point for reasons of style and content, i.e. the ritual exorcisms which he assumed to be typical for period 1 (1970:20-23).It turned out to be wrong, as similar exorcisms occurred, though much rarer, in other periods. Xu Jinxiong (Hsü Chin-hsiung) by contrast confirms their dating in period four on account of the types of hollows on the reverse side of the bone (1970:3-4).

Some diviners lasted over several periods. One, named Great (person standing, seen from in front) did his job from Wu Ding's time (1a) all the way to Geng Ding (3) and died in respectable old age. He must have been an adaptable character, as within his lifetime, divination changed a lot. Diviner Mouth was busy in period 2b and 3. Diviner Carrying (man carrying a hoe) appears in period 1a, 1b and 3 but is absent in 2a and 2b. It looks like two, perhaps three persons with the same name. Another two diviners used the name Emerger (foot coming out of a pit), they were active in period 1a, 2b and 3. These four are not enough to confuse things much. The grand result is a catalogue of nine distinct phases. Not that the details are accepted by everyone. Chang Tsung Tung has a fascinating discussion about the dating of a group of inscriptions lacking diviner names, which used to be attributed to periods 4a and 4b, and which he attributes to periods 1b and 2a (1970:24-27). Sorry, but it would go beyond the scope of this book.

A new and highly useful tool for dating is the study of the hollows and notches on the back of plastrons and scapulae. Here I shall use the summary by Hsü Chin-hsiung, 1970:4-7, and the excellent illustration of hundreds of hollows illustrated by the same author (here written Xu Jinxiong) in *Dong Zuobing Xian Sheng Shi Shi Si Zhou Nian Ji Nian Kan,* Taibei, 1978, 110-136. For a start, there are two basic types of hollows. One of them is roughly circular; the other is lengthy, ovoid and has a notch running from top to bottom. In some cases the notch has two further outlets at the end. In most cases, only one of the two was used. However, in some periods the two were combined. Simply read on.

The Five Periods

Let's have a general summary of the criteria for each period. Of course this is a very simplified account. It may give you a general idea on what happened when, and how a given inscription can be roughly dated. Of course there are also ways of fine tuning the dating. I cannot go into these, as they are very special cases. For instance, in period three the sign of bird Peng was sometimes accompanied by the sail meaning wind. Or the way the sign for the Yellow River changed in period three. Or the simplification of the sign for the drum-sacrifice. Here we are dealing with general issues. I list the names of kings and (known) queens and try to say something about the length of the reign. It isn't easy. T.T. Chang (1970:21) gives two widely different estimates by Dong Zuobin and Chen Mengjia, while David Keightley offers a third (2006:240-241). The latter is based on the present scholarly assessment that Wu Ding reigned around 1200 BCE and possibly for quite a while before, and that the Shang ended in 1045.

Period 0 (move to Xiaotun, Anyang, new capital.)
0: possible but unattested oracle bone inscriptions of Pan Geng, no queen known.
The same from Xiao Xin (Zu Xin), no queen known.
The same from Xiao Yi (Di Yi) and Queen Bi Geng.

Possibly period 0 did not exist at all, and Wu Ding built the capital.

Period 1

1a: King Wu Ding (Di Ding) and queens Bi Gui, Bi Xin and Bi Wu. Allegedly 59 years rule.

1b: End of Wu Dings reign. Possibly (but not likely) King Zu Ji. No queen known, if ever there was one.

In period one, hollows appear in four types: round hollow in long hollow, both chiselled. Round hollow near long hollow, both chiselled. Drilled round hollow without long hollow. Chiselled long hollow without round hollow. Wu Ding's time is characterised by experimentation. Most long hollows measure 15-20 mm and are made with great care.

Characters are written carefully and generally large. The scribes had a strong sense of calligraphy and beauty.

Ritual: 'Old School': a huge range of ritual and religious inscriptions. Sacrifices follow no steady pattern but are made when needed. Topics are: ancestors, gods, Di, nature deities, directional deities, Yi Yin, mythical ancestors and ghosts. Dreams, ritual exorcisms, music, oaths, curses, hosting, ascension rites, harvest, ritual messages, pilgrimage, burning of drought sacrifices, priests, fu ladies, wu etc.. Oracles were made for many members of the nobility.

Weather, childbirth, hunting, war, travel, treaties, new cities, building, fiefs, inspection tours, commands, tribute, luck of the week. Divination is genuine, there are bad as well as good outcomes. Many diviners are employed.

Period 2

2a: Zu Geng and Queen Bi (Mu) Yi. 7 to 10 years on the throne.

'Old School': Divination topics as in Wu Ding's time.

2b: Zu Jia (Di Jia) and Queen Bi Wu. 19 to 33 years.

'New School': massive change in religious practice. Strict ritual schedule granting each notable ancestor and ancestress five special sacrifices each year. Hosting of ancestors. New calendar. Change of introduction of the intercalary month.

Weather, hunting, war, travel, commands, luck of the week and of the night.

Divination topics are much reduced and results of divination are more expectably positive. The amount of ancestors who receive sacrifices is narrowed down. Gods, nature deities, mythical ancestors, Yi Yin etc. receive no sacrifices any more.

Hollows like period 3, see below.

2b or 3: possibly King Lin Xin (Fu Xin). Questionable. No queen known, if any. Regency between 0 and 8 years.

Period 3

3: Geng Ding (Geng Zu Ding) and Queen Bi Xin. Ruled between 8 and 16 years.

Religious reform: reintroduction of *'Old School'* divination, ritual and sacrifice. Gods, Di etc. receive offerings again, sacrifices are made when required, Zu Ji's ritual schedule is cancelled (or we have no evidence for it). Other topics as in period 1a and b. But oracles are not quite as common as in period 1. Human sacrifices are either not as excessive as under Wu Ding or not recorded in such detail.

Hollows in periods 2 and 3: Long hollows are preferred. Some are rounded at the edges which makes them similar to period 1. Others are pointed at top and bottom. The hollows of these periods are large and rather coarsely made, most are longer than 20 mm. Another typical element are large, scorched spaces. Evidently, a new method of heating was explored.

Period 4

4a: Wu Yi and Queen Bi Wu. 4 to 40 years.

4b: Wen Ding (Wen Wu Ding, Di Ding) and Queen Bi Gui. 10 to 13 years.

'Old School' continues. Writing is much as in period 1, large and carefully executed. Style often resembles period 1, but there are new signs showing more complex line-work.

General topics as in period 1.

Return of the round hollow. Most hollows are long, but a few have a round hollow at the side. The change from 3 to 4 is fluent, making it hard to date the pieces. Sizes and shapes of the hollows vary a lot. Often the hollows are made in a sloppy and careless way. It gets worse towards the end of period 4. Often, hollows of different sizes appear on the same bone. In general the hollows shrink, some to under 10 mm, as does the size of the scorched section.

Period 5

5a: Di Yi (Fu Yi), no queen known. 18 to 35 years.

Return to *'New School'*. Five sacrifice schedule reintroduced. Few original inscriptions. Some concern about hunting and war. Hunts were always divined on days 2, 4, 5, 8 and 9 of the week. Topics like rainfall, angry ancestors, deities, disease, dreams, harvest, assignation of officers, concerns of the nobility etc. disappear. Divination is a predictable routine and the answers, so far as known, are always positive. The cracks per piece of bone are reduced.

Writing is tiny and cramped; many bones arc filled from bottom to top with routine questions about the auspiciousness of a night or week. The period 5 sacrifice calendar is so crammed that the entire ritual schedule of all ancestors could be reconstructed. References to months increase.

Very few diviners, the king usually divines himself, and sticks to a minimum.

5b: Zhòu Xin, Zhòu Wang, Di Xin and Queen Da Ji (?). 33 to 63 years.

The change from Di Yi to Zhòu Xin is difficult to observe. So far, we only have divinations from the first decade of this king's regency. In all likeliness, he stopped divining, just as he abandoned the burdensome five ritual schedule. It was not replaced by *'Old School'* ritualism. The king simply wasn't interested any more. Or maybe he continued divining in Zhaoge, where he allegedly built a new capital. The sacrificial schedule had become so burdensome that divination is reduced to weather, hunting, war and the auspiciousness of weeks and nights. The campaigns of his early years are documented. The results of divinations are always good.

Writing is tiny and hard to read. The signs show great uniformity, as they were made by only one or two scribes. There were very few diviners beside the king, who divined as little as possible. Hunting divination is always performed on the same days of the week.

The dating by hollows poses problems as not much material exists from the end of the Shang. Size varies, some have rounded hollows next to the long hollow, and many are made in a sloppy fashion. Zhòu Xin didn't care.

Forgeries

used to be a problem in the first years when chaotic excavations were made by profit hungry amateurs. The many inscriptions which Frank Chalfant copied between 1904 and 1914, many of them the cherished property of private collectors and museums in Britain, Scotland, Germany and the United States, contain a considerable amount of forgeries. Of the 2178 pieces published in the *Couling-Chalfant Collection of Inscribed Oracle Bones*, (1935, 1938, 1939) Dong Zuobin and Chen Mengjia identified 116 forgeries. It's the worst score in Oracle bone literature.

There are several types of forgeries.

The most harmless type is an exact copy of an original inscription. It may alter the statistic, but it does no damage to the understanding of the Shang. And, who knows, if the original was destroyed or lost during the war, it saved a piece of valuable information. Such forgeries, if they exist, are impossible to identify at the time being. The age of the bone is no criteria, as so many large scapula had wide empty spaces which simply waited for someone to fill them in.

If the forgery consisted of a single fragment of bone or shell with only one word on it cannot be identified, unless that character is very badly written or raises suspicion by being otherwise unknown.

There are many other forgeries in evidence, and most of them are very easy to identify. The forgers were enthusiastic amateurs. Most had no knowledge of archaic Chinese. Many of them were illiterate. Imagine skilled carvers who know a couple of signs, or a few combinations, and carve them on a handy piece of ancient bone. Or who added writing to a large piece which didn't have much genuine text, thus improving the value.

In many cases, the forgery is a wild mixture of genuine characters, badly copied characters and entirely imaginative elements. They do not follow the usual structure of a question or charge. Instead, we find fragments of dates and diviner names, which should be in the beginning of a given text, somewhere mixed up in the writing. And just as the forgers did not know what they wrote, or how it should be structured, they were not aware of the grammar. Anachronisms, i.e. the blend of different handwritings or the use of characters from different periods in a single inscriptions are another clue. Sometimes topics collide, such as hunting, sacrifice and war in a single short text. Finally, there is an aesthetic element which often gives forgeries away. Many forgers were simply too self-conscious and careful. They created inscriptions which looked extra good. Many are placed right in the centre of a piece. There is something deliberate to them, unlike the writing and carving of people who spend years and years doing a routine job. And finally, the forgers often showed off by compiling as many different characters as possible in a single text. All of which paid well. The early collectors, many of them acquiring bones at extreme prices, were attracted to inscriptions with many and varied signs, mysterious, well executed and, in a way, magnificent little works of art.

Nowadays, the issue of forgery only comes up from time to time when popular books show illustrations the author couldn't read. The archaeological excavations in Anyang were strictly disciplined and henceforth, amateur digging came to an end. While collections in Europe and America still exhibited the odd forgery, the scholarly standard in China and Japan ensured that very few forgeries, if any, made it into the books. The only flaws which still appeared occurred when a piece was drawn. Some drawings have fine lines missing or added, depending on how scratched and time-worn the original was. Such errors are quite understandable when you look at rubbings. Too many genuine pieces are badly eroded and leave lots of space for guesswork.

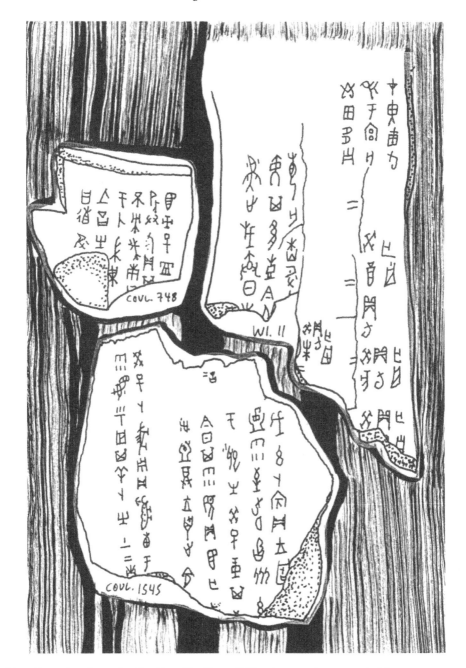

*Two forgeries from the Couling-Chalfant Collection. and one partial forgery
from the Richard Wilhelm collection
(The text on the bottom right and centre is genuine)*

The great collection made by Hu after the war has a very few drawings where one or two signs were overlooked or misdrawn. But considering the amazing wealth of research in his volumes, such minor errors should be excused. On the whole, the matter of forgery has become a curiosity of the past. One day, it will be considered a form of early twenty century art and evaluated by standards of calligraphy and inventiveness.

Structural elements

Modern Chinese signs are usually a composition of several items, the so called radicals. Radicals are root-signs of the language, i.e. small units of meaning and sound. Think of them as basic atoms out of which more complex characters are created. Or think the other way around: radicals are the units into which a given sign can be divided. They make it slightly easier to use a Chinese dictionary. Sometimes you can even guess what an unknown character refers to when you look at the radicals. Like the radical shui (water), which appears in many fluid-related characters. Or the radical *'ge'* (originally a dagger-axe), which tends to appear in martial contexts. It's a general thing with plenty of exceptions. In many signs, a given radical does not appear for its meaning (the picture of a thing or idea) but for its phonetic value. Here, it tells us how something else is pronounced.

In such matters, Shang period writing was not very refined. It was making a few starts, but given that the pronunciation of archaic Chinese remains highly enigmatic, we can't really be sure. However, most Shang characters are more than simple pictures.

Take the sign *'bell'* (p.737). It shows a somewhat bell-shaped thing, not a precise rendering how Shang bells looked. This character had some additional meanings. It could signify south, or Deity South, or the South People, I.e. the southern neighbours of the Shang. The south also signifies warmth and light, as it is from this direction that the sun shines strongest. It implies expansion, just like the tone of a bell spreads out. Bells are bright, and though the old Shang bells acquired a thick patina over the millennia, originally the bronze was polished and shone like the sun. And finally, it seems that when a noble received the right to govern a district, city of fief, s/he received a bell or bells as a sign of status. All of these ideas can be found in the character. At the top there is a small trident. This is the proto-radical *'growth'*, which appears in such characters as wood, tree, grass. It signifies expansion, be it of the tone, of warmth, of royal authority. Shang bells did not have such a thing. Neither did they contain a square with a dot or line in the centre. It's the character *'sun'* or *'day'*, and shows the brightness of the metal and the direction south. In short, the unrealistic image contains a lot of secondary symbolism. In a similar way the character *'cloud'* or Deity Cloud is a combination of the proto-radicals *'turbulence'* and *'up, high'* or *'upper deity'*. Sarah Allan (1991:46-50) offers a beautiful interpretation of the complex character *'east'* which has been interpreted as a bag of grains or a bundle of wood. But it could also be, as she suggests, a mixture of the proto-radicals *'wood, tree'* and *'sun'*. They capture the idea of the growing, or rising sun and may even symbolise the mythical Fu Sang tree growing in the very east of the world.

As you can see, it's valuable to look into the characters very closely and to consider which graphical elements might be meaningful. I have found it a highly stimulating meditation. I often look at arrangements of Shang images when I make music or simply empty my mind prior to meditation or prayer. It's amazing what emerges from the deep. Now I wouldn't claim that every bit of symbolism you can dream up was actually intended by the scribes. But when symbolism suits word and meaning, I'm quite in favour of it. Discovering the depths of ancient symbols is more than a creative reconstruction. A good character can convey a huge amount of insight when you open up and stare, wonder, receive and enjoy.

Finale:
The Chemistry of Culture

The Shang came to a violent end. You read about it earlier. People have told and retold the story so many times. They have turned it into a moral fable, they invested King Wen and King Wu with a remarkable amount of reinforced extra virtue and turned the doomed tyrant into the evil guy par excellence. Few have bothered to look at it as a case study in brain chemistry. Much of what we call culture is based on keeping the brain chemistry satisfied. By transforming tryptophan, your body naturally manufactures serotonin, an all round chemical with many varied uses in your system. From serotonin, dopamine is manufactured. It's one of the keys to human alchemy. The substance is essential for your attention, your alertness, your all-round feelings of being well and satisfied. Dopamine stimulates the so called pleasure centres and is essential for motivation strategies. It is also a substance that causes plenty of addiction. People get a dopamine rush when they consume soft and hard drugs, be it tobacco, alcohol, hashish, opium, amphetamines, heroin and others. Sure, the rush is bigger or smaller, depending on the amount of dopamine it raises (either by releasing it or by slowing down the re-absorption), and much depends on the individual neural makeup. Also, each of these drugs is a complex blend of molecules that create a lot of extra effects. But dopamine isn't only amplified when drugs are consumed. People get similar increases in available dopamine from making love, from sex, risk sports, hunting, gambling, crime and similar activities. All of them can be habit forming. There is chemistry to pleasure. It also appears in refined cooking. Just remember how cunning Yi Yin convinced Tang becoming a ruler would mean much finer food on the table. *Lüshi Chunqiu* (14.2) takes several pages to recount Yi Yin's lesson. Tang learned that there are 5 tastes, 3 materials, 9 ways of cooking and 9 changes in the materials. There are ape lips, tails of young swallows, marrow of buffaloes and elephants, phoenix eggs, the six legged scarlet turtle, flying fish and algae from Mount Kunlun. Yi Yin praised the specialities of each country and district, and when he was done Tang was hungry for the empire. Few people are aware that, beyond simple nourishment, food is full of drugs. Lettuce contains opiates, tomatoes tryptamine and serotonin (especially catsup, as vinegar amplifies the effect), soy sauce flavour enhancer; beans and meat provide tryptamine; cheese offers bufotenin, dimethyltryptamin (DMT) and opiates; sausages amphetamines, haemamphetamines and opiates; chocolate contains cannabiols and opiates; wheat and meat provide opiates. Ginger seems to interact with serotonin receptors. Spices like long pepper, cinnamon, ginger, nutmeg, aniseed, cloves, fennel, galangal and cardamom, especially when mixed with alcohol and/or heated, produce amphetamines and some of them release mild hallucinogens. Heated alcohol with spices, perfumes, honey and herbs was a common offering and beverage among the Shang. They usually used the three legged, beaker shaped jue or four legged jia vessels for the job. Fu Hao's tomb contained 12 huge jia beakers; eight of them are more than 60cm high with a weight around 20kg. She also had 53 drinking vases, called gu; imagine the sort of life she intended to lead in the otherworld. While the Shang did not have access to all the spices listed above, they certainly had more tropical plants than the people in northern China nowadays. They may even have used plants and fungi that have long become extinct.

MAO blockers appear in grilled meat, soy sauce, Asian fish sauce, balsamic vinegar, bananas and various mushrooms. They reduce the reabsorbtion of serotonin and nor-adrenaline; hence raise the level of both. Remember that serotonin is an multi-tasking chemical with a wide range of uses in body, mind and intestines, and people who have too little of it tend to feel badly aligned, disorganised and depressed. The SAD disorder that affects so many during the dark days of winter is closely related to a lack of serotonin. Many SAD patients develop a craving for sugar, and indeed sugar provides a short burst of endorphins. These act as self-made pain-killers. It's not the same thing as a dopamine rush to the reward and pleasure centres, but at least it keeps a person moderately serene. Serotonin is also essential for the production of dopamine: when your serotonin level drops, so does the level of dopamine. Nor-adrenaline is good for excitement. So are the amphetamines in blood. Many of them survive cooking, and concentration is highest in blood sausage. The Shang frequently offered and ate raw meat, which, freshly slaughtered, contained even more of the stuff. It also contains vitality. I recall a goodbye meal in rural Kurdistan. A goose had its head cut off. The children of the family came running and each of them was anointed with a drop of fresh blood on the forehead. Within seconds, they all went wild with excitement.

Refined cuisine involves a vast amount of consciousness changing drugs (Pollmer, 2010; Alberts & Mullen, 2003). Some call it culture; while neuro-chemists might speak of drug indulgence. Then there is art. Some people get a kick from the visual system. It's the reason why we decorate our homes and appreciate pictures, or, in the Shang's case, temples and tombs painted in bright red, decorated with black and blue, and bronze cauldrons of high refinement. Others get a dopamine release from being emotionally stimulated by music. Sure, music is just tones, rhythms and perhaps lyrics, just as pictures are basically photons processed by the retina and the visual cortex, but what makes them valuable is the activity they produce in the mind. Again, responses differ. In most people, the acoustic cortex is more intensely connected to the limbic system (which makes feelings and emotions) than the visual cortex. However, each of us is unique, and as we grow up we gain culture (i.e. learn which sense experiences and behaviour patterns exactly gives us a kick). Call it human existence: once we are over the stage where we have to struggle to survive, we devote our time and energy to playing around with our neural systems. In the physical realm, this quest is based on neural clusters and pathways, on electric transmission, brain waves, electric impulses, chemistry and a lot of other factors we haven't discovered yet. Fashionable clothes and jewellery, symbols of might, glory and attractiveness...you name it, they stimulate glands and cause the head to buzz with activity. Then there is love. That's a tough one. While love may be a spiritual activity that allows you to discover yourself in another and the other in yourself, on the physical plane there is plenty of chemistry involved. Let's take a look at the last culture junkie of the Shang. As Zhòu Xin noticed, *'falling in love'* is one of the strongest self induced drug states. Let me simplify this a bit. We are looking at a case history which is more than 3000 years old. First of all: the patient. Zhòu (Tyrant) Xin, a rich lad from a difficult family. Dad hardly cared about him, his elder brothers ignored him (until they disappeared somehow) and most of his relations are dead, hungry and pretty demanding. All he has is good looks, physical power, a clever head, great wealth and the uncanny ability to ruin a dynasty. He is a passionate hunter, an uncompromising warlord and a heavy drinker. Recently he has given up worshipping the ancestors as there are better things to do. What happens when people fall in love? Young Mr. Tyrant did just that. One fateful moment in the temple, a fluttering curtain and he is in love with the picture of Nüwa. Love can be like this: it does not necessarily require mutual attraction. And there we have our young regent, tossing around in bed with nothing but despair and longing on his mind. Thinking of your beloved day and night: it's a sure sign of drug addiction. Now for a serious comment. Diviner Swimmer explains: the process is by no means completely explored yet, but some of it goes like this: the serotonin level drops, the adrenaline level rises, endorphins are released and so is, in most people, oxytocin. Add a lot of other chemicals, many of them yet undiscovered. It's a complex mixture with steadily changing ingredients. But our tyrant is not only in love, he is also in heat. The oracle says: Day jia-zi of a long, long story. Crack making indeed, the divination reveals: lust is not quite the same as love. Lucky people gain one; get the other for free. Men and women release testosterone, and the level of serotonin, dopamine and nor-adrenaline rises (Alberts & Mullen, 2003:19-25). No blame. Lust involves not quite the same chemistry as love, but the mind is good at making fluid changes. And it can make them fast. Especially when a tyrant wants something more tangible than a remote, unattainable and thoroughly angry goddess. Nüwa is just now sending him a proper bride. She's a pretty girl from a noble family, looks like the goddess, well versed in art, music and courteous behaviour. Perhaps she could have exerted a good influence on Zhòu Xin. Tough luck that she never got a chance. The poor thing is obsessed by a fox, but as she uses a strong deodorant and keeps her tail out of the way the monarch may not notice. Daji arrives at the royal court, casting cow eyes at the tyrant as she collapses gracefully at his feet. It surely gets his attention. Back to the real world: another interesting chemical is PEA (phenethylamine). This stuff, typically released when people fall in love, is very similar to amphetamine. Its effects are not completely explored, but it seems to increase the dopamine level and to cause excitement, euphoria and intensifies perception. At the same time, it increases the amount of available energy. It's simply great if you want to be up all night and feel really good. Now it's party time in Anyang. Nobody dares to go to bed, the torches burn all night and in the morning the administrators feel wrecked. Not so our young tyrant and his shyly blushing bride: time distortion and additional energy reserves are typical side effect of fresh love, lust and sexual activity. Associated and disassociated perception vary a lot. Nor is he likely to notice that she pounces on mice when he isn't looking. Love is confusing all the way; we are just beginning to work out what we do within ourselves to create some of the greatest experiences our system can produce. That is, excluding serious people and loyal ministers. Oracle news: there may well be, as Milkman & Sunderwirth (2010:240-241) propose, several undiscovered neurotransmitters involved. One of them might be similar to the so called *'love drug'* MDA or its close cousin MDMA (Ecstasy). Such substances may be involved in the more spiritual aspects of love, the almost psychedelic intensification of perception and the sense of intense unity and sharing. It raises the question what happens in people who experience religious love, the bliss of devotion and the love that comes flooding from the heart when you radiate joy. Well, it doesn't happen to Zhòu Xin so we can reserve that observation for refined people, most of whom are trying to get a huge distance between themselves and the capital at the moment. Our young sweethearts are very much in love. They share beds, they share jokes and they especially share their little hobbies. Being freshly in love often involves very rapid learning; lovers easily embrace their partner's taste in music, movies, art, cannibalism, torture and ingenious executions. It may remind you of the *'imprinting'* phenomenon that often characterises acid trips.

But this is just the start. In a typical relationship, the period of *'falling in love'* is characterised by strong emotionality, great ups and downs, obsessive behaviour, excitement, scatterbrainedness, lack of appetite and so on. It's a wonderful but also a weakening state of mind. After weeks or months, the subconscious decides that the fireworks can't go on forever. Over-the-top chemistry is not beneficial for a normal life. It may be a good idea to get a regular meal or a night of sleep occasionally. From time to time you have to think about politics, or at least about the ministers who are supposed to do it for you. So the intoxication is brought to a more reasonable level, once in a while, and this may cause withdrawal symptoms. Regarding the PEA, the level rises until it seems to reach a plateau. You already guessed this: the couple habituates. As the level is not changing much, passion isn't perceived so strongly as before. Some people show the typical symptoms of amphetamine withdrawal and experience a reduction of dopamine. In other words: they become miserable, dissatisfied and generally difficult. Tyrants tend to invent ingenious tortures and new taxes. They hunt and gamble in excess, and swill their wine faster than the liver can handle it. Anything for more dopamine. Or they decide that shifting the capital would be fun, especially when it allows you to leave the ancestral cemetery behind, and maybe some huge idiotic building projects will add a little glamour to life. Or happy couple moves to Zhaoge and watches how the population toils. Each night they sit under the stars and drink. After the initial the excitement, many people seem to generate oxytocin. This remarkable chemical seems to be involved in generating feelings of trust, comfort and safety. Many people on oxytocin tend to become more trusting and less cautious, which may easily result in pregnancy. The oxytocin effect may be amplified by endorphins, making our lovers feel soothed, comforted and happily at home. (Milkman & Sunderwirth, 2010:234-238) And while the general love-craze gives way to calm and serene domestic happiness, we observe a situation that is ideally suited to the rearing of children. Mind you, it does not work that way in all people. It definitely does not work with Zhòu Xin, who didn't have a trusting day in all of his life. Nor does it work in Daji, who could think of nicer prospects than digging a hole to have a litter of yelping cubs. It has been hypothesised that some people (especially tyrants) have less access to oxytocin, which makes it harder for them to handle lasting relationships. Some people move from one partner to another as soon as the initial excitement is over. Others begin a quarrelling relationship. It's so easy to accuse the partner for not making the right chemistry flow. Love and lust can be addictive. A stimulus (the partner) that used to produce the desired rush of excitement and intoxication may cease to function that way. People who use drugs habituate. And when the rush gets weaker the stupid ones accuse each other of having changed. Someone really clever could have told them that feelings can be made, once you realise the responsibility is yours. A clever wu might have said: It's not the partner who stimulates your glands, it's yourself, using the partner and a lot of highly specific thinking. However, there is no-one clever around at the moment. The middlish clever ones were all tortured to death while the really clever ones have long moved to Mount Kunlun for immortality training. It involves keeping out of human affairs whenever possible.

Sad news, that Zhòu Xin isn't good at making oxytocin. But Daji has a trick for that. She pouts, she makes scenes, runs to her apartments and makes him wait. It raises expectations. One of the fun things about human beings is that you can get the same dopamine kick when you expect something good to happen than when it actually happens (Wolfram Schultz in von Schönburg, 2006:170). People are so good at expectations: the entire advertisement industry lives from endless hopes and no fulfilment. Daydreaming is a neat trance that provides access to plenty of feelings. You imagine good things to happen and feel good, next you imagine them to be better and feel wonderful. Even if they don't, you still had a great time expecting them, and nobody comes around and tells you to give back the good feelings. It's only after several disappointments that the expectation, hence the dopamine kick run down. And Da Ji is cunning and will not let this happen. Instead, she asks for another couple of towers, terraces and palace buildings and her darling is sure to have them built. Nothing is as soothing as watching little conscript citizens pounding earth the whole night through. But Zhòu Xin is still a difficult husband. He hunts, he drinks and ages rapidly. Soon Da Ji notices that even ingenious make up doesn't get her any further. Oracle news: clever fox lady introduces two concubines, both of them dangerous spirits, who keep the lust besotted monarch under her control. At this point, in the king's overdue far-too-much ritual year, terrible omens appear. One of them is the allied army under the command of King Wu which happens to camp in front of the new capital and is simply too big to be overlooked. Fighting ensues and goes on for a long time, what with so many officers trying for fast promotion. Our tyrant remains, bleary eyed, tired and tragic on the deer terrace and wonders where all the good times went. Final oracle news: the dynasty is coming to a full stop; another high culture down the drain due to dopamine addiction.

Short Glossary

(For deities, royal persons etc please consult the index).

Anyang: place in Henan, northern China. The nearby village Xiaotun was the location of the last Shang capital, otherwise known as Yin. Yin here is a place name, do not confuse with Yin/Yang.

Bamboo Annals: a historical work of the early and middle Zhou period which was recorded on long bamboo slips, each of them inscribed with forty words. The work was discovered in a Warring State period tomb in the third century and caused a stir among the scholars of the period, as it provided a history that was frequently at odds with the carefully edited histories of the late Zhou and Han periods. In consequence, many historians dismissed it as unreliable, or even as a forgery. There are two versions, one of them possibly edited after the Song Dynasty and another that was reconstructed from quotations in early sources. Nowadays, the Bamboo Annals are considered a valuable source work.

Chuci: Words or Songs of the State of Chu. A collection of magnificent songs once attributed to Qu Yuan (who may have composed and compiled a few). The earliest songs were written in the fourth C. BCE, but the entire collection was not completed in its present form until the second C. AD. Much of the material focuses on cosmology, myth, ritual and the ceremonies of the wu.

Chunqiu: Spring and Autumn. A general term that may refer to a period and to a number of encyclopaedic texts. As between spring and autum lies the whole year, the term expresses a totality.

Cong: an enigmatic jade cylinder. Congs are usually round on the outside but have a square hole running through the centre. Presumably the roundness symbolised heaven and the square shape earth. Some have more or less stylised taotie faces on the outside. Congs were extremely valuable ritual offerings. Whether they actually served a function remains uncertain.

Da (Tian) Yi Shang: the Great (or Heavenly) City Shang. Name of the capital in the late Shang period.

Daodejing: the Book of the Dao and the De, a fourth or third century BCE compilation attributed to Laozi. Presently, there are four distinct versions. The well known classic version comes from Wang Bi in the third century, two versions were discovered in the Han period Mawangdui tomb library and an even earlier and much shorter version, the Guodian Laozi dates from the Warring

States period. The book is one of the fundamental texts of Daoism.

Daoism: a general term for a wide range of philosophical, meditative and religious systems that are based, to a greater or smaller extent, on the teachings attributed to Laozi, Zhuangzi, Liezi and even the yellow Emperor Huangdi. Key ideas of philosophical Daoism are that people should cultivate their original nature by a return to softness, stillness, simplicity and silence; that the perfect sage/regent achieves everything by doing as little as possible; and that cleverness, saintliness and the Confucian virtues do harm to the natural development of things. Some Daoist movements were highly political while others developed a wide range of meditative, alchemical, sexual, magical or ritual practices.

Di: a complex term for what may have been the supreme deity or deities of the Shang. Also used as a general word for *'deity'* and as a posthumous title for a selection of late Shang kings.

Dizhi: Earthly Stem, a late term for the twelve signs that the Shang combined with the Tiangan to achieve a ritual cycle (ganzhi) of sixty days. See Tiangan.

Erligang: name of a Bronze Age culture that existed near modern Zhengzhou; where a Shang capital is being unearthed.

Erlitou: name of a Bronze Age culture that may represent the ancestors of the Shang culture. Frequently identified with the hypothetical Xia *'Dynasty'*.

Feng Shen Yan Yi: Account of the Name Giving (or: installation) of the Gods. A late Chinese novel describing in great and wonderfully anachronistic detail the fall of the Shang and the triumph of the Zhou. The story is full of wonder tale elements, Daoist lore, and bizarre characters, and has been filmed many times. Unlike traditional history, it claims that the end of the Shang involved endless battles until finally two long chapters are devoted to the ceremony that changes fallen heroes and immortals into Zhou period stellar gods.

Fangshi: method masters. A class of ritualists that became popular around the late Zhou period who combined intellectual study and writing, magical ritual, talisman sorcery and a profound knowledge of classical history. They largely replaced the wu ritualists, who were more inclined to ecstatic performances, and had a strong influence on early Daoism.

Ganzhi: the ritual cycle of sixty days.

Guanzi: a middle of the fourth century BCE work that contains much material on statecraft. Between these sections, a few chapters provide some of the earliest material on self cultivation by breathing exercise, meditation and stillness. These texts come from the earliest phase of what became Daoism later on and address themselves to immortality seekers.

Guben Zhushu Jinian: see Bamboo Annals.

Gui: Ghost or spirit. in Shang usage, a general term for any sort of ghost. In modern usage, a ghost or somebody else's ancestor, usually malevolent.

Guoyu: a Warring States work on history, containing earlier material.

Han Dynasty: two periods that initiated a cultural renaissance in China. The Former Han governed from 206 BCE to 8 CE; the later Han from 25 CE- 220 CE. In between, the Xin Dynasty usurped the throne.

Hangtu: a method of building firm terraces, house foundations and city walls by pounding earth.

Houji: Lord Millet, otherwise known as Qi, the Abandoned. Not to be confused with Qi as in vitality, breath, etc. Agricultural deity, culture hero and primal ancestor of the Zhou.

Huainanzi: an encyclopaedic work composed by Liu An (c. 179–122 BCE), king of Huainan, and a group of scholars. The work combines statecraft, a ritual calendar, cosmology, geography, astronomy, ecology, mythology, early history, war strategy, proverbs and numerous other items in a semi-Daoist setting. Liu An hoped that it would become the ultimate manual for the enlightened king. Sadly, his king Hanwudi was not very enlightened and Liu An, after being accused of having imperial ambitions, committed suicide.

Jiaguwen: Oracle Bone Inscriptions.

Jiandi: the mother of Xie, ancestress of the Zi clan and the Shang.

Jinben Zhushu Jinian: *'Modern'* Bamboo annals. See Bamboo Annals.

Kongzi (551-479 BCE): Confucius. A sage, scholar and statesman who had enormous influence on Chinese culture. His system is based on ritual conduct, benevolence, love for humanity and insists on a strict stratification of society. While Kongzi insisted that he was merely teaching the lore of the sages of antiquity, he was actually creating a new system of human behaviour. His teachings were not merely aimed at the kings and aristocrats but aimed at every person willing to make an effort to improve her- or himself.

Kui: a one legged dragon-monster. Two of them combine to form a single taotie. Also, a mysterious one legged water beast. The Yellow Emperor caught one and used its hide for the first drum.2. a historical one legged music master, famed for his bad manners but great loyality.

Laozi: literally Old Sage or Old Boy. 1. A mythical philosopher who lived in Kongzi's time and developed the rudiments of Daoism. 2. Possibly a title for a fourth or third century sage who developed Daoism. 3. The name of the book by that author, otherwise known as the Daodejing.

Legalism: a philosophy based on the teachings of Lord Shang, Xunzi and Li Si. It postulates that extreme punishments will make the world peaceful and crime-free, that everyone should spy on their neighbours, that laziness and failure should be punished and that people cannot be trusted. Very popular in the State of Qin and during the short lived Qin Dynasty.

Liji: the Book of Rituals. One of the Confucian Classics. A late Zhou compilation, subsequently edited and expanded during the Han Dynasty. The book describes at great length the foundation of ritual, custom and conduct. It also contains sections of the lost *Classic of Music* and a number of texts attributed to Kongzi and like minded philosopher-sages. In relating the origin of customs, the *Liji* contains numerous fascinating details on worship and ritual in antiquity, some of them authentic, others distorted or completely fanciful.

Liezi:1.a fascinating compilation of myth, Daoist metaphor and bizarre odds and ends. Some sections may come from the fourth century BCE or are based on earlier works; others were made up and added up to the fourth century AD. As the resulting muddle is hard to date or to use as a serious source, many scholars ignore the work or underestimate it. 2. The title of a Daoist who allegedly composed parts of the work or at least appears in it.

Lisao: Encountering Trouble or Undergoing Tribulation. A magnificent poem by statesman and poet Qu Yuan, included in the *Chuci*, describing how its author was wronged and misunderstood at the court, retired to the remote countryside and took up wu practices. The poem includes 'shamanic' elements such as heavenly flight and the search for a spirit mate.

Lü Buwei (290 - 235 BCE): Prime Minister of Qin, guardian of the future First Emperor and the richest merchant of his time. Also, the only merchant who had such an amazing degree of power and influence in Chinese history. He controlled a vast network of trade and intelligence, and used his influence to set his protégée on the throne. Lü was a great patron of art and literature, and invited thousands of scholars to his home, where, after much entertainment, he asked them to compose short essays. These texts are the source of the *Lüshi Chunqiu*. Also look for *Lüshī*, as this is the popular short name.

Lüshi Chunqiu: The Spring and Autumn Annals of Master Lü. A fascinating encyclopaedic work compiled and edited by Prime Minister Lü Buwei in the last years of the Warring States Period. A book on statecraft combining Confucian, Daoist and Legalist ideas, plus essays on music, conduct, agriculture, history and an invaluable ritual calendar, composed to educate the king of Qin, the future *'First Emperor'*. Qin Shihuangdi, under the influence of hard core legalist Li Si did not give a damn for Lü's attempts to recommend virtue, moderation and traditional thought nor did he much appreciate his council that kings ought to listen to their ministers. Eventually, he banished Lü, who took the hint and suicided.

Lunyü: the *Annalects*, a work containing brief sayings attributed to Kongzi (Confucius).

San Huang: a branch of Daoism that focuses on the worship of the Three August Ones, the emperors of Heaven, earth and the middle realm.

Mengzi (fourth century BCE): a sage philosopher who did much to elaborate and popularize Confucian thought. His lore emphasizes that people are basically good, that the king should provide an example of virtue and that the population should be treated with benevolence.

Qi: during the Shang period, a multipurpose term indicating, among many other things, motion, horizontal motion, exchange and so on. During the Zhou period, the sign began to signify the basic substance of everything. All that exists is an expression of qi on some level of density. Later writers narrowed down the meaning of qui to mean vitality, life energy, breath, breath energy and so on.

Qin Dynasty: 221-207 BCE. The first dynasty that governed a unified China. Reign of the *'First Emperor'* Qin Shihunagdi and his son.

Sanxingdui: a place in Sichuan that provided overwhelming evidence for a bronze casting, highly evolved culture, contemporary with the late Shang that was organized along different lines, had another religion, and was completely unknown to the historians. Its discovery ended the earlier assumption that Chinese civilization evolved only around the Yellow River.

Shang: excellent, supreme, exalted. Name of a period, state and *'dynasty'* that allegedly started after the fall of the Xia around 1700 or 1600 BCE and lasted until c. 1045 BCE.

Shangshu: Documents of the Shang. A section of the *Shujing* purporting to contain original Shang speeches. In prosaic reality, some of these texts may have been based on Shang materials, but they were repeatedly rewritten, edited or even forged by the historians of the late Zhou and Han Dynasty.

Shanhaijing: The *Book of Mountains and Seas*. A bizarre compendium, accumulated at various periods between the third century BCE and the third century CE. The book describes the geography of ancient China and the four dangerous outlandish regions. Some of it is based on more or less reliable accounts by travelers, but the greatest part deals with entirely fictional lands peopled by spirits, deities and all sorts of odd beings. These sections can be considered as a travelling guide for the spirit journeys of wu ritualists.

Shen: a useful word for the divine, the gods, spirits and benevolent ancestors, and to a quality of sacredness in general.

Shiji: The Account of History by Grand Historian Sima Qian of the Han Dynasty. A groundbreaking attempt to record the entire history of China from the mythical Yellow Emperor to Sima's days. It contained and critically evaluated most historical texts that had survived the great book burning of the First Emperor. In his work, Sima created a model for historical research that remained in use for two thousand years.

Shijing: The *Book of Songs*. A Confucian Classic. This collection contains some of the earliest literature of China. The material was composed after the seventh or sixth century BCE and offers invaluable insights into ritual hymns, sacrificial odes and folk songs. Several songs are based on material that comes from the Shang and early Zhou periods. Allegedly, Kongzi (Confucius) himself collected and edited the songs. In court ritual, the songs had an essential function. Kings ordered special songs to be played to make subtle statements, and likewise, a guest could make a request or statement by asking for a specific song.

Shujing: The *Book of Documents*. One of the venerated Confucian Classics. The book is a collection of historical documents, usually speeches and proclamations, that purport to come from all periods of early Chinese history. Some sections are attributed to the speeches of Yao, Shun and Yü in earliest antiquity; others tell you what Tang the Successful told his troops, how Yi Yin admonished the heir, what King Wen and King Wu said when they overthrew the Shang and what the early regents of the Zhou had in mind. While sections of the documents can be traced to the early Western Zhou, the majority of the material was compiled, edited or invented by well meaning scholars of the late Zhou and Han Dynasty. These historians wanted to create a history as it ought to have been. Especially the 'early' sections are full of Han period fabrications. Chinese scholars venerated the *Shujing* until the late19th century, when it became increasingly obvious that the texts could not be as old as tradition claimed.

Shuowen Jiezi: The earliest surviving Chinese dictionary. An enormously influential work of the early second century composed with the intent to clear up the origin of old words, and to eradicate a number of miswritings. Its author, Xu Shen, ordered and glossed 10,516 characters under the heading of 540 radical signs. The book was so functional that it remained in use until 1717.

Sima Qian (145 -? BCE): the Grand Historian of the Han, author of the Shiji.

Sima Zhen: eighth century descendant of Sima Qian, who added several chapters on ancient prehistory to the work of his illustrious ancestor.

Suoshenji: A work by fourth century historian Gan Bao that contains anecdotes about immortals (xian), spirits, omina, sorcery, unusual historical events, incredibly unlikely tales and so on. The author seriously believed in his stories and provides an invaluable insight into the beliefs of the fourth century.

Taotie: according to Lü Buwei the word means glutton. It was used since the Song Dynasty to describe the highly symmetrical faces of monsters, dragons, animals and people that grace Shang and early Zhou art. Usually, a taotie can be split in the centre, so that each half shows a one legged kui dragon.

Tian: Heaven. Most of the Shang did not venerate Heaven, though the last regents of period 5 may have acknowledged the idea. Heaven was highest deity of the Zhou. After the fall off the Shang, the Zhou identified the Shang deity/s Di with their own Tian; later on both were identified with the Jade Emperor, the heavenly regent of folk religion.

Tiangan: Heavenly Stem. A late term to describe the ten days (suns) that make up the Shang ritual week (xun). Not to be confused with the xun ocarīna. When the Heavenly Stems and Earthly Branches (dizhi) are combined, they yield the ganzhi ritual cycle of sixty days.

Wu: a ritualist, often female, who mediates between the human and divine realm. Not to be confused with day name '*wu*' and King Wu Dīng. The word could be translated as shaman, exorcist, spirit medium, sacrificer and so on. Unlike many Central Asian shamans, the wu frequently enjoyed a high status at the court and participated in state rituals. Also, a place name and a term for the deity of a given quadrant, or for the deities of the four quadrants.

Wu Di: Five Emperors or Five Thearchs. The mythical regents who followed the Three August Ones.

Wu Xing: Five Movers, Five Transformers. A Zhou concept that is usually and wrongly translated as the Five Elements (wood, fire, earth, metal, water). While the Greek Elements describe the basic materials out of which things are composed, the wu xing are five expressions of qi and symbolize the forces of change, transformation, becoming, being and destruction. During the late Zhou and Han period, the system of the wu xing was elaborated to mind blowing perplexity.

Xia: the name of a real or imaginary dynasty that preceded the Shang. Nowadays, some scholars use the term Xia to describe the Neolithic Erlitou culture in the Shang homeland. According to the Zhou historians, the Xia '*Dynasty*' was founded by Yü the Great directly after the flood. Traditionally, it governed from c. 2100 – c. 1700 or 1600 BCE.

Xiaotun: Little Hamlet. A village near Anyang, Henan, where the ruins of the last Shang capital were discovered.

Xibeigang: Northwest High Ground. The royal cemetery near Xiaotun, on the other side of the river.

Xie: the son of Lady Jiandi, King Di Ku and a black bird. Ancestor of the Zi clan and the Shang.

Xun: the ritual week of the Shang, consisting of ten days (or suns). On the last day of each xun, a divination was made for the next.

Yijing: Classic of Changes, also known as the *Zhoujing* (the Changes of the Zhou) or *Xijing* (the Changes of Fuxi). A Confucian Classic. The book consists of sixty-four chapters and is used for divination using yarrow stalks or, more recently, coins. This type of divination was a product of the Middle Western Zhou, and some of the texts date from this period. According to legend, the book was written by the first Zhou regents, Wen Wang and Wu Wang. Though the two appear in the book, the language is younger. The text incorporates poems, sayings, proverbs and literary fragments from many centuries. The classical version, occasionally celebrated as *'the oldest book in the world'* was compiled during the Tang Dynasty! Fragments of the *Yijing* from the stone classics, bamboo books or quoted in the *Zuozhuan* indicated that earlier versions must have been different. Then, the Mawangdui tomb library provided a *Yijing* that dated from the early Han Dynasty. A quarter of the characters differed from the classical version, and so did the order of the text.

Yin Benji: Basic Annals of the Yin (Shang). A section of the *Shiji*.

Yinxu: the Waste (or: Ruins) of Yin. Another name for the countryside around Xiaotun.

Yin: a name for the Shang that was popular among the Zhou and Han historians. Some scholars use the term Yin for the late Shang who dwelled near Xiaotun, Anyang. Whether the Shang ever used the term Yin for themselves remains unknown.

Yin & Yang: two symbols expressing a primal polarity that became highly popular during the Zhou period. Originally, yang signified the sunny side of a hill and yin the dark side of a hill. Later generations added an enormous amount of extra meanings to the terms.

Zhuangzi: the name of a book and a sage philosopher who probably contributed to it. The work consists of six *'inner chapters'* that may come (largely) from the fourth or third century BCE and a range of later additions that combine early material with later texts, including some that contain Confucian and Legalist thought. It is possible that the *Zhuangzi*, as we have it, was compiled and edited at the court of Liu An. The *Zhuangzi* is one of the Daoist classics and a wonderful book full of crazy anecdotes and bizarre jokes.

Zhongren: The Many People. A much discussed designation for the Shang citizens. Some early researchers assumed the term to indicate serfs or slaves, contemporary researchers have shown that the zhongren, unlike the ren (humans, people) did have rights and status.

Zhou Period: the time from the fall of the Shang, nowadays dated 1045 BCE until the fall of the *'dynasty'* in 221. Zhou should not be confused with tyrant Zhòu, the last king of the Shang. It is divided into a Western Zhou period (1045? - 771? BCE) and an Eastern Zhou period that began after 771 BCE. The first part of the Eastern Zhou is called the Spring and Autumn period (771?-481), the second the Warring States period (481 – 221 BCE). During the Eastern Zhou, the Zhou regents had little power and influence, and functioned as religious figureheads while the royal relations, each of them heading their own states, fought it out with each other.

Zhouli: the *Rites of the Zhou*. A work on Zhou period ritual, compiled towards the end of the period.

Zhushu Jinian: see Bamboo Annals.

Zi Clan: the royal family of the Shang.

Zuozhuan: *Zuo's Tradition*. A Warring States History book.

Appendices

Introduction to the Inscriptions

In the following pages you will find a selection of oracle bone inscriptions that is by no means typical. You will read very common inscriptions, dealing with rain, hunting, the Five Rituals and the luck of the coming ten day week, side by side with extremely rare items on cult for unusual deities, ghosts, trees, and highly specific rituals. Some common topics, like war and travel, appear only on occasion. Hence, the selection gives a useful summary on religious affairs, but is by no means typical for the sort of oracles that were asked most of the time. Another untypical element is the length of the texts: as they are so badly damaged, nowadays most oracle bones only contain fragments of a given divination.

To make a translation, I had to make a few basic decisions which may or may not be appropriate. Like many Chinese scholars, I have chosen to treat the inscriptions as if they were questions. As you hopefully read earlier on, this choice is a convenience and by no means undisputed. A range of excellent oracle bone scholars prefer to see the inscription as charges, and where it comes to inscriptions from the bureaucratically minded periods 2b and 5, put forward that these may have constituted propositions of what the future should be like. However, the bulk of the inscriptions on the next pages are from periods 1, 2a, 3 and 4, when divination was the real intent of the ritual, and the king was actually interested in what the ancestors and gods were telling him. As genuine divination is a form of asking, I consider the question-format more suitable.

Another peculiarity is the way in which I translated the character jin, which means, at the most basic level, *'now'* (p.769). It looks like a roof with a supporting horizontal beam. When placed next to the sun, moon, ten-day week etc it becomes a time word and means the present day, night, month, week etc. Jin plus sun means literally *'now/day'* i.e. *'today'*. We also see it as *'now/night'*, *'now/xun-week'*, *'now/season'* and so on. All of this is accurate but sounds terribly clumsy. To make the inscriptions a little easier to comprehend, I have often taken the liberty of translating *'this/day'*, *'this/week'* and so on. True, it's not accurate. It's a convenience to create readable English and should not mislead you that the character means *'this'* in general.

I am sure you will find some of the translations a little rugged. I have frequently avoided smoothing them as this would have necessitated invention and creative additions to a textual material that is often unspecific and very sparse, if not in shorthand.

Last, my readings contain, as every other oracle bone translation, a number of assumptions and personal preferences. Many inscriptions contain uncertain bits, and when we want to turn them into meaningful phrases we have to decide what seems to be the likeliest interpretation. It could be wrong. That's the reason for the dictionary. Please look up words and consider alternate interpretations. Reading the bones is still a fairly young science and will undergo numerous reinterpretations in the next centuries. I offer my interpretations in all humility and look forward to better studies in the years to come.

Common Routine Divinations

Bing-shen (day 33) / crack-making / divination / this / night / not have / disaster? (Sun, 1937 #12)

Gui-wei (day 20) / crack-making / divination: / this / night / disaster? Eighth month. (Menzies S0448, 2482)

Gui-wei (day 20) / crack-making / diviner Temple of Ancestress / divines: / (*this*) xun week / not have / disaster? Fourth month. (Li, 1981 #150)

Gui-you (day 10) / crack-making / king / divines: / (*this*) xun week / not have / misfortune? / In / tenth month. (Li, #148)

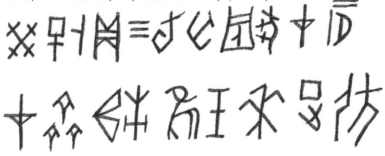

Gui-si (day 30) / crack-making / divination / third / xun week: / not have / disaster / in / twelfth month / in / PLN ? / resting place (=camp) / it is / king / coming / (*on*) punitive expedition / (*against*) Man / State (Li, 1981 #181)

Weather #1

Ji-chou (day 26) / crack-making / diviner Separate / divines: / this / day /
perhaps / rain? Divination: / this / day / no / rain? (Chen: 1970 # 3)

Yi-you (day 22) / crack-making / diviner Great / divines: / until / this /
second moon / (*will*) have/ great / rain? Luo, 1913: 3, 19a,#2)

Possibly / (*at*) day's / centre (= *noon*) / have / great / rain?
(Menzies, B1846 3555)

Wu-shen (day 45) / crack-making: / pacify / rain? / This / day / Xin / arrive
/ (*in the*) afternoon / rain? (Hu, 5 #70)

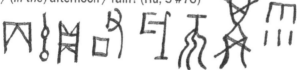

Bing-wu (day 43) / divination: / (*shall the offer to*) Ding / Father / (*by*)
killing with axe / not / (*make us*) meet / rain? (Hu, 5 #93)

Xin-you (day 58) / crack-making: / divination: /possibly / rain? This / day /
not / rain. / This is / (*occasion for*) ritual purification? (C-C, 3 #602)

Weather #2

Perhaps / (*offering*) piglets / five / receive / rain? (Hu, 5 #112)

Gui-chou (day 50) / crack-making / diviner Turbulence / divines: / also (*will there be*) / lasting / rain? (C-C, 1 #1559)

Not / perhaps / shit / rain? (JGWZD p.944)

Yi-you (day 22) / crack-making / diviner Temple of Ancestress / divines: / next / ding-hai (day 24) / not / perhaps / grant / sunshine?
(Li, 1981 # 266)

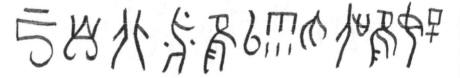

Cloud / at / north / thunders. / It is / bringing / rain. / (*Is this*) not / blame / (*but*) perhaps / good? (T.T. Chang, 1970: 213 # 15.6)

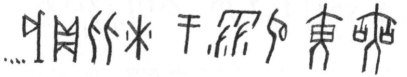

...-xu / divination: / following / (*a*) burned offering / for / Deity Snow / present / (*to*) Yi-Yin / dancing? (JGWZD p. 1243 & C-C, 1 #1533)

Weather #3

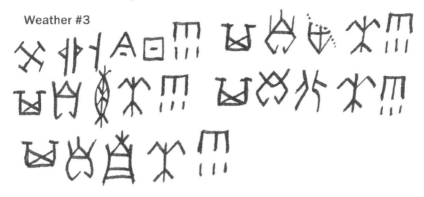

Gui-mao (day 40) / crack-making / this / day / rain? / Perhaps / at / west? come / rain? / Perhaps / at / east / come / rain? / Perhaps / at / north / come / rain? Perhaps / at / south? / come rain? (Li, 1981 #225)

....diviner Temple of Ancestress / divines: / thunder / not / perhaps / (*means*) misfortune? (T.T. Chang, 1970: 213 #15.5)

Bing-wu (day 43) / crack-making / diviner Separate / divines: / birth (*of*) / ten moon (*new moon of the tenth month*) / rainy? / Perhaps / it is / hailshower (*or* heavy rain)? (Li, 1981 # 258)

Jia-xu (day 11) / crack-making / (*ritual*) stand / (*in the*) centre / grants / sunshine? Yi-hai (day 12) / indeed (*it*) / raised / sunshine. (Li, 1981 # 269)

Perhaps / unknown offering / not have / great / rain / (*but*) goes (*to*) / clear up? (Li, 1981 #264)

Hunting #1

King / perhaps / cross river / river Excellent / (*with*) archers (*or:* to shoot) /... / deer, / not have / misfortune? (Menzies, B2017 , 1906)

Ren-xu (day 59) / shall not / hunt / perhaps / misfortune? Perhaps / encounter / great (*or:* heavenly) rain? (Menzies B1890, 1999)

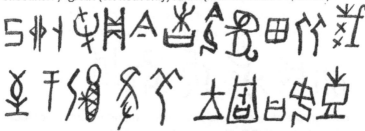

Ji-mao (day 16) / crack-making / diviner Quarrel (?) / divines: / this / (*unknown*) season / order / hare (person? animal?) / hunt/ follow / (*to*) STN / arrive / at / Turtle River. / Catch / Qiang? / King / prognosticates / says / (*there will be*) misfortune. (Li, 1981 #451 & JGWZD 1374)

Ren-yin (day 39) / king / makes cracks / (*and*) divines: / hunt / (*at*) PLN / advance /... / not have / misfortune / king / prognosticates / (*and*) says: / here /ritual purification. / Received / fox / deer / hornless deer (*or:* does?). (Li, 1981 #447)

Hunting #2

King / will / shoot / rhino. / Not have / accident? (Hu, 5 #388)

Ren-wu (day 19) / crack-making / diviner Temple of Ancestress / divines: / catch / tiger? (Hu, 3,2 #16)

Divination: / hares / not / it is / many / (*will be*) caught? (Sun, 1937 #750)

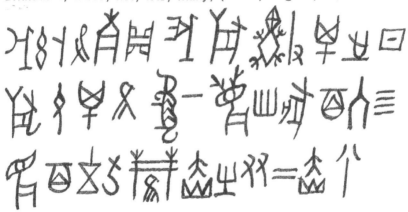

Wu-wu (day 55) / crack-making / diviner Bell-Stroke / divines: / we (shall) /winter hunt (battue hunting) / (*at*) PLN / hunt? /(*At the*) end / (*of the*) day / (*of*) battue hunting / indeed / caught / it is: / tiger: / one, / deer: / forty, / fox: / 164, / small deer: / 159 / pheasant (?) / red / received / armload double-red (birds): / 18. (Hentze, 1967:64; Haarmann, 1991: 109)

Receive (= catch) / elephant? (Luo, 1913, 3, 31b #1)

Hunting #3

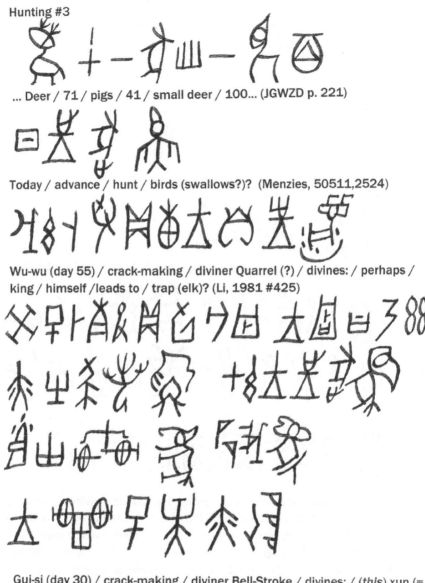

... Deer / 71 / pigs / 41 / small deer / 100... (JGWZD p. 221)

Today / advance / hunt / birds (swallows?)? (Menzies, 50511,2524)

Wu-wu (day 55) / crack-making / diviner Quarrel (?) / divines: / perhaps / king / himself /leads to / trap (elk)? (Li, 1981 #425)

Gui-si (day 30) / crack-making / diviner Bell-Stroke / divines: / (*this*) xun (= week) / not have / misfortune? / King / prognosticates / says / it is (*or:* you) / this / also / have / disaster / like / (unknown divination estimate)./ Jia-wu (day 31) / king / advances / (*to*) hunt / rhinos. / Small ministers / cooperate (PEN?) / chariot / horse / collide. / Driver (of) / royal / chariot / Prince Shoulderpack / also / falls. (Li, 1981 #505 & JGWZD p. 1035)

Harvest

Wu-wu (day 55) / crack-making / diviner Temple of Ancestress / divines: / spill libation / pray (*for*) / harvest / at / Deity Mount Yue / Deity Yellow River / Ancestor Monkey? (Luo, 1913, 7, 5a #2)

It is / ? / pray (*for*) / harvest / Deity Mount One (*or*: High, Celestial). / In / PLN: Mulberry Tree / field / give (*offering*)? (Menzies, B1814, 184)

...-yin / crack-making / diviner ? / divines: / rainbow (*appeared*) / perhaps / harvest? (Li, 1981 #292)

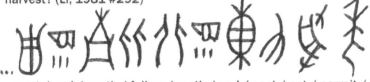

...west / and / south / follow / north / and / east / not / permit / harvest? (Hu, 3, 2#46)

Geng-chen (day 17) / crack-making / diviner Turbulence / divines: / frontier states / permit / harvest? (Li, 1981 #284)

West / states / permit / millet (*harvest*)? / North / states / permit / millet (*harvest*)? / Gui-mao (day 40) / divination: / east / permit / millet (*harvest*)?... (Li, 1981 #291)

Scapula and Plastron

Divination: / turtles / not / perhaps / Southerners / bring (*them*)? (Luo, 1913, 4, 54b #1)

Divination: / STN: Hunting Net / ... / come / king / ... / perhaps / come / ... / indeed / arrive / import / turtle (specific species) / eight / (and another species)/ 500 / fourteenth moon. (JGWZD p. 636)

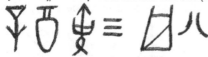

Xin-you (day 58) / turtle shells / three / scapula / eight... (JGWZD p.1587)

Wu-zi (day 25) / Fu ? / consecrates / three / pair (*of scapula or plastrons*) / (*in the presence of*) Deity Mount Yue. (JGWZD p.1027)

Fu Tree-Snake / consecrates / gives / (a) pair / (*in the presence of*) diviner Temple of Ancestress. (JGWZD p.648

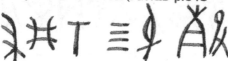

Fu Jing / consecrates / four / pair / (*in the presence of*) diviner Bell-Stroke (Hu, 3,1 #15)

Stars and Possible Stars

End / (*of the*) night / ... / (*constellation?*) dragon / also / great (*or: heavenly*) / star? (JGWZD p. 743)

Jia- / day / ji-si (day 6) / night / to (geng-wu; day 7) / ... / have / new / great / star (= nova) / next to / Fire (= fire star; Mars or Antares) / ... / not / auspicious? / ... / misfortune / perhaps / come / disaster? (Li, 1981 #213)

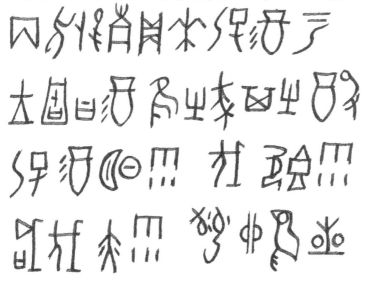

Bing-shen (day 33) / crack-making / diviner Bell-Stroke / divines: / coming / yi-si (day 42) / spill libation (*or:* perform beautifully) / (*for*) Xia Yi ? / King / prognosticates / says: / spill libation (*or:* perform beautifully) / perhaps / have / misfortune (*or:* kill, cut)? / Perhaps / have / wine-offering by breaking vessel (*or:* anomalous weather phenomenon; *or:* thunder)? / Yi-si (day 42) / wine spilling (*or:* perform beautifully) / (*at*) daybreak / rain. / Human decapitation: / cease (*or:* already) / rain. / (*For?*) Tang (*or:* for all *or:* at completion) / decapitation / also / rain. / (*We*) beat a snake / (*and*) split (*it*) / (*for*) bird (*or:* quickly) / star (*or:* cleared up and sunny). (T.T. Chang, 1970: 203 #14.28; translation after Chang, Keightley, Li & Takashima)

Deities of the Directions #1

Ren-shen (day 9) / crack-making / divination: / offering / to / East / Woman (*or* Mother) / (*and*) West / Mother / agreed? (JGWZD, p. 662 & T.T. Chang 1970: 202 # 14.27)

Ji-you (day 46) / crack-making / diviner Bell Stroke / divines: / burned offering / for / East / Mother / nine / bovines? (JGWZD, p. 1300 & T.T. Chang, 1970: 201 # 14.25)

Divination: / burned offering / for / East / Woman (*or* Mother) / three / pigs? (T.T. Chang, 1970: 201, # 14.23)

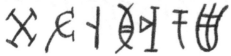

Gui-chou (day 50) / crack-making:/ unknown ritual / for / Deity West? (Hu, 4,4,#160)

For / North Deity / pig (*or* dog?)? (T.T. Chang, 1970: 201 # 14.23)

Possibly / (Deity) West / direction / cursed / me (*or* us)? (T.T. Chang, 1970: 200 #14.19)

Deities of the Directions #2

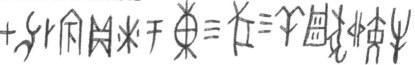

Jia-shen (day 21) / crack-making / diviner Temple of Ancestress / divines: / burned offering / for / Deity East / three / pigs / three / sheep / (and a) black / dog / (and) split / yellow / bovine? (Li, # 536 & T.T. Chang: 1970: 199, # 14.6)

Divination: / burned offering / for / Deity West / shall not / soothe? (C-C. 3, # 618)

Geng-xu (day 47) / crack-making: / pacification / for / four / directions: / (*offer*) perhaps / five / dogs? (Hu, 2,# 487 & JGWZD p. 552 & 954)

Offering / for / Deity West / ten / bovines? / Divination: / not have / misfortune? / (*Has*) Father / Yi / cursed / (*the*) king? (*should there be*) ritual information / for / Tang (or everyone)? / Offering to Di / in the / West? (C-C, 3, #391)

...crack-making / perhaps / Lady Hairpin / (*should*) pray (*for*) / rain / from / southern / direction? (T.T. Chang, 1970: 200, # 14.21)

Divine Cloud/s

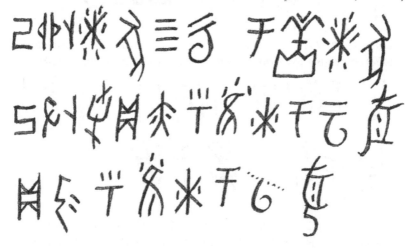

Gui-you (day 10) / crack-making / give / burned offering / for / for (*sic*) / six / Divine Clouds: / five / pigs / split / five / sheep?
Gui-you (day 10) / crack-making / give / burned offering / for / six / Divine Clouds: / six / pigs / split / sheep / six? (T.T.Chang, 1970: 206, #14.32)

Ji-mao (day 16) / crack-making / burned offering / a pig / (*for*) four / Divine Clouds / (and) for / Deity Mount Yue / burned offering / a pig?
Ji-chou (day 26) / crack-making / diviner Quarrel (?) / divines: / also / call / General Little Bird (Sparrow?)/ (to make) burned offering / for / Divine Cloud: / (a) leopard?
Divination: / do not / call / General Sparrow / (to make) burned offering / for / Divine Cloud: / (a) leopard? (C-C, 1,#972 & T.T. Chang, 1970: 206, #14.33)

Deity Peng: the Stormwind #1

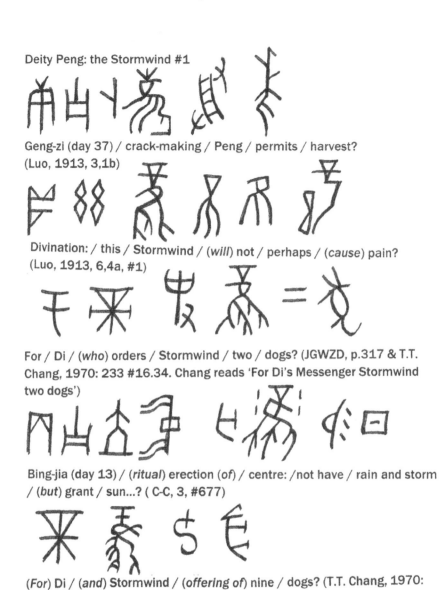

Geng-zi (day 37) / crack-making / Peng / permits / harvest?
(Luo, 1913, 3,1b)

Divination: / this / Stormwind / (*will*) not / perhaps / (*cause*) pain?
(Luo, 1913, 6,4a, #1)

For / Di / (*who*) orders / Stormwind / two / dogs? (JGWZD, p.317 & T.T.
Chang, 1970: 233 #16.34. Chang reads 'For Di's Messenger Stormwind
two dogs')

Bing-jia (day 13) / (*ritual*) erection (*of*) / centre: /not have / rain and storm
/ (*but*) grant / sun...? (C-C, 3, #677)

(*For*) Di / (*and*) Stormwind / (*offering of*) nine / dogs? (T.T. Chang, 1970:
233 # 16.35)

Perhaps / (*we will*) meet / Stormwind? (Hu, 1, 1,#55. A period 3 inscription:
note the sail for wind that accompanies bird Peng).

Deity Peng: the Stormwind #2: Names of Directions and Winds

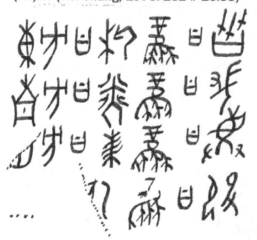

Divination: / Di Offering / at / East /direction / called / Splitter / wind / called / Harmoniser / pray (for) / harvest? Divination: / Di Offering / at / West /direction / called / Shrinker (?) / wind / called / ? / pray (for) / harvest? /Divination: / Di Offering / at / South /direction / called / Long Growth (?) / wind / Human (?) / pray (for) / harvest? / First moon. Divination: / Di Offering / at / North /direction / .... called / Slayer / pray (for)...? (T.T. Chang, 1970: 232 # 16.33)

East / direction / called / Splitter / wind / called / Harmoniser. / South / direction / called / ? / wind / called / Long Growth (?). /West / direction / called / ? / wind / called / Shrinker (?)/ ... ?/ wind / called / Slayer. (Li, 1981 # 204, see also 205)

Goddesses or Early Ancestresses

Geng-zi (day 37) / diviner Zi / crack-making / perhaps / pair of lambs / (*and*) ritual purification / (*at*) Mother Tiger? (JGWZD p. 1331)

Perhaps / pray (*for*) / harvest / at / Mother Wood-Tiger / (*and conduct*) ding cauldron ritual...? (Hu, 2 #461 & JGWZD p. 1332)

Geng-zi (day 37) / diviner Zi / crack-making / perhaps / (*offer*) pair of lambs / (*and*) ritual purification / (*at*) Mother Dragon? (JGWZD p. 1262)

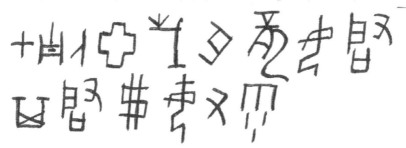

Jia-zi (day 1) / crack-making / ancestral tomb (*place or person?*) / misfortune / ear (*person or state?*) / (*should*) Mother Dragon / receive report ? / Is it / (*if she*) receives report / not / Mother (*Dragon*) / give / rain? (Li, 1981# 531& JGWZD p. 1287)

Shall (I) / pray (*before*) / Bi Gui, / Mother ?,/ Bi Jia / (&) Mother Venerable Dragon / perhaps...? (C-C, 1 #1716)

Deity Er (Child with Open Fontanel)

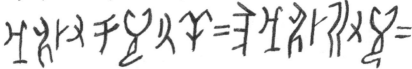

Wu-shen (day 45) / crack-making: / offering / for / Deity Er / raise / (a) sheep / (and) two / dogs (or pigs)? / Wu-shen / crack-making / shall not / offer / (to) Deity Er / two? (Chen, 1970 #54)

...-wei / crack-making: / perhaps / request / rain / at / Deity Er? (Hu. 2 #420)

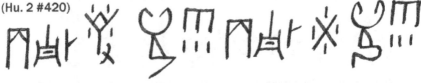

Bing-zi (day 13) / crack-making: / fire-ritual / (for) Deity Er / (causes) rain? Bing-zi / crack-making: / burned offering / (for) Deity Er / (causes) rain? (Hu, 5 #110)

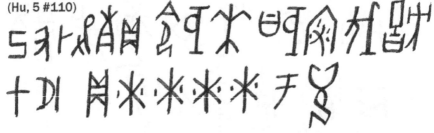

Ji-chou (day 26) / crack-making: / diviner Bell-Stroke / divines: / (shall the king) order / Round Axe (State and personal name)/ (to) come / (and) authorise / (general) STN / PEN / (to) war / (against) Chin-Beard / fang-state / in /month / ten? Divination: / burned offering / burned offering / burned offering / burned offering /for / Deity Er? (C-C, 3 #525)

Ji-wei (day 56) / Divination: / (on) geng-shen (day 57) / spill libation / (and) burned offering / for / Deity Er / two / pair of lambs / butchered and laid out / large / pair of cattle / (causes) rain? (Li, 1981 # 6)

Deity Huang He: The Yellow River #1

Pray / at / Yellow River / (*offer*) three / pairs of sheep. / Pacification?
(Chen, 1970 #58)

Wu-wu (day 55) / crack-making / diviner Quarrel (?) / divines: / this / xin-you (day 58) / assemble / (*for*) libation spilling / (*for*) Yellow River?
(Luo, 1913, 32a #3)

Burned offering / for / Yellow River / one / pair of sheep / bury / two / pair of sheep? (Luo, 1913: 32b #1)

Geng-zi (day 37) / crack-making / diviner Quarrel (?) / divines: /perhaps/ end of the ritual year (*celebration*): / at (for) / Yellow River / bring (*offerings*) / (*for all*) Great / Deities / all the way / to / many / younger generations (*of ancestors*)? (Menzies 50091,2332)

Divination: / shall not / dance / (*for*) Yellow River / not have / perhaps / rain? (JGWZD p. 1186 & T.T. Chang, 1970: 171 #12.13)

Geng-chen (day 17) / divination: / solar / eclipse. / Perhaps / ritual report / for / Deity Yellow River?
(JGWZD p.1366 & T.T. Chang, 1970: 175 #12.22)0

Deity Huang He: The Yellow River #2

Geng-xu (day 47) / crack-making / diviner Bell-Stroke / divines: / for / Yellow River / offer / thanks (*ritual*)? (JGWZD p. 1185)

...cattle / drowning / for / Yellow River / request / harvest? (C-C, 1 #86)

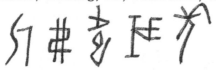

Yellow River / not / (*has*) cursed / my (*our*) / harvest? (C-C, 1 #407)

Ren-yin (day 39) / crack-making / diviner Bell-Stroke / divines: / (*has the*) Yellow River / cursed / (*the*) king? (T.T. Chang, 1970: 172 #12.16)

Xin-wei (day 8) / crack-making / diviner Bell-Stroke / divines: / (*shall the*) king / not / go / (*to*) war (against) Chin-Beard / Fang...? Ren-shen (day 9) / crack-making / diviner Bell-Stroke / divines: / at / Yellow River / beg (*for help*) / (*against*) / Chin-Beard / Fang? (T.T. Chang, 1970: 173 #12.17)

Xin-chou (day 38) / crack-making: / for / Yellow River / (*offer*) concubine? (T.T. Chang, 1970: 177 # 12.31)

River Gods

Wu-wu (day 55) / crack-making: / king / (*make*) burned offering / (*for*)
Deity Turtle River? (Hu, 1, 1 #20)

...pray (for) / millet / at / Deity River Excellent (*today: River Zhang*) / (*will*)
give / great / (*rain*)? (Hu, 5 #123 & T.T. Chang, 1970: 181 #12.43)

King / perhaps / offer / for / Deity River Excellent / on / right / cliff / burn
offering on a pyre: / gives / rain? (T.T. Chang, 1970: 183 #12.45)

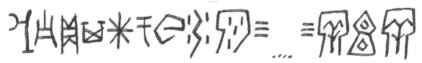

Wu-zi (day 25) / divination: / perhaps / burned offering / for / Deity River
Turbulence (*today: Heng Shui*) / (*at the*) source / three / .... / three / pair of
sheep / butchered and lay out / pair of sheep? / (Li, 1981 # 61. The second
part of the divination repeats the question offering pairs of cattle)

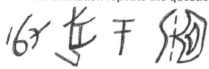

....beat to death / dog / for / Deity River Ear? (JGWZD p.1210 & T.T. Chang,
1970: 183 #12.50)

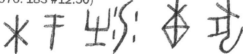

Burned offering / for / Deity River Have (*River Wei, perhaps a river south of
the Shang domain*) / perhaps / dog? (T.T. Chang, 1970: 183 #12.49 &
JGWZD p.1184)

Deity Mount Yue (Sheep Mountain) #1

Ding-si (day 54) / crack-making / diviner Temple of Ancestress / divines: / burned offering / for / Deity Mount Yue? / Not have / disaster? (Luo, 1913,51a #1)

Gui-you (day 10) / crack-making / divination: / burned offering / for / Deity Mount Yue / pair of lambs / split / three / pair of sheep? Luo, 1913, 7, 25b #2)

Divination: / request (*help against*) / Chin-Beard / Fang: / for / Deity Mount Yue / one / bovine? Divination: / assemble / (*for*) war / (*against*) Chin-Beard / Fang? (Gu Wen Zi Yan Jiu (3), 1980, ill. p.59 #480)

Gui-you (day 10) / crack-making / perhaps / receive (*or:* ear offering) / rain / (*from*) Deity Mount Yue? (Hu, 2 #422)

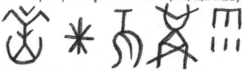

Wu-wu (day 55) / crack-making / diviner Separate / divines: / pray (*for*) / harvest / at / Deity Mount Yue? (Hu, 1,2 #13)

(*Give to*) Deity Mount Yue / burned offering. / Not / encounter / rain? (Hu, 5 #91)

Deity Mount Yue (Sheep Mountain) #2

Ji-you (day 46) / divination: / xin-hai (day 48) / perhaps / burned offering /
for / Deity Mount Yue / one / pair of sheep / split / one / bovine: / rain? /
Ji-you (day 46) / divination: / xin-hai (day 48) /perhaps /burned offering /
for / Deity Mount Yue: / rain? / Perhaps / burned offering / for / Deity
Mount Yue / three / pair of sheep (Hu, 5 #89)

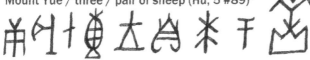

Geng-xu (day 47) / crack-making: / perhaps / king / himself / prays / at /
Deity Mount Yue? (Hu, 5 #118 & T.T. Chang, 1970: 187 #13.10)

At / Deity Mount Yue's / temple / pour libation / have / rain? (T.T. Chang,
1970: 188 #13.15)

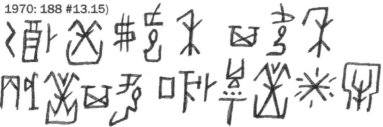

Yi-you (day 22) / crack-making / Mount Yue / (has) not / cursed / (the)
millet? Perhaps / cursed / millet? / Bing-xu (day 23) / Mount Yue /
perhaps / cursed? Ding-hai (day 24) crack-making: /pacify / Mount Yue
/(with) burned offering / pair of cattle? (T.T. Chang, 1970: 186 #13.3)

Mountain Deities #1

(due to varied writing of the characters of mountain and fire, some of the more obscure deities may actually be related to fire).

Gui-si (day 30) crack-making / burned offering / (*for*) Deity Mount Eye? (C-C, 1 #1130; USB #146; JGWZD p.1128; T.T. Chang 1970: 189 #13.17)

Burned offering / (*for*) Deity Mount Yue / (*and*) burned offering / (*for*) Deity Mount Axe? (T.T. Chang, 1970: 189 #13.18 & JGWZD p.1119)

(Day) -bing / burned offering / (*for*) Deity Mount Yue / (*and*) Deity Mount Tilted Head? (T.T. Chang, 1970: 189 #13.19, see also 'Rare Deities #2')

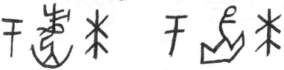

At / Deity Mount Hairpin / pray? / At / Deity Mount Child / pray? (T.T. Chang, 1970: 190 #13.20 & JGWZD p.1126)

Deity Mount (*or:* Fire?) Palace Gate / burned offering / perhaps / pair of lambs? (JGWZD p.1113)

Gui-si (day 30) / divination: / perhaps / burned offering / (*for*) Deity Jade Mountain / (*gives*) rain? (T.T. Chang, 1970: 190 #13.22)

Mountain Deities #2 and Hill Deities

Deity One (*or:* Celestial) Mountain / and / Deity Mount Step (*or:* Trample) / perhaps / (*offer*) pair of lambs / (*will*) give / great / rain? (JGWZD 1126 & T.T. Chang, 1970: 190 #13.21)

Perhaps / pray (*for*) / harvest / (*at*) Deity One (*or:* Celestial) Mountain / (*and*) Deity Mount Step (*or:* Trample) / (*and*) at / Small Mountain (*or* Small Fire): / blood spilling on altar / (*one*) piglet? (JGWZD p. 1131)

Ding-chou (day 14) / crack-making / give / for / five / Mountain Deities / in / PLN / second / moon / crack-making? (T.T. Chang, 1970: 190 #13.23)

Xin- / ..../ divination: / .... / burned offering / for / ten / Mountain Deities? (T.T. Chang, 1970: 191 #13.24)

Divination: / set up libation in vessel / for / Deity Hill Work? (Chen, 1970 #17, also Li, 1981 # 9 & T.T. Chang, 1970: 191 #13.26)

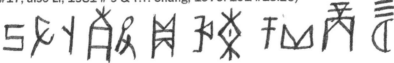

Ji-chou (day 26) / crack-making / diviner Bell-Stroke / divines: / unknown ritual / for / Deity Hill Shang (=Excellent) / (*in the*) fourth / moon? (T.T. Chang, 1970: 191 #13.25. Perhaps an elevated section of the capital?)

531

Di #1

Geng-wu (? *Ought to be geng-xu, day 47*) / crack-making / divination: / (we) have / locusts / perhaps (*it is*) / Di's / order? (Luo, 1913, 5, 25a #1)

Xin-hai (day 48) / crack-making / diviner ? / divines: / this / first / moon / Di / (*will*) not / perhaps / order / rain? (JGWZD p.574)

Geng-xu (day 47) / crack-making / divination: / Di / perhaps / (*makes*) descend / Drought? JGWZD p. 1511 & T.T. Chang, 1970: 213 #15.8)

Crack-making / diviner Quarrel (?) / High / Di / (*makes*) descend / . Drought? (Hu, 3, 1 #31 & T.T. Chang, 1970: 214 #15.10)

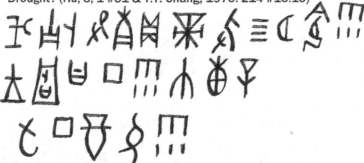

Wu-zi (day 25) / crack-making / diviner Bell-Stroke / divines: / (*will*) Di / up to / fourth / night / order / rain? / King / prognosticates / (*and*) says / day ding / rain. / Not / it is / day xin. / (*Next*) xun-week / ding-you (day 34) / indeed / rain. (Li, 1981 #224 & T.T. Chang, 1970: 212 #15.3)

Di #2

Divination: / Di / perhaps / up to / this / 13th / month / order / thunder? / Di / perhaps / at / birth / (of) first / moon / order / thunder? (T.T. Chang, 1970: 212 #15.4)

Divination: / shall not / (in the) war / (against the) Chin-Beard (state) / Di / not / me (us) / perhaps / grant / support? (Luo, 1913, 6, 58a #4; Li 1981 #388 & T.T. Chang, 1970: 216 #15.16)

Divination: / foreigners / (do) harm / (they) surround (us) / perhaps / Di / ordered / (to) make / us / misfortune? Third month. (C-C, 3 #486 & T.T. Chang, 1970: 215 #15.14)

(*Does*) Di / damage / Tang's / city? (JGWZD p..96)

I§†⌂⺆☆⺚⺭⊞⺬⺚⺆⺬⺛

Ren-yin (day 39) / crack-making / diviner Temple of Ancestress / divines: / as / there is / no / rain / (is) Di / perhaps / (with) this / Dragon City / not / in agreement? (JGWZD p.676 & T.T. Chang, 1970: 218 #15.22)

Xin-mao (day 28) / crack-making / diviner Bell-Stroke / ... / Di / damages / this / city? (C-C, 2, B32 = 28)

Di #3

Xin-chou (day 38) / crack-making / diviner Bell-Stroke / divines: / Di / agrees (*with*) / (*the*) king? (JGWZD p. 676)

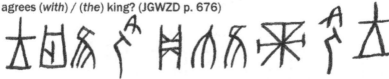

King / (*has*) misfortune / perhaps / (*he is*) reprimanded? / Divination: / not / perhaps / Di / reprimands / (*the*) king? (T.T. Chang, 1970: 221 #15.29)

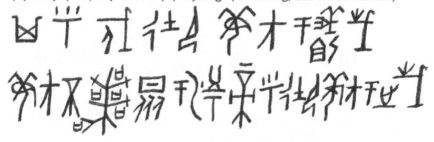

Perhaps / call / frontier-guard / (*to*) resist / Qiang / tribe / at / PLN? / (*Should we*) harm / Qiang / tribe / (*so we*) don't / lose / citizens? / At / Peaceful River / Di / call / to resist / Qiang tribe? / At / this (*place?*) / harm (*them*)? (T.T. Chang, 1970: 224)

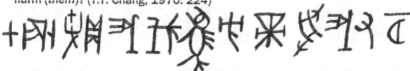

Jia-chen (day 41) / crack-making / diviner Quarrel (?) / divines: / I (*or:* we) / wage war / (*against*) Horse State / (*will*) Di / grant / me (us) / support? / First Month. (T.T. Chang, 1970: 216 #15.15)

Divination: / burned offering / for / Di / Cloud? (Di's cloud? Or Di and Deity Cloud?) (JGWZD p. 1252)

Di #4

Di (*offering*) / at / west? (*or:* Deity West?) (JGWZD p. 1277 see also Menzies B2338, for 'Di North' and 'Di South')

Divination: / Di of the Directions / one / Qiang / two / dogs / split / one / bovine? (or: Di (offering) in all directions; possibly even: to Foreign Di) (JGWZD p. 955)

Geng-wu (day 7) / divination: / locusts / great (*many*) / reside (*here*). / For / Di's / Five / Jade / Ministers / pacification (*ritual*) / in / Zu Yi's / temple / crack-making? (T.T. Chang, 1970: 234 #16,39)

King / gives / offering with axe-cut / for / Di's / Five / Ministers / ritual (to restore order) / perhaps / not have / rain? (JGWZD p.321)

Gui-you (day 10) / divination: / Di's / five / jade (*ministers*) / perhaps / three / pair of bovines...? (Li, 1981 #210)

Yi-mao (day 52) / crack-making / perhaps / give / offering with axe-cut / for / Di Ding (= Wu Ding) / one / pair of bovines? (Hu, 1, 1 #62)

Di #5

Divination: / Tang / (*gives*) host ritual / for / Di? / Divination: / Ta Jia / (*gives*) host ritual / for / Tang? /Divination: /Zu Yi / (*gives*) host ritual / for / Di? (T.T. Chang, 1970: 227 #16.14)

Divination: / Di (*offering*)/at (=with) / Wang Hai? (T.T. Chang, 1970: 227 #16.15)

Di offering / at (*or for* = with) / deity Yellow River? (T.T. Chang, 1970: 228, #16.19)

Ding-si (day 54) / crack-making / divination: / Di ritual offering / bird sacrifice? / Divination: Di ritual offering / bird sacrifice / three / sheep / three / pigs / three / dogs? (Luo, 1913: 4, 17b #3)

Jia-xu (day 11) / shall not / Di ritual offering / (one) dog? / Ding-chou (day 14) / crack-making / king / shall not / offer to Di / (one) tiger? (JGWZD p. 528 & T.T. Chang, 1970: 223 #16.2)

(Geng-)xu (day 47) /crack-making / General Panther /shall not (*perform*) / Di ritual / at / Turtle River: / (*shall there be*) rain? (JGWZD p.1438 & T.T. Chang, 1970: 228 #16.20)

Di #6

Divination: / Di ritual offering / at / east / bury / black / dog / burned offering / three / pair of sheep / split / yellow / cattle (skull?)? (Hu, 3, 2 #5 & T.T. Chang, 1970: 229 #16.22)

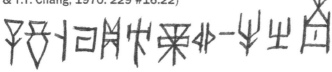

Xin-you (day 58) / crack-making / diviner Turbulence / divines: / directional / Di offering ritual / split / one / bovine / give / South? (Luo, 1913: 7, 1a #1; South = 'to the south', 'to Deity South' or a member of the South state).

Yi-hai (day 12) / crack-making / diviner Quarrel (?): / Di ritual offering / at (or: for) / west? / Auspicious. (C-C, 3 #362)

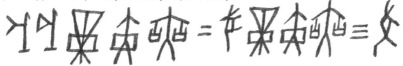

Wu-xu (day 35) / Di ritual offering / (*together with*) Yi Yin / dancing / (*and*) two / dogs? Di ritual offering / (*together with*) Yi Yin / dancing / (*and*) three / dogs? (Luo, 1913: 6, 21a #2 & T.T. Chang, 1970: 228 #16.18)

Divination: / directional / Di ritual offering / it is / pour libation / (*at, for or with*) Deity Mount Yue? (Menzies #B1112,729)

Gui-wei (day 20) / crack-making / Di ritual offering / (*together with*) Xia Yi?
Gui-wei / crack-making / offer / axe-sacrificed / bovine / for / Xia Yi?
(T.T. Chang, 1970: 227, 16.17)

Earth Deities #1

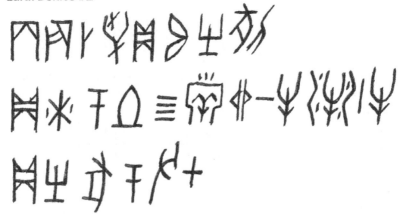

Bing-chen (day 53) / crack-making / diviner Quarrel (?) / divines / (*the*) army / has / suffered losses? Divination: / burned offering / for / Earth deity: / four / pairs of lambs / split / one / bovine / drown / ten / bovines? Divination: / offer / pig / for / Father / Jia?
(Chen, B. #17, Li, 1981 # 9 & JGWZD p. 1204)

Gui-hai (day 60) / crack-making / give / Earth Deity / burned offering / (a) Qiang prisoner of war / (*and*) one / pair of lambs / butchered and laid out raw. (Li, 1981, #10)

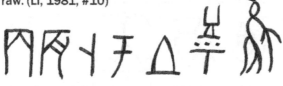

Bing-chen (day 53) / crack-making / at / Earth Deity / pacification / (*of the*) stormwind? (T.T. Chang, 1970: 192 # 14.4)

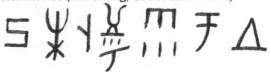

Ji-wei (day 56) / crack-making / pacification / (*of the*) rain / at / Earth Deity? (T.T. Chang, 1970: 192 # 14.2)

Earth Deities #2

Divination: / shall not / pray (*for*) / harvest / at / State (PLN) / Earth Deity?
(JGWZD p. 711 & T.T. Chang, 1970: 197 # 14.4)

Jia-wu (day 31) / crack-making / diviner Endurer (*or* Goer?) /divines: /
eastern / Earth Deity / grants / harvest? (Li, 1981: 273. See also Li 275 for
western Earth Deity and 276 for northern earth Deity granting harvest).

Northern / Earth Deity / grants / harvest? / Auspicious. Western / Earth
Deity / grants / harvest? Auspicious. /Southern / Earth Deity / grants /
harvest? Auspicious. Eastern / Earth Deity / grants / harvest? (Li, 1981 #
277. A period 5b inscription, note writing of 'earth' as 'male')

Ren-shen (day 9) / crack-making / (*shall we make*) music / (*for*) four /
Earth Deities / (*and*) for / deity or state name ...? (Hu, 3,1,#131)

Gui-chou (day 50) / crack-making / (*we*) shall / make offerings / (*for*) PLN
Bo (*Tang's residence*) / Earth Deity. / Perhaps / (*make*) divine /goodness?
(T.T.Chang, 1970: 197 # 14.13 proposes that the last signs should be read
'harmonization ritual')

Deity, Deities or Ancestor/s Double Snake

Xin-mao (day 28) / crack-making: / burned offering / for / Double Snakes?
(Luo, 1913, 4, 52b #1)

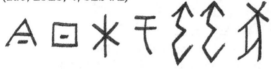

This / day / burned / offering / for / Double Snakes / (*a*) pig?
(Luo, 1913, 4, 55a#3)

Geng-xu (day 47) / crack-making / diviner: Bell-Stroke / divines: / Double
Snakes / (*have*) not / me (or us) / cursed? (JGWZD p. 1427)

Ren-chen (day 29) / crack-making / next / jia-wu (day 31) / burned offering
/ for / Double Snakes / goat / and / castrated pig?
(T.T. Chang, 1970: 207, #14.37 & JGWZD # 1427)

Divination: / *PEN:* To Taste / (*conduct at*) Yellow River / burned offering /
for / Double Snakes / receive / rain? / Divination: / call / to dance / for /
Double Snakes? (T.T. Chang, 1970: 206, #14.34)

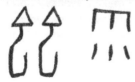

Double Snakes / (*grant?*) rain? (Menzies, #S0403, 3278)

Rare Deities #1

Divine: / at / centipede (?) / deity / request / harvest? (JGWZD, p. 1432)

Crack-making / perhaps / ask (*for*) / harvest / at / centipede (?) / deity / gives / great / rain? (JGWZD, p. 1432)

Gui-hai (day 60, *last day of the cycle*) / crack-making / perhaps / wine spilling / (*for*) deity spider (?) / at (*or together with?*) / Yellow River deity? (JGWZD 1446)

At / drum ritual / clothes offering / indeed / give (to) / spider (?) deity. / King / receives / support? (JGWZD, p. 1446)

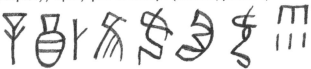

Offering / (*by the*) king / (*for*) deity Tilted Head / decapitate / three (*people?*) / split / pair of sheep? (JGWZD, p. 1164)

Xin-you (day 58) / crack-making / perhaps / Woman (*deity or ancestress*) ? / (*has*) cursed / (*the*) rain? (JGWZD, p.1302)

Rare Deities #2

Burned offering / sheep / twenty / for / unknown deity / agreed? (JGWZD p.1013)

At / ding-hai (day 24) / music making (*for*) / unknown deity / not / (*have*) rain? (JGWZD p. 1374)

...-you / pray (*for*) / millet / at / unknown deity? (C-C, 1 # 1644)

Pray (*for*) / harvest / at / unknown deity? (T.T. Chang, 1970: 208 # 14.39)

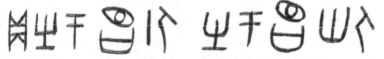

Divination: / offer / for / unknown deity / ten / humans? / Offer / for / unknown deity / thirty / humans? (T.T. Chang, 1970: 208 # 14.41)

...-shen / crack-making / (*deity*) Fu / (*grants*) rain? (Hu, 5 # 108)

...you / (*deity*) Fu / (*grants*) rain? (Hu, 5 #109)

Rare Deities, Ancestors or Spirits #3

Yi-mao (day 52) / divination: / raise / human decapitation offering / turtle deity (*or*: ancestor?) / five / Qiang / three / pair of bovines? (Hu, 2 #495)

Ji-wei (day 56) / crack-making / purification ritual / (*for*) Prince / PÉN? / at / (*deity or ancestress*) Woman Owl? (JGWZD p. 409)

Divination: / burned offering / for / Deity Tree / three / castrated pigs / three / sheep? (Hu, 3,1 #50 & JGWZD p. 640)

Ji-chou (day 26) / divination: / for / Wood / (*at*) night / spill libation? (JGWZD p.667)

Three / pair of bovines / (*for*) Great Forest? (JGWZD p. 669)

Offering (?) / named: / one thousand / Great Forest / king / (*performs*) unknown ritual / at the end / (*offers*) eight / dogs / eight / castrated pigs / ... / three / sheep, / Southerners / four? / Split / for / east / direction / (*called*) Splitter / three / bovines / three / sheep? / South... (C-C, 3 #472)

Unspecified Deities and Ancestors

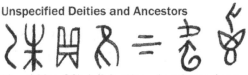

Yi-wei (day 32) / divination: / perhaps / upper and lower gods / (*have*) cursed / PEN? (JGWZD p.6)

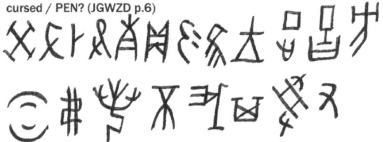

Gui-chou (day 50) / crack-making / diviner Bell-Stroke / divines: / shall not / perhaps / (*the*) king / restore order (= punitive expedition) / (*against*) Chin-Beard / State? / Upper and lower gods / (*do*) not / agree / (*and do*) not / myself (*or:* us) / perhaps / grant / support? (JGWZD p.6)

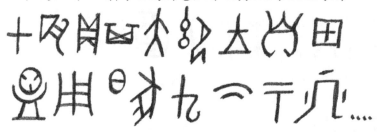

Jia-chen (day 41) / divination: / perhaps / great / ritual purification / (*of the*) king / at / Shang Jia! / blood offering in bowl / use / white / boar / nine / high / gods / (*receive*) blood on the altar...? (JGWZD p. 749)

Ji-mao (day 16) / divination / request / at / Shang Jia / (*and*) six / gods? (Hu, 2, #530)

...-mao / crack-making / request / rain / (from) nine / gods? (T.T. Chang, 1970: 100 #6.16)

Ghosts & Unspecified Ancestors

Ding-wei (day 44) / crack-making / king / divines: / many / ghosts / (*in my*)
dreams / not have / coming / disaster? (USS, #217; C-C, 1, # 1213)

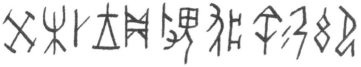

Gui-wei (day 20) / crack-making / king / divines: / ghost-fear / (*in my*)
dreams / (*should*) I / not / (*have a*) ritual purification? (JGWZD,p.1024)

Divination: / (*is*) possibly / auspicious / (*the*) eleventh Moon?
Divination: / (*will there be*) possibly / ghosts? (USS # 359; C-C, 1,#1354)

Divination: / ancestral tombs / many / ghost / dreams; / (*will I*) not have /
dreams / fourth moon? (Luo, 1913: 4, 18a, #2; also Li # 501. Li reads
'disease' instead of 'dreams'.)

Crack-making / divination: / ghost / not / (*bring*) misfortune?
(Hu, 1,5,#221)

Divination / (*is there a*) ghost ? Divination / (*is it*) auspicious?
(Hu, 4, 2, #170)

Early Ancestors #1

Ren-xu (day 59) / king / speaks: / Ancestor Monkey / thanks-giving (*ritual*) / (*one*) bovine? / First / moon. (C-C, 1 #1298)

(*before*)...Ancestor Monkey / and/ Shang Jia / perhaps / purification ritual? (JGWZD p.623)

Divination: / pray (*for*) / harvest / at / Ancestor Monkey / (*offer*) nine / bovines? (T.T. Chang, 1970: 94 #6.2)

(*Should*) Wang Hai / (*receive*) four / sheep / four / pigs / five / sheep? ... (USB #92)

Gui-mao (day 40) / divination: / should not / bring / (*to*) remote / grandfather / Wang Hai / rhino horn offering (?) / (*and*) perhaps / burned offering? (JGWZD p.482)

Jia-chen (day 41) / crack-making / diviner Bell-Stroke / divines: / (*on the*) coming / xin-hai (day 48) / burned offering / for / Wang Hai / thirty / bovines? (Li, 1981 #17)

Early Ancestors #2

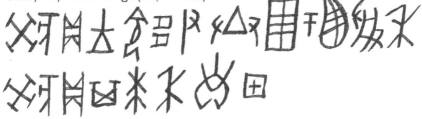

Ding-mao (day 4) / divination: / STN / bring / Qiang (*captives*). / Perhaps /
use (*them*) / for / Shang Jia / blood on the altar / (*and for all ancestors*)
until / to / father Ding? (Hu, 5 #119)

Gui-Hai (day 60) / divination: / king / orders / many / administrators /
agricultural work / (*at the*) fields / in / west / receive / grains? / Gui-hai /
divination: / request / harvest / at / Shang Jia? (T.T. Chang, 1970: 97 #6.8)

Yi-you (day 22) / (*for*) Di / human decapitation / at (= with) Shang Jia?
(Hu, 2, #520 & T.T. Chang, 1970: 227 #16.16)

Geng-chen (day 17) / crack-making: / offer: / raise / human decapitation /
for / Shang Jia / three / Qiang / (and) nine / pair of lambs? (Hu, 2 #512)

Divination: / ritual report / (*about*) Chin-Beard / State / for / Shang Jia? /
Divination: / for / Tang / ritual report? / Divination: / King / follows /
General Wash Feet / Shield (*to war*)? (T.T. Chang 1970: 112 #7.10)

Early Ancestors #3

Ji-si (day 6) / divination: / (*on*) hai (day 12) / offering / for / Tang / three / pair of sheep? (Hu, 3,1 #37)

Divination: / make / great / city / at / Tang's / earth (= former domain)? (C-C, 3 #611)

Jia-zi (day 1) / king / makes cracks / (*and*) speaks: / next / yi-chou (day 2) / perhaps / spill libation / (*and perform*) feather dance / for / Tang? (Li, 1981 #48)

Yi-hai (day 12) / crack-making / diviner Carrier / divines: / hosting / (*of*) Tang / offer cooked grains / not / encounter / rain / (*in the*) seventh month? (T.T. Chang, 1970: 155 #10.24)

Ji-chou (day 2) / crack-making / in / small / temple / offering / raise / a sacrifice with axe-cut / for / Ta Yi (=Tang)... (Li, 1981 #131)

Divination: / ritual purification / at / Tang / Tai Jia / Tai Ding / (and) Grandfather Yi / (*offer*) / one hundred / Qiang / (and) one hundred / pair of sheep? Divination: / ritual purification / perhaps / (*offer*) bovines / three hundred? (T.T. Chang, 1970: 88 #5.20)

Early Ancestors #4

Yi-wei (day 32) / crack-making / shall not / use (= sacrifice) / Qiang / for / Tang? (JGWZD p. 1553)

Divination: / Tai Jia / host ritual / for / Tang? (JGWZD p. 1536)

Xin-chou (day 38) / crack-making / king / perhaps / offer / raise / human decapitation / (for) Tai Yi / perhaps / (*fulfil*) old / promise of the crown prince / use (= sacrifice) / humans / fifteen? (T.T. Chang, 1970: 128 #8.8)

Divination: / perhaps / extend (*or:* go to) / ritual purification / at / Tai Wu / share a meal (*with the ancestor*)? (JGWZD p. 1014)

Next / yi-you (day 22) / offer / human decapitation / for / five / deities: / Shang Jia / Tang / Tai Ding / Tai Jia / (*and*) Zu Yi? (JGWZD p. 1553)

Yi-you (day 22) / crack-making / divination: / give / burned offering / for / Tai Yi / Tai Ding / Tai Jia? (Hu, 3,1 #135)

Early Ancestors #5

Tai Ding / cursed / us? (T.T. Chang 1970: 83 #5.7)

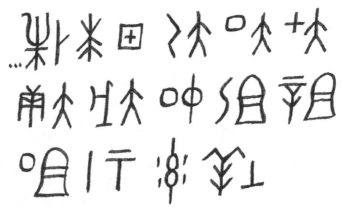

...-wei / crack-making / request / (*from*) Shang Jia / Tai Yi / Tai Ding / Tai Jia / Tai Geng / Wu Geng / Zhong Ding / Zu Yi / Zu Xin / Zu Ding / (*all in all*) ten / gods / (*make offering*) strangle / male sheep? (T.T. Chang, 1970: 100 #6.15; similar inscriptions Li, 1981 #22 & 23)

Ding-hai (day 24) / crack-making / diviner Bell-Stroke / divines: / past / yi-you (day 22) / preparation / return (of the army?) / ritual purification / ..../ (*for*) Tai Ding / Tai Jia / Zu Yi / (*offer*) one hundred / cups of spiced wine / one hundred / Qiang / split / three hundred... (Li, 1981 #54)

Early Ancestors #6

Divination: / for / Tai Jia / ritual report / Chin-Beard / State / (has) emerged (= invaded us)? / Ritual report / (about the) Chin-Beard / for / Yi Yin? (T.T. Chang, 1970: 111 #7.9)

Divination: / Chin-Beard / State / (has) emerged / perhaps / Yi Yin / cursed / us? (Hu, 2 #57 & T.T. Chang, 1970: 83 #5.6)

Xin-you (day 58) / crack-making / offering / (to) Yi Yin / human decapitation? (Menzies S0104, 2084)

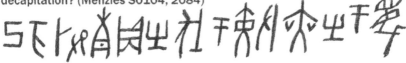

Ji-hai (day 36) / crack-making / diviner Bell-Stroke / divines: / offer / human decapitation / for / Yi Yin / dance? / Offer / at (or: for) / old administrators (or: unknown ancestor)? (Luo, 1913, 52b #1)

Jia-xu (day 11) / crack-making / it is / prayer (for) / rain. / For / Yi Yin / dance? (JGWZD p.1175.)

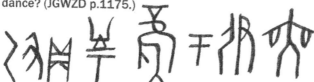

Yi-chou (day 2) / divination: / pacify / Deity Stormwind. / For / Yi Yin / dance? (T.T. Chang, 1970: 86 #5.15)

Royal Activities #1

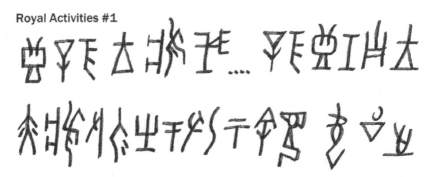

Night to / xin-hai (day 48) / king / dreams: / I /.... / Xin-hai (day 48) / night to / ren-zi (day 49) / king / also / dreams: / Yi Yin / offer / .... / for (*or:* at) Father Yi / ancestral tablet (?) / I / observe (*or:* receive *or* hold audience)? / Curse / ? / stop? (Luo, 1913: 7, 33a #1)

Wu-yin (day 15) / crack-making / diviner Command / divines: / king / unknown ritual / perhaps / auspicious? (Menzies # S0289, 2730)

Perhaps / king / prays? (Menzies #B2411, 395)

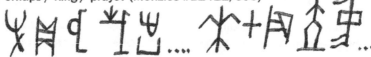

Diviner Quarrel (?) / divines: / STN Round Axe / misfortune / emerges / ... / coming / jia-chen (day 41) / erect / centre/ ...? (C-C, 3 #503)

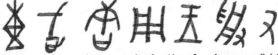

Perhaps / temple name (*selection for deceased*)/ Geng pronounced / use. / King / grants / support? (JGWZD 1365)

King / gives / offering with axe blow / for / High Di's / Five / Ministers / establish order / perhaps / not have / rain? (JGWZD p.1529)

Royal Activities #2

...hai / crack-making / diviner Command / divines: / king / (*performs*)
unknown ritual / swallows / here / today / perhaps / auspicious? Eighth
month / good luck / swallows. (Luo, 1913, 6, 43b #2 & JGWZD p.1259)

Ren-zi (day 49) / (crack-making) / diviner Temple of Ancestress / divines: /
Chin-Beard / State / (*has*) emerged. / King / (*performs*) drink offering? /
Fifth month. (Hu, 3 #162)

Divination: / king / unwell / perhaps / (*offer?*) female tiger? (JGWZD p. 81)

Geng-xu (day 47) / crack-making / I / (*have*) ear / singing. / Have / ritual
purification / at / Zu Geng...? (T.T. Chang, 1970: 54 #3.9)

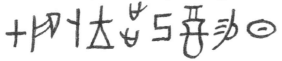

Jia-chen (day 41) / crack-making: / king / goes / ji-you (day 46) / grant /
sun? (Hu, 5 #12. King has good weather or grants boons?)

Ding-mao (day 4) / divination: / king / it is / raise / Jade cong /(*and*)
burned offering: / three / pair of bovines, / split ...? (Hu, 2 #537 & JGWZD
p.430)

Royal Activities #3

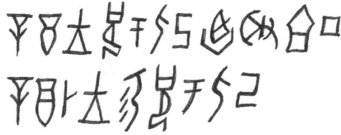

Wu-yin (day 15) / crack-making / diviner Troop / divines: / king / hosts /
Tai Wu / eclipse (*occurs*). / Not have / misfortune? (JGWZD p.1141)

Xin-you (day 58) / king / prays / at / Bi Ji / ? / ear-offering / (*for*) Zu Ding?
Xin-you / crack-making / king / shall not / pray / at / Bi Ji? (Li, 1981 #80)

Yi-chou (day 2) / crack-making: / (*king*) spill libation / (*and have*) ritual
purification / at / Bi Geng? / Decapitate humans / twenty / (*offer*) spiced
wine / thirty (*cups*)? (T.T. Chang, 1970: 78 #4.27)

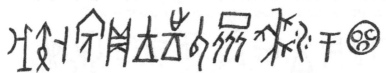

Divination: / inspect / cattle / hundred?/ Divination: / shall not / advance /
inspect cattle? / Divination: / king / advances / inspects / cattle? (Luo,
1913, 3, 23a #2)

Wu-yin (day 15) / crack-making / diviner Temple of Ancestress / divines: /
king / leads / brings / citizens / (*to plant?*) water millet / at / PLN Window
(T.T. Chang, 1970: 253 #18.26)

Royal Activities #4

Geng-xu (day 47) / crack-making / diviner Bell-Stroke / divines: / king / erects (= plants) / water millet. / Receive / harvest? (T.T. Chang, 1970: 253 #18.24)

Geng-zi (day 37) / crack-making / divination: /king / perhaps / observe / ploughing (with fork-plough)? Perhaps / lead / twelfth month? (T.T. Chang, 1970: 254 #18.27)

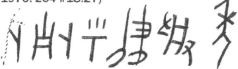

Bing-zi (day 13)/ crack-making: / call / ... / (for) ploughing? / Receive / (*good*) harvest? (Luo, 1913, 7, 15b #1)

...at / PLN ? / not have / disaster? / At / PLN Mulberry Tree / not have / disaster? / At / PLN ? / not have / disaster? (Li, 1981 #343)

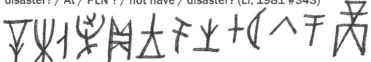

Xin-wei (day 8) / crack-making / diviner Quarrel (?) / divines: / king / at / birth / (*of*) seventh month / enter / at / Shang (city or state)? (Luo, 1913, 2, 1a #2)

Ji-you (day 46) / crack-making / king / shall not / perhaps / die / ninth month? Ji-you / crack-making: / king / not / die? (Li, 1981 #445)

Royal Activities #5

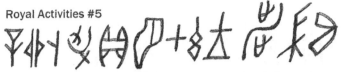

Xin-mao (day 28) / crack-making / diviner Quarrel (?) / divines / next / jia-wu (day 31) / king / crosses river / returns (with the army)? (Luo, 1913, 5, 29a #1, similar in Hu, 2 #219)

Ding-you (day 34) / crack-making / diviner Bell-Stroke / divines: / this / (*unknown*) season / king / raises / people / five thousand / (*to*) set things right (=punitive expedition) / (*against*?) Earth / State / grant / have / support? / Third moon. (Li, 1981 #384)

King / perhaps / Dragon / State / (*wage*) war? (*Or*) king / perhaps / STN Man / punitive expedition? / Divination: / king / follows / General Far Seeing High Climber / (*to*) war? / King / perhaps / (*go with*) General Wash Feet Shield? / For / Tang/ ritual report / (*and to all ancestors up to*) arriving / at / (*Zu*) Ding / ritual report? /(*Or*) for Shang Jia / and / Tang (*only*)? (T.T. Chang, 1970: 115 #7.15)

Ding-wei (day 44) / crack-making / diviner ? / divines: / Man / State / promise / (*to*) see / new / family. / Now / autumn / king / perhaps / follows? (JGWZD p. 409)

Ritualist Lady E; possibly a sister of King Wu Ding.

Ji-you (day 46) / crack-making / (the) king / divines: / Ē / gives birth /
indeed / it is / in (the) / first / moon...? (JGWZD, # 1311)

Divination: / shall not / at / ding (day) / (be a) prayer (for) / harvest /
(made by) E? (Hu, 6, 2, #11)

Divination: / (I) dreamed: / (of) E. / Not / perhaps / (have) misfortune? (T.T.
Chang, 1970: 39; #1.13)

Jia-zi (day 1) / crack-making / diviner Temple of Ancestress / divines: /
(should) in the evening / (there be a) prayer / (for) rain / (by) E / at (or of) /
Deity Yellow River? (T.T. Chang, 1970: 179, # 12.37)

Jia-zi (day 1) / crack-making / diviner Temple of Ancestress / divines: /at /
Yue Mountain / prayer (for) / rain / (by) E? (T.T. Chang, 1970: 188, #13.14)

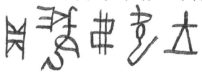

Divination: / E / (has) not / cursed / (the) king? (JGWZD, p.1311)
After her death, Lady E became a dangerous ancestress. She received
offerings (Chang, 1970: 70) and ritual reports (JGWZD p. 1311)

Fu Hao #1

Fu Hao / perhaps / offer / (*at the*) spring? (Hu, 2 #243)

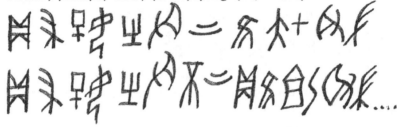

Divination: / Fu Hao / offer / ear-sacrifice / (*to*) upper gods./ Perhaps / Tai Jia / (*receives*) ear sacrifice / (*of the*) fu? Divination: / Fu Hao / offers / ear-sacrifice / not / upper gods? / Divination: / is it / Zu Yi / (*receives*) ear-sacrifice / fu...? (USB #45 & C-C, 1, 1020)

Jia-xu (day 11) / crack-making / diviner Turbulence / divines: / ritual purification / (*of*) Fu Hao / at / Father Yi / promise / offer a servant? (C-C, 1 #1701)

Ji-mao (day 16) / crack-making / diviner Bell-Stroke / divines: / ritual purification / (*of*) Fu Hao / at / Father Yi / (*offer*) bowl / (*of*) sheep (*meat*) / (*and*) thirty / pigs / (*and*) promise / ten / pair of sheep? (JGWZD p. 522)

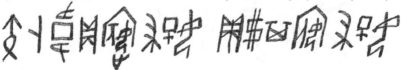

...-yin / crack-making / diviner Separate / divines: / hosting ritual / (*performed by?*) Fu Hao? Divination: shall not / perhaps / hosting ritual / (*be performed by*) Fu Hao? (Luo, 1913,7,27b #2)

Fu Hao #2

Divination: / call / Fu Hao / inspect (*or*: grant audience) / many / fu (=ladies) / at / PLN: Three Sheep? (Menzies, B1128, 542)

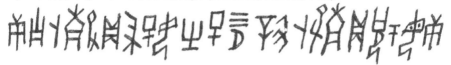

Geng-zi (day 37) / crack-making / diviner Bell-Stroke / divines: / Fu Hao / has / child (*or*: prince) third month? Xin-chou (day 38) / crack-making / diviner Bell-Stroke / divines / pray / at / Mother Geng? (Li, 1981 #129 & T.T. Chang, 1970: 101 #6.19 & Gu Wen Zi Yan Jiu, 3, 1980: 53 #387)

Ren-xu (day 59) / crack-making / diviner Temple of Ancestress / divines: / Fu Hao / (*gives*) birth / (to a) son? (Hu, 2 #244)

Divination: / Fu Hao / has / disease / perhaps / (*she*) has / (*been*) cursed? Divination: / perhaps / Father Yi / reprimands / Fu Hao? (T.T. Chang, 1970: 43 #1.21)

Divination: Fu Hao / (*was exposed to*) disastrous / wind / (*she*) has / disease? (T.T. Chang, 1970. 45 #1.26)

...Diviner Quarrel (?) / divines: / Fu Hao / (*has?*) dragon? (JGWZD p.1261)

Fu Hao #3

Divination: / Bi Ji / cursed / Fu Hao's / child (*or:* son)? (T.T. Chang, 1970: 44 #1,23)

Divination: / perhaps / Fu Hao / calls / (*for*) ritual purification / frontier guard / administrators? (Luo, 1913, 6, 6a #3)

Ren-shen / crack-making / diviner Quarrel / divines: / order / Fu Hao / follows / general Wash Feet Shield / (*to*) war / (*against*) Prayer / State / grant / (*he*) has / support? (JGWZD p. 1313)

Yi-you (day 22) / crack-making / diviner Quarrel / divines: / shall not / call / Fu Hao / to advance / (*and*) raise / people (=troops) / at / STN: Dragon Temple? (C-C, 3 #709 & JGWZD p. 976, compare Luo, 1913, 7, 30b #2)

Xin-si (day 18) / crack-making / divination: / raise / Fu Hao / three thousand men / (*and let her*) raise / (*further*) troop / ten thousand / call / (*to*) war? (C-C, 1 #310)

Divination: / king / dreams: / Fu Hao / not / perhaps / wounded (*or:* pain)? (T.T. Chang, 1970: 49, 2.10)

Fu Jing #1

Gui-mao (day 40) / crack-making / diviner Temple of Ancestress / divines /
Jing (= well, shaft) / State (*representatives*) / at / Tang's / temple /
(*sacrifice*) wild boar? (JGWZD p.555)

Divination: / next / xin-hai (day 48) / call / Fu Jing / (*for*) butchering and
laying out meat (*offerings*) / at / Soundstone-Stroke's / tomb-temple?
(JGWZD p. 598)

Wu-yin (day 15) / crack-making / diviner Temple of Ancestress / divines: /
ritual purification / (*of*) Fu Jing / at / (*ancestress*) Mother Geng? (Hu, 3,
#121 & T.T. Chang, 1970: 55 #3.14)

....Mother Bing / cursed / Fu Jing? (T.T. Chang, 1970: 43 #1.20)

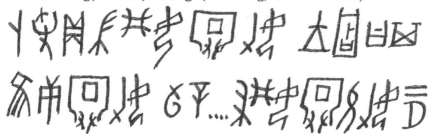

Crack-making / diviner Quarrel (?) / divines / Fu Jing / (*gives*) birth / (*to*) a
son? / King / prognosticates / says / perhaps / (*if*) it is / (*on*) day geng /
(*the*) birth / (*will be*) a son. / (*next*) xun-week / day xin / ... / Fu Jing / (*gives*)
birth / indeed / a son. / Second moon. (Li, 1981 #480)

Fu Jing #2

Call / Fu / to / PLN ? / at / Zu Xin / ritual purification? /Divination: / call /
Fu Jing / (to) hunt / at / PLN? (Luo, 1913,2, 45a #1 & Li 1981 #460)

Divination: / Fu Jing / ill / perhaps / (she) has (been) / cursed? (JGWZD p.
555)

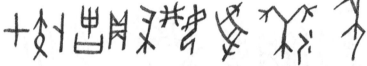

Fu Jing / water millet / not / perhaps / inspect? (JGWZD p. 555)

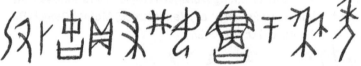

Jia-yin (day 51) / crack-making / diviner ? / divines: / Fu Jing / permits /
water millet / harvest? (Li, 1981 #288)

Yi-chou (day 2) / crack-making / diviner ? / divines: / Fu Jing / (performs)
unknown ritual / for / millet / harvest? (Hu, 3, 2 #27)

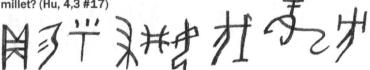

Divination: / shall not / call (= order) / Fu Jing / (to) go / harvest / water
millet? (Hu, 4,3 #17)

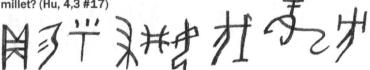

Divination: / shall not / call (= order) / Fu Jing / (to wage) war / (against)
Dragon / State? JGWZD p.1261)

Wu: Ritualists, Place Name, Sacred Quadrant #1

Wu-zi (day 25) / crack-making: / pacify / Deity Stormwind / (*by or at*) / north / wu...?. (Hu, 2 #49. Probably the northern quadrant or the place).

Gui-you (day 10) / perhaps / share a meal / (*with*) wu ? (Menzies, S0110, 2351. Either with the ritualists or with the directional deities).

Yi-chou (day 2) / crack-making: / spill libation / decapitate human / (*on*) xin-wei (day 8) / at (*or:* for) / wu? (Hu, 1,4 #1 Place or deities of the quadrants?)

Yi-si (day 42) / crack-making / wu / damage (= PEN?) / in / PLN: Tiger(?) River...? (JGWZD p.1192)

Divination: / wu / PEN: Woman Bed / not / (*have? perform?*) ritual purification? (JGWZD p. 1317)

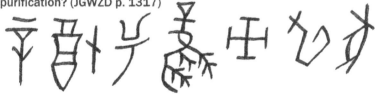

Xin-you (day 58) / crack-making: / pacify / Deity Stormwind / wu / (*offer*) nine / pigs? (USB 18; C-C, 1 #992)

Wu: Ritualists, Place Name, Sacred Quadrant #2

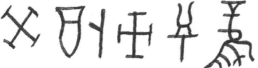

Gui-you (day 10) / crack-making: / wu / pacify / Deity Stormwind? (T.T. Chang, 1970: 226 #16.12)

....divination: / wu / millet? (Hu, 5, 233. A harvest ritual, an offering or a payment in food?)

Geng-xu (day 47) / wu / (*offer*) Di / one / sheep / one dog? Geng-xu (day 47) / crack-making: / offer / for / Deity Mount Yue / pray (*for*) / millet? (Hu, 5 #76 & T.T. Chang, 1970: 225 #16.10)

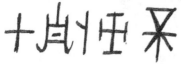

Jia-zi (day 1) / crack-making: / wu / Di (*offering?*)? (Hu, 5 #349)

Gui-hai (day 60) / divination: / this / day / Di offering / at / sacred quadrants (*or:* deities of the directions *or:* place wu) / pig / one / dog / one? (T.T. Chang, 1970: 226 #16.11 & JGWZD p. 496)

(*Shall the*) wu / (*offer*) Di / one / dog? (T.T. Chang, 1970: 225 #16.18)

Wu: Ritualists, Place Name, Sacred Quadrant #3

Wu-yin (day 15) / crack-making: / wu / offer / decapitate human / (*ensures*) this / night (*or*: month) / rain? Ji-mao (day 16) / crack-making: / burned offering / pig /(*for*) Deity Four Clouds? (C-C, 1 #972)

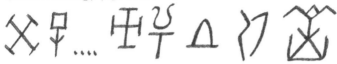

Gui-si (day 30) / ... / wu / pacify / Earth Deity, / Deity Yellow River / (*and*) Deity Mount Yue? (T.T. Chang, 1970: 226 #16.13 & JGWZD p.552)

Divination: / unknown ritual (*or*: PEN) / bring / wu? (JGWZD p.496)

Divination: / unknown ritual (*or*: PEN) / bring / wu? (JGWZD p.496)

Ji-mao (day 16) / divination: / ritual report / for / Father Ding? / Divination: / not / disaster / (*for the*) king / perhaps / wu (*ritual?*) ? (C-C, 1 #992 & JGWZD p. 496)

Jia-chen (day 41) / crack-making: / burn human / Woman Berry (?)? / Burn human / Woman Berry (?) / (*on*) ding-wei (day 44)? Ding-wei / crack-making: (*will there be*) rain? (T.T. Chang, 1970: 250 #18.18. A wu burned as a drought sacrifice?)

Disease

Divination: Mother Bing / not have (caused my) / worms? (JGWZD p.1429)

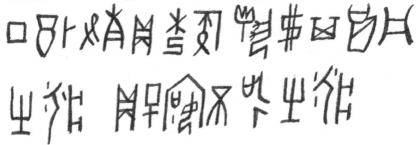

Ding-you (day 34) / crack-making / diviner Bell-Stroke / divines: / Marquis PEN: ? / (*at the*) time to light torches / not / perhaps / misfortune / wind / has / disease? / Divination: / Prince PEN: ? / (*has*) not / come. / Has / disease? (Li, 1981 #502)

Divination: / diseased / teeth / (*should I have*) purification ritual / at / Father Yi? / Not / purification ritual? (Li, 1981 #493)

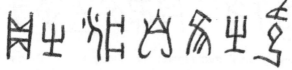

Divination: / have / diseased / nose / perhaps / have / curse? (Li, 1981 #495 & T.T. Chang, 1970: 37 #1.5)

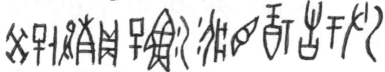

Gui-si (day 30) / crack-making / diviner Bell-Stroke / divines: / Prince Fisher / (*has*) diseased / eye. / Drink offering / (*and*) ritual report / for / Father Yi? (Hu, 3,2 #53; Li, 1981 #497 & T.T. Chang, 1970: 110 #7.3)

Curses #1

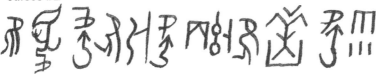

Perhaps / Ancestor Monkey / (*has*) cursed (*us*)? / Perhaps / Deity Yellow River / cursed? / Bing-wu (day 49) / crack-making / is it / Deity Mount Yue / (*who*) cursed / (*the*) rain? (C-C, 3, #201)

Geng-yin (day 27) / crack-making / perhaps / Ancestor Monkey / cursed / (*the*) millet? (T.T. Chang, 1970: 82 #5.2)

Divination: / perhaps / Di / cursed / our / harvest? (JGWZD p.1426)

Divination: / not / perhaps / Tai (= great) / gods / (*who*) cursed / (*the*) king? (JGWZD p.1141)

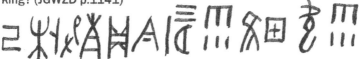

Ji-wei (day 56) / crack-making / diviner Bell-Stroke / divines: / now / thirteenth month / rain. / Perhaps / Shang Jia / cursed / (*the*) rain? (T.T. Chang, 1970: 82 #5.3)

Geng-shen (day 57) / crack-making / diviner Swimmer / divines: / Deity Yellow River / cursed / (*the*) rain? / Divination: / Deity Yellow River / did not / curse / (*the*) rain? (T.T. Chang, 1970: 167 #12.2)

Curses #2

Father Xin / (*has*) not / cursed? Not / perhaps / Pan Geng / (*who*) cursed / (*the*) king? / Perhaps / I (*or:* we) / have / made / misfortune? (Luo, 1913, 27b #2)

Xin-you (day 58) / crack-making / diviner Quarrel (?) / divines: / this / day / king / goes / to / PLN? / not have / curse? (Luo, 1913, 2, 26a #2)

Perhaps / Zu ... / cursed? / Perhaps / Zu Yi / cursed? / Perhaps / Zu Xin / cursed? / Perhaps / Zu Geng / cursed? (Gu Wen Zi Yan Jiu, 3, 1980: 77, #2)

Gui-chou (day 50) / crack-making / ... / divines: / (*for*) upper and lower gods / pour libation / ... / (*for*) Tai Yi / clothes offering / up to / (*the*) many / younger generations. / Not have / curse? (Gu Wen Zi Yan Jiu 3, 1980: 67 #471)

Divination: / my / families / old / blind and sick / minister / not has / cursed / me (*or:* us)? (T.T. Chang, 1970: 40 #1.15)

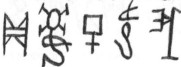

Divination: / STN /(*late*) prince / cursed / me (*or:* us)? (Hu, 3,2,137)

Curses #3

Bi (= Grandmother) Gui / (*brought*) disaster / (*to the*) king? (JGWZD p. 1568)

Mother PLN: Dagger-axe Woman / (*has*) not / cursed / (*the*) king? (T.T. Chang, 1970: 40 #1,14)

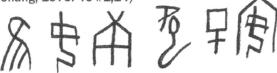

Perhaps / Mother Geng / cursed / Prince PEN: Peaceful Life? (JGWZD p. 1300)

Xin-chou (day 38) / crack-making / diviner Bell-Stroke / divines: / (there *was a*) hailstorm (*or:* heavy rain). / (Did) Woman Snake / not / (*cause this*) misfortune? (JGWZD p. 1305)

Divination: / king / (*suffers from*) ear-screaming (=tinnitus) / it is / painful. / (*Has*) Mother Ji / cursed / (*the*) king? (T.T. Chang, 1970: 37 #1.4)

Divination: / perhaps / (*the*) many / mothers (= ancestresses) / (*have*) cursed (us)? (C-C, 1 #663)

Disasters #1 Deluge, Earthquake & Fire

....diviner Bell-Stroke / divines / Deity River Turbulence / perhaps / makes / this / city / disaster? T.T. Chang, 1970: 180 # 12.42)

Yi-mao (day 52) / crack-making / divination: / this / (*unknown*) season / (*to the*) spring / come (*for ritual*) / (*as the*) river / floods? (Li, 1981 #308)

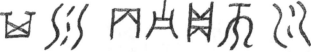

Perhaps / (*there will be a*) deluge? Bing-zi (day 13) / divination: / not / deluge? (Hu, 6, 1 #482)

Ji-hai (day 36) / crack-making / diviner Temple of Ancestress / divines: / king / arrives / at / this / deluge / (*shall he make a*) burned offering / for / Deity Yellow River / three / pair of lambs / (*and*) drown / three / bovines? (JGWZD p. 1124)

Ren-xu (day 59)/crack-making / (*in*) PLN Ancient / standing / divination / (*by*) king: / this / moon (= night, month) / not / earthquake? (Hu, 2 #828)

Crack-making: / perhaps / ritual report / (*about the*) fire / for / younger generation / Grandfather Ding?
(Hu, 2 #599 & T.T. Chang, 1970: 122 # 7.29)

Disasters #2 Locusts

Geng-shen (day 57) / crack-making / diviner Quarrel (?) / divines: / this / year/ locusts / (*will*) not / arrive / (*at*) this / (*state and city*) Shang ? / Second / moon. (Sun, 1937 #687)

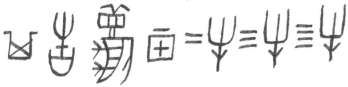

Perhaps / (*we shall*) ritually inform / (*that*) locusts (*are coming*) / (*ancestor*) Shang Jia / (*and offer*) two bovines? Three bovines? Four bovines? (T.T. Chang, 1970: 122 #7.28)

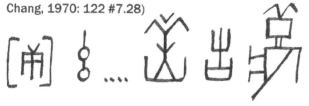

....-wu / .... / Deity Mount Yue / (*should be*) ritually informed / (*about*) locusts? (T.T. Chang, 1970: 187 #13.9 reads geng-wu (day 7)).

Jia-shen (day 21) / crack-making / diviner Temple of Ancestress / divines: / ritual report / locusts /for / Deity Yellow River? (JGWZD p. 784)

Divination: / perhaps / pacification / (*of*) locusts / coming / xin-mao (day 28) / (*by*) spilling libation? (JGWZD p. 784)

Disasters #3 Drought (Spirit or Deity) and Drought Sacrifices

....-yin / crack-making / I (*or*: we) / not (*have*) / Drought? (Li, 1981 # 306)

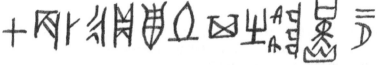

Jia-chen (day 41) / crack-making / diviner Swimmer / divines: / west /
earth / perhaps / have / descending (*upon them*) / Drought / (*in the*)
second moon? (Li, 1981 #303 & JGWZD p. 1112)

Perhaps / use (=sacrifice) / burn hunchback / (*and*) bovine? (T.T. Chang,
1970: 249 #18.15)

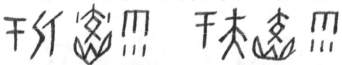

Divination: / burn human / son / have / following / rain? / Divination: /
shall not / burn human / not have / perhaps / rain? (Luo, 1913: 5, 33a #2)

For / Deity Yellow River / burn human / (*causes*) rain? / For / Heaven /
burn human / (*causes*) rain? (Menzies B1834, 314)

Divination: / burn human / PEN: Pair of Sheep Woman / have / rain? Shall
not / burn human / PEN: Woman Here In / not have / perhaps / rain?
(T.T. Chang, 1970: 250 #18.17)

Ritual: Stand in the Centre or Erect the Centre

Geng-yin (day 27) / crack-making / divination: / king / perhaps / centre / erect / agreed (agreement)? (Hu, 2 #221)

Jia-yin (day 51) / crack-making: / stand (or: erect) / centre? (Hu, 2 #524)

Jia-xu (day 11) / crack-making / erect / centre / grant / sun (sunshine? Or: bestow boons?)? Yi-hai (day 12) / indeed / grant sun. (Li, 1981 #269)

Gui-mao (day 40) / crack-making / diviner Quarrel (?) / divines: / next / ... / centre / not have / storm and rain / bing-zi (day 13) / ... / indeed / not have... (Li, 1981 #222.)

...erect / centre / indeed / not have / storm and rain / ... / diviner Turbulence / divines: / next / ding-hai (day 24) / grant / sun ? / Bing-xu (day 23) / hailstorm (or: heavy rain) ... (Li, 1981: 220 see also C-C, 3 #677 in section on bird Peng)

Divination: / this / (unknown) season / shall not / march (against) / Earth / State? / Divination:/erect (or: stand) / centre? (C-C, 3 #604, see also Li, 1981 #333 for the 'shall not' version)

Dreams #1

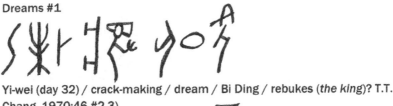

Yi-wei (day 32) / crack-making / dream / Bi Ding / rebukes (*the king*)? T.T. Chang, 1970:46 #2.3)

Divination: / king / dreams / perhaps / end / (*of the*) pain? (Hu, 4, 5#40)

Divination: / king / dreams / (*deceased*) Brother Ding /not / perhaps / (*causes*) misfortune? (JGWZD p. 464)

Divination: / king / (*is*) unwell / maybe / (*he has*) worms (*or: parasites*)? / Divination: / Fu Hao / dreams / not / perhaps / Father Yi (*is responsible*)? Divination: / perhaps / Father Yi / (*made*) unwell / (the) king? (T.T. Chang, 1970: 49 #2.9)

Divination: king / dreams / perhaps / misfortune? Divination: / king (*has*) / perhaps / disease / (*of the*) eye? (T.T. Chang, 1970: 47 #2.6)

Dreams #2

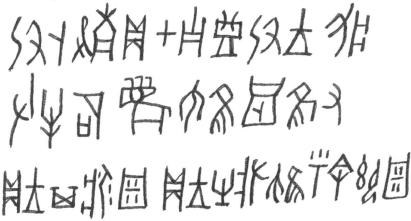

....king / prognosticates / speaks / (we) have / misfortune / (I) have / dreamed. / Perhaps / have / coming / disaster? / Seventh / day / ji-chou (day 26) / indeed / have / coming / disaster / at / ... / ? / grant / call / ? / ... / foreign state / advance to the frontier / at / our / ... (Li, 1981 #433)

Yi-chou (day 2) / crack-making / diviner Bell-Stroke / divines: / Jia-zi (day 1) / night to / yi-chou (day 2) / king / dreamed / (*he*) herded / (*a*) stone / elk. / (*Is this*) not / it is / misfortune: / is it / helpful? / Divination: / king / perhaps / (has) disease / (is it) misfortune? / Divination: / king / has / dream: / (is it) not / perhaps / (a) call / (for) himself / (to be) ritually purified / (of) misfortune? (T.T. Chang, 1970: 257 #19.4)

Ascension Ritual #1

...coming / hay harvest / ascend / at / West / Deity? (JGWZD p. 1510)

King / perhaps / ascend? / This / used (=was done). (JGWZD p. 1510)

Perhaps / ascend / at (= to *or*: for) / Tai Yi / Zu Yi? (JGWZD p. 1510)

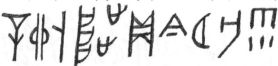

...Tai (*or*: ten great ancestors? / ritual purification / perhaps / ascend / at / distant / grandfather /(Wang) / Hai / bring / drink sacrifice (?)? (Hu, 2, #472)

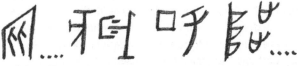

Zu Yi / for / Tai Yi / perhaps / ascend? (Hu, 2 #537)

Xin-mao (day 28) / crack-making / diviner Ascender / divines: / this / night (*or*: month?) / not have / rain? (C-C, 1 #1188)

...diviner Troop / ... / -hai / sacrifice with axe blow / (*to*) Father Ding / ascend... (C-C, 1, #1388)

Ascension Ritual #2 and Hosting Ritual

Wu-chen (day 5) / offer / decapitate human / at / ascension / split / pair of
sheep / (*for*) divine Mother Geng (C-C, 3 #481)

Xin-you (day 58) / divination: / drink offering / (*and*) ritual report / ? / for /
Mother Xin? / Divination: / ascend / at / (*to?* Father or day) Ding / use (*or:*
sacrifice)? (C-C, 3 #462)

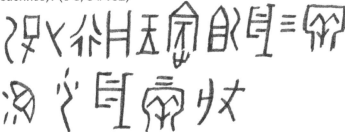

Yi-si (day 42) / crack-making / diviner Crossroad / divines: / king / hosts /
Zu Yi / kills with axe / three / pair of sheep / and / (*for*) Xiao Yi / kills with
axe / two / pair of sheep / not have / blame? (Gu Wen Zi Yan Jiu 3, 1980,
ill. p. 29 #232)

Xin-si (day 18) / crack-making / divination: / king / hosts / Mother Xin /
kills with axe / pair of sheep... (USS 236)

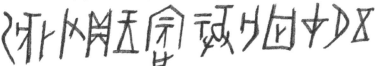

Yi-hai (day 12) / crack-making / diviner ? / divines: / king / (*performs*)
hosting / (*with*) drink offering? / Not have / disaster / in / fifth month?
(Sun, 1937 #404)

Diverse Rituals #1

Gui-hai (day 60) / divination: / Spike / State / bring / cattle / perhaps / raise cups / at / coming / jia-shen (day 21)? (Hu, 2 #499)

Yi-wei (day 32) / crack-making / diviner Quarrel (?) / divines: / coming / xin-hai (day 38) / spill libation / drink and pour wine / (*in*) thanksgiving / for / Zu Xin? / Seventh month. (T.T. Chang, 1970: 128 #8.7)

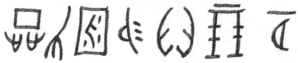

Advance to the frontier (*or*: siege) / not / in peril? / Grant / cowries (=money) / (and) jade (*ornaments or*: cong) / first month? (Hu, 4, 3 #81)

Geng-xu (day 47) / ... / divination: / grant / many / mothers: / give / cowries / (&) jade cong? (JGWZD pl 702)

Ji-hai (day 36) / crack-making / (*for*) Mother Ji / offering with axe blow / perhaps / male / bovine? (Hu, 5 #226)

Perhaps / cook and offer / rhino / (*to*) Zu Ding? Perhaps / two / rhinos? (Hu, 5 #193)

Diverse Rituals #2

Wu-chen (day 5) / crack-making / divination: / next / yi-si (day 42) / (at the) time to light torches / give / for / Mother Geng / pair of sheep? (Menzies, S0157, 3235)

Xin-si (day 18) / divination: / it is / pray (for) / birth / at / Bi Geng / (and) Bi Bing. (*Offer*) male bovine / male sheep / white / boar? (T.T. Chang, 1970: 102 #6.22 & JGWZD p. 688)

Gui-wei (day 20) / crack-making / (for?) Fu Shu (= Lady Mouse): / Fu Shu / offers / (to) Bi Geng / (one) sheep / (one) pig? (C-C, 1 #1606)

Ritual purification / (of) Fu shu's / child / at / Bi Ji? (T.T. Chang, 1970: 58 #3.22)

Divination: / not / bird (?) offering / promise / ten (?) / (for) Zu Yi ? (JGWZD p. 433)

Ding-si (day 54) / crack-making / give / burned offering / for / Father Ding / 100 / dogs / 100 / pigs / split / 100 / bovines? (T.T. Chang, 1970: 136 #9.12)

Diverse Rituals #3

Three / hundred / Qiang / use (=sacrifice) / for / Ding? (JGWZD p. 1549)

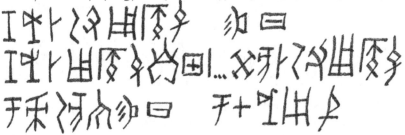

Ren-xu (day 59) / crack-making: / yi-chou (day 2) / use (= sacrifice) /
Marquis Bud? / Grant / sun?/ Ren-xu / crack-making: / sacrifice / Marquis
Bud / for / Shang Jia / ten (?)...Gui-hai (day 60) / crack-making: / yi-chou
(day 2) / sacrifice / Marquis Bud? / At / coming / yi-hai (day 12) / not /
grant / sun? / At / jia-xu (day 11) / sacrifice / Bud...? (USB #34, see also
USB #81 and C-C, 1 #1009, 1053, 1126 & 1153 for same topic)

At / gui-hai (day 60) / inspect / elephants / grant / sun (= give boons?
Have sunshine?)? (Li, 1981 #332)

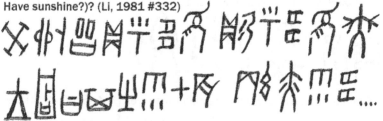

Gui-mao (day 40) / crack-making / diviner To Show / divines: / call / many
/ blind musicians / Divination: / shall not / call / many /musicians / (for)
dance? / King / prognosticates / says / perhaps / have / rain / jia-chen
(day 41)? Bing-wu (day 49) also / rain / many ... (Li 1981 #248 & T.T.
Chang, 1970: 243 #18.1)

Dancing

Ji-wei (day 56) / crack-making / diviner Bell-Stroke / divines: / (*shall*) I (= the king. *Or: we*) / dance? (Chen, 1937 #877)

Perhaps / (*in the*) wood / dance / offering / set things right? (Menzies B1825, 943)

Jia-chen (day 41) / crack-making / next / yi-si (day 42) / I (*or: we*) / ... / music / dance / (*until*) arriving / at / bing-wu (day 43)... (C-C, 3 #502)

Dance / (*for or: at*) Deity Mount Yue / (*receive*) rain? (JGWZD p. 631)

Perhaps / rain dance / (*at*) Grass-Snake / burial temple / gives / rain? (JGWZD p. 631)

Bing-chen (day 53) / crack-making / divination: / this / day / music / (*and*) dance. / Have / following / rain? (T.T. Chang, 1970: 93 #5.27 & 244 #18.3)

Ritual Purification

...-xu / crack-making: / ritual purification / (of) Prince Shoulderpack / before / Mother Ji. / (Sacrifice) two / pair of lambs? (Hu, 1, 5 #134)

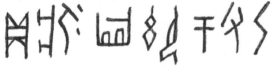

Divination: / (I have) diseased / teeth. Ritual purification / before / Father Yi? (Luo, 1913: 25a, 1)

Gui-wei (day 20) / crack-making / in / PLN? / divination: / this / night / army (camp) / (should) not / tremble (earthquake?). / Is it / (occasion for) ritual purification? (JGWZD p.195)

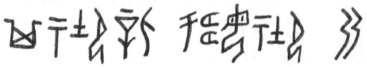

Is it / ritual purification / (before) Bi Xin? / Before / Many Mothers (=ancestresses) / ritual purification? / (Or) not? (T.T. Chang, 1970: 61 #3,31)

Geng-xu (day 47) / crack-making: / I / (should) myself / ritually purify? (T.T. Chang, 1970: 61 #3.32)

Ding-chou (day 14) / crack-making / diviner Temple of Ancestress / divines: / Prince Imperial Palace Garden / perhaps / ritually purify / king / before / (Zu) Ding's / Wife / (the) second / Bi Ji? (T.T. Chang, 1970: 62 #3.33)

Five rituals #1

Jia-zi (day 1) / king / makes cracks / (*and*) speaks: / next / yi-chou (day 2) / it is / pour libation / (*and perform*) yi ritual (*feather dance*) / (*for*) Tang. / Not / (*have*) rain? (T.T. Chang, 1970: 153 #10.19, period 2b)

Gui-chou (day 50) / crack-making / divination: / king / hosts / Zhong Ding's / wife / Bi Gui / (*performs*) yi ritual / not have / blame? (JGWZD p. 373)

Perhaps / offer / raise / sacrifice by axe-blow / for / Shang Jia / together (*with*) / yi ritual? (Hu, 2 #522)

Gui-mao (day 40) / king / makes cracks / (*and*) divines: / spill libation / (*and*) yi ritual / for / Shang Jia / (*and all*) up to / many / younger generations / clothes offering / not have / curse? Myself (*have*) / misfortune / in / ninth / month? /(*fill word: it is*) / king's / fifth / (cult year). (T.T. Chang, 1970: 157 #10.27 typical for period 5b)

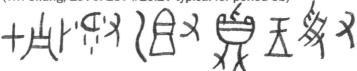

Jia-zi (day 1) / crack-making / chi ritual (*raw meat offering*) / (*for*) Zu Yi / give / food offering (*cooked in a ding vessel*). King / grants / support? (Hu, 5 #1)

Five rituals #2

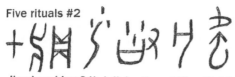

Jia-shen (day 21) / divination: / Xiao Yi / (*receives*) chi ritual / (*shall we*) not have/ curse? (Hu, 5 #88 & T.T. Chang, 1970: 146 #10.6)

Jia-xu (day 11) / crack-making / diviner Crossroad / divines: / next / yi-hai (day 12) / chi ritual / for / Zu Yi / not have / curse / in / eighth moon? (C-C, 1 #1032)

Ji-chou (day 26) / crack-making / divination: / king / hosts / Zu Ding / (*with*) zai ritual (*offering cooked grains*)? (Hu, 6, 3 #245)

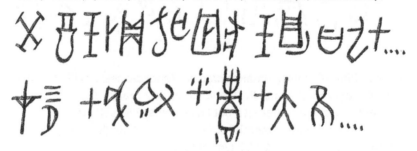

Xin-you (day 58) / crack-making / divination: / king / hosts / Geng Ding's / wife / Bi Xin / (*with a*) zai ritual / not have / blame? (Li, 1981 #102)

Gui-you (day 10) / king / makes cracks / (and) divines: / this xun week / not have / disaster? / King / observes cracks / speaks: / Bi Jia / ... / in / third moon. / Jia shu (day 11) / chi ritual / (*for*) Xiao Jia / (*and*) zai ritual / (*for*) Tai Jia / perhaps... (C-C, 1 #1661)

Five rituals #3

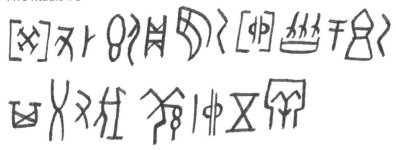

(Gui)-chou (day 50) / crack-making / diviner ? / divines: / next / yi-(mao) (day 52) / xie ritual (*harmonisation ritual*) / for / Zu Yi / perhaps / encounter (*rain?*)? / Offer /decapitation / (*of*) Qiang / ten / (*and*) split / five / pair of sheep? (T.T. Chang, 1970: 151 #10.15)

Ren-shen (day 9) / crack-making / diviner Troop / divines: / king / hosts / Bi Ren / (*for*) xie ritual? / Not have / blame / in / eighth month? (C-C, 3 #79)

Bing-chen (day 53) / crack-making / diviner Troop / divines: / next / ding-si (day 54) / xie ritual / for / Zhong Ding / (*with*) clothes offering. / Not-have / curse / in / eighth moon? (T.T. Chang, 1970: 152 #10.16)

Gui-hai (day 60) / crack-making / divination: / Tai Yi / rong (*drum ritual*) / (*and*) shared meal? / Zu Ding / with / ... / shared meal? (Li, 1981 #42)

Five rituals #4 & Branch Offering

Gui-wei (day 20) / king / makes cracks / (*and*) divines: / spill libation / rong ritual / day (21) / at / Shang Jia / up to / for / many / younger generations / clothes sacrifice / not have / curse?/ I / (*have*) disaster / in / fourth month? / (fill word: it is) / king's / second / ritual year (Li, 1981 #124 & T.T. Chang, 1970: 157 #10.26)

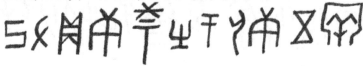

Gui-hai (day 60) / crack-making / divination: / king / hosts / Bi Gui / rong ritual / today. / Not have / blame? (Hu, 6,2 #125)

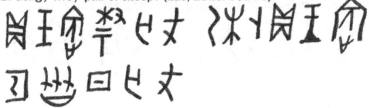

Ji-chou (day 26) / divination: / geng (day 27) /branch offering / give / for / Bi Geng / five / pair of sheep? (Luo, 1913: 36a #3)

Divination: / king / hosts / (*with*) branch offering / not have / blame? Yi-wei (day 32) crack-making / divination: / king / hosts / Bao Yi / xie ritual / today / not have / blame? (Li, 1981 #35, see also Gu Wen Zi Yan Jiu, 3, 1980 ill. p. 5:41)

State Names 1

State Names 2

State Names 3

State Names 4

State Names 5

State Names 6

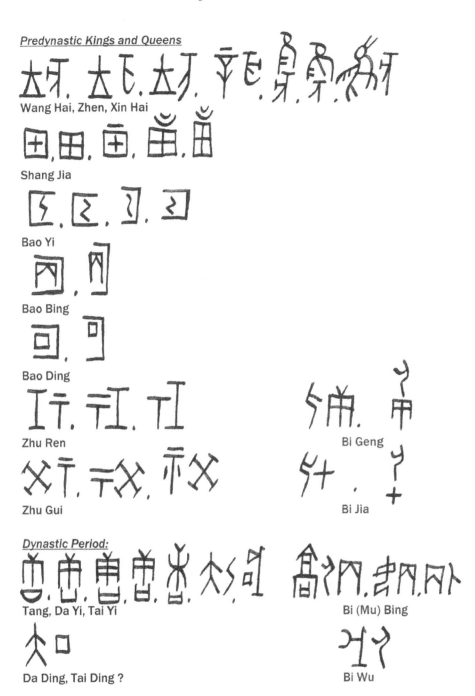

Predynastic Kings and Queens

Wang Hai, Zhen, Xin Hai

Shang Jia

Bao Yi

Bao Bing

Bao Ding

Zhu Ren

Bi Geng

Zhu Gui

Bi Jia

Dynastic Period:

Tang, Da Yi, Tai Yi

Bi (Mu) Bing

Da Ding, Tai Ding ?

Bi Wu

Regents 1

Wai Bing, Bu Bing

Prime Minister Yi Yin

Yi Yin's Wife

Zhong Ren, Nan Ren?

Tai Jia, Da Jia

Bi Xin

Wo Ding?

Bu Bing?

Tai Geng, Da Geng

Bi Ren

Xiao Jia

Yong Ji, Lü Ji (Yu Ru?)

Bi Ji (Yu Bi?)

Regents 2

Tai Wu, Da Wu

Bi Ren

Zhong Ding

Bi Ji

Bi Gui

Wai Ren, Bu Ren

He Dan Jia

Zu Yi, Xia Yi

Bi Geng

Bi Ji

Zu Xin

Bi Ren

Bi Geng

Bi Jia

Wo Jia, Qiang Jia

Mu Geng

Zu Ding

Bi Geng

Bi Xin

Bi Ji

Bi Gui

Nan Geng

Regents 3

Xiang Jia, Hu Jia, Yang Jia

Pan Geng

Xiao Xin, Zu Xin

Xiao Yi, Di Yi

Bi Geng

Oracle Bones Period 1:

Wu Ding, Di Ding

Bi Wu

Bi Xin

Bi Gui

Zu Ji?

Oracle Bones Period 2a:

Zu Geng

Bi (Mu) Yi

Regents 4

Oracle Bones Period 2b:

Zu Jia, Di Jia

Lin Xin, Fu Xin?

Bi Wu

Oracle Bones Period 3:

Geng Ding, Geng Zu Ding

Bi Xin

Oracle Bones Period 4a:

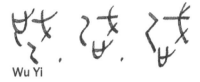

Wu Yi

Bi Wu

Oracle Bones Period 4b:

Wen Ding, Wen Wu Ding, Di Ding

Bi Gui

Oracle Bones Period 5a:

Fu Yi, Di Yi

Oracle Bones Period 5b:

Zhòu Xin, Zhòu Wang, Di Xin

Da Ji

Regents 5

Prototypes of the 'Celestial Stems'

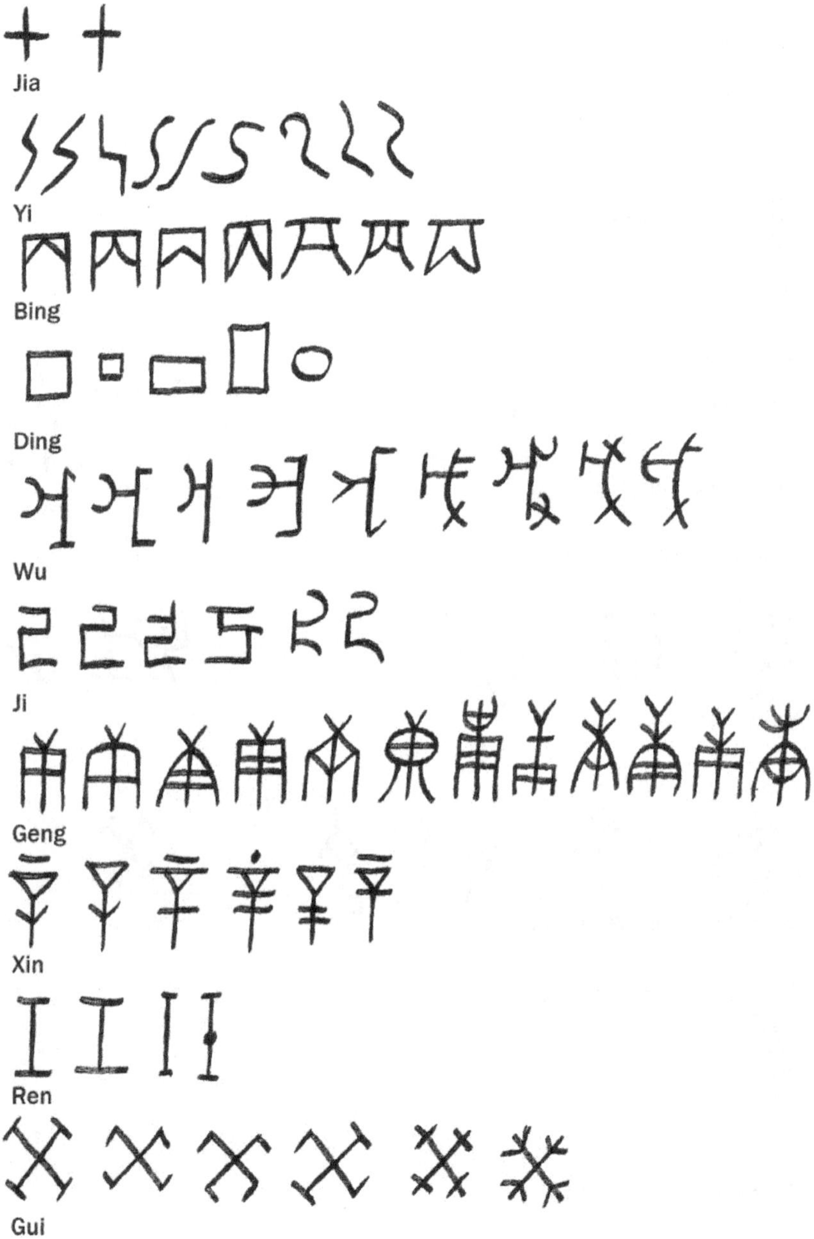

Jia

Yi

Bing

Ding

Wu

Ji

Geng

Xin

Ren

Gui

Prototypes of the 'Earthly Branches'

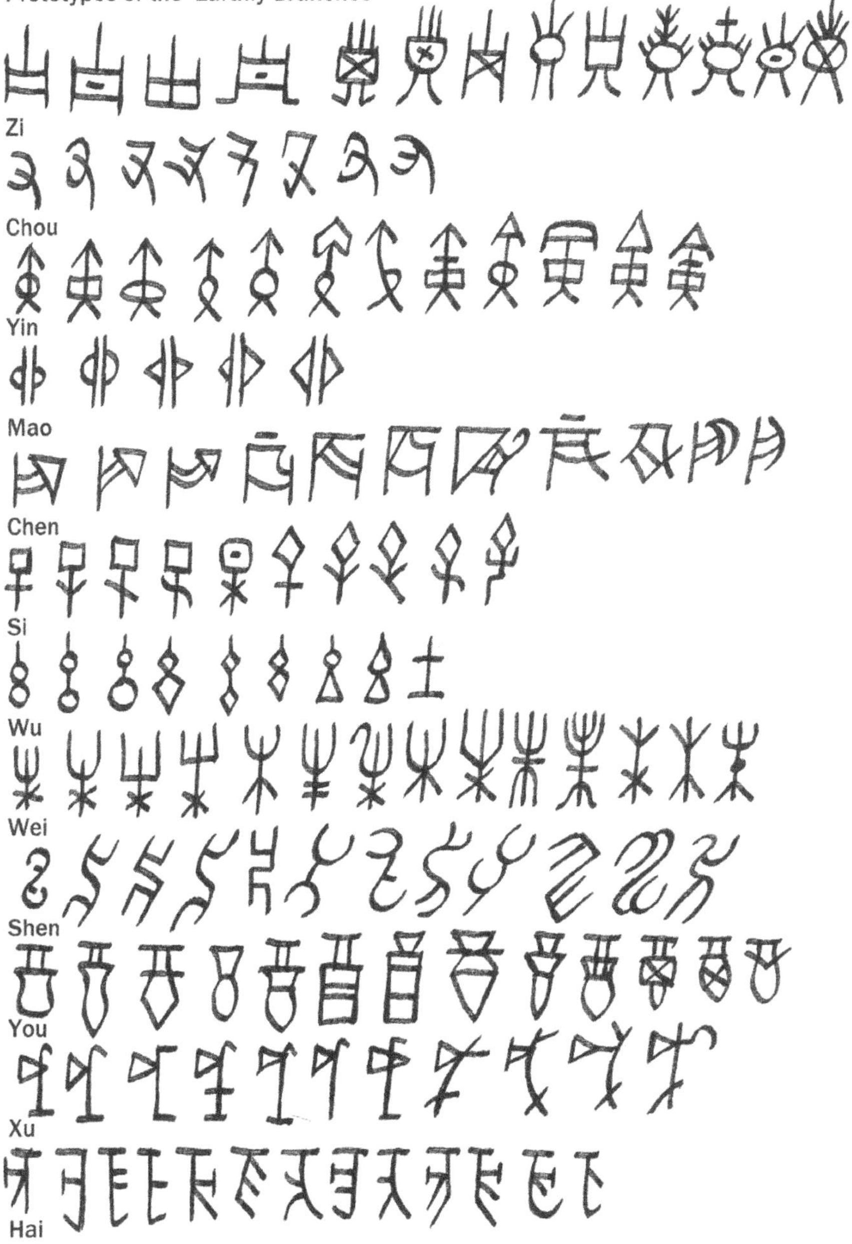

Zi

Chou

Yin

Mao

Chen

Si

Wu

Wei

Shen

You

Xu

Hai

Diviners according to Shima Kunio

Diviners 1

③ BING-XIN (?)
GENG-DING

④a WU-YI

④b WEN-
WU-
DING

⑤a DI-YI

⑤b DI-XIN

① or ④

Diviners 2

The Oracle Bone Dictionary

On the next pages you will find a modest dictionary of common Jiaguwen characters. I have selected basic signs which have a meaning in everyday language. You can use them to write birthday greetings or poetry, you can enjoy them when you practice calligraphy and, if you are into exploring consciousness, you can use them in meditations, trance journeys and spell-writing. The oracle bone characters are excellently suited for these purposes. However, they do have limitations. Languages and consciousness are closely connected. It's easier to think about phenomena that you have words for, which explains why humans make up more and more words and languages expand infinitely. Ancient Chinese had a rich and detailed vocabulary. However, we do not understand even half of it. There is a huge range of signs which are simply personal, place and state names and which I have not included. Plus maybe some two thousand signs which are incomprehensible at the time being. You won't find them here. If you want to see a pretty complete account, look them up in *Jiaguwen Zidian*. But even when you use the characters of this dictionary, you will soon learn that some topics are hard to express. To this day, there are no characters for many emotions, social customs, human relationships or abstract thought, and even some very basic everyday activities. The oracle bones only record topics for divination. We are lucky that kings like Wu Ding insisted on divining about such a wide range of topics. I am sure the Shang used a lot more characters when they wrote documents, planned campaigns or did the book keeping for the palace, recorded extended hunting trips and military campaigns. With a bit of luck, future excavations will extend the scope of what we know and understand.

Before you make use of the dictionary (or find yourself confused by the organisation of the thing) let me give a brief introduction on **how to find a character**. In the past, oracle bone dictionaries generally made use of the order of radicals given by the *Shuowen* dictionary. This was a convenient choice, as serious scholars of Chinese were well acquainted with the order of the 540 basic signs. It also had the advantage that any new dictionary could make use of an organising structure that was widely known among the literati. Things are different in contemporary China. The amount of basic radicals has been reduced considerably, so that modern Chinese dictionaries generally only use around 200 root-signs to organise their characters, and even these pose problems to the many unhappy people not busy learning Chinese. While learning the order of 200 radicals is easier than 540, it still remains hard to memorize the sections where you can hope to find a given character. To make things easy for you, I have replaced the traditional organisation by one based on groups of filters. In this system, each section has priority over the sections following it. So, when you wish to find a certain sign, you have to acquaint yourself with a few simple groups, which are organised in a hierarchical way. Let me explain. In the first section, you find all signs which include an **animal**. The order is based on biology, i.e. there are wild mammals, domestic mammals, birds, reptiles, amphibians, fish and small animals. It provides you with a good overview about the animals so essential for Shang religion, clan-organisation and daily life and reveals a lot about animal husbandry and the ecosystem.

Many signs in this section are of a composite nature. Elephant plus hand, pig plus foot, dog plus axe and so on. When you look for a sign showing a foot stepping on a snake (=curse), you will find it in the animal section, not in the section on feet. Sheep plus mountain is in the mammal section, dragon and house among the reptiles. I did not want to burden the dictionary by listing composite characters in two or three different sections. So when you want to look up a character including an animal, it will appear in the animal section, no matter what other signs accompany it.

Now that we have excluded all animal related characters, we come to the next section. The next filter is the sign **standing human, in profile**. Here you find any character including the standing human in profile, except for those including animals.

Then follows **standing human from in front**. It gives all signs with standing, frontal human figures except for those including animals and standing humans in profile.

Next is **kneeling woman** followed by **kneeling man**. Kneeling, by the way, was not a sign of subservience: the Shang simply did not use chairs. Then follows **child**, it's a very brief section. Next we continue with **parts of the body**, the **vegetation**, **nature**, **settlements** and finally **objects**, **tools** and **household utensils** and unidentifiable stuff that won't fit anywhere.

It sounds more complicated than it is. If you want to identify an unknown character you simply have to look at the simple key to the signs and remember that each heading has a priority. Hand and elephant will appear under *'animals'* as animals have priority one. *'Sideways human kicked by foot'* appears under human in profile, as that heading has priority over foot.

To keep things functional I have made a few exceptions. A few important characters are listed in several sections. And some characters, which contain varied elements, had to be shown in all related sections. But on the whole, I have aimed at keeping this short and simple.

Each character may appear in several **graphical variations**. The order which you see does NOT necessarily show the development of the character. That's because there is no simple step-by-step development where it comes to Shang writing. In the final 250 years of the Shang period, some signs remained unchanged and others were written in many, many different ways. Writing was not standardized yet and many scribes improvised or developed their very own aesthetic preferences. Variation is greatest in period 1, when any topic was divined and more diviners and scribes were busy at the job than ever. I have collected more than twenty ways of writing *'Yellow River'*, more than twenty for *'little bird without tail'*, more than 35 for *'Ding cauldron: to divine'*, and roughly twenty for ancestor monkey, divine dragon and tiger each. Some of these come from datable inscriptions, but many others are from small fragments that cannot be dated with reasonable certainty. Given such a wide range of variations, and such a short period of time, it would be absurd to postulate that one sign neatly developed into another. Different scribes preferred different renderings. Or maybe it was the diviners who had their personal preferences; possibly even the kings had their say. Dating oracle bones would be much easier if writing had been standardised and each period nicely followed a set of conventions.

More so, there are misspellings. When a sign lacks a horizontal element it could well be that the scribe or carver forgot it. In ancient Chinese writing, vertical lines were carved first, then the bone was turned and the diagonal and horizontal lines incised. Given that some inscriptions were made in a hurry, the occasional missing line has to be expected. Some inscriptions were made with loving care and others hurriedly scratched and simplified. It doesn't always mean that a simple sign is a sloppy expression of a more elaborate one. When writing develops, there are many influences at work. Some scribes prefer elaboration and aesthetic beauty; others go for simplicity, functionality and speed. During the late Shang, we observe them all. Periods 1 and 2a favoured inscriptions that are well written, large and bold. Period 2b, with its more bureaucratic approach to divination, often shows more standardised inscriptions. Period 3 retained much of period 1 and 2 and elaborated many characters while retaining elder forms. Period 4 produced new forms but also re-introduced forms that are exactly like those of period 1. Consequently, period 1 and period 4 provide much space for scholarly disagreement. Period 5 downsized the divination business so much that only a handful of diviners and scribes did the job. Given that very few carvers engraved the bones, and that the topics of divination were much reduced, there are fewer variations on record than in earlier times. They probably existed in the bamboo scroll documents of historians, archivists, administrators and officials, but as these are lost, we get the misleading impression that period 5 writing was standardised.

I would like to point out that some variations are very common and others appear very rarely. I have selected many variations as they add to the visual richness of the character. By examining the variations, you can get a feeling for the range of possible developments and sense the essence of each grapheme. A study of the original inscriptions will tell you which forms of writing were the most common.

In many cases a given sign is not known from all periods. Here, we encounter the limits of our source material. Further excavations will help us close the gaps. A sign that appears only in period one and five obviously wasn't forgotten in the meantime. However, it may have been used with a different meaning. Rivers provide a good example. In period 1, several rivers were venerated as deities. In period 2b, their veneration stopped, and when you encounter a river in a divination, it is merely a place name. In period 3 and 4, a range of period 1 deities were revived and the river name may imply worship again. In period 5, it will be a place name. So, when you read that a given character can be a deity or a state name, place name or personal name, it does not follow that it was all of these at all times. And when a deity only appears in period 1 inscriptions it does not imply that the deity went out of business in periods 2 b to 5. It simply ceased to be a topic of divination. Probably it continued to be worshipped, but the king simply did not bother to ask about it anymore. The bones and turtle shells do not tell us everything: they only reveal what was divined about.

If you want to **date inscriptions**, I suggest you look up the table of diviners and consider the topic of the divination. There are also a few signs which definitely only occur in a specific period which may give good estimations. Nevertheless, a measure of caution is needed. Every scholar who translates ancient writing is in danger of running around in small circles chasing her or his own tail. You date a give variation in period one because it the diviners name fits that time, well and good. Then you find a fragment where that sign appears without much further writing. Sure, it's tempting to date such a fragment in period one. It could be wrong. The fragment could come from some conservative writer in another period. Maybe your generalisation is wrong. It could be an exception to your rule, only you will never notice when you are feeling too certain. And things won't improve by scholarly consent. A majority decision is no guarantee that something is true. It merely indicates that a given group of people from a specific period, university or country feels moderately sure (or agrees with the authorities). In a hundred years, other scholars might call the majority decision of today an outdated fashion of the turn of the twenty first century and discard it with a snigger. In dealing with ancient history (or with any other aspect of science, life, religion or reality), we are handling degrees of probability. We will never be absolutely certain.

Likewise, the **meanings** of each sign have to be taken with a dose of caution. In many cases, I listed several interpretations. It's not my job (nor am I competent) to decide which oracle bone scholar is *'right'*. With most characters, several readings are possible, and even these are often vague.

Take the matter of evaluation. There is a range of signs meaning something like *'good, auspicious, lucky, beneficial'*, but we do not know what they mean exactly. No doubt to the Shang they were more precise, ranging from not bad, to good, great, to miraculously wonderful. We simply can't tell the difference.

The same applies to the many characters meaning something like *'misfortune, accident, disaster, catastrophe'*. Take war divination. The kings divined about strategy, and this means that they asked specific questions. When you ask *'will there be defeat'*, the word *'defeat'* is not helpful. There are many ways of being defeated in war. You can be beaten at once or slowly over many years, your supplies can break down, the costs of a campaign can destroy the economy, generals can be assassinated, fear, weather, climate or plague can finish the army. Maybe a chariot wheel breaks and you end head first in a ditch. Disaster can come in many shapes. The Shang kings did not need to know if a general would meet defeat, they wanted to know about specific types of defeat. Some signs for *'disaster'* appear typically in war-divination, and we can be sure they referred to specific types of disaster. Other signs for disaster are more common in hunting divination, weather forecasts or regard rituals. It's only our modern ignorance that attaches a vague *'disaster, inauspicious'* to a wide range of probably rather specific calamities. And it gives the mistaken impression that the Shang asked vague questions. They didn't. We just can't read them precisely.

Where it comes to the graphemes, we often have a **literal meaning** of an image, such as the sign *'basket'* and its **sound**, which was identical with the word for *'it is; this is; is it? Perhaps?; will it be?'*; plus the third person: *'he, she'*. Maybe a symbolism was involved but certainly the main reason was phonetic. In oracle bone divination, nobody gave a damn about baskets. Here, the sign is always used phonetically and refers to a useful grammatical particle. This does not necessarily mean that the sign had ceased to be used for basket. Somewhere in the royal household administrators calculated the amount of baskets that was needed every few months. Their records have not survived. But given the amount of planning and administration the Shang needed to control their domain, I am sure that someone was busy keeping count of baskets, brooms, knives, spoons, stone tools, chopping boards and other everyday objects. In studying the Shang, we have to take into account that the common oracle bone writing and the much rarer writing on bronze objects are both reflections of an earlier script which was used for all sorts of purposes. It was, in all likeliness, written on bamboo strips, and went to rot in the soil. What we know from the oracle bones and from a few bronze vessels is just a selection which survived. The Shang wrote letters, contracts and documents. They had an eye on imports, tributes, war-payments and the like. And when you build a city from scratch you need a lot of administrators to calculate work-force, costs, tools, food and resources. The same goes for those who organise armies, and plan campaigns that may take half a year or more. The administrators and scribes must have used a lot more characters than we are aware of nowadays. And to give plain original signs like *'basket'* their due, I have included them in the range of meanings. To show that they were not used for *'basket'* in the oracle bones, they appear in brackets. Wherever a sign can be identified as something which it was not used for in the oracle bone script (such as chopping board, wooden spade, stalk of grass etc) the item appears in brackets. This estimate may change. Maybe we will discover a divination regarding an owl one day.

Composite characters often tell a story. A foot kicking a head (=reprimand), a sleeper struggling in bed (=dream vision, nightmare) or a foot stepping on a serpent (=curse) are symbolism. Shang writing started out that way and contains a much larger amount of ideographic characters than modern Chinese. But even among the Shang, characters did include **phonetic elements**. When you have a picture of two items, it could be *'meaning of picture one, pronounced as picture two'*. Anyone looking for symbolism in such a grapheme will be confused by the phonetic element. Many characters seem to appear in variation as the scribes differed in their choice of phonetic elements. Nowadays spoken Chinese only has a little over 400 different syllables; hence many words have the same or similar sounds. If you have several signs to indicate the same pronunciation, you may experiment and develop several forms of the written character. Take the character written knife (or knife spade) plus ax-blade. It means *'to request, beg'* (p.782). Obviously, the story told by the ax and the knife has little to do with the meaning. However, some scribes improvised. When you distort the character *'knife'* a little, it looks like *'human standing in profile'* (p.656). Hence, you get: to request = human threatened by axe blade. Those scribes who favoured this writing had a funny (or realistic) idea about how things are requested, but the majority of scribes did not agree and the variation remained a rarity.

Classification of **gods** can be difficult. With the more common gods, the matter is easy. Sure, we often don't really know if a god is a nature god, a deified early ancestor, a deified culture hero or a nature- or place-god who incarnated in human form to be deified once again after death. In Chinese myth, all of these and more are possible. Distinctions between humans, animals and deities are often very fluid. We can identify the better known gods by the fact that they receive prayer and sacrifices, and that people worry if they have cursed the harvest. But what about the *'lesser'* gods? When a god only appears in two or three inscriptions, many interpretations are possible. It could be a minor and unimportant god, it could be a very important but highly specialised god, it could be an important god who didn't need to be divined about, or it could be a god of one of the many states or tribes that made up the Shang domain, with more followers in the country than in the capital. Maybe we haven't found the really important inscriptions regarding the deity yet, or maybe they were destroyed over the last centuries. All of this is possible. There are quite a range of such gods in the inscriptions. Mostly, we only know that something is a deity because it received a sacrifice. Here, grammar provides great fun. We can have an inscription like *'sacrifice three dogs for/at X'*. The sign for/at is the problem. It could be a sacrifice *for* a deity or a sacrifice *at* a place. Some places were sacred to the Shang, and when the sign X only appears in two or three fragmentary inscriptions, we will never be entirely sure whether X is a deity or a sacred place. Or the deity of a place; as the Shang believed in a sacred landscape. If we are lucky we also come upon an inscription like *'shall we hunt for/at X?'* That settles the matter. The Shang did not hunt for anyone, and X must be a place. Eminent dictionaries, like *Jiaguwen Zidian*, take a cautious approach and favour reading *'sacrifice at X'*, so that they arrive at a great range of place names, some of which may yet turn out to be deities.

Last, there is the question **how many characters are there**? Take a look at the sign *'dancing'* (p.662). It shows a human from in-front, with outstretched arms, from which a range of objects are dangling. Some, like cattle-tails, can be identified. They are still in use in some shamanic dances. Others look like buckets, sacks, baskets, triangles or completely defy identification. Here, the price-winning question is: is this a single ideogram? T.T. Chang treated it as one character meaning *'dancing'* and *'queen, royal mate'*; *Jiaguwen Zidian* divides it into two distinct characters, namely: 1. *'ritual dance (for female ancestors?)'* & *'Wife of a king or Yi Yin'*; and 2. *'to dance'* (in general) & a state name. Is this all there is to the sign? With a little imagination we could discover or invent several distinct dances, by treating every odd shape as a distinct ritual costume. Maybe we are not dealing with one or two character groups but with a dozen definite characters, each of them with a very specific meaning. It could even be true. Likewise, some scholars consider the sign *'ding cauldron'* as a single character with multiple variations, while others prefer to make a difference between the angular ding and the rounded one, and propose that the round ding refers to a cauldron sacrifice. Not that this works out for all inscriptions. There are always exceptions. And once again, regardless what we argue, we can't be sure.

PEN is **Personal Name**. It can be a personal name, it might even be a title, but in many cases it is a clan name or the name of a family from a location. Lady Mouse came from the Mouse clan, Lady Well/Shaft from the Well/Shaft clan. It also happens to be the name of a state and a district. Hence, personal names go beyond what people are nowadays named for. In many cases, the personal names seem to be clan names. However, we cannot be sure that this is always the case. Titles and nick-names are just as possible. There is even the possibility that people had several names during their lives, such as birth names, call names, adult names, scholarly names and so on. In China, among the Han and many minorities, multiple names are a common custom. A person may even change her or his name to end a streak of bad luck or to begin a new period in life. In particular the diviner's names are worth studying. Some, like *'Great'*, *'Revealer'*, *'Drummer'*, *'Bell-Stroke'*, *'Ascender'*, *'Mouth'*, *'Invoker'*, *'Temple of Ancestress'* could easily be acquired names or honourary titles. Others, such as *'Pass Through Fields'*, *'City'*, *'Swimmer'*, *'Dog'*, *'Crossroad'*, *'Turbulence'*, *'Separate'* are less flattering and may be clan names chosen for phonetic reasons, or nick names referring to special events.

PLN is **Place Name**. It can be a part of the palace or the capital, a town, settlement, district, sacred site or general location. In many cases, we can't tell which. We can sometimes observe that a given place is popular for hunting, or is regularly used for army camps, but in most cases details are lacking.

STN is **State Name**. This is a vague term for any people, tribe or culture the Shang were in contact (or conflict) with. Some of them were foreign fang-States. Here, fang means foreign. A fang state may be hostile or bound to an alliance. Occasionally, fang states joined the Shang domain. In this case, they usually disappear from the list of foreign states and are not subject to divination any more. Or they broke away from the Shang and became enemies once again. The neighbours of the Shang were a varied lot. Alliances were flexible, allies could turn into enemies and enemies become friends. Some fang states were high cultures, civilised, with large cities and metal technology. Others were simple tribal groups making a living by hunting and gathering, or migrated with herds of cattle and sheep. In many cases, we can't tell the difference. It's a difficult specialist problem and I leave it to the specialists. Hence, I have used the general term *'state'* for any of them, no matter how powerful or insignificant.

(   ) signifies what the sign originally meant, or shows, or might have shown. The brackets indicate that in the highly specialised oracle bone inscriptions, the sign was not used in its original sense, but for phonetic reasons, or as a composite character. (Broom) =royal lady; (hand plus stone tool) =father; (chopping board) =grandfather; (spoon) = grandmother etc all appear in brackets, as the divinations do not refer to brooms, stone tools, chopping boards or spoons. These words did exist in Bronze Age Chinese writing, but they never appear in that sense in the oracle bone inscriptions.

By contrast, the word *'tiger'* is not in brackets. It could be a reference to a deity or a state, but as tigers appear in sacrifices and hunting inscriptions, they have no brackets. The word *'Lady Tigermonster'* (a deity or ancestress) does appear in brackets, as it is a composite made up of two glyphs. Likewise, a river written *'tiger plus water'* is in brackets. We cannot know whether the Shang thought of it as a Tigerriver, or meant *'river pronounced like tiger'* or both.

? Signifies that a meaning is highly doubtful.

Mammals

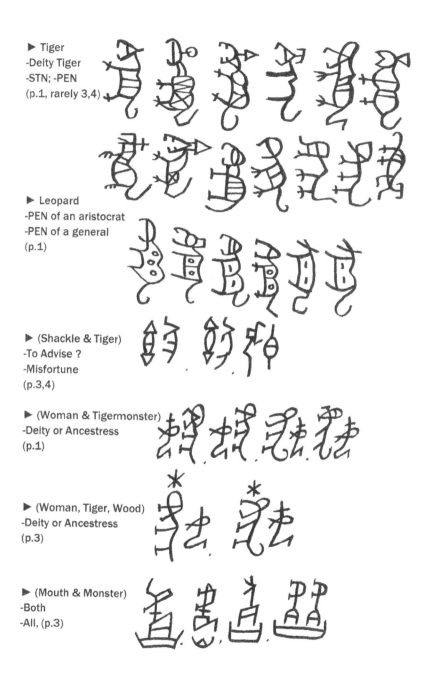

▶ Tiger
-Deity Tiger
-STN; -PEN
(p.1, rarely 3,4)

▶ Leopard
-PEN of an aristocrat
-PEN of a general
(p.1)

▶ (Shackle & Tiger)
-To Advise ?
-Misfortune
(p.3,4)

▶ (Woman & Tigermonster)
-Deity or Ancestress
(p.1)

▶ (Woman, Tiger, Wood)
-Deity or Ancestress
(p.3)

▶ (Mouth & Monster)
-Both
-All, (p.3)

► (Vessel & Cat)
-Tribute payment
-PLN
(p.1,3)

► (Tiger, ?)
a Ritual
-Cut
-STN; -PLN; -PEN
(p.1,3)

► (Tiger, Water)
-a River
-River Deity
(p.1)

► (Blade: Not-have, Dog)
-Fox
(p.1,3,5)

► Wolf
(p.1)

► Hare
- STN; -PLN; -PEN
(p.1,2,5)

► King Tu (Yang) Jia
(p.1)

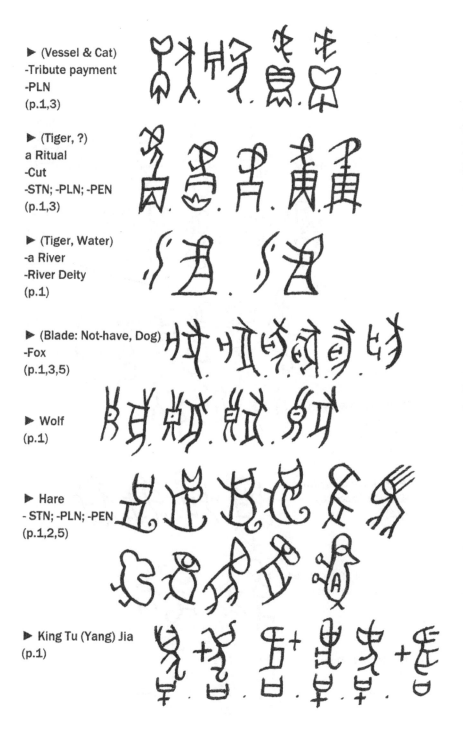

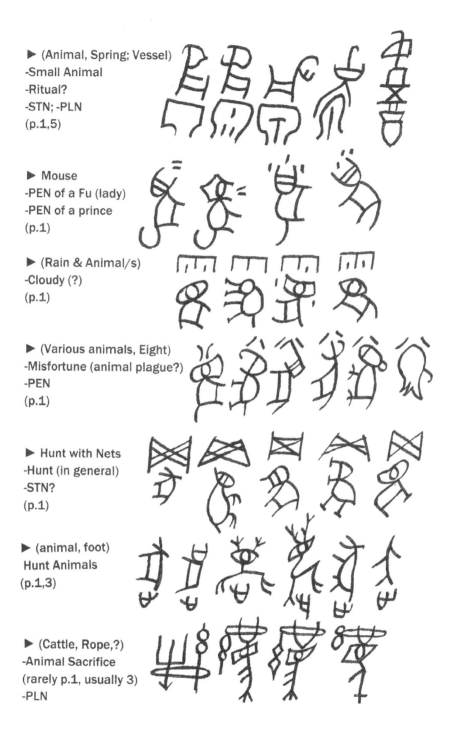

▶ (Animal, Spring; Vessel)
-Small Animal
-Ritual?
-STN; -PLN
(p.1,5)

▶ Mouse
-PEN of a Fu (lady)
-PEN of a prince
(p.1)

▶ (Rain & Animal/s)
-Cloudy (?)
(p.1)

▶ (Various animals, Eight)
-Misfortune (animal plague?)
-PEN
(p.1)

▶ Hunt with Nets
-Hunt (in general)
-STN?
(p.1)

▶ (animal, foot)
Hunt Animals
(p.1,3)

▶ (Cattle, Rope,?)
-Animal Sacrifice
(rarely p.1, usually 3)
-PLN

▶ (Animal, Mouth)
-Trap, to trap
-PEN
(p.1, rarely 3)

▶ (Two Animals, Mouth)
-(preparation for?) Animal Sacrifice
-PLN; -PEN
(p.1)

▶ Elephant
-STN
(p.1)

▶ (Elephant, Hand)
-Help
-Make, Build
-Deity or PEN
(p.1)

▶ Rhinoceros
-PLN
(p.1,2,3,4,5)

▶ (Horn, Human)
-Rhino people
-STN, see people
(p.1)

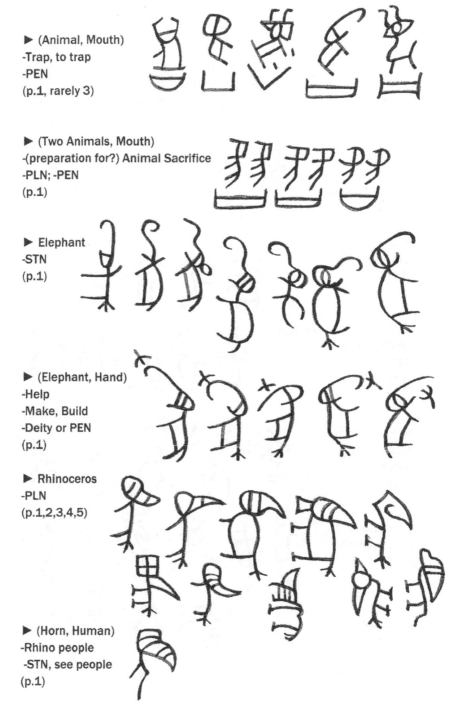

▶ Monkey
-Deity Monkey (?)
-Primal Ancestor
Nau, Chi or Ji
(p.1,2,3,4)

▶ unknown Animal
(p.1)

▶ Red Panda?
(p.1)

▶ (mouth, river, animal)
-unknown Animal
-A Ritual
(p.3)

▶ unknown Animal

▶ unknown Animal

▶ Chinese Elk
- STN; -PEN
(mostly p.1, also 3,5)

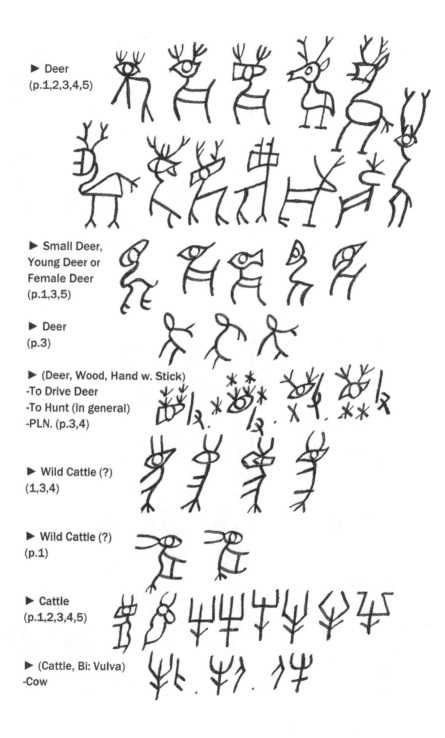

▶ Deer
(p.1,2,3,4,5)

▶ Small Deer,
Young Deer or
Female Deer
(p.1,3,5)

▶ Deer
(p.3)

▶ (Deer, Wood, Hand w. Stick)
-To Drive Deer
-To Hunt (in general)
-PLN. (p.3,4)

▶ Wild Cattle (?)
(1,3,4)

▶ Wild Cattle (?)
(p.1)

▶ Cattle
(p.1,2,3,4,5)

▶ (Cattle, Bi: Vulva)
-Cow

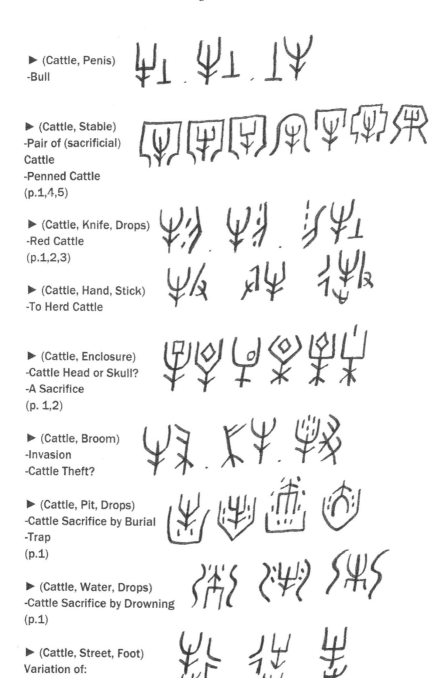

► (Cattle, Penis)
-Bull

► (Cattle, Stable)
-Pair of (sacrificial)
Cattle
-Penned Cattle
(p.1,4,5)

► (Cattle, Knife, Drops)
-Red Cattle
(p.1,2,3)

► (Cattle, Hand, Stick)
-To Herd Cattle

► (Cattle, Enclosure)
-Cattle Head or Skull?
-A Sacrifice
(p. 1,2)

► (Cattle, Broom)
-Invasion
-Cattle Theft?

► (Cattle, Pit, Drops)
-Cattle Sacrifice by Burial
-Trap
(p.1)

► (Cattle, Water, Drops)
-Cattle Sacrifice by Drowning
(p.1)

► (Cattle, Street, Foot)
Variation of:
-To Arrive, (p. 1,4)

▶ Sheep, Goat
-PLN; -PEN
(p.1,2.3,4,5)

▶ (Goat/Sheep, Vulva)
-Female Goat/Sheep

▶ (Goat/Sheep, Penis)
-Male Goat/Sheep

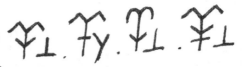

▶ (Goat/Sheep, Stable)
-Pair of (sacrificial)
Goat/Sheep
-Penned Sheep
(p. 1,2,3,4,5)

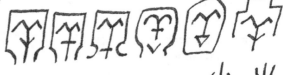

▶ (Goat/Sheep, Stable, Drops: Small)
-Pair of (sacrificial) Lambs
(p.1,3,4)

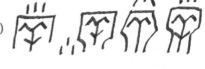

▶ (Goat/Sheep, Stable, Woman)
-A Pair of (sacrificial) Female
Goat/Sheep?
-A Drought Sacrifice or
-PEN of a woman chosen as drought
Sacrifice (a Wu?) (p.1)

▶ (Goat/Sheep, Mountain)
-Deity Yue Shan
-The Peak
(holiest mountain of the Shang)
(mainly p.1, occ. 3,4)

▶ (Goat/Sheep, ?)
-Deity Sheep (variation of Yue Shan?)
-STN
(p.1)

▶ (Goat/Sheep, Hand)
-A Gift, to Present
(p.2,3,4)

▶ (Goat/Sheep, Hand, Stick)
-To Herd Goat/Sheep
-A Sort of Sheep
-Goat/Sheep Sacrifice
-PLN (p.1, occas. 4)

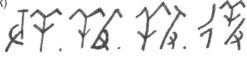

▶ (Goat/Sheep, Foot, Road, ?)
-To Herd Goat/Sheep?
-To Go
-PEN
(p. 3,5)

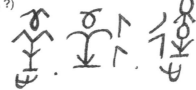

▶ (Goat/Sheep, Drops)
-Goat/Sheep Sacrifice

▶ (Goat/Sheep, Pit, Drops)
-Goat/Sheep Sacrifice
by Burial
-Trap
(p.1)

▶ (Goat/Sheep, Drops, Water)
-Goat/Sheep Sacrifice
by Drowning
(p. 1)

▶ (Double Goat/Sheep, Drops)
-Goat/Sheep Sacrifice
-PEN of a diviner p.2
(p.1,2,3)

▶ (Raising a Sheep/Goat)
-A Sacrifice (usually for rain)
(p.1)

▶ (Sheep/Goat, loop?, grass: birth)
-A Sacrificial Animal
(p.1)

▶ (Goat/Sheep, Bowl)
-To Share a (sacrificial) Meal
with people, ancestors or gods.
-PLN
(p. 1)

▶ (Goat/Sheep, Human)
-STN: the Qiang people
See: people (p.1,3)

▶ King Wo (Qiang) Jia

▶ A Sort of Goat/Sheep
(p.1)

▶ (Goat/Sheep, Triangle)
-A Ritual
(mainly p.1, occ.4)

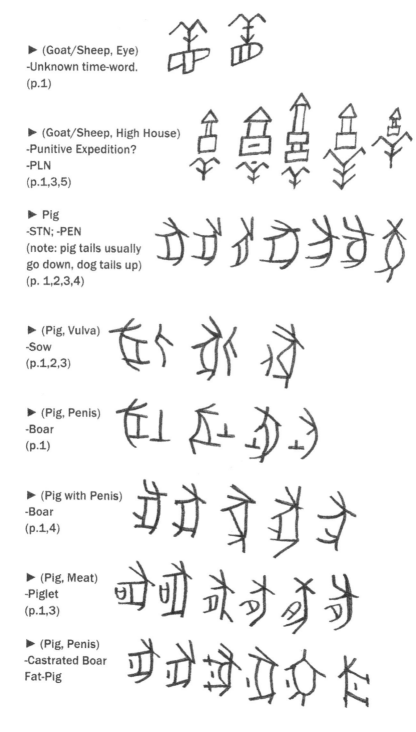

▶ (Goat/Sheep, Eye)
-Unknown time-word.
(p.1)

▶ (Goat/Sheep, High House)
-Punitive Expedition?
-PLN
(p.1,3,5)

▶ Pig
-STN; -PEN
(note: pig tails usually
go down, dog tails up)
(p. 1,2,3,4)

▶ (Pig, Vulva)
-Sow
(p.1,2,3)

▶ (Pig, Penis)
-Boar
(p.1)

▶ (Pig with Penis)
-Boar
(p.1,4)

▶ (Pig, Meat)
-Piglet
(p.1,3)

▶ (Pig, Penis)
-Castrated Boar
Fat-Pig

▶ a Type of Pig?
-Unknown animal
-Phonetic particle
(p.1,2)

▶ (Pig, Hands)
-A Ritual
-Offering?
(p. 1,2)

▶ (Pig, Hand, ?)
-to Go Towards something
-A Ritual
-PEN, (p. 1)

▶ (Pig, Knife)
-To Cut a Pig
-Hurt, Harm, Damage
(mainly p.1, occ.4)

▶ (Pig, Pit, Drops)
-Sacrifice of a Pig by
Burial
(p.1)

▶ (Pig, Enclosure)
-To Surround a Place
-Battue Shooting
-Pig Paddock, (p.1)

▶ (Pig, House)
-Family
-Home
(p.1.2.3.4)

▶ (Pig, Snake)
-A Ritual Object
or Offering, (p.3)

► (Pig, Arrow)
-Wild Boar
-Boar Hunt?
-A Sacrifice
-PLN (p. 1)

► Dog
(+ 'many') Admin. Rank
STN;-PEN
(p.1,3,4)

► (Dog, ?)
A Type of Dog
PEN
(p.2)

► (Dog, Ritual Post?)
To Hunt
Hunting Ritual
Battue Shooting?
Winter Hunt?
(p.1,3,4)

► (Dog, Pit)
Dog Sacrifice by Burial
(p.1)

► (Dog, Vessel)
Tribute Payment
PLN
(p. 1,3)

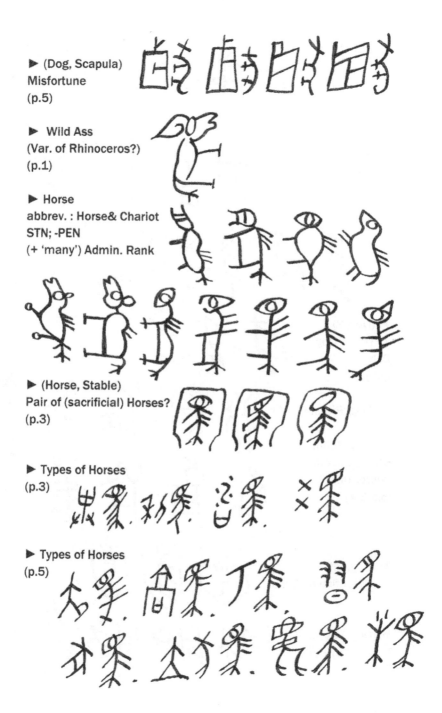

▶ (Dog, Scapula)
Misfortune
(p.5)

▶ Wild Ass
(Var. of Rhinoceros?)
(p.1)

▶ Horse
abbrev. : Horse& Chariot
STN; -PEN
(+ 'many') Admin. Rank

▶ (Horse, Stable)
Pair of (sacrificial) Horses?
(p.3)

▶ Types of Horses
(p.3)

▶ Types of Horses
(p.5)

Birds

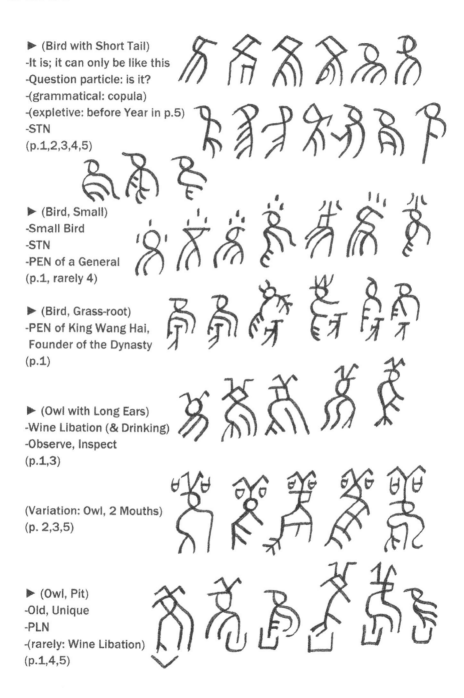

▶ (Bird with Short Tail)
-It is; it can only be like this
-Question particle: is it?
-(grammatical: copula)
-(expletive: before Year in p.5)
-STN
(p.1,2,3,4,5)

▶ (Bird, Small)
-Small Bird
-STN
-PEN of a General
(p.1, rarely 4)

▶ (Bird, Grass-root)
-PEN of King Wang Hai,
 Founder of the Dynasty
(p.1)

▶ (Owl with Long Ears)
-Wine Libation (& Drinking)
-Observe, Inspect
(p.1,3)

(Variation: Owl, 2 Mouths)
(p. 2,3,5)

▶ (Owl, Pit)
-Old, Unique
-PLN
-(rarely: Wine Libation)
(p.1,4,5)

► (Bird, Wood?, Foot)
-Unknown Bird
(p.1,4)

► (Bird, Net)
-Catch
-Receive
-STN
(p.1)

► (Bird, Net, Arrow)
- Catch Birds
(p. 1)

► (Bird, Hand-net)
- Get, Receive
-PEN of Diviner
(p.1)

► (Bird, Hand)
-Catch
-Receive
-PLN;-PEN
(p.1)

► (Bird, Arrow)
-Unknown Bird
-Hurt or Killed
(p. 1,2,3,5)

► (Bird, Roof)
-Cloudy, Overcast
-Foggy?
-Tomb?
-(phonetic), (p.1)

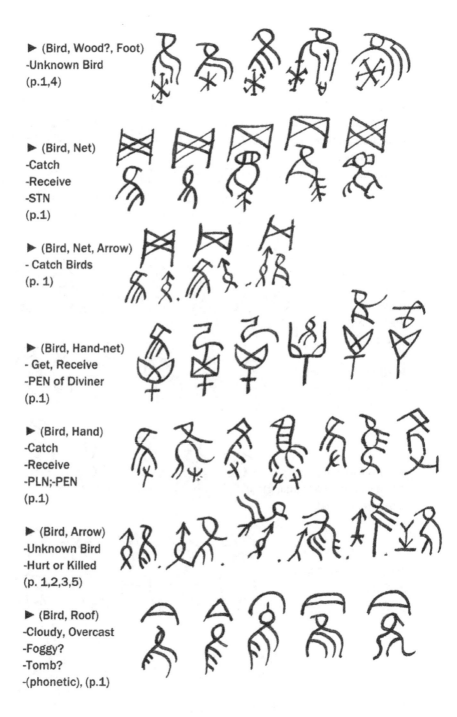

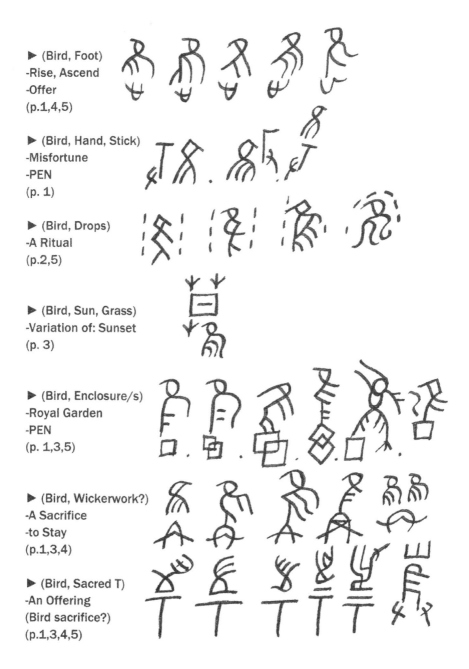

▶ (Bird, Foot)
-Rise, Ascend
-Offer
(p.1,4,5)

▶ (Bird, Hand, Stick)
-Misfortune
-PEN
(p. 1)

▶ (Bird, Drops)
-A Ritual
(p.2,5)

▶ (Bird, Sun, Grass)
-Variation of: Sunset
(p. 3)

▶ (Bird, Enclosure/s)
-Royal Garden
-PEN
(p. 1,3,5)

▶ (Bird, Wickerwork?)
-A Sacrifice
-to Stay
(p.1,3,4)

▶ (Bird, Sacred T)
-An Offering
(Bird sacrifice?)
(p.1,3,4,5)

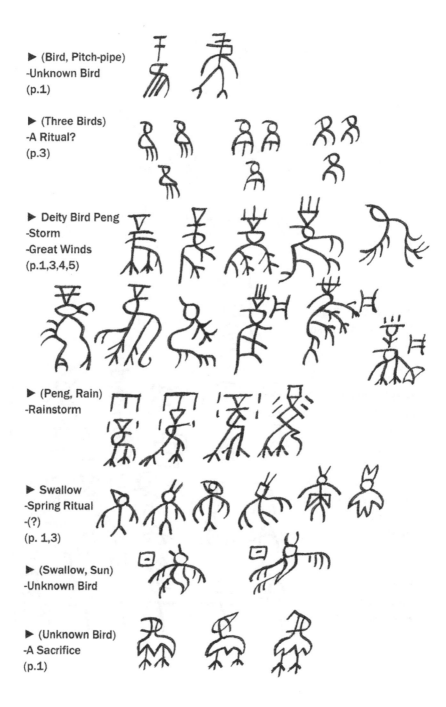

► (Bird, Pitch-pipe)
-Unknown Bird
(p.1)

► (Three Birds)
-A Ritual?
(p.3)

► Deity Bird Peng
-Storm
-Great Winds
(p.1,3,4,5)

► (Peng, Rain)
-Rainstorm

► Swallow
-Spring Ritual
-(?)
(p. 1,3)

► (Swallow, Sun)
-Unknown Bird

► (Unknown Bird)
-A Sacrifice
(p.1)

▶ (Bird w. Throat Cut
or Hanging)
-Bird Sacrifice
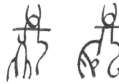

▶ (Raven, Crow)
-Finally?
-Swiftly?
-PLN,-PEN
(p.1)

▶ (Raven, Star)
-Constellation Bird Star?
-Weather finally cleared up?
(p1)

▶ (Raven, Hand, Grass)
-Chick, Young Bird
(p.1)

▶ (Raven?,?)
-Constellation
(p.1)

▶ Unknown Bird
(p.3)

▶ (Woodpecker)
-PLN
(p.1)

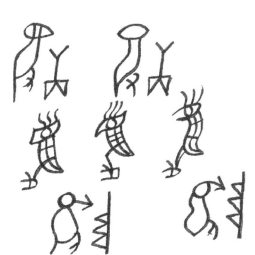

► Cockerel
-PLN; -PEN
(p.1,3)

► (Cock, Mouth)
-Sing
-PEN
(p.1,3,5)

► (Cock, Mouth, Ear)
-Variation of: Tinnitus
(p.1)

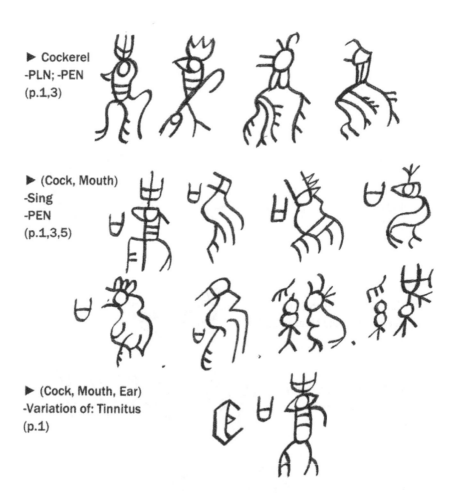

Reptiles

▶ Dragon
-Deity Dragon
-Misfortune?
-Luck, Healing?
-STN;-PLN;-City-name
(p.1,3,4)

▶ (Dragon, Hands)
-Deity Dragon, Veneration
-STN;-PLN;-PEN
(p.1)

▶ (Dragon, House)
-Shrine for Deity Dragon?
-STN;-PEN
(P.1)

▶ (Dragon, Hands, Woman)
-Deity or Ancestress
(p.1)

▶ Ancestor Long Jia

▶ Wingless Dragon
-Crocodile?
-Misfortune, Disaster
-Deity or Spirit
(p.1,2,3)

▶ (Wingless Dragon, Mouth)
-unknown Worm, Insect
or Pest of the Fields
(p.4)

▶ (Double Headed Dragon)
-Rainbow
-Misfortune?
(p.1)

▶ Snake
-Misfortune, Death
Ending, Otherworld
-Relation of the King
-Variation of: Cult Year
-PLN;-PEN
(p.1,2)

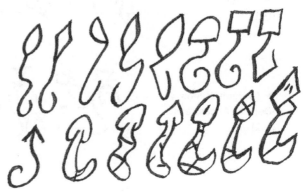

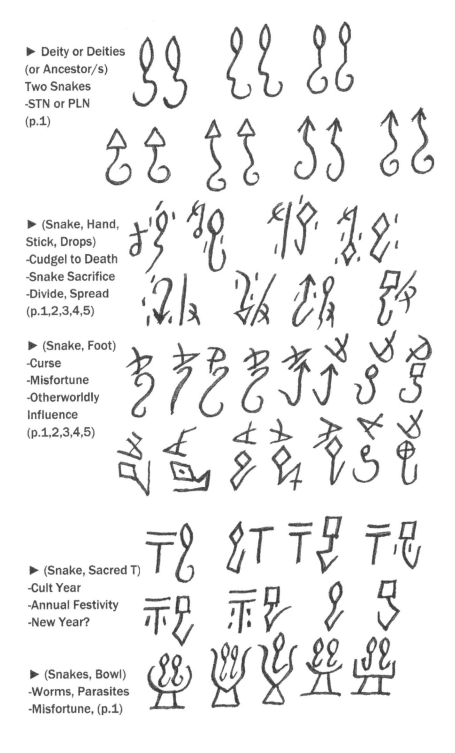

▶ Deity or Deities
(or Ancestor/s)
Two Snakes
-STN or PLN
(p.1)

▶ (Snake, Hand,
Stick, Drops)
-Cudgel to Death
-Snake Sacrifice
-Divide, Spread
(p.1,2,3,4,5)

▶ (Snake, Foot)
-Curse
-Misfortune
-Otherworldly
Influence
(p.1,2,3,4,5)

▶ (Snake, Sacred T)
-Cult Year
-Annual Festivity
-New Year?

▶ (Snakes, Bowl)
-Worms, Parasites
-Misfortune, (p.1)

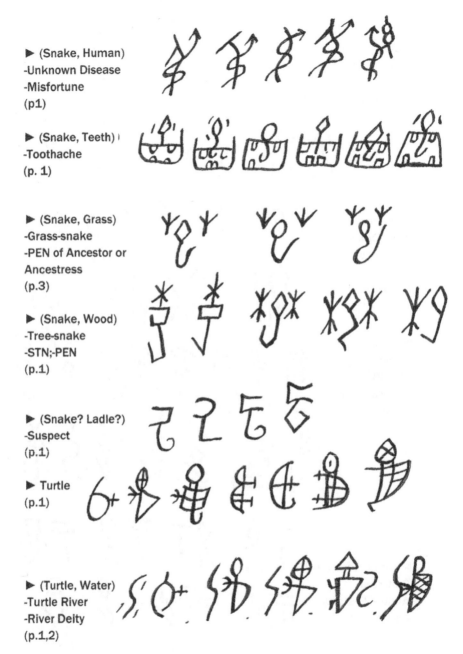

▶ (Snake, Human)
-Unknown Disease
-Misfortune
(p1)

▶ (Snake, Teeth)
-Toothache
(p. 1)

▶ (Snake, Grass)
-Grass-snake
-PEN of Ancestor or
Ancestress
(p.3)

▶ (Snake, Wood)
-Tree-snake
-STN;-PEN
(p.1)

▶ (Snake? Ladle?)
-Suspect
(p.1)

▶ Turtle
(p.1)

▶ (Turtle, Water)
-Turtle River
-River Deity
(p.1,2)

Reptiles, Amphibians

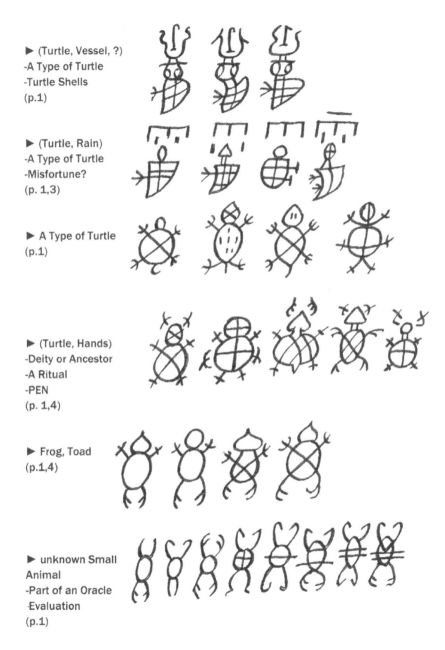

▶ (Turtle, Vessel, ?)
-A Type of Turtle
-Turtle Shells
(p.1)

▶ (Turtle, Rain)
-A Type of Turtle
-Misfortune?
(p. 1,3)

▶ A Type of Turtle
(p.1)

▶ (Turtle, Hands)
-Deity or Ancestor
-A Ritual
-PEN
(p. 1,4)

▶ Frog, Toad
(p.1,4)

▶ unknown Small
Animal
-Part of an Oracle
-Evaluation
(p.1)

Fish

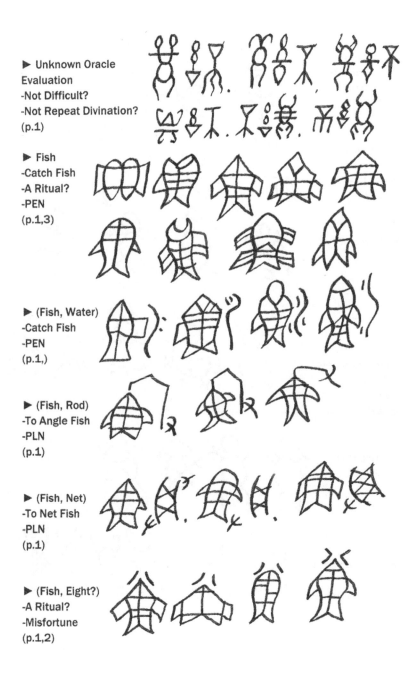

► Unknown Oracle
Evaluation
-Not Difficult?
-Not Repeat Divination?
(p.1)

► Fish
-Catch Fish
-A Ritual?
-PEN
(p.1,3)

► (Fish, Water)
-Catch Fish
-PEN
(p.1,)

► (Fish, Rod)
-To Angle Fish
-PLN
(p.1)

► (Fish, Net)
-To Net Fish
-PLN
(p.1)

► (Fish, Eight?)
-A Ritual?
-Misfortune
(p.1,2)

Fish, Small Animals

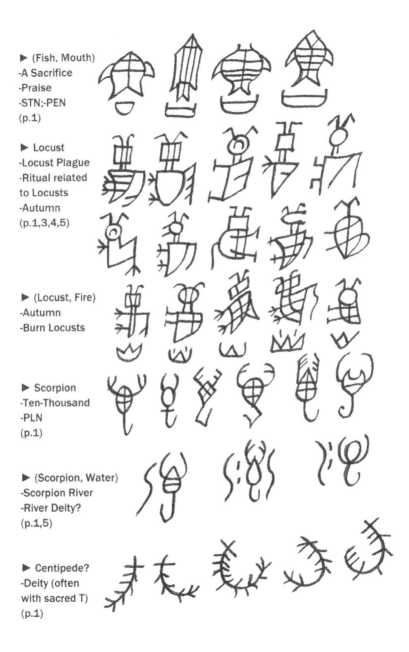

► (Fish, Mouth)
-A Sacrifice
-Praise
-STN;-PEN
(p.1)

► Locust
-Locust Plague
-Ritual related
to Locusts
-Autumn
(p.1,3,4,5)

► (Locust, Fire)
-Autumn
-Burn Locusts

► Scorpion
-Ten-Thousand
-PLN
(p.1)

► (Scorpion, Water)
-Scorpion River
-River Deity?
(p.1,5)

► Centipede?
-Deity (often
with sacred T)
(p.1)

Small Animals

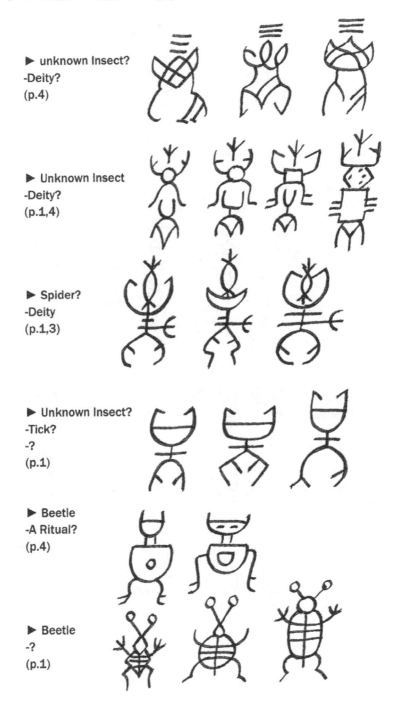

▶ unknown Insect?
-Deity?
(p.4)

▶ Unknown Insect
-Deity?
(p.1,4)

▶ Spider?
-Deity
(p.1,3)

▶ Unknown Insect?
-Tick?
-?
(p.1)

▶ Beetle
-A Ritual?
(p.4)

▶ Beetle
-?
(p.1)

▶ Grasshopper?
-?
(p.1)

▶ Snail?
-?
(p.1)

▶ Shell?
-Fungus?
-5th of 12
-STN
(p.1,2,3,4,5)

▶ (Shell? Foot)
-Tremble
-Earthquake
(p.1,4,5)

▶ (Shell?, Wood)
-Morning Sacrifice
-Admin. Rank (w. 'many')
-STN
(p.1,2)

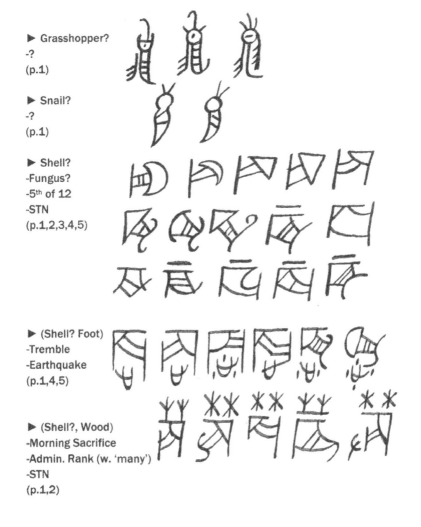

▶ Cowrie Shell
-Valuable, Rare
-Money
-An Offering
(p.1,3)

▶ (Cowrie, Vessel)
-STN or Admin. Rank
-PEN
(p.1, rarely 3)

▶ (Cowrie, Hand,
Stick, Mouth)
-Futile
-Unsuccessful
-Misfortune
(p.1)

▶ (Cowrie, Hand, Street)
-Obtain, Receive
-PEN
(1, rarely 3)

▶ (Cowrie, Arrows)
-Animal Sacrifice
-STN
(p. 1)

▶ (Cowrie, Sacred T, Hand)
-A Ritual

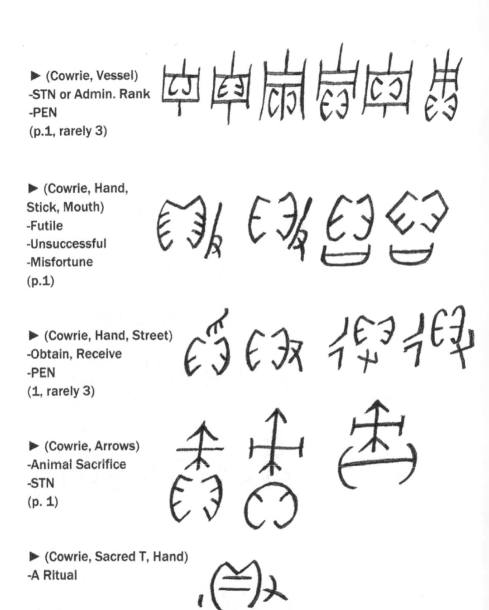

Human

▶ Human
-One Thousand
-STN
(p.1,2,3,4,5)

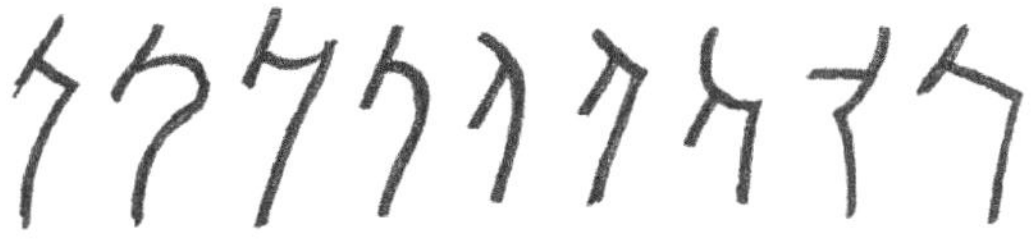

▶ One Thousand

▶ (Spoon, Shovel)
-(Bi) Ancestress
-Female (Animal)
-Vulva
(p.1,2,3,4,5)

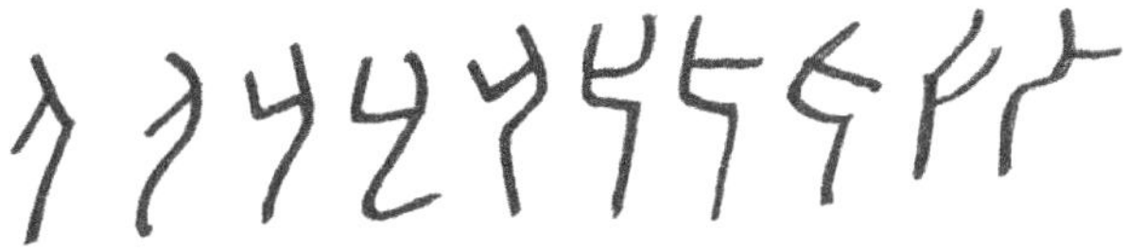

▶ (Human, ?)
-A Ritual
-PEN
(p.1,3)

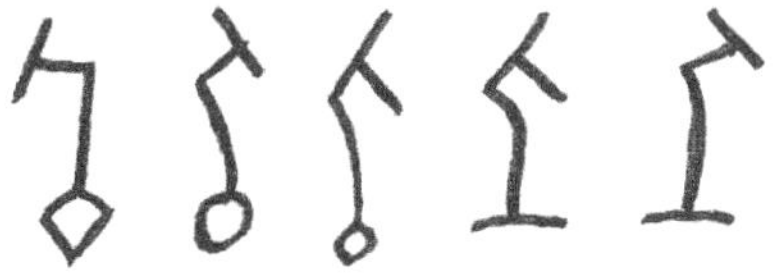

▶ (Two Persons)
-Follow
-From
(p.1,2,3,4,5)

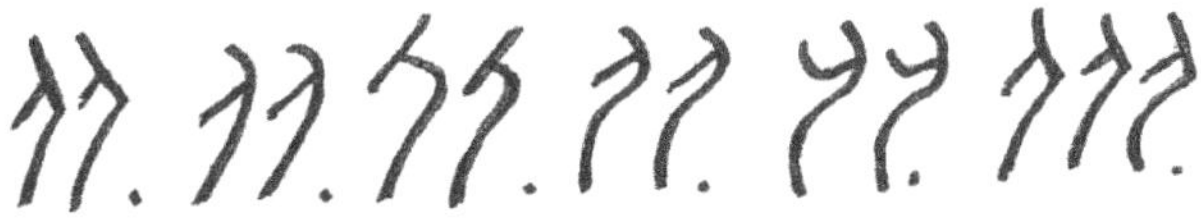

▶ (Follow, Flag)
-Troop
-PEN
-PEN of Diviner (p.2)
(p.1,2,3)

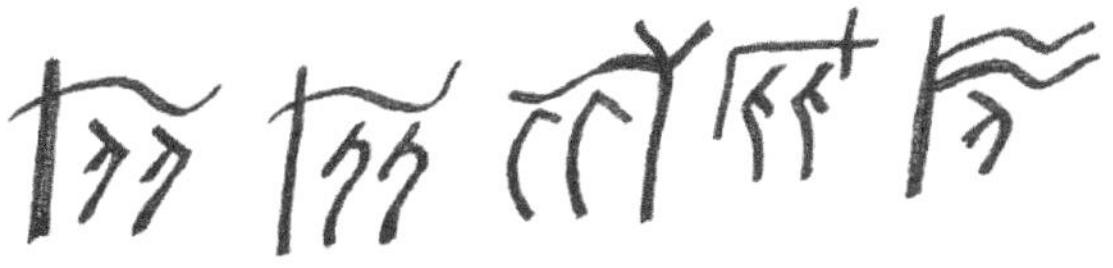

▶ (Follow, Line)
-Put Together
-Combine
-PLN
(1,3,4)

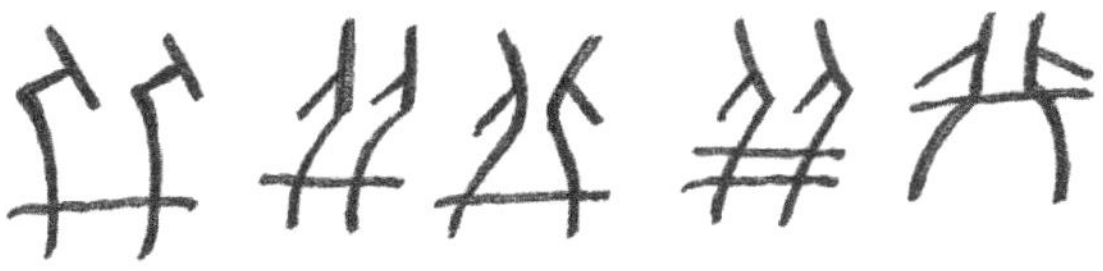

▶ (Road, Follow, Foot)
-Go To
-PLN
(p.1)

▶ (Human, Kneeling Person)
-Deity
-PLN
(p.1)

▶ (People, Sun)
-'The Many'
-Citizens
-Higher Clans
(p.1,2,3,4)

▶ (Pin, People)
-A Ritual
-?
(p.1,3)

▶ (People Back to Back)
-Back
-North
-Deity North
-Northern States
PLN (p.1,2,3,4,5)

▶ (Separate)
-Negation:
Is Not
-STN?-PLN?
(p.1,2,3,4)

▶ (People Fighting)
-Fight?
-PLN
(p.1)

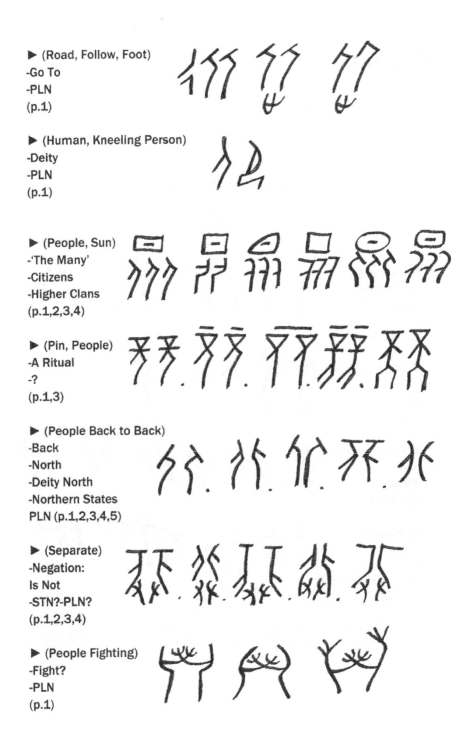

▶ Variation of:
Female, Woman,
Daughter
(p.1)

▶ Belly
-Body
-rarely: pregnant
(p.1)

▶ Pregnant
(p.1)

▶ (Long Hair)
-Long
Enduring, Old
-Name of the South
and the Southwind
-STN or PEN
-PLN? (p.1,3,5)

▶ (Human, High)
-Beginning, The First
-Original
-Great
-STN, -PLN
(p.1,2,3)

▶ (Human, ?)
-Important
-Intense
-Climax?
(p.1)

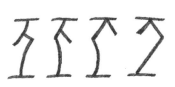

▶ (Human, Drops)
-Ask, Beg, request
-Male Relation of
Father's Family (p.1)

▶ (Human, Drops)
-Scales, Scale Armour
-PEN of King Pan Geng
(p.1)

▶ (Human, Drops:
To urinate)
-Weak
(p.1)

▶ (Human, Drops)
- Shit
-Manure
(p.1)

▶ (Human, Drops)
-Variation of: Sick
-Disease
(p.1)

▶ (Human, Drops, Boat)
-Variation of:
Flood, Deluge
(p.1)

▶ (Human, Snake)
-Variation of:
Unknown Disease
-Misfortune, (p.1)

▶ (Human, Death Mask?)
Variation of: Ghost
(p.1)

▶ (Ghost, Stick)
-Fear
-Ghost-Visitation
(p.1)

▶ (Human, Sheep)
-STN of the Qiang
Nomads
-PLN (p. 1,3)

▶ (Human, Monkey)
-Variation of: Primal ancestor
Nau, Chi or Ji
-Monkey
(p.1)

▶ (Human, Horn)
-Rhino-People
-STN
(p.1)

▶ (Woman, Human, Child)
-Soothe, Calm
-Stabilise
-(Part of a Name)
(p.1)

▶ (Woman, Child, Drops:
Freshly Born)
-Next
-Younger (Generation)
-with 'many': the Many
Younger Generations
(p.1,2,3,4,5)

▶ (Hand catches Human)
-Reach
-Until, To, As Far As
(p.1,2,3,4)

▶ (Human, Hand, Stick)
-Plague
-Forced Labour?
-PEN (p.1)

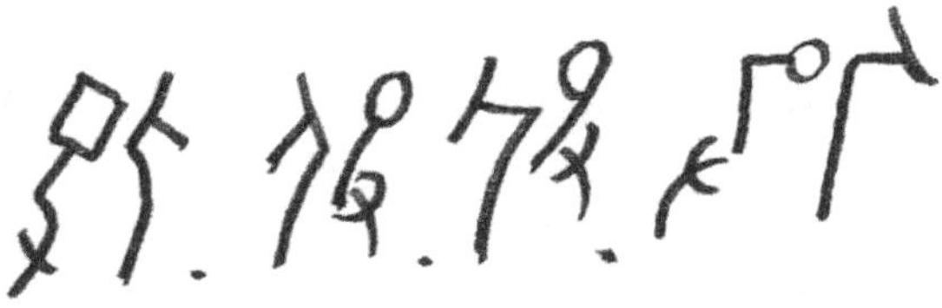

▶ (Human, Hand, Stick)
-A Sacrifice
(p.3)

▶ (Human, Hand, Stick)
-Steward, Administrator
-PEN of Yi Yin
(p.1,2,3,4)

▶ (Yi Yin, Dance or Wife)
-Yi Yin's Wife?
-Dance Offering for Yi Yin?
(p.2,3,4)

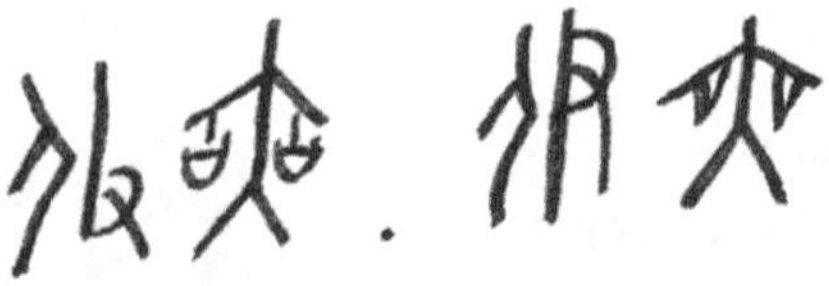

▶ (Human, Hand, Road)
-Rescue
(p.1)

▶ (Human, Mouth, Hand)
-Extend
-Delay
-A Ritual (p.1, mainly 3)

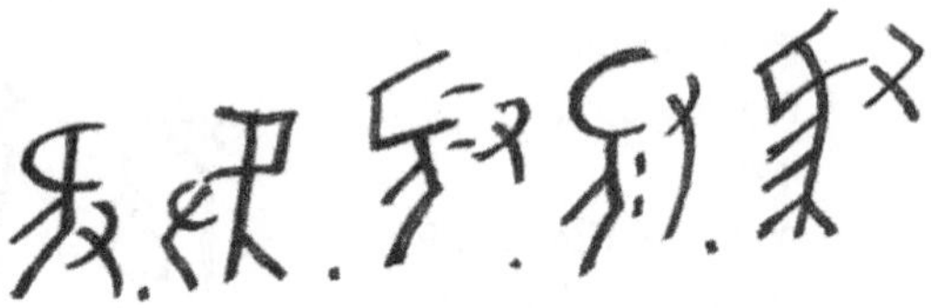

▶ (Woman, Foot)
-Born, Birth
(p.1)

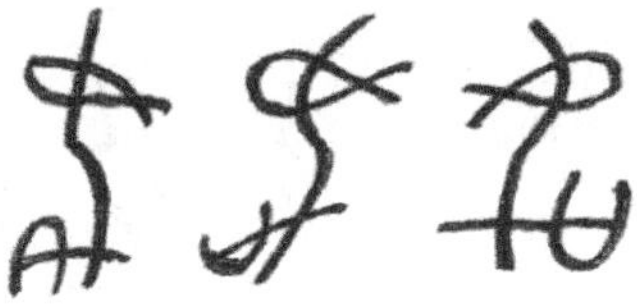

▶ (Human, Foot)
-To Observe from a
High Place
-A Ritual
-Pray for Rain?
(p.1,4)

▶ (Human, Foot)
-Advance, Lead
-Earlier (Generation)
-A Ritual?
(p.1,4)

▶ (Human, Foot:
Kick Head)
-Rebuke, Criticism
-Rebuke by Ancestors
-Misfortune
-A Ritual?(p.1,3)

▶ (Human, Foot, Road)
Variation of:
-Aristocratic Rank
-A Ritual
-Defend?
-STN;-PLN;-PEN (p.1)

▶ (Human, Foot, Plow)
-Till the Soil, Sow, Plough
-Ritual of first Ploughing
-with 'Administrator':
Manage Arable Land
(p.1, rarely 4)

▶ (Human, Mouth)
-Elder Brother
(p.1,2,3)

▶ (Human, Mouth,?)
-Unknown Part of
the Body
(p.1)

▶ (Human, Mouth)
-Call (People)
-Taste
-STN;-PEN
(p.1)

▶ (Human, Mouth, Vessel)
-Offer and Drink Alcohol
(p.1)

▶ (Human, Mouth, Ear)
-Listen
-Wise?
(p.1)

▶ (Woman, Mouth, Rope)
-Question Female Prisoner
-Enslave?
(p.1,5)

▶ (Human, Eye)
-To Gaze into the
Distance
-PEN of a General
-An Offering
-PLN; -PEN (p.1,4)

▶ (Human, Eye)
-Observe, Inspect
-Inspection Tour
-Grant Audience
-STN;-PEN (p.1)

▶ (Human, Eye, Axe)
-Old Administrator
-Rain-related Ritual or
Deity
-PEN
(p.1)

▶ (Human, Eye, Water)
-Variation of:
Before Dawn
(p.3)

▶ (Human, Eye, Axe)
-Ambush
-Wage War
-PEN of
Early Ancestor
(p.1,3,4)

▶ (Head, Negation, Human)
-Deity or Ancestor?
(p.1)

▶ (Human, Brush)
-Tail
-A Sacrifice
(p.1)

▶ (Human, Nose)
-Variation of:
Animal sacrifice
(p.1)

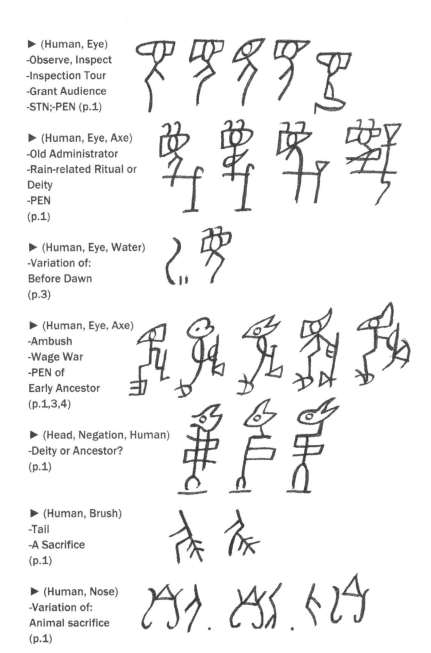

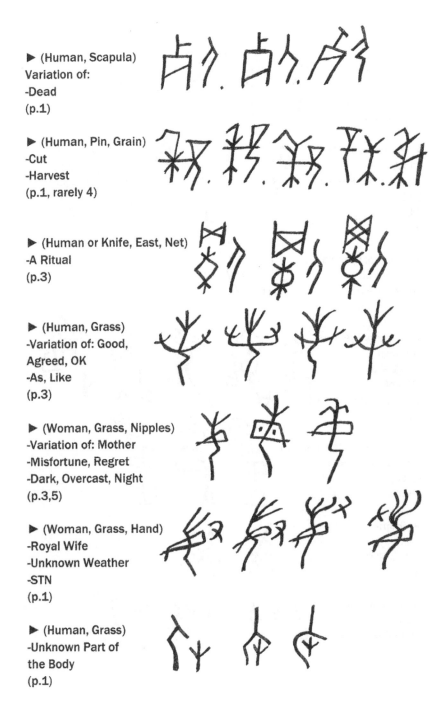

▶ (Human, Scapula)
Variation of:
-Dead
(p.1)

▶ (Human, Pin, Grain)
-Cut
-Harvest
(p.1, rarely 4)

▶ (Human or Knife, East, Net)
-A Ritual
(p.3)

▶ (Human, Grass)
-Variation of: Good,
Agreed, OK
-As, Like
(p.3)

▶ (Woman, Grass, Nipples)
-Variation of: Mother
-Misfortune, Regret
-Dark, Overcast, Night
(p.3,5)

▶ (Woman, Grass, Hand)
-Royal Wife
-Unknown Weather
-STN
(p.1)

▶ (Human, Grass)
-Unknown Part of
the Body
(p.1)

▶ (Human, Plant)
-Grains (Millet?)
-Harvest
-Agricult. Year
(p.1,3)

▶ (Human, Grain, Knife)
-Verb related to Agriculture
(p.1)

▶ (Human, Tree)
-Rest, Stop
-Blessing
-PLN (p.1)

▶ (Human, Grass, East)
-Name of a Disease or
-A part of the Body
(p.1,4)

▶ (Human, Sun)
-Variation of:
Second Meal
(p.3)

▶ (Human, Sun)
-A Ritual?
(p.1)

▶ (Human, Road, Drops)
-Swim
-PEN of a Diviner
-PLN;-PEN (p.1,2,3,5)

▶ (Human, Wickerwork?)
-Unknown Oracle Evaluation
-PEN
(p,1)

▶ (Human, Wickerwork?, Grain)
-Soldier's Barracks
-PEN
(p.1)

▶ (Human, Pin,
Earth-Heap, Wickerwork)
-Unknown Vegetable or Grain
(p.1)

▶ (Human, 1000, House)
-March
-Move Troops
-? (p.1)

▶ (Human, Wickerwork?, House)
-A Ritual?
(p.1)

▶ (Human, Drops, House)
-With 'Many': Administrative Rank
or Group of People
-PLN;-PEN
(p.1, mainly3)

▶ (Human, Mat, House)
-Variation of:
Complete, Finished
-A Ritual?
-Continuously? Overnight? (p.1,3)

▶ (Human, Stick, House)
-House Servant or Labourer
(p.1)

▶ (Human, Well, Shaft)
-Imprisoned
-Distress
(p.1)

▶ (Human in Coffin)
-Burial
-Death?
(p.1)

▶ (Human or
Concubine, Pit, Drops)
-Human Sacrifice by Burial?
(p.1)

▶(Human, Hat)
-Administrative Rank
-A Ritual
-STN
(p.1)

▶ (Human, Hat, Stick)
-Old
-Blind?
-Musician
-PLN (p.1,2,5)

▶ (Human, Hat, Stick, Bed)
-Old, Blind and Sick

▶ (Human, Bed, Drops)
General Term for:
-Disease
(p.1,4)

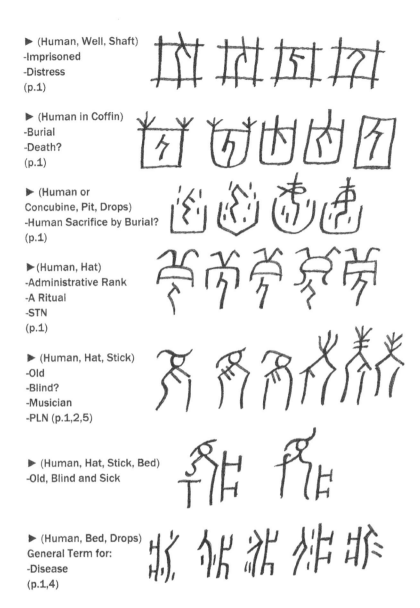

▶ Foot Disease
▶ Knee Disease
▶ Head Disease

▶ Mouth Disease
▶ Tongue Disease
▶ Pregnancy Disease

▶ Heel Disease
▶ Nose Disease
▶ Tooth Disease

▶ (Human, Hand, Bed)
-Body Disease
-Healing Body Disease
-STN;-PLN
(p.1, rarely 4)

▶ (Scapula, Wind,
Hand, Human, Bed)
-Misfortune Wind
Have Disease
(p.1)

▶ (Human, Bed, Rain)
-Disease or Misfortune
(Heavy Sweating?)
(p.1)

▶ (Human, Eye, Bed)
-Dream Vision
-Nightmare
-Misfortune
(p.1,3)

▶ (Human, Arms, Bed:
-Dreaming with strong motions)
-Dream Vision
-Nightmare
(p.1)

▶ (Human, Hoe)
-Carry
-PEN of Diviner/s (p.1 &3)
-With 'Water': Variant of
Huang He, Yellow River (p.3)
-Deity of Yellow River (p.3)

▶ (Human, Bag)
-Give, Bring
-Receive, Import
(p.1,3,4)

▶ (Human or Woman, Rope)
-Prisoner, Captive
- Dark Woman (Xuan Nü)?
-PLN;-PEN
(p.1)

▶ (Human, Handcuffs)
-Arrest
-Prisoner
-STN or PEN
(p.1,3,4,5)

▶ (Human, Carpenter's Square)
-Administrative Rank
-PEN
(p,1)

▶ (Human, Child, Ladder)
-Fall
(p.1)

▶ (Human, Hand-net)
-Catch People?
-PEN of a General (p.1)
-STN
(p.1, rarely 4)

▶ (Human, Bell)
-A Ritual?
(p.1)

▶ (Human, Axe)
-Wage War
-Sacrifice Human
-Decapitate
(p.1,3,4,5)

▶ (Human under Axe)
-Defend
-Station troops
-Border-guards
(p.1,3)

▶ (Human, Blade)
-Variation of:
Ask, Request
(p.1,2,4)

▶ (Human?, Pit or Vessel)
-Wine Vessel
-Long (Time)
(p.1,3)

▶ (Human, Vessel)
-Animal sacrifice?
(p.3)

▶ (Human, Vessel, drops)
-Ritual Bath
(p.1,2)

▶ (Human, Vessel, Mouth)
-A Ritual
(p. 5)

▶ (Human, Vessel?, Foot)
-Belly
-Digestion?
?
(p.1,3)

▶ (Human, Cauldron, Foot)
-Cook
-Food Offering
(p.1,3,5)

Great

▶ (Human)
-Great, Large
-Title: Great
-Royal Name Element
-Heaven (p.5)
-PEN of a Diviner (p.1,2,3)
(p.1,2,3,4)
▶ Great City Shang
Heavenly City Shang
-Name of the Capital
(p.1,2,3,5)

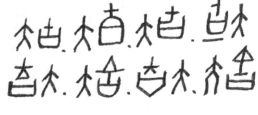

▶ (Great, Mouth, ?)
-Great and Good
-Auspicious Omen
(p.1,3)

▶ A Deity?
(p.1)

▶ (Human, ?)
-Name of the South
and the South Wind
(p.1)

▶ (Human, Enclosure)
-Ritual?
-Clan Sign?
(p.1,2,4)
▶ (Human, Ground)
-Erect
-Stand
-To Place
-A Ritual
PEN (p.1,3,4)

▶ (Human, Ground)
-Variation of: Arrive
(p.1,3,4)

▶ (Human or King, ?)
-Variation of:
Borderland
-STN
(p.1,3)

▶ (Two Humans)
-Both
-Together, With, And
PLN;-PEN (p.1,3)

▶ (Human, Axe Blade?)
-King
(p.1,2,3,4,5)

▶ (Human, Ornament
or Tattoo?)
-Beautiful
-Element of Names and
Placenames (p.1,2,3,4,5)

▶(Human, Tilted Head)
-Deity or Ancestor
-with 'Mountain':
a Mountain deity
(p.1)

▶ (Human, ?)
-Vulva
(p.1)

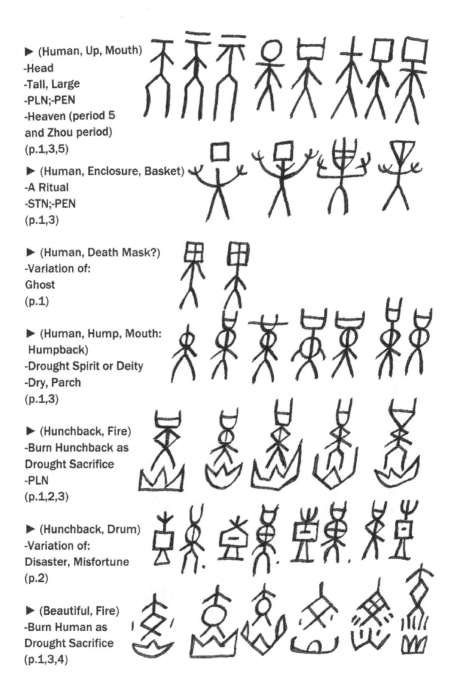

▶ (Human, Up, Mouth)
-Head
-Tall, Large
-PLN;-PEN
-Heaven (period 5
and Zhou period)
(p.1,3,5)

▶ (Human, Enclosure, Basket)
-A Ritual
-STN;-PEN
(p.1,3)

▶ (Human, Death Mask?)
-Variation of:
Ghost
(p.1)

▶ (Human, Hump, Mouth:
 Humpback)
-Drought Spirit or Deity
-Dry, Parch
(p.1,3)

▶ (Hunchback, Fire)
-Burn Hunchback as
Drought Sacrifice
-PLN
(p.1,2,3)

▶ (Hunchback, Drum)
-Variation of:
Disaster, Misfortune
(p.2)

▶ (Beautiful, Fire)
-Burn Human as
Drought Sacrifice
(p.1,3,4)

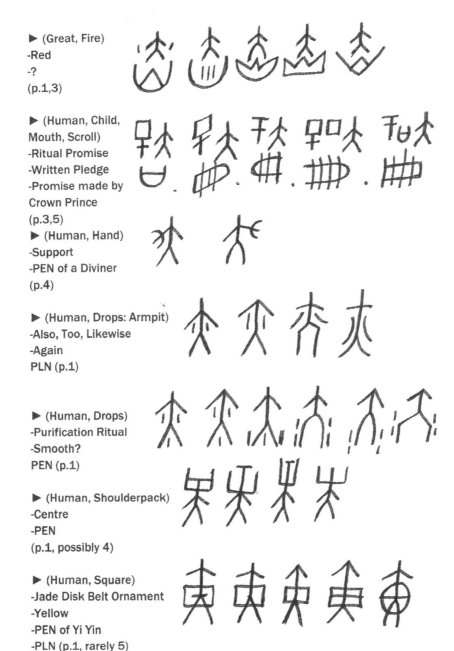

▶ (Great, Fire)
-Red
-?
(p.1,3)

▶ (Human, Child, Mouth, Scroll)
-Ritual Promise
-Written Pledge
-Promise made by Crown Prince
(p.3,5)

▶ (Human, Hand)
-Support
-PEN of a Diviner
(p.4)

▶ (Human, Drops: Armpit)
-Also, Too, Likewise
-Again
PLN (p.1)

▶ (Human, Drops)
-Purification Ritual
-Smooth?
PEN (p.1)

▶ (Human, Shoulderpack)
-Centre
-PEN
(p.1, possibly 4)

▶ (Human, Square)
-Jade Disk Belt Ornament
-Yellow
-PEN of Yi Yin
-PLN (p.1, rarely 5)

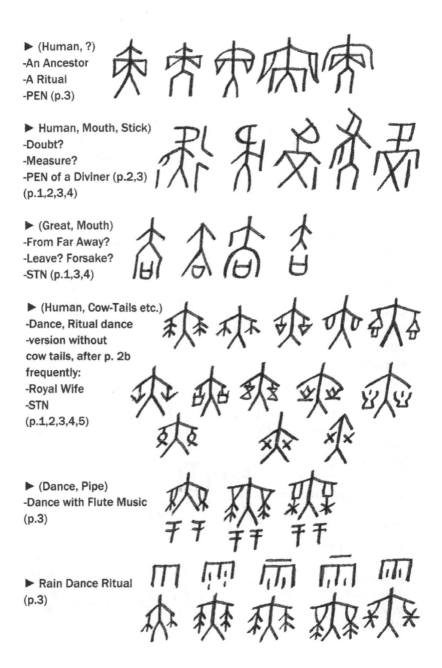

▶ (Human, ?)
-An Ancestor
-A Ritual
-PEN (p.3)

▶ Human, Mouth, Stick)
-Doubt?
-Measure?
-PEN of a Diviner (p.2,3)
(p.1,2,3,4)

▶ (Great, Mouth)
-From Far Away?
-Leave? Forsake?
-STN (p.1,3,4)

▶ (Human, Cow-Tails etc.)
-Dance, Ritual dance
-version without
cow tails, after p. 2b
frequently:
-Royal Wife
-STN
(p.1,2,3,4,5)

▶ (Dance, Pipe)
-Dance with Flute Music
(p.3)

▶ Rain Dance Ritual
(p.3)

▶ (Dance, Feet, Enclosure)
-Circle Dance Ritual
(p.1)

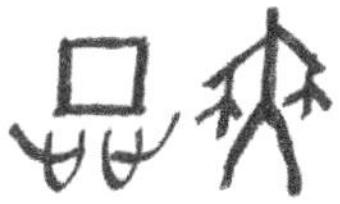

▶ (Human, Mouth, ?)
-Dance Ritual?
(p.1)

▶ (Human, Mouth, Triangle)
-Dance Ritual?
(p.1)

▶ (Human, Mouth, Rope)
-Ritual?
(p.1)

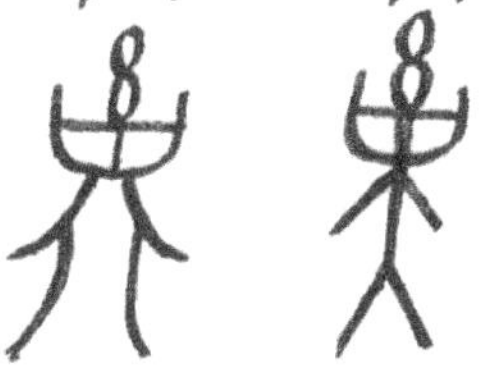

▶ (Stand, Feather)
-Next (Day, Night,
Week, Month)
-Variation of:
Feather Dance Ritual
PEN (p.1,2,3,4,5)

▶ (Human, Hand,
Leaves or Fruit)
-Early Morning
(p.1)

▶ (Human, Tree or
Treetrunk)
-Climb, Ascend
-PEN of a General
(p.1, perhaps 4)

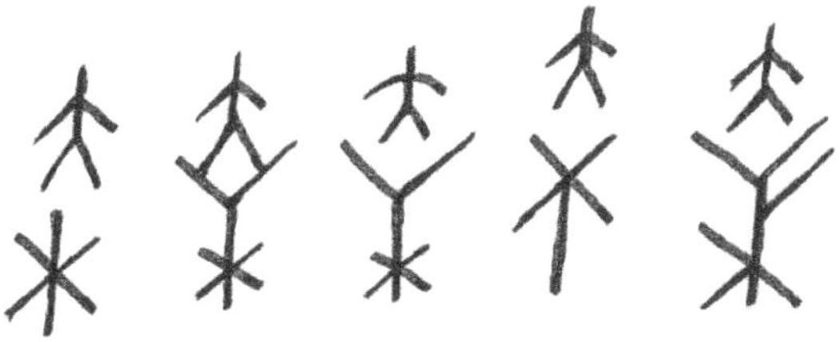

► (Human, Sun)
-Afternoon
-Second Meal
(p.1,3)

► (Human, Street, Foot)
-Meet, Advance Towards
-Greet, Greeting Ritual
?
STN;-PEN
(p.1,4)

► (Human, House)
-A Side-chamber or Hall
in the Royal Palace
-Great Hall?
(p.3)

► (Human, Ship)
-Ford
-Cross River
(p.1)

► (Two Humans, Enclosure)
-A Ritual?
(p.1)

► (Human, Rope, Hand)
-Captive
-PLN
-PEN?
(p.1,5)

► (Human, Arrow)
-Wound
-Disease
-PEN
(p.1)

▶ (Human, Bow)
-Archer
-PEN of Diviner (p.4)
-PEN (p.1,4)

▶ (Human, Axe, Shield)
-Take up Arms ?
(p.1)

▶ (Woman, Axe)
-Ritual to Cross a River
(p.1)

▶ (Human, Saw)
-Punishment:
Foot Amputation
(p.1)

▶ (Human, Vessel)
- Ho Vessel
-Vessel for Baby Burial?
(p.1)

▶ (Human, Cross-Roads,
Vessel)
-A Ritual
(p.3)

Woman

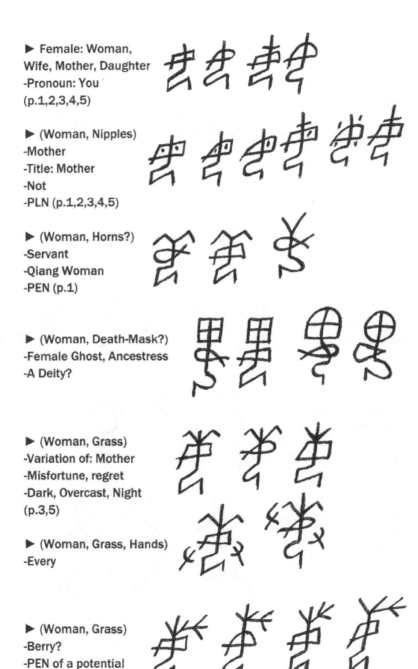

▶ Female: Woman,
Wife, Mother, Daughter
-Pronoun: You
(p.1,2,3,4,5)

▶ (Woman, Nipples)
-Mother
-Title: Mother
-Not
-PLN (p.1,2,3,4,5)

▶ (Woman, Horns?)
-Servant
-Qiang Woman
-PEN (p.1)

▶ (Woman, Death-Mask?)
-Female Ghost, Ancestress
-A Deity?

▶ (Woman, Grass)
-Variation of: Mother
-Misfortune, regret
-Dark, Overcast, Night
(p.3,5)

▶ (Woman, Grass, Hands)
-Every

▶ (Woman, Grass)
-Berry?
-PEN of a potential
Drought Sacrifice
(a Wu?) (p.1)

▶ (Woman,
Hair-Ornament)
-A Ritual?
-PEN
(p.3)

▶ (Woman,
Hair-Ornament,
 Fire or Mountain)
-A Deity
(p.3)

▶ (Woman, Saw-Axe)
-A Deity (E Huang) ?
-PEN of Lady E
(Sister of Wu Ding?)
(p.1)

▶ (Woman, Hat, Collar?)
-Mother (Royal Concubine)
-Concubine
-Palace Woman
(p.1, rarely 4)

▶ (Palace Woman, Man)
-Human Sacrifice
 (Attendants for
an Ancestor or God)
(p.1)

▶ (Woman, Rope)
-Variation of: Captive
-Dark Woman
(Xuan Nü)?
-?
-PLN; -PEN (p.1)

▶ (Woman, Child)
- Good, Beautiful
-PEN of Queen Fu Hao:
-Woman Good
-or: Woman of the Zi Clan
(p.1,4)

▶ (Woman, Child:
Freshly Born)
Variation of:
-Next
-Younger (Generation)
-With 'many': the Many
Younger Generations
(p.1,3,4)

▶ (Woman, Grass, Child)
-A Deity?
(p.3)

▶ (Woman, Embryo)
-Variation of:
Pregnant
(p.1)

▶ (Woman, Digging Stick)
-Beauty
-Good, Lucky
-Birth of a Son
-PEN (p.1)

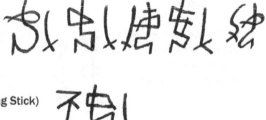

▶ (Woman, Snake?, Digging Stick)
-Birth of a Daughter
-?
(p.1)

▶ (Woman, Mouth, Foot)
-Arrive
(p.1)

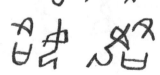

► (Woman, Mouth)
-Advantageous
-Auspicious
-Obey, Follow Instructions
(p.1)

► (Woman, Mouth,
Knife: Food)
-Food Mother: Nurse
(p.3)

► (Woman, Tree)
-Timeword for short Periods?
-STN;-PEN
-(Zhou period: Young Woman)
(p.1,3,5)

► (Woman, Drum)
-Misfortune
-Military Disaster
(p.1,2)

► (Woman, Leaves or Berries)
-Overly Intimate?
-PEN
(p.1)

► (Woman, Sapling: Here)
-Local Woman (a potential
Drought Sacrifice)
(p.1)

▶ (Woman, Earthwork?)
-A Deity or Ancestress
-A Ritual (p.3,4,5)

▶ Concubine, Field,
Digging Stick)
-Woman or Concubine
with High Status
(p.3,5)

▶ (Woman, Well)
-PEN of Queen Fu Jing
(p.1)

▶ (Woman, House)
-Living Peacefully
-Settled Circumstances
-PLN;-PEN
(p.1,3)

▶ (Woman, House, Foot)
-Variation of: Bin Ritual
Being Guest or Receiving Guest
(Human, Ancestor or Deity)
-PEN
(p.1)

▶ (Woman, Broom: Fu Lady)
-Royal Wife
-PEN
(p.1)

▶ (Woman, Bed)
-PEN of a Wu (Shamaness)
(p.1)

▶ (Woman, Mat)
Variation of:
-Complete, Finished
-A Ritual?
-Continuously? Overnight?
(p.1)

▶ (Woman, Axe)
Variation of:
-Tribute Payment
-Making a Gift to a Superior
(p.1)

▶ (Woman, East)
-Deity Woman/Mother East
(p.1)

▶ (Woman, West)
-Deity Woman/Mother West
(p.1)

▶ (Woman, North)
-Deity Woman/Mother North?
(p.1)

Kneeling

▶ (Human, Brush, Small)
-Palace Servant
(p.1)

▶ (Woman, Child, Nipple)
-Suckle
(p.1)

▶(Kneeling Person)
-A Ritual or Meditation
in Presence of
Ancestors or Deities
(p.1, rarely 4)

▶ (Two Humans)
-Human Sacrifice
-PEN
-PEN of a Diviner (p.3)
(p.1,3,4)

▶ (Child with Open Fontanel)
-Deity Er
-Unknown Early Ancestor?
(p.1,3,4)

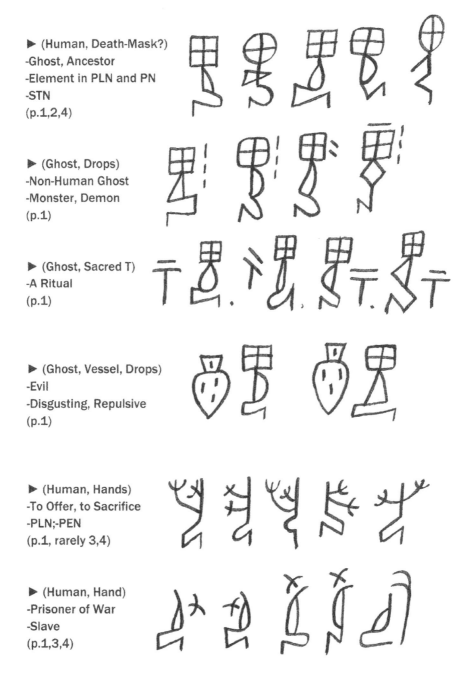

▶ (Human, Death-Mask?)
-Ghost, Ancestor
-Element in PLN and PN
-STN
(p.1,2,4)

▶ (Ghost, Drops)
-Non-Human Ghost
-Monster, Demon
(p.1)

▶ (Ghost, Sacred T)
-A Ritual
(p.1)

▶ (Ghost, Vessel, Drops)
-Evil
-Disgusting, Repulsive
(p.1)

▶ (Human, Hands)
-To Offer, to Sacrifice
-PLN;-PEN
(p.1, rarely 3,4)

▶ (Human, Hand)
-Prisoner of War
-Slave
(p.1,3,4)

▶ (Human, Hand, Pit)
-Human Sacrifice
by Burial?
-Burial Ritual?
(p.1, rarely 3)

▶ (Human, Hand, Stick)
-Slay
-Name of the North Wind
(p.1)

▶ (Human, Hand, Shackles)
-Arrest
-Revenge
(p.1,3)

▶ (Human, Hand, Vessel)
-Capture (of Qiang)
-Domesticate?
(p.4)

▶ (Human, Hand, Food)
-Enter
-Carry Something In?
-?
(p.1)

▶ (Human, Hand, Grass)
-Variation of: Good,
Agreed, OK
-As, Like
(p.1,2,3,4)

▶ (Human, Hand, Tree)
-Time of Lighting Torches
-Evening
-A Ritual
(p.1,2,3,4)

▶ (Human, Mouth, Sacred T)
-Pray, Invoke, Worship
-A Ritual
-Title: Priest
-STN
(p.1,2,3,4)

▶ (Human, Mouth, Drops)
-Flood, Deluge
-A Ritual
(p.1, rarely 4)

▶ (Human, Mouth, Ear)
-News, Message
-Report
-Receive a Report
-PEN
(p.1)

▶ (Human, Mouth,
-Vessel, Drops)
-Ritual Face
Washing?
-PEN (p.1,5)

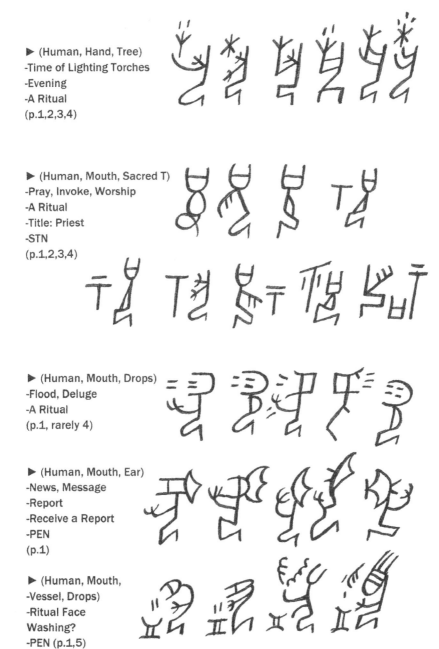

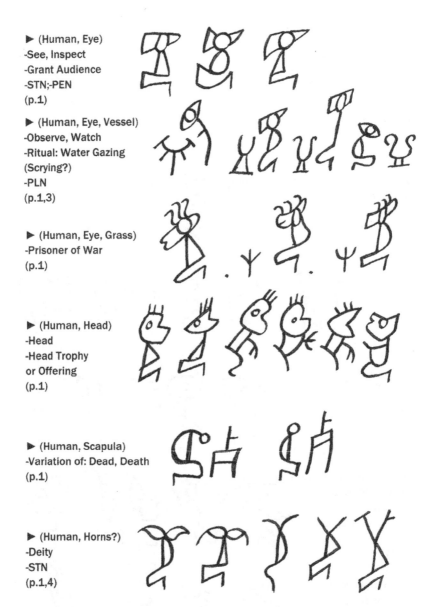

► (Human, Eye)
-See, Inspect
-Grant Audience
-STN;-PEN
(p.1)

► (Human, Eye, Vessel)
-Observe, Watch
-Ritual: Water Gazing
(Scrying?)
-PLN
(p.1,3)

► (Human, Eye, Grass)
-Prisoner of War
(p.1)

► (Human, Head)
-Head
-Head Trophy
or Offering
(p.1)

► (Human, Scapula)
-Variation of: Dead, Death
(p.1)

► (Human, Horns?)
-Deity
-STN
(p.1,4)

▶ (Human, Moon)
-Earlier, Before
-A Ritual?
-STN
(p.1, rarely 3)

▶ (Human, Enclosure)
-City
-Large Settlement
-?
-PEN
(p.1,2,3,5)

▶ (Human, House, Grave)
-Visit Ancestral Temple
-A Ritual
(p.1)

▶ (Human, Roof)
-Order, Command
-PLN
-(Zhou period:
Mandate of Heaven,
'Fate') (p.1,2,3,4,5)

▶ (Human, Rope)
-Ritual of Self-Purification
-Exorcism in the Presence
of Deities or Ancestors
-PLN?
-STN
(p.1,3,4)

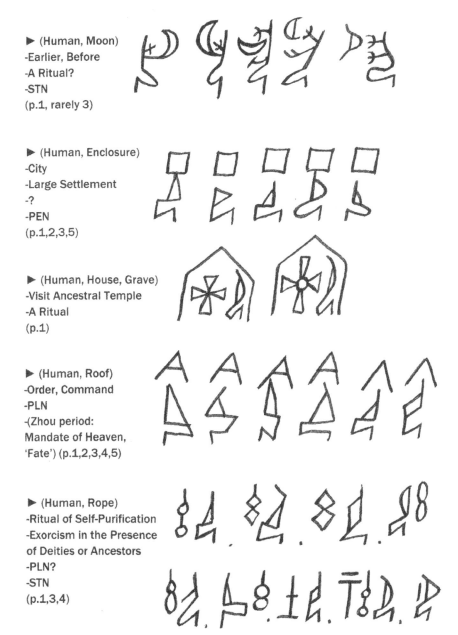

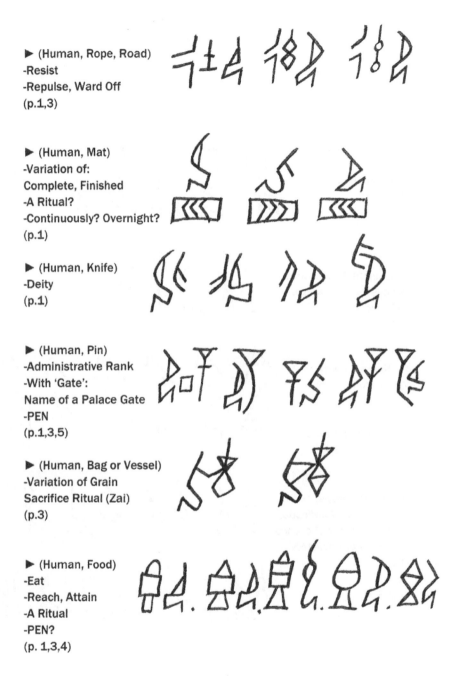

▶ (Human, Rope, Road)
-Resist
-Repulse, Ward Off
(p.1,3)

▶ (Human, Mat)
-Variation of:
Complete, Finished
-A Ritual?
-Continuously? Overnight?
(p.1)

▶ (Human, Knife)
-Deity
(p.1)

▶ (Human, Pin)
-Administrative Rank
-With 'Gate':
Name of a Palace Gate
-PEN
(p.1,3,5)

▶ (Human, Bag or Vessel)
-Variation of Grain
Sacrifice Ritual (Zai)
(p.3)

▶ (Human, Food)
-Eat
-Reach, Attain
-A Ritual
-PEN?
(p. 1,3,4)

▶ (Human, Mouth, Food:
Well Fed Person)
-Already, Now
-Complete
-A Ritual
(p.1,3,4)

▶ (Two Humans, Food)
-Feast, Banquet
-Eat Together with People,
Ancestors or Deities
-Hometown
(p.1,3,4)

Child

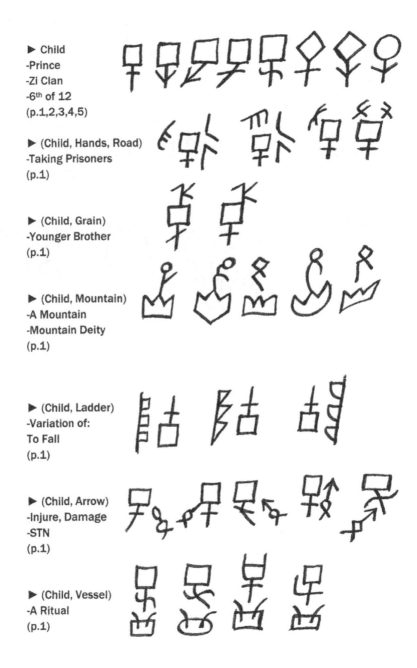

▶ Child
-Prince
-Zi Clan
-6th of 12
(p.1,2,3,4,5)

▶ (Child, Hands, Road)
-Taking Prisoners
(p.1)

▶ (Child, Grain)
-Younger Brother
(p.1)

▶ (Child, Mountain)
-A Mountain
-Mountain Deity
(p.1)

▶ (Child, Ladder)
-Variation of:
To Fall
(p.1)

▶ (Child, Arrow)
-Injure, Damage
-STN
(p.1)

▶ (Child, Vessel)
-A Ritual
(p.1)

Claw

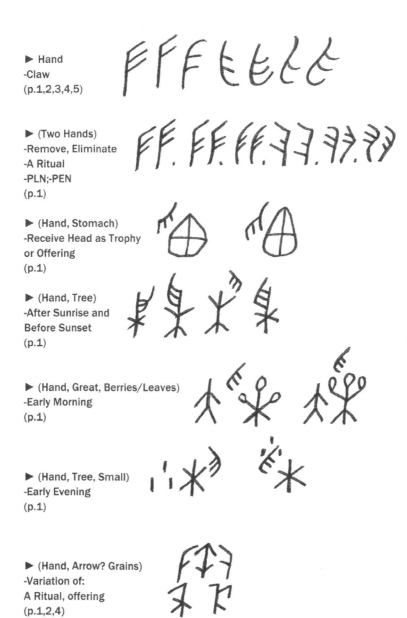

► Hand
-Claw
(p.1,2,3,4,5)

► (Two Hands)
-Remove, Eliminate
-A Ritual
-PLN;-PEN
(p.1)

► (Hand, Stomach)
-Receive Head as Trophy
or Offering
(p.1)

► (Hand, Tree)
-After Sunrise and
Before Sunset
(p.1)

► (Hand, Great, Berries/Leaves)
-Early Morning
(p.1)

► (Hand, Tree, Small)
-Early Evening
(p.1)

► (Hand, Arrow? Grains)
-Variation of:
A Ritual, offering
(p.1,2,4)

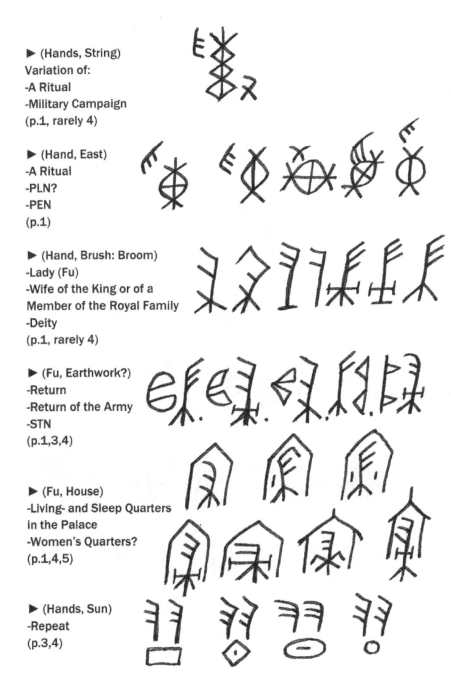

► (Hands, String)
Variation of:
-A Ritual
-Military Campaign
(p.1, rarely 4)

► (Hand, East)
-A Ritual
-PLN?
-PEN
(p.1)

► (Hand, Brush: Broom)
-Lady (Fu)
-Wife of the King or of a
Member of the Royal Family
-Deity
(p.1, rarely 4)

► (Fu, Earthwork?)
-Return
-Return of the Army
-STN
(p.1,3,4)

► (Fu, House)
-Living- and Sleep Quarters
in the Palace
-Women's Quarters?
(p.1,4,5)

► (Hands, Sun)
-Repeat
(p.3,4)

▶ (Hands, Rain)
-Snow
-Deity
(p.1)

▶ (Hands, Earth)
-Variation of: Work the Earth
-Arable Land
-A Ritual?
-Set Traps
-PLN (p.1,5)

▶ (Hands, Earth, Wall)
-Variation of: Wall
-Use, Sacrifice
-Has Been Done
(p.1,5)

▶ (Hand, Wickerwork?)
Variation of:
-Lift, Raise
-A Ritual
-PEN
(p.1,3,4,5)

▶ (Hand, Scroll, Wickerwork?)
-Ritual: Raise Document
-Record Ceremony
(p.1)

▶ (Hand, Stick, Eight?)
Variation of:
-Stick into the Earth
-STN
(p.1)

▶ (Hand, Stick)
Abbreviated Form of:
-Yi Yin
-Steward
-Administrator
(p.1,2,3,4)

▶ (Hands, Stick)
Variation of:
-A Ritual
-And, Together, With
(p.1,3)

▶ (Hands, Stick)
Variation of: Offering of Valuables (Silk?)
-Measure
-PLN of a Cultplace
-PEN
-?
(p.1)

▶ (Hand, Stick, Sail
or Boat:
Boat Repair)
-Variation of:
Pronoun: I, We, Mine, Ours
(p.1,2,3,4,5)

▶ (Hands, Bed)
Variation of:
-Regulate
-Lead or Station a Troop
-An Offering?
(p.1,3,4)

▶ (Hand, Vessel)
-A Ritual
-Wash Hands?
(p.1)

▶ Hands, Vessels,
Mouth, Fire, Thunder)
-Cast Metal
(p.5)

Hand

▶ (Hand)
-Have, Give, Offer
-Allow, Permit
-And, With, Again
-PLN
(P.1, rarely p.2,3,4)

▶ (Hand, River)
-A River
-River Deity
(p.1)

▶ Hand, Claw
-Have, Give, Offer
-Support, Help, Protection
-And, With
-2nd of 12
(p.1,2,3,4,5)

▶ Right Hand
-Right

▶ Left Hand
-Left

▶ (Hand, Thumb Crossed)
-Blame, Error, Mistake
-Negation: Don't Do
-Exceptional?
(p.1,3,5)

▶ Arm
-STN?
(p.1)

▶ (Two Hands)
-Raise (Troops, Offerings etc.)
-Offer, Dedicate
Gather, Collect
-PEN
(p.1,4,5)

▶ (Two Hands)
-Divine Protection
-Friendly
-PEN
(p.1)

▶ (Hand, Stick, Foot)
-A ritual
(p.1,4)

▶ (Hand, Foot, String, Vessel)
-A Ritual
(p.5)

▶ (Hand, Foot, House)
-Reach
(p.3)

▶ (Hand, Mouth, Drops;
here: Piece of Meat)
-Raw Meat Sacrifice
-Second Ancestral Festival (Chi)
-General Term for: Offering
-STN; -PEN
(p.1,2,3,4,5)

▶ (Hand, Mouth, Stick)
-Name of Yi Yin
-Steward
-Administrator
(p.1)

▶ (Hand, Eye, Scapula)
- to Divine
-Examine Scapula
-King Prognosticates
(p.1)

▶ (Hands, Eye, Net)
-A Ritual related to the
Bin Guesting Ceremony
(p.3, mainly 5)

▶ (Hand, Ear)
-Ear Offering
(symbolic for the
whole animal)
-Receive, Take
(p.1,3,4)

▶ (Hand, Grass)
-Hay Harvest
-Good, Joy
-Offering a
Domestic Animal
(p.1)

▶ (Hand, Brush)
-A Ritual
(p.1)

▶ (Hand, Grass, Earth)
-A Ritual
(p.1,3)

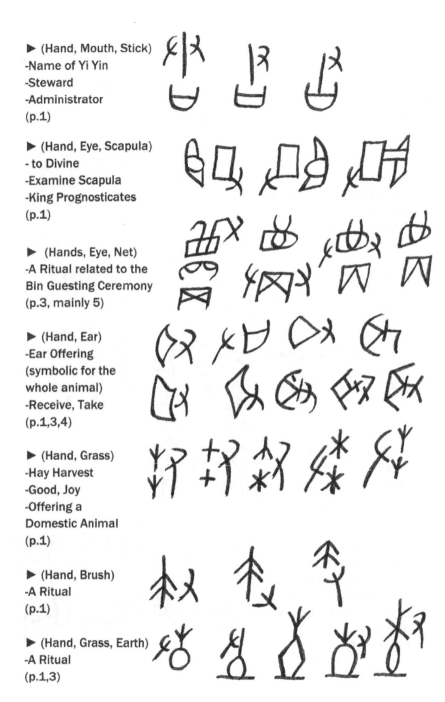

► (Hands, Wood?
Cow Tail?)
-Make or Conduct
Ritual Music
-Ask, Pray, Request
(p.1,2,3)

► (Hand, Bell)
-Bell Music
-PEN of diviner
(p.1)

► (Hand, Jade-Chime)
-Jade-Chime Music
-Animal Sacrifice
-STN;-PLN
-PEN?
(p.1,3,5)

► (Hand, Drum)
-Drum Music Offering
-Fifth Ancestral Festival (Rong)
-PEN of Diviner (p.4a)
-STN;-PEN
(P.1,2,3,4,5)

► (Drumstrokes)
-Variation of Drum Offering
(p.1,2,5)

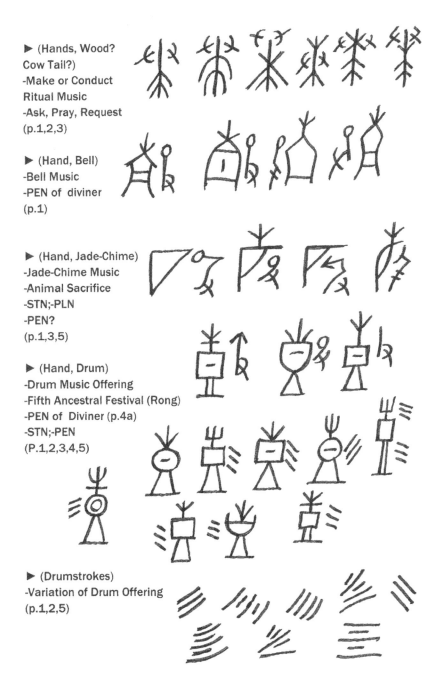

▶ (Hand, Sun, Vessel, Grass)
-Offering Cooked Grains
-Third Ancestral Festival (Zai)
-PLN
(p.1,2,3,4,5)

▶ (Hands, Fire, Wood)
-Burn
-Burn Frontier Land
-Burn Land for Cultivation
-Hunt with Fire
(p.3)

▶ (Hand, String, Fire)
-A Ritual
-PLN
(p.1)

▶ (Hand, String, Stick)
-Unknown Group of People
(p.1)

▶ (Hand, String, Drops)
-A Ritual
-Military Campaign
(p.1, rarely 4)

▶ (Hands, String, Millet)
-A Ritual?
(p.1,2,4)

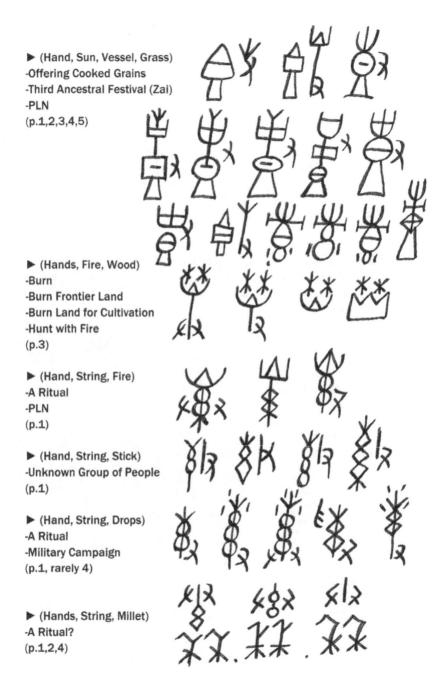

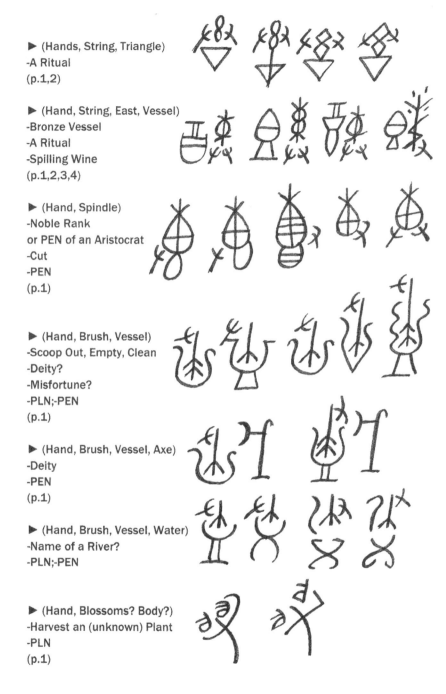

▶ (Hands, String, Triangle)
-A Ritual
(p.1,2)

▶ (Hand, String, East, Vessel)
-Bronze Vessel
-A Ritual
-Spilling Wine
(p.1,2,3,4)

▶ (Hand, Spindle)
-Noble Rank
or PEN of an Aristocrat
-Cut
-PEN
(p.1)

▶ (Hand, Brush, Vessel)
-Scoop Out, Empty, Clean
-Deity?
-Misfortune?
-PLN;-PEN
(p.1)

▶ (Hand, Brush, Vessel, Axe)
-Deity
-PEN
(p.1)

▶ (Hand, Brush, Vessel, Water)
-Name of a River?
-PLN;-PEN

▶ (Hand, Blossoms? Body?)
-Harvest an (unknown) Plant
-PLN
(p.1)

▶ (Hand, Sun, ?)
-A Ritual
(p.3)

▶ (Hand, Sun, Door)
-Weather Clears Up
-Sunny
-PLN
(p.3)

▶ (Hand, Door)
-Open, Access
-Sky Clears Up?
(p.1,2,4)

▶ (Hand, Door, Mouth)
-Make a Report
-STN or PLN
-PEN
(p.3)

▶ (Hand, Sun, Loom)
-Solar Eclipse
(p.1,3,4)

▶ (Hands, Sail/Wind)
-Raise, Lift
-A Ritual
-STN
(p.1,2,3,4)

▶ (Hand, Sail, Stick)
-Turn, Rotate
-PEN of Pan Geng
(p.1,2)

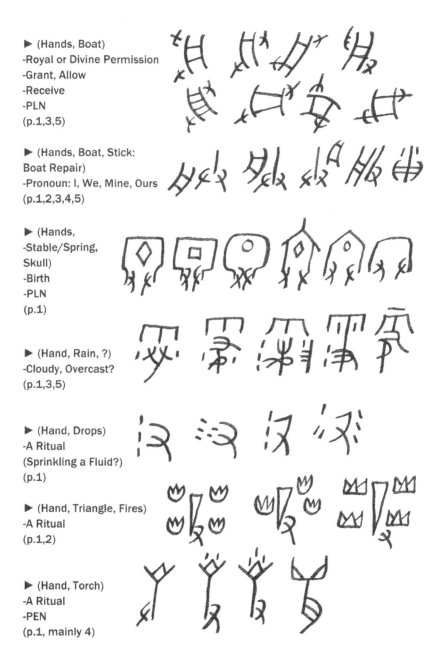

► (Hands, Boat)
-Royal or Divine Permission
-Grant, Allow
-Receive
-PLN
(p.1,3,5)

► (Hands, Boat, Stick:
Boat Repair)
-Pronoun: I, We, Mine, Ours
(p.1,2,3,4,5)

► (Hands,
-Stable/Spring,
Skull)
-Birth
-PLN
(p.1)

► (Hand, Rain, ?)
-Cloudy, Overcast?
(p.1,3,5)

► (Hand, Drops)
-A Ritual
(Sprinkling a Fluid?)
(p.1)

► (Hand, Triangle, Fires)
-A Ritual
(p.1,2)

► (Hand, Torch)
-A Ritual
-PEN
(p.1, mainly 4)

► (Hand,
Mountains,
House, Jade,
Pin, West)
-Jade Mine
-Gain Jade
(p.1)

► (Hand, Jade)
-Offer Jade?
-PLN;-PEN
(p.1)

► (Hand, Jade, ?)
-Make, Do
-Lift
-Afterwards
-PEN
(p.1,3,4,5)

► (Hand,
Earthwork? Mouth)
-A Ritual
(p1,2,3)

► (Hands, Earth)
-Variation of: Work the Earth
-Arable Land
-A Ritual?
-Set Traps
-PLN (p.1,3,4,5)

► (Hands, Field)
-To Grant Land?
-STN
(p.1)

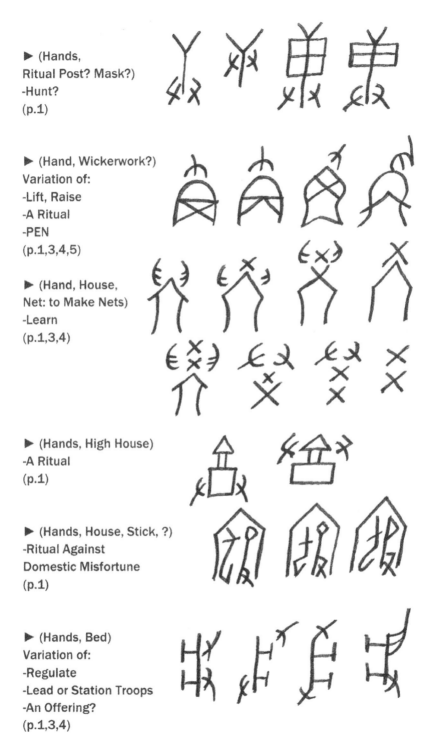

▶ (Hands,
Ritual Post? Mask?)
-Hunt?
(p.1)

▶ (Hand, Wickerwork?)
Variation of:
-Lift, Raise
-A Ritual
-PEN
(p.1,3,4,5)

▶ (Hand, House,
Net: to Make Nets)
-Learn
(p.1,3,4)

▶ (Hands, High House)
-A Ritual
(p.1)

▶ (Hands, House, Stick, ?)
-Ritual Against
Domestic Misfortune
(p.1)

▶ (Hands, Bed)
Variation of:
-Regulate
-Lead or Station Troops
-An Offering?
(p.1,3,4)

► (Hand, Sacred T, Drops)
-Protection, Help
-A Ritual
(p.1,2,3,4)

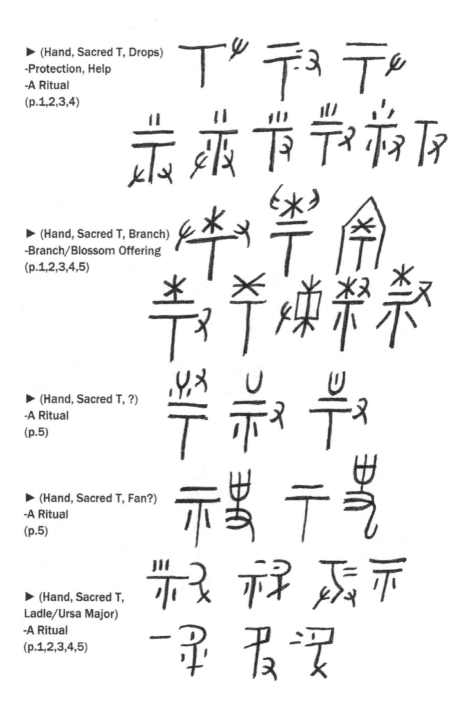

► (Hand, Sacred T, Branch)
-Branch/Blossom Offering
(p.1,2,3,4,5)

► (Hand, Sacred T, ?)
-A Ritual
(p.5)

► (Hand, Sacred T, Fan?)
-A Ritual
(p.5)

► (Hand, Sacred T,
Ladle/Ursa Major)
-A Ritual
(p.1,2,3,4,5)

▶ (Hands, Sacred T, Vessel?)
-A Ritual
(p.3)

▶ (Hands, Sacred T, Scroll)
-Blessing a Document
(p.1)

▶ (Hands, Scroll)
-Consecrate a Document
-PLN
(p.1,2,3,4,5)

▶ (Hands, Scroll, Mouth/Box)
-Proclaim a Document
-Seal a Document in a Box
(p.1)

▶ (Hand, Jacket)
-A Ritual
Variation of:
-Clothes Offering?
(p.1,4)

▶ (Hands, Loop?)
-A Ritual?
(p.1)

▶ (Hand, Stick, Mouth)
-PEN of Yi Yin
-Steward
-Administrator
-STN (p.1,2,3,4)

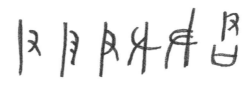

► (Hand, Stone Tool)
-Father
-Title: Father
-Uncle
(p.1,2,4)

► (Hands, Stick)
-Conjunction: With, And
(p.1,3)

► (Hand, Stick, Wind, ?)
-Unknown Musical Instrument
(p.3)

► (Hand, Stick, Bow)
-A Ritual
(p.1, rarely 3)

►(Hands, Stick or Mat)
-Measure
-Sacrifice of Valuables (Silk?)
-Name of a Cult Place
-PEN
(p.1,2,3,4)

► (Hand, Digging Sticks)
-A Ritual
(p.1)

► (Hand, Fan?)
-Order, Command
-Despatch an Official
-Low Administrative Rank
-Grant Promotion
-PEN of a Diviner (p.1)
-PLN;-PEN (p. 1,3,4,5)

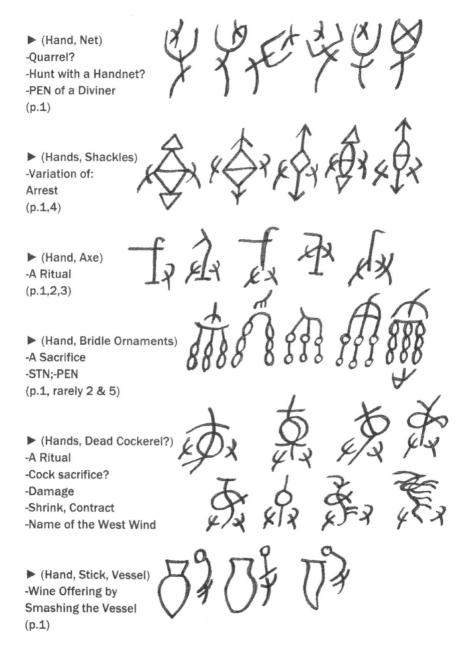

► (Hand, Net)
-Quarrel?
-Hunt with a Handnet?
-PEN of a Diviner
(p.1)

► (Hands, Shackles)
-Variation of:
Arrest
(p.1,4)

► (Hand, Axe)
-A Ritual
(p.1,2,3)

► (Hand, Bridle Ornaments)
-A Sacrifice
-STN;-PEN
(p.1, rarely 2 & 5)

► (Hands, Dead Cockerel?)
-A Ritual
-Cock sacrifice?
-Damage
-Shrink, Contract
-Name of the West Wind

► (Hand, Stick, Vessel)
-Wine Offering by
Smashing the Vessel
(p.1)

▶ (Hand, Stick, Pin?)
-Ominous Weather
Phenomenon
-Thunder?
(p.1)

▶ (Hands, Food)
-Raise
-Dedicate, Offer
-Food Offering
(p.1,4)

▶ (Hand, Stick, Food)
-Food Offering
-Animal or Human Sacrifice
(p.1,2,3,5)

▶ (Hands, Bowl, Grains)
-Various Grain Offerings
(p.3,5)

▶ (Hand, Cauldron)
-A Ritual?
-PLN?
-PEN
(p.1,4,5)

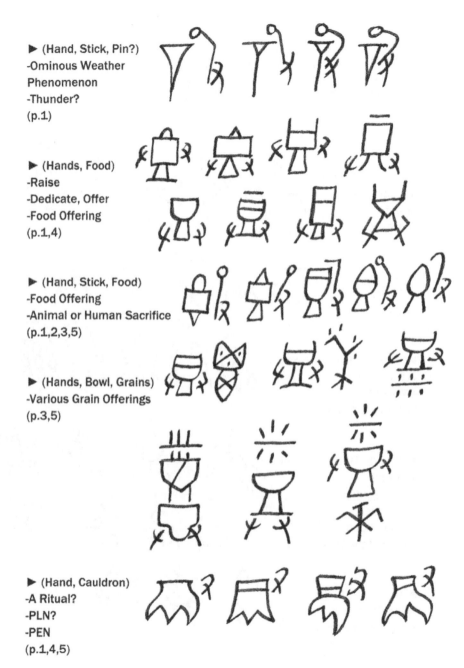

► (Hands, Vessel, Ladder)
-Drink Offering
(p.1,2,3,4)

► (Hands, Chopping Board, Ladder)
-Make a Gift
(p.2)

► (Hand, Zun Vessel)
-A Ritual
(p.1)

► (Hands, Vessel, Sacred T)
-Variations of:
Wine Offering
(p.1,2,3,4,5)

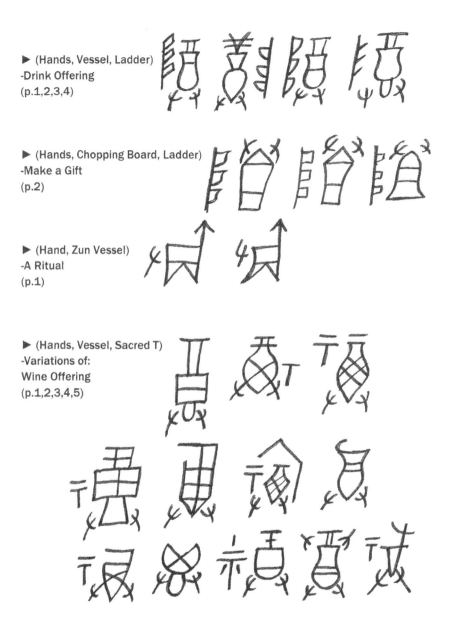

Foot

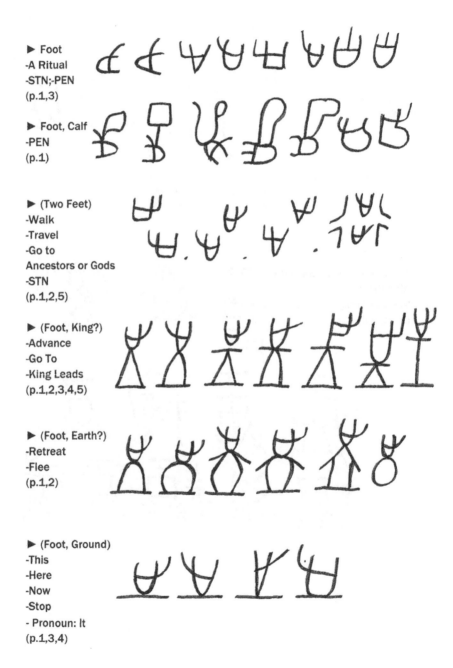

► Foot
-A Ritual
-STN;-PEN
(p.1,3)

► Foot, Calf
-PEN
(p.1)

► (Two Feet)
-Walk
-Travel
-Go to
Ancestors or Gods
-STN
(p.1,2,5)

► (Foot, King?)
-Advance
-Go To
-King Leads
(p.1,2,3,4,5)

► (Foot, Earth?)
-Retreat
-Flee
(p.1,2)

► (Foot, Ground)
-This
-Here
-Now
-Stop
- Pronoun: It
(p.1,3,4)

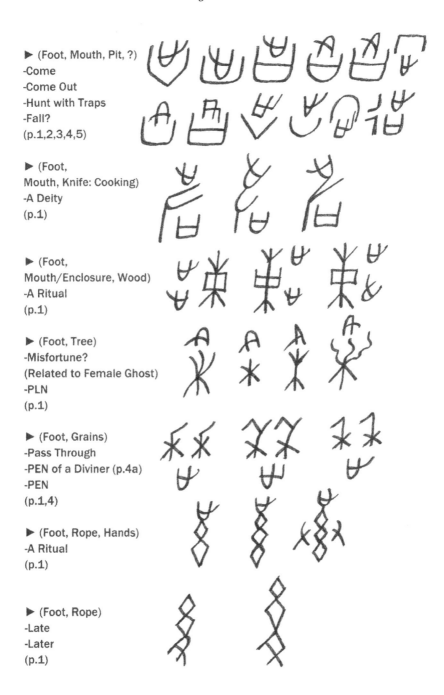

► (Foot, Mouth, Pit, ?)
-Come
-Come Out
-Hunt with Traps
-Fall?
(p.1,2,3,4,5)

► (Foot,
Mouth, Knife: Cooking)
-A Deity
(p.1)

► (Foot,
Mouth/Enclosure, Wood)
-A Ritual
(p.1)

► (Foot, Tree)
-Misfortune?
(Related to Female Ghost)
-PLN
(p.1)

► (Foot, Grains)
-Pass Through
-PEN of a Diviner (p.4a)
-PEN
(p.1,4)

► (Foot, Rope, Hands)
-A Ritual
(p.1)

► (Foot, Rope)
-Late
-Later
(p.1)

► (Foot, Wheat)
-Grain (Wheat?)
-STN;-PLN
(p.1,2,3)

► (Foot, Grass-Hut)
-Attack
-Advance Against
-PEN
(p.1,4)

► (Foot, Sun, Pit)
Variation of:
-Arise, Appear
-Sunrise
(p.1)

► (Foot, Wind,
Basin, Drops)
-Ritual Foot Washing
-STN
(p.1)

► (Feet, Water)
-Ford
-Cross Water
(p.1,3)

► (Feet, Water)
-A Ritual
(p.1)

► (Foot, Drops)
-Ritual Feet Washing?
-STN;-PLN;-PEN
(p.1)

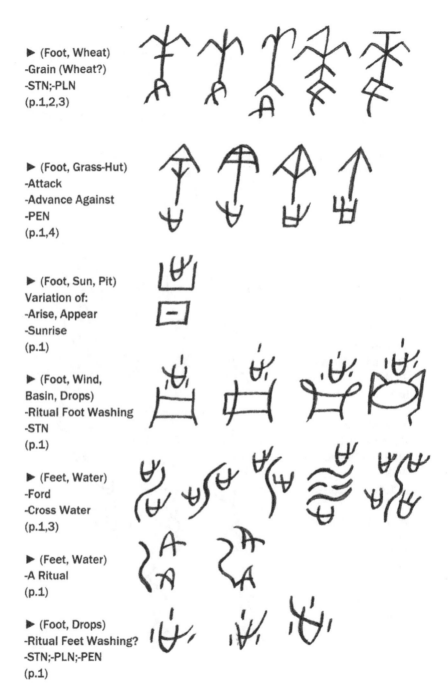

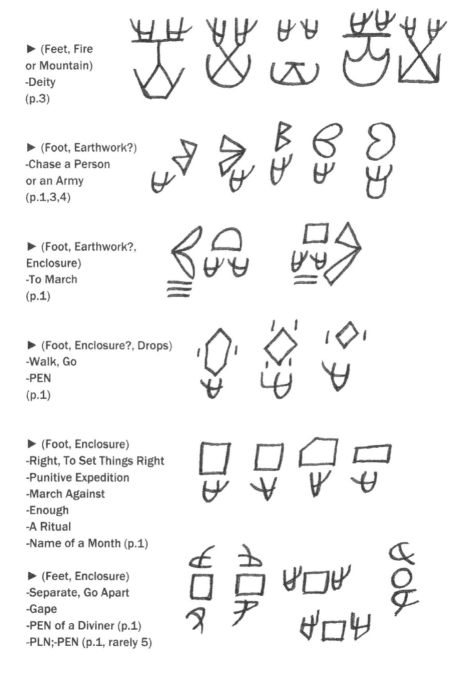

▶ (Feet, Fire
or Mountain)
-Deity
(p.3)

▶ (Foot, Earthwork?)
-Chase a Person
or an Army
(p.1,3,4)

▶ (Foot, Earthwork?,
Enclosure)
-To March
(p.1)

▶ (Foot, Enclosure?, Drops)
-Walk, Go
-PEN
(p.1)

▶ (Foot, Enclosure)
-Right, To Set Things Right
-Punitive Expedition
-March Against
-Enough
-A Ritual
-Name of a Month (p.1)

▶ (Feet, Enclosure)
-Separate, Go Apart
-Gape
-PEN of a Diviner (p.1)
-PLN;-PEN (p.1, rarely 5)

▶ (Feet, Enclosure)
-Advance to Frontier
-Surround, Encircle
-Besiege
-STN;-PLN
(p.1)

▶ (Feet, Enclosure)
-Encircle?
-City Guard
(p.1)

▶ (Foot, Road)
-Long Duration
-Extend, Prolong
-Go
-A Ritual
-PEN (p.1)

▶ (Foot, Road, Thunder)
-Ritual Supplication
(p.3)

▶ (Foot, Road, Wall)
Variation of:
-A Ritual
-STN
(p1,4)

▶ (Foot, Crossroad)
-Continuously
-Long Durations
-PEN
(p.1)

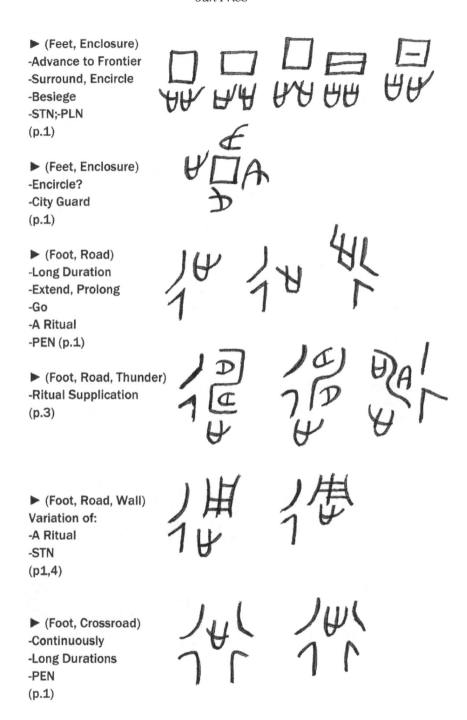

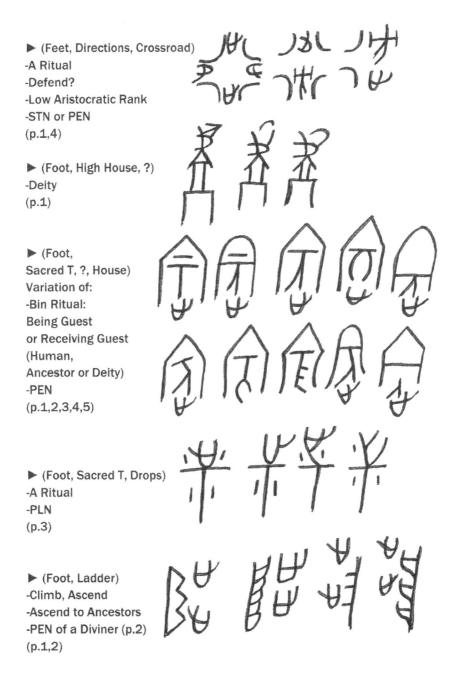

► (Feet, Directions, Crossroad)
-A Ritual
-Defend?
-Low Aristocratic Rank
-STN or PEN
(p.1,4)

► (Foot, High House, ?)
-Deity
(p.1)

► (Foot,
Sacred T, ?, House)
Variation of:
-Bin Ritual:
Being Guest
or Receiving Guest
(Human,
Ancestor or Deity)
-PEN
(p.1,2,3,4,5)

► (Foot, Sacred T, Drops)
-A Ritual
-PLN
(p.3)

► (Foot, Ladder)
-Climb, Ascend
-Ascend to Ancestors
-PEN of a Diviner (p.2)
(p.1,2)

▶ (Foot, Ladder)
-Descend
-Lower, Let Down
(Di/s let/s
something down)
(p.1,2)

▶ (Foot, Flag, Street, Sun)
-Return
-Return of the Army
-PEN
(p.1,3)

▶ Foot-Shackle
-Pursue, Catch
(p.1)

▶ (Foot, Axe)
-Temple Name
for Posthumous Worship
-STN
(p.1,5)

▶ (Foot Above Axe)
-A Ritual
(p.1)

▶ (Foot, Axe)
Variation of:
-Kill with Axe
-A Sacrifice
-Year
(p.1)

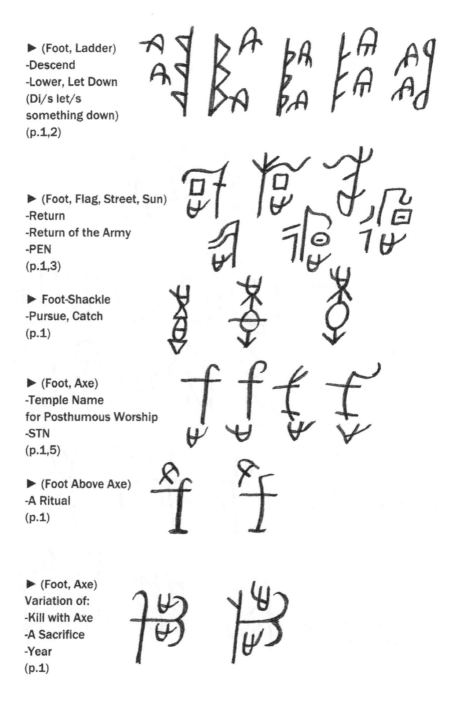

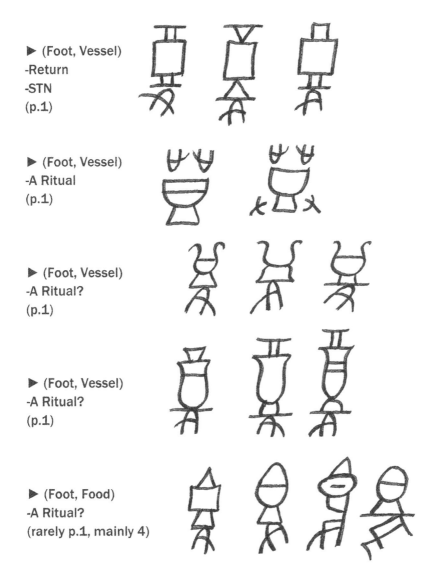

▶ (Foot, Vessel)
-Return
-STN
(p.1)

▶ (Foot, Vessel)
-A Ritual
(p.1)

▶ (Foot, Vessel)
-A Ritual?
(p.1)

▶ (Foot, Vessel)
-A Ritual?
(p.1)

▶ (Foot, Food)
-A Ritual?
(rarely p.1, mainly 4)

Mouth

▶ Mouth
-Misfortune?
-PEN of a Diviner (p.1)
(p.1)

▶ (Mouth, Line)
-To Name
-Speak, Proclaim
-Question: Is It?
Perhaps?
(p.1)

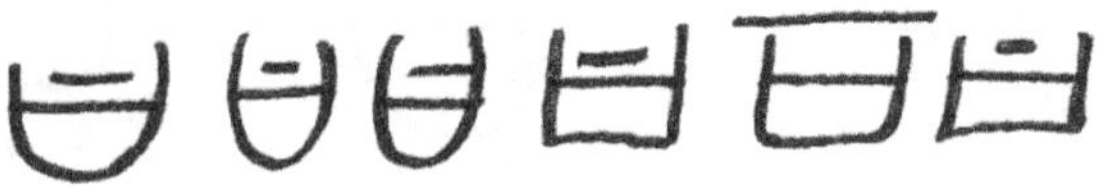

▶ (Three Mouths)
-A Ritual
(p.1,2,4,5)

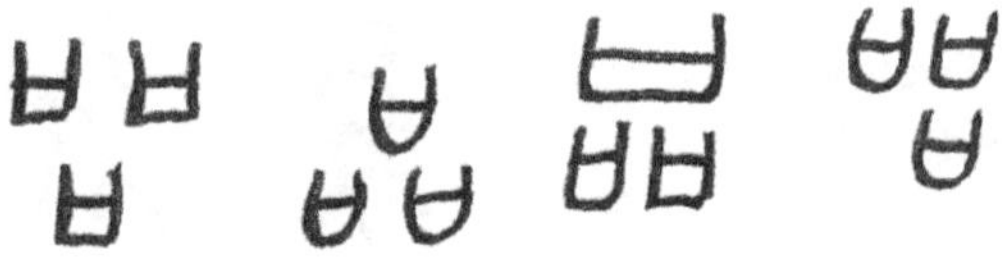

▶ (Three Mouths, Cliff?)
-A Ritual?
-PLN
(p.1,4)

▶ (Two Mouths)
-Scream
(p.1)

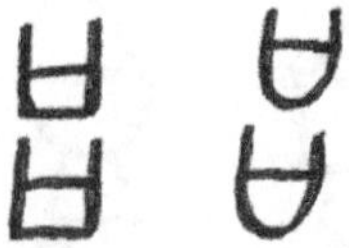

▶ (Scream, Ear)
-Tinnitus
-STN
(p.1)

▶ (Mouth, Ear)
-King Listens
-Listen
(p.1)

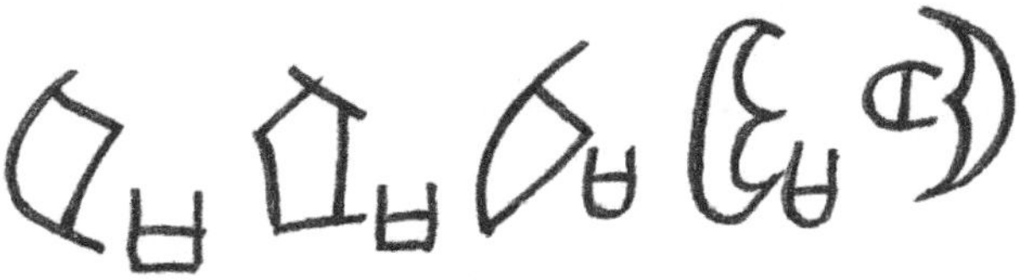

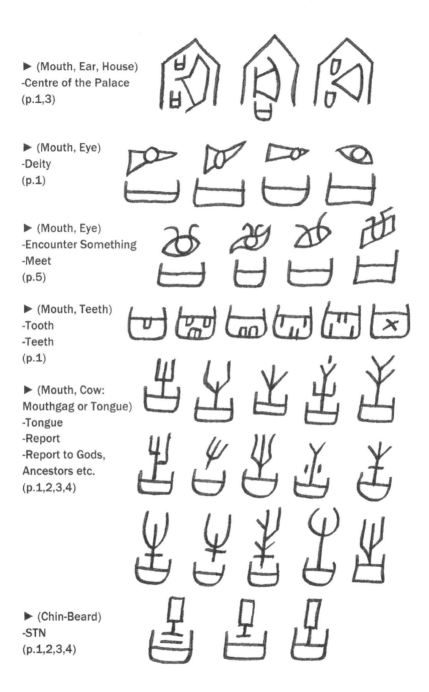

▶ (Mouth, Ear, House)
-Centre of the Palace
(p.1,3)

▶ (Mouth, Eye)
-Deity
(p.1)

▶ (Mouth, Eye)
-Encounter Something
-Meet
(p.5)

▶ (Mouth, Teeth)
-Tooth
-Teeth
(p.1)

▶ (Mouth, Cow:
Mouthgag or Tongue)
-Tongue
-Report
-Report to Gods,
Ancestors etc.
(p.1,2,3,4)

▶ (Chin-Beard)
-STN
(p.1,2,3,4)

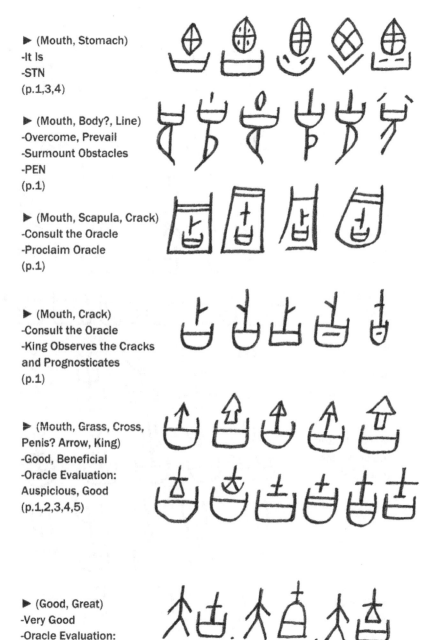

▶ (Mouth, Stomach)
-It Is
-STN
(p.1,3,4)

▶ (Mouth, Body?, Line)
-Overcome, Prevail
-Surmount Obstacles
-PEN
(p.1)

▶ (Mouth, Scapula, Crack)
-Consult the Oracle
-Proclaim Oracle
(p.1)

▶ (Mouth, Crack)
-Consult the Oracle
-King Observes the Cracks
and Prognosticates
(p.1)

▶ (Mouth, Grass, Cross,
Penis? Arrow, King)
-Good, Beneficial
-Oracle Evaluation:
Auspicious, Good
(p.1,2,3,4,5)

▶ (Good, Great)
-Very Good
-Oracle Evaluation:
Very Auspicious (p.1,3)

► (Good, Small)
-Oracle Evaluation:
Moderately Auspicious
(p.1)

► (Good, ?)
-Exceptionally Good
-Oracle Evaluation:
Extremely Auspicious
(p.1, rarely 5)

► (Mouth, Seedling)
-Variation of: Here, In, At
-Now
-To Be In
(p.1,2,3,4,5)

► (Mouth, Seedpod?)
-PEN of Tang/Da Yi
(p.1,3)

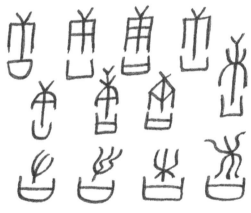

► (Mouth, Growth)
-Timeword for the
3-5th Month and
the 11-13th Month
(p.1)

► (Mouth, Millet)
-A Ritual
-?
(p.1)

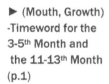

► (Mouths, Tree)
-Mulberry Tree
-Lose
-Waste Away, Die
-PLN
(p.1,2,3,4,5)

► (Mouth, Wind)
-Meet, Encounter
-A Ritual?
-?
(p.2,3,5)

► (Mouth, Flood)
-Misfortune?
(p.1)

► (Mouth, Drops)
-Piece of Raw Meat
-Cut Meat
(p.1)

► (Two Pieces
of Meat)
-Much, A Lot, Many
-Very
(p.1,2,3,4,5)

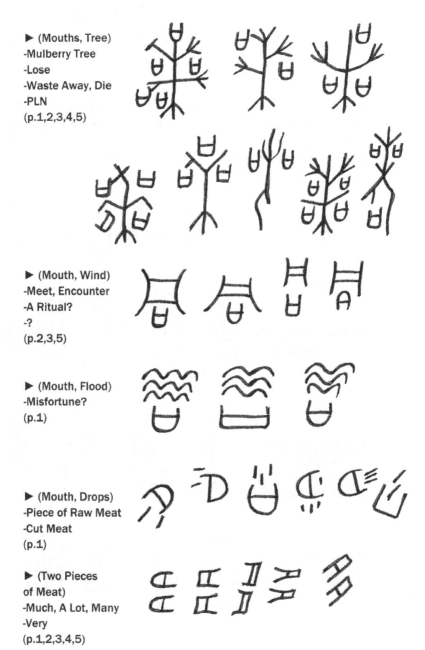

► (Two Pieces of Meat): -Much, A Lot, Many ; -Very
-A Group, such as People, Ancestors or Ghosts
-Administrator, Administrative Rank

► Many Younger
Generations
► Many Mothers
► Many Fathers
► Many Fu Ladies

► Many Ancestresses
► Many Princes
► Many Musicians
► Many Ghosts

► Many Births
(Newcomers?)
► Many Guests?
► Many Administrators

► Many Bows
Administrator/s
► Many Dogs
Administrator/s
► Many Horses
Administrator/s
► Many
(Morning Sacrifices)?

► Many Fields
(Administrator/s)
► Many Grains
Administrator/s
► Many Clothes?
► Many ?

▶ (Mouth, Moon)
-A Ritual?
-PLN
(p.1)

▶ (Mouth, Lightning)
-Thunder
-STN;-PLN;-PEN
(p.1)

▶ (Mouth, Water?
Lightning?)
-Variation of:
Cast Metal
-STN;-PLN
(p.1, rarely 3)

▶ (Mouth, Cliff)
-Stone
-Deity
-STN;-PEN
(p.1)

▶ (Mouth, Enclosures)
-Show
-Exhibit
-PEN of a Diviner
(p.1)

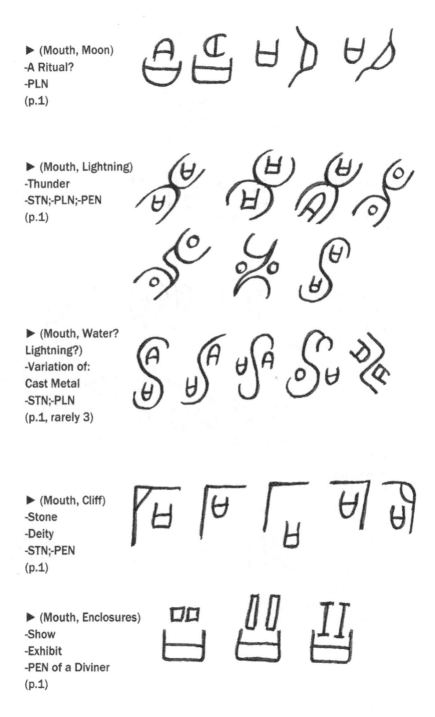

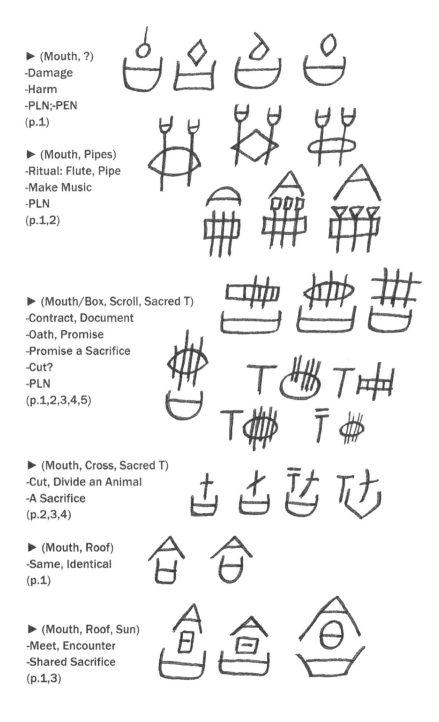

▶ (Mouth, ?)
-Damage
-Harm
-PLN;-PEN
(p.1)

▶ (Mouth, Pipes)
-Ritual: Flute, Pipe
-Make Music
-PLN
(p.1,2)

▶ (Mouth/Box, Scroll, Sacred T)
-Contract, Document
-Oath, Promise
-Promise a Sacrifice
-Cut?
-PLN
(p.1,2,3,4,5)

▶ (Mouth, Cross, Sacred T)
-Cut, Divide an Animal
-A Sacrifice
(p.2,3,4)

▶ (Mouth, Roof)
-Same, Identical
(p.1)

▶ (Mouth, Roof, Sun)
-Meet, Encounter
-Shared Sacrifice
(p.1,3)

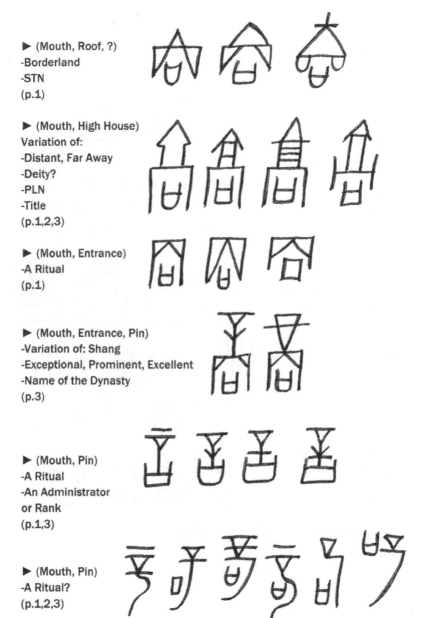

► (Mouth, Roof, ?)
-Borderland
-STN
(p.1)

► (Mouth, High House)
Variation of:
-Distant, Far Away
-Deity?
-PLN
-Title
(p.1,2,3)

► (Mouth, Entrance)
-A Ritual
(p.1)

► (Mouth, Entrance, Pin)
-Variation of: Shang
-Exceptional, Prominent, Excellent
-Name of the Dynasty
(p.3)

► (Mouth, Pin)
-A Ritual
-An Administrator
or Rank
(p.1,3)

► (Mouth, Pin)
-A Ritual?
(p.1,2,3)

▶ (Mouth, Pin, Axe: Loom)
-Weave
-Brown or Yellow
-Dry Meat
-Eclipse of Sun or Moon
-PEN
(p.1,3,4)

▶ (Mouth, Eight?)
-Male
-Name-particle:
The Earlier
(p.2,4,5)

▶ (Mouth, Flag)
-Return
-A Ritual?
(p.1,3)

▶ (Mouth, Line)
-Variation of: Cooperation
(p.1)

▶ (Mouth,
Digging Sticks)
-Cooperation
-Harmonise
-Fourth Ancestral
Festival (Xie)
-PEN
(p.1,2,3,4,5)

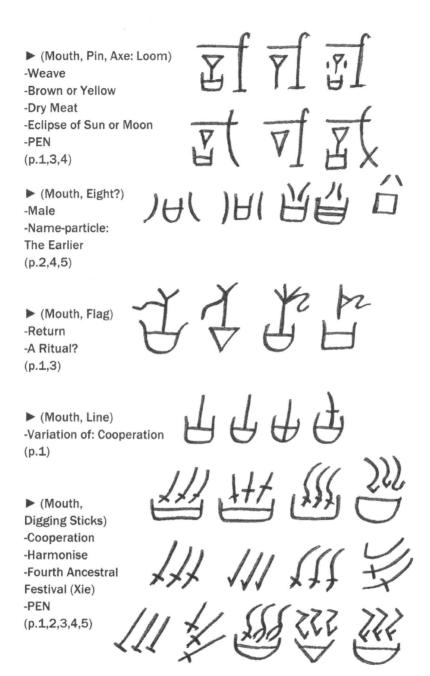

▶ (Mouth, Knife)
-Food, Food Offering
-Kitchen Deity?
-Ritual Week (Zi)?
(p.1,2,3,4,5)

▶ (Mouth, Rope, Knife)
-Animal sacrifice
(p.4)

▶ (Mouth, Arrow)
-Turtle Plastron
-PEN
(p.1,4)

▶ (Mouth, Shackle)
-Arrest
-A Ritual?
(p.1)

▶ (Mouth, Shackle, Enclosure)
-Prison
-Custody
-Phonetic element
(p.1, rarely 5)

▶ (Mouth, Five?)
-A Ritual
(p.4)

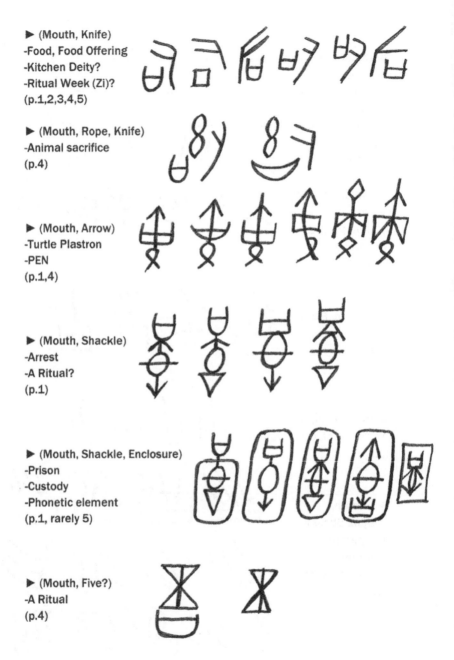

▶ (Mouth, Axe?)
-Agreement
-Auspicious
-STN
(p.1, rarely 3)

▶ (Mouth, Axe)
-Title of Tang/Da Yi
-All, Every
(p.1,4)

▶ (Enclosure, Axe)
-Title of Tang/Da Yi
-Complete
-Fulfil
(p.1,4)

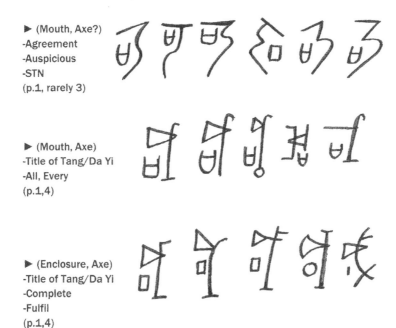

Eye

▶ Eye
-STN;-PLN
(p.1,3,4)

▶ (Eye, Line)
-Now
(p.1,4)

▶ (Eye)
-Administrator
-Overseer
-Minister
(p.1,2,3,4,5)

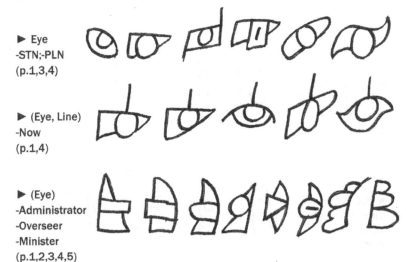

▶ Di's Five
Jade Ministers
A Group of Deities,
possibly Planets,
Winds, Mountains,
Directions etc.
(p.2a,3)

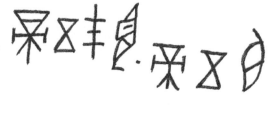

▶ (Eye, Eyebrows)
-Eyebrow
-Wide Eyed Vision
-Look Closely
(p.1)

▶ (Eye, Grass)
-Watch
-Inspect
(p.1,3,5)

▶ (Eye, Wood)
-Observe
(p.1, rarely 5)

► (Eye, Rain)
-Observe
-STN
(p.1,5)

► (Eye, Rain, Axe)
-Shield
-PLN;-PEN
(p.1)

► (Eye, Drops)
-Tears
-Until
-With, And
-STN or PEN
(p.1,3,4)

► (Wide-Open-Eye, Water)
-Before Dawn
(p.3,4,5)

► (Eye, Water)
-Water Meadow
-PEN of Shang Jia
(p.1)

► (Eye, Mountain)
-A Mountain
-Mountain Deity
(p.1,3)

► (Eye, House)
-Continuously?
-Administrative Rank?
(p.1)

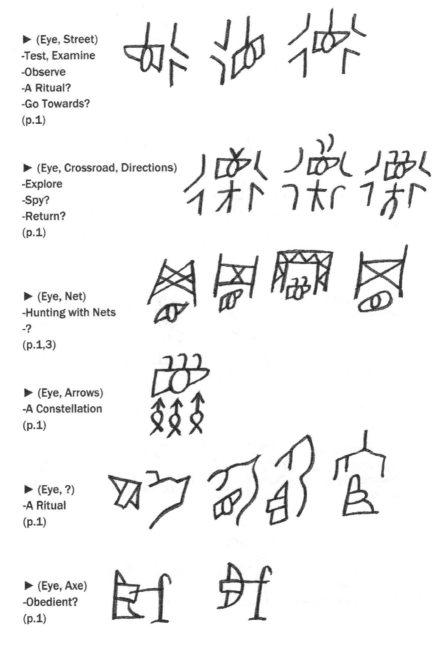

► (Eye, Street)
-Test, Examine
-Observe
-A Ritual?
-Go Towards?
(p.1)

► (Eye, Crossroad, Directions)
-Explore
-Spy?
-Return?
(p.1)

► (Eye, Net)
-Hunting with Nets
-?
(p.1,3)

► (Eye, Arrows)
-A Constellation
(p.1)

► (Eye, ?)
-A Ritual
(p.1)

► (Eye, Axe)
-Obedient?
(p.1)

Ear, Nose, Stomach

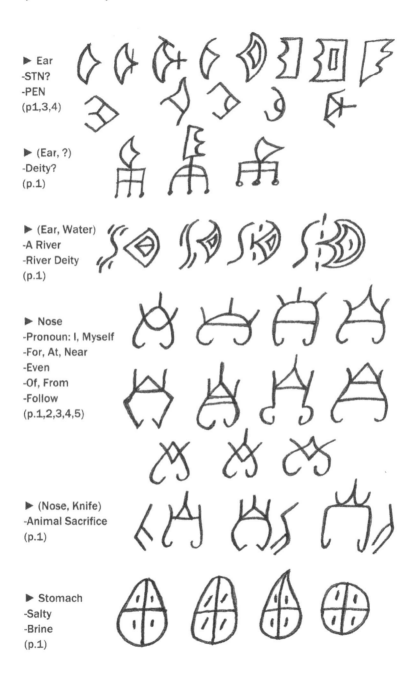

▶ Ear
-STN?
-PEN
(p1,3,4)

▶ (Ear, ?)
-Deity?
(p.1)

▶ (Ear, Water)
-A River
-River Deity
(p.1)

▶ Nose
-Pronoun: I, Myself
-For, At, Near
-Even
-Of, From
-Follow
(p.1,2,3,4,5)

▶ (Nose, Knife)
-Animal Sacrifice
(p.1)

▶ Stomach
-Salty
-Brine
(p.1)

Bone

▶ Scapula
-Bone
-Misfortune
-PLN;-PEN
(p.1,2,3,4,)

▶ (Scapula, Dog)
-Misfortune
(p.5)

▶ (Broken
-Scapula, Crack)
-Exhibit, Show
-Death

▶ (Scapula, Water)
-Variation of:
Interpret the Oracle
(p.1)

▶ (Scapula, Hollows)
-Misfortune
-Unwell, Sick
-Black, Dark (Scorched?)
-A Cult Vessel?
(p.1)

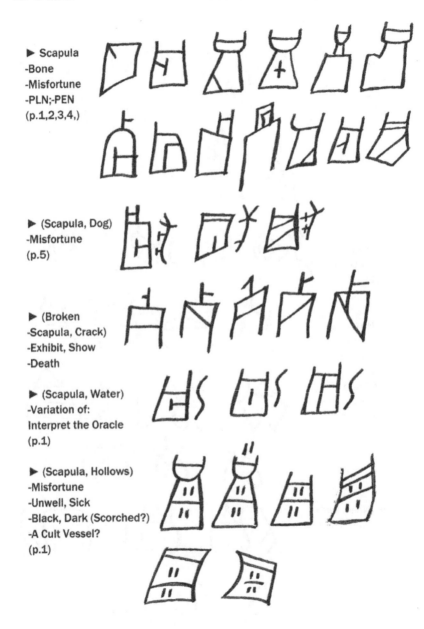

Head, Penis

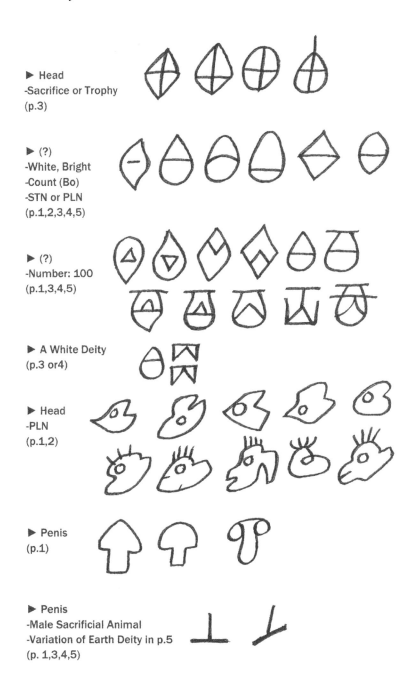

▶ Head
-Sacrifice or Trophy
(p.3)

▶ (?)
-White, Bright
-Count (Bo)
-STN or PLN
(p.1,2,3,4,5)

▶ (?)
-Number: 100
(p.1,3,4,5)

▶ A White Deity
(p.3 or4)

▶ Head
-PLN
(p.1,2)

▶ Penis
(p.1)

▶ Penis
-Male Sacrificial Animal
-Variation of Earth Deity in p.5
(p. 1,3,4,5)

Plants

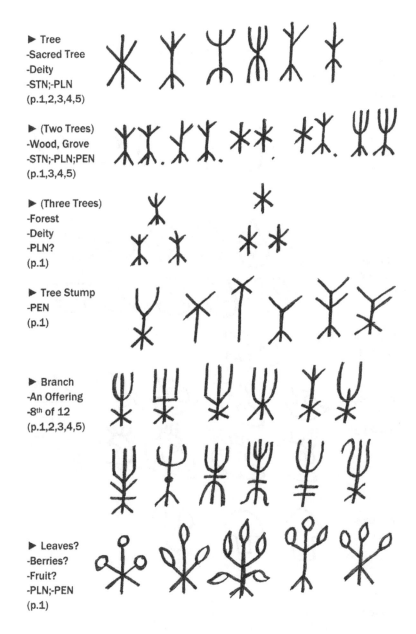

▶ Tree
-Sacred Tree
-Deity
-STN;-PLN
(p.1,2,3,4,5)

▶ (Two Trees)
-Wood, Grove
-STN;-PLN;PEN
(p.1,3,4,5)

▶ (Three Trees)
-Forest
-Deity
-PLN?
(p.1)

▶ Tree Stump
-PEN
(p.1)

▶ Branch
-An Offering
-8th of 12
(p.1,2,3,4,5)

▶ Leaves?
-Berries?
-Fruit?
-PLN;-PEN
(p.1)

► (Blossoms?)
-PLN
-PEN
-(p.1,5)

► (Tree, Enclosure)
-A Ritual
-Burned Offering?
-PEN
(p.1,4)

► (Fur-Cloak)
-Variation of :
Ask, Pray, Request
-Blame
-Disaster
-Not Yet
(p.1,2,3,4,5)

► (Plant?)
-A Ritual
-?
(p.1)

► (Plant?)
-Variation of:
Timeword for
3-5th Month and
11-13th Month
(p.1, rarely 4)

▶ (Bundle of Branches?)
-(Sun behind Fusang Tree?)
-(Bag of Seeds?)
-East
-Deity East
-PLN
(p.1,2,3,4,5)

▶ (East, House)
-Eastern Hall or
Courtyard
(p.1)

▶ (East, Net, Knife)
-Ritual
(p.3)

▶ (East, Axe)
-Ritual for Deities,
Yi Yin etc.
(p.1)

▶ (Tree, Enclosure)
-Variation of:
Branch Offering
(p.1,3,4)

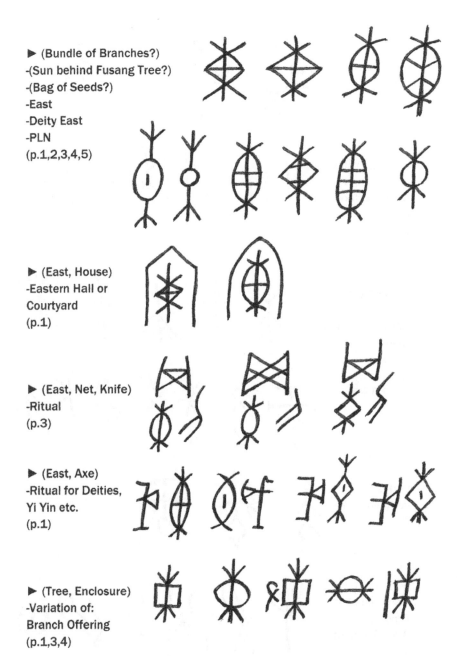

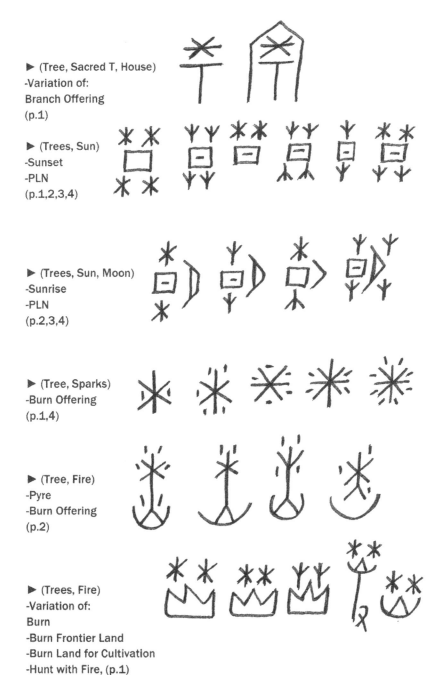

▶ (Tree, Sacred T, House)
-Variation of:
Branch Offering
(p.1)

▶ (Trees, Sun)
-Sunset
-PLN
(p.1,2,3,4)

▶ (Trees, Sun, Moon)
-Sunrise
-PLN
(p.2,3,4)

▶ (Tree, Sparks)
-Burn Offering
(p.1,4)

▶ (Tree, Fire)
-Pyre
-Burn Offering
(p.2)

▶ (Trees, Fire)
-Variation of:
Burn
-Burn Frontier Land
-Burn Land for Cultivation
-Hunt with Fire, (p.1)

▶ (Trees, Fire, House)
-Administrative Rank
or Function
-PLN
(p.1,2,4)

▶ (Trees, House)
-Temple in a Grove
-Temple of Tang / Da Yi
(p.1)

▶ (Trees, Earth or Penis)
-A Ritual
-STN
(p.1,3)

▶ (Tree?)
-Sacrifice?
(p.1,2,3)

▶ (Tree, Grass-Hut?)
-Change, Transform
-PLN
(p.1,3,4,5)

▶ (Tree, Axe?)
-Split, Splitter
-Name of the Eastern
Deity and Direction
(p.1)

▶ (Tree, String)
-Early String Instrument?
(Guzheng or Qin)
-PLN
-PEN of a Diviner (p.1)
(p.1,4,5)

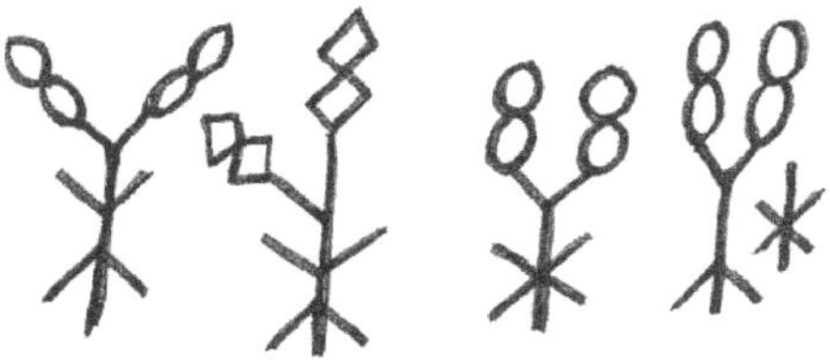

▶ (Tree, Vessel)
-Variation of:
Drink Offering
(p.1,4)

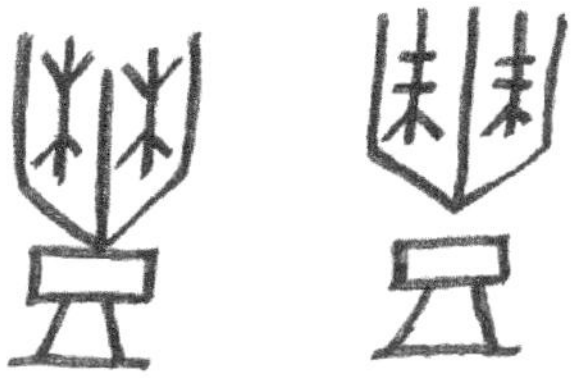

▶ Grass, Hay
(p.1,2,3,4)

▶ (Grass Emerging)
-Birth
-New, Fresh
-Life
(p.1,2,3,4)

▶ New Moon
-New Month

▶ (Grass, Suns)
-Star
-Constellations
-Sunny?
(p.1)

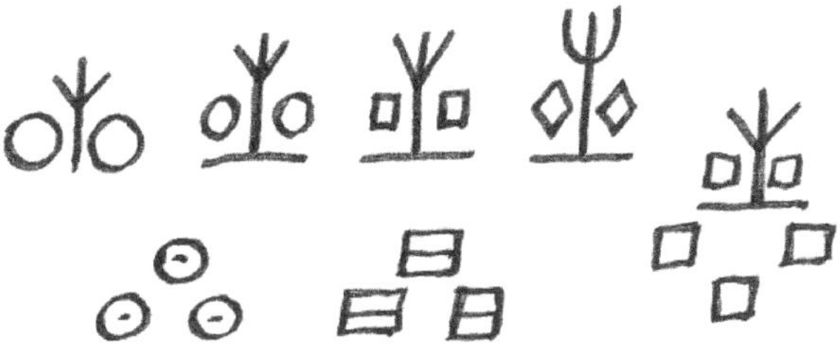

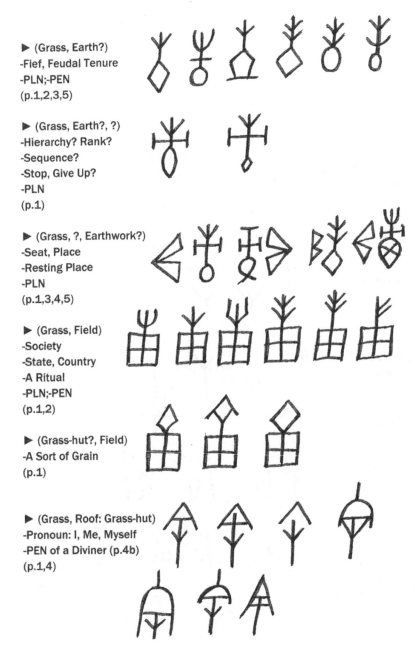

▶ (Grass, Earth?)
-Fief, Feudal Tenure
-PLN;-PEN
(p.1,2,3,5)

▶ (Grass, Earth?, ?)
-Hierarchy? Rank?
-Sequence?
-Stop, Give Up?
-PLN
(p.1)

▶ (Grass, ?, Earthwork?)
-Seat, Place
-Resting Place
-PLN
(p.1,3,4,5)

▶ (Grass, Field)
-Society
-State, Country
-A Ritual
-PLN;-PEN
(p.1,2)

▶ (Grass-hut?, Field)
-A Sort of Grain
(p.1)

▶ (Grass, Roof: Grass-hut)
-Pronoun: I, Me, Myself
-PEN of a Diviner (p.4b)
(p.1,4)

▶ (Spindle)
-Question Particle:
Is it? Will it be?
-(grammatical copula)
(p.1,2,3,4,5)

▶ (Spindle)
-A Ritual
-PEN
(p.1)

▶ Spindle, Beads?)
-Variation of:
Bridle Ornament?
-STN or PLN
(p.1,4)

▶ (Grass, String)
-Variation of:
String

▶ (Grass, String)
-Administrative Rank
(p.1)

▶ (Grass, String, Knife)
-Work
(p.1)

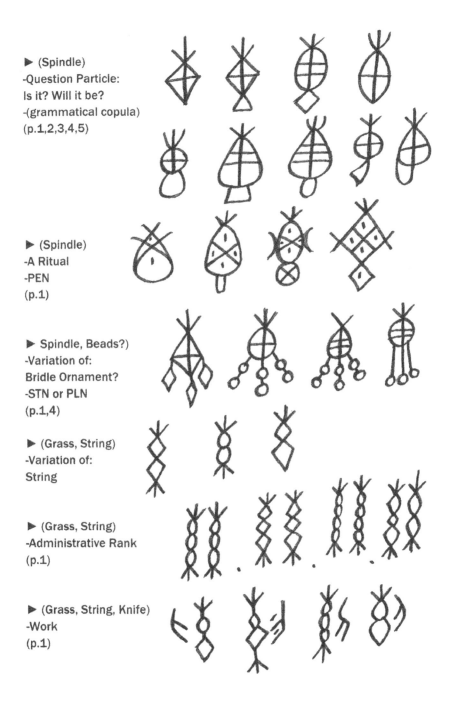

Jan Fries

► (Hill, Work)
-Name of a Hill
-Deity
(p.1)

► Drum
Variation of:
-Drum Music Offering
-Fifth Ancestral
Festival (Rong)
-STN;-PEN
(p.1,2,3,4,5)

► (Grass, Vessel, Fire)
-Variation of:
Offering Cooked Grains
(p.1,3,4)

► (Grass, Vessel, Mouth)
Variation of:
-Offering Cooked Grains
-Third Ancestral Festival (Zai)
-PLN
(p1,2,3,4, especially 5)

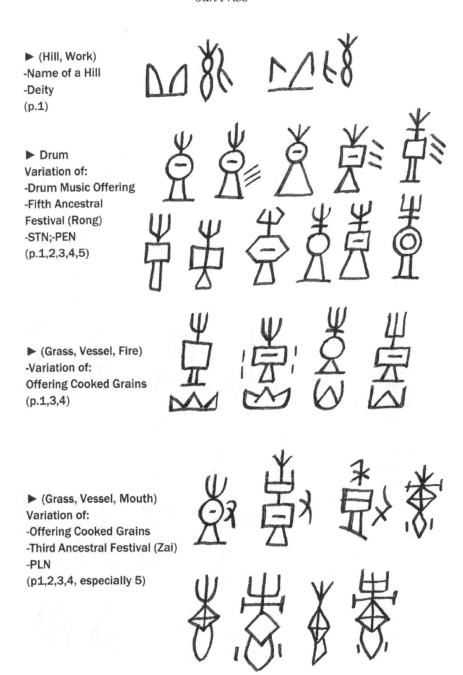

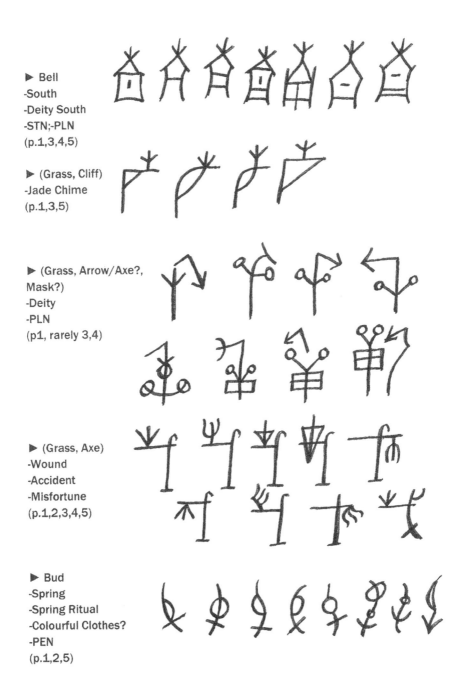

► Bell
-South
-Deity South
-STN;-PLN
(p.1,3,4,5)

► (Grass, Cliff)
-Jade Chime
(p.1,3,5)

► (Grass, Arrow/Axe?,
Mask?)
-Deity
-PLN
(p1, rarely 3,4)

► (Grass, Axe)
-Wound
-Accident
-Misfortune
(p.1,2,3,4,5)

► Bud
-Spring
-Spring Ritual
-Colourful Clothes?
-PEN
(p.1,2,5)

▶ Bud
-Pair
-Pair of Scapula or Plastrons
for Divination
(p.1)

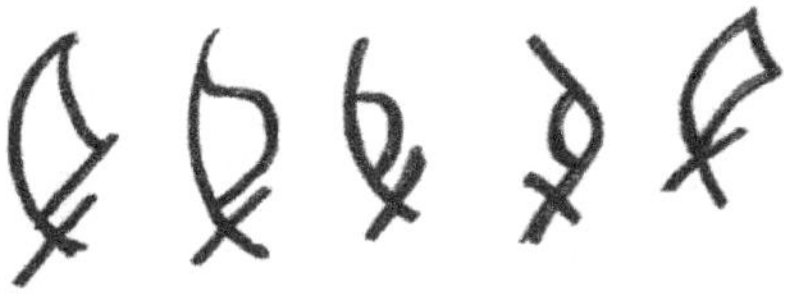

▶ (Bud, sacred T)
-Ritually Prepare
1, 3 & 5 pairs of
Scapula or Plastrons
(p.1)

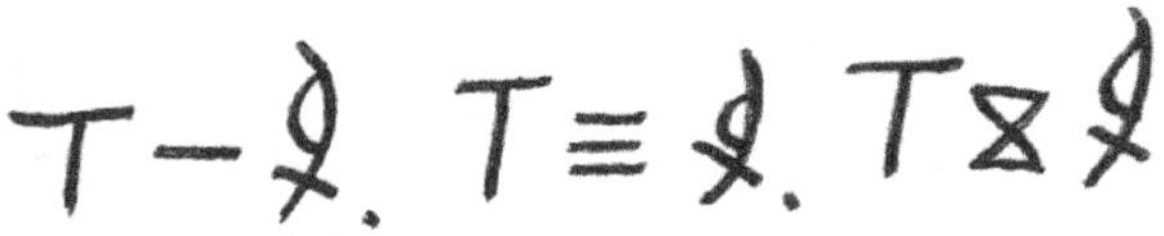

▶ (Bud, Grass,
Trees, Sun)
-Spring
-Spring Ritual
-Courtship or
Marriage Ritual?
-PLN
(p.1,3, rarely 5)

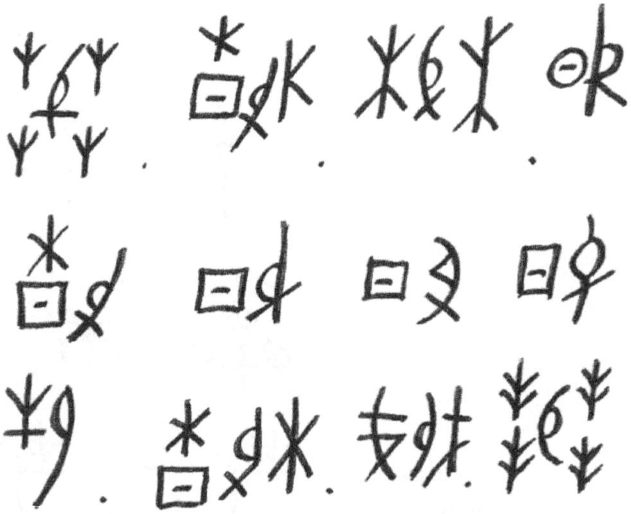

▶ (Bud, Cross)
-A Ritual?
(p.1,3)

▶ Brush
-(Sign Element)
(p.1,2,3,4,5)

▶ (Brush, Rain?)
-Pronoun: You
-STN
-PEN?
-?
(p.1, rarely 3)

▶ (Seed-Bud?)
(Root?)
-Negation: No, Not
-Question Particle
at the end of a
charge: Isn't it?
-STN;-PLN
(p.1,2,3,4,5)

▶ (Root, Digging Stick)
-A Ritual?
-STN
(p.2,3,5)

▶ (Brush, Jacket)
-A Ritual?
(p.4)

▶ (Root?, Earthwork)
-Administrative
Rank or Function
(p.1)

▶ Bamboo Shoot?
-Decade, Ten-Day Week (Xun)
-Divination for a Xun
-PLN
(p.1,2,3,4,5)

▶ (Hook? Tendril?)
-Number: Nine
(p.1,4,5)

▶ (?)
-Deity
(p.4)

▶ Grains
-Millet?
-Rice?
-Sowing?
-Harvesting?
-STN;-PEN
(p.1,4)

▶ Panic Millet
(p.1)

▶ (Millet, Water)
-A Type of Millet
-To Plant Millet
-Millet Harvest?
-A Ritual
(p.1,3,4)

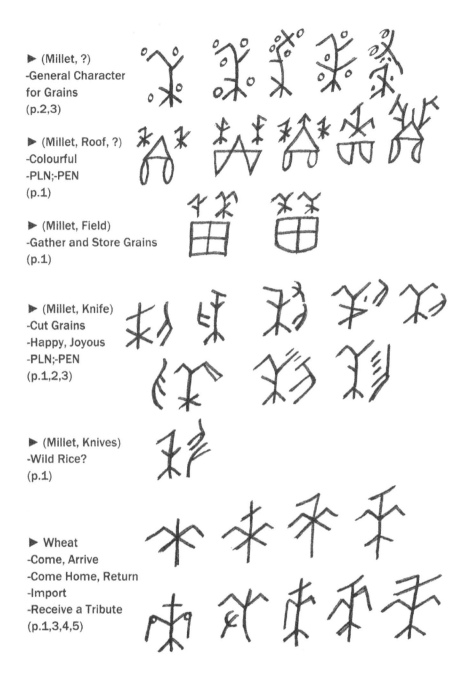

▶ (Millet, ?)
-General Character
for Grains
(p.2,3)

▶ (Millet, Roof, ?)
-Colourful
-PLN;-PEN
(p.1)

▶ (Millet, Field)
-Gather and Store Grains
(p.1)

▶ (Millet, Knife)
-Cut Grains
-Happy, Joyous
-PLN;-PEN
(p.1,2,3)

▶ (Millet, Knives)
-Wild Rice?
(p.1)

▶ Wheat
-Come, Arrive
-Come Home, Return
-Import
-Receive a Tribute
(p.1,3,4,5)

▶ (Seed Husk?)
-7th of 10
(p.1,2,3,4,5)

▶ (Seed-Husk?, Seeds?)
-Variation of Seed-Husk?
-Chaff
-Name Element
(p.5)

▶ (Seed Husk, Wind)
-Musical Instrument
(p1,3)

▶ (Grass, Jade)
-Variation of:
Jade Ornament
-Offering
-PLN? PEN?(p.1)

▶ (Seedling)
Variation of:
-Here, In, At
-Now
-To Be In
(p.1,2,3,4,5)

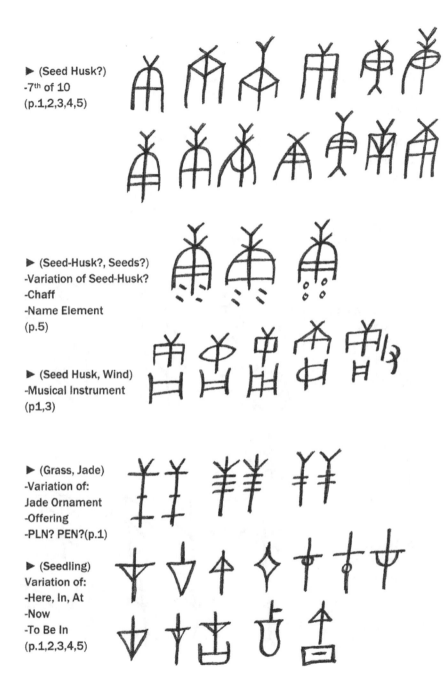

Nature

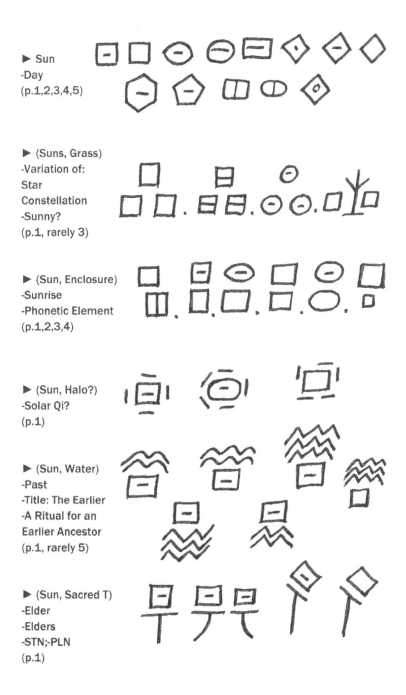

▶ Sun
-Day
(p.1,2,3,4,5)

▶ (Suns, Grass)
-Variation of:
Star
Constellation
-Sunny?
(p.1, rarely 3)

▶ (Sun, Enclosure)
-Sunrise
-Phonetic Element
(p.1,2,3,4)

▶ (Sun, Halo?)
-Solar Qi?
(p.1)

▶ (Sun, Water)
-Past
-Title: The Earlier
-A Ritual for an
Earlier Ancestor
(p.1, rarely 5)

▶ (Sun, Sacred T)
-Elder
-Elders
-STN;-PLN
(p.1)

► (Sun, To Raise)
-Sky Clears Up
-Sun Emerges
-Grant a Boon
(p.1)

► (Sun, Feather)
-Feather Dance Ritual
-First Ancestral Festival (Yi)
- Next Day (if followed
by a day sign)
(p.1,2,3,4,5)

► (Sun, Moon)
-Dawn, Morning
-Bright
-PLN
(p.1)

► Moon
-Month
-Evening
-Evening Sacrifice
-Night
(Evening & Night
often with a dot)
(p.1,2,3,4,5)

► (Sun, Centre)
-Noon
(p.1,3)

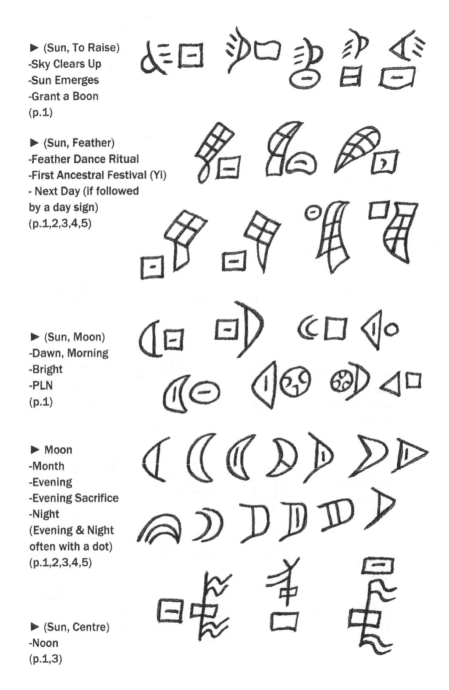

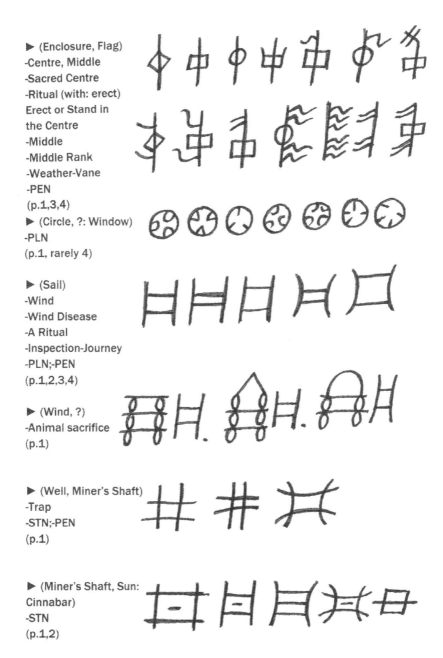

► (Enclosure, Flag)
-Centre, Middle
-Sacred Centre
-Ritual (with: erect)
Erect or Stand in
the Centre
-Middle
-Middle Rank
-Weather-Vane
-PEN
(p.1,3,4)

► (Circle, ?: Window)
-PLN
(p.1, rarely 4)

► (Sail)
-Wind
-Wind Disease
-A Ritual
-Inspection-Journey
-PLN;-PEN
(p.1,2,3,4)

► (Wind, ?)
-Animal sacrifice
(p.1)

► (Well, Miner's Shaft)
-Trap
-STN;-PEN
(p.1)

► (Miner's Shaft, Sun:
Cinnabar)
-STN
(p.1,2)

► (Wind, ?)
-Deity or Ancestor
(p.3,4)

► (Ladle)
-Ursa Major
(p.1)

► (Ladle, Drops: Bushel)
-A Ritual
-Deity?
-Ursa Major?
-PLN
(p.1,2,3,5)

► River
-2nd of 10
(p. 1,2,3,4,5)

► Various Rivers

► (River, Drops)
-Water
-River
-Flood
(p.1,3,4)

▶ (3 Rivers, Seedling)
-Disaster
-Flood?
(p.1,2,3,4,5)

▶ (River, Digging Stick Handle)
-Huang He, the Yellow River
-River Deity
(p.1,2,4)

▶ (River, Carry)
-Huang He, the Yellow River
-River Deity
(p.3,4)

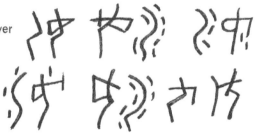

▶ (River, Turbulence)
-River Heng Shui
-River surrounding the Capital
-River Deity
(p.1,2,3,4)

▶ Turbulence
-PLN;-PEN
-PEN of a Diviner (p.1)
(p.1,3,4)

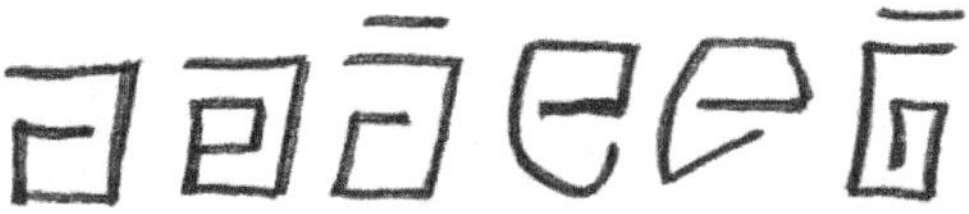

▶ (Turbulence, Above)
-Cloud
-Cloudy, Overcast
-Deity or Deities Cloud:
3 Clouds, 4 Clouds,
6 Clouds, Di Cloud
(p.1,4)

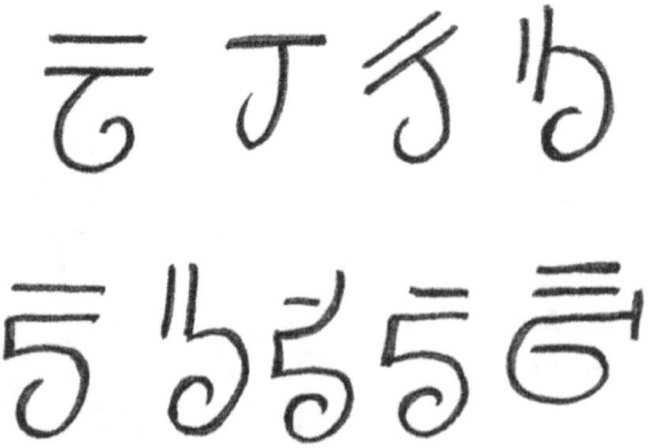

▶ (River, Road)
-Disaster
-Flooded Road?
-PEN of a Diviner (p.1 or 4)
-PEN
(p.1,4)

▶ (River, Boat)
-Float
-Swim
(p.1)

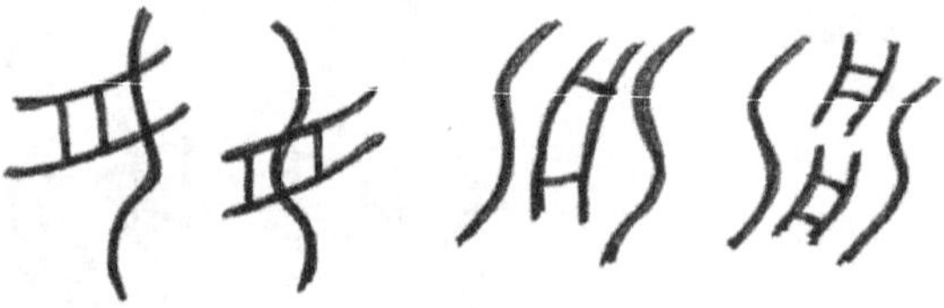

▶ (River, Scroll, Mouth)
-Sink Document
In River (i.e. give
Document or make
a promise to River Deity)
(p.1)

► (Rivers, Pole?)
-Name of the West
-Name of the Westwind
-?
(p.1)

► (Rivers, Administrator)
-Administrator or
Administrative Rank
-PEN
(p1)

► Lightning
-9th of 12
(p.1,2,3,4,5)

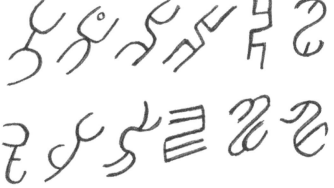

► (Lightning, Mouth,
Wheel)
-Thunder
-Thunderstorm
-STN;-PLN;-PEN
(p.1,2,4)

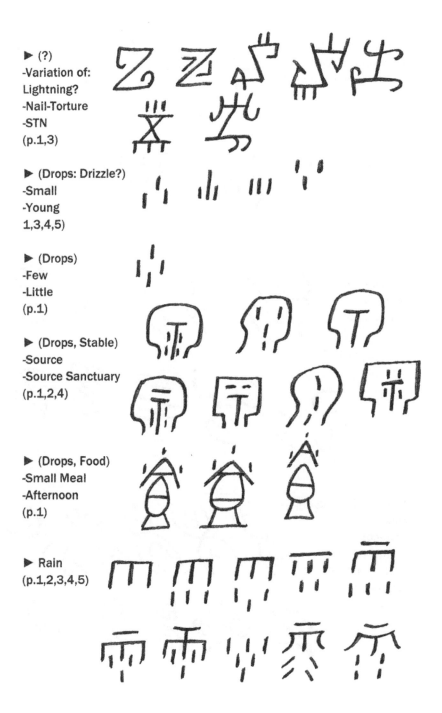

▶ (?)
-Variation of:
Lightning?
-Nail-Torture
-STN
(p.1,3)

▶ (Drops: Drizzle?)
-Small
-Young
1,3,4,5)

▶ (Drops)
-Few
-Little
(p.1)

▶ (Drops, Stable)
-Source
-Source Sanctuary
(p.1,2,4)

▶ (Drops, Food)
-Small Meal
-Afternoon
(p.1)

▶ Rain
(p.1,2,3,4,5)

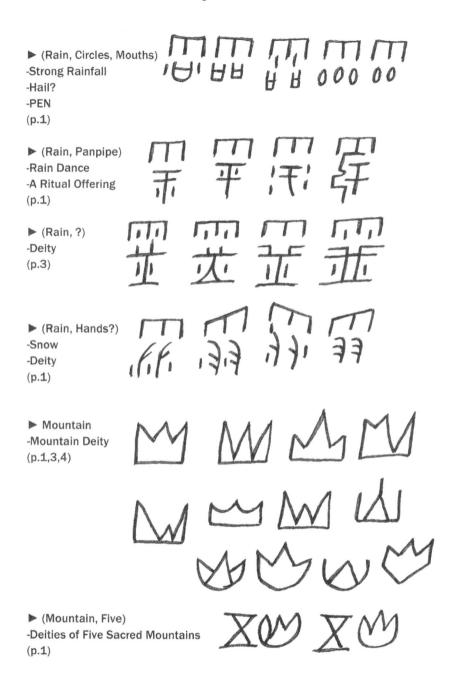

▶ (Rain, Circles, Mouths)
-Strong Rainfall
-Hail?
-PEN
(p.1)

▶ (Rain, Panpipe)
-Rain Dance
-A Ritual Offering
(p.1)

▶ (Rain, ?)
-Deity
(p.3)

▶ (Rain, Hands?)
-Snow
-Deity
(p.1)

▶ Mountain
-Mountain Deity
(p.1,3,4)

▶ (Mountain, Five)
-Deities of Five Sacred Mountains
(p.1)

► (Mountain, Ten)
-Deities of Ten Sacred Mountains
(p.1)

► Mountains and
Mountain Deities
(may include some
Fire Deities!)
(p.1,3,4)

► (Mountain or Fire, String)
-Dark
-Black
(p.1,3)

► Fire
-Fire Star
(Mars? Antares?)
-PEN
(p.1,3,4)

► (3 Fires)
-Ritual
-Burn Qiang? (p.1)

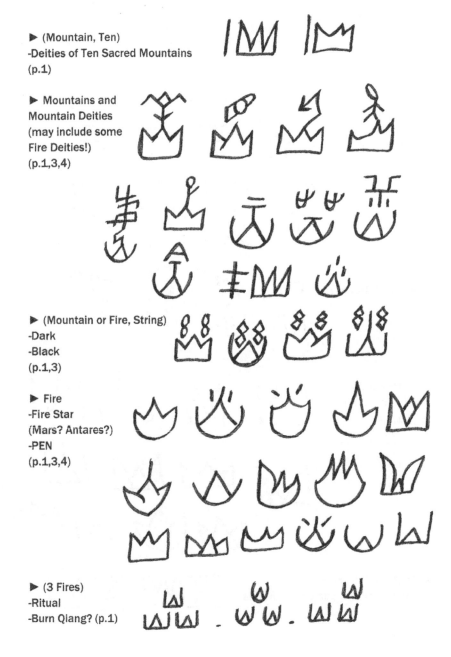

▶ Hill
-Hill Deity
-Elevated District
of a Settlement
-PLN
(p.1,2)

▶ (Hill, Shang)
-Supreme Hill
-Hill Deity
(p.1)

▶ (Hill, Work)
-Hill
-Hill Deity
(p.1)

▶ (Heaps of Earth?)
-Earthwork?
-Fortification
-Fortified Camp
-Army
-PEN
(p.1,2,3,5)

▶ (Earthwork?, Below)
-Stop
-Rest
(p.1)

▶ (Earthwork, House)
-Dwell, Inhabit
-Inn?
-Army Building?
(p.1)

▶ (Mound, Earth Altar or Standing Stone)
-Earth
-Earth Deity
-Earth Deity of a Place
-STN
(p. 5: written as: ⊥ Male, Penis)
(p.1,3,4,5)

▶ (Ladder, Steps)
-PEN
(p.1)

▶ (Stone, Cliff)
-Stone
-Deity
-STN;-PEN
(p.1)

▶ (Cliff, Sacred T)
-A Ritual
(p.1)

▶ (Cliff, Axe)
-Collide
-Meet?
(p.1)

▶ Jade
-A Unit of Jade
(p.1)

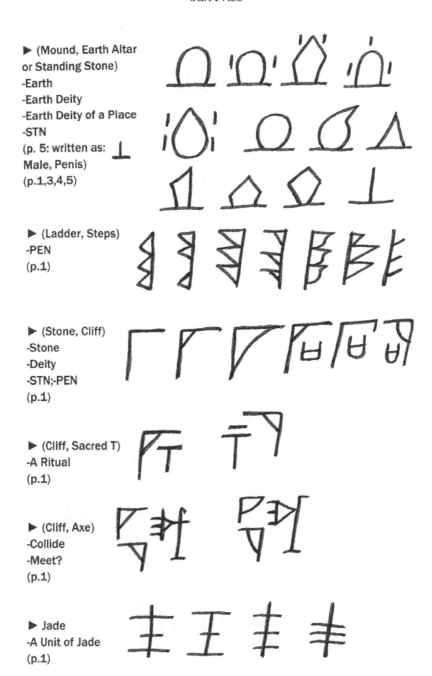

754

▶ (2 Jades)
-Jade Sacrifice
-PLN? PEN?
(p.1,3)

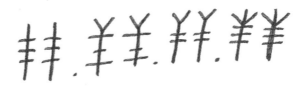

▶ Jade Cong
-Offering a Sacred
Jade Cylinder
-Royal Gift
(p.1,2,4)

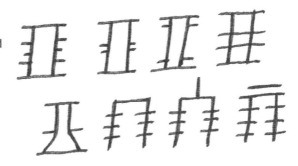

Field

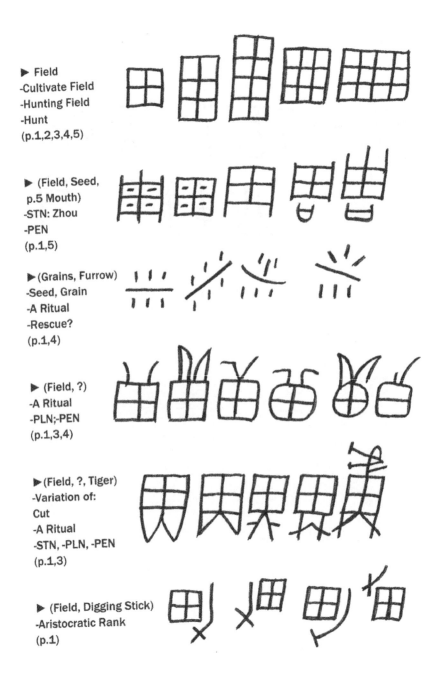

▶ Field
-Cultivate Field
-Hunting Field
-Hunt
(p.1,2,3,4,5)

▶ (Field, Seed,
  p.5 Mouth)
-STN: Zhou
-PEN
(p.1,5)

▶(Grains, Furrow)
-Seed, Grain
-A Ritual
-Rescue?
(p.1,4)

▶ (Field, ?)
-A Ritual
-PLN;-PEN
(p.1,3,4)

▶(Field, ?, Tiger)
-Variation of:
Cut
-A Ritual
-STN, -PLN, -PEN
(p.1,3)

▶ (Field, Digging Stick)
-Aristocratic Rank
(p.1)

Field, Wall, Road

▶ (Cross, Enclosure, Above)
-PEN of Shang Jia
(p.1,2,3,4,5)

▶ (Earth Wall)
Use, Apply
Sacrifice

▶ (Earth Wall, Two Strings= This, Here)
-Done, Completed, Fulfilled
(p.1,3,4,5)

▶ (Earth Wall, Street, Foot)
-A Ritual?
-STN
(p.1,4)

▶ (Street)
(p.1,2,3,4,5)

▶ (Crossroad)
-Go, Travel
-PEN of a Diviner (p.2,3)
-STN;-PEN (p.1,2,3)

Road, Pit, Structure

► (Crossroad, String)
-Lead, Guide
(p.4)

►Pit
-Trap
-Mortar
(p.1)

► (Box, Chest)
-Thank
-Thanksgiving Ritual
-Reward Good
-Name Element in
Predynastic Titles
(p.1,3,4)

► PLN of a Temple
or Sanctuary
(p1)

► (Wickerwork?)
(p.1,2,3,4)

► (Double Wickerwork?,
Road: Scaffolding)
-Encounter, Meet, Unite
-Come Together
-Arrive, Happen
-A Ritual
-STN;-PEN
(p.1,3,4,5)

House

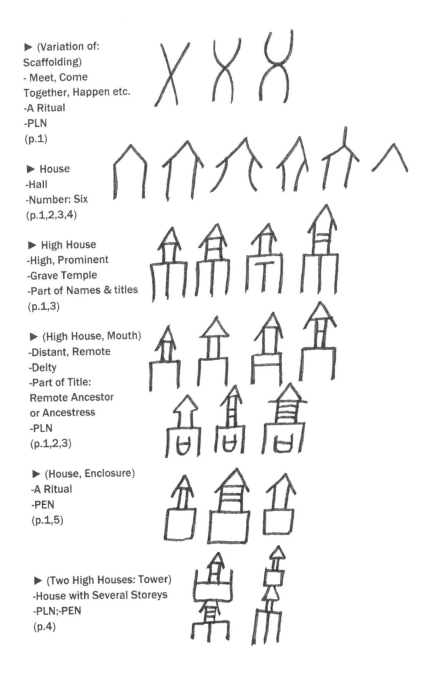

▶ (Variation of: Scaffolding)
- Meet, Come Together, Happen etc.
-A Ritual
-PLN
(p.1)

▶ House
-Hall
-Number: Six
(p.1,2,3,4)

▶ High House
-High, Prominent
-Grave Temple
-Part of Names & titles
(p.1,3)

▶ (High House, Mouth)
-Distant, Remote
-Deity
-Part of Title:
Remote Ancestor
or Ancestress
-PLN
(p.1,2,3)

▶ (House, Enclosure)
-A Ritual
-PEN
(p.1,5)

▶ (Two High Houses: Tower)
-House with Several Storeys
-PLN;-PEN
(p.4)

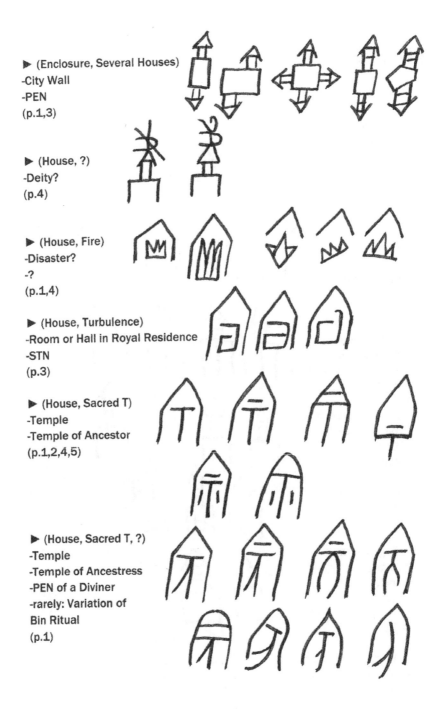

▶ (Enclosure, Several Houses)
-City Wall
-PEN
(p.1,3)

▶ (House, ?)
-Deity?
(p.4)

▶ (House, Fire)
-Disaster?
-?
(p.1,4)

▶ (House, Turbulence)
-Room or Hall in Royal Residence
-STN
(p.3)

▶ (House, Sacred T)
-Temple
-Temple of Ancestor
(p.1,2,4,5)

▶ (House, Sacred T, ?)
-Temple
-Temple of Ancestress
-PEN of a Diviner
-rarely: Variation of
Bin Ritual
(p.1)

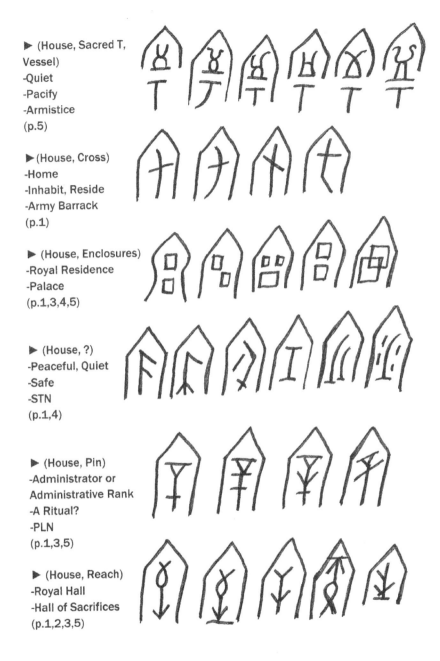

▶ (House, Sacred T, Vessel)
-Quiet
-Pacify
-Armistice
(p.5)

▶(House, Cross)
-Home
-Inhabit, Reside
-Army Barrack
(p.1)

▶ (House, Enclosures)
-Royal Residence
-Palace
(p.1,3,4,5)

▶ (House, ?)
-Peaceful, Quiet
-Safe
-STN
(p.1,4)

▶ (House, Pin)
-Administrator or Administrative Rank
-A Ritual?
-PLN
(p.1,3,5)

▶ (House, Reach)
-Royal Hall
-Hall of Sacrifices
(p.1,2,3,5)

House, Chopping Board, Enclosure

▶ (House, Vessel)
-Variation of:
Drink Sacrifice
(p.1,2)

▶ (Chopping Board
Or: Burial Urn)
-Grandfather
-Man of Grandfather's
Generation
-Ancestral Title
(p.1,2,3,4,5)

▶ (Chopping
Board, Meat)
-to Slaughter
-Ritual: Offer
Fresh Meat
On Chopping
Board
(p.1,3,4,5)

▶ (Chopping Board,
Knife, Meat)
-Cut Meat
-Animal or
Human Sacrifice
(p.1,3,4,5)

▶(Stable, Enclosure)
- with sheep, lamb or cattle:
A Pair of Sacrificial Animals
or: a Penned Animal
-Stabled, Domesticated
(p.1,2,3,4,5)

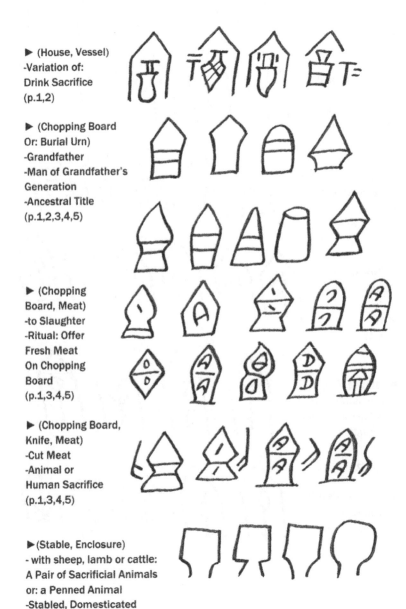

Enclosure, Lines

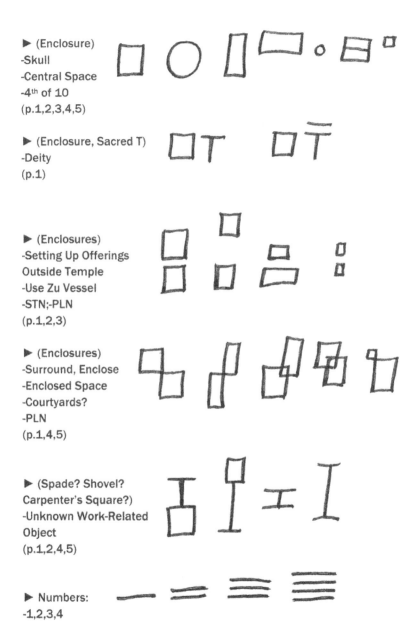

▶ (Enclosure)
-Skull
-Central Space
-4th of 10
(p.1,2,3,4,5)

▶ (Enclosure, Sacred T)
-Deity
(p.1)

▶ (Enclosures)
-Setting Up Offerings
Outside Temple
-Use Zu Vessel
-STN;-PLN
(p.1,2,3)

▶ (Enclosures)
-Surround, Enclose
-Enclosed Space
-Courtyards?
-PLN
(p.1,4,5)

▶ (Spade? Shovel?
Carpenter's Square?)
-Unknown Work-Related
Object
(p.1,2,4,5)

▶ Numbers:
-1,2,3,4

Lines

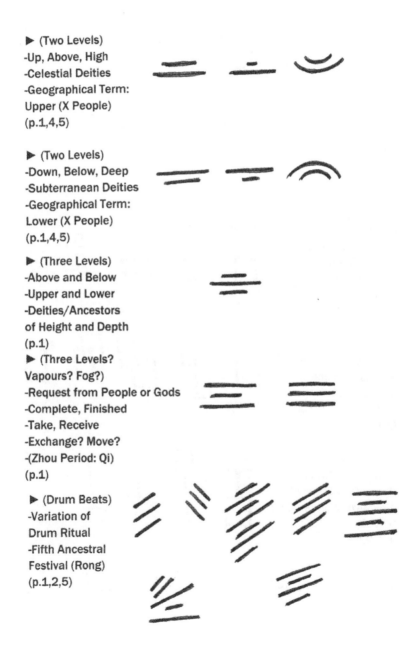

▶ (Two Levels)
-Up, Above, High
-Celestial Deities
-Geographical Term:
Upper (X People)
(p.1,4,5)

▶ (Two Levels)
-Down, Below, Deep
-Subterranean Deities
-Geographical Term:
Lower (X People)
(p.1,4,5)

▶ (Three Levels)
-Above and Below
-Upper and Lower
-Deities/Ancestors
of Height and Depth
(p.1)

▶ (Three Levels?
Vapours? Fog?)
-Request from People or Gods
-Complete, Finished
-Take, Receive
-Exchange? Move?
-(Zhou Period: Qi)
(p.1)

▶ (Drum Beats)
-Variation of
Drum Ritual
-Fifth Ancestral
Festival (Rong)
(p.1,2,5)

Lines, Crack

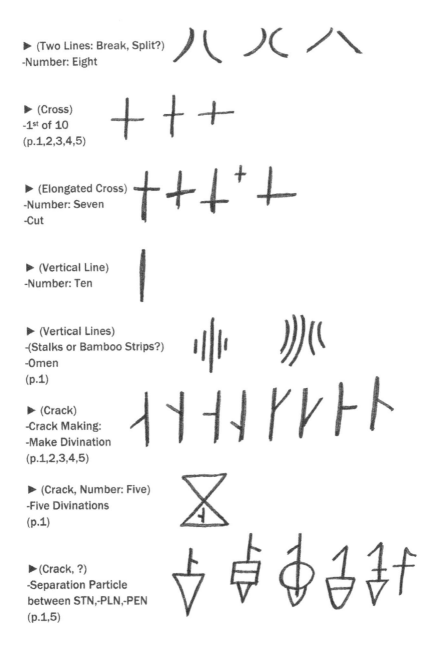

▶ (Two Lines: Break, Split?)
-Number: Eight

▶ (Cross)
-1st of 10
(p.1,2,3,4,5)

▶ (Elongated Cross)
-Number: Seven
-Cut

▶ (Vertical Line)
-Number: Ten

▶ (Vertical Lines)
-(Stalks or Bamboo Strips?)
-Omen
(p.1)

▶ (Crack)
-Crack Making:
-Make Divination
(p.1,2,3,4,5)

▶ (Crack, Number: Five)
-Five Divinations
(p.1)

▶ (Crack, ?)
-Separation Particle
between STN,-PLN,-PEN
(p.1,5)

Sacred T

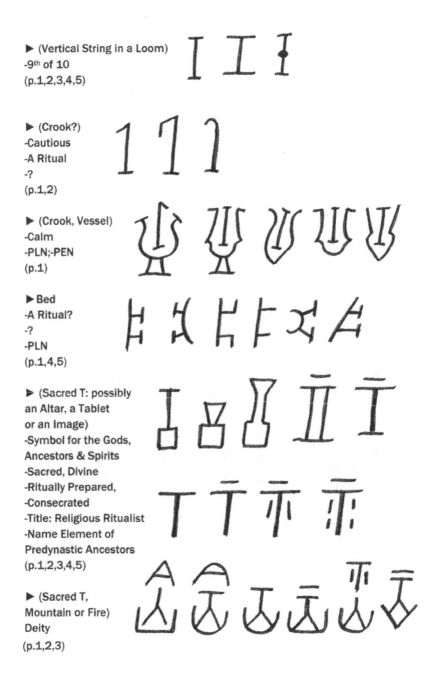

▶ (Vertical String in a Loom)
-9th of 10
(p.1,2,3,4,5)

▶ (Crook?)
-Cautious
-A Ritual
-?
(p.1,2)

▶ (Crook, Vessel)
-Calm
-PLN;-PEN
(p.1)

▶ Bed
-A Ritual?
-?
-PLN
(p.1,4,5)

▶ (Sacred T: possibly
an Altar, a Tablet
or an Image)
-Symbol for the Gods,
Ancestors & Spirits
-Sacred, Divine
-Ritually Prepared,
-Consecrated
-Title: Religious Ritualist
-Name Element of
Predynastic Ancestors
(p.1,2,3,4,5)

▶ (Sacred T,
Mountain or Fire)
Deity
(p.1,2,3)

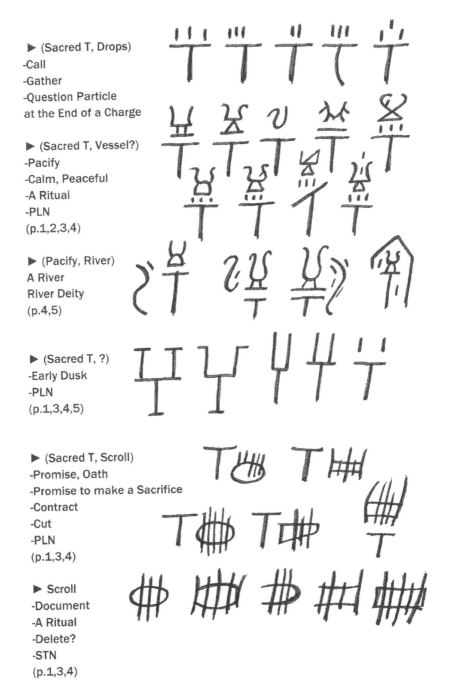

▶ (Sacred T, Drops)
-Call
-Gather
-Question Particle
at the End of a Charge

▶ (Sacred T, Vessel?)
-Pacify
-Calm, Peaceful
-A Ritual
-PLN
(p.1,2,3,4)

▶ (Pacify, River)
A River
River Deity
(p.4,5)

▶ (Sacred T, ?)
-Early Dusk
-PLN
(p.1,3,4,5)

▶ (Sacred T, Scroll)
-Promise, Oath
-Promise to make a Sacrifice
-Contract
-Cut
-PLN
(p.1,3,4)

▶ Scroll
-Document
-A Ritual
-Delete?
-STN
(p.1,3,4)

► (Scroll, Vessel)
-A Ritual
(p.1,2)

► (Sacred T, Ladle)
-Variation of:
Ursa Major?
-A Ritual
-PLN
(p.1,4)

► (Sacred T, Food)
-A Ritual?
(p.1,4)

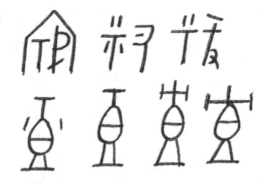

► (Sacred T, Vessel)
-Variation of Drink Sacrifice
(p.1,2,3,4)

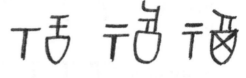

► (Sacred T in all Directions)
-Wu: 'Shaman', Ritualist,
Medium, Invoker, Exorcist
-Ritualist of Di?
-Four Directions
-Deities of Four Directions
-Sacred Quadrant
-STN;-PLN;-PEN
(mainly p.1, rarely 2a,5)

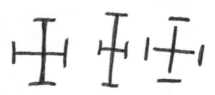

Environment

▶ (Sacred T, Knife
or Forked Spade)
-Fang: Square, Quarter, Direction
-Sacred Directions & Deities
-Foreign People & Countries
(p.1,2,3,4,5)

▶ Royal Tomb
-Title: Ancestor or Ancestress
-Royal Relations
-a Rank or Office?
-PEN of a Diviner (p.1 or 4)
-PEN
(p.1,3,4)

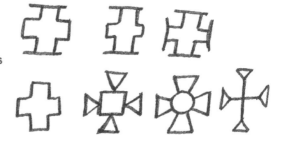

▶ (Panpipe or
Pitch Pipe)
-For, To
-At, Near
-rarely: With, And
-To Go To
(p.1,2,3,4,5)

▶ (Pipe, Vessel)
-Bowl for Food or Drink
-STN;-PLN
(p.3,5)

▶ (Roof, High)
-Now
-Today
-This (Day, Night, Week, Month)
(p.1,2,3,4)

▶ (Entrance)
-Enter
-Inside
-Import
-3rd of 10
-PLN
(p.1,2,3,4,5)

▶ (Roof, ?)
-Variation of: Frontier Land
-STN
(p.1,4)

▶ (Roof, Food)
-Food, Eat
-Second Meal
-Lunar Eclipse
-PLN
-?
(p.1,3,4,5)

▶ (Roof, Food, Small)
-Afternoon
-Small meal
(p.1)

▶ (Rope)
-Enter
-Inside
-Return
-PLN
(p.1,3)

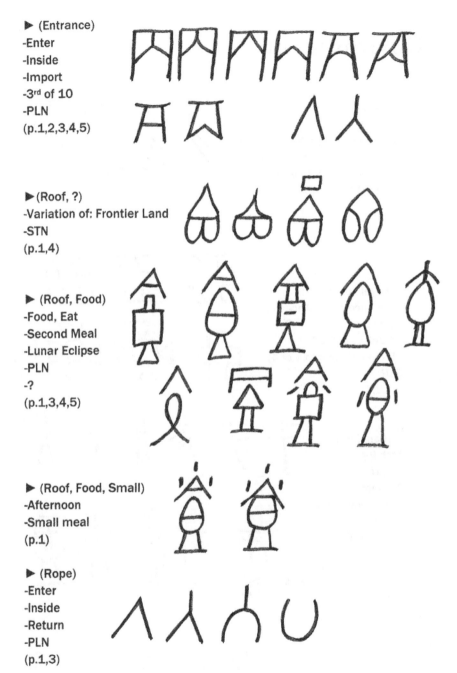

▶ (Rope Ends)
-Finish, End
-Complete
(p.1,4,5)

▶ (Rope Loop?)
-Agreement
-Confirmation
-Indeed, Truly
(p.1,2,3,4)

▶ Door
-PLN (Three Doors)
(p.1,2,3)

▶ Palace Gate
-PLN (Three Gates)

▶ (Mask on Pole?)
-Hunting Fetish?
-PLN Element
(p.1,2,3,4)

▶ (Altar? Scapula?)
(p.1,4)

▶ (Altar, Drops)
-Blood Offering on Altar
(p.1,4)

Di

► (Altar?, ?)
-A Ritual
-Cult Vessel
-STN
(p.1,5)

► (Blossom? Stem Pod?)
-(Masked Ritualist?)
-(Tree, Carpenter's Square, Above?)
-(Sacred T, Eight Directions?)
-Deity or Deities Di
-Posthumous Title of a few
Late Shang Kings
-(in Zhou Period:
interchangeable
with
Tian: the
Divine Sky)
(p.1,2,3,4,5)

► (Di, Enclosure)
-Di Ritual
-Offering to Di
-Di Offering to
Directions
of the World
(p.1)

► (Di, Small)
-A Di Ritual
(p.4)

Household Utensils

▶(Pin, Needle)
-(Symbol of High Rank?)
-(Tattooing Needle?)
-8th of 10
(p.1,2,3,4,5)

▶ (Bent Needle)
-A Spirit
-STN;-PLN;-PEN
(p.1,2,rarely 4)

▶ (Bent Needle, Mouth)
-A Ritual
(p.1,2,3)

▶ (Needle,
Earthwork?)
-Pain
-Hurt,
Inflict Pain
(p.1,3)

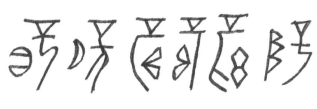

▶ (Pin, Axe?:
Fresh Wound?)
-New, Fresh
-A Ritual
-PLN
(p.1,3,4)

►(Pin, Axe: Loom)
-Dry Meat
-A Ritual
-Yellow or Light Brown
-Eclipse
-Animal sacrifice
-PEN
(p.1,3,4,5)

► (Pin, Entrance, Mouth)
-Name of the Shang Dynasty
-Exceptional, Prominent,
Excellent
-PLN of the Capital City
-PLN of a Hill
-PEN
(p.1,3,5)

► (Shang, River)
-A River
-River Deity
(p.1,2)

► Arrow
-3rd of 12
-PEN of Yi Yin
(p.1,2,3,4,5)

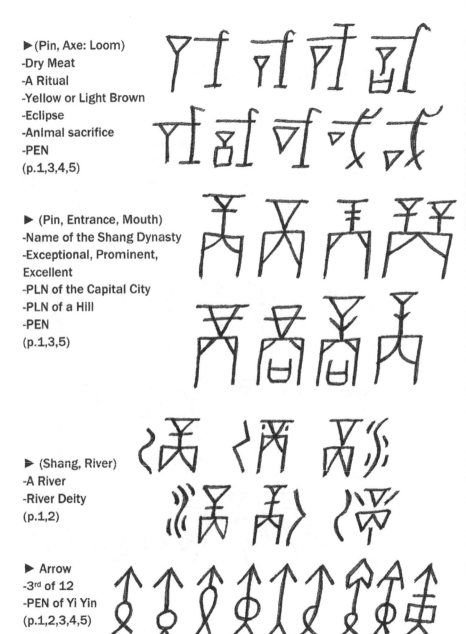

▶ (Arrow, Hook)
-Variation of:
Serpent
–Deity or Deities
  Two Serpents
(p.1,2,3)

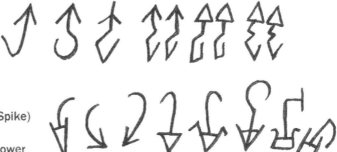

▶ (Arrow, Curve: Spike)
-PLN
-STN (Upper and Lower
Spike People)
 (p.1,4,5)

▶ (Rhino Horn)
-Drinking Horn
-A Ritual
(p.1)

▶ (Two Arrows)
-Hurt, Harm
(p.1,3)

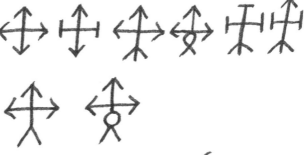

▶ (Arrows, Cross)
-Animal sacrifice
-STN;-PEN
(p.1,3,4)

▶ (Arrows, Cross)
-Palace Guard
-PLN
(p.1)

▶ (Arrow, Cliff: Shooting Range)
-Aristocratic Rank: Marquis
(p.1,4)

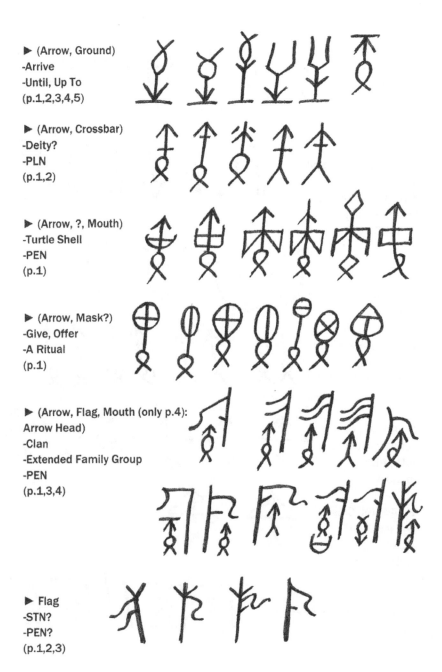

▶ (Arrow, Ground)
-Arrive
-Until, Up To
(p.1,2,3,4,5)

▶ (Arrow, Crossbar)
-Deity?
-PLN
(p.1,2)

▶ (Arrow, ?, Mouth)
-Turtle Shell
-PEN
(p.1)

▶ (Arrow, Mask?)
-Give, Offer
-A Ritual
(p.1)

▶ (Arrow, Flag, Mouth (only p.4):
Arrow Head)
-Clan
-Extended Family Group
-PEN
(p.1,3,4)

▶ Flag
-STN?
-PEN?
(p.1,2,3)

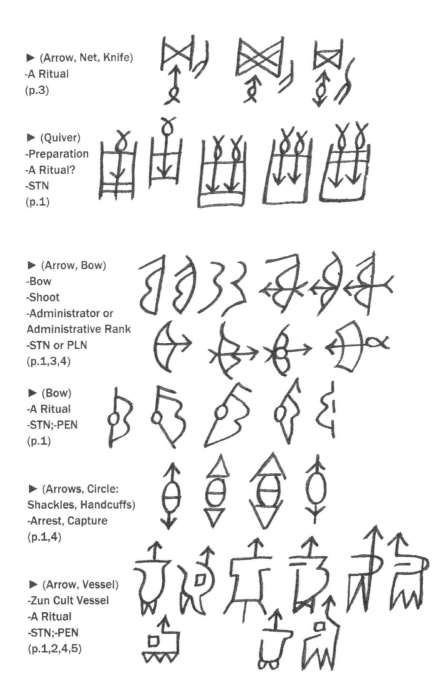

▶ (Arrow, Net, Knife)
-A Ritual
(p.3)

▶ (Quiver)
-Preparation
-A Ritual?
-STN
(p.1)

▶ (Arrow, Bow)
-Bow
-Shoot
-Administrator or
Administrative Rank
-STN or PLN
(p.1,3,4)

▶ (Bow)
-A Ritual
-STN;-PEN
(p.1)

▶ (Arrows, Circle:
Shackles, Handcuffs)
-Arrest, Capture
(p.1,4)

▶ (Arrow, Vessel)
-Zun Cult Vessel
-A Ritual
-STN;-PEN
(p.1,2,4,5)

► (Arrows, Cauldron)
-Jia Cult Vessel
-?
(p.1)

► (Serpent, Pole)
-Little Brother
-?
(p.1,2)

► (Weft)
-6th of 10
(p.1,2,3,4,5)

► (Textile)
-Negation: No, Not
(p.1,2,3,4)

►(Textile, Knife)
-End, Finish
-Omit
-PEN
(p.1)

► (Two Silk Cocoons:
String, Rope)
-Bind
-Lead
-Dark, Mysterious
-7th of 12
(p.1,2,3,4,5)

► (Two Strings)
-This
-Here
(p.1,2,3,4,5)

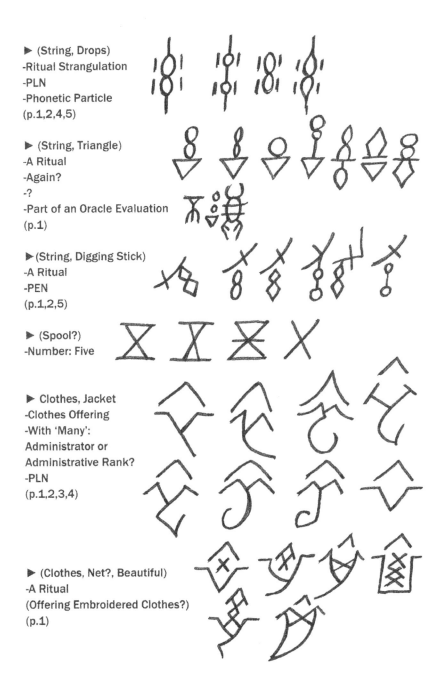

► (String, Drops)
-Ritual Strangulation
-PLN
-Phonetic Particle
(p.1,2,4,5)

► (String, Triangle)
-A Ritual
-Again?
-?
-Part of an Oracle Evaluation
(p.1)

►(String, Digging Stick)
-A Ritual
-PEN
(p.1,2,5)

► (Spool?)
-Number: Five

► Clothes, Jacket
-Clothes Offering
-With 'Many':
Administrator or
Administrative Rank?
-PLN
(p.1,2,3,4)

► (Clothes, Net?, Beautiful)
-A Ritual
(Offering Embroidered Clothes?)
(p.1)

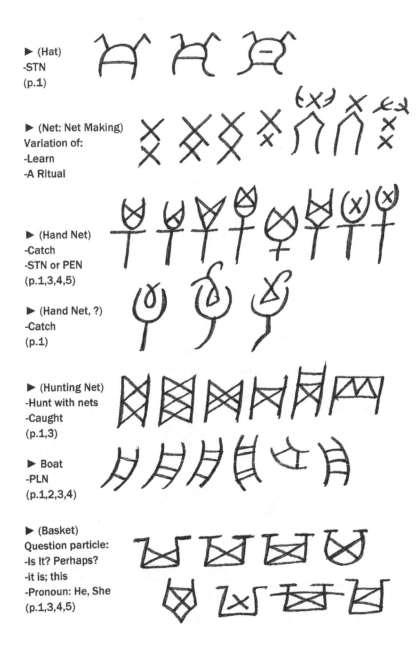

▶ (Hat)
-STN
(p.1)

▶ (Net: Net Making)
Variation of:
-Learn
-A Ritual

▶ (Hand Net)
-Catch
-STN or PEN
(p.1,3,4,5)

▶ (Hand Net, ?)
-Catch
(p.1)

▶ (Hunting Net)
-Hunt with nets
-Caught
(p.1,3)

▶ Boat
-PLN
(p.1,2,3,4)

▶ (Basket)
Question particle:
-Is It? Perhaps?
-it is; this
-Pronoun: He, She
(p.1,3,4,5)

► (River, Basket, Small)
A River
River Deity
(p.1)

► (Cinnamon Blossom?)
-(Dangerous
In-Between Directions?)
-10th of 10
-End of the Ten-Day Week
-Weekly Divination
(p.1,2,3,4,5)

► (Large Basket?
Nest?)
-West
-Deity West
(p.1,2,3,4,5)

► (Feather)
-Next
-Next (Day, Night, Week, Month)
(p.1,2,3,4,5)

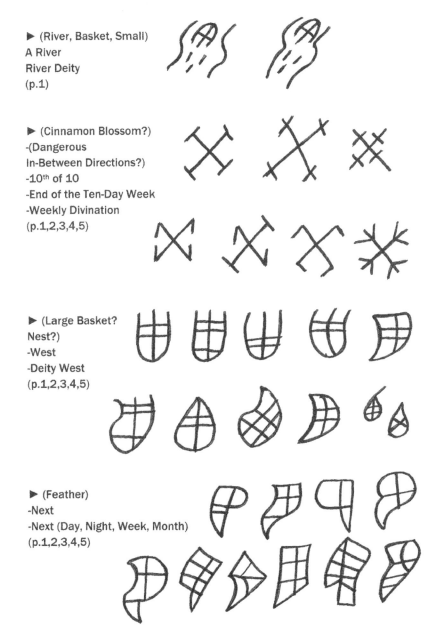

► Chariot
-Military Unit?
(p.1)

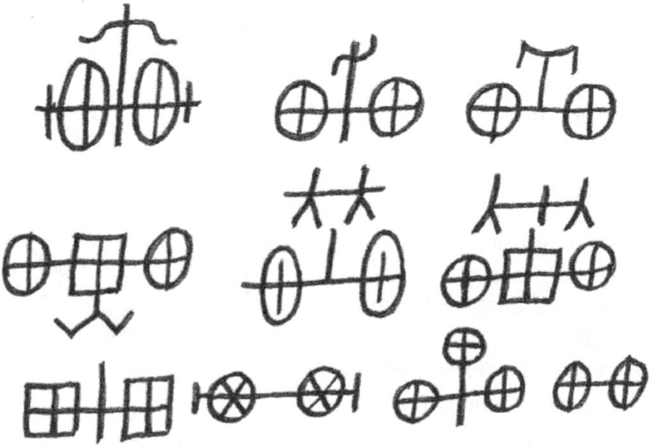

► (Knife)
-(Forked Spade)
-Cut
-STN;-PEN
(p.1)

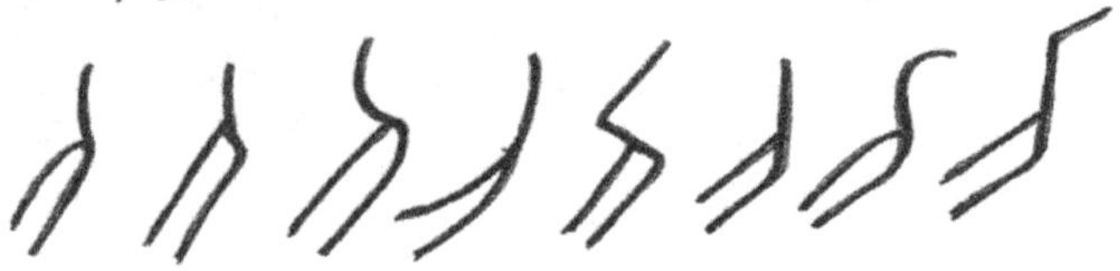

► (Knife, Drops)
-Colourful
-Red?
(p.1,2,4)

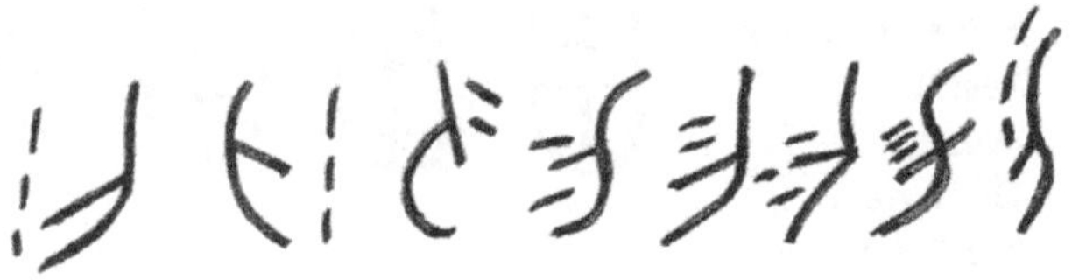

► (Knife, Edge)
-Request, Beg
-Phonetic Element
(p.1,2,4)

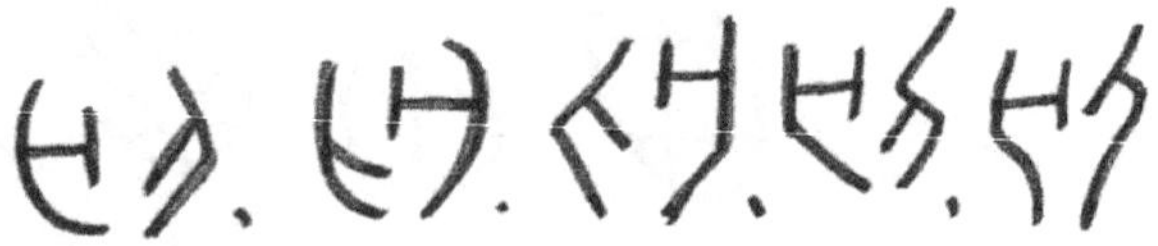

► (Edge)
-Negation: Not,
Not Have
(p.1,2,3,4,5)

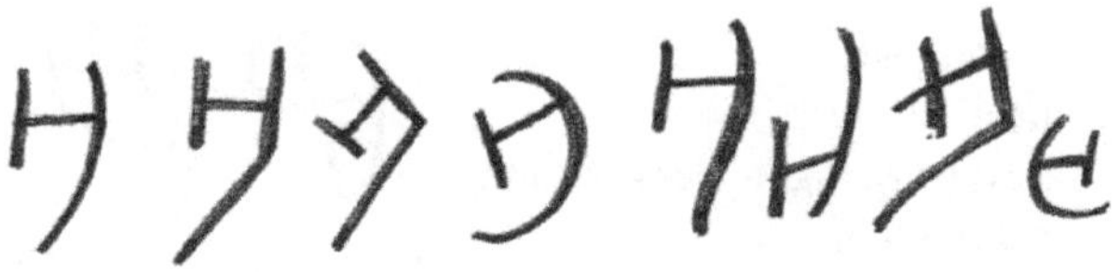

► (Two Edges)
-A Ritual
(p.3)

▶ (Grass Root)
-12th of 12
(p.1,2,3,4,5)

▶ (Dagger Axe)
-Deity
-STN;-PEN
(p.1)

▶ (Two Dagger Axes)
-Invasion, Conquest
(p.1,5)

▶ (Dagger Axe, Shield)
-Strike, Hit
-Start
-Do, Make
-A Ritual
(p.1,3)

▶ (Dagger Axe, Shield)
-A Military Activity
-Misfortune
-STN
(p.1)

▶ (Axe with Triangular Blade)
-Harm
-Kill
11 of 12
(p.1,2,3,4,5)

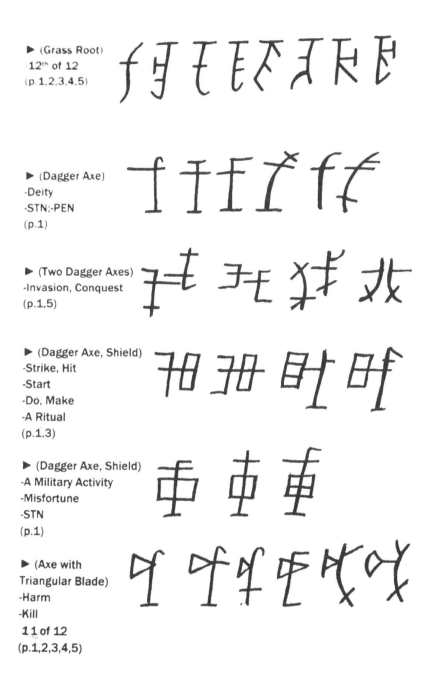

▶ (Axe. Enclosure. Dot (p.3))
-Title of Tang/Da Yi
-Complete
-Fulfil
(see also Axe. Mouth)
(p1,3,5)

▶ (Axe with
Round Blade)
-War
-5th of 10
(p.1,2,3,4,5)

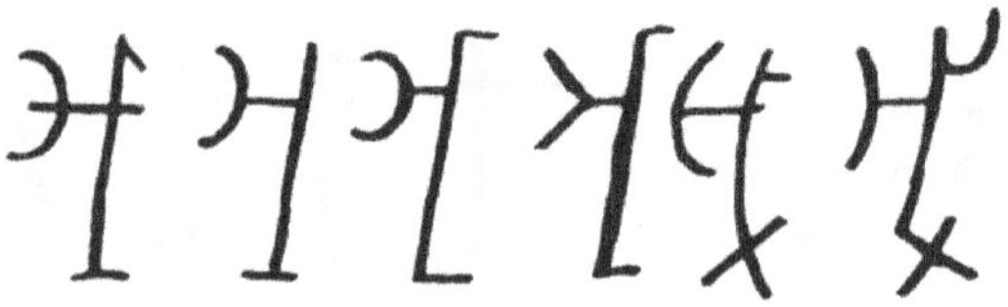

▶ (Jade Double Axe?)
-Split, Spread
-Cut to Pieces
-4th of 12
-PLN;-PEN
(p.1,2,3,4,5)

▶ (Axe?)
-Deity
(p.1,2)

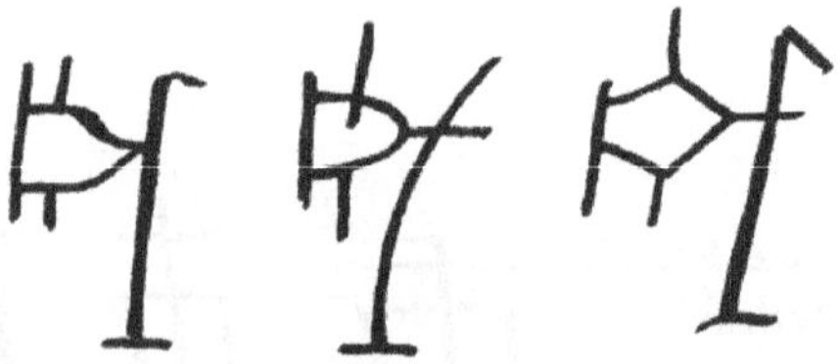

▶ (Axe with Broad Blade, Dots)
-Kill with Axe
-Sacrifice
-Year
(p.1,2,3,4,5)

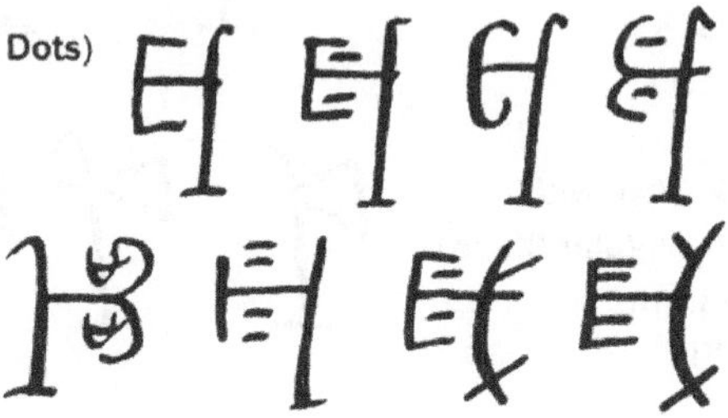

▶ (Axe, Trident: Saw?)
-Pronoun: I, We, Us
-Mine, Our
(P.1,2,3,4,5)

▶ (Saw Axe, Sheep)
-Observe
-PEN of Zu Jia
(p.1,3,5)

▶ (Digging Stick)
-Son
-A Ritual
(p.1,2)

▶ (Three Digging Sticks)
Variation of:
-Cooperation
-Harmonise
-Fourth Ancestral
Festival (Xie)
-PEN
(p. 4)

▶ (Spade)
-Give, Bring
-Receive, Import
(p.1,2,3,4,5)

▶ (Knee Spade?)
(p.1)

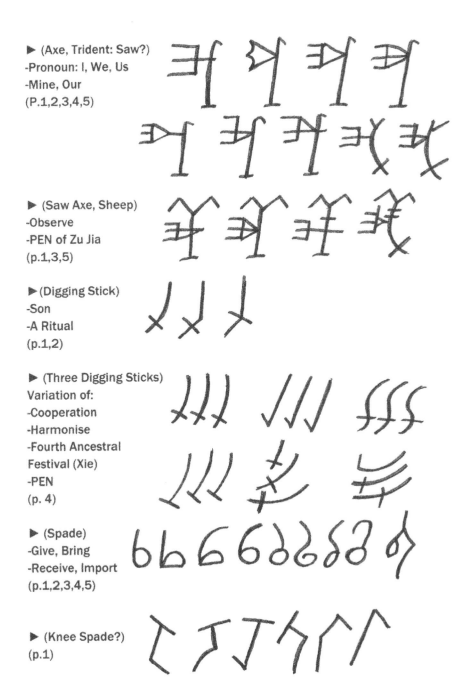

▶ (?)
-Pronoun: You
-It Is
-?
(p.1,3)

▶ (?)
-Prohibition:
Shall Not
-STN;-PEN
(p.1,2,3,4,5)

▶ (?, Drops: Signal Flag)
-Strong Prohibition:
Should Not,
Do Not
-Colourful
(p.1,3,4)

▶ (?)
-Very
-Extremely
-A Ritual
-Flood?
-PLN;-PEN
(p.1)

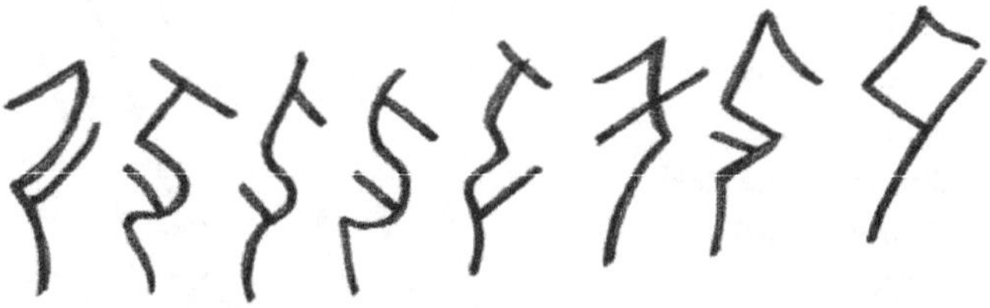

▶ (Grain Measure)
-Raise, Gather
-Lift
-Sacrifice on a
High Location
(p.1,2,3,4,5)

► Melt Metal
-Tin
-Cloudy, Overcast
-Transform, Change
-Grant
-A Ritual
-PLN
(p1: Two Vessels
p.1,2,3,4,5:
Abstract Version)

► Bowl or Cup
-An Offering
-The Night between
Two Day Dates
-STN
(p.1)

► (Bowl, ?)
-Blood
-Blood Sacrifice
-Relationship (a Bloodline)
-PLN
(p.1,2,3,4,5)

► (Bowl, ?)
-An Offering
(p.1)

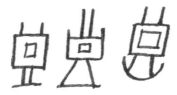

▶ (Bowl, ?)
-An Offering
-?
-PLN
(p.1,2)

▶ (Bowl, Food)
-Food
-Food Offering
(p.1,2,3,4)

▶ (Bowl, Jade, Herbs)
-A Special Wine Sacrifice
(p.1,3,4)

▶ (Bowl, Ladle? Body?)
-Variation of: Wine Vessel
-Long
-Long Duration
(p.1,3,5)

▶ (Vessel?)
-A Ritual
(p.1)

▶ (Bowl, Hair)
-Elder? Aged?
-Beard?
-PLN
(p.1)

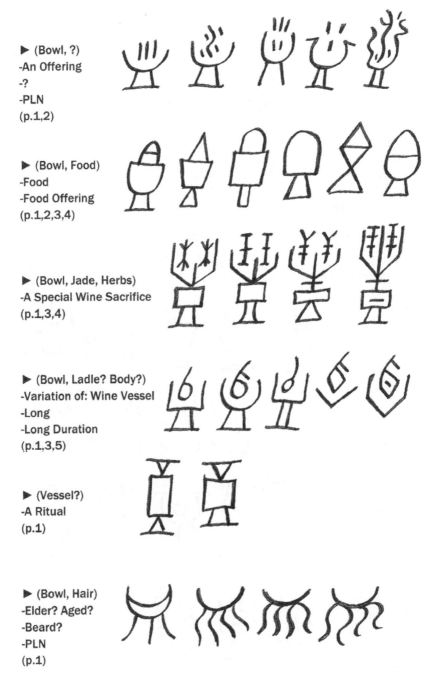

▶ Cult Vessel Type Ho
-Vessel for Baby Burial?
(p.1)

▶ Cult Vessel
Xian
-A Ritual
-STN
(p.1,3,4,5)

▶ Ding Cauldron
-Divination Ritual
-to Divine
-Ask, Test, Question
-to Regulate
-to Make Come True
-Cauldron Ritual
-Cook
-Prefer
(p.1,2,3,4,5)

▶ (Ding, ?)
-Cook
-Food Offering
(p.1,3,5)

▶ (Cult Vessel)
-(Child)
-1st of 12
(p.1,2,3,4,5)

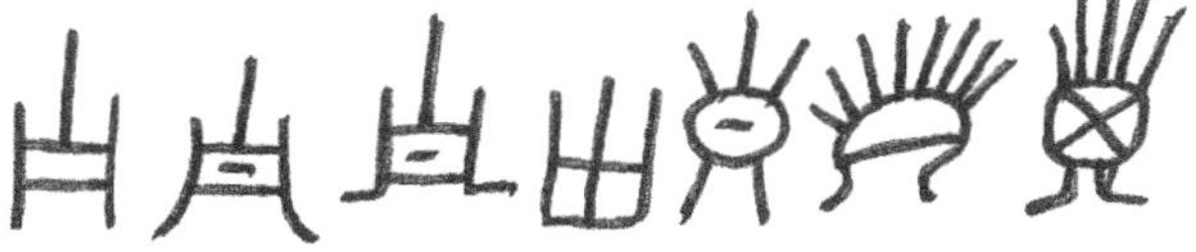

▶ (Cult Vessel?)
-Barn, Grain Storage
-With 'Many': Administrator
or Administrative Rank
(p.1,2,3,4)

▶ Wine Vessel
-Drink Sacrifice
-10th of 12
(p.1,2,3,4,5)

▶ (Wine Vessel, Drops)
-Wine Sacrifice involving
Spilling & Drinking
(p.1,2,3,4,5)

▶ (Wine Vessel, Ground)
-Wine Offering by Setting
up a Vessel for Evaporation
(p.1,2,5)

▶ (Wine Vessel, Five)
-A Ritual
(p.1)

▶ (Wine Vessel,
Grains)
-Probably: Rice
-Beans?
-Millet?
-?
-PLN
(p.1,5)

▶ (Cup)
-Drink Sacrifice
-Variation of:
Spiced Wine?
(p.1,3)

▶ (Cup, Drops)
-Wine with Spices,
Perfumes or Drugs
-An Offering
(p.1,3,5)

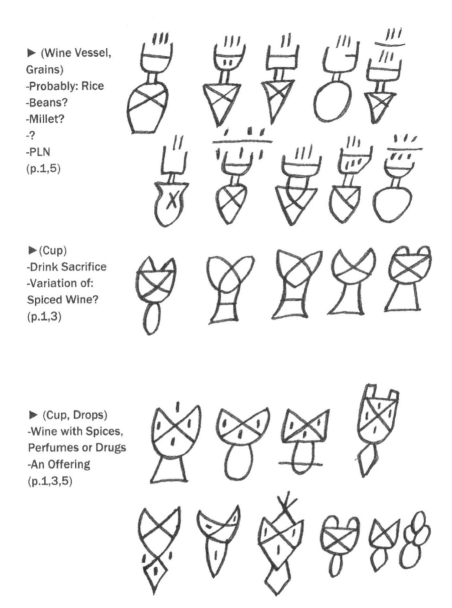

Bibliography

100 Tang and Song Ci Poems, translation Xu Yuan-Chong, 1991

Alberts, Andreas & Mullen, Peter: *Aphrodisiaka aus der Natur*. Kosmos Verlag, Stuttgart, 2003

Allan, Sarah: *The Shape of the Turtle: Myth, Art and Cosmos in Early China*; State University of New York Press; Albany; 1991

Allan, Sarah: *The Way of Water and Sprouts of Virtue*. State University of New York Press, Albany, 1997

Allan, Sarah and Williams, Crispin (editors): *The Guodian Laozi, Proceedings of the International Conference, Dartmouth College, May 1998*; University of California, Berkeley, 2000

Allan, Sarah: *On the Identity of Shang Di and the Origin of the Concept of a Celestial Mandate (Tian Ming)*. University of California, Berkeley. Early China, Vol. 31, 2007,

Altchinesische Hymnen. Aus dem 'Buch der Lieder' und den 'Gesängen von Ch'u'; (*Shijing & Chu Ci*) translation Peter Weber-Schäfer; Verlag Jakob Hegner; Köln; 1967

Bagley, Robert: *Ancient Sichuan, Treasures from a Lost Civilization*; Seattle Art Museum, Princeton University Press; 2001

Barnard, Noel: *New Approaches and Research Methods in Chin-Shih-Hsüeh*. Toyo bunka kenkyusho kiyo (Memoirs of the Institute for Oriental Culture), Tokyo University, Band 19.1959

Bächtold-Stäubli, Hanns & Hoffmann-Krayer: *Handwörterbuch des deutschen Aberglaubens*, Weltbild, Augsburg, 2000 (1927-1942, 10 volumes)

Bandler, Richard: *Richard Bandler's Guide to Trance-formation. How to Harness the Power of Hypnosis to Ignite Effortless and Lasting Change*. Health Communications, Inc, Deerfield Beach, 2008

Bandler, Richard: *Get the Life you Want. The Secrets to Quick and Lasting Life Change with Neuro-Linguistic Programming*. Health Communications, Inc, Deerfield Beach, 2008

Behr, Wolfgang: *Xià: Etymologisches zur Herkunft des ältesten chinesischen Stammesnamens*. Asiatische Studien / Études Asiatiques, LXI, 3, 2007 Peter Lang Verlag, Bern, 2007

Birrell, Anne: *Chinese Mythology, An Introduction*; The John Hopkins University Press, Baltimore & London, 1993

Blacker, Carmen: *The Catalpa Bow. A Study of Shamanistic Practices in Japan*. Unwin, London, 1986

Book of Songs, an unexpurgated translation of. (*Shijing*) translation Xu Yuanzhong, Panda Books, Beijing, 1994.

Breggin, Peter: *Toxic Psychiatry, Drugs and Electroconvulsive Therapy: The Truth and Better Alternatives*, HarperCollins, 1993

Brinker, Helmut und Goepper, Roger: *Kunstschätze aus China, 5000 v. Chr. bis 900 n. Chr. Neuere archäologische Funde aus der Volksrepublik China*, Katalog, Kunsthaus Zürich, 1980

Buddruss, Adolf & Georg: *Schamanengeschichten aus Sibirien*. Verlag Clemens Zerling, Berlin, 1987

Cahill, Suzanne E. : *Transcendence and Divine Passion. The Queen Mother of the West in Medieval China*. Stanford University Press; Stanford; 1993

The Cambridge History of Ancient China. From the Origins of Civilization to 221 B.C. Edited by Michael Loewe and Edward L. Shaughnessy, Cambridge University Press 2006

The Cambridge History of China. The Ch'in and Han Empires 221 B.C. - A.D. 220. Edited by Denis Twitchett and Michael Loewe. Cambridge University Press, reprinted by Caves Books, Taipei, Taiwan, 1987.

Carter, Rita: *Atlas Gehirn*; Schneekluth Verlag, München, 1999

Chinese Health Qigong Association: *Wu Qin Xi.* Foreign Language Press, Beijing, 2007

Cleary, Thomas: *Vitality, Energy, Spirit. A Taoist Sourcebook.* Shambhala Publications, Boston, 1991

Three Treatises on Inscribed Oracle Bones. Drawn by Frank H. Chalfant. Published by Britton, R.S..

1. *The Couling Chalfant Collection.*

2. *Seven Collections* (Tientsin Anglo-Chinese College; Shanghai Museum; Bergen Collection; Princeton University; Richard Wilhelm Collection; Sun Collection; Royal Asiatic Society of London).

3. *The Hopkins Collection.* Shanghai 1935, New York 1938 und New York 1939.

Chang, Kwang-chih: *The Archaeology of Ancient China.* Yale University Press, New Haven, revised edition, 1971

Chang, Kwang-chih: *Shang Civilization.* Yale University Press; New Haven, 1980

Chang, Kwang-chih: *Art, Myth and Ritual. The Path to Political Authority in Ancient China.* Harvard University Press; Cambridge; 1983

Chang, Kwang-chih (Editor): *Studies of Shang Archaeology. Selected Papers from the International Conference on Shang Civilization.* Yale University press; New Haven, 1986

Chang, Kwang-chih (and others): *The Formation of Chinese Civilization: an archaeological perspective.* Edited by Sarah Allan, with contributions by K. C. Chang, Xu Pingfang, Lu Liancheng, Shao Wangping, Wang Youping, Yan Wenming, Zhang Zhongpei, Xu Hong, Wang Renxiang and Peter Ucko. Yale University Press, New Haven, 2005

Chang, Tsung-tung (Zhang, Cong Dong): *Der Kult der Shang Dynastie im Spiegel der Orakelinschriften. Eine paläographische Studie zur Religion im archaischen China.* Otto Harrassowitz; Wiesbaden, 1970

Chang, Tsung-tung (Zhang, Cong Dong): *Die Bildungsregeln und Strukturen der altchinesischen Schriftzeichen* (Extended paper given at the 22. International Sinologist Congress in Stockholm 2. 9. 1970) in Münchner Studien zur Sprachwissenschaft, Heft 30, R. Kitzinger Verlag, München 1972

Chen Bahghai: *Jiaguwen Lingshi*; Tianjin People's Press, 1970 (1919)

Chen Zhi: *From Exclusive Xia to Inclusive Zhu-Xia: The Conceptualisation of Chinese Identity in Early China.* Journal of the Royal Asiatic Society, Third Series, Vol. 14, Part 3, November 2004, Cambridge University Press, Cambridge 2004

Chinese Characters. A Genealogy and Dictionary. Rick Harbaugh; Han Lu Book & Publishing; Taipei, 1998

Cho Hung-Youn: Koreanischer Schamanismus. Hamburgisches Museum für Völkerkunde, 1982

Chou, Hung-hsiang: *Oracle Bone Collections in the United States*; University of California Press; Berkeley, 1976

Chuang Tzu, the Complete Works of. translation Burton Watson; Columbia University Press; New York; 1971 (1968)

Chuang Tsu: *Inner Chapters*. translation Gia-Gu Feng and Jane English, Random House, New York, 1974

Chu Ci. The Songs of the South. An Ancient Chinese Anthology of Poems by Qu Yuan and other Poets. translation David Hawkes; Penguin; London; 1985

Chun Shin-yong (ed.): *Kultur des koreanischen Schamanismus.* Iudicium Verlag, München, 2001

Clements, Jonathan: *The First Emperor of China.* Sutton Publishing, 2007

Confucius, *The Annalects.* (Kong Zi, *Lun Yü*). Translation D. C. Lau, Penguin Books, London, 1979

Creation of the Gods. (Feng Shen Yan Yi.) Translation Gu Zhizhong; New World Press; Beijing; 1992

Das Alte China. Menschen und Götter im Reich der Mitte; catalog, Kunsthaus Zürich; 1996

The Classic of Mountains and Seas (Shan Hai Jing). Translation Anne Birrell, Penguin; London; 1999

Despeux, Catherine and Kohn, Livia: *Women in Daoism*, Three Pines Press, Cambridge MA, 2003

Deusen, Kira van: *The Flying Tiger. Woman Shamans and Storytellers of the Amur.* McGill-Queen's University Press, Montreal 2001

Dian. Ein versunkenes Königreich in China. Catalogue, Museum Rietberg, Zürich, 1986

Ding, Wangdao (translation) *100 Chinese Myths and Fantasies*; Beijing; 1990

Dong Zuobing Xian Sheng Shi Shi Si Zhou Nian Ji Nian Kan; Publisher Yi Wen Yin Shu Guan; Taipei, 1978

Frühling und Herbst des Lü Bu We. Translation Richard Wilhelm; Diederichs; München; 1979

Eno, Robert: *Deities and Ancestors in Early Oracle Inscriptions.* In: Lopez, Donald (ed.) *Religions of China in Practice*; Princeton University Press; Princeton; 1996

Eskildsen, Stephan: Asceticism in Early Taoist Religion. State University of New York Press, Albany, 1998

Evans, Dylan: *Placebo. Mind over Matter in Modern Medicine.* Harper/Collins, London, 2004

Feng Menglong & Luo Guanzhong: *Der Aufstand der Zauberer (Pingyaozhuan)*, Translation M. Porkert, Insel Verlag, Frankfurt/M, 1986

Flessel, Klaus: *China*, in: *Die Grosse Weltgeschichte*, Volume 3 (pages 74-268), 'Frühe Kulturen in Europa', Weltbild Verlag, Augsburg, no year.

Friedländer, Ludwig: Sittengeschichte Roms. Bertelsmann Lesering, no year

Fries, Jan: *Cauldron of the Gods. A Manual of Celtic Magick.* Mandrake Press, Oxford, 2003

Fries, Jan: *Helrunar. A Manual of Rune Magick.* Third, revised edition, Mandrake of Oxford, 2006

Fries, Jan: *Kālī Kaula*, Avalonia Books, 2010

Fries, Jan: *Living Midnight. Three Movements of the Tao.* Mandrake Press; Oxford; 1998

Gan Bao, *Anecdotes about Spirits and Immortals (Suo Shen Ji)*, two volumes, translation Huang Diming & Ding Wangdao, Foreign Language Press, Beijing 2004

Girardot, N.J.: *Myth and Meaning in Early Taoism*; University of California Press: Berkeley; 1988

Granet, Marcel: *Das chinesische Denken*; Piper Verlag, München, 1963

Groot, J.J.M. de: *The Religious System of China*, 6 volumes, reprinted by Ch'eng-wen Publishing Co; Taipei; 1967

Guo, Jue: *Reconstructing Fourth Century B.C.E. Chu Religious Practices in China*, University of Wisconsin, Madison, Proquest, UMI Microfilm, 2009

Guofeng. Das Liederbuch der Chinesen. (*Shiji*) Translation Heide Köser, edited by Armin Hetzer; Insel Verlag, Frankfurt 1990

Gu Wen Zi Yan Jiu (*Journal of Ancient Writing Studies*), published by Xu Zhong Shu, Beijing, vol.3, 1980; vol.6, 1981.

Han Shan, *150 Gedichte vom Kalten Berg*, Diederichs, Köln, 1974

Haarmann, Harald: Universalgeschichte der Schrift. Campus Verlag, Frankfurt, Sonderausgabe für Parkland Verlag Köln, 1998

Hartlieb, Johannes: *Das Buch der verbotenen Künste*, Diederichs, München, 1998

He Xingliang: *Totemism in Chinese Minority Groups*, China Intercontinental Press, 2006

Henricks, Robert G.: *Lao Tzu's Tao Te Ching, A Translation of the Startling New Documents Found at Guodian*; Columbia University Press, New York, 2000

Hertzer, Dominique: *Das alte und das neue Yijing*, Diederichs Verlag, München, 1996

Hertzer, Dominique: *Das Mawangdui Yijing*, Diederichs Verlag, München, 1996

Hessler, Peter: *Oracle Bones. A Journey between China and the West.* John Murray Publishers, London, 2007

Hori Ichiro: *Folk Religion in Japan.* The University of Chicago Press, Chicago, 1968

Hu Bin: *A Brief Introduction to the Science of Breathing Exercise*, revised edition, Hai feng Publishing Company, Hong Kong, 1983

Hu, Hou Xuan: *Zhan Hou Suo Jian Jia Gu Lu* (Survey of Bone-Inscriptions after the War). 6 Volumes. Beijing 1951, Reprinted in Taipei, no year.

Huainanzi, chapters three, four and five, translation and commentary: John S. Major: *Heaven and Earth in early Han Thought*; State University of New York Press; 1993

Hsü Chin-hsiung: *The Menzies Collection of Shang Oracle Bones*, 2 vol., The Royal Ontario Museum, Toronto, 1970

Huangdi Neijing Suwen Jizhu. Der Klassiker des Gelben Kaisers zur Inneren Medizin. Translation Wolfgang G. A. Schmidt. Herder Verlag, Freiburg, 1993

The I Ching or Book of Changes, translation R. Wilhelm & C. Baynes, Routledge & Kegan Paul, London, 1977

Keightley, David N.: *Sources of Shang History, The Oracle Bone Inscriptions of Bronze Age China*, University of California Press, Berkeley, 1978

Keightley, David N.: *The Ancestral Landscape. Time, Space and Community in Late Shang China*; Univ. of California, Berkeley, 2002 (2000)

Kendall, Laurel: *The Life and Hard Times of a Korean Shaman.* University of Hawaii Press, Honolulu, 1988

Klöpsch, Volker & Müller, Eva: *Lexikon der chinesischen Literatur*, Beck, München, 2004

Kohn, Livia and Yoshinobu Sakade (editors*): Taoist Meditation and Longevity Techniques*, University of Michigan, 1989

Kramer, Samuel Noah: *Sumerian Mythology*, revised edition. University of Pennsylvania Press, Philadelphia, 1972

Kramer, Samuel Noah: *History begins at Sumer. Thirty-nine Firsts in Recorded History*, revised edition. University of Pennsylvania Press, Philadelphia, 1981

Kryukov, M.V. : *The Language of Yin Inscriptions*. U.S.S.R. Academy of Sciences, Nauka Publishing House, Moscow 1980

Laotse: *Tao Te King. Nach den Seidentexten von Mawangdui.* Translation H-G Möller Fischer Verlag, Frankfurt, 1995

Lao Zi: *The Book of Tao and Teh.* Translation Gu Zhengkun, Chinese-English Classic Series, Peking University Press, Beijing, 1995

Lao Tse*: Tao Te Ching, The Book of the Way and Its Virtue*, translation J.J.L. Duyvendak, John Murray Publishers, London, 1954

Lao Tzu's Tao Te Ching, A Translation of the Startling New Documents Found at Guodian, trans., ed. & commentary by Henricks, Robert G., Columbia University Press, New York, 2000

Leick, Gwendolyn: *Sex and Eroticism in Mesopotamian Literature.* Routledge, London, 2003

Liä Dsi: Das wahre Buch vom quellenden Urgrund. Translation Richard Wilhelm; Diederichs; München; 1996

Liang, Shou-Yu & Wu, Wen-Ching: *Qigong Empowerment. A Guide to Medical, Taoist, Buddhist, Wushu Energy Cultivation.* The Way of the Dragon Publishing, Rhode Island, 1997

Liang, Shou-Yu & Dr. Yang, Jwing-Ming: *Xingyiquan. Theory, Applications, Fighting Tactics and Spirit.* YMAA Publication Center, Boston, 2002

Li Chi: *Anyang, a chronicle of the discovery, excavation and reconstruction of the ancient capital of the Shang Dynasty*; University of Washington Press, Seattle, 1977

Li Ch'ing-chao: Complete Poems, translation Kenneth Rexroth und Ling Chung; New Directions; New York; 1979

Lienert, Ursula: *Typology of the Ting in the Shang Dynasty. A tentative Chronology of the Yin-hsü Period.* 2 volumes, Franz Steiner Verlag, Wiesbaden, 1979

Liezi; translation Liang Xiaopeng; Zhonghua Book Company, Beijing, 2005

Li Gi. Das Buch der Riten, Sitten und Gebräuche. Translation Richard Wilhelm; Diederichs, München; 1997

Li He: *Goddesses, Ghosts, and Demons. The Collected Poems of Li He (790 - 816)*; translation J. D. Frodsham; Anvil Press Poetry, London, 1983

Li Ju-Chen: *Flowers in the Mirror*, translation Lin Tai-Yi, Yilin Press, 2005

Li Ki (Liji), trans. J. Legge, 2 vol. Motilal Banarsidass Publishers, Delhi, 2008 (1885)

Li, Pu: *Jiaguwen Xuan Du*; publisher Hua Dong Shi Fan Da Xue; Shanghai, 1981

Li Song: *Chinese Bronzeware. A Mirror of Culture.* China Intercontinental Press, 2009

Liu An, King of Huainan: *The Huainanzi.* Ed. & trans. John s. Major, Sarah A. Queen, Andrew Seth Meyer, Harold D. Roth, Columbia University Press, New York 2010

Liu E, *Die Reisen des Lao Can*; translation Hans Kühner; Insel Verlag, Frankfurt, 1989

Liu Hua Yang: *Hui-ming-ging. Das Buch von Bewußtsein und Leben.* Translation by Richard Wilhelm in: *Das Geheimnis der Goldenen Blüte*, Diederichs Verlag, Köln, 1986

Li Leyi: *Entwicklung der chinesischen Schrift am Beispiel von 500 Schriftzeichen*; Verlag der Hochschule für Sprache und Kultur; Beijing; 2001

Li Xueqin: *Chinese Bronzes. A General Introduction.* Foreign Language Press, Beijing, 2007

Luo Zheng Yu: *Yin Xu Shu Qi Qian Bian* vol. 1-8, Kyoto, 1913

Mathieu, Christine & Ho, Cindy (editors): *Quentin Roosevelt's China: Ancestral Realms of the Naxi.* Rubin Museum of Art, New York, Arnoldsche Art Publishers, Stuttgart, 2011

Miller, Lucien (ed.): *South of the Clouds. Tales from Yunnan.* University of Washington Press, Seattle and London;,1994

Puett, Michael J.: *To become a God. Cosmology, Sacrifice, and Self-Divinization in Early China.* Harvard-Yenching Institute: Harvard University Press; Cambridge; 2002

Pritchard, James B. (editor): *Ancient Near Eastern Texts Relating to the Old Testament*, third edition with supplement, Princeton University Press, Princeton, 1969

Qu Yuan, *Selected Poems of Chü Yuan*, translation and commentary Sun Dayu, SFLEP Bilingual Chinese Culture Series, Vol. 1, 2007

Qu Yuan: *Li Sao and other poems by Qu Yuan*; translation Yang Xianyi & Gladys Yang, Foreign Language Press, Beijing 1980

The Rig Veda. Translation Doniger O' Flaherty, Penguin Books, London, 1981

The Rig Veda. Translation Griffith, book of the Month club, NY, 1992

Rock, Joseph F.: *The Na-khi Naga Cult and Related Ceremonies*, 2 vols., Instituto Italiano per il Medio ed Estremeo Oriente, Rome, 1952

Rossi, Ernest: *The Psychobiology of Mind Body Healing.* Norton, NY, 1986

Roth, Harold D.: *Original Tao, Inward Training (Nei-yeh) and the Foundations of Taoist Mysticism*; Columbia University Press, New York, 1999

Saggs, H.W.F.: *The Might that was Assyria.* Sidgwick & Jackson, London, 1984

Saso, Michael: *The Teachings of Taoist Master Chuang.* Yale University Press; New Haven; 1978

Saso, Michael*: Blue Dragon White Tiger, Taoist Rites of Passage*; The Taoist Center, Washington D.C., 1990

Saso, Michael: Taoism and the Rite of Cosmic Renewal, Washington State University Press, 1990 (second edition)

Saso, Michael*: The Gold Pavilion, Taoist Ways to Peace, Healing and Long Life*, Charles E. Tuttle, Boston, 1995 (incorporating the *Gold Pavilion Classic* by Wei Huacun)

Scarpari, Maurizio: *Das antike China.* Verlag Karl Müller; Köln; 2001

Schafer, Edward H.: *The Divine Woman. Dragon Ladies and Rain Maidens.* North Point Press, San Francisco, 1980

Schafer, Edward H.: *The Vermillion Bird. T'ang Images of the South.* University of California Press, Berkeley, 1985

Schuessler, Axel: *ABC Etymological Dictionary of Old Chinese*, University of Hawa'i' Press, Honolulu, 2007

Seagrave, Sterling: *Dragon Lady – The Life and Legend of the Last Empress of China.* Alfred A. Knopf, New York, 1992

Shan Hai Ching. Legendary Geography and Wonders in Ancient China. Trans. Hsiao-Chieh Cheng, Hui-Chen Pai Cheng & Kenneth Lawrence Thern, National Institute for Compilation and Translation, Taipei, 1985

Shaughnessy, Edward L.: *Before Confucius. Studies in the Creation of the Chinese Classics.* State University of New York Press, Albany: 1997

Shaw, Miranda: *Passionate Enlightenment. Women in Tantric Buddhism.* Princeton University Press, New Jersey, 1994

Shi Er Jia Ji Jin Tu Lu (Twelve Family Luck Metal Picture Collection), collection Shang Jun Yang, Taipei, 1973

Shu Ching, Book of History, (Shujing) translation James Legge & Clae Waltham, George Allan & Unwin, London; 1972

Ssuma Ch'ien (Sima Qian) *Including History of the Hsia Dynasty and Yin Dynasty,* translation Herbert J. Allen; 1894-1895, Forgotten Books, no year

The Shih King, (Shijing) translation James Legge, Sacred Books of the East, Vol. 3; 1879

Ssu-ma Ch'ien: *The Grand Scribe's Records,* vol.1; ed. W. Nienhauser Jr., Indiana University Press, Bloomington, 1994

Stolz, Alfred: *Schamanen. Ekstase und Jenseitssymbolik.* Dumont Verlag, Köln, 1988

Störig, Hans Joachim: *Kleine Weltgeschichte der Philosophie,* Knaur Verlag, München, 1964

Strassberg, Richard E : *A Chinese Bestiary.* University of California Press, Berkeley, 2002

Sun Haibo: *Jia Gu Wen Lu;* Henan Tongzhi Wen Wu Zhi; Beijing 1937 or 1938

Szuma Chien: *Selections from Records of the Historian.* translation von Yang Hsien-Yi und Yang, Gladis; Foreign Language Press, Beijing, 1979

Takashima, Ken-Ichi: *A Study of the Copula in Shang Chinese.* Reprinted from The Memoirs of the Institute of Oriental Culture, University of Tokyo, No. 112, 1990, privately printed.

Takashima, Ken-Ichi: Placement of Inscriptions on Oracle Bone Plastrons as a Guide to Decipherment. Asiatische Studien / Études Asiatiques, LIX, 1, 2005 Peter Lang Verlag, Bern, 2005

The Oracle Bone Journal, vol. 10: Japan Oracle Bone Institute, Tokyo, 1964

The Tso Chuan, selections from China's oldest narrative history; translation Burton Watson; Columbia University Press, New York; 1989

Ungnad, Arthur: *Die Religionen der Babylonier und Assyrer,* Diederichs, Jena 1923

Vos, Frits: *Die Religionen Koreas.* Verlag W. Kohlhammer, Stuttgart, 1977

Walls, Jan & Yvonne: *Classical Chinese Myths,* Joint Publishing Co., Hongkong, 1984

Waley, Arthur: *Die neun Gesänge. Eine Studie über Schamanismus im alten China.* Marion von Schröder Verlag, Hamburg, 1957

Wen Fong (editor): *The Great Bronze Age of China, An Exhibition from the People's Republic of China,* Metropolitan Museum of Art, New York, 1980

Werner, E.T.C.: *Myths and Legends of China.* Dover Publications; New York; 1994 (1922)

Wei Boyang: *Cantong Qi. The Secret of Everlasting Life.* Translation R.Bertschinger, Element, Shaftesbury, 1994

White, David Gordon: *The Alchemical Body. Siddha Traditions in Medieval India.* Universtity of Chicago Press, 1996

Whittaker, Gordon*: Calendar and Script in Protohistoric China and Mesoamerica. A comparative Study of Day Names and Their Signs.* Holos Verlag, Bonn, 1991

Wilhelm, Richard: *Chinesische Märchen.* Rohwolt, Hamburg, 1994

Wilhelm, Richard, translation Baynes, Cary: *The I Ching or Book of Changes.* Routledge, London1977

Xu Zhong Shu (editor)*: Jia Gu Wen Zi Dian,* Si Chuan, Ci Shu, Chu Ban She; 1990 & 2006

Yang, Xiaoneng: *Reflections of Early China. Decor, Pictographs, and Pictorial Inscriptions.* Nelson-Atkins Museum of Art; University of Washington Press; Seattle; 2000

Yü Chün-Fang: *Kuan-Yin. The Chinese Transformation of Avalokiteśvara.* Columbia University Press, New York, 2001

Zhang Zhenxiang: *Fu Hao - eine königliche Gemahlin und ihre letzte Ruhestätte,* in *Das alte China,* Zürich, 1996

Zheng, Chantal: *Mythen des alten China*; Diederichs, München; 1990

Zhouyi, The Book of Changes. A New Translation with Commentary by Rutt, Richard, Routledge Curzon, London, 2002

General Index

C

H

L

Dictionary Index

Note that the heading *'deity'* includes other types of shen, such as ancestors, sacred rivers, mountains etc.

C

calf (of a leg) 702
call (people) 648
call 767
calm 645, 766, 767
camp, fortified 753
captive 655, 664, 667
capture (of Qiang) 674
capture 777
carpenter's square? 763
carry something in? 674
carry 655
cast metal 685, 716, 787
catch birds 626
catch people? 656
catch 626, 708, 780
cattle head or skull? 617
cattle sacrifice (burial) 617
cattle sacrifice (drowning) 617
cattle theft? 617
cattle 616
caught 780
cautious 766
centipede? 637
central space 763
centre of the palace 711
centre 661, 745
chaff 742
change 732, 787
chariot 782
chase a person or army 705
chest 758
chi offering 687
chick 629
child 680, 789
chin beard 711
chopping board 762
cinnabar 745
cinnamon blossom? 781
citizens 642
city guard 706
city wall 760
city 677
clan sign('Enclosure')? 658
clan 776
claw 681
clean 691
cliff 754
climax? 643
climb 663, 707
clothes offering? 697, 779
clothes, colourful? 737
cloud 748

cloudy? 613, 693
cloudy 626, 748, 787
cock sacrifice? 699
cockerel 630
collect 687
collide 754
colourful 741, 782, 786
combine 641
come out 703
come together 758, 759
come 703, 741
command 677, 698
complete 652, 671, 678, 679, 721, 764, 771, 784
completed 757
concubine, high ranking 670
concubine 667
confirmation 771
cong 755
conjunction: also, too, likewise, again 661
conjunction: and, together, with 684, 723, 769
conjunction: and, with 686
conjunction: and 698
conjunction: with, and, both, together 659
conjunction: with 659, 684, 686, 698, 723, 769
conquest 783
consecrated 766
constellation (unidentified) 629, 724
constellation Bird Star? 629
constellation 733, 743
continuously? 652, 671, 678, 723
continuously 706
contract 699, 717, 767
cook 657, 789
cooperation 719, 785
country 734
courtship ritual? 738
courtyards? 763
cow 616
cowrie shell ritual 640
cowrie shell 639
crack-making 765
criticize 647
crocodile 632
crook? 766
cross river 664
cross water 704
cross 765

crossroad 757
crow 629
cudgel to death 633
cult year 632, 633
cultivate field 756
cultivate the soil 694
cup 787
curse 633
custody 720
cut meat 714, 762
cut textile 778
cut to pieces 784
cut 612, 650, 717, 756, 767, 782

D

dagger axe (halberd) 783
damage 622, 680, 699, 717
dance (circle dance) 663
dance offering (for Yi Yin?) 646
dance 662
dangerous directions? 781
dark 650, 666, 726, 752, 778
daughter 643, 666
dawn 744
day name: 1 of X: jia 765
day name: 1 of XII: zi 789
day name: 2 of X: yi 746
day name: 2 of XII chou 686
day name: 3 of X: bing 770
day name: 3 of XII: yi 774
day name: 4 of X: ding 763
day name: 4 of XII: mao 784
day name: 5 of X: wu 784
day name: 5 of XII: chen 639
day name: 6 of X: ji 778
day name: 6 of XII, si 680
day name: 7 of X, geng 742
day name: 7 of XII: wu 778
day name: 8 of X: xin 773
day name: 8 of XII: wei 728
day name: 9 of X: ren 766
day name: 9 of XII: shen 749
day name: 10 of X: gui 781
day name: 10 of XII: you 790
day name: 11 of XII: xu 783
day name: 12 of XII: hai 783
day 743
dead, death 632, 650, 676, 726
death? 653
decapitate 656
dedicate 687, 700
deep 764

deer 616
defend? 647, 707
defend 656
deities (in general) 766
deities Di's Five Ministers 722
deities Double Snake 633, 775
deities Five Mountains 751
deities Four Directions 768
deities of Directions 769
deities of fire? 752
deities of height and depth 764
deities Ten Mountains 752
deities, celestial 764
deities, subterranean 764
deity (of cooking?) 703
deity (unidentified) 642, 649, 691, 763, 707, 737, 740, 746, 759
deity Arrow? 776
deity Axe 784
deity Bird Peng 628
deity Bird Star? 629
deity Centipede? 637
deity Child Open Fontanel 672
deity Dagger Axe 783
deity Dark Woman? 655, 667
deity Dragon 631
deity Dragon-Woman 631
deity Drought (Ba) 660
deity E Huang? 667
deity Earth 727, 754
deity East/Wind (name) 732
deity East 730
deity Elephant? 614
deity Er 672
deity Forest 728
deity Fu 682
deity Hill Shang 753
deity Hill Work 736, 753
deity Hill 753
deity Monkey? 615, 645
deity Mount Child 680
deity Mount Eye 723
deity Mount Sacred T 766
deity Mount Step (or: Trample) 705
deity Mountain 751
deity Mouth-Eye 711
deity North Wind (name) 674
deity North 642
deity of a mountain 659
deity of the kitchen? 720
deity or deities Cloud 748
deity or deities Di 772

Lightning Source UK Ltd.
Milton Keynes UK
UKOW06f2327250815

257507UK00001B/1/P